PREFACE

Petri Nets represent a long and sustained effort to develop concepts, theories and tools to aid in design and analysis of concurrent systems. They are used in many areas of computer science including software engineering, data base and information systems, computer architecture and operating systems, communication protocols and computer networks, process control, and socio-technical systems such as office communication and man-machine interaction. Quite substantial theory has been developed for Petri Nets. It reflects all major problem areas of concurrent distributed systems and covers many successfully applied principles and analysis techniques for systems organisation.

Since the time that C. A. Petri has presented his original ideas, a rich body of knowledge has been developed – a recent bibliography (in *Advances in Petri Nets 1987*) includes more than 2000 entries. Already in 1979 an *Advanced Course on Petri Nets* was organized in Hamburg, West Germany, aiming at systematizing the existing knowledge and making it well accessible to a wide audience of computer scientists interested in theory and applications of concurrent systems. This course has turned out to be successful in the sense that it has initiated a lot of new research into applications and theory of Petri Nets. This had led to another *Advanced Course* in 1986 in Bad Honnef, West Germany – where during two weeks more than 30 lectures were presented covering the most important current developments in the area of Petri Nets. These two courses have not only led to make the existing knowledge more systematic and better accessible to the broad community of computer scientists but they also have helped to clarify the basic philosophy underlying the Petri Net approach.

The books (2 volumes) that we present now are based on lectures given during the Advanced Course in Bad Honnef. They address those who are

- interested in systems design and would like to learn to use Petri Nets,
- familiar with subareas of the theory or the applications of nets and wish to become acquainted with the whole area,
- interested in learning about recent results presented within a unified framework,
- going to learn about successfully applying Petri Nets in various practical situations,
- interested in the relationship of Petri Nets to other models of concurrent systems.

The book is organized in two parts. The first part presents a number of central Petri Net models and their properties setting a firm formal basis for developing the theory of Petri Nets and for the numerous efforts to adopt Petri Nets to a wide range of applications.

The second part discusses tools supporting the design of Petri Nets as well as their modification and analysis, presents quite a variety of applications of Petri Nets and it also covers the relationship of Petri Nets to other models of concurrency.

There were more than 160 participants coming from all over the world attending the Advanced Course on Petri Nets in Bad Honnef. Clearly this book cannot reflect the very stimulating and friendly atmosphere of the course where a lot of new ideas and friendships were born, and where discussions went often deep into the night (with local wine and beer helping essentially in getting insight into each others ideas). There has been also a permanent exhibition of software based Petri Net tools – one of the most popular spots during the course. A definite highlight for the participants of the course was a festive colloquium to honour the 60th birthday of C. A. Petri, organized at the nearby Birlinghoven Castle by the board of directors of the Gesellschaft für Mathematik und Datenverarbeitung. The participants of the course have been invited to attend this colloquium. (Another issue of *Advances in Petri Nets* is devoted to this special occasion.)

As it was said already, the course in Bad Honnef was a successor to the Advanced Course in Hamburg in 1979. In addition to stimulating a lot of research in the area of Petri Nets, the Hamburg course instigated many activities helping to organize the life of the Petri net community. These have led (among others) to:

1. The annual *European Workshop on Application and Theory of Petri Nets.* The organization of the workshop is coordinated by the Steering Committee (H. J. Genrich, K. Jensen, C. A. Petri – honorary member, G. Roucairol, and G. Rozenberg – chairman) that also takes care of many other matters concerning the Petri Net community. The sites of the workshop were: Strasbourg, France – 1980, Bad Honnef, Germany – 1981, Varenna, Italy – 1982, Toulouse, France – 1983, Aarhus, Denmark – 1984, Helsinki, Finland – 1985, Oxford, England – 1986, Zaragoza, Spain – 1987.

2. The publication of the *Petri Net Newsletter* published by the Special Interest Group on Petri Nets and Related System Models of the Gesellschaft für Informatik, three times a year. The *Newsletter* is edited by O. Herzog, W. Reisig and R. Valk.

3. The publication of the *Advances in Petri Nets* by Springer-Verlag within the *Lecture Notes in Computer Science* series. The *Advances* are edited by G. Rozenberg. The intention of these volumes is to present the most significant recent results in the application and theory of Petri Nets to the broad computer science community.

It is rather symbolic that this year, when the current volumes appear, it is 25 years ago that Petri's seminal thesis "Kommunikation mit Automaten" has appeared. Hence we have found it rather natural to "bracket" our book between a "Prologue" and an "Epilogue" by C. A. Petri. Both contributions are based on his lectures during the Advanced Course in Bad Hònnef.

St. Augustin, February 1987

W. Brauer,
W. Reisig,
G. Rozenberg

ACKNOWLEDGEMENTS

First of all, we acknowledge the cooperation of G. Roucairol and P. S. Thiagarajan for the planning of the course and of this proceedings.

Our special thanks go to the lecturers. They have not only given lectures during the course and provided lecture notes on time, but after the course they took the trouble to revise their texts according to the feedback received from the course participants and the critical comments of referees. We are obliged to the referees.

We are very indebted to the participants of the course for creating such a nice atmosphere during the course and for being so eager to learn (more) about Petri Nets.

The course and the production of these volumes could not have been achieved without the support of numerous institutions, scientific organizations, and companies. In particular we are grateful to

- the Gesellschaft für Mathematik und Datenverarbeitung (GMD) for being the institution organizing the course and supporting it financially;
- the Gesellschaft für Informatik (GI) for organizational support;
- the Deutsche Physikalische Gesellschaft (DPG) for supporting the local arrangements at Bad Honnef;
- the city of Bad Honnef for offering the "Kursaal";
- Siemens AG, IBM Deutschland, Honeywell-Bull, PSI, Actis, and Meta Software for their donations;
- Springer-Verlag for its cooperation in the production of these volumes.

Finally we want to express our gratitude to all members of the course staff, especially to Mrs. Ch. Harms, for the excellent job they have done before, during and after the course, and to E. Smith for preparing a verbatim account of C. A. Petri's improvised lecture in Bad Honnef so that we could include it as an epilogue in Part II of this proceedings.

CONTENTS OF PART I

CONTENTS OF PART II

Section 8: Relationship to other Models of Concurrency

Epilogue

INTRODUCTION TO PART I

In Part I of this book a number of central Petri Net models is presented and their properties discussed. In this way a firm formal basis is set for developing the theory of Petri Nets as well as for the numerous efforts to adopt Petri Nets to a wide range of applications.

In the first section *elementary net systems (EN systems)* are considered. This class of nets (together with *condition/event systems*) forms the underlying system model of the net theory. Many fundamental notions and phenomena of concurrent systems – as modeled by Petri Nets – are formulated and analysed on the level of EN systems.

In modelling concurrent systems one is often led to generalizations of EN systems. *Place/transition systems (P/T-systems)* have been introduced in this way. Section 2 considers the basic theory of P/T systems.

The modelling of concurrent systems encountered in practice often leads to EN systems or P/T systems of unmanagable size. To overcome this problem – very crucial for successful applications of Petri Nets – various kinds of the so called *high level nets* are considered. They are discussed in Section 3.

Section 4 presents a number of research lines concerning models discussed in the first three sections. The topics discussed are concerned with the design and analysis of various Petri Net models and include structural as well as behavioural properties of them.

When dealing with specific application problems one is often led to the formulation of quite specialized Petri Net models. Such models are presented in Section 5. They include various types of *stochastic nets* (originating mostly in connection with using Petri Nets in performance evaluation) and *FIFO nets.*

PROLOGUE

C. A. Petri: *Concurrency Theory*

Concurrency Theory

Carl Adam Petri

GMD

A great amount of work is being done today in the area of parallel information processing and supercomputation, and it is no longer considered extravagant to talk of 64 K or more processors being concurrently active at a single task. All technical problems of interconnecting many processors seem to be essentially solved, but it remains difficult to distribute and to organize a large task so as to extract the full advantage from the availability of a multitude of processors.

Under these circumstances, it seems that the notion of Concurrency should attract some attention, since it is the only basic notion which distinguishes sequential processing from multiprocessing. Let us first outline the specific notion of concurrency which refers to the lowest possible level, in order to attain full generality: let us consider the unique historical record of an execution of a process described in the greatest possible detail. We collect the elements of this occurrence structure in a set X . In general, X is distributed over time and space.

We assume now that the historical record gives the set X some structure by means of a binary relation $<$ which indicates causal dependence. We define: $x < y$ if and only if a physical signal starts out from $x \in X$ and arrives at $y \in X$; x must be different from y.

The speed of physical signals is limited by the speed of light, c , as far as we know; if we chose to introduce a coordinate system for spacetime, and Δr were the spatial distance between x and y , and Δt their time difference, we would have to assert

$$x < y \Rightarrow (\Delta r)^2 \leq c^2(\Delta t)^2 \wedge \Delta t > o$$

but we must firmly resist the temptation to infer $x < y$ from $\Delta t > o$.

The signal relation $<$ must, of course, be independent of the choice of a coordinate system; that is precisely why we are interested in it. The "historical record", an occurrence structure, should show invariant and physically implemented relations only, because we are considering real-world processes and their inherent structure exclusively.

From the verbal definition of $<$, we can assert very little indeed about its properties; only that the structure of $(X,<)$ is a strict partial order: $SPO\,(X,<)$

$$\text{Def:} \quad SPO\,(X,<) \;:\Leftrightarrow\; \bigwedge xy : x<y \Rightarrow x\in X \wedge y\in X$$
$$\wedge \bigwedge x\in X : \neg(x<x)$$
$$\wedge \bigwedge x,y,z\in X : x<y \wedge y<z \Rightarrow x<z$$

in words: $<$ is an irreflexive, transitive relation in X ;

in shorthand: $SPO\,(X,<) :\Leftrightarrow\; < \subseteq X\times X,\quad < \cap\, id = \emptyset,\quad <^2 \subseteq <.$

By "id" we denote the set $\{(x,x) \mid x\in X\}$.

We will have to rely on this kind of shorthand to keep our theory intelligible; presently, it consists of some 500 statements on concurrency, which, together with the proofs of their interdependencies, could not be understood if written out in full, in addition to the explanations, examples and modes of application, which are necessary because so many of the statements are contrary to intuition. For the same reason, we confine ourselves here to those statements which might be candidates for axioms, irrespective of their strong interdependence.

In any strict partial order, we can define the disorder relation "neither $x<y$ nor $y<x$" . We define our basic relation, concurrency, as the disorder belonging to the signalling relation:

$$x \text{ co } y \;:\Leftrightarrow\; x,y\in X \wedge \neg(x<y) \wedge \neg(y<x)$$

or for short $\quad co := \overline{< \cup >}$

all complements, denoted by $\overline{\quad}$, being taken relative to X resp. to $X\times X$, as context will indicate.

If co is thus derived from an $SPO\,(X,<)$, it follows that co is (totally) reflexive and symmetric :

$$id \subseteq co \quad , \quad co = co^{-1} \quad \text{where} \quad R^{-1} := \{(y,x) \mid (x,y)\in R\} .$$

A structure (X,co) with these properties is called a Similarity.

Whether or not co is derived from $(X,<)$, we put down as axioms, or basic assumptions, that (X,co) is a non-trivial similarity :

(A o)	$\|X\| > 1$
(A 1)	$id \subseteq co$
(A 2)	$co = co^{-1}$

Concurrency theory would now lead into well-trodden roads if co were transitive : a transitive similarity is an equivalence relation; X would be partioned into equivalence classes of co , and these would be fully ordered if an SPO (X,<) was originally given. End.

Let us remark that a full ("linear") ordering can be defined by strengthening (A1) : $id \subseteq co$ into $id = co$:

$$FO(X,<) :\Leftrightarrow SPO(X,<) \wedge \underline{co = id} .$$

In our context, an SPO can (but should not) be viewed as a collection of maximal full orders, the signal trajectories, shortly called L i n e s . On each line, co is trivially transitive, being equal to identity. The "points" (elements) of a line are totally interconnected by the relation $li := \langle \cup\, id\, \cup \rangle$

and we introduce in general the definition of li in terms of co :

Def: $$li := \overline{co} \cup id$$

li is obviously a similarity, like co ; we have

$$id \subseteq li , \quad li = li^{-1} , \quad li \cap co = id , \quad li \cup co = X \times X .$$

On each line, li is transitive, but not necessarily on a collection of lines.

We now assert that, in general, co is not transitive :

$$\neg(co^2 \subseteq co) , \quad \text{or} \quad \boxed{co^2 - co \neq \emptyset}$$

So we explicitly state and explain our opinion that the (mostly implicit) assumption "$co^2 \subseteq co$" is based on misconceptions.

The first misconception is the firmly entrenched idea that all points of a process execution occur, in reality, at a well-defined point "in time", that is, on a linear absolute Newtonian time scale, common to all observers : Time : $X \longrightarrow \mathbb{R}$

As Einstein has conclusively shown, this function Time is by no means independent of the observer; the transformation of $Time_1$ to $Time_2$ between different observers is not even homomorphic (order-preserving). Still many people think that fast signals behave like slow signals, and admit the false idealization

$$x \text{ co } y \Leftrightarrow \text{Time}(x) = \text{Time}(y)$$

dovetailing splendidly with the idea of arbitrary interleaving for $x \neq y$:

$$x \text{ co } y \Rightarrow \text{Time}(x) \neq \text{Time}(y)$$

With the idealization "concurrency is equitemporality", co is of course transitive. We have to reject this idea.

The measurement of time, like all other measurement, is based on observation, and observation is based on the combination of physical signals. We should not refer to time measurement when we study the combinatorics of signals.

The second misconception also refers to observation. In the theories of observation and measurement, a basic predicate is

" x cannot be distinguished from y , by observation, with respect to a specified order $<$ "

The specified order may refer to amounts of time, length, mass etc. Anyway, the "indifference" relation is a similarity like co . It is often called an "approximate equality", and is denoted by "$\approx$". We shall continue to denote it by "co".

Now many people assume, while recognizing that indifference is not transitive, that it is impossible to calculate successfully with a mere similarity, in contrast to the easy use of transitive relations like equality and order. They tend to manipulate the basic phenomenon of indistinguishability, which relates immediately to their experience, and twist it until it becomes transitive.

Norbert Wiener has given ([1]) the following recipe to achieve this purpose. Non-transitivity of co shows up completely in three-point diagrams of the form

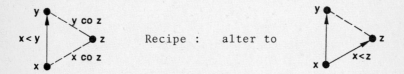

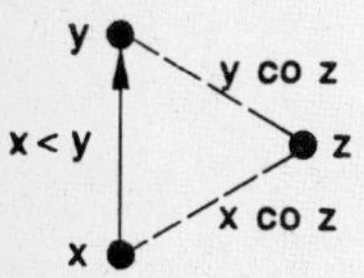

Recipe : alter to

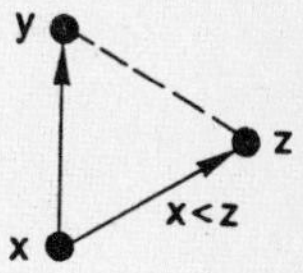

Wiener gives the following justification for this falsification of experience (condensed from [1]) : X is fully ordered in reality.

Therefore $co \neq id$ is an illusion, not reflecting reality but the shortcomings of the observer (poor eyes, lack of microscope etc.). Further, it cannot be that $z < x$, since then also $z < y$, and "an indifference interval (z,y) cannot overlap a difference interval (x,y)". Also, z cannot be equal to x, since $x < y$ excludes x co y. Therefore, $x < z$.

However :
If the argument is valid, it yields the stronger conclusion

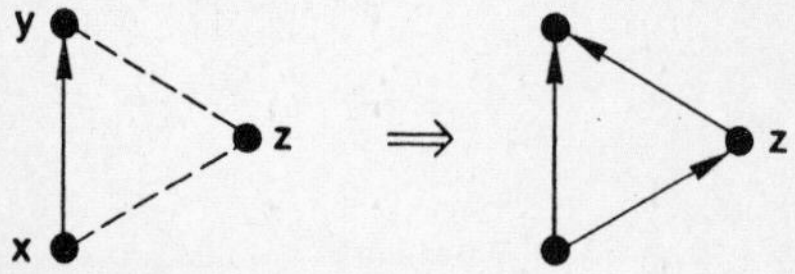

: $\underline{x < z < y}$

As the recipe stands, its result depends on the direction of $<$, whereas the axioms of order remain unchanged if $<$ is replaced by $>$. Anyway, by Wiener's argumentation, his recipe might as well be :

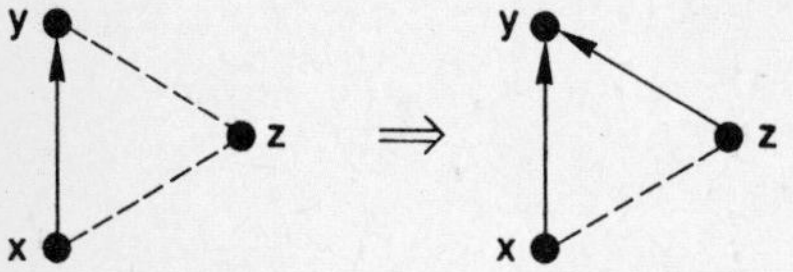

, with different result.

More importantly, the result of the recipe can be contradictory, or can depend on the sequence of its individual applications :

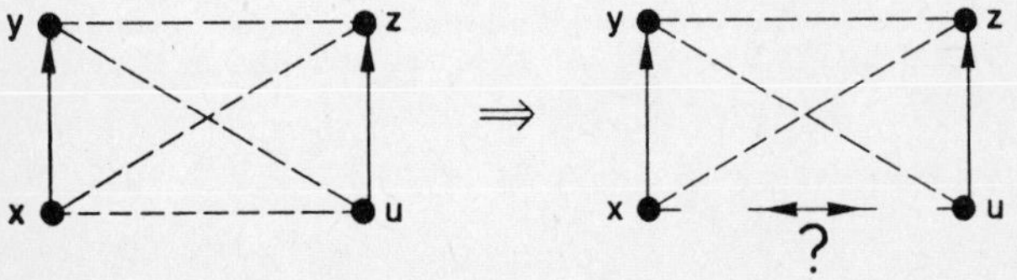

While Wiener would argue that this diagram does not occur in reality, we know from experience that it does.
Moreover, Wiener's construction fails to achieve its proper aim : while his residual indifference is in fact transitive and permits the formation of equivalence classes of indifference, we see that across the border between neighboring equivalence classes we can make arbitrarily fine distinctions. If the equivalence classes are densely ordered, we can make arbitrarily fine distinctions everywhere; both cases are contrary to experience.

Finally, we reject Wiener's fundamental premiss that X is fully ordered in reality. It is true that we can select lines, as subsets of X, on which the points are fully ordered, but then we have selected something corresponding to a <u>single</u> signal and cannot enter signal combinatorics, and cannot speak of the interaction of sufficiently many signals which give rise to the concept of a real-world process.

To sum up, we reject Wiener's recipe in total.

We shall not dare to tamper with the relation of indifference, we shall acknowledge the possibility that it is not transitive in a sufficiently large context; where the experienced reality, our universe, is the largest context in question. But we shall look out for transitive relations expressible in terms of co ; the result will be Concurrency Theory, along with a <u>calculus of indifference and other similarities</u>.

We return to mathematics now, giving substance to those verbal considerations.

Our first step resembles, in purpose and in effect, the introduction of the weakest separation axiom ("T_0") in topology. Let "opensets (x)" denote the set of all open sets which contain the point $x \in X$.

The relation

$$x \text{ isotopic } y \ :\Leftrightarrow \ \text{opensets}(x) = \text{opensets}(y)$$

is clearly an equivalence. It means that x and y are indistinguishable by the constructions of the topology.

The axiom

$$T_0 : \ \text{opensets}(x) = \text{opensets}(y) \Rightarrow x = y$$

lifts the burden of making topologically irrelevant distinctions from all further topological considerations. It is of great mathematical value, and it does no harm since it can be revoked whenever there are reasons, from outside a specific topological space, to do so.

Analogously, let us call $\dot{Co}(x)$ the set of points which are in relation co with the point $x \in X$. Again, the relation

Def: $$x \ \widetilde{co} \ y \ :\Leftrightarrow \ Co(x) = Co(y)$$

is an equivalence; it is the transitive kernel of co , and we call it "co-congruence". Of course, $\widetilde{co} \subseteq co$.

We demand : $$Co(x) = Co(y) \Rightarrow x = y$$

That is, we declare that we are not interested in distinctions which cannot be expressed in terms of co , and which are irrelevant in the structure (X,co) which is our only concern in concurrency theory. We express this in the form

(A 3) $\widetilde{co} = id$ and likewise

(A 4) $\widetilde{li} = id$ meaning

$$Li(x) = Li(y) \Rightarrow x = y \quad \text{where} \quad Li(x) := \{y \mid x \text{ li } y\}$$

We can deduce A 3 and A 4 from A 5 :

(A 5) $\widetilde{co} = \widetilde{li}$

since $\widetilde{co} \subseteq co$, $\widetilde{li} \subseteq li$, and $co \cap li = id$. Explicitly :

(A 5)' $Co(x) = Co(y) \Leftrightarrow Li(x) = Li(y)$

" <u>(X,co) is irreducible</u> "

Note that if X is a line (i.e. co=id), all points of it are in relation $\widetilde{li}$ to each other; on a line, A 4 implies $|X| = 1$, in contradiction to A o : $|X| > 1$.

If we want to see what A 5 , the "axiom of irreducibility", means for the study of program structures, we have in the first place to distinguish between control structure and the much larger signalling structure implied by the execution of a program. When we consider the control structure only of a parbegin-parend clause comprising unbranched sequences, then, if A 4 is to be valid, each unbranched sequence must be reduced to a single element; this is not unusual in theories of program structure. But further, if A 3 is to be valid, all those "parallel" elements must be "co-reduced" into one single element, and subsequent li-reduction collapses the whole parbegin-parend clause into a single point.

But this is not in the least a reason to reject A 5 and all elegance of concurrency theory with it. Rather, we should keep in mind that the abstraction of control structure, without precise indication of the possibilities or impossibility of mutual influence of "parallel" substructures, is inherently dangerous.

Let us check the consequences of assuming co to be transitive in addition to A 5 . They are :

$$\widetilde{co} = co \ , \quad \widetilde{li} = li \ , \quad co = li \ , \quad co = li = id$$

and therefore $|X| = 1$, contrary to A o .

Having inspected the <u>transitive kernel</u> of the similarities co and li , let us inspect their <u>transitive hull</u>.

Def: $co^* := \bigcup_{n \in \mathbb{N}} co^n = id \cup co \cup co^2 \cup co^3 \cup \ldots$

co^* and li^* are clearly equivalence relations. We demand now that they are total in X :

(A 6) $co^* = X \times X$

(A 7) $li^* = X \times X$

We can deduce A 6 and A 7 from A 8 :

(A 8) $co^* = li^*$

("(X,co) is coherent")

We call a relational structure (X,R) coherent iff all of X is connected by $R \cup R^{-1}$ and also connected by $\overline{R \cup R^{-1}}$.
So if co is the disorder of an SPO $(X,<)$, and (X,co) is coherent, then $(X,<)$ is also coherent, and vice versa.

A 7 says that, in a sufficiently large context (e.g. the accessible universe), X is connected by signals. li^*, $= (\overline{co} \cup id)^*$, is an equivalence; it partitions X into li-connected subsets, and there is no signal flow between different such subsets. They would represent separate universes which are inaccessible from each other.
By A 7 , we declare that we are interested in one universe only, ours.

A 6 , $co^* = X \times X$, is valid in Minkowski spacetime (not in Galilean, or Newtonian spacetime). Minkowski spacetime gives a framework for possible signalling, and a fortiori for actual physical signalling which is our topic. I feel, however, that a stronger reason should be given for maintaining A 6 , to convince those who believe relativity is nonsense. The similarity relation co may always be interpreted as an indifference relation. A 6 can then be stated as saying :
From any point x , we can reach any other point y in a finite number of imperceptibly small steps. This is an important intuitive aspect of "continuity" of (X,co) resp. $(X,<)$. It is also a main aspect of the inherent imprecision of measurement. When we go from signal combinatorics to signal mechanics (not in this paper), by endowing signal occurrences with mass, energy, momentum, charge, spin etc., A 6 will be connected to Heisenberg's Uncertainty Principle. -

A 8 is the short rewriting of the conjunction of A 6 and A 7 ; it serves to focus attention onto the notion of coherence.

The smallest non-trivial (A o) coherent structure is

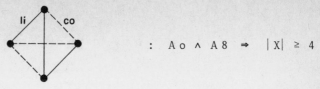

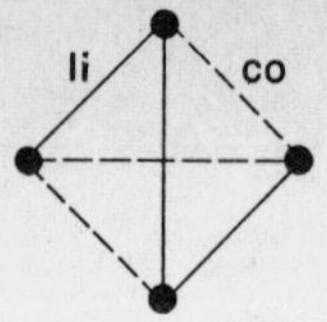

: $A_0 \wedge A8 \Rightarrow |X| \geq 4$

It is irreducible and plays a central role in concurrency theory. Observe that no two points of the four can be identical, even though li and co include identity. Further, if we choose an orientation $<$ on any one of the li-connections, there is exactly one way to orient all li-connections consistently :

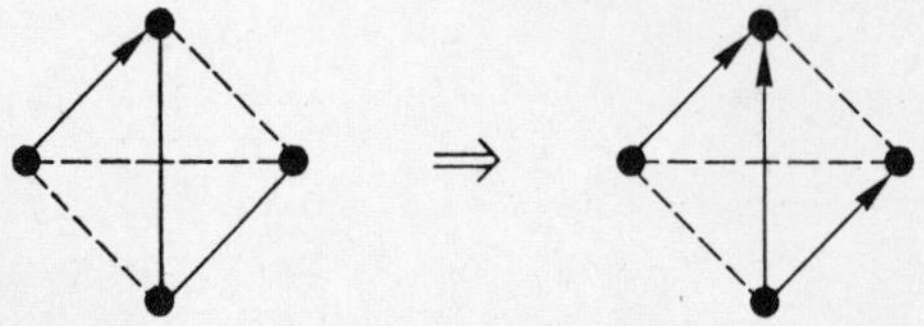

We call an SPO $(X,<)$ with this property a natural order, and its corresponding structure (X,co) a natural disorder.

(A 9) : (X,co) is a natural disorder
i.e. $\overline{co}$ can be consistently oriented in exactly two ways, if co is the disorder $\overline{<\cup>}$ of an SPO $(X,<)$.

In general, we shall call a similarity (X,co) a natural disorder iff the relation G (see below), the finest granulation of $\overline{co}$, can be oriented consistently by a flow relation F (that of a net (S,T;F)) in exactly two ways : F and F^{-1}, with $F \cap F^{-1} = \emptyset$ and $F \cup F^{-1} = G$.

The "iff" definition is much more general : it accommodates not only SPO's but also cyclic arrangements, e.g. synchronization graphs.

We shall not justify this global assumption here, but shall base it below on local properties of (X,co) . However, if A 9 holds, all order is derivable from disorder, all observable signal structure from indifference statements.
"Cosmos arises out of Chaos" are not my words; but in view of A 9 I am surely justified in calling concurrency a fundamental relation, since all signalling can be constructed from it.

Let us now continue the search for transitive aspects of the non-transitive co . We ask : what are the largest subsets of X within which co is transitive and connected, i.e. a full relation ?
We call such subsets "Kens of co" and define in general, for all relational structures (X,r) with $r \subseteq X \times X$

$$\text{Ken}\,(a,r) :\Leftrightarrow \quad \bigwedge x,y \in a : (x,y) \in r \cup r^{-1} \cup id$$
$$\wedge \bigwedge x \in \bar{a} \ \bigvee y \in a : (x,y) \notin r \cup r^{-1} \cup id$$

$$\text{Kens}\,(r) := \{a \mid \text{Ken}\,(a,r)\}$$

For similarities, $r \cup r^{-1} \cup id$ equals r . If r is moreover transitive, the Kens of r are simply its equivalence classes in X . Thus, Kens are the closest possible substitutes for equivalence classes and are especially useful for similarities. Two Kens may overlap, two different equivalence classes may not.
Given now a similarity (X,co) :

Def: $\quad$ cut (c) :⇔ Ken (c,co)
Def: $\quad$ line (l) :⇔ Ken (l,li) $\qquad$ (⇔ Ken $(l,\overline{co})$)

A cut is, in our main interpretation, a "time slice" extended over all space. In terms of causal order, cuts do not in general form a sequence, but a lattice : of two cuts c_1, c_2 , part of c_1 may lie before c_2 , another part of c_1 may lie after c_2 .
Easier to see is, that the union of all cuts equals X , and that

$$co = \{(x,y) \mid \bigvee c : \text{cut}\,(c) \wedge x,y \in c\}$$

Therefore, all signalling can be constructed, on the "natural disorder" assumption, from the <u>unordered</u> set of <u>presents</u> (cuts), each "present" being a maximal disorder (chaos) in X .

A cut may also be viewed as a "snapshot" of a developing process. Considering <u>lines</u> to be the longest signals (e.g. persistent physical particles), it appears to be a matter of course that each line leaves a trace on each snapshot; each line must meet every cut.

$$\text{cut}(c) \wedge \text{line}(l) \Rightarrow c \cap l \neq \emptyset$$

Def: $\quad$ K dense (X,co) :⇔ $\quad$ Ken (c,co) ∧ Ken (l,li) ⇒ $c \cap l \neq \emptyset$

(A 10) $\qquad$ <u>K dense (X,co)</u>

The smallest structure which is <u>not</u> K dense is the N-shaped figure already mentioned as the smallest coherent order :

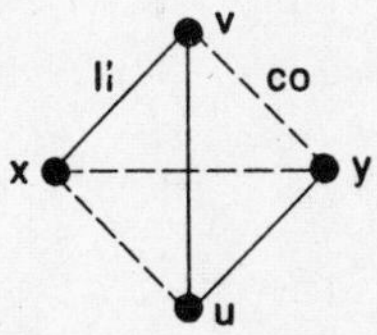

x and y form a cut, u and v form a line, and this line does not

intersect this cut : $\{x,y\} \cap \{u,v\} = \emptyset$. Whichever way we orient the li-relation, there must be an element z between u and v if the figure is to be K dense , and z must form a cut $\{x,y,z\}$.
We demand :

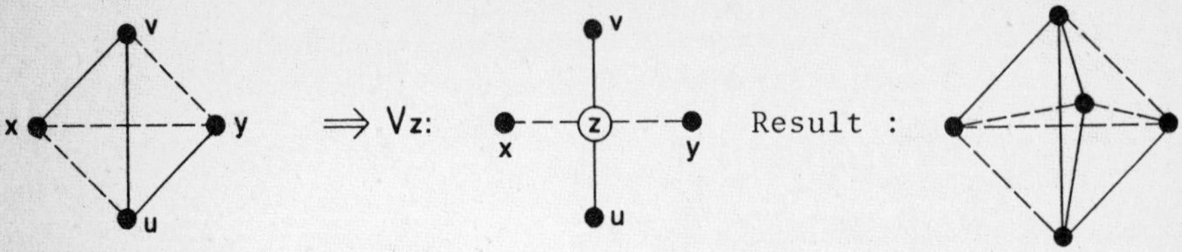

The result is again a natural disorder, giving rise to exactly two S P O's which are natural orders. Formally :

Def: N dense (X,co) $:\Leftrightarrow$ $\bigwedge x\,y\,u\,v \in X$: (x li v li u li y $\wedge$ u co x co y co v
$\Rightarrow \bigvee z \in X$: u li z li v $\wedge$ x co z co y)

If a structure contains a diagram which is not N dense , it cannot be K dense : K dense (X,co) $\Rightarrow$ N dense (X,co)

N density is thus the local aspect of the global K density , which takes its name from "Ken" (old German, Scottish, Japanese : a bounded region (of knowledge, of power)) and from the fact [2] that K density can be most easily proved or disproved by drawing a K-shaped figure, where the vertical stroke of the K indicates a line, and the area between the oblique strokes of the K indicates a cut. The question is then: does (must) the central point of the K belong to the cut ?

If all cuts are finite, K density is equivalent to N density [4] (Plünnecke). In that case, local tests are sufficient to prove the fundamentally important property of K density .
We propose therefore

(A 11) N dense (X,co)

for the case that A 10 cannot be verified, and also because the N density **construction** will be the basis for the two generalizations of Dedekind continuity we shall require for signal structures.

Within cuts and lines, both co and li are transitive.
Let us go on to look for further transitive constructions.

Def: x Cl y $:\Leftrightarrow$ Li x $\subseteq$ Li y $\wedge$ $x,y \in X$

Cl is obviously reflexive and transitive.
x Cl y means that all lines passing through x must also pass through y . Cl is our bridge from similarity relations to topology.

Let a be an arbitrary subset of X :

Def: Closure of a := Cl [a] $:= \left\{ y \mid \forall x \in a : x \text{ Cl } y \right\}$

As a closure operation, the relational image under Cl fulfils all the axioms of an elementary topology [2]. To ensure that the topology (X,Cl) is T_0 , i.e. distinguishes the points of X topologically, we define <u>proximity P</u> and <u>gross proximity G</u> :

Def: P := Cl - id , $G := P \cup P^{-1}$ with

(A 12) $P^2 = \emptyset$

(A 13) $G^* = X \times X$

We have, using A 5 (irreducibility) :

$x\,P\,y \Leftrightarrow \text{Li}\,x \subsetneqq \text{Li}\,y$, $\text{Cl} = P \cup \text{id}$, $\text{Cl} \subseteq \text{li}$, $G \subseteq \overline{\text{co}}$,

$\text{Cl} = \overline{\text{li}\,\overline{\text{li}}}$, $P = \overline{\text{li}}\,\text{li} - \text{li}\,\overline{\text{li}} = \overline{\text{co}} - \overline{\text{co}}\,\overline{\text{li}}$, $G = \overline{\text{li}}\,\text{li} \oplus \text{li}\,\overline{\text{li}}$

domain $P \cap$ range $P = \emptyset$, domain $P \cup$ range $P = X$.

All of these statements give or deepen our interpretation of P : P means "is changed by" . Explicitly :
<u>x P y means "the occurrence x of a state of a signal begins or ends by the occurrence y of an interaction of that signal with another signal"</u> .

Def: S := domain P ; T := range P

Consequence : (S,T;P) is an undirected (A 12) , connected (A 13) <u>net</u>.

The structure (X,co) is equivalent to a pair of nets (S,T;F) and (S,T;F') where $F' = F^{-1}$, $S \cup T = X$.
These nets are special in that

$\bigwedge s \in S : |{}^{\bullet}s| = |s^{\bullet}| = 1$ (e.g. by (A 19, below))
$\bigwedge t \in T : |{}^{\bullet}t| > 1 \wedge |t^{\bullet}| > 1$ by (A 12)
and $\bigwedge s_1\, s_2 \in S : ({}^{\bullet}s_1 = {}^{\bullet}s_2 \wedge s_1^{\bullet} = s_2^{\bullet}) \Rightarrow s_1 = s_2$ by (A 5)

They are special occurrence nets or synchronization nets (graphs).
We have $F \cup F^{-1} = P \cup P^{-1} = G$; this justifies the term "vicinity" in

Def: vic (x) := vicinity of x $:= \left\{ y \mid x\,G\,y \right\}$

Note that $x \notin \text{vic}(x)$ even though $x \in \text{Cl}\,[\{x\}]$
We use vic (x) to ensure the essence of the "natural order"

assumption A 9, a global assumption which seems to be an expression of mere wishful thinking to some, and a brazen imputation to others. For those, it will be easier to accept that in the vicinity of each element, co is transitive (A 14) and partitions that vicinity of x into exactly two equivalence classes (A 15), namely the points "immediately before" x and those "immediately after" x, without saying which class is which, but enabling us to propagate an orientation F given on one element of G through the whole of X (using A 13) :

(A 14) $\bigwedge x$: Within vic (x), $co^2 \subseteq co$ (local transitivity)

(A 15) $\bigwedge x$: Within vic (x), $\emptyset \neq \overline{co}^2 \subseteq co$ (local orientability)

A consistent orientation of G is an F with $F \cap F^{-1} = \emptyset$,

$$F^2 \subseteq \overline{co}\ , \quad F\,F^{-1} \subseteq co\ , \quad F^{-1}\,F \subseteq co\ ,$$

and of course $F \cup F^{-1} = G$. -

As a counterpart of Cl we can formulate

Def: $x\ Cl'\ y\ :\Leftrightarrow\ Co\ x \subseteq Co\ y$

Cl' is another reflexive and transitive relation; it forms the closure operation of a different elementary topology over X, different because $Cl \subseteq li$, $Cl' \subseteq co$.
Analogously to P and G, we define

Def: $D := Cl' - id\ , \quad H := D \cup D^{-1}$

We have, using A 5 (irreducibility) :

$x\ D\ y \Leftrightarrow Co\ x \subsetneqq Co\ y\ , \quad Cl' = D \cup id\ , \quad Cl' \subseteq co\ , \quad H \subseteq \overline{li}$

$Cl' = \overline{co\ \overline{co}}\ , \quad D = \overline{co}\ co - co\ \overline{co} = \overline{li} - \overline{li}\ \overline{co}\ , \quad H = \overline{co}\ co \oplus co\ \overline{co}$

$x\ D\ y \Rightarrow (\ \bigwedge c : \text{cut}\ c \wedge x \in c \Rightarrow y \in c \wedge x \neq y\ )$

Therefore D might be called a strict implication within cuts; we interpret rather, since x might be an interaction and not a state :

x D y means " x is a detail of y "

The range of D turns out to lie in domain of P, namely S :
For the constructions of signal combinatorics, it is sufficient to assume

((A 16)) $D^2 = \emptyset$

((A 17)) $D^2 = P^2$

(A 18) $\qquad H^* = X \times X$

A 16 is a logical consequence of A 17, since $D \cap P = \emptyset$.
We "assert" A 16 (and therefore A 17) with less confidence than A 18, since it has been only formally, but not yet physically justified.

As a consequence of A 18 : $H^* = (D \cup D^{-1})^* = X \times X$, every point of X <u>is or has</u> a detail. According to A 3, this idea of detailing is not a trivial one : $D \cap \widetilde{co}$ is even empty, D contains no trivial subrelation.

The main point of importance for having details is the following : A cut ("time slice") c may contain a point x which denotes an interaction between signals. Then we cannot make, at that "time" c, any proposition about the occurrence of <u>states</u> on those signals; rather, all the states immediately related to the interaction x lie in the vicinity of x and are just undergoing a change in x, i.e. some of them cease to hold in x, the rest are beginning to hold, but not yet holding, in x. x can, by A 5, be precisely defined by the beginning and ending of states in its vicinity, and no state can begin and end at the same point x. We refer to this as to the

<u>Extensionality Principle of Elementary Changes</u> .

Now we want to ensure, beyond this principle, that every change (interaction) x should be accompanied by a propositionally assertable state y, guaranteed to be an element of every cut containing x, i.e. $x D y$. y must lie outside of the vicinity of x, since $D \subseteq \overline{li}$. In addition to this, we would like to ensure (by $D^2 = \emptyset$) that such a state element y defines as narrowly as possible the position of x on one of the lines passing through x.

$x D y$:

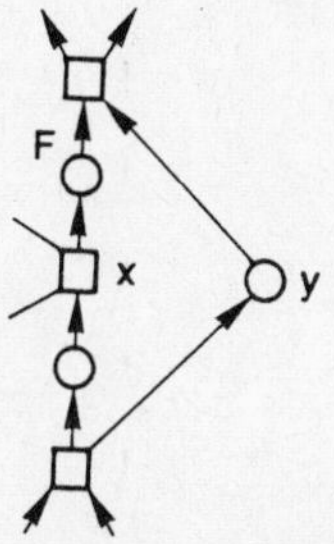

: $Co\, x \subsetneqq Co\, y$

In other words, we want every transition to be accompanied by a state in such a way that, if we are <u>uncertain</u> whether the transition is just about to occur, just occurring, or has just occurred, we <u>are</u> certain that the accompanying state does hold.

It is obvious that we can always construct such states; we know that such states do exist in some physical signal structures; but we can only surmise that every interaction in a given physical system is indeed accompanied by a position-limiting state. Anyway, we have to have <u>some</u> method (e.g. "operational topology", [2]) to deal with uncertainty, especially in boundary situations. We can view the mathematics of concurrency theory as a general way to deal with uncertainty of classification; witness the concentration on mere similarities and on their Kens. -

The following three last assumptions A 19, A 20, A 21 will be formulated in terms of strict partial orders only, even though they can be rewritten in terms of (X,co) and then be applied to finite "cyclic ropes" [3], too. But this rewriting is somewhat cumbersome and would obscure the close relationship to well-known parts of mathematics : order theory and Dedekind continuity. Given an SPO $(X,<)$:

Def: $\quad CIP(X,<) :\Leftrightarrow \bigwedge x,y \bigvee u,v \; : \; u \leq x \leq v \wedge u \leq y \leq v$

This is the " cone intersection property " (CIP) :
let us call $\{ z \mid z \leq x \}$ the <u>precone</u> of x , etc.

The CIP can now be described thus :
For any two points $x,y \in X$, the precones of x and of y intersect, and also the postcones of x and of y intersect. Note that not even maximal u's or minimal v's are necessarily unique. Intent as we are to keep our assumptions free from trivialities, we observe that for $x \, li \, y$, CIP holds trivially: $u = Min \{x,y\}$, $v = Max \{x,y\}$. We formulate the assumption that real-world signals have the CIP as the assumption that the <u>Lozenge Axiom</u> applies to them :

(A 19) $\quad \bigwedge x\, y \; : \; x \, \overline{li} \, y \Rightarrow \; \bigvee u,v \; : \; u < x < v \wedge u < y < v$

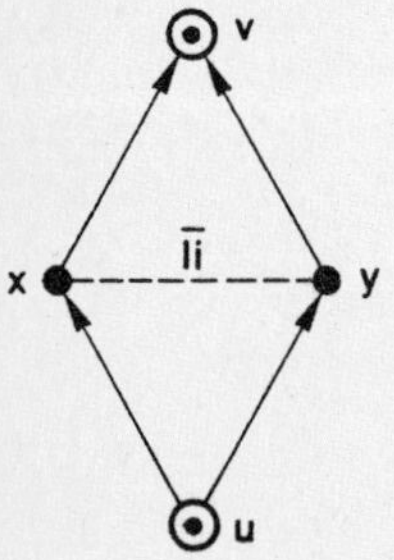

← Lozenge Axiom

obviously <u>not</u> → immediately expressible in co

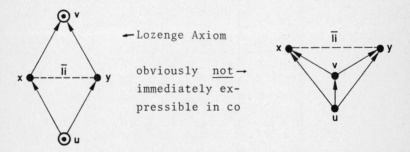

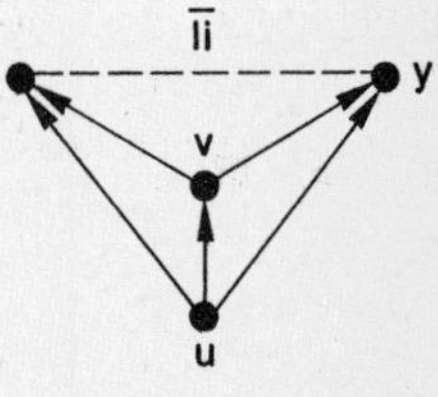

since the right-hand figure has the same co-structure.

To indicate a sufficient, though not necessary condition for A 19 in terms of co , and to pave the way for an equivalent to A 19 given in terms of co using A o - A 18 , we proffer :

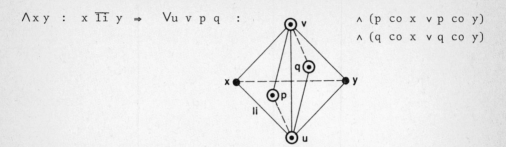

$\bigwedge x y \;:\; x \; \overline{li} \; y \Rightarrow \bigvee u\, v\, p\, q \;:$

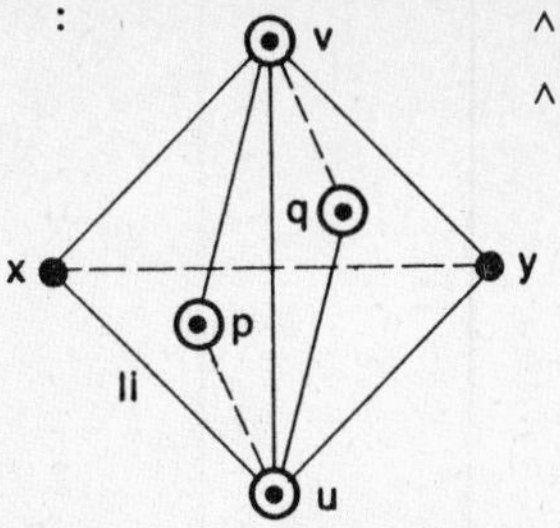

$\wedge\ (p \text{ co } x \vee p \text{ co } y)$
$\wedge\ (q \text{ co } x \vee q \text{ co } y)$

Note that all four indicated structures are coherent, irreducible natural disorders.

Finally we turn to the decisive property of Dedekind continuity of signal structures $(X,<)$, which is implied by S P O $(X,<)$ and A o - A 19 . We give it, nevertheless, as independent assumptions A 20, A 21 because they, in turn, imply the essence of A o - A 19 ; because they shed a new light on the relationship between "discrete" and "continuous" mathematical modelling, and because they open a new wide range for the application of net theory.

In short, the cuts ("time slices") of certain S P O's can be likened to real numbers, because their S P O's contain no jumps and no gaps; this is Dedekind's well-known requirement of continuity. In fact, for co = id , A 20 or A 21 reflect, as can easily be observed when they are written out in full [2], the original Dedekind idea of continuity.

For our purpose, we have to generalize the notions of "jump" and of "gap" from full orders to partial orders.
Jumps present no difficulty : our "new" definition is equivalent to the classical one.

Def: Jump $(x,y) :\Leftrightarrow x < y \wedge \bigwedge z : x < z \Rightarrow y \leq z$
$\wedge \bigwedge z : z < y \Rightarrow z \leq x$

Jumps are excluded by A 4 : Jump$(x,y) \Rightarrow x \; \widetilde{\overline{li}} \; y$ and thus $x = y$.
We have: If Jump (x,y), then there is no z between x and y , and y is the unique immediate successor of x .
We denote immediate successorship by $\lessdot$

Def: $\lessdot := < - <^2$

The non-trivial part of generalized Dedekind continuity is, that it can occur in <u>combinatorial</u> orders, often called <u>discrete</u> orders. Therefore, we will formulate A 20, A 21 <u>for combinatorial orders only</u>.

Def: Combinatorial S P O $(X,<)$:⇔ S P O $(X,<) \wedge \leq = \lessdot^*$

For non-combinatorial orders, the trivial generalization G o is applicable : An S P O $(X,<)$ is G o D continuous iff all Lines (= Kens (1i)) are D continuous in the classical Dedekind sense. Then $\lessdot = \emptyset$: $(X,<)$ is everywhere dense.

(A 20) $(X,<)$ is a combinatorial K dense S P O without jumps and without G1 gaps ;

(A 21) $(X,<)$ is a combinatorial K dense S P O without jumps and without G2 gaps .

We call $(X,<)$ "G1 D continuous" if it conforms to A 20
We call $(X,<)$ "G2 D continuous" if it conforms to A 21

It remains to define G1 gaps and G2 gaps , and to give the gap-filling constructions corresponding to that of Dedekind [2].

G 1 gap :

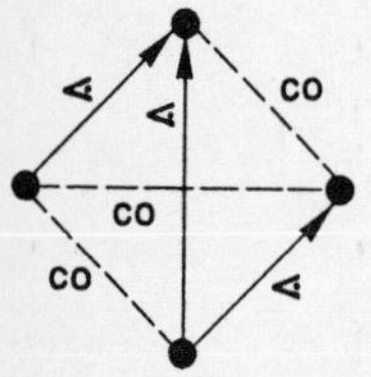

G 2 gap :

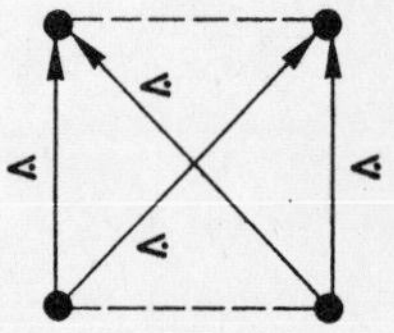

A G1 gap is nothing else but an infringement of N density and therefore of K density . It can be filled by inserting the z element required by the definition of N density above.
That is, a K dense S P O cannot have G1 gaps anyway :

(A 20)' : $(X,<)$ is an S P O with A 4, A 10, and A 13.

We have mentioned G1 gaps because they show clearly how the local test for Dedekind completeness works :
If we omit an S-detail from X , it is filled in again uniquely by the simple and reasonable construction given by requiring N density , and

not by the infinite regress initiated when we seek to implement density $(\lessdot \subseteq \lessdot^2)$ constructively.

A G 2 gap arises if we remove a T-element from X ; namely in the vicinity of that T-element. First, we observe that the order restricted to the vicinity must remain N dense . For this purpose, we rewrite the definition of N density equivalently :

$$\text{N dense } (X,\lessdot) \Leftrightarrow \bigwedge x,y,u\,v : (x \lessdot v \wedge u \lessdot v \wedge u \lessdot y \wedge x \text{ co } u \wedge v \text{ co } y \wedge \neg \bigvee z : u \lessdot z \lessdot v) \Rightarrow x \lessdot y$$

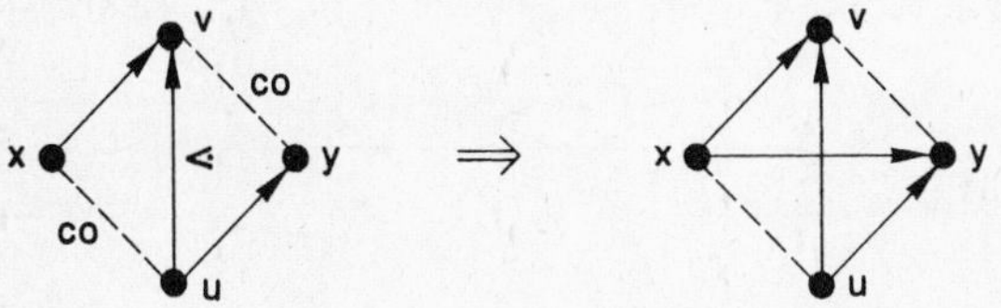

("If there is no z between u and v , the diagram can not be N-shaped")

Yet, the resulting diagram constitutes a G 2 gap, i.e. a gap according to an old generalization of Dedekind completeness, to be found in mathematical dictionaries, and explained in [2].

The gap-filling construction for G 2 gaps proceeds as follows :

Given 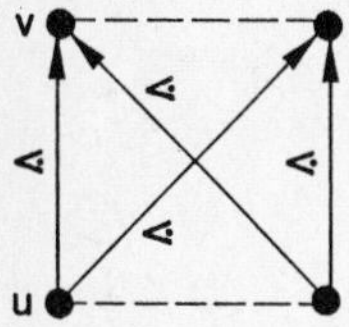

, fill in a point z between u and v

such that

1. z becomes $\lessdot$ all immediate successors of u
2. all immediate predecessors of v become $\lessdot$ z

graphically : replace the maximal $\lessdot$ diagrams

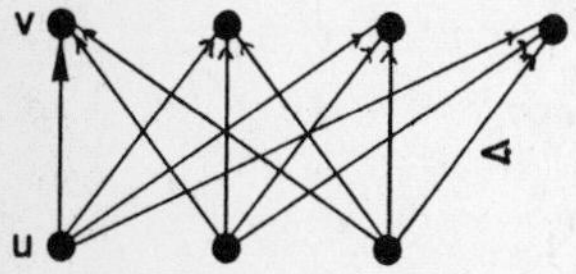

by the $\lessdot$ diagram

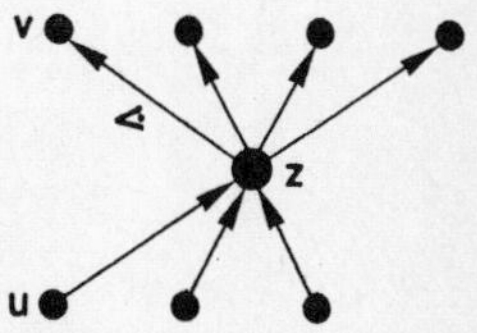

Note that the removal of z from the right diagram yields again the left diagram, and that both diagrams are N dense .

This construction is essential for a fundamental theory of change, applicable to the introduction of "changing truth value" into the logic of assertions on the holding of states :
Assume that we know nothing about changes, transitions or interactions. This amounts to having, instead of the rich structure $(X,<)$, only the structure $(S, < \cap S \times S)$.

N density (in its rewritten version) places an important restriction on that structure. But if it is N dense , the construction of filling all G 2 gaps restitutes the full $(X,<)$ by adding all changes T in accord with the extensionality postulate.

This means : If we want continuous temporal logic, we need Space (co ≠ id) and not infinitesimal time-"steps", accompanied by an uncountable infinity of states. -

Engineers will admit that the accuracy of measurement ends, in all kinds of practice, in indistinguishability (a similarity relation like co) and not in infinitesimality. We have tried to capture this insight of experience in our theory. -

We have proposed 21 highly interdependent assumptions on physical concurrency; while their number can be diminished, we have not done so, as we wanted to show the many conceptual facets of concurrency separately. We have not fixed an upper bound for the number of signals which may take part in a single interaction $t \in T$; we admit different bounds for different applications.

Could the 21 assumptions constitute a contradiction-free axiom system? Yes, for the graphical symbols of this Advanced Course are models of A o - A 18 , the infinite figure indicated is a model of A o - A 21 , and is the cycle-free unwinding of the finite figure.

As a matter of course, substructures of a structure (X,co) which fulfils A o - A 21 do not necessarily fulfil all those assumptions. In application, we do not consider, as a rule, the totality of all signals. Of what use, then, can be concurrency theory in the practice of applications, where many of the given assumptions do not hold, or cannot be verified ?

Answer : the theory tells how a given signal structure is connected with the environment, or how it must be refined to fit into some environment. We see, that in this respect, our assumptions play the very same role as the laws of physics play in engineering.

Is concurrency theory in some sense complete, at the present time ?
No : the assumptions on the dimension and topology of Space and Statespace are missing entirely. This remains a topic for future research.

How can concurrency theory contribute to the problem area of multiprocessing ?

1. By pointing out, in a formally precise way, many new conceptual facets of concurrency, including its truly fundamental nature;
2. By giving a physical basis for net theory (all concurrency structures with A_0 - A_{21} are nets) and by directing attention to the physically meaningful classes of nets;
3. By way of general net theory which permits, through continuous net mappings, to go to any desired higher level of description and to formulate the necessary high-level concepts.

The remark is in order here that all combinatorial topologies of arbitrary dimension can be constructed as quotient topologies of nets. This justifies the hope that all implementable signalling structures, discrete as well as continuous (digital as well as analog) may be completely described in terms of concurrency, using combinatorial mathematical tools only.
Under this aspect, today's problems of multiprocessing appear to be extremely specialized. Could it be that this is the real reason why they are so difficult to solve ?

References :

[1] N. Wiener : A New Theory of Measurement :
A Study in the Logic of Mathematics
Proceedings of the London Mathematical Society,
Vol.19, 1919, pp.181-205 London 1921

Modern Usage in e.g. :

J. Pfanzagl : Die axiomatischen Grundlagen einer
allgemeinen Theorie des Messens.
Physica Verlag Würzburg 1959

[2] C.A. Petri : Concurrency and Continuity
7th European Workshop on Petri Nets,
Oxford, June 1986
Extended version to appear in:
Advances in Petri Nets 1986
Springer L N C S , 1987

[3] C.A. Petri : Concurrency
In: W.Brauer (Ed): Net Theory and Applications
L N C S Vol.84, pp.251-260.
Berlin, Heidelberg, New York - Springer Verlag 1980

[4] H. Plünnecke : K-density, N-density and Finiteness Properties
In: G.Rozenberg (Ed.): Advances in Petri Nets 1984
L N C S Vol.188, pp.392-412
Berlin, Heidelberg, New York, Tokyo -
Springer Verlag 1985

SECTION 1

ELEMENTARY NET SYSTEMS – FUNDAMENTALS

P. S. Thiagarajan: *Elementary Net Systems*

G. Rozenberg: *Behaviour of Elementary Net Systems*

C. Fernández: *Non-sequential Processes*

ELEMENTARY NET SYSTEMS

P.S. Thiagarajan

The Institute of Mathematical Sciences
Madras - India

ABSTRACT Our aim will be to introduce and discuss the basic system model of net theory called Condition/Event Systems. We shall start with a brief discussion of the twin notions of states and transitions as viewed within net theory. This will motivate the restrictions placed on the Condition/Event System model. We shall then introduce nets and construct Condition/Event Systems with the help of nets.

A major objective will be to use our system model to formalize the fundamental situations associated with the behaviour of a distributed system. In particular, we shall consider phenomena such as conflict (choice), concurrency and confusion. This will then lead to the identification of a number of interesting behavioural sub-classes of Condition/Event Systems.

Key words: Elementary Net Systems, Conditions, Events, Transition Systems, Sequence, Choice, Concurrency, Confusion, C/E-systems

CONTENTS

0. INTRODUCTION

A major part of net Theory may be viewed as a theory of distributed systems and processes. Here we shall introduce some basic aspects of this part of net theory. More precisely, we shall construct a simple model of distributed systems called Elementary Net Systems (abbreviated as EN systems from now on). We can then sketch some of the foundational aspects of net theory with the help of this model.

The focus of interest here is distributed systems. The net theoretic view of processes is presented in this course elsewhere (in particular, see the contributions by C.Fernândez, C.A.Petri, G.Rozenberg and G.Winskel). In the next section we discuss briefly how states and changes-of-states are viewed at a primitive level in our theory. It turns out that nets are the appropriate mathematical objects for capturing this view of states and changes-of-states. Hence, in Section 2, we present nets and develop some related notions and terminology. This will lead - in Section 3 - to the definition of the EN system model. In Section 4 we justify the assumptions made in net theory at the foundational level regarding states and changes-of-states. We do this by viewing EN systems as transition systems. (To the uninitiated reader: Transition systems are a simple and general system model in which practically no assumptions are made regarding the relationship between states and changes-of-states.) We show that EN systems are, in principle, transition systems that satisfy a strong extensionality principle with regards to changes-of-states.

Section 5 contains the essence of our presentation. In this section we define, with the help of the EN system model, the three fundamental concepts underlying the study of distributed systems: causal dependence, choice and concurrency. We point out how net theory is ideally suited for defining these concepts in a simple and precise manner. Moreover, we show how the main source of difficulty in the study of distributed systems - namely, the interplay between choice and concurrency - can be identified in our theory both formally and graphically in a direct fashion.

In the last section we introduce a system model called Condition/Event Systems (C/E systems, for short). Wherein net theory is viewed in a larger perspective - as opposed to the narrower approach taken here - C/E systems are better suited to serve the role of the basic system model. A C/E system is essentially an EN system which satisfies some additional restrictions. We conclude by discussing the motivations underlying these additional restrictions.

1. CONDITIONS AND EVENTS

A theory of distributed systems is distinguished by the way it chooses to formulate the twin notions of states and changes-of-states (henceforth referred to as transitions). The guiding principles adopted by net theory in formulating these two notions are :

(i) States and transitions are two intertwined but distinct notions that deserve an even-handed treatment.

(ii) Both states and transitions are distributed entities.

(iii) The extent of change caused by a transition is fixed; it does not depend on the state at which it occurs.

(iv) A transition is enabled to occur at a state if and only if the fixed extent of change associated with the transition is possible at that state.

Here we wish to discuss, in an informal fashion, the first two of these principles. In Section 3 and 4 it will become clear that the EN system model is a simple formalization of all the four principles.

At the basic level of system description, we start with a set of atomic states called conditions denoted B and a set of atomic transitions called events denoted E. By setting $B \cap E = \emptyset$ we agree to treat states and transitions as distinct entities.

A (distributed) state is defined to be a set of conditions holding concurrently. A (distributed) transition is defined to be a set of events occurring concurrently. In net theory, at this basic level, states are referred to as cases and transitions are referred to as steps. A transition relation then specifies how cases are transformed into cases by the occurrences of steps. Here is an example.

Example 1.1

$$B = \{b_1,b_2,b_3,b_4,b_5\}$$

$$E = \{e_1,e_2,e_3\}$$

$$C = \{\{b_1,b_2\},\{b_2,b_3\},\{b_1,b_4\},\{b_3,b_4\},\{b_5\}\}$$

$$U = \{\{e_1\},\{e_2\},\{e_1,e_2\},\{e_3\}\}$$

Here C is the set of cases and U is the set of steps. We have specified the transition relation graphically. For example, in this system the case $\{b_1,b_2\}$ can be transformed into case $\{b_3,b_4\}$ by the occurrence of the step $\{e_1,e_2\}$. Stated differently, the event e_1 and

e_2 can occur concurrently at the case in which the conditions b_1 and b_2 hold (and no other condition holds). When both e_1 and e_2 have occurred, the system ends up in the case $\{b_3,b_4\}$.

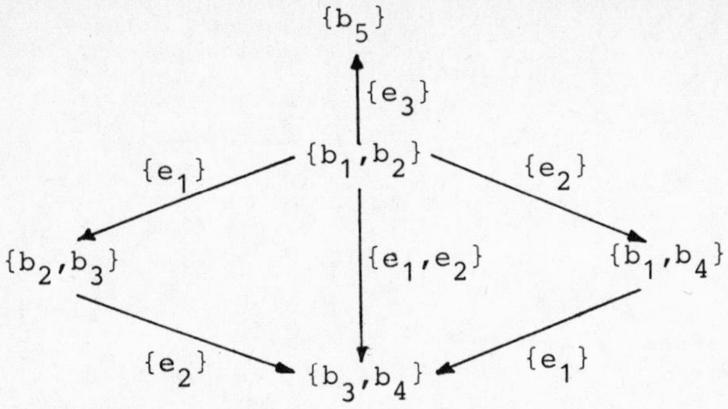

Figure 1.1

Two key questions that now arise are :

(i) When can a step (i.e. a set of events) occur (concurrently) at a case ?

(ii) What is the resulting case when a step occurs at a case ?

Net theory provides elegant answers to these questions by postulating a <u>fixed</u> neighbourhood relationship between the conditions and the events. This then leads to a "structural" transition relation that relates potential cases to potential cases via potential steps. As a result, a system can be specified by naming the conditions, the events, the neighbourhood relationship - called <u>the flow relation</u> - between the elements of B and E and an initial case denoted c_{in} . The set of actual cases, the set of actual steps and transition relation associated with the system then all become <u>derived</u> notions.

Our aim now is to formalize and explicate these informal ideas. The first step is to introduce the mathematical objects called <u>nets</u> using which one can model the fixed neighbourhood relationship between the conditions and the events.

2. NETS

<u>Definition 2.1</u> A <u>net</u> is a triple $N = (S,T;F)$ such that

(i) $S \cup T \neq \emptyset$ and $S \cap T = \emptyset$.

(ii) $F \subseteq (S \times T) \cup (T \times S)$.

(iii) $\underline{dom}(F) \cup \underline{ran}(F) = S \cup T$ where

$\underline{dom}(F) = \{x \in S \cup T \mid \exists y \in S \cup T .\ (x,y) \in F\}$ and

$\underline{ran}(F) = \{y \in S \cup T \mid \exists x \in S \cup T .\ (x,y) \in F\}$.

Thus a net may be viewed as a non-empty bipartite directed graph without any isolated nodes. Let $N = (S,T;F)$ be a net. Then S is the set of S-elements, T is the set of T-elements and F is the flow relation of N. $X = S \cup T$ is the set of elements of N. We shall denote as S_N (T_N, X_N) the set of S-elements (T-elements, elements) of the net N. The flow relation of the net will be denoted as F_N. Often, the subscript N will be dropped if the net under question is clear from the context.

In diagrams, the S-elements will be drawn as circles, the T-elements as boxes and the members of the flow relation will be indicated through appropriate directed arcs. Here is an example of a net specified in its graphical form.

Example 2.2

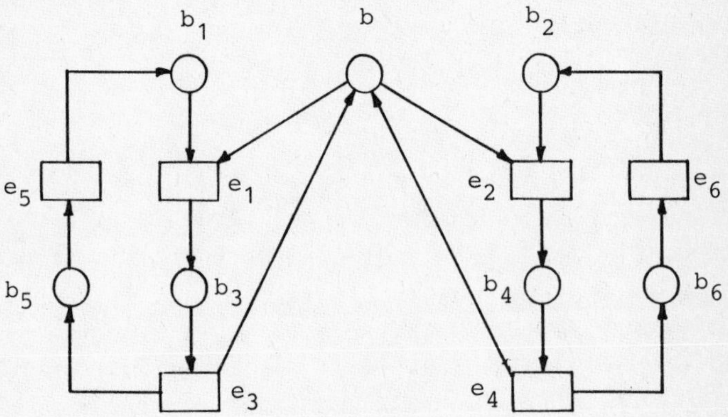

Figure 2.1

In this net, (b_1,e_1), (e_3,b_5) and (b,e_1) are members of the flow relation. (b,e_3) is not in the flow relation.

A very useful notational aid that captures a "local" fragment of the flow relation can be defined as follows.

Definition 2.3 Let $N = (S,T;F)$ be a net, $x \in X_N$ and $Y \subseteq X_N$.

(i) ${}^{\bullet}x = \{y \in X_N \mid (y,x) \in F\}$ is the pre-set of x.

(ii) $x^{\bullet} = \{y \in X_N \mid (x,y) \in F\}$ is the post-set of x.

(iii) $\cdot Y = \bigcup_{x \in y} \cdot x$ and $Y^{\cdot} = \bigcup_{x \in y} x^{\cdot}$.

In Example 2.2, $b^{\cdot} = \{e_1, e_2\}$, $e_3^{\cdot} = \{b_5, b\}$ and $\{e_5, e_6\}^{\cdot} = \{b_1, b_2\}$. This dot notation is often used for imposing certain syntactic restrictions on nets. To illustrate, we present two such restrictions.

Definition 2.4 Let $N = (S,T;F)$ be a net.

(i) N is pure iff $\forall x \in X_N . \; \cdot x \cap x^{\cdot} = \emptyset$.

(ii) N is simple iff $\forall x, y \in X_N . \; \cdot x = \cdot y \wedge x^{\cdot} = y^{\cdot} \Rightarrow x = y$.

The net shown in Figure 2.1 is pure and simple.

Depending on the intended applications, a wide range of interpretations can be attached to the elements of a net. In this course, a net will be predominantly viewed as a representation of the underlying structure of a distributed system. As a result, the S-elements will be interpreted as the local states and the T-elements will be interpreted as the local transitions of a system. The flow relation would then capture the neighbourhood relationship between the local states and local transitions.

In the present work we shall use the S-elements to represent the conditions and the T-elements to represent the events in order to arrive at the basic model. Consequently, throughout what follows, we will work with nets of the form $N = (B,E;F)$. Moreover, $\cdot e$ will be called the set of pre-conditions and $e^{\cdot}$ will be called the set of post-conditions of the event e .

We now wish to associate a "structural" transition relation with a net using which potential cases can be transformed into potential cases via potential steps. This will then at once lead us to the EN system model. We shall first develop the transition relation we are after through a sequence of informal steps (no pun intended).

Let $N = (B,E;F)$ be a net, $c \subseteq B$ and $e \in E$. We now ask : When can e occur at c ? The answer provided by net theory is : e can occur at c iff all the pre-conditions hold at c and none of the post-conditions hold at c . In other words, $\cdot e \subseteq c$ and $e^{\cdot} \cap c = \emptyset$.

Returning to Example 2.2, let $c = \{b_5, b, b_6\}$. In diagrams, a case will be shown by marking (i.e. by placing a small darkened circle) just those conditions that are members of c .
Here is the case $\{b_5, b, b_6\}$ marked on the net of Example 2.2.

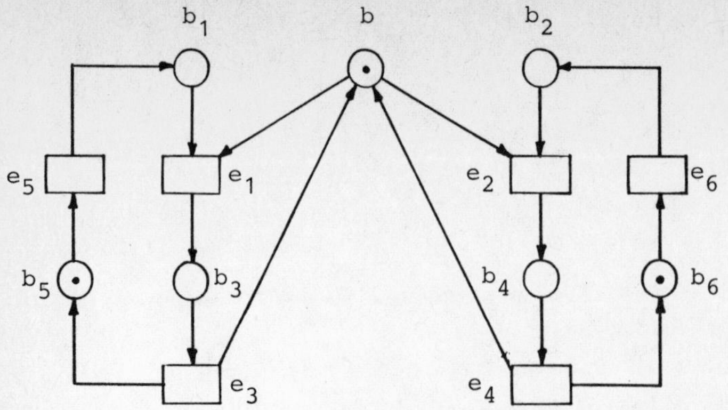

Figure 2.2

At this case both e_5 and e_6 are enabled. No other event is enabled at this case.

Let $N = (B,E;F)$ be a net, $c \subseteq B$ and $e \in E$ such that e can occur at c. We now ask: What is the result of e occurring at c? The net theoretic answer is: When e occurs at c, the pre-conditions of e cease to hold and the post-conditions of e begin to hold. The remaining parts of the case remain unaffected. Consequently, the resulting case is $(c - {}^{\bullet}e) \cup e^{\bullet}$.

In this sense, the change-of-state produced by an event occurrence is confined strictly to its immediate neighbourhood.

At the case shown in Figure 2.2, e_5 can occur. When e_5 occurs, the resulting case is $\{b_1,b,b_6\}$.

Let $N = (B,E;F)$ be a net, $c \subseteq B$ and $u \subseteq E$. We now ask: When can the events in u occur concurrently at c? In other words, when can the step u occur at c? The answer provided by net theory is: u can occur at c iff the events in u can individually occur at c without interfering with each other.

As we have seen, the effect of an occurrence of the event e is confined to ${}^{\bullet}e \cup e^{\bullet}$. Hence the requirement that the occurrences of the events in u should not interfere with each other can be formalized as:

$$\forall e_1, e_2 \in u \,.\; e_1 \neq e_2 \Rightarrow ({}^{\bullet}e_1 \cup e_1^{\bullet}) \cap ({}^{\bullet}e_2 \cup e_2^{\bullet}) = \emptyset \,.$$

At the case shown in Figure 2.2, the step $\{e_5,e_6\}$ is enabled to occur.

Finally, let $N = (B,E;F)$ be a net, $c \subseteq B$ and $u \subseteq E$ such that the step u is enabled to occur at c. We ask: What is the result of u occurring at c ? The answer is: The result is the "sum" of the results of the events in u occurring individually at c. Stated differently, when u occurs at c the resulting case c' is given by :

$$c' = (c - {}^{\bullet}u) \cup u^{\bullet} .$$

In the example shown in Figure 2.2, when $\{e_5,e_6\}$ occurs at $\{b_5,b,b_6\}$, the resulting case is $\{b_1,b,b_2\}$. At this case both e_1 and e_2 are enabled. However $\{e_1,e_2\}$ is not a step at this case.

The three definitions to follow will formalize these ideas. The alert reader might have noticed that the ideas sketched above confirm to the principles laid down at the beginning of Section 1. We will return to this point in Section 4.

Definition 2.5 Let $N = (B,E;F)$ be a net and $u \subseteq E$. Then,

$$\underline{Ind}(u) \overset{def}{\Longleftrightarrow} \forall e_1,e_2 \in u \, . \; e_1 \neq e_2 \Rightarrow ({}^{\bullet}e_1 \cup e_1^{\bullet}) \cap ({}^{\bullet}e_2 \cup e_2^{\bullet}) = \emptyset$$

$\underline{Ind}(u)$ denotes the fact that u constitutes a set of (pair-wise) independent events.

Definition 2.6 Let $N = (B,E;F)$ be a net. $c \subseteq B$ and $u \subseteq E$.

Then u is (a step) enabled at c iff $\underline{Ind}(u)$ and ${}^{\bullet}u \subseteq c$ and $u^{\bullet} \cap c = \emptyset$.

We let $c[u>_N$ denote the fact that u is enabled at c . If $u = \{e\}$ is a singleton then we shall write $c[e>_N$ instead of $c[\{e\}>_N$.

Finally, we can put down the definition we are after. In what follows, we let $P(Y)$ denote the set of subsets of the set Y .

Definition 2.7 Let $N = (B,E;F)$ be a net. Then $\longrightarrow_N \; P(B) \times P(E) \times P(B)$ denotes the (elementary) transition relation associated with N and is given by :

$$\longrightarrow_N = \{(c,u,c') \mid c[u>_N \wedge c' = (c - {}^{\bullet}u) \cup u^{\bullet}\} .$$

We will often write $c[u>_N c'$ instead of $(c,u,c') \in \longrightarrow_N$. Where N is clear from the context we will drop the subscript N and simply write $c[u>c'$. As before, if $u = \{e\}$ is a singleton, then we shall write $c[e>c'$ instead of $c[\{e\}>c'$. We conclude this section with two simple but very useful observations.

Theorem 2.8 Let $N = (B,E;F)$ be a net, $c,c' \subseteq B$ and $u \subseteq E$ such that $c[u>c'$. Suppose $\{u_1,u_2\}$ is a partition of u (i.e. $u_1 \cup u_2 = u$ and $u_1 \cap u_2 = \emptyset$) . Then there exists $c'' \subseteq B$ such that

$c[u_1>c''$ and $c''[u_2>c'$. (In fact, $c'' = (c - {}^{\bullet}u_1) \cup u_1^{\bullet})$.

Proof Follows easily from the definitions.

Theorem 2.9 Let $N = (B,E;F)$ be a net, $c \subseteq B$ and $e \in E$ such that $c[e>$. Then ${}^{\bullet}e \cap e^{\bullet} = \emptyset$.

Proof Follows at once from ${}^{\bullet}e \subseteq c$ and $e^{\bullet} \cap c = \emptyset$.

3. ELEMENTARY NET SYSTEMS

Definition 3.1 An Elementary Net System (EN system) is a quadruple $\mathcal{N} = (B,E;F,c_{in})$ where $(B,E;F)$ is a net called the underlying net of and $c_{in} \subseteq B$ is called the initial case of $\mathcal{N}$.

Figure 2.2 is the graphical representation of an EN system with the initial case marked in the diagram.

Let $\mathcal{N} = (B,E;F,c_{in})$ be an EN system. Then $N_{\mathcal{N}}$ will denote the underlying net of $\mathcal{N}$. Where $\mathcal{N}$ is clear from the context (as it will almost always be) we will write just N instead of $N_{\mathcal{N}}$. $B_{\mathcal{N}}$ ($E_{\mathcal{N}}$, $F_{\mathcal{N}}$, $X_{\mathcal{N}}$) will denote the set of conditions (events, flow relations, elements) of $\mathcal{N}$. Now as promised in Section 1, we can quickly derive the state space (i.e. the set of cases), the set of steps and the transition relation associated with the EN system $\mathcal{N}$ from $\longrightarrow_N$.

Definition 3.2 Let $\mathcal{N} = (B,E;F,c_{in})$ be an EN system. Then $C_{\mathcal{N}}$ denotes the set of cases of $\mathcal{N}$ and is the least subset of $P(B)$ satisfying :

(i) $c_{in} \in C_{\mathcal{N}}$.

(ii) If $c \in C_{\mathcal{N}}$, $u \subseteq E$ and $c' \subseteq B$ such that $(c,u,c') \in \longrightarrow_N$ (recall that $N = (B,E;F)$), then $c' \in C_{\mathcal{N}}$.

For the EN system shown in Figure 2.2, $\{b_3,b_2\}$ is a case of the system but $\{b_3,b_4\}$ is not a case of the system.

Definition 3.3 Let $\mathcal{N} = (B,E;F,c_{in})$ be an EN system. Then $U_{\mathcal{N}}$ denotes the set of steps of $\mathcal{N}$ and is given by :

$$U = \{u \subseteq E \mid \exists c,c' \in C_{\mathcal{N}} . \ (c,u,c') \in \longrightarrow_N\}$$

(Once again, $N = (B,E;F)$.)

Definition 3.4 Let $\mathcal{N}$ be an EN system. Then $\longrightarrow_{\mathcal{N}}$ is the transition relation of $\mathcal{N}$ and is $\longrightarrow_N$ (where $N = N_{\mathcal{N}}$) restricted to $C_{\mathcal{N}} \times U_{\mathcal{N}} \times C_{\mathcal{N}}$.

The fact that steps can be broken up into sub-steps for nets (as stated in Theorem 2.8) holds also for EN systems.

Theorem 3.5 Let N be an EN system and $(c,u,c') \in \longrightarrow_N$. Suppose $\{u_1,u_2\}$ is a partition of u . Then there exists $c'' \in C_N$ such that (c,u_1,c'') , $(c'',u_2,c') \in \longrightarrow_N$.

Proof Follows easily from the definition of C_N .

At this stage we have a simple system model using which the fundamental notions of net theory can be defined and explained. However it will be very convenient - from a purely technical standpoint - to impose a restriction on our model before we proceed to develop the theory. Fortunately, it turns out that imposing this restriction does not involve any loss of generality.

The point is that in an EN system the requirement for deciding whether or not an event e can occur at a case c has both an "input" component (all the pre-conditions of e must hold at c) and an "output" component (none of the post-conditions of e can hold at c). By demanding a property called contact-freeness we can obtain a model in which for the event e to occur at a case c , it is sufficient that all the pre-conditions of e hold at c .

There are a number of reasons for demanding contact-freeness. Firstly the fundamental situations - to be discussed in Section 5 - that can arise in the history of an EN system are easier to classify if we assume contact-freeness. Secondly, the notion of a non-sequential process generated by an EN system (see the contribution by G.Rozenberg) can be formulated in a clean way only for contact-free EN systems. Finally, it is contact-free EN systems that can be generalized smoothly to arrive at a more expressive model commonly known as Petri nets.

Definition 3.6 Let $N = (B,E;F,c_{in})$ be an EN system. Then N is contact-free iff $\forall e \in E \,.\, \forall c \in C \,.\, {}^\bullet e \subseteq c \Rightarrow e^\bullet \cap c = \emptyset$.

The EN system shown in Figure 2.2 is contact-free. Figure 3.1 is a system which is not contact-free.

We will now show how to transform an EN system N into a contact-free EN system N' , such that N and N' are behaviourally equivalent in a strong sense. The idea is to add to N the "complement" of every condition in N . We first illustrate the idea with an example before giving the formal definition.

Example 3.1

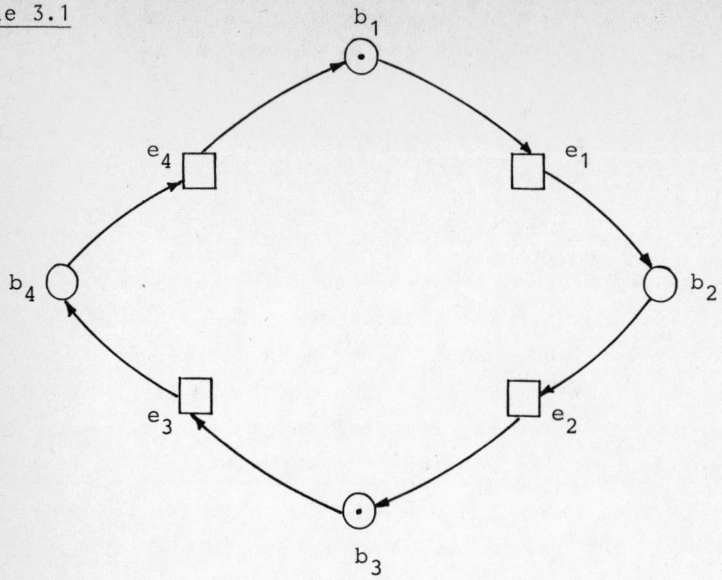

Figure 3.1

In Figure 3.2 we have shown the EN system obtained by applying our transformation to the EN system shown in Figure 3.1. It might be instructive to verify that the new system is contact-free.

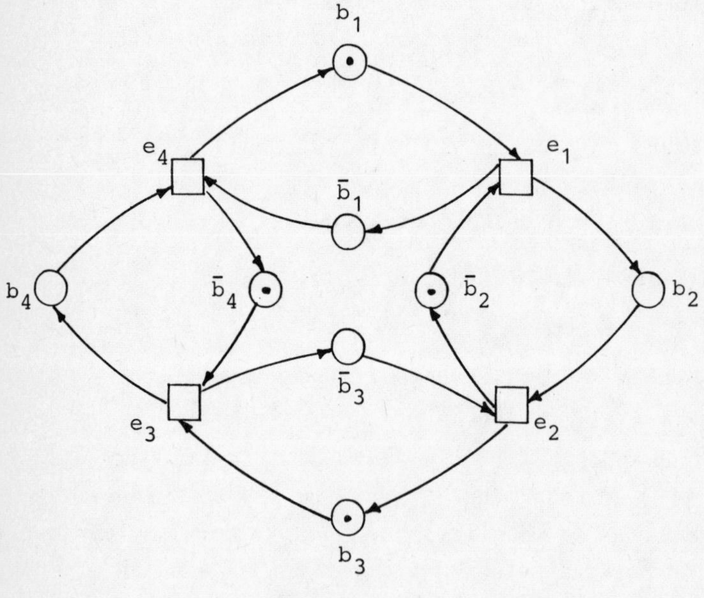

Figure 3.2

Definition 3.7 Let $N = (B,E;F,c_{in})$ be an EN system. Let $\overline{B}$ be a set disjoint from $B \cup E$ and $f: B \to \overline{B}$ be a bijection. (Throughout what follows, we denote $f(b)$ as $\overline{b}$ for every $b \in B$.) Then the S-complementation of N relative to $(\overline{B},f)$ is $N' = (B',E';F',c_{in})$ where

(i) $B' = B \cup \overline{B}$

(ii) $E' = E$

(iii) $F' = F \cup \{(e,\overline{b}) \mid e \in E \wedge (b,e) \in F\}$
$\cup \{(\overline{b},e) \mid e \in E \wedge (e,b) \in F\}$

(iv) $c'_{in} = c_{in} \cup f(B - c_{in})$

We now wish to show that the effects of applying this transformation are quite pleasant. For doing so, it will be convenient to first transport the notion of a step being enabled at a case to EN systems.

Definition 3.8 Let $N = (B,E;F,c_{in})$ be an EN system, $c \in C_N$ and $u \subseteq E$. Then u is enabled at c iff there exists $c' \in C$ such that $(c,u,c') \in \longrightarrow_N$.

We will let $c[u>_N$ denote the fact that u is enabled at c in the EN system N. Often we will drop the subscript N if N is clear from the context. For $u = \{e\}$, we will write $c[e>_N$ instead of $c[\{e\}>_N$.

We can now state the effects of applying the transformation specified in Definition 3.7.

Theorem 3.9 Let $N = (B,E;F,c_{in})$ be an EN system. Let $\overline{B}$, f and $N' = (B',E';F',c'_{in})$ be as specified in Definition 3.7. Then

(i) N' is an EN system.

(ii) $C_{N'} = \{c \cup f(B-c) \mid c \in C_N\}$.

(iii) $U_{N'} = U_N$.

(iv) $(c_1,u,c_2) \in \longrightarrow_N$ iff $(c_1 \cup f(B-c_1), u, c_2 \cup f(B-c_2)) \in \longrightarrow_{N'}$.

(v) N' is contact-free

Proof Clearly $N' = (B',E';F')$ is a net and $c'_{in} \subseteq B'$. Hence N' is an EN system. This establishes (i). We will not prove the remaining parts. We will however take the first step required for doing so.

Let $N = (B,E;F)$. We will use $\cdot$ to denote the dot relation associated with N and use $^\circ$ to denote the dot relation associated with N'. Thus ${}^{\bullet}x = \{y \in X_N \mid (y,x) \in F\}$ for $x \in X_N$ and $x^{\circ} = \{y \in X_{N'} \mid (x,y) \in F'\}$ for $x \in X_{N'}$, etc. It follows from the definition of N' that $\forall e \in E$. ${}^{\circ}e = {}^{\bullet}e \cup f(e^{\bullet})$ and $e^{\circ} = e^{\bullet} \cup f({}^{\bullet}e)$. The key step in the proof is to establish the following

<u>Claim</u> Let $c_1 \in C_N$ and $c_1' \in C_{N'}$, such that $c_1' = c_1 \cup f(B - c_1)$ Then

(i) $\forall e \in E$. $c_1[e\rangle_N$ iff $c_1'[e\rangle_{N'}$.

(ii) If $e \in E$ is enabled at c_1 then $(c_1' - e) \cup e = c_2 \cup f(B - c_2)$ where $c_2 = (c_1 - {}^{\bullet}e) \cup e^{\bullet}$

<u>Proof of Claim</u> (i) Let $c_1[e\rangle_N$. Then ${}^{\bullet}e \subseteq c_1$ and $e^{\bullet} \cap c_1 = \emptyset$. We need to show that ${}^{\circ}e \subseteq c_1'$ and $e^{\circ} \cap c_1' = \emptyset$. We know that ${}^{\circ}e = {}^{\bullet}e \cup f(e^{\bullet})$. Now ${}^{\bullet}e \subseteq c_1 \subseteq c_1 \cup f(B - c_1) = c_1'$. Since $e^{\bullet} \cap c_1 = \emptyset$ we have $e^{\bullet} \subseteq B - c_1$. Hence $f(e^{\bullet}) \subseteq f(B - c_1) \subseteq c_1 \cup f(B - c_1) = c_1'$. We now have ${}^{\circ}e \subseteq c_1'$.

Since $e^{\bullet} \cap c_1 = \emptyset$ and $e^{\bullet} \subseteq B$ and $B \cap f(B) = \emptyset$ we have $e^{\bullet} \cap c_1' = \emptyset$. Now ${}^{\bullet}e \subseteq c_1$ implies that ${}^{\bullet}e \cap (B - c_1) = \emptyset$. Since f is a bijection $f({}^{\bullet}e) \cap f(B - c_1) = \emptyset$. Clearly $f({}^{\bullet}e) \cap c_1 = \emptyset$. From $e = e^{\bullet} \cup f({}^{\bullet}e)$ is now follows that $e \cap c_1' = \emptyset$.

By a similar argument one can show that $c_1'[e\rangle_{N'}$ implies that $c_1[e\rangle_N$.

(ii) Assume that e is enabled at c_1. Then by part (i) of the claim, e is also enabled at c_1'. We must show that $(c_1' - {}^{\circ}e) \cup e^{\circ} = c_2 \cup f(B - c_2)$ where $c_2 = (c_1 - {}^{\bullet}e) \cup e^{\bullet}$.

$$c_1' - {}^{\circ}e = (c_1 \cup f(B - c_1)) - ({}^{\bullet}e \cup f(e^{\bullet}))$$
$$= (c_1 - {}^{\bullet}e) \cup (f(B - c_1) - f(e^{\bullet})).$$

Since $e^{\circ} = e^{\bullet} \cup f({}^{\bullet}e)$ we then have

$$(c_1' - {}^{\circ}e) \cup e^{\circ} = (c_1 - {}^{\bullet}e) \cup (f(B - c_1) - f(e^{\bullet})) \cup (e^{\bullet} \cup f({}^{\bullet}e))$$
$$= ((c_1 - {}^{\bullet}e) \cup e^{\bullet}) \cup ((f(B - c_1) - f(e^{\bullet})) \cup f({}^{\bullet}e)).$$

But $(c_1 - {}^{\bullet}e) \cup e^{\bullet} = c_2$. Hence we must know that $(f(B - c_1) - f(e^{\bullet})) \cup f({}^{\bullet}e) = f(B - c_2)$.

Suppose $\bar{b} \in f(B - c_1) - f(e^{\bullet})$. Then $b \in B - c_1$ and $b \notin e^{\bullet}$. But $b \in B - c_1$ implies that $b \notin c_1$ which in turn implies that $b \notin c_1 - {}^{\bullet}e$. We now have $b \notin c_1 - {}^{\bullet}e$ and $b \notin e^{\bullet}$. Hence $b \notin (c_1 - {}^{\bullet}e) \cup e^{\bullet} = c_2$. Thus $f(b) = \bar{b} \in f(B - c_2)$.

Suppose that $\bar{b} \in f({}^{\bullet}e)$. Then $b \in {}^{\bullet}e$ and hence $b \notin c_1 - {}^{\bullet}e$. Since ${}^{\bullet}e \cap e^{\bullet} = \emptyset$, we have $b \notin e^{\bullet}$ also.

Thus $b \notin (c_1 - {}^\cdot e) \cup e^\cdot = c_2$ and once again we have shown that $f(b) = \bar{b} \in f(B - c_2)$. This establishes $(f(B - c_1) - f(e^\cdot)) \cup f({}^\cdot e) \subseteq f(B - c_2)$.

To show inclusion in the other direction, consider $\bar{b} \in f(B - c_2)$. Hence $b \in B - c_2$. From $b \notin c_2$ it follows that $b \notin c_1 - {}^\cdot e$ and $b \notin e^\cdot$. Suppose $b \in c_1$. Then $b \in {}^\cdot e$ so that $f(b) = \bar{b} \in f({}^\cdot e)$.

If $b \notin c_1$ then $b \in B - c_1$ so that $f(b) = \bar{b} \in f(B - c_1)$. We already know that $b \notin e^\cdot$ and hence $f(b) = \bar{b} \notin f(e^\cdot)$. Therefore $b \notin c_1$ implies that $\bar{b} \in f(B - c_1) - f(e^\cdot)$ and we now have the required inclusion. This establishes the claim.

The remaining parts of the proof consists of observing that $c'_{in} = c_{in} \cup f(B - c_{in})$ followed by a bit of induction with repeated appeals to the claim established above.

It turns out that $\mathcal{N}$ and $\mathcal{N}'$ - as in Definition 3.7 - are equivalent to each other in the strongest possible behavioural sense. The interested reader is invited to consider the notion of behavioural equivalence called case graph isomorphism introduced by G.Rozenberg in his contribution. Thus demanding contact-freeness does not involve any loss of generality. To conclude this section, we shall verify that the enabling requirements for the event occurrences are indeed simpler for contact-free EN systems. To do so, we first introduce an "input-only" version of an independence set of events.

<u>Definition 3.10</u> Let $N = (B,E;F)$ be a net and $u \subseteq E$. Then

$$\underline{ind}(u) \overset{def}{\Longleftrightarrow} \forall e_1, e_2 \in u \,.\; e_1 \neq e_2 \Rightarrow {}^\cdot e_1 \cap {}^\cdot e_2 = \emptyset .$$

Clearly $\underline{Ind}(u)$ implies $\underline{ind}(u)$ but the converse is in general false.

<u>Theorem 3.11</u> Let $\mathcal{N} = (B,E;F,c_{in})$ be a contact-free EN system, $c \in C_{\mathcal{N}}$ and $u \subseteq E$. Then $c[u\rangle_{\mathcal{N}}$ iff $\underline{ind}(u)$ and ${}^\cdot u \subseteq c$.

<u>Proof</u>

$\Rightarrow$ By definition there exist $c' \in C_{\mathcal{N}}$ such that $(c,u,c') \in \longrightarrow_{\mathcal{N}}$. This implies that $(c,u,c') \in \longrightarrow_N$ where N is the underlying net of $\mathcal{N}$. From the definition of $\longrightarrow_N$ it now follows that ${}^\cdot u \subseteq c$ and $\underline{Ind}(u)$. But $\underline{Ind}(u)$ at once implies $\underline{ind}(u)$.

$\Leftarrow$ We will first show that $u^\cdot \cap c = \emptyset$. Consider $e \in u$. Since ${}^\cdot u \subseteq c$, we have ${}^\cdot e \subseteq c$. $\mathcal{N}$ is contact-free. Hence $e^\cdot \cap c = \emptyset$. This establishes $u^\cdot \cap c = \emptyset$.

Next we show that $\underline{\text{Ind}}(u)$. To this end, consider $e_1, e_2 \in u$ with $e_1 \neq e_2$. We must verify that $({}^\bullet e_1 \cup e_1^\bullet) \cap ({}^\bullet e_2 \cup e_2^\bullet) = \emptyset$. ${}^\bullet e_1 \cap {}^\bullet e_2 = \emptyset$ follows from $\underline{\text{ind}}(u)$. ${}^\bullet e_1 \cap e_2^\bullet \neq \emptyset$ would imply that $e_2^\bullet \cap c \neq \emptyset$ because ${}^\bullet e_1 \subseteq c$. But then we also have ${}^\bullet e_2 \subseteq c$. Now ${}^\bullet e_2 \subseteq c$ and $e_2^\bullet \cap c \neq \emptyset$ contradict the contact-freeness of N . Hence ${}^\bullet e_1 \cap e_2^\bullet = \emptyset$. By symmetry ${}^\bullet e_2 \cap {}^\bullet e_1 = \emptyset$.

Suppose that $e_1^\bullet \cap e_2^\bullet \neq \emptyset$. We know that ${}^\bullet e_1 \subseteq c$ and $e_1^\bullet \cap c = \emptyset$. Hence $(c, e_1, c_1) \in \longrightarrow_N$ where $c_1 = (c - {}^\bullet e_1) \cup e_1^\bullet$ and N is the underlying net of N . But $c \in C_N$. Hence $c_1 \in C_N$. Since ${}^\bullet e \cap {}^\bullet e_2 = \emptyset$ we have ${}^\bullet e_2 \subseteq c_1$. Therefore, $e_1^\bullet \cap e_2^\bullet \neq \emptyset$ would lead to $e_2^\bullet \cap c_1 \neq \emptyset$ because $e_1^\bullet \subseteq c_1$. And this contradicts the contact-freeness of N .

We now have proved $\underline{\text{Ind}}(u)$ and $u^\bullet \cap c = \emptyset$; ${}^\bullet u \subseteq c$ by hypothesis. Hence $(c, u, c') \in \longrightarrow_N$ where $c' = (c - {}^\bullet u) \cup u^\bullet$. From $c \in C_N$ it follows that $c' \in C_N$. Therefore $(c, u, c') \in \longrightarrow_N$. We now have $c[u>$.

In contrast, the enabling requirement for EN systems in general looks as follows :

<u>Theorem 3.12</u> Let $N = (B, E; F, c_{in})$ be an EN system (not necessarily contact-free). Let $c \in C$ and $u \subseteq E$. Then $c[u>_N$ iff $\underline{\text{Ind}}(u)$ and ${}^\bullet u \subseteq c$ and $u^\bullet \cap c = \emptyset$.

<u>Proof</u> Trivial .

Thus contact-freeness does yield a simpler enabling criterion.

4. EN SYSTEMS VIEWED AS TRANSITION SYSTEMS

In this section we wish to show that the EN system model satisfies the principles (in particular the last two) stated at the beginning of Section 1. This is best done by embedding EN systems in a more general framework that permits a wide range of assumptions regarding states and transitions. This more general framework is called transition systems.

<u>Definition 4.1</u> A <u>transition system</u> is a quadruple $TS = (S, A, \rightarrow, s_0)$

where (i) S is a set of <u>states</u>

(ii) A is a set of <u>actions</u>

(iii) $\rightarrow \subseteq S \times A \times S$ is the <u>transition relation</u>

(iv) $s_0 \in S$ is the <u>initial state</u> .

Example 4.2 $TS = (S,A,\to,s_0)$ with $S = \{s_0,s_1,s_2,s_3,s_4\}$, $A = \{a,b,c\}$ and $\to = \{(s_0,a,s_1)\ ,\ (s_0,a,s_2)\ \ (s_1,b,s_3)\ \ (s_2,c,s_4)\}$. Here is a graphical representation of TS following some obvious conventions.

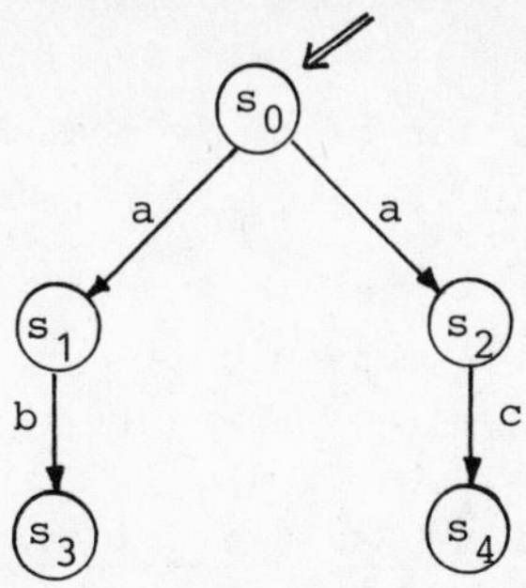

Figure 4.1

An EN system may be viewed as a transition system in the following sense.

Definition 4.3 Let $N = (B,E;F,c_{in})$ be an EN system. Then TS_N denotes the transition system associated with N and is the quadruple $TS_N = (C\ ,U\ ,\to_N,c_{in})$.

Clearly TS_N is a transition system. Below we show an EN system together with the transition system associated with it. (Throughout what follows, we will often write - both in diagrams and in text - the singleton $\{x\}$ as x . This should cause no confusion.)

Example 4.4

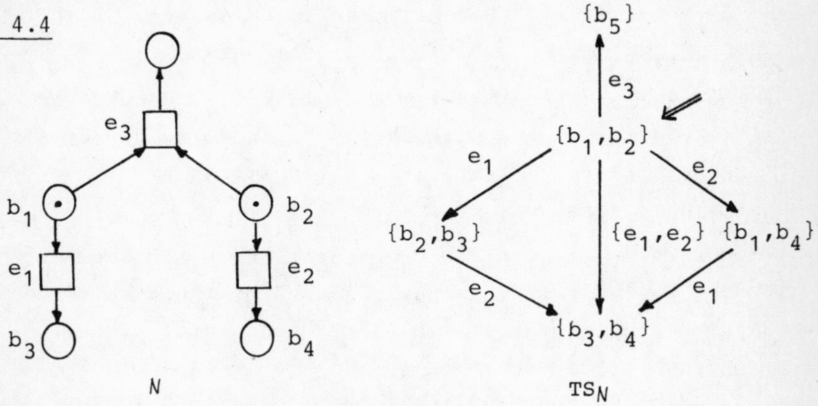

Figure 4.2

As the above example shows, the transition system associated with an EN system can be graphically represented as an edgelabelled directed graph with an initialized node. Such a directed graph - quite apart from its graphical representation - can be viewed and handled as a mathematical object in its own right. When one takes this approach w.r.t. the transition system associated with an EN system, the resulting object is called the case graph of the EN system.

Case graphs yield some appealing notions of behaviour and play a dominant role in the study decidability issues associated with marked nets (which are a generalization of EN systems). For more information concerning case graphs see the contribution by G.Rozenberg.

In order to evaluate the EN system model in the context of transition systems, it will be convenient - and in fact more or less necessary - to add some structure to transition systems.

Definition 4.5 A Condition / Event transition system (abbreviated as C/E transition system) is a 6-tuple $TS = (B,E,S,A,\rightarrow,s_0)$ where

(i) B is a set of conditions and E is a set of events such that $B \cap E = \emptyset$.

(ii) $S \subseteq P(B)$ and $A \subseteq P(E)$.

(iii) $(S,A,\rightarrow,s_0)$ is a transition system (in the sense of Definition 4.1)

Thus a C/E transition system is a transition system whose states are composed out of sets of conditions and whose actions are composed out of sets of events. The following observation is obvious.

Theorem 4.6 Let $N = (B,E;F,c_{in})$ be an EN system. Then $TS_N = (B,E,C_N,U_N,\rightarrow_N,c_{in})$ is a C/E transition system.

From now on, for the EN system N, TS_N will denote the C/E transition system associated with N (as defined in Theorem 4.6). Moreover, unless otherwise stated, by a transition system we will mean a C/E transition system.

Let $TS = (B,E,S,A,\rightarrow,s_0)$ be a transition system and $(s,a,s') \in \rightarrow$. Now what is the change caused by the occurrence of the action a at s which results in s'? One natural measure of the change produced by this occurrence of a is : $(s-s', s'-s)$. After all, $s-s'$ are the conditions that cease to hold and $s'-s$ are the conditions that begin to hold as a result this occurrence of a which transforms s into s'. In general, different occurrences of a can produce different "amounts" of changes. Here is a trivial example.

Example 4.7

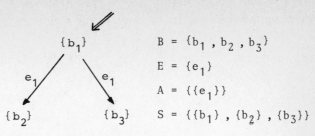

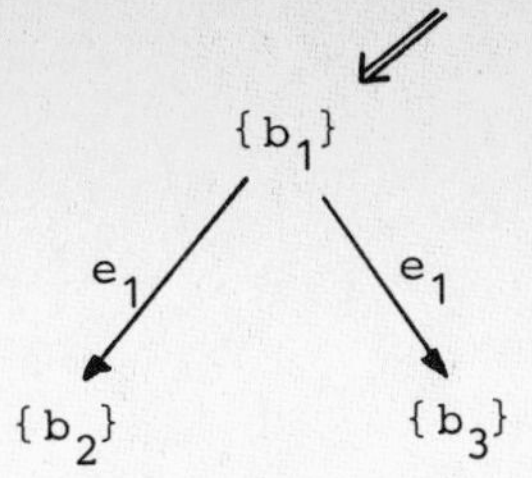

$B = \{b_1, b_2, b_3\}$

$E = \{e_1\}$

$A = \{\{e_1\}\}$

$S = \{\{b_1\}, \{b_2\}, \{b_3\}\}$

Figure 4.3

When e_1 occurs at $\{b_1\}$ to lead to $\{b_2\}$, the change produced is $(\{b_1\}, \{b_2\})$ but when e_1 occurs at $\{b_1\}$ to lead to $\{b_3\}$, the change produced is $(\{b_1\}, \{b_3\})$!
This cannot happen for transition systems associated with EN systems.

Theorem 4.8 Let TS_N be the transition system associated with the EN system $N = (B,E;F,c_{in})$.

(i) $\forall e \in E \,.\, (c_1,e,c_2), (c_3,e,c_4) \in \longrightarrow_N \Rightarrow (c_1-c_2, c_2-c_1) = (c_3-c_4, c_4-c_3)$.

(ii) In fact $\forall u \in U_N$.
$(c_1,u,c_2), (c_3,u,c_4) \in \longrightarrow_N \Rightarrow (c_1-c_2, c_2-c_1) = (c_3-c_4, c_4-c_3)$

Proof

(i) Let $e \in E$ and $c,c' \in C_N$ such that $(c,u,c') \in \longrightarrow_N$.
We shall show that $c-c' = {}^\bullet e$ and $c'-c = e^\bullet$.
From $(c,e,c') \in \longrightarrow_N$ it follows that $c' = (c - {}^\bullet e) \cup e^\bullet$.
Let $b \in c-c'$. Then $b \notin c'$ and therefore $b \notin c - {}^\bullet e$ (and $b \notin e^\bullet$).
But $b \in c$. Hence $b \in {}^\bullet e$ and we have $c-c' \subseteq {}^\bullet e$.
Now let $b \in {}^\bullet e$. $(c,e,c') \in \longrightarrow_N$ implies that $c[e>$ which in turn implies that ${}^\bullet e \subseteq c$ and $e^\bullet \cap c = \emptyset$. Hence from $b \in {}^\bullet e$ we have $b \in c$. ${}^\bullet e \subseteq c$ and $e^\bullet \cap c = \emptyset$ together imply that ${}^\bullet e \cap e^\bullet = \emptyset$. Hence from $b \in {}^\bullet e$ we can deduce $b \notin e^\bullet$.
Since $b \in c$ and $b \in {}^\bullet e$, we also have $b \notin c - {}^\bullet e$. Thus $b \notin e^\bullet$ and $b \notin c - {}^\bullet e$ which leads to $b \notin c'$.
Finally, from $b \in c$ we conclude $b \in c-c'$ so that ${}^\bullet e \subseteq c-c'$.
We now have $c-c' = {}^\bullet e$. By a similar argument one can also show $c'-c = e^\bullet$ and we omit it. Now let (c_1,e,c_2), $(c_3,e,c_4) \in \longrightarrow_N$. Then, by the above argument, $c_1-c_2 = {}^\bullet e = c_3-c_4$ and $c_2-c_1 = e^\bullet = c_4-c_3$.

(ii) Let $(c_1,u,c_2), (c_3,u,c_4) \in \longrightarrow_N$.
Then using (i) it is easy to show that

$$c_1-c_2 = {}^\bullet u = c_3-c_4 \quad \text{and} \quad c_2-c_1 = u^\bullet = c_4-c_3$$

Thus in transition systems that "correspond" to EN systems, the change caused by an action does not depend on the state at which it occurs. It will be convenient to identify this subclass of transition systems.

Definition 4.9 Let $\mathcal{TS}$ denote the class of all transition systems, $\mathcal{TS}_1$ the class of C/E transition systems. Then

$$\mathcal{TS}_2 = \{TS \in \mathcal{TS}_1 \mid TS \text{ satisfies } \underline{A1}\} \quad \text{where}$$

A1 (with $TS = (B,E,S,A,\rightarrow,s_0)$)

$$(s_1,a,s_2),(s_3,a,s_4) \in \rightarrow \;\Rightarrow\; (s_1-s_2, s_2-s_1) = (s_3-s_4), s_4-s_3) \;.$$

Clearly for every EN system N, TS_N is a member of $\mathcal{TS}_2$ (due to Theorem 4.8). Now let $TS = (B,E,S,A,\rightarrow,s_0)$ satisfy A1. Then with TS we can associate two functions $\underline{pre}_{TS} : A \rightarrow \mathcal{P}(B)$ and $\underline{post}_{TS} : A \rightarrow \mathcal{P}(B)$ such that :

$$\forall (s,a,s') \in \rightarrow . \quad \underline{pre}_{TS}(a) = s-s' \text{ and } \underline{post}_{TS}(a) = s'-s$$

In other words, whenever a occurs, $\underline{pre}_{TS}(a)$ cease to hold and $\underline{post}_{TS}(a)$ begin to hold. From now we shall write just pre and post without subscripts. This should cause no confusion.

Let TS_N be the transition system associated with the EN system N. Clearly for TS_N the associated functions pre and post satisfy : $\forall u \in U_N . \;\; \underline{pre}(u) = {}^\bullet u$ and $\underline{post}(u) = u^\bullet$

Let $TS = (B,E,S,A,\rightarrow,s_0)$ be a transition system, $s \in S$ and $a \in A$. We now ask : When can the action a occur at the state s ? Formally we have :

Definition 4.10 Let $TS = (B,E,S,A,\rightarrow,s_0)$ be a transition system, $s \in S$ and $a \in A$. Then a is enabled at s - denoted $\underline{en}(a,s)$ - iff there exists $s' \in S$ such that $(s,a,s') \in \rightarrow$.

For $\mathcal{TS}_2$, there is a nice necessary condition stating when an action is enabled at a state.

Theorem 4.11 Let $TS = (B,E,S,A,\rightarrow,s_0) \in \mathcal{TS}_2$. Let $s \in S$ and $a \in A$. If $\underline{en}(a,s)$ then $\underline{pre}(a) \subseteq s$ and $\underline{post}(a) \cap s = \emptyset$.

Proof Assume that a is enabled at s . Then for some $s' \in S$, we have $(s,a,s') \in \rightarrow$. TS satisfies A1, and hence by the definitions of pre and post, we have $s-s' = \underline{pre}(a)$ and $s'-s = \underline{post}(a)$. Clearly this implies that $\underline{pre}(a) \subseteq s$ and $\underline{post}(a) \cap s = \emptyset$.

This necessary criterion is, in general, not sufficient.

This can be brought out through an example.

Example 4.12

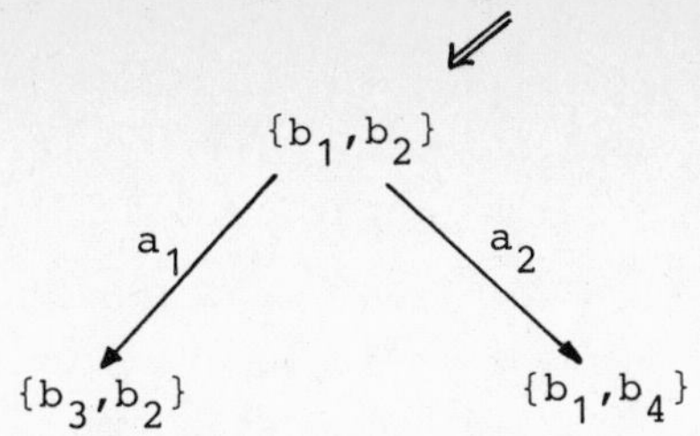

Clearly this is a transition system which vacuously satisfies A1 and hence is a member of TS_2. In this system, $\underline{pre}(a_1) = \{b_1\}$, $\underline{post}(a_1) = \{b_3\}$, $\underline{pre}(a_2) = \{b_2\}$ and $\underline{post}(a_2) = \{b_4\}$. At the state $s = \{b_1, b_4\}$ we have $\underline{pre}(a_1) \subseteq s$ and $\underline{post}(a_1) \cap s = \emptyset$. But a_1 is not enabled at s.

The distinguishing feature of EN systems is that - viewed as transition systems - the necessary criterion of Theorem 4.11 is also sufficient.

Theorem 4.13 Let N be an EN system so that $TS_N = (B, E, C_N, U_N, \rightarrow_N, c_{in})$. Then (in TS_N !) $\forall c \in C_N$, $\forall u \in U_N$, $\underline{en}(u,c)$ if and only if $\underline{pre}(u) \subseteq c$ and $\underline{post}(u) \cap c = \emptyset$.

Proof Necessity follows from Theorem 4.11. So assume that $c \in C_N$ and $u \in U_N$ such that $\underline{pre}(u) \subseteq c$ and $\underline{post}(u) \cap c = \emptyset$. But $\underline{pre}(u) = {}^\bullet u$ and $\underline{post}(u) = u^\bullet$. Hence $c' = (c - {}^\bullet u) \cap u^\bullet \in C_N$. Moreover $(c, u, c') \in \rightarrow_N$. Therefore u is enabled at c.

It is this property of EN systems which gives it the strong flavour of a "flow" model. This has far-reaching consequences in the development of the theory. In particular, because of this property, linear algebra can be used to develop quantitative analysis tools for this model and its suitable extensions (see the contributions by K.Lautenbach).

We can now conclude that the EN system model does indeed incorporate the principles stated at the beginning of Section 1.

5. FUNDAMENTAL SITUATIONS

We now wish to define some of the basic concepts of net theory with the aid of the EN system model. In doing so, we shall assume every EN system we encounter to be contact-free.

At a case c of an EN system N, two events e_1 and e_2 can be related to each other in (at least) three ways.

(i) (Sequence) e_1 can occur at c but not e_2. However, after e_1 has occurred e_2 can occur.

(ii) (Choice) e_1 and e_2 can occur individually at c but not both. In other words, $\{e_1\}$, $\{e_2\}$ are steps at c while $\{e_1,e_2\}$ is not a step at c.

(iii) (Concurrency) Both e_1 and e_2 can occur at c with no order specified over their occurrences. In other words, $\{e_1,e_2\}$ is a step at c.

A nice feature of net theory is that it not only separates these relationships conceptually (as indicated above) but also graphically and mathematically.

Sequence

Here is a graphical representation of sequencing of events in an EN system.

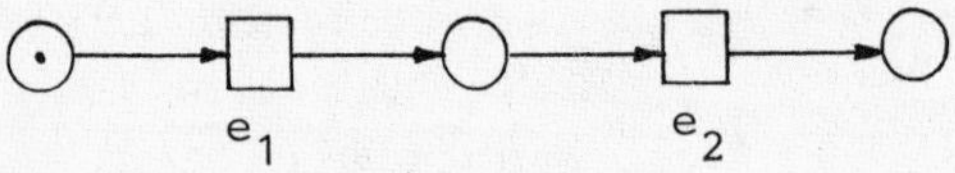

Figure 5.1

At the case shown, the occurrence of e_2 must be preceded by that of e_1.

Formally we have the following definition.

Definition 5.1 Let $c \in C_N$ and $e_1, e_2 \in E$ where N is an EN system. We say that e_1 and e_2 are in sequence at c iff $c[e_1>$ and $\neg(c[e_2>)$ and $c'[e_2>$ where $c[e_1>c'$.

Choice (conflict)

Here is a graphical representation of a conflict situation in an EN system.

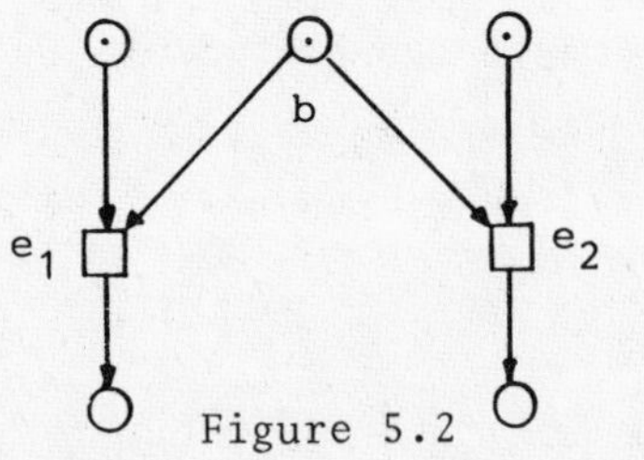

Figure 5.2

At the case shown, e_1 and e_2 can occur individually; but due to the "shared" condition b, $\{e_1,e_2\}$ is not a step. Note however, whether e_1 will occur or e_2 will occur is left unspecified. Thus EN systems can exhibit non-determinism.

Formally we have the following definition.

Definition 5.2 Let e_1 and e_2 be two events and c a case of an EN system N. e_1 and e_2 are in conflict at c iff $c[e_1>$ and $c[e_2>$ but not $c[\{e_1,e_2\}>$.

Concurrency

Here is a graphical representation of concurrency in an EN system.

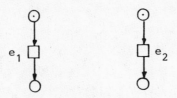

Figure 5.3

At the case shown, both e_1 and e_2 can occur without interfering with each other. Moreover, no order is specified over their occurrences. Hence, in general, the occurrences of events and the resulting holdings of conditions will be partially ordered; EN systems can exhibit non-sequential behaviour.

Definition 5.3 Let e_1 and e_2 be two events and c a case of the EN system N. e_1 and e_2 can occur concurrently at c iff $c[\{e_1,e_2\}>$.

We move now to consider a situation called confusion which results from the mixture of concurrency and conflict.

Confusion

Here is a graphical representation of a confusion in an EN system.

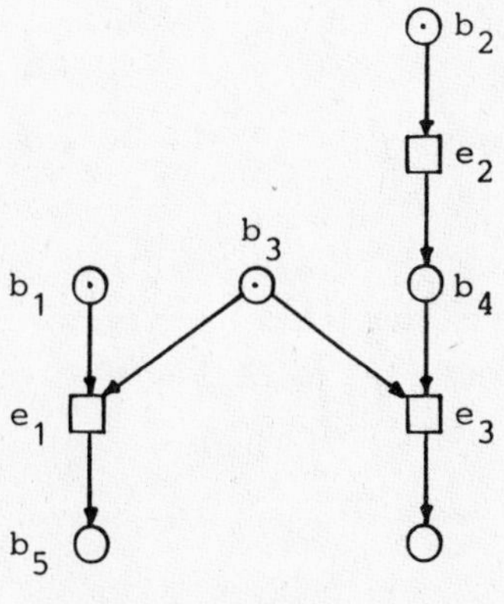

Figure 5.4

Let $c = \{b_1,b_2,b_3\}$ and $c' = \{b_4,b_5\}$ so that $c[\{e_1,e_2\}>c'$. Here there could be disagreement over whether or not a conflict was resolved in going from the case c to c' via the step $\{e_1,e_2\}$. Two honest sequential observers O_1 and O_2 could report :

O_1 : e_1 occurred first without being in conflict with any other event. And then e_2 occurred.

O_2 : e_2 occurred first. As a result e_1 and e_3 got in conflict. This conflict was resolved in favour of e_1 which then occurred.

This is a confused situation. Confusion arises whenever concurrency and conflict "overlap". This phenomenon appears to be basic in nature and appears under various disguises depending on the chosen level and mode of description of a distributed system. At the level of switching circuits confusion appears as the glitch problem which is also known, more appropriately, as the synchronisation failure problem. At this level, it appears to be difficult - if not impossible - to obtain a "correct" implementation.

Systems exhibiting confusion are also difficult to analyse. This is due to the fact that the "intermediate" cases determined by the elements of a step could differ radically from each other in terms of choices available regarding system behaviour. Consequently one cannot take advantage of concurrency and analyse the cases generated by just <u>one</u> possible sequentialisation of a step; one must analyse <u>every</u> possible sequentialisation.

Net theory suggests that it is not the combination of choice and concurrency as such that causes difficulties. Rather, it is those combinations of choice and concurrency resulting in confusion that cause trouble. The contribution by E.Best deals with a class of net-based systems in which choice and concurrency are combined in a confusion-free manner so that the resulting class of systems admits a nice theory.

Unfortunately, it is not always possible to avoid confusion. For example consider the system shown in Figure 2.2 which models the solution to a primitive mutual-exclusion problem. It is easy to check that this system exhibits confusion.

We now wish to formalize the notion of confusion.

<u>Definition 5.4</u> Let $N = (B,E;F,c_{in})$ be an EN system, let $c \in C$ and let $e \in E$ be such that $c[e>$. The <u>conflict set of</u> e (<u>at</u> c), denoted <u>cfl</u>(e,c), is the set $\{e' \in E \mid c[e'>$ and not $c[\{e,e'\}>\}$.

Thus the conflict set of e at c is the set of all events that are in conflict with e at c.

Definition 5.5 Let $N = (B,E;F,c_{in})$ be an EN system, let $c \in C_N$ and let e_1, e_2 be two distinct events in E such that $c[\{e_1,e_2\}>$. The triplet (c,e_1,e_2) is a confusion (at c) if $\mathrm{cfl}(e_1,c) \neq \mathrm{cfl}(e_1,c_2)$, where $c[e_2>c_2$. We say that N is confused at c iff there is a confusion at c.

Thus a triplet (c,e_1,e_2) is a confusion if $\{e_1,e_2\}$ is a step at c and the occurrence of e_2 at c changes the conflict set of e_1.

Example 5.6 Consider the EN system given in Figure 5.4. For $c = \{b_1,b_2,b_3\}$ we have $\mathrm{cfl}(e_1,c) = \emptyset$. Then (c,e_1,e_2) is a confusion because $\mathrm{cfl}(e_1,c) = \emptyset \neq \{e_3\} = \mathrm{cfl}(e_1,c_2)$, where $c_2 = \{b_1,b_3,b_4\}$.

It is natural to distinguish between the following two types of confusions.

Definition 5.7 Let N be an EN system, $c \in C_N$, $e_1,e_2 \in E_N$. Let $\gamma = (c,e_1,e_2)$ be a confusion and let $c[e_1>c_2$.

(i) γ is a conflict-increasing confusion, abbreviated ci confusion, iff $\mathrm{cfl}(e_1,c) \subset \mathrm{cfl}(e_1,c_2)$.

(ii) γ is a conflict-decreasing confusion, abbreviated cd confusion, iff $\mathrm{cfl}(e_1,c_2) \subset \mathrm{cfl}(e_1,c)$.

Example 5.8

(i) Consider the EN system and the confusion (c,e_1,e_2) from the previous example. Since $\mathrm{cfl}(e_1,c) \subset \mathrm{cfl}(e_1,c_2)$, (c,e_1,e_2) is a ci confusion.

(ii) Consider the following EN system :

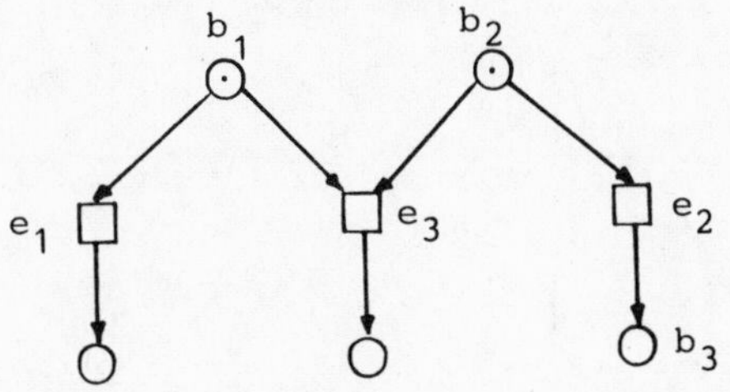

Figure 5.5

For $c = \{b_1,b_2\}$, (c,e_1,e_2) is a confusion because

$\underline{cfl}(e_1,c) = \{e_3\} \neq \emptyset = \underline{cfl}(e_1,c_2)$, where $c_2 = \{b_1,b_3\}$. Since $\underline{cfl}(e_1,c_2) \subset \underline{cfl}(e_1,c)$, (c,e_1,e_2) is a cd confusion.

(iii) Consider the following EN system :

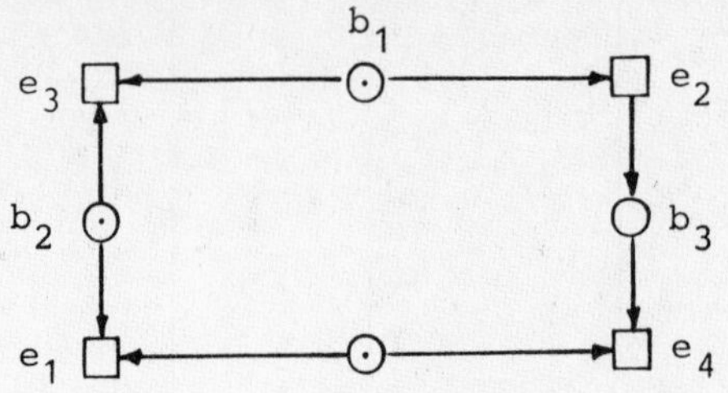

Figure 5.6

For $c = \{b_1,b_2,b_4\}$, (c,e_1,e_2) is a confusion because $\underline{cfl}(e_1,c) = \{e_3\} \neq \{e_4\} = \underline{cfl}(e_1,c_2)$, where $c_2 = \{b_2,b_3,b_4\}$. Note that (c,e_1,e_2) is neither a ci confusion nor a cd confusion.

As we have seen from the above example, the distinction between ci and cd confusion is not "exhaustive" - there exist confusions that are neither ci nor cd. In the literature ci confusions are often referred to as <u>asymmetric</u> confusions and cd confusions as <u>symmetric</u> confusions.

Based on the notions of conflict, concurrency and confusion, we can identify a number of interesting subclasses of EN systems.

<u>Definition 5.9</u> Let $N = (B,E;F,c_{in})$ be an EN system.

(i) N is <u>sequential</u> iff $(\forall u \in U_N)\ [|u| = 1]$

(ii) N is <u>deterministic</u> iff $(\forall c \in C)\ (\forall e_1,e_2 \in E)$ $[c[e_1> \ \&\ c[e_2> \Rightarrow c[\{e_1,e_2\}>]$.

(iii) N is <u>confusion-free</u> iff there is no confusion in N .

<u>Example 5.10</u>

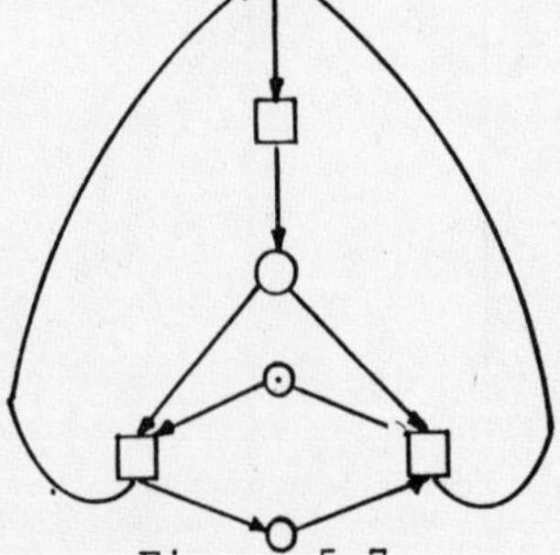

Figure 5.7

This system is both sequential and deterministic.

<u>Example 5.11</u>

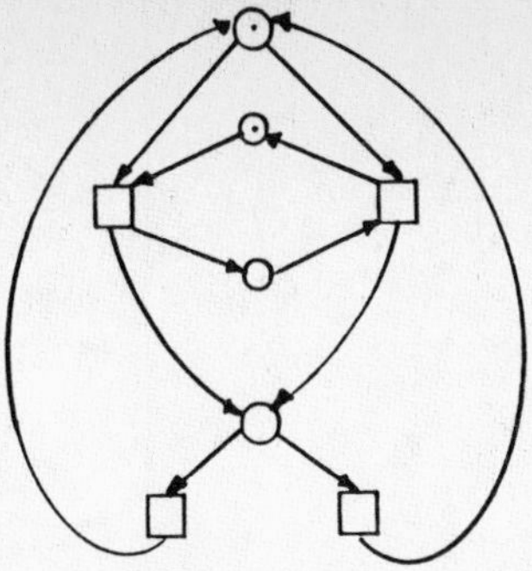

Figure 5.8

This system is sequential but non-deterministic.

<u>Example 5.12</u>

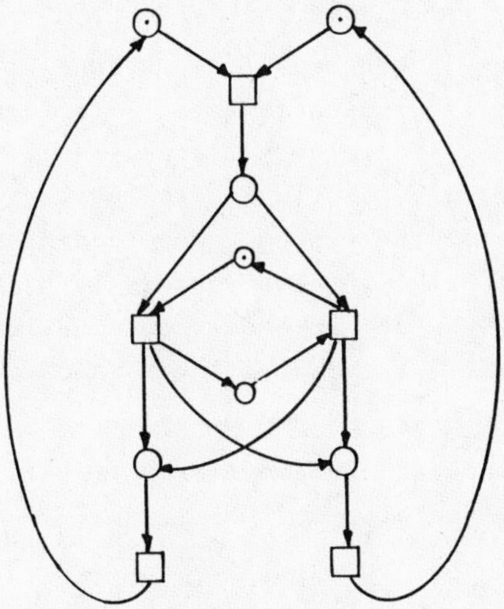

Figure 5.9

This system is non-sequential but deterministic.

<u>Example 5.13</u>

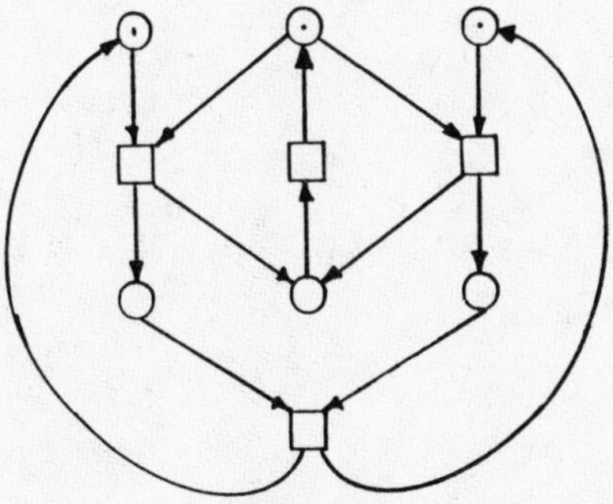

Figure 5.10

This system is non-sequential and non-deterministic but confusion-free.

Example 5.14

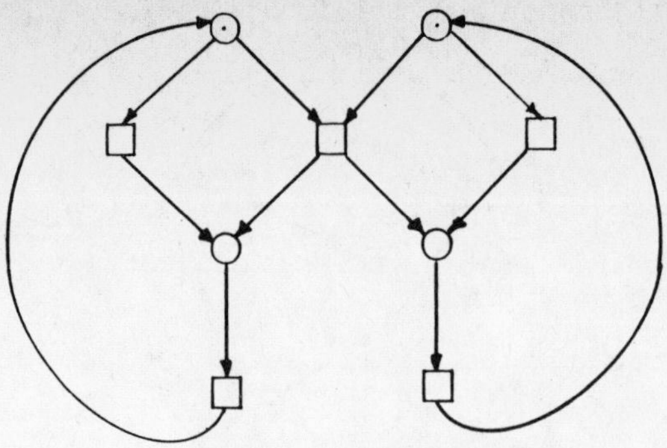

Figure 5.11

This system is non-sequential and non-deterministic and exhibits both forms of confusion.

The alert reader might wonder at the unnecessary complexity of the preceding examples. The reason is this : It turns out that the behavioural properties of determinacy, sequentiality and confusion-freeness can be guaranteed by placing suitable structural restrictions on the underlying net of an EN system. (Once again, see the contribution by E.Best.) Unfortunately, these restrictions are merely sufficient and not necessary. Hence, in order to emphasize that for all the behavioural subclasses, the underlying nets can be arbitrarily complex, we have chosen the above examples.

From the definitions and the above examples it is now easy to establish the following hierarchy of EN systems.

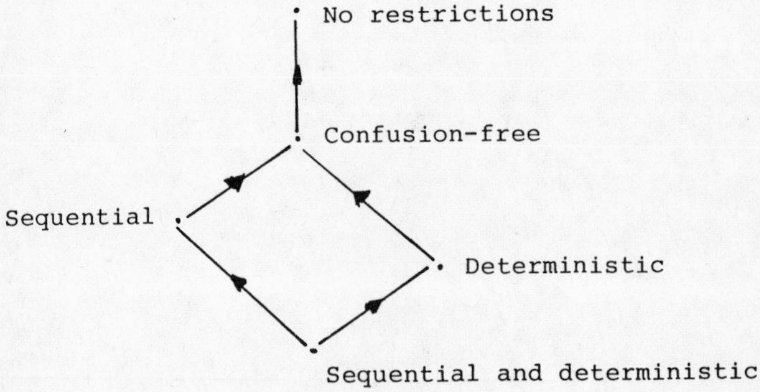

Figure 5.12

6. CONDITION / EVENT SYSTEMS

In this last section we consider a net-based model of systems called Condition/Event Systems (abbreviated as C/E systems).
This model has traditionally served as the starting point for constructing system models in net theory. We shall first define a C/E system. We shall then bring out the salient features of this model by comparing it with the EN system model.

The first point of departure is that the state space of a C/E system is a "full" case class rather than just a "forward" case class as in the case (!) for EN systems.

Definition 6.1 Let $N = (B,E;F)$ be a net and $c \subseteq B$.

(i) $[c\rangle_N$, the forward case class generated by c is the least subset of $\mathcal{P}(B)$ satisfying :

(i.a) $c \in [c\rangle_N$

(i.b) If $c' \in [c\rangle_N$ and $u \subseteq E$ and $c'' \in \mathcal{P}(B)$ such that $(c,u,c') \in \longrightarrow_N$ then $c'' \in [c\rangle_N$

(ii) $\langle c]_N$, the backward case class generated by c is the least subset of $\mathcal{P}(B)$ satisfying :

(ii.a) $c \in \langle c]_N$

(ii.b) If $c' \in \langle c]_N$ and $u \subseteq E$ and $c'' \in \mathcal{P}(B)$ such that $(c'',u,c') \in \longrightarrow_N$, then $c'' \in \langle c]_N$

(iii) $[c]_N$, the full case class generated by c is the least subset of $\mathcal{P}(B)$ satisfying :

(iii.a) $c \in [c]_N$

(iii.b) If $c' \in [c]_N$ and $u \subseteq E$ and $c'' \in \mathcal{P}(B)$ such that $(c',u,c'') \in \longrightarrow_N$ or $(c'',u,c') \in \longrightarrow_N$ then $c'' \in [c]_N$

(iv) $C \subseteq \mathcal{P}(B)$ is a full case class of N iff there exists $c \subseteq B$ such that $C = [c]_N$

Let $\mathcal{N} = (B,E;F,c_{in})$ be an EN system. Then $C_{\mathcal{N}} = [c_{in}\rangle_N$ where N is the underlying net of $\mathcal{N}$. In this sense, we consider a forward case class - namely, the one generated by c_{in} - as the state space of an EN system.

Example 6.2

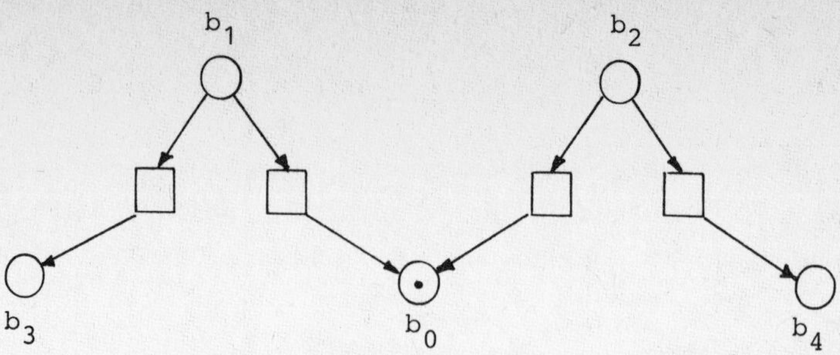

Figure 6.1

Let $c_i = \{b_i\}$ for $i = 0,1,2,3,4$. Then $[c_0\rangle = \{c_0\}$, $\langle c_0] = \{c_0,c_1,c_2\}$ and $[c_0] = \{c_0,c_1,c_2,c_3,c_4\}$. Notice that $c_1 \in \langle c_0]$ (and hence $c_0 \in [c_1\rangle$) but $c_0 \notin \langle c_1]$ (and hence $c_1 \notin [c_0\rangle$).

The key property of full case classes is that they partition the powerset of the conditions.

Theorem 6.3 Let $N = (B,E;F)$ be a net. Define $\sim_N \subseteq \mathcal{P}(B) \times \mathcal{P}(B)$ as :

$$c \sim_N c' \text{ iff } c \in [c']_N$$

Then,

(i) $\sim_N$ is an equivalence relation.

(ii) $\forall c,c' \subseteq B$. $c \sim_N c'$ iff $[c]_N = [c']_N$

(iii) $C \subseteq \mathcal{P}(B)$ is a full case class of N iff it is an equivalence class under the (equivalence) relation $\sim_N$.

Proof Follows easily from the definitions.

We are now prepared to present the C/E system model.

Definition 6.4 A Condition/Event system is a quadruple $\Sigma = (B,E;F,C)$ where

(i) $(B,E;F)$ is a simple net called the underlying net of Σ and is denoted as N_Σ .

(ii) $C \subseteq \mathcal{P}(B)$ is a full case class of N_Σ called the set of cases of Σ .

(iii) $\forall e \in E . \exists c \in C . c[e\rangle_{N_\Sigma}$.

Due to Theorem 6.2, to specify a C/E system Σ , it is sufficient to specify N_Σ and one representative member of the set of cases of Σ . Figure 6.1 may now be viewed as the graphical representation of a C/E system.

We now wish to briefly motivate the three (main) components of the definition of a C/E system.

(i) <u>The set of cases is a full case class</u> .

This demand is motivated by the desire to facilitate <u>backward reasoning</u> concerning the past history of a system (given its present state). It is often useful to determine the choices that have been made in the past of a system's behaviour - which have lead to the current state; one can then determine the alternative ("possible") current states that have been excluded.

For the system shown in Figure 6.1, suppose we are given the state c_0 (recall that $c_i = \{b_i\}$ by convention) to be the current state. Viewed as the initial state of an EN system, nothing interesting can be said about this system. But viewed as the current state of a C/E system we can conclude - through backward reasoning - that this system must have reached the current state either from c_1 or c_2 . Consequently, c_4 or c_5 are possible current states that have been excluded, through the decisions that have been taken in the past.

To inject a note of controversy, we feel that the demand for full case class does not always capture the intuition that one must be able to reason about the past behaviour of a system. Consider the C/E system of Figure 6.1 but with a different "current" state as shown below.

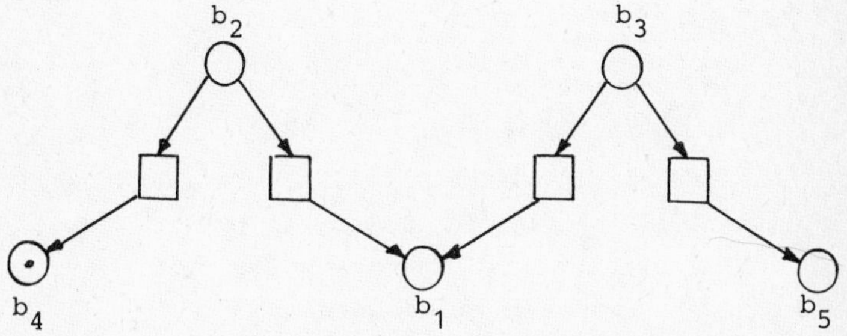

Figure 6.2

Viewing c_4 as the current state - through backward reasoning - we can conclude that this state must have been reached from c_2 . Through forward reasoning (at c_2), we can conclude that the system might have - instead of choosing c_4 - gone to the state c_1 . But it seems that we must stop at this stage; the states c_3 and c_5 should not be "accessible" through this process of "zig-zag" reasoning if we start from c_4 !

One possibility is to identify a "current" case c_{in} - just like we identify an initial case for EN systems, and define the set of cases to be the set :

$$\bigcup \{[c\rangle \mid c \in \langle c_{in}]\}$$

Unfortunately, such state spaces will not enjoy the properties stated in Theorem 6.2. And this might have some unpleasant consequences in the subsequent development of the theory. We now wish to consider the second restriction placed on a C/E system.

(ii) <u>The underlying net is simple</u>.

Let $\Sigma = (B,E;F,C)$ be a C/E system with $N = (B,E;F)$ Then it is easy to see that the change caused by an event occurrence is the same in every context. In other words,

$$\forall e \in E \,.\, (c_1,e,c_2),(c_3,e,c_4) \in \longrightarrow_N \Rightarrow (c_1-c_2, c_2-c_1) = (c_3-c_4, c_4-c_3)$$

This can be rephrased as :

$$\forall e_1,e_2 \in E \,.\, (c_1,e_1,c_2),(c_3,e_2,c_4) \in \longrightarrow_N \Rightarrow$$
$$(e_1 = e_2 \Rightarrow (c_1-c_2, c_2-c_1) = (c_3-c_4, c_4-c_3))$$

By demanding N_Σ to be simple we guarantee a stronger version of this principle.

<u>Theorem 6.5</u> Let $\Sigma = (B,E;F,C)$ be a C/E system. Then

$$\forall e_1,e_2 \in E \,.\, \forall (c_1,e_1,c_2),(c_3,e_2,c_4) \in \longrightarrow_{N_\Sigma} .$$
$$(e_1 = e_2 \Leftrightarrow (c_1-c_2, c_2-c_1) = (c_3-c_4, c_4-c_3))$$

<u>Proof</u> As preceding remarks indicate, necessity is merely an observation. So let $(c_1,e_1,c_2),(c_3,e_2,c_4) \in \longrightarrow_{N_\Sigma}$ such that $(c_1-c_2, c_2-c_1) = (c_3-c_4, c_4-c_3)$. Then $c_1-c_2 = {}^\bullet e_1 = c_3-c_4 = {}^\bullet e_2$ and $c_2-c_1 = e_1^\bullet = c_4-c_3 = e_2^\bullet$. Since N_Σ is simple, we then have $e_1 = e_2$.

The alert reader might have noticed that to guarantee this stronger "extensionality" principle regarding changes caused by event occurrences, it is sufficient to demand simplicity of events. More precisely, it is sufficient to demand :

$$\forall e_1,e_2 \in E \,.\, {}^\bullet e_1 = {}^\bullet e_2 \wedge e_1^\bullet = e_2^\bullet \Rightarrow e_1 = e_2 .$$

So why demand it for the conditions also ? The answer can be given as follows :

<u>Theorem 6.6</u> Let an <u>E-simple C/E system</u> be defined as a quadruple $\Sigma = (B,E;F,C)$ satisfying :

(i) $N_\Sigma = (B,E;F)$ is a net such that $\forall e_1,e_2 \in E$. ${}^\bullet e_1 = {}^\bullet e_2 \wedge e_1^\bullet = e_2^\bullet \Rightarrow e_1 = e_2$.

(ii) C is a full case class of N_Σ.

(iii) $\forall e \in E \,.\, \exists c \in C \,.\, c[e\rangle_{N_\Sigma}$.

Suppose $b_1, b_2 \in B$ such that $^{\bullet}b_1 = {^{\bullet}b_2}$ and $b_1^{\bullet} = b_2^{\bullet}$. Then $\forall c \in C\ (b_1 \in c \Leftrightarrow b_2 \in c)$.

Proof We will merely sketch the proof idea.

Suppose $b_1, b_2 \in B$ with $^{\bullet}b_1 = {^{\bullet}b_2}$ and $b_1^{\bullet} = b_2^{\bullet}$. If $b_1 = b_2$ there is nothing to be proved. So assume that $b_1 \neq b_2$. Now suppose that $c \in C$ such that $b_1 \in c$ but $b_2 \notin c$. Then no event in $^{\bullet}b_1$ can occur at c because $b_1 \in c$. At the same time no event in $b_2^{\bullet}$ can occur at c because $b_2 \notin c$. Hence no event in $^{\bullet}b_1 \cup b_1^{\bullet} = {^{\bullet}b_2} \cup b_2^{\bullet}$ can occur at c. Let $e \in {^{\bullet}b_1} \cup b_1^{\bullet}$. ($^{\bullet}b_1 \cup b_1^{\bullet} \neq \emptyset$ because N_Σ is a net.) Then it is easy to verify - by induction - that $\forall c' \in C$. e is not enabled at c'. And this contradicts the definition of an E-simple C/E system.

Thus once the simplicity of events is imposed, we cannot distinguish - within the state space C - between the holdings (and non-holdings) of two conditions b_1 and b_2 that satisfy $^{\bullet}b_1 = {^{\bullet}b_2}$ and $b_1^{\bullet} = b_2^{\bullet}$. Thus nothing is lost - and some mathematical elegance is gained - by demanding N_Σ itself to be simple .

(iii) Every event has an occurrence .

Consider the following EN system

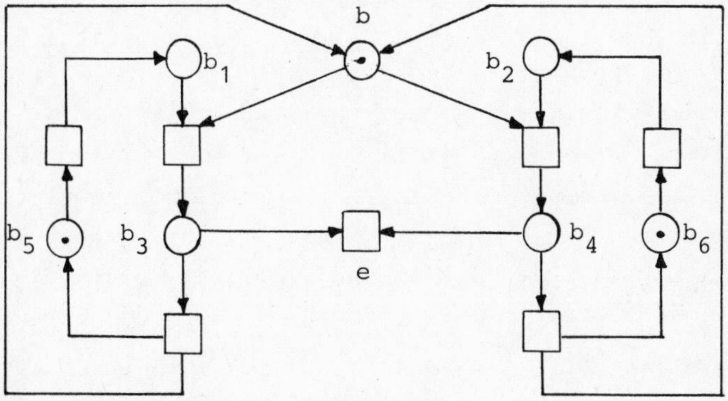

Figure 6.3

In this system the event e is "dead". In other words, e is not enabled at any case of the system. There is a positive view of interpreting this fact. Namely, e models an invariant property of the state space of this EN system $N : \forall c \in C\ .\ (b_3 \notin c \vee b_4 \notin c)$.

Hence dead T-elements can be used for representing certain invariant properties concerning condition holdings over the state space.

Thus by demanding that every event should have an occurrence somewhere in the state space, we have the possibility of augmenting the language of condition holdings and non-holdings with the help of dead T-elements. The invariant properties represented by such T-elements are called facts. There is a net-based calculus of facts which is sound and complete.

There is an interesting historical sequence of developments leading from the calculus of facts to the construction of the Predicate/Transition system model (see the contribution by H.J.Genrich).

There is a second reason for demanding that every event should have an occurrence somewhere in the state space. It turns out that a nice metric called synchronic distance can be defined over the event occurrences. Now synchronic distances come out to be metrics only if we guarantee that every event has an occurrence somewhere in the state space. (See the contribution by U.Goltz.)

Finally, even for EN systems, notions of behavioural equivalence work properly only if we first "filter out" the dead events; but it is time to stop.

7. BIBLIOGRAPHICAL NOTES

Most of this material is based on [RT] which contains a fairly complete survey of the basic aspects of net theory. An earlier survey which devotes a considerable amount of space to Petri's approach to the study of distributed systems can be found in [GLT1]. Yet another - and more accessible (compared to [GLT1]) - introduction to the fundamentals is [R].

The net theoretic view of states and transitions was first put down by Petri with the help of a transition system model called substitution systems [P1]. A more detailed account of substitution systems and their relationship to net theory can be found in [GLT2].

Fundamental situations were first classified by Petri in [P2]. A.W.Holt was, as far as we know, the first to pinpoint confusion as a deep source of difficulties.

The behavioural properties of sequentiality, determinacy and confusion-freeness can be - in a sufficient but not necessary sense - captured syntactically. EN systems based on a subclass of nets called S-graphs (T-graphs, Free Choice nets) are guaranteed to be sequential (deterministic, confusion-free). There is a rich theory for each of these subclasses of systems. The main results can be found in [RT]. See also the contribution by E.Best in this course.

More material concerning C/E systems can be found in [GLT1] and [R].

8. REFERENCES

(LNCS is an abbreviation for Springer Lecture Notes in Computer Science.)

[GLT1] H.J.Genrich, K.Lautenbach, P.S.Thiagarajan : Elements of General Net Theory LNCS 84 (1980), pp. 21-163

[GLT2] H.J.Genrich, K.Lautenbach, P.S.Thiagarajan : Substitution Systems: A Family of System Models based on Concurrency. LNCS 88 (1980), pp.698-723

[P1] C.A.Petri : Concepts of Net Theory Mathematical Foundations of Computer Science. Proceedings of Symposium and Summer School, High Tatras (1973), pp. 137-148

[P2] C.A.Petri : General Net Theory Proceedings of the Joint IBM University of Newcastle upon Tyne Seminar on Computing System Design (1976)

[R] W.Reisig : Petri Nets, An Introduction EATCS Monographs on Theoretical Computer Science, Springer-Verlag (1985)

[RT] G.Rozenberg, P.S.Thiagarajan : Petri Nets: Basic Notions, Structure and Behaviour. LNCS 224 (1986), pp. 585-668

BEHAVIOUR OF ELEMENTARY NET SYSTEMS

G. Rozenberg

Department of Computer Science
University of Leiden
Leiden, The Netherlands

and

Department of Computer Science
University of Colorado at Boulder
Boulder, Colorado, U.S.A.

ABSTRACT. We consider two ways of recording the behaviour of an elementary net system (EN system): via *sequential observations* and via *non-sequential* observations. In the sequential point of view each record of the behaviour of an EN system is a string of event occurrences (called a *firing sequence)* as registered by a sequential observer. In the non-sequential point of view we can define the behaviour of an EN system by either extracting causal order of events from firing sequences (obtaining *firing traces)* or by recording all non-sequential observations of event occurrences *and* of resulting holdings of conditions (each such record is called a *process)*. In our contribution we discuss each of the three approaches and then relate them to each other.

Key words: Petri nets, elementary net systems, state space, case graph, firing sequences, theory of traces, dependence graphs, firing traces, processes, labeled partial orders of events.

CONTENTS:

0. INTRODUCTION

The aim of this paper is to discuss the behaviour of elementary net systems which were presented as a simple model of distributed systems in the contribution by P.S. Thiagarajan.

There are at least two reasons for formalizing the notion of the behaviour of an EN system. First of all one should be able to express formally what a given EN system does (how does it behave). Secondly, one gets a formal tool for comparing EN systems with each other.

Clearly, the question "What is the behaviour of an EN system ?" is strongly related to the question "How can the behaviour of an EN system be observed ?". The relationship of these two questions is strongly reflected in our lecture.

Actually our point of departure is to distinguish between *sequential* and *non-sequential* observations and then to identify records of such observations with the system behaviour.

In the sequential point of view each record of the behaviour of an EN system is a string of event occurrences (called a *firing sequence*) as registered by a sequential observer.

In the non-sequential point of view one can either record all non-sequential observations of event occurrences (called *firing traces*) or proceeding in a more detailed fashion one can record all non-sequential observations of event occurrences together with the resulting holdings of conditions; such records are called *processes.*

During the lecture we discuss the two approaches and compare them with each other.

Our way of defining the behaviour of EN systems is not the only one discussed in the literature. Some of the other approaches will be discussed in the contributions by C. Fernandez, M. Jantzen, and R. Valk. Even within the above sketched methodology *we consider finite behaviours only ; consequently we will consider finite words and finite nets only.* Some aspects of extending our considerations to the infinite case (infinite stretches of behaviour) will be discussed in the contributions by C. Fernandez and R. Valk.

We end this introduction by noting that our contribution directly continues the contribution by P.S. Thiagarajan - hence we build on notions and notations introduced there.

1. PRELIMINARIES

Although we assume the reader to be familiar with basic mathematical notions (sets, graphs, bipartite graphs, node- and edge-labeled graphs, graph isomorphisms, etc.) we recall a number of them in this section in order to establish our notation and terminology and also because some of these notions are used in our paper in a specific way.

When dealing with sets *we will often identify a singleton set* $\{x\}$ *with its element* x - this however should not lead to confusion. For a set X, $|X|$ denotes its cardinality. For sets X, Y and a function $\phi: X \rightarrow Y$, we use $\phi(X)$ to denote the set $\{\phi(x) \mid x \in X\}$.

For an alphabet Σ, Σ^* denotes the set of all finite words over Σ and Λ denotes the *empty word.*

We will deal with various kinds of graphs. Instead of adopting one general definition, it will be more convenient to develop various notions of graphs and introduce a specific notation for each notion.

A (*directed*) *graph* is an ordered pair $g = (V, Y)$ where V is the set of *nodes* and $Y \subseteq V \times V$ is the set of *edges. Unless explicitly stated otherwise we deal with nonempty graphs only* (i.e., we assume that $V \neq \emptyset$). A (*directed*) *path* in g is a sequence of nodes $\pi = v_0, \cdots, v_n$, $n \geq 1$, such that $(v_i, v_{i+1}) \in Y$ for all $0 \leq i < n$; if $v_0 = v_n$ then π is a (*directed*) *circuit.* g is said to be *acyclic* iff no path in g is a circuit.

We discuss now other kinds of graphs used in these notes.

A *bipartite graph* is a triplet (V_1, V_2, Y) where $V_1 \neq \emptyset$, $V_2 \neq \emptyset$, $V_1 \cap V_2 = \emptyset$, $(V_1 \cup V_2, Y)$ is a graph and $Y \subseteq (V_1 \times V_2) \cup (V_2 \times V_1)$.

Remark 1.1. Our definition of a bipartite graph differs somewhat from the conventional definition mostly used in the literature : we consider the two sets partitioning the set of all nodes to be an ordered pair (V_1, V_2) *so that we can distinguish between (and unambiguously refer to) them. This slight definitional difference is quite crucial when we use bipartite graphs to deal with nets. To stress this difference we will often (especially in the context of concepts from net theory) write a specification of a bipartite graph in the form* $(V_1, V_2 ; Y)$ *rather than* (V_1, V_2, Y).

The terminology concerning paths is carried over to a bipartite graph (V_1, V_2, Y) by viewing it as a graph $(V_1 \cup V_2, Y)$.

Let $g = (V_1, V_2, Y)$ be a bipartite graph and let $W \in \{V_1, V_2\}$. The *W-contraction of* g, denoted $ctr_W(g)$, is the graph $\{(V_1 \cup V_2) - W, Y_W\}$, where $(v, v') \in Y_W$ iff there exists a $w \in W$ such that $(v, w) \in Y$ and $(w, v') \in Y$.

Let Σ be an alphabet. A *node* Σ*-labeled graph* is a triplet (V, Y, ϕ), where (V, Y) is a graph and $\phi : V \rightarrow \Sigma$ is the (*node*) *labeling function.* A *node* Σ-labeled bipartite graph is a 4-tuple (V_1, V_2, Y, ϕ) where $(V_1 \cup V_2, Y, \phi)$ is a node Σ-labeled graph such that $\phi(V_1) \cap \phi(V_2) = \emptyset$. An *edge* Σ*-labeled initialized graph* is a triplet $g = (V, Y, v_{in})$ where $V \neq \emptyset$ is the set of *nodes,* $Y \subseteq V \times \Sigma \times V$ is the set of Σ*-labeled edges* and $v_{in} \in V$ is the *initial node; rlab*(g) denotes the set $\{\sigma \in \Sigma \mid (v, \sigma, v') \in Y$ for some $v, v' \in V\}$. In all the terminology above we may replace " Σ-labeled" by "labeled" whenever Σ is clear from the context.

Let $g_1 = (V_1, Y_1, \phi_1)$ be a node Σ_1-labeled graph and $g_2 = (V_2, Y_2, \phi_2)$ a node Σ_2-labeled graph.

We say that g_1 and g_2 are *isomorphic,* written g_1 *isom* g_2 iff

there exists a bijection $\alpha : V_1 \rightarrow V_2$ such that

$(\forall v \in V_1)[\phi_2(\alpha(v)) = \phi_1(v)]$ and

$(\forall v, v' \in V_1)[(v, v') \in Y_1$ iff $(\alpha(v), \alpha(v')) \in Y_2]$.

We say that g_1 and g_2 are *label-isomorphic* and write g_1 *lisom* g_2 iff there exist bijections $\alpha : V_1 \rightarrow V_2$ and $\beta : \phi_1(V_1) \rightarrow \phi_2(V_2)$ such that

$(\forall v \in V_1)[\phi_2(\alpha(v)) = \beta(\phi_1(v))]$ and

$(\forall v, v' \in V_1)[(v, v') \in Y_1$ iff $(\alpha(v), \alpha(v')) \in Y_2]$.

Let $g_1 = (V_1, V_2, Y_1, \phi_1)$ be a node Σ_1-labeled bipartite graph and $g_2 = (W_1, W_2, Y_2, \phi_2)$ a node Σ_2-labeled bipartite graph. We say that g_1 and g_2 are *label-isomorphic,* written g_1 *lisom* g_2 , iff there exist bijections

$\alpha : V_1 \cup V_2 \to W_1 \cup W_2$ and $\beta : \phi_1(V_1 \cup V_2) \to \phi_2(W_1 \cup W_2)$ such that

$(\forall v \in V_1 \cup V_2)[\, v \in V_1$ iff $\alpha(v) \in W_1 \,]$,

$(\forall v \in V_1 \cup V_2)[\, \phi_2(\alpha(v)) = \beta(\phi_1(v)) \,]$ and

$(\forall v, v' \in V_1 \cup V_2)[\, (v, v') \in Y_1$ iff $(\alpha(v), \alpha(v')) \in Y_2 \,]$.

Let $g_1 = (V_1, Y_1, v_1)$ be an edge Σ_1-labeled initialized graph and $g_2 = (V_2, Y_2, v_2)$ be an edge Σ_2-labeled initialized graph. We say that g_1 and g_2 are *label-isomorphic,* written g_1 *lisom* g_2, iff there exist bijections

$\alpha : V_1 \to V_2$ and $\beta : \mathit{rlab}(g_1) \to \mathit{rlab}(g_2)$ such that

$\alpha(v_1) = v_2$

$\beta(\mathrm{rlab}(g_1)) = \mathrm{rlab}(g_2)$, and

$(\forall v, v' \in V_1)(\forall \sigma \in \mathit{rlab}(g_1))[\, (v, \sigma, v') \in Y_1$ iff $(\alpha(v), \beta(\sigma), \alpha(v')) \in Y_2 \,]$.

In these notes we will deal with *partially ordered sets* (*posets*) and with *labeled partially ordered sets* (*labeled posets*).

A *poset* is a graph $g = (V, Y)$ such that Y is a transitive, antisymmetric and reflexive relation. A *Σ-labeled poset* is a node Σ-labeled graph $g = (V, Y, \phi)$ such that (V, Y) is a poset. Whenever Σ is clear from the context we may use the phrase "labeled" rather than "Σ-labeled".

With each acyclic graph $g = (V, Y)$ we associate the poset (V, Y^*) where Y^* is the transitive and reflexive closure of Y; this poset is denoted by $\leq_g$. Similarly with each Σ-labeled acyclic graph $g = (V, Y, \phi)$ we associate the labeled poset (V, Y^*, ϕ) which we also denote by $\leq_g$.

Remark 1.2. For the sake of notational simplicity we will sometimes write $x \leq_g y$ (where $x, y \in V$ and $V, g, \leq_g$ are as above) rather than to write $x\, Y^*\, y$; this however should not lead to confusion. □

In this lecture we will often consider the set of all (node-labeled) graphs isomorphic to a given (node-labeled) graph g ; this set is denoted by $\bar{g}$ and it is referred to as an ***abstract* (*node−labeled*) *graph.*** To avoid set theoretical difficulties we will assume that the nodes of all (node-labeled) graphs we consider are taken from one fixed countable set of elements.

2. ON THE SIMILARITY OF EN SYSTEMS

In this section we will be concerned with establishing criteria for the "similarity" of EN systems *without* defining first their behaviour. Rather, we do it by considering two basic components of an EN system - the ***static structure*** and the ***distributed state space.***

For an EN system N its static structure is given by the underlying set N_N and so the notion of the structural similarity of EN systems is based on the standard notion of isomorphism of bipartite graphs.

Definition 2.1. Let $N_1 = (B_1, E_1; F_1, C_1)$ and $N_2 = (B_2, E_2; F_2, C_2)$ be EN systems. We say that N_1 and N_2 are ***structurally similar,*** denoted $N_1 \equiv N_2$,

iff there exists a bijection $\alpha : X_{N_1} \rightarrow X_{N_2}$ such that

$(\forall x, y \in X_{N_1})[\ (\ x \in B_1 \text{ iff } \alpha(x) \in B_2\ ) \text{ and } ((x, y) \in F_1 \text{ iff } (\alpha(x), \alpha(y)) \in F_2\ )\ ]$
and

$\alpha(C_1) = C_2$. □

The distributed state space of an EN system N is given by its case graph. The notion of the case graph of an EN system was discussed already in the contribution by P.S. Thiagarajan - we given now the formal definition.

Definition 2.2. Let $N = (B, E; F, C_{in})$ be an EN system. The ***case graph of** N*, denoted CG_N, is the initialized edge-labeled graph (V, Y, v_{in}), where

$V = C_N$, $Y = \{(C_1, U, C_2) \mid C_1[U > C_2\}$ and $v_{in} = C_{in}$. □

The notion of the state space similarity is based on the (label-) isomorphism of case graphs.

Definition 2.3. EN systems N_1, N_2 are *state space similar,* denoted

$N_1 \cong N_2$, iff CG_{N_1} *lisom* CG_{N_2}. □

Now we return to the "complement construction" discussed in the contribution by P.S. Thiagarajan. This construction converts an arbitrary EN system into a contact-free EN system and it was argued that the resulting system is "equivalent" to the original system. Now we can formalize this claim.

Theorem 2.1.

(1) Let N be an EN system and let N' be the EN system obtained by applying the complement construction to N. Then $N \cong N'$.

(2) For every EN system N there exists a contact-free EN system N' such that $N \cong N'$.

□

In the sequel of these notes, unless explicitly stated otherwise, we will consider contact-free EN systems only. This restriction is quite essential and we will discuss it in more detail in Section 6.

3. SEQUENTIAL OBSERVATIONS OF EVENT OCCURRENCES

Perhaps the simplest way to define the behaviour of an EN system is through *sequential observers.* Each record of an observation by a sequential observer is a string of event occurrences (called a firing sequence). The collection of all such records represents the behaviour of the system.

Definition 3.1. Let $N = (B, E; F, C_{in})$ be an EN system. $\rho \in E^*$ is a *firing sequence of N* iff

either $\rho = \Lambda$

or $\rho = e_1 \cdots e_n$, $n \geq 1$, $e_1, \cdots, e_n \in E$ and there exists a sequence of cases $C_0, C_1, \cdots, C_n$ in C_N such that $C_0 = C_{in}$ and $C_{j-1} [e_j > C_j$ for $1 \leq j < n$. □

We will use $\mathbf{FS}(N)$ to denote the set of firing sequences of N .

Firing sequences can be interpreted as walks in the restricted state space of an EN system. In order to formalize this statement we need the following notion.

Definition 3.2. Let $N = (B, E; F, C_{in})$ be an EN system. The *sequential case graph of N*, denoted SCG_N , is the edge-labeled initialized graph

(V, Y, v_{in}) where

$V = C_N$,

$Y = \{(C_1, U, C_2) \mid C_1 [U > C_2 \text{ and } |U| = 1\}$ and $v_{in} = C_{in}$. □

Now we can interpret firing sequences as follows:

ρ is a firing sequence of an EN system N iff ρ is the sequence of edge-labels corresponding to a path in SCG_N starting from its initial node (recall our convention that we often identify singleton sets with their elements).

Example 3.1. Consider the following EN system $N_1 = (B_1, E_1; F_1, C_1)$, where $C_1 = \{b_1, b_2\}$:

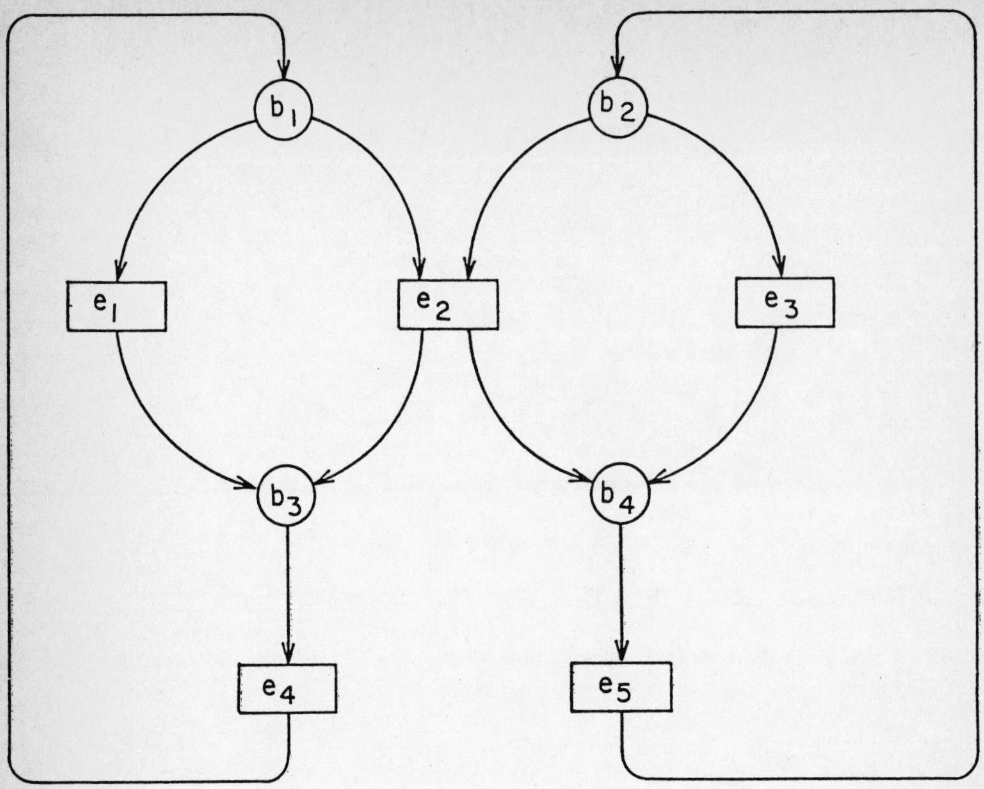

Figure 3.1

Then CG_{N_1} is as follows :

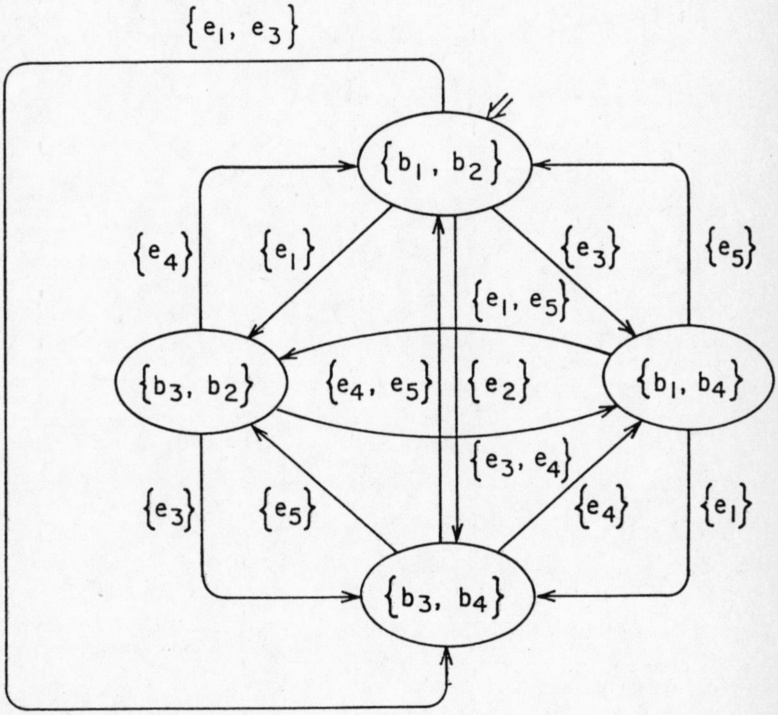

Figure 3.2

and SCG_{N_1} is as follows :

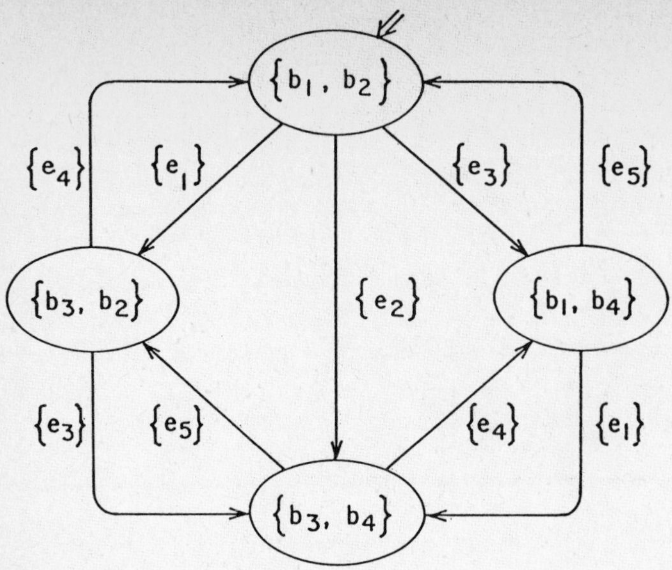

Figure 3.3

Since we have

$\{b_1, b_2\} [e_1 > \{b_3, b_2\}$,

$\{b_3, b_2\} [e_3 > \{b_3, b_4\}$,

$\{b_3, b_4\} [e_5 > \{b_3, b_2\}$, and

$\{b_3, b_2\} [e_4 > \{b_1, b_2\}$,

each of the following strings :

Λ, e_1, e_1e_3, $e_1e_3e_5$, $e_1e_3e_5e_4$

is a firing sequence of N_1 ; it is easily seen that each of these strings is the sequence of edge labels corresponding to a path in SCG_{N_1} . □

SCG_N has a finite number of nodes and a finite number of edges labeled by events from N (actually by singleton sets consisting of events from N - but this difference is neglected in our considerations). Hence one can consider SCG_N to be the transition diagram of a finite state automaton where the initial node corresponds to the initial state of the automaton and all the nodes (states) are terminal.

Thus the following result is obvious.

Theorem 3.1. For an EN system N, the set $\mathbf{FS}(N)$ is a prefix closed regular language. □

Clearly, representing the behaviour of an EN system N via its firing sequences provides an important insight - e.g., it tells us about all the "sequential walks" (trajectories) in the state space of N. However there are some serious problems concerning this representation. A firing sequence records an observation by a *sequential observer* of a system that (in general) is basically *non-sequential.* It may happen that within a firing sequence there is a subsequence $e_1 e_2$ while in the system considered (observed) these two occurrences are cconcurrent. Thus the linear order of event occurrences in a firing sequence does not necessarily reflect the causal order enforced by the system on event occurrences.

Consequently, the description of the system behaviour via firing sequences will be really valuable if the causal (in general partial) order of events can be extracted from firing sequences. In order to do so one has to augment the "observational" description of the system with some structural information about the system (i.e. information based on the underlying net of the system only).

An elegant approach to this problem is provided by the *theory of traces.*

4. TRACES AND DEPENDENCE GRAPHS

In this section we will briefly review the basic notions of the theory of traces to the extent that they are needed for our purpose. More advanced issues of this theory are discussed in the contribution by A. Mazurkiewicz.

Definition 4.1.

(i) Let Σ be an alphabet. An *independence relation* (*over* Σ) is a symmetric and irreflexive binary relation over Σ . A *dependence relation* (*over* Σ) is a symmetric and reflexive binary relation over Σ .

(ii) A *reliance alphabet* is a triple (Σ, I, D), where Σ is an alphabet, I is an independence relation over Σ , and D is a dependence relation over Σ such that $I \cup D = \Sigma \times \Sigma$ and $I \cap D = \emptyset$. □

An independence relation over Σ induces two important relations over Σ^* .

Definition 4.2. Let $Z = (\Sigma, I, D)$ be a reliance alphabet.

(i) The relation $\doteq_I \subseteq \Sigma^* \times \Sigma^*$ is defined by :

$(\forall \rho, \rho' \in \Sigma^*)[\rho \doteq_I \rho'$ iff

$(\exists \rho_1, \rho_2 \in \Sigma^*)(\exists (a, b) \in I)[\ \rho = \rho_1 a b \rho_2$ and $\rho' = \rho_1 b a \rho_2\ ]\ ]$.

(ii) The relation $\overset{*}{=}_I \subseteq \Sigma^* \times \Sigma^*$ is the least equivalence relation over Σ^* containing $\doteq_I$. □

In the notation as above we say that ρ and ρ' are *I-equivalent* iff $\rho \overset{*}{=}_I \rho'$. We use $[\rho]_I$ to denote the equivalence class of $\overset{*}{=}_I$ containing ρ and we use $\Theta(I)$ to denote the set of all equivalence classes of I.

Remark 4.1. In the above we have used the notations like $\doteq_I, \overset{*}{=}_I$, and $[\rho]_I$ which formally speaking are not correct; rather one should use the notations like $\doteq_Z$, $\overset{*}{=}_Z$, and $[\rho]_Z$, respectively. However we have decided on this slight abuse of notation for didactical reasons. In the context of a given reliance alphabet $Z = (\Sigma, I, D)$ some of the notions we will consider will explicitly depend on I while other will explicitly depend on D - to make this apparent we will subscript our notation for the former by I and for the latter by D . □

Example 4.1. Consider the reliance alphabet $Z_1 = (\Sigma_1, I_1, D_1)$, where $\Sigma_1 = \{a, b, c, d\}$

and

$I_1 = \{(a,b), (b,a), (a,d), (d,a), (b,c), (c,b)\}$,

and the string $\rho_1 = a\,b\,c\,a\,d$.

Then

$\rho_1 \doteq_{I_1} b\,a\,c\,a\,d \doteq_{I_1} b\,a\,c\,d\,a$ and consequently $\rho_1 \overset{*}{\doteq}_{I_1} b\,a\,c\,d\,a$.

As a matter of fact

$[\rho_1]_{I_1} = \{abcad, bacad, bacda, abcda, acbda, acabd, acbad\}$. □

We are ready now to define the notions of a trace and a trace language.

Definition 4.3. Let $Z = (\Sigma, I, D)$ be a reliance alphabet. An element of $\Theta(I)$ is called a *trace* (*over* I) and a subset of $\Theta(I)$ is called a *trace language* (over I) . □

For a reliance alphabet $Z = (\Sigma, I, D)$, a string language $K \subseteq \Sigma^*$ may be partitioned by $\overset{*}{=}_I$ in either a "consistent" or an "inconsistent" way.

Definition 4.4. Let $Z = (\Sigma, I, D)$ be a reliance alphabet and let $K \subseteq \Sigma^*$. We say that K is I - *consistent* iff

$(\forall t \in \Theta(I))[$ either $t \cap K = \emptyset$ or $t \subseteq K]$. □

Example 4.2. Consider the reliance alphabet Z_1 from Example 4.1 and consider the language $K = \{abcad, acabd, daa\}$. Then K is *not* I_1-consistent because $[\rho_1]_{I_1} \cap K \neq \emptyset$ while $[\rho_1]_{I_1} \not\subseteq K$ (where $\rho_1 = abcad$).

On the other hand,

$K' = \{abcad, bacad, bacda, abcda, acbda, acabd, acbad, cbd, bcd\}$

is Z_1-consistent since $K' = [\rho_1]_{I_1} \cup [cbd]_{I_1}$. □

Given a reliance alphabet $Z = (\Sigma, I, D)$ a string language $K \subseteq \Sigma^*$ induces a trace language over Z as follows.

Definition 4.5. Let $Z = (\Sigma, I, D)$ be a reliance alphabet and let $K \subseteq \Sigma^*$. The *trace language of* K (*over* I) denoted $[K]_I$ is the trace language

$\{[x]_I \mid x \in K\}$. □

Now we can use classes of string languages to define classes of trace languages. In particular we can transfer the notion of regularity of string languages into the framework of trace languages as follows.

Definition 4.6. Let $Z = (\Sigma, I, D)$ be a reliance alphabet and let $T \subseteq \Theta(I)$. We say that

T is *regular* iff there exists a regular $K \subseteq \Sigma^*$ such that $T = [K]_I$. □

Example 4.3. Let Z_1, K, K′ and ρ_1 be as in Example 4.2. Then

$[K]_I = \{[\rho_1]_I, [daa]_I\}$ and $[K']_I = \{[\rho_1]_I, [cbd]_I\}$;

since, both K and K′ are regular (even finite),

$[K]_I$ and $[K']_I$ are regular trace languages. □

Each trace may be viewed as an abstract acyclic node-labeled directed graph and consequently as an abstract labeled poset. This fact is crucial in applying the theory of traces to define the non-sequential behaviour of EN systems.

Definition 4.7. Let $Z = (\Sigma, I, D)$ be a reliance alphabet and let $\rho \in \Sigma^*$.

(i) If $\rho = \Lambda$ then the *canonical dependence graph of* ρ is the empty graph and the *canonical labeled poset of* ρ is the empty poset.

(ii) Let $\rho = \sigma_1 \dots \sigma_n$ for some $n \geq 1, \sigma_1, \dots, \sigma_n \in \Sigma$.

The *canonical dependence graph of* ρ is the Σ-labeled graph (V, Y, ϕ) defined by:

(1) $V = \{1, \dots, n\}$,

(2) $(\forall i \in \{1, \dots, n\})[\ \phi(i) = \sigma_i\ ]$,

(3) $(\forall i,j \in \{1, \dots, n\})[\ (i,j) \in Y$ iff $(i < j$ and $(\sigma_i, \sigma_j) \in D)\ ]$.

The *canonical labeled poset of* ρ is the labeled poset determined by the canonical dependence graph of ρ . □

The canonical dependence graph of ρ is denoted by $<\rho>_D$ and the canonical labeled poset of ρ is denoted by $<<\rho>>_D$.

Remark 4.2. It is important to notice that while D is reflexive, $<\rho>_D$ is irreflexive. □

The basic property of the above construction is the following.

Lemma 4.1. Let $Z = (\Sigma, I, D)$ be a reliance alphabet and let $\rho, \rho' \in \Sigma^*$. Then $<\rho>_D$ *isom* $<\rho'>_D$ iff $[\rho]_I = [\rho']_I$. □

Thus for a trace $t = [\rho]_I \in \Theta(I)$, $<\rho>_D$ is an "isomorphic invariant" of t - it does not depend (up to an isomorphism) on the choice of a representative of t.

Example 4.4. Let Z_1 and ρ_1 be as in Example 4.1.
Then $<\rho_1>_{D_1}$ is as follows :

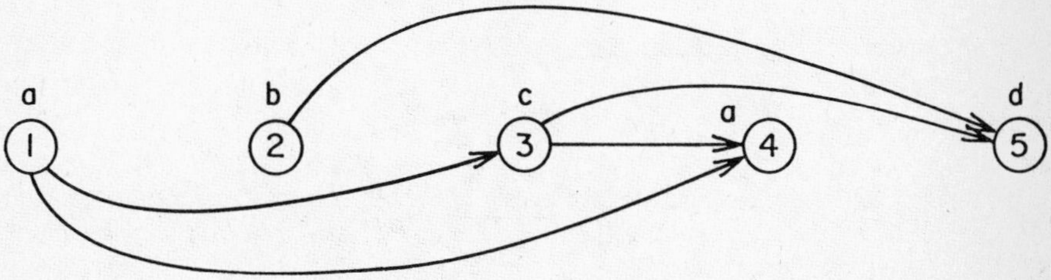

Figure 4.1

For $\rho_2 = \text{bacda}$, $<\rho_2>_{D_1}$ is as follows :

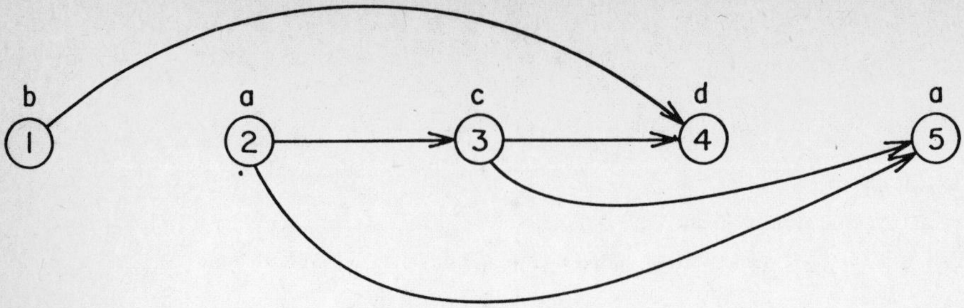

Figure 4.2

We notice that $\rho_1 \overset{*}{=}_I \rho_2$ (see Example 4.1) and indeed, according to Lemma 4.1, we have $< \rho_1 >_{D_1}$ *isom* $< \rho_2 >_{D_1}$; to see this consider the bijection α between the nodes of $< \rho_1 >_{D_1}$ and the nodes of $< \rho_2 >_{D_1}$ defined by :

$\alpha(1) = 2, \alpha(2) = 1, \alpha(3) = 3, \alpha(4) = 5$ and $\alpha(5) = 4$.

Clearly, $<< \rho_1 >>_{D_1}$ is as follows :

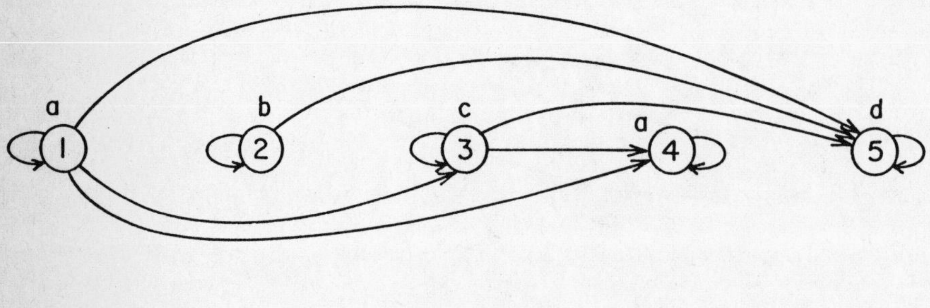

Figure 4.3

while $<< \rho_2 >>_{D_1}$ is as follows :

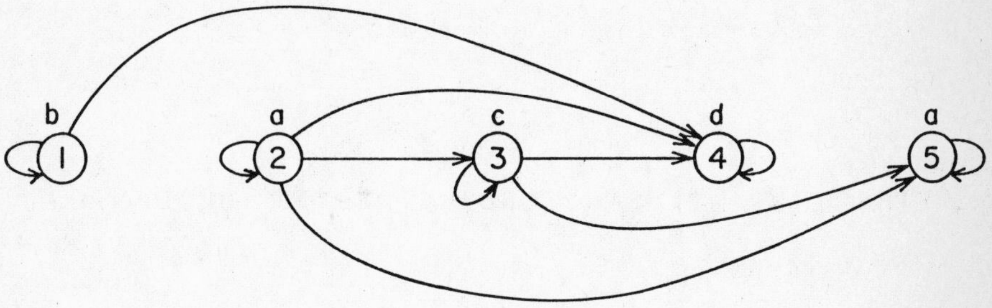

Figure 4.4

□

Definition 4.8. Let $Z = (\Sigma, I, D)$ be a reliance alphabet

(i) Let $t \in \Theta(I)$.

The *abstract dependence graph of* t, denoted *adg*(t) , is the abstract node-labeled graph $\overline{<\rho>_D}$, where $\rho \in t$.

The *abstract labeled poset of* t , denoted *alp*(t) , is the abstract labeled poset $\overline{<<\rho>>_D}$, where $\rho \in t$.

(ii) Let $T \subseteq \Theta(I)$.

The *set of abstract dependence graphs of* T, denoted **ADG**(T), is the set $\{adg(t) \mid t \in T\}$.

The *set of abstract labeled posets of* T, denoted **ALP**(T), is the set $\{alp(t) \mid t \in T\}$. □

Remark 4.3.

(1) Note that Lemma 4.1 guarantees that the notions of the abstract dependence graph and of the abstract labeled poset of a trace are well-defined; i.e., given $\rho, \rho' \in t$, $\overline{<\rho>_D} = \overline{<\rho'>_D}$ and $\overline{<<\rho>>_D} = \overline{<<\rho'>>_D}$.

(2) Since we are mostly interested in *abstract* dependence graphs and *abstract* labeled posets

we will often skip the adjective "abstract" and talk simply about dependence graphs and labeled posets of traces. Whenever we need to talk about a representative of the abstract dependence graph (abstract labeled poset) of a trace we will use the adjective "concrete" ; thus a concrete dependence graph of a trace t is an element of *adg*(t) - in particular, $<\rho>_D$ for a ρ in t is a concrete dependence graph of t . □

5. EXTRACTING CAUSAL ORDERS FROM SEQUENTIAL OBSERVATIONS

Within the theory of traces a concurrent system S is modeled through the notion of a trace system which consists of (contains) an information about the "structure" of S and an information about sequential observations of S. The former is formalized via a reliance alphabet $Z = (\Sigma , I , D)$, where Σ is the set of events of S and the latter is formalized via a language $K \subseteq \Sigma^*$. Formally we have the following definition.

Definition 5.1. A *trace system* is an ordered pair $S = (Z , K)$ where $Z = (\Sigma , I , D)$ is a reliance alphabet and $K \subseteq \Sigma^*$. □

Given a trace system $S = (Z , K)$ one uses Z to extract causal, in general partial, order of events from strings of K using techniques described in Section 4. In order to model an EN system $N = (B , E ; F , C_{in})$ by a trace system one has to define the corresponding reliance alphabet $Z_N = (\Sigma , I_N , D_N)$ and the corresponding string language K_N. The first steps of this modelling are rather obvious: Σ is the set of events E and K_N is the set of firing sequences **FS**(N). The remaining step is to define the independence relation I_N.

Definition 5.2. Let $N = (B, E, F, C_{in})$ be an EN system. The *independence relation induced by N*, denoted I_N , is the binary relation over E defined by:

$(\forall e_1 , e_2 \in E)[(e_1 , e_2) \in I_N \text{ iff } ({}^\bullet e_1 \cup e_1^\bullet) \cap ({}^\bullet e_2 \cup e_2^\bullet) = \emptyset]$.

The *reliance alphabet induced by* N, denoted Z_N, is the triplet (E, I_N, D_N) where $D_N = E \times E - I_N$ is the *dependence relation induced by* N . □

One can easily verify that Z_N is indeed a reliance alphabet (i.e. that I_N is a symmetric and irreflexive relation) .

The independence relation I_N for an EN system N is well-chosen in the following sense.

Theorem 5.1. Let N be an EN system. Then $\mathbf{FS}(N)$ is I_N-consistent. □

Hence if a firing sequence ρ is observable in N then so is every firing sequence that is I_N-equivalent with ρ !

Example 5.1. Consider the EN system N_1 from Example 3.1. Then

$I_{N_1} = \{(e_1,e_3),(e_3,e_1),(e_1,e_5),(e_5,e_1),(e_3,e_4),(e_4,e_3),(e_4,e_5),(e_5,e_4)\}$,

$D_{N_1} = (E_1 \times E_1) - I_{N_1}$,

and

$Z_{N_1} = (E_1, I_{N_1}, D_{N_1})$.

Clearly, $e_1 e_3 e_5 e_4 e_2 \in \mathbf{FS}(N_1)$.

It is easily verified that

$$[e_1e_3e_5e_4e_2]_{I_{N_1}} = \{e_3e_5e_1e_4e_2,\ e_3e_1e_5e_4e_2,\ e_1e_3e_5e_4e_2,\ e_3e_1e_4e_5e_2,\ e_1e_3e_4e_5e_2,\ e_1e_4e_3e_5e_2\} .$$

By Theorem 5.1, $[e_1e_3e_5e_4e_2]_{I_{N_1}} \subseteq \mathbf{FS}(N_1)$ and indeed it is easily verified that each element of $[e_1e_3e_5e_4e_2]_{I_{N_1}}$ is the sequence of edge labels corresponding to a path in SCG_{N_1} (see Example 3.1) and thus is a firing sequence of N_1 . □

Now we can transform the set of firing sequences of an EN system into its set of traces, the set of abstract dependence graphs and the set of abstract labeled posets.

Definition 5.3. Let N be an EN system.

(i) The set of *firing traces of* N, denoted $\mathbf{FT}(N)$, is the trace language $[\mathbf{FS}(N)]_{I_N}$.

(ii) The set of *abstract firing dependence graphs of* N, denoted $\mathbf{AFD}(N)$, is the set $\mathbf{ADG}(\mathbf{FT}(N))$.

(iii) The set of *abstract firing labeled posets of* N, denoted $\mathbf{AFLP}(N)$, is the set $\mathbf{ALP}(\mathbf{FT}(N))$.

Example 5.2. Let N_1 be the EN system from Example 3.1. The following are some of the concrete firing dependence graphs of N_1 (see Example 5.1 for D_{N_1}) :

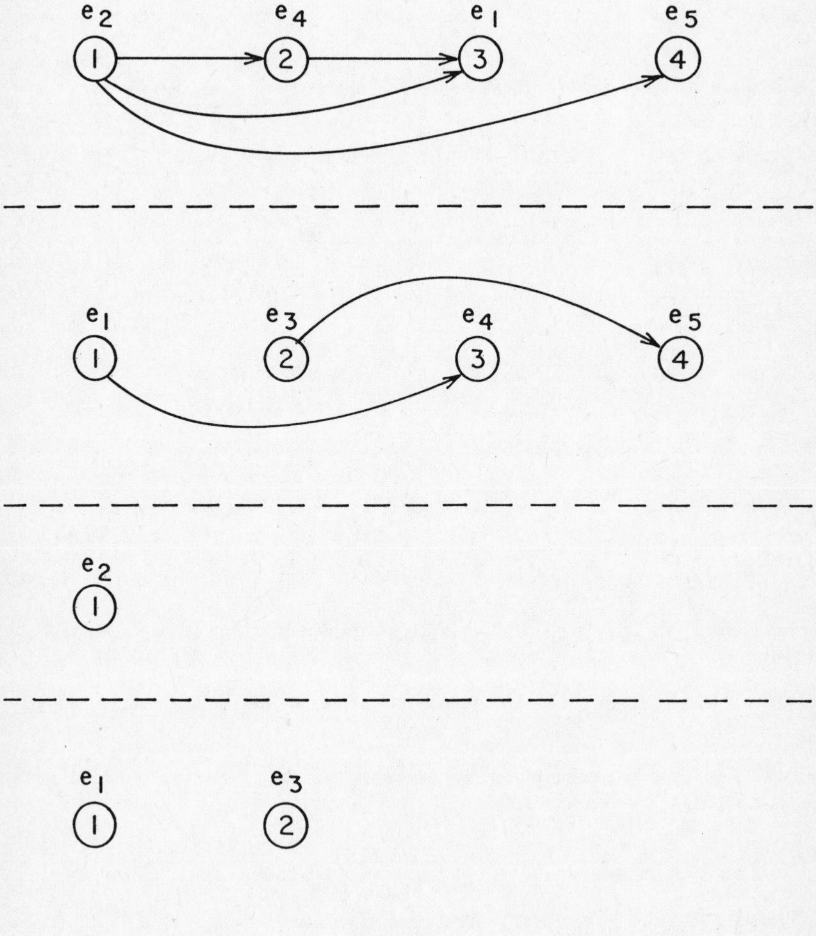

Figure 5.1

The corresponding concrete labeled posets are:

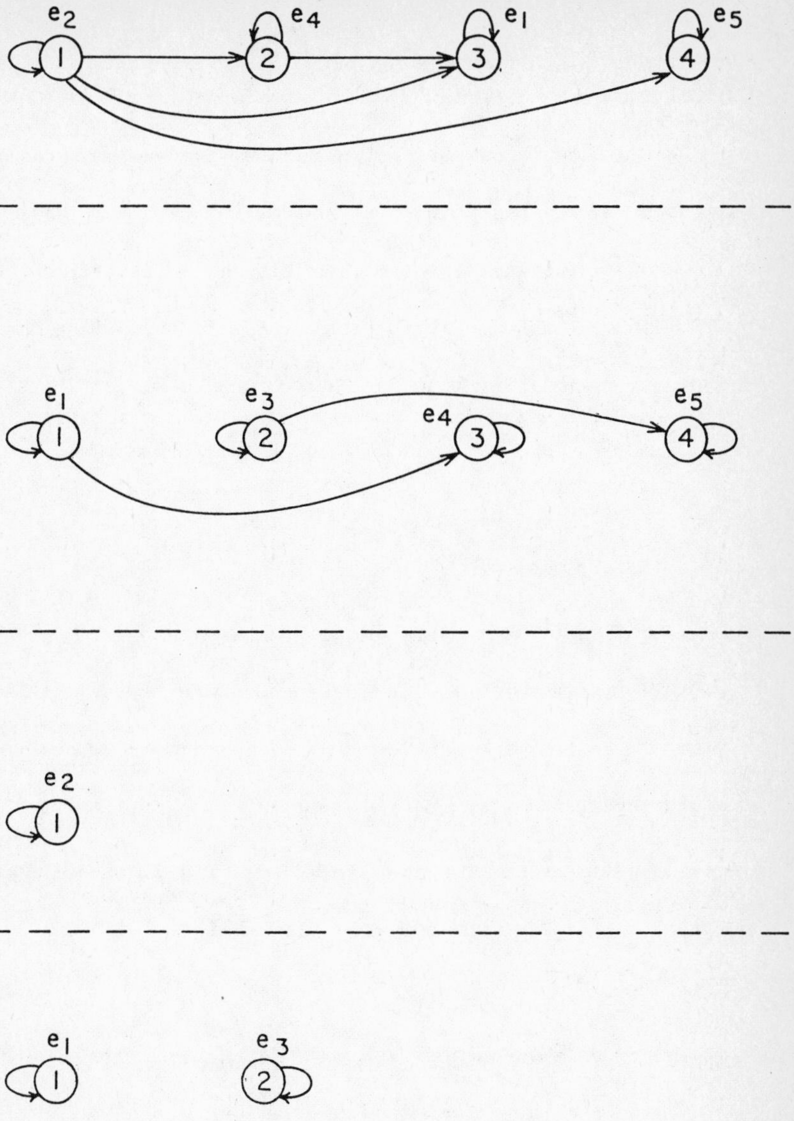

Figure 5.2

The following result follows directly from Theorem 3.1.

Theorem 5.2. $\mathbf{FT}(N)$ is regular for each EN system N . □

6. NON-SEQUENTIAL OBSERVATIONS OF EVENT OCCURRENCES AND CONDITION HOLDINGS

We will consider now a representation of the non-sequential behaviour of an EN system that is more detailed than the one obtained via firing traces. The idea is to "run" the system - resolving conflicts in an arbitrary fashion as and when they arise - and record non-sequential occurrences by events *together with* the resulting holdings of conditions during such a run. Now the records are non-sequential to start with and the resulting objects (called *processes*) are based on a special kind of nets called occurrence nets.

Definition 6.1. An *occurrence net* is a net N = (S , T ; F) which satisfies

(i) $(\forall s \in S)[\,|{}^\bullet s| \leq 1$ and $|s^\bullet| \leq 1\,]$.

(ii) $(\forall x,y \in X_N)[\,(x,y) \in F^+ \Rightarrow (y,x) \notin F^+\,]$. □

An occurrence net is meant to model a non-sequential stretch of history and hence it is required to be acyclic. In such a history - where all conflicts have been resolved - every condition begins (ceases) to hold as the result of a unique event occurrence. Consequently every condition is required to be non-branching both at the input and output side.

Also, we do not consider events with empty output sets. *Thus for the sequel we will additionally assume that* if N = (S , T ; F) is an occurrence net then:

(iii) $(\forall t \in T)[\,t^\bullet \neq \emptyset\,]$.

Since an occurrence net is a bipartite graph the notion of a node-labeled occurrence net should be clear. Now we can define a process of an EN system as a node-labeled occurrence net satisfying certain "consistency requirements". We will use $^\circ N$ to denote the set $\{x \in X_N \mid {}^\bullet x = \emptyset\}$.

Definition 6.2. Let $N = (B,E;F,C_{in})$ be an EN system and $N = (S,T;H,\phi)$ a node-labeled occurrence net.

N is a *process of* N iff

(i) $\phi(S) \subseteq B$ and $\phi(T) \subseteq E$.

(ii) $(\forall s_1,s_2 \in S)[\phi(s_1) = \phi(s_2) \Rightarrow$ either $s_1 \leq_N s_2$ or $s_2 \leq_N s_1]$.

(iii) $(\forall t \in T)[\phi({}^\bullet t) = {}^\bullet\phi(t)$ and $\phi(t^\bullet) = \phi(t)^\bullet]$.

(iv) $\phi({}^\circ N) \subseteq C_{in}$. □

We use $\mathbf{P}(N)$ to denote the set of all processes of N .

It is easily seen that if N is a process, then ${}^\bullet t \neq \emptyset$ for every $t \in T_N$.

Example 6.1. Consider the EN system N_1 from Example 3.1. Then the following node-labeled occurrence net $N_1 = (S_1, T_1; H_1, \phi_1)$:

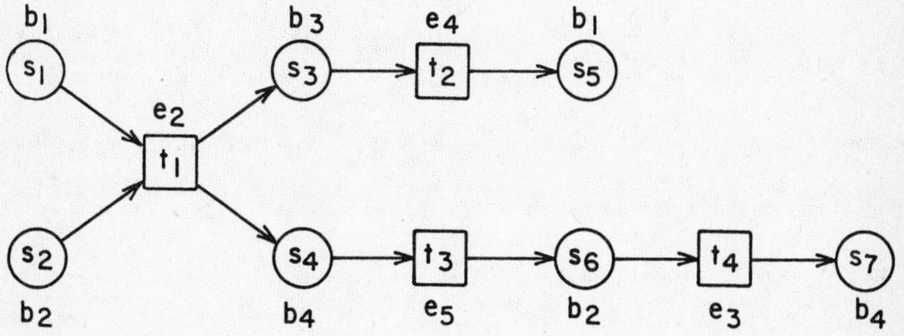

Figure 6.1

is a process of N_1 ; here we use the graphical convention that the identity of an element of N_1 (an S-element or a T-element) is indicated within a node representing it (a circle or a box respectively) while the label of the element (i.e., the value of ϕ_1) is written next to the node representing the element.

It is easily seen that the labeling ϕ_1 of the occurrence net $(S_1,T_1;H_1)$ satisfies conditions (i) through (iv) of the above definition.

N_1 records non-sequential occurrences of events e_2, e_4, e_5, e_3 together with the holdings of appropriate conditions during a run of N_1 transforming the case $\{b_1,b_2\}$ into the case $\{b_1,b_4\}$.

Also the following occurrence net $N_2 = (S_2,T_2;H_2,\phi_2)$:

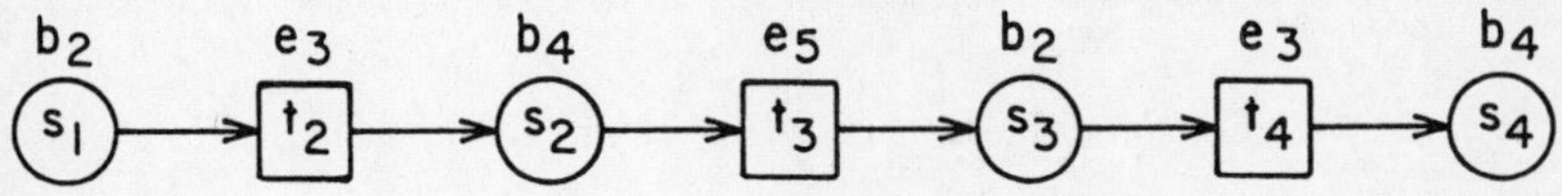

Figure 6.2

is a process of N_1. It records sequential occurrences of events (an occurrence of e_3 followed by an occurrence of e_5 followed by an occurrence of e_3) together with the holdings of appropriate conditions during a run of N_1 transforming the subcase $\{b_2\}$ (of the case $\{b_1,b_2\}$) into the subcase $\{b_4\}$ (of the case $\{b_1,b_4\}$) .

□

A useful intuition behind the notion of the process is this : if we mark the conditions in ^{o}N and play the token game on N , then this particular game should also be "permitted" by N . This intuition is formalized as follows. (A *slice* of an occurrence net N, or of a node labeled occurrence net N, is a maximal anti-chain consisting of S-elements only.)

Theorem 6.1. Let N be an EN system, $N = (S,T;F,\phi)$ a process of N and S' a slice of N. Then there exists a $C \in C_N$ such that $\phi(S') \subseteq C$. □

The notion of a process as a formalization of a behaviour of an EN system is too detailed : it turns out that two EN systems without "redundant events" with label-isomorphic sets of processes are structurally similar.

In order to formalize the notion of an EN system without "redundant events" we need the following definition.

Definition 6.3. Let N be an EN system. The set of *active events of* N, denoted ev(N), is the set $\bigcup_{U \in \mathcal{U}_N} U$. If $E_N = ev(N)$, then N is *reduced.* □

It is easily seen that, in general, ev(N) may be a strict subset of E_N .

The label-isomorphism of sets of processes is understood as follows. Let W_1 be a set of node Σ_1-labeled bipartite graphs and W_2 be a set of node Σ_2-labeled bipartite graphs. We say that W_1 and W_2 are *label-isomorphic* iff there exists a function $\gamma : \Sigma_1 \rightarrow \Sigma_2$ and a bijection $\delta : W_1 \rightarrow W_2$ such that for each $g \in W_1$, g and δ(g) are label-isomorphic where the bijection involved between the labels of g - say Σ_g - and the labels of δ(g) is γ restricted to Σ_g .

We are ready now to formalize the above mentioned result.

Theorem 6.2. Let N_1 and N_2 be reduced EN systems. Then $\mathbf{P}(N_1)$ is label-isomorphic with $\mathbf{P}(N_2)$ iff $N_1 \equiv N_2$. □

Although the process representation of the behaviour of an EN system is too detailed (as manifested by the above result) the *notion* of a process is very useful. Indeed a theory of non-sequential processes based on occurrence nets can be built up without tying ourselves down to a system model. This theory is discussed in the contribution by C. Fernandez.

To overcome the rather undesirable identification of an EN system with its (process) behaviour one tries to get rid of too detailed information recorded within a process. The obvious way to do it is to dispose of recording of the holdings of conditions during a run of the system.

This leads us to the following definition.

Definition 6.4. Let N be an EN system and let $\mathrm{N} = (S,T;F,\phi)$ be a process of N.

(i) The S-contracted version of N is a *contracted process of N* ; the set of all contracted processes of N is denoted by **CP**(N).

(ii) The *elementary event structure of* N, denoted *ees*(N), is the labeled poset $\leq_{ctr_S(N)}$; the set of all elementary event structures of processes of N is denoted by **EES**(N) . □

By considering contracted processes, rather than processes, one disposes of the identification of an EN system with its behaviour. Now a given behaviour can be realized by (essentially) different EN systems.

Theorem 6.3. There exist reduced EN systems N_1 and N_2 such that **CP**(N_1) is label-isomorphic with **CP**(N_2) while it is not true that $N_1 \equiv N_2$. □

In developing the theory of behaviour of EN systems we have assumed that we deal with contact-free systems only. Now we can, somewhat informally, give (some of the) reasons for this assumption.

Consider the EN system N_2 with the following N_{N_2}:

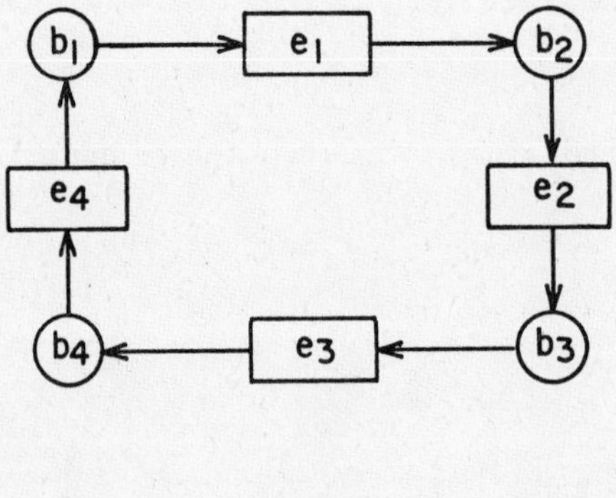

Figure 6.3

and the initial case equal $\{b_1 , b_3\}$. It is clear that this system can have arbitrarily long stretches of behaviour (e.g. the sequence of steps $\{e_1,e_3\}$, $\{e_2,e_4\}$ may be repeated arbitrarily many times).

On the other hand, if we would like to apply our definition of a process to N_2 then we get only a finite set of abstract processes for N_2 !

Here they are (since we consider abstract processes we indicate only the labels of the elements of the occurrence nets) :

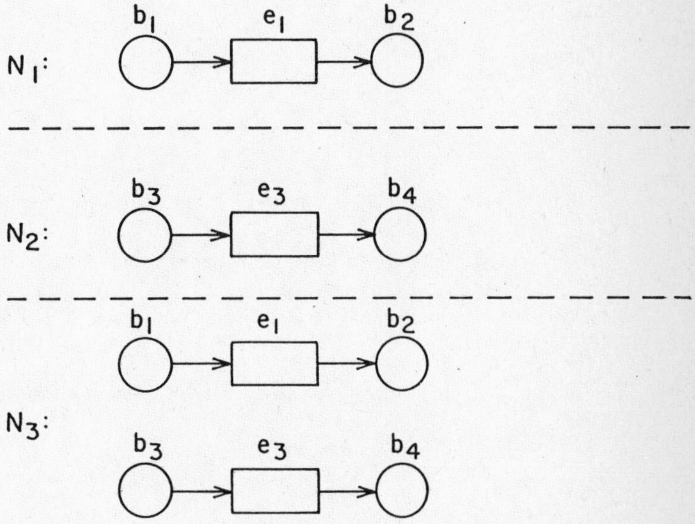

Figure 6.4

We note that, e.g., if we consider two possible "elementary" extensions of N_3 :

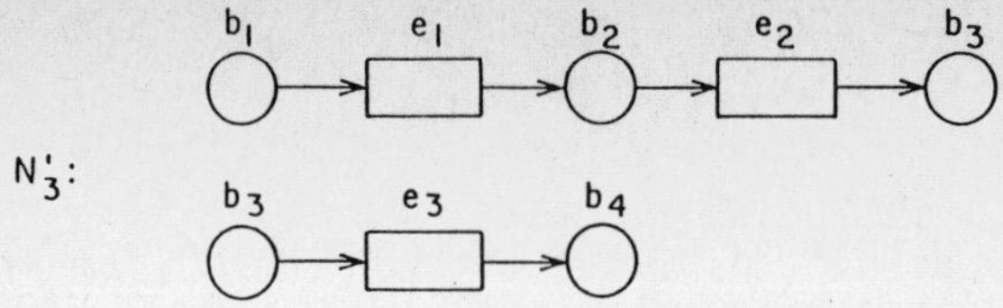

and

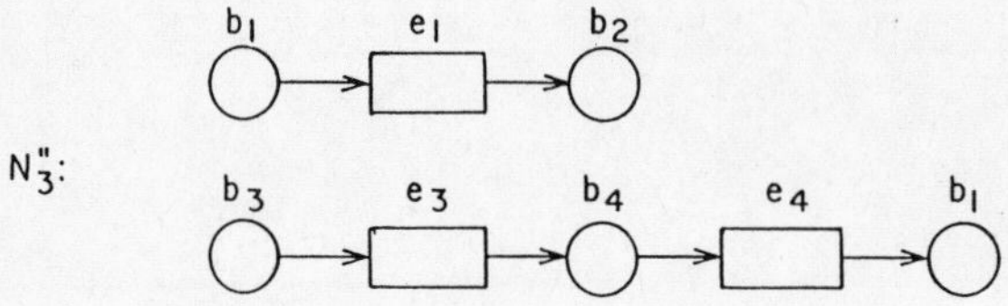

Figure 6.5

then we get node-labeled occurrence nets which are not processes of N_2 ; condition (ii) of Definition 6.2 is violated : in N_3' we have two places labeled by b_3 which are not ordered in $\leq_{N_3'}$, and in N_3'' we have two places labeled by b_1 which are not ordered in $\leq_{N_3''}$.

On the other hand if we apply the standard complement construction to N_2 we obtain the EN system N_2' with the following underlying net:

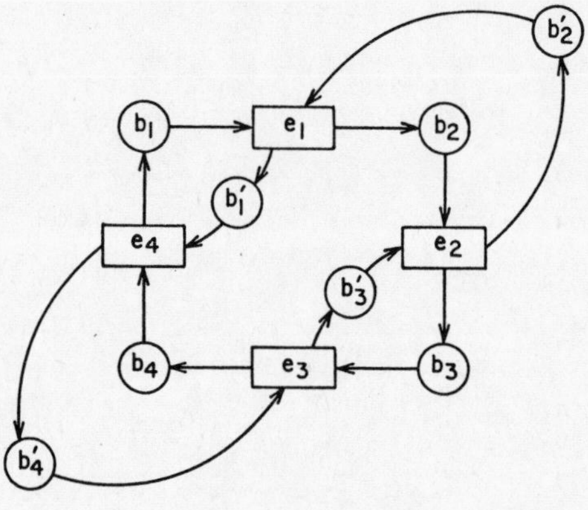

Figure 6.6

and with the initial case equal $\{b_1, b'_2, b_3, b'_4\}$. Now the set of processes is infinite.

Here, e.g., the process "corresponding to" the node-labeled occurrence net N_3' is the following node-labeled occurrence net $\tilde{N}_3$:

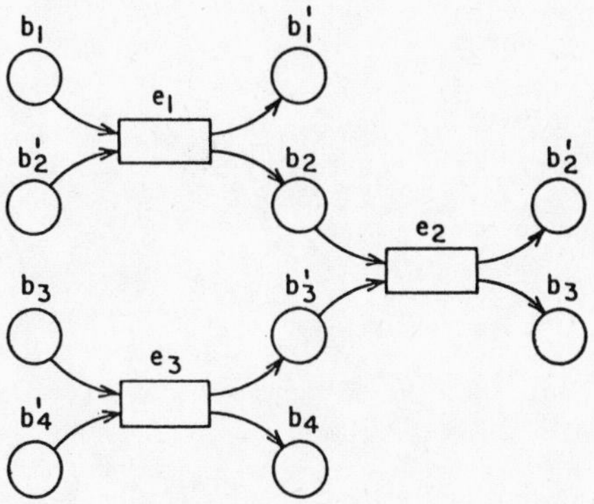

Figure 6.7

Now the two places labeled by b_3 are ordered in $\leq_{\tilde{N}_3}$!

7. COMPARING SEQUENTIAL AND NON-SEQUENTIAL APPROACHES

We have discussed two essentially different ways (methodologies) of representing the behaviour of an EN system N.

(1) Obtain the firing sequences of the system. Then use the dependence relation D_N to break these strings into dependence graphs of N to obtain **AFD**(N) and subsequently **AFLP**(N).

This methodology can be illustrated as follows:

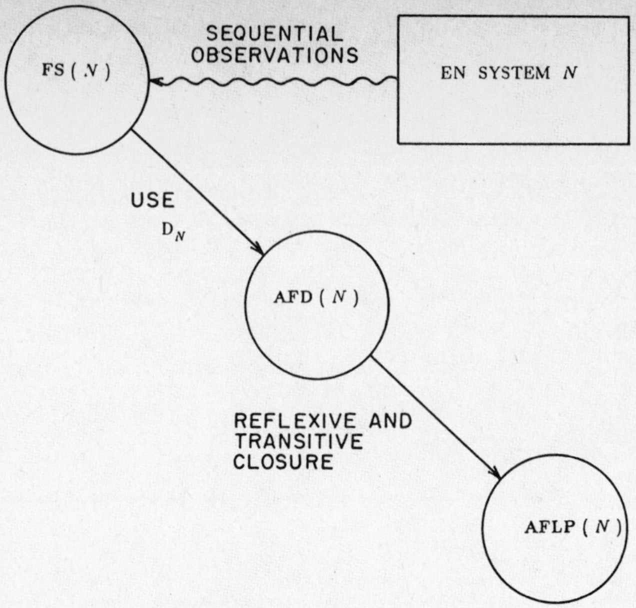

Figure 7.1

(2) Obtain the processes of N. Then use the (S-)contraction to obtain **CP**(N) and consequently **EES**(N) .

This methodology can be illustrated as follows:

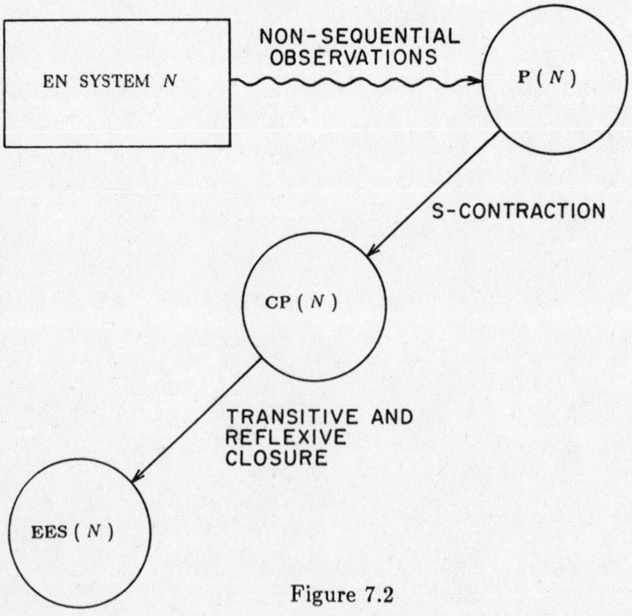

Figure 7.2

The following result provides the comparison of these approaches (in what follows, $\stackrel{\lambda}{=}$ denotes the equality of two sets of node labeled graphs modulo the empty graph λ).

Theorem 7.1.

(1) There exists an EN system N such that $\mathbf{AFD}(N) \stackrel{\lambda}{\neq} \mathbf{CP}(N)$.

(2) For each EN system N, $\mathbf{AFLP}(N) \stackrel{\lambda}{=} \mathbf{EES}(N)$. □

Hence we have the following situation:

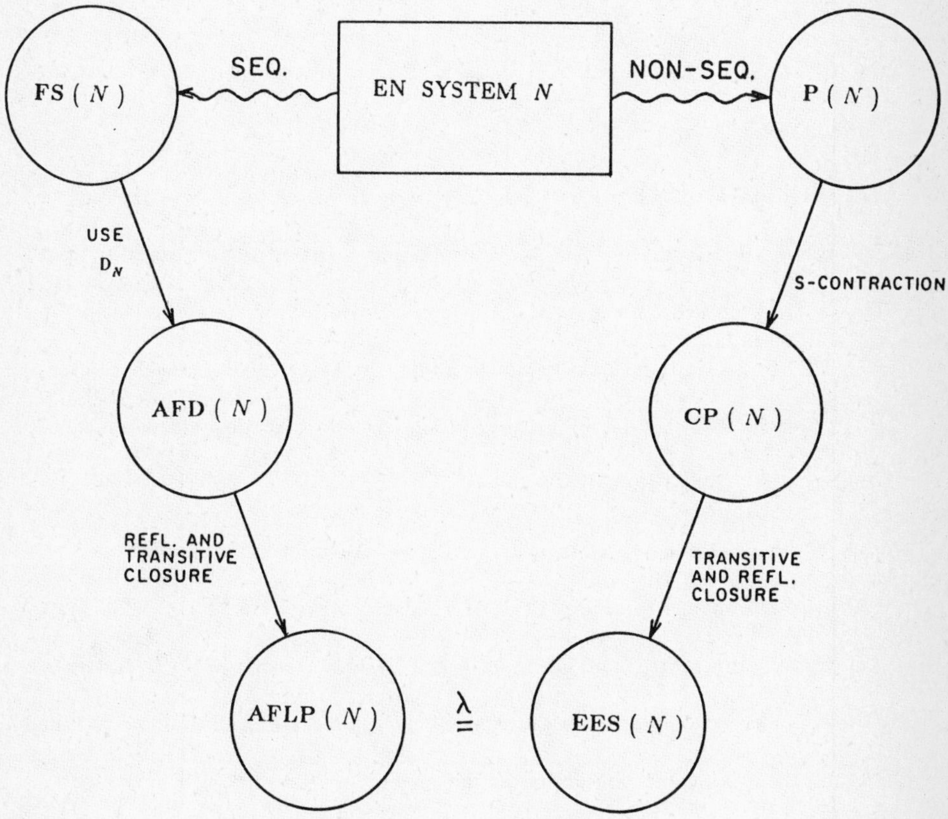

Figure 7.3

ACKNOWLEDGEMENTS

The author is indebted to IJ.J. Aalbersberg, I. Keesmaat and P.S. Thiagarajan for useful comments on the first version of theses notes, and to H. Ortiz and M. Powell for the superb typing of the manuscript in a very short time. THe author gratefully acknowledges the support by National Science Foundation grant number MCS-8305245.

8. BIBLIOGRAPHICAL NOTES

The material presented here follows very closely [RT] where also the notion of an EN system was formulated.

Expressing the behaviour of Petri nets by the sets of firing sequences was the topic of very extensive investigation in 1970's. The major work that initiated this research is due to Hack [H]. Typical work on firing sequences and their generalizations is presented in [J], [JV], [P], [RV], and [S1]. Unfortunately little is known about the sets of firing sequences of EN systems (or C/E systems). The topic of firing sequences is discussed in more depth in the contribution by M. Jantzen and R. Valk.

The theory of traces is due to A. Mazurkiewicz [M1]. An interesting application of the theory of traces to the problem of decomposition of C/E systems is presented in [M2]. A survey of the theory of traces stressing the relationship to the theory of C/E systems is presented in [AR]. The basic properties of dependency graphs are studied in [ER]. The major issues of the theory of traces are presented in the contribution by A. Mazurkiewicz.

The notion of a process (for C/E systems) was introduced by C.A. Petri in [Pt]. Typical work on the theory of processes is presented in [B], [FT], [R], and [S2]. The notion of a process for P/T systems is formulated in [GR]. The contribution by C. Fernandez investigates many important issues in the theory of processes.

Elementary event structures were formulated in [NPW].

The relationship between the sequential and the non-sequential behaviour as discussed in our paper (and illustrated by the final diagram of Section 7) is established in [AR] (for the case of C/E systems). Related work - mainly for P/T systems - is presented in [BF].

9. REFERENCES

[AR] IJ.J. Aalbersberg and G. Rozenberg, Theory of traces, Institute of Applied Mathematics and Computer Science, University of Leiden, Techn. Rep. No. 86-16 (1986).

[B] E. Best, A theorem on characteristics of non-sequential processes, *Fundamenta Informatica* III.1 (1980), pp. 77-94.

[BF] E. Best and C. Fernandez, Concurrent systems and processes, GMD Internal Report (1985).

[ER] A. Ehrenfeucht and G. Rozenberg, On the structure of dependency graphs, Computer Science Department, University of Colorado at Boulder, Boulder, Colorado, USA, Tech. Rep. No. CU-CS-329-86 (1986).

[FT] C. Fernandez and P.S. Thiagarajan, D-continuous causal nets: a model of non-sequential processes, *Theoretical Computer Science* 28 (1984), pp. 171-196.

[GR] U. Goltz and W. Reisig, The non-sequential behaviour of Petri nets, *Information and Control* 57 (1983), pp. 125-147.

[H] M.H.T. Hack, Petri net languages, Computation Structures Group Memo 124, Project MAC, M.I.T., Cambridge, Massachusetts, USA (1976).

[J] M. Jantzen, On the hierarchy of Petri net languages, *RAIRO Theoretical Informatics* 19 (1979), pp. 19-30.

[JV] M. Jantzen and R. Valk, Formal properties of Place/Transition systems, *Lecture*

Notes in Computer Science 84 (1980).

[M1] A. Mazurkiewicz, Concurrent program schemes and their interpretation, Computer Science Deparatment, Aarhus University, Aarhus, Denmark, Techn. Rep. No. PB-78 (1978).

[M2] A. Mazurkiewicz, Semantics of concurrent systems: a modular fixed-point trace approach, *Lecture Notes in Computer Science* 188 (1984), pp. 353-375.

[NPW] M. Nielsen, G. Plotkin and G. Winskel, Petri nets, event structures and domains, Part I, *Theoretical Computer Science* 13 (1981), pp. 85-108.

[P] J.L. Peterson, Computation sequence sets, *Journal of Computer and System Sciences* 13 (1976), pp. 1-24.

[Pt] C.A. Petri, Non-sequential processes, GMD, St. Augustin, W. Germany, Internal Report GMD-ISF-77.5 (1977).

[R] W. Reisig, *Petri nets: An Introduction,* EATCS Monographs on Theoretical Computer Science, Springer-Verlag, Heidelberg (1985).

[RT] G. Rozenberg and P.S. Thiagarajan, Petri nets: basic notions, structure, behaviour, *Lecture Notes in Computer Science* 224 (1986), pp. 585-668.

[RV] G. Rozenberg and R. Verraedt, Subsets languages of Petri nets, Part I, *Theoretical Computer Science* 26 (1983), pp. 301-326.

[S1] P. Starke, Free Petri net languages, *Lecture Notes in Computer Science* 64 (1978), pp. 506-515.

[S2] P. Starke, Processes in Petri net, *Electronische Informationsverarbeitung und Kybernetik* 17 (1981).

NON-SEQUENTIAL PROCESSES

César Fernández

Gesellschaft für Mathematik und Datenverarbeitung mbH
Postfach 1240, Schloß Birlinghoven
D-5205 St. Augustin 1
Federal Republic of Germany

ABSTRACT. This paper present a selection of some properties of a non-sequential process.
Three types of properties are studied, namely: discreteness properties, density properties and the D-continuity property.
Relations between these properties are established.

Key words: Occurrence net, line, cut, poset, dense, combinatorial, discreteness properties, N-density, K-density, D-continuity.

CONTENTS

1. Introduction

Net theory uses a uniform language to talk about systems and processes. In order to investigate the properties of a system we use "marked nets". A behaviour of a marked net - i.e. a behaviour of a system - can be recorded in different ways. One way is to record the condition holdings and the event occurrences of the system. In the frame of net theory, what we get is called a non-sequential process.

Non-sequential processes can also be studied using nets; in this case, a particular type of nets is needed. We call them "occurrence nets". The specific properties of an occurrence net allow us to attach to each occurrence net a partially ordered set (poset, for short). In the last seven years a lot of research has been done in the area of non-sequential processes. The main motivation of the work done in those years has been the previous work of C.A. Petri exposed - for instance - in [9] and [10]. The idea of this paper is to present - using posets - some properties of a non-sequential process.

The selection of the properties presented here corresponds to the particular taste of the author of this paper, but - without any doubt - the choosing has been strongly influenced by the work done by C.A. Petri.

The paper is organized as follows:
In the next section we introduce some basic terminology. In section 3 we analyze three types of properties of a non-sequential process, namely: discreteness properties, density properties and the D-continuity property.

In section 4, we study some relations between the properties introduce in section 3.

The last section is devoted to some final remarks.

2. Occurrence Nets

We start with the concept of a net.

Definition 2.1 A triple $N = (S,T;F)$ is called a net iff

(a) $S \cap T = \emptyset$

(b) $F \subseteq (S\times T) \cup (T\times S)$

(c) $S \cup T \neq \emptyset$

(d) $\mathrm{dom}\, F \cup \mathrm{cod}\, F = S \cup T$

where:

$\mathrm{dom}\, F = \{x \in S \cup T \mid \exists y \in S \cup T : (x,y) \in F\}$

$\mathrm{cod}\, F = \{x \in S \cup T \mid \exists y \in S \cup T : (y,x) \in F\}$.

As always, S is the set of S-elements (drawn as circles in diagrams); T is the set of T-elements (drawn as boxes in diagrams) and F is the flow relation. In diagrams, the elements of F are denoted by directed arcs.
$X = S \cup T$ is the set of elements of the net.
We use the following notations:

$^{\bullet}x = \{y \in X \mid (y,x) \in F\}$ (Pre-set of $x \in X$)

$x^{\bullet} = \{y \in X \mid (x,y) \in F\}$ (Post-set of $x \in X$)

$F^{+} = \cup\{F^{n} \mid n \in \mathbb{N} - \{0\}\}$ $\mathbb{N} = \{0,1,2,3,\ldots\ldots\}$.

$F^{*} = F^{+} \cup \mathrm{id}$.

Let us consider an example. Figure 1 shows a system which is modelled by a net. The state of the system is represented by the marking shown in the figure. The well known transition rule tell us how a marking changes under the occurrence of one T-element.

In this example the T-elements are called events. The set of events are denoted by E.

The S-elements are called conditions and the set of conditions is denoted by B.

Our net (representing the concurrent system) is then N = (B,E;F) where:

$B = \{b_1, b_2, b_3, b_4, b_5, b_6, b_7\}$

F : As indicated in the figure

$E = \{e_1, e_2, e_3, e_4, e_5, e_6\}$.

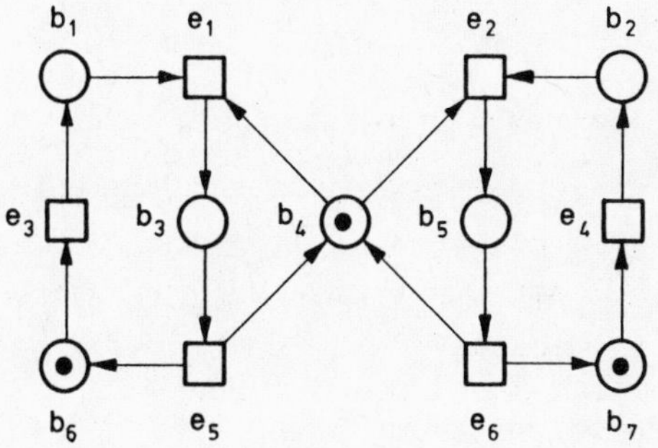

Figure 1

If we produce a run of a system, i.e. if we record the condition-holdings and the event-occurrences of the system then we get the net of figure 2.

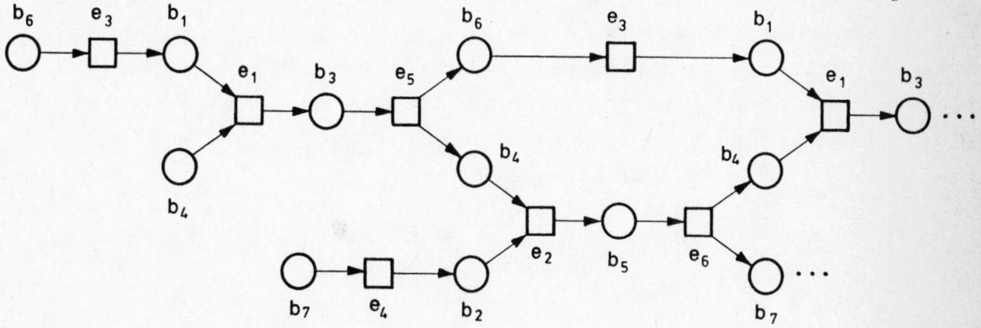

Figure 2

We say that the net in figure 2 is a non-sequential process of the system given in figure 1.

In the process of figure 2, the conflict between e_1 and e_2 (in the system) is solved, i.e. the net of figure 2 has no conflict.

Furthermore, this net has no cycles and for this reason we can - as we shall see later - attach to this type of net a partially ordered set (poset, for short).

This special kind of nets, with no cycles and no conflict, are called occurrence nets.

Formally, we have:

Definition 2.2 A net $N = (B,E;F)$ is called an occurrence net iff:

(a) $\forall b \in B : |{}^{\bullet}b| \leq 1 \wedge |b^{\bullet}| \leq 1$

(b) $\forall x,y \in B \cup E : (x,y) \in F^+ \Rightarrow (y,x) \notin F^+$

In an occurrence net the S-elements are called conditions and the T-elements, events. If $N = (B,E;F)$ is an occurrence net, then we can associate to it a structure PO_N or $PO=(X;<)$ - when no confusion arises - where $X = B \cup E$ and $< := F^+$.

Notation If $< = F^+$ then we can also use:

$\leq = F^+ \cup id = F^*$

$> = <^{-1}$

It is not difficult to see that the structure $PO = (X;<)$ is a partially ordered set, i.e. a set together with an irreflexive and transitive relation. Posets are an adequate and elegant mathematical machinery to study non-sequential processes. We shall consider posets in general; however, we must always remember that the poset attached to an occurrence net is a very particular one and this is the main concern of our study. We are going to need some basic concepts about posets. These are given in the next two definitions.

Definition 2.3 Let $PO = (X;<)$ be a poset. Then:

(a) $x \lessdot y \Leftrightarrow x < y \wedge \nexists z \in X : x < z < y$.

(b) For $x \in X$: ${}^{\bullet}x = \{y \in X | y \lessdot x\}$ and $x^{\bullet} = \{y \in X | x \lessdot y\}$

(c) PO is called dense iff $\lessdot = \emptyset$

(d) PO is called combinatorial iff $< = (\lessdot)^+$

<u>Remarks.</u>

(1) The notation introduced in definition 2.3(b) is consistent with the notation introduced after definition 2.1.

(2) Part (c) of the previous definition means that if $x < y$ then there exists always a $z \in X$ such that $x < z < y$.

(3) Part (d) of definition 2.3 means that if $x < y$ then there exists a finite set $\{x_1, x_2, \dots, x_n\} \subseteq X$ such that

$x = x_1 \lessdot x_2 \lessdot x_3 \lessdot \dots\dots\dots \lessdot x_n = y$.

(4) Clearly the poset attached to an occurrence net is combinatorial and for this reason, in what follows, we shall consider mainly combinatorial posets. We shall always assume $X \neq \emptyset$.

(5) If $x \lessdot y$ we shall use the graphical notation

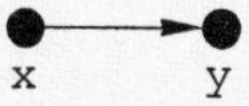

If $x < y$, but not necessarily $x \lessdot y$, we shall use the graphical notation 

(6) Finally we would like to point out that the poset attached to an occurrence net is not only combinatorial but has also some other specific properties. In some papers these type of posets have been called "occurrence posets" (see for instance [1]). Important is that the set of the posets attached to occurrence nets is a subset of the set of combinatorial posets.

We introduce now the relation co together with some other important concepts for posets.

<u>Definition 2.4</u> Let $PO = (X;<)$ be a poset. Then:

(a) $li = < \cup > \cup id$.

(b) $co = (X \times X - li) \cup id$

(c) $l \subseteq X$ is a li-set (chain) iff $\forall x,y \in l : (x,y) \in li$

(d) $l \subseteq X$ is a line (maximal chain) iff l is a li-set and $\forall z \in X-l \; \exists x \in l : (x,z) \notin li$.

(e) We denote with $L(X;<)$ - or L when no confusion arises - the set of lines of $(X;<)$.

(f) $c \subseteq X$ is a co-set (antichain) iff $\forall x,y \in c : (x,y) \in co$.

(g) $c \subseteq X$ is a cut (maximal antichain) iff c is a co-set and $\forall z \in X - c \; \exists x \in c : (x,z) \notin co$.

(h) We denote with C(X;<) - or C when no confusion arises - the set of cuts of (X;<).

<u>Example</u> Consider the infinite occurrence net (and its attached poset) given in figure 3.

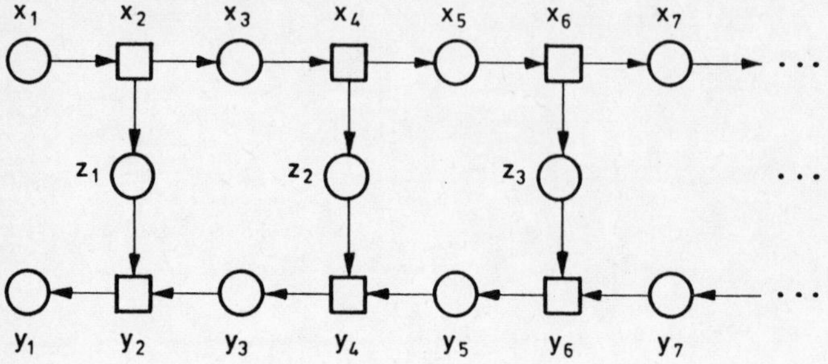

Figure 3

x_1 li x_3 (in fact $x_1 < x_3$); x_5 co z_2.

$\{x_1,x_2,x_7\}$ is a finite li-set which is not a line.

$\{x_i \mid i \in \mathbb{N} - \{o\}\}$ is an infinite li-set which is not a line.

$\{x_1,x_2,z_1,y_2,y_1\}$ is a finite line.

$\{x_i \mid i \in \mathbb{N} - \{o\}\} \cup \{y_i \mid i \in \mathbb{N} - \{o\}\}$ is an infinite line.

$\{z_1,z_2\}$ is a finite co-set which is not a cut.

$\{z_i \mid i \in \mathbb{N} - \{o\} \wedge i \text{ odd}\}$ is an infinite co-set which is not a cut.

$\{z_1,z_2,z_3,x_7\}$ is a finite cut.

$\{z_i \mid i \in \mathbb{N} - \{o\}\}$ is an infinite cut.

In what it follows we shall assume the axiom of choice. As a consequence, for every li-set (co-set) there is a line (cut) which contains the li-set (co-set). We proceed now to the next section where we shall introduce some properties of posets.

3. Some properties of a poset.

In this section we shall introduce three main types of properties of posets. We start with the so called discreteness properties.

(a) Discreteness properties of a poset.

In order to motivate the first discreteness property, let us consider again the example in figure 3.
As we know the poset attached to this occurrence net is combinatorial, which means that between any two ordered elements we can find a finite chain. For instance, $x_4 < y_4$ and we could choose the finite set $\{x_4, x_5, x_6, z_3, y_6, y_5, y_4\}$ such that

$$x_4 \lessdot x_5 \lessdot x_6 \lessdot z_3 \lessdot y_6 \lessdot y_5 \lessdot y_4.$$

However, between x_4 and y_4 there exists also an infinite chain, namely $\{x_4, x_5, x_6, \ldots\} \cup \{y_4, y_5, y_6, \ldots\}$.
If we do not allow the existence - in a poset - of an infinite chain between two elements then the poset has a particular property called "weak discreteness". Formally:

Definition 3.1 A poset $(X;<)$ is weakly discrete iff

$$\forall x,y \in X \quad \forall l \in L: \; | \, [x,y] \cap l \, | \in \mathbb{N}$$

where $[x,y] = \{z \in X \mid x \leq z \leq y\}$

Remarks.

1) If a poset $(X;<)$ is weakly discrete then it is combinatorial.

2) The poset of figure 3 is combinatorial but not weakly discrete.

Example In figure 4 we have an example of a weakly discrete poset.

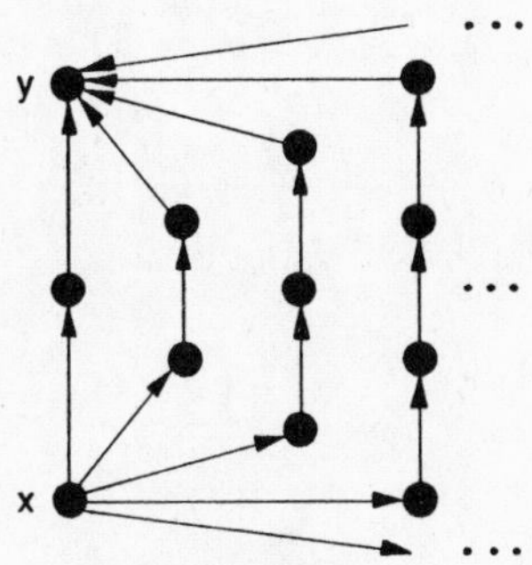

Figure 4

Here we have, for instance $x < y$ and for all $l \in L, [x,y] \cap l$ is finite. We have seen that the poset of figure 4 is weakly discrete. However there is no bound for the length of the chains between x and y. If we impose the property that there is always a bound on the length of the chains between two given points, then we get a new type of discreteness called bounded discreteness (b-discrete, for short). Formally we have the following definition.

Definition 3.2 A poset $(X;<)$ is boundedly discrete (b-discrete, for short) iff $\forall x,y \in X \;\; \exists n \in \mathbb{N} : \forall l \in L: |\,[x,y] \cap l\,| \leq n$.

Remarks.

(1) It is clear from the definition that the poset of figure 4 is not b-discrete.

(2) From the definition 3.1 and 3.2 it follows trivially that:

Theorem 3.3 If a poset $(X;<)$ is b-discrete then it is weakly discrete.

Proof. Follows from definitions 3.1 and 3.2. □

(3) The poset of figure 4 shows that the converse of the theorem 3.3 is - in general - not true.

In figure 5, a poset is shown which is weakly discrete and also b-discrete.

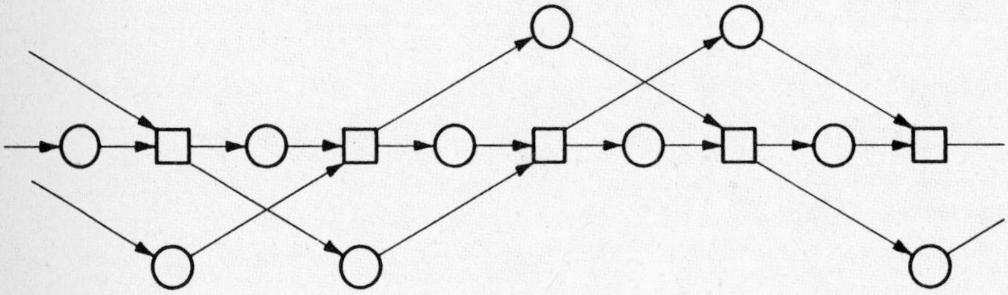

Figure 5

Looking again at the example of figure 4 one might think that the reason that this poset is not b-discrete depends on the fact that the post-set of x and the pre-set of y are infinite sets. In fact, if we impose the condition that for every element $x \in X$ we must have that the pre-set and the post-set of x are finite sets, then b-discreteness and weak discreteness are exactly the same. Formally:

Theorem 3.4 Let $(X;<)$ be a poset such that

$\forall x \in X : |{}^{\bullet}x| \in \mathbb{N}$ and $|x^{\bullet}| \in \mathbb{N}$. Then, $(X;<)$ is b-discrete if and only if it is weakly discrete.

Proof. See, for instance [2] □

Remark.

The concept of b-discreteness is close related to the notion of observability as defined in [11]. A process is observable if we can assign an integer "time" point to every element so that the assignment respects the causal ordering. Formally, we have:

Definition An observer f of $(X;<)$ is a function $f: X \to \mathbb{Z}$ such that $\forall x,y \in X: x < y \Rightarrow f(x) < f(y)$. In this case we say that $(X;<)$ is observable.

The relation between observability and b-discreteness is given by the following theorem:

Theorem (Winskel, [11])

(a) If a poset $(X;<)$ is observable then it is boundedly discrete.

(b) If X is countable and $(X;<)$ is boundedly discrete then $(X;<)$ is observable.

Observability and bounded discreteness are closely connected with the fact that - in a sense - the process must be "finitely realizable". Readers interested in this topic may consult [7].

Finally, we would like to introduce a third type of discreteness. Let us consider the examples given in figure 6 (a) and (b).

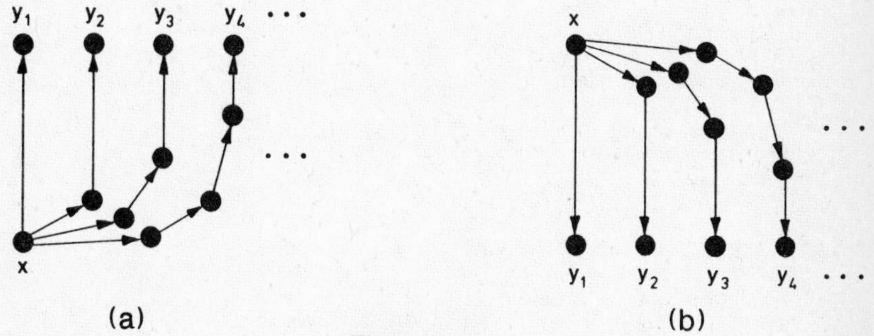

Figure 6

Both posets are not only weakly discrete but also b-discrete. However, in both examples the lines going through x have no bound (in their longitude).

We introduce then the concept of discreteness with respect to a cut.

<u>Definition 3.5</u> Let $(X;<)$ be a poset and $c \in C(X;<)$. $(X;<)$ is discrete with respect to c iff

$\forall x \in X \;\; \exists n \in \mathbb{N} : \forall l \in L : |[c,x] \cap l| \leq n \wedge |[x,c] \cap l| \leq n.$

Where:

$[c,x] = \{z \in X \mid \exists y \in c : y \leq z \leq x\}$

$[x,c] = \{z \in X \mid \exists y \in c : x \leq z \leq y\}.$

<u>Remark.</u> Clearly the two examples of figure 6 are not discrete with respect to the cut $c = \{y_i \mid i \geq 1\}$.

Discreteness with respect to a cut is a stronger property than b-discreteness. In fact, we have the following theorem:

<u>Theorem 3.6</u> Let $(X;<)$ be a poset.

If there exist a cut c such that $(X;<)$ is discrete with respect to c then $(X;<)$ is boundedly discrete.

<u>Proof.</u> Let $x,y \in X$. We have to show that there exists $n \in \mathbb{N}$ such that for all $l \in L$ we have $|[x,y]| \cap l| \leq n$.

If $x \text{ co } y$ then choosing $n = o$ we get the result.

Without loss of generality we can assume $x < y$. We consider three cases.

<u>Case 1</u> $\exists z \in c : z \leq x$ (see figure)

In this case we have:

$[x,y] \subseteq [c,y]$

Then, $\forall l \in L : [x,y] \cap l \subseteq [c,y] \cap l$

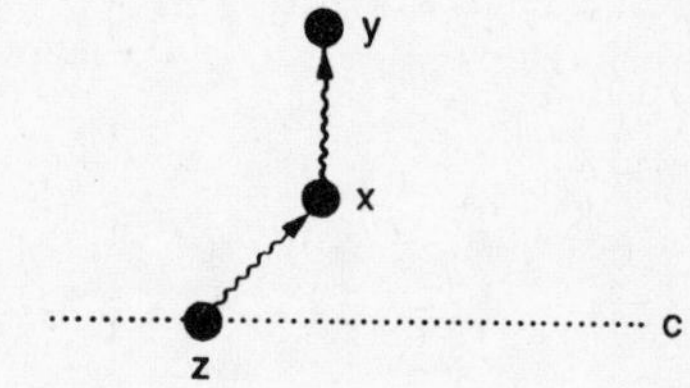

But since $(X;<)$ is discrete with respect to c, there exists $n \in \mathbb{N}$ such that for all $l \in L$ we have:

$|[x,y] \cap l| \leq |[c,y]| \cap l| \leq n$

and we are done.

<u>Case 2</u> $\exists z \in c : y \leq z$ (see figure)

In this case we have:

$[x,y] \subseteq [x,c]$

and the result follows similarly as in case 1.

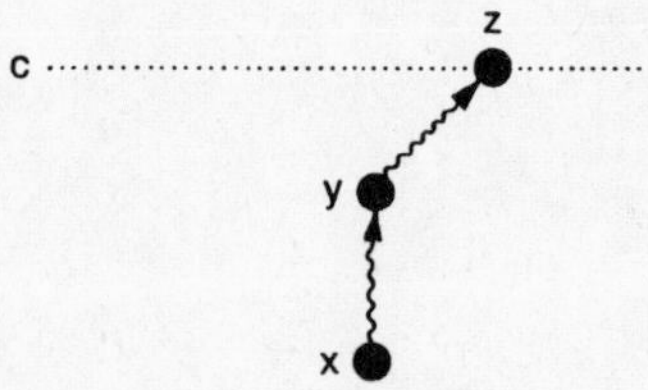

<u>Case 3</u> $\exists z_1, z_2 \in c : x < z_1 \wedge z_2 < y$

In this case, it is not difficult to see that:

$[x,y] \subseteq [x,c] \cup [c,y]$

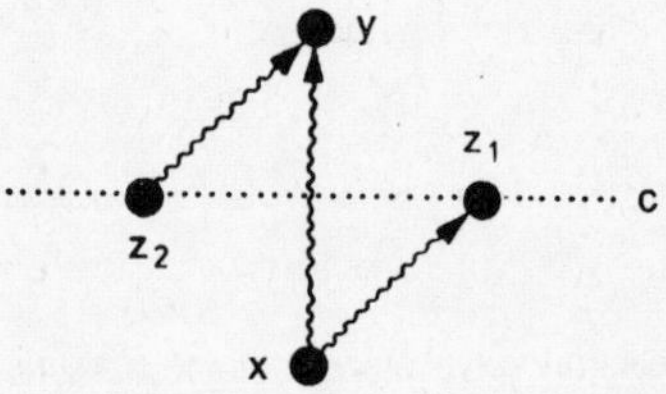

Then, $\forall l \in L$ we have:

(1) $[x,y] \cap l \subseteq ([x,c] \cup [c,y]) \cap l = ([x,c] \cap l) \cup ([c,y] \cap l)$

Since $(X;<)$ is discrete with respect to c, there exist $n_1, n_2 \in \mathbb{N}$ such that $|[x,c] \cap l| \leq n_1 \wedge |[c,y] \cap l| \leq n_2$.

From (1) follows that $\exists n = n_1 + n_2 \in \mathbb{N}$ such that

$$|[x,y] \cap l| \leq n \quad \text{for all } l \in L$$ □

and again we are done.

The reciprocal of theorem 3.6 is - in general - not true. Counterexamples are not easy. One counterexample is found in [7] page 30. The proof that this is a counterexample requires the notion of observability and it is out of the scope of this paper. The reciprocal of theorem 3.6 is true if $(X;<)$ is countable, but again the proof requires concepts which are not considered in this work. The interested reader may consult [11] and [7]. We have proved the implications shown in figure 7

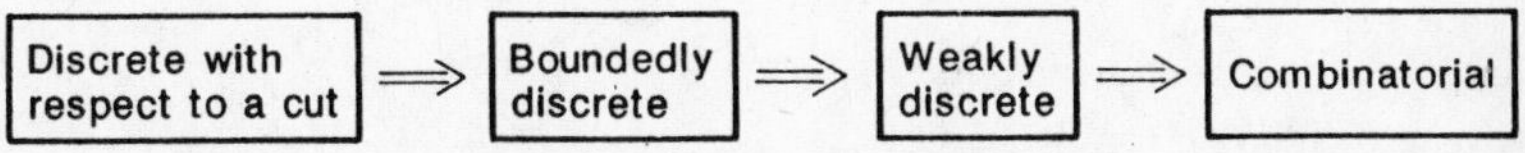

Figure 7

and furthermore we know that the implications in the other direction are - in general - not true. We shall study next two density properties of a poset.

b) Density properties of a poset.

Since we are considering only combinatorial posets, these posets can not have the density property established in definition 2.3 (c). In fact the density property defined in definition 2.3 (c) is "opposite" to the notion of combinatorialness.

We would like to introduce now two types of density - introduce by Petri in [9] - which are meaningful for combinatorial posets. In fact these two density properties are also meaningful for general posets. We start with the notion of N-density.

Informally, N-density means that in an N-shaped diagram as the one indicated in figure 8(a), there must exist a point z between x and y (as indicated in figure 8(b)).

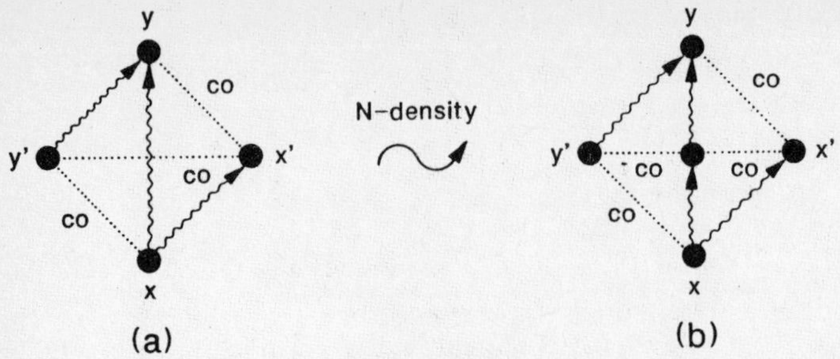

Figure 8

Formally:

Definition 3.7 Let (X;<) be a poset. (X;<) is N-dense iff

$$\forall x,y,x',y' \in X : x < y \wedge x < x' \wedge y' < y \wedge (x \text{ co } y' \text{ co } x' \text{ co } y) \Rightarrow \exists z \in X : x < z < y \wedge (x' \text{ co } z \text{ co } y')$$

Remarks.

1) The finite combinatorial poset of figure 9 is not N-dense.

2) The poset indicated in figure 10 is N-dense.

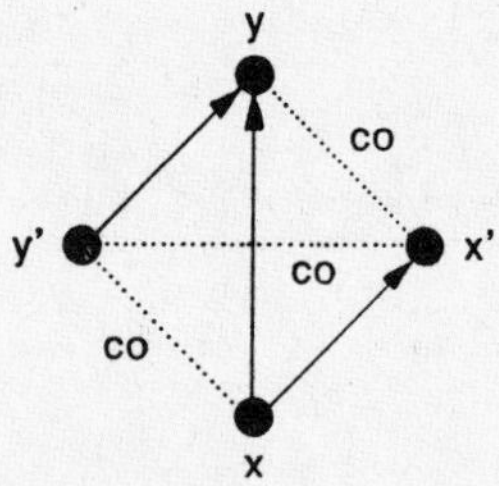

Figure 9

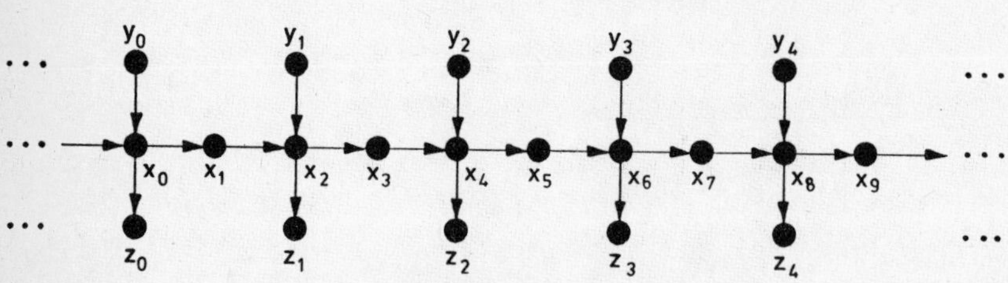

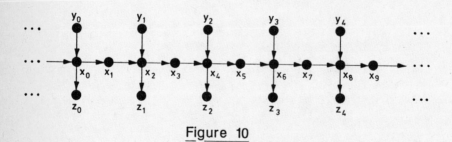

Figure 10

The other type of density we would like to introduce, which is also compatible with the combinatorial characteristic of the poset, is called K-density (K : from the German word "Kombinatorisch").

We usually interprete lines as sequential subprocesses of the process modelled by (X;<).

Cuts are interpreted as states of the process (X;<). K-density postulates that every element of a sequential subprocess (line)of (X;<) must be in a definitive state (cut). Formally:

Definition 3.8 Let (X;<) be a poset.
(X;<) is K-dense iff $\forall c \in C\ \forall l \in L : c \cap l \neq \emptyset$.

Remarks.

(1) Clearly $|c \cap l| = \begin{cases} 0 \\ 1 \end{cases}$ for all cuts c and all lines l.
Then $c \cap l \neq \emptyset$ is equivalent to say that $|c \cap l| = 1$.
K-density says then that each cut and each line intersect in one point.

(2) The two posets in figure 9 and 10 are not K-dense.

The relation between K-density and N-density is given by the following theorem.

Theorem 3.9 Let (X;<) be a poset.
If (X;<) is K-dense then (X;<) is N-dense.

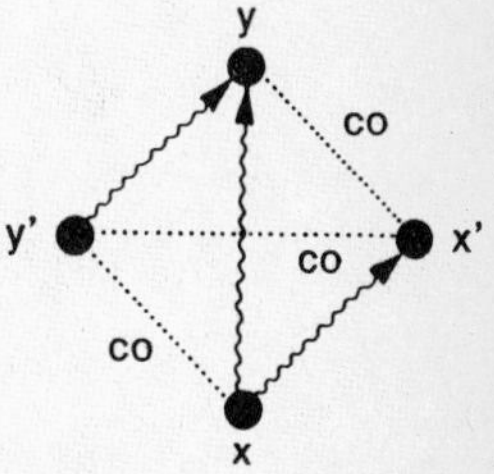

Proof. Let $x,y,x',y' \in X$ such that

$x < y \wedge x < x' \wedge y' < y \wedge (x \text{ co } y' \text{ co } x' \text{ co } y)$

We have to prove that $\exists z \in X$ such that

$x < z < y \wedge (x' \text{ co } z \text{ co } y')$

Now, $\{x',y'\}$ is a co-set. Let $c \in C$ such that $\{x',y'\} \subseteq c$.

$\{x,y\}$ is a li-set. Let $l \in L$ such that $\{x,y\} \subseteq l$.

Since (X;<) is K-dense, we have $\exists z \in X$ such that $l \cap c = \{z\}$.

We have $x' \text{ co } z \text{ co } y'$ since $z,y',x' \in c$ and $c \in C$.

We have to show only that $x < z < y$.

Now, $x,y,z \in l$.

If $z \leq x$ then $z < x'$, a contradiction since $z \text{ co } x'$.

i.e. $x < z$

Now, if $z \geq y$ then $y' < y \leq z$, a contradiction since $y' \text{ co } z$.

i.e. $z < y$.

So, we have $\exists z \in X : x < z < y \wedge (x' \text{ co } z \text{ co } y')$ and we are done.

□

We have proved that:

K-density $\Longrightarrow$ **N-density**

Figure 11

The implication in the other direction is not true since the example of figure 10 is N-dense but $c \cap l = \emptyset$ where

$c = \{y_i \in X \mid i \in Z\}$ and $l = \{x_i \in X \mid i \in Z\}$,

i.e. it is not K-dense.

We have seen that a combinatorial poset could be N-dense (an example is given in figure 10) or not (an example is given in figure 9). However we can show that the posets attached to occurrence nets are always N-dense. We have, then, the following theorem:

<u>Theorem 3.10</u> Let $N = (B,E;F)$ be an occurrence net and $(X;<)$ its attached poset. Then $(X;<)$ is N-dense.

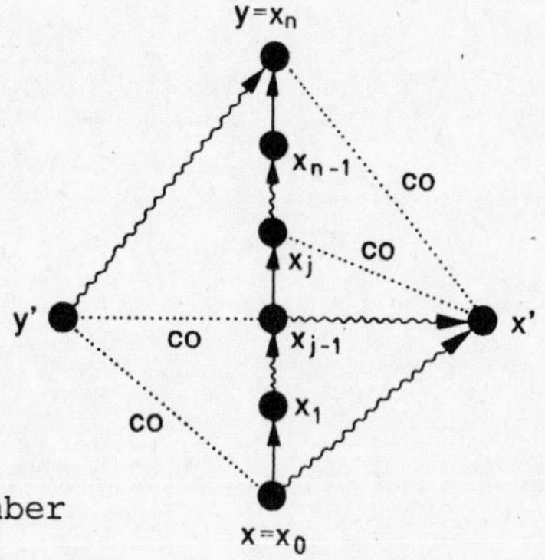

<u>Proof.</u> Let $x,y,x',y' \in X$ such that

$x < y \wedge x < x' \wedge y' < y \wedge$

$(x \text{ co } y' \text{ co } x' \text{ co } y)$

Since $(X;<)$ is combinatorial we have

$\exists x_o, x_1, \ldots, x_n$ such that:

$x = x_o F x_1 F x_2 F \ldots F x_{n-1} F x_n = y$

Let $j : 1 \leq j \leq n$ be the smallest natural number such that $x_j \text{ co } x'$. (j exists since $y = x_n \text{ co } x'$)

By the election of j, it is clear that x_{j-1} li x'; $x' < x_{j-1}$ implies $x' < y = x_n$, a contradiction since $x' \text{ co } x_n$.

So we must have $x_{j-1} < x'$.

Now, $x_{j-1} < y'$ implies $x = x_o < x_{j-1} < y'$, a contradiction since $x = x_o \text{ co } y'$.

$y' < x_{j-1}$ implies $y' < x_{j-1} < x'$ a contradiction since $y' \text{ co } x'$.

So, we must have $y' \text{ co } x_{j-1}$ (see figure).

Clearly, $x_{j-1} \in E$ and then $x_j \in B$.

Now $x_j < y'$ implies $x = x_o < x_j < y'$, a contradiction since $x = x_o \text{ co } y'$.

$y' < x_j$ is a contradiction since $y' \text{ co } x_{j-1}$ and $x_j \in B$.

This means that $x_j \text{ co } y'$.

So, we have found a $z = x_j$ such that $x < z = x_j < y \wedge y' \text{ co } z \text{ co } x'$,

and this means that $(X;<)$ is N-dense. □

Let us now consider a "continuity" property of a poset.

(c) D-continuity property of a poset

The D-continuity property we would like to analyze is a generalization to posets of the well known completeness (continuity) property of the set of real numbers.

We follow here the main ideas introduced by R. Dedekind in his way to construct the reals starting with the rationals [5].

Let $(X;<)$ be a totally ordered set, i.e. $(X;<)$ is a poset for which every two elements are comparable. Formally, $(X;<)$ is a poset such that $\forall x,y \in X : x \text{ li } y$. A Dedekind cut of $(X;<)$ is a partition $(A,\bar{A})$ $(\bar{A} = X-A)$ of X, such that every element in A is smaller than every element in $\bar{A}$.

Formally we have the following definition:

Definition 3.11 Let $(X;<)$ be a totally ordered set.
$(A,\bar{A})$ - where $\bar{A} = X-A$ - is a Dedekind cut (D-cut, for short) iff

(1) $A \neq \emptyset$; $\bar{A} \neq \emptyset$

(2) $\forall x \in A \ \forall y \in \bar{A} : x < y$

The set of D-cuts of $(X;<)$ is denoted by $D(X;<)$ or simply D when no confusion arises.

Let us consider a couple of examples.

Let $A = \{x \in \mathbb{Z} \mid x \leq o\}$

$\bar{A} = \{x \in \mathbb{Z} \mid x > o\}$.

$(A,\bar{A})$ is clearly a D-cut in the totally ordered set $(\mathbb{Z};<)$.

It is easy to see that $\text{Max } A = \{o\}$

$\text{Min } \bar{A} = \{1\}$.

Calling $M(A) = \text{Max } A \cup \text{Min } \bar{A} = \{0,1\}$, we have $|M(A)| = 2$

Now if $A = \{x \in \mathbb{Q} \mid x < o \vee x^2 < 2\}$

$\bar{A} = \mathbb{Q} - A$

Then $(A,\bar{A})$ is a D-cut of $(\mathbb{Q};<)$.

In this case, Max $A = \emptyset$ and $M(A) = \emptyset$, i.e. $|M(A)| = 0$.
Min $\overline{A} = \emptyset$

It is also easy to see that for all $(A,\overline{A}) \in D(\mathbb{R};<)$ - i.e. for all D-cuts in the reals - we have $|M(A)| = 1$. This property is what we want to capture in posets. Usually we say that $|M(A)| = 2$ represents a "jump" and $|M(A)| = 0$ represents a gap (hole). We say that $|M(A)| = 1$ represents "continuity" (completeness). Formally we have the following definition of D-continuity.

Definition 3.12 Let $(X;<)$ be a totally ordered set and $(A,\overline{A})$ be a D-cut of $(X;<)$.

(a) Max $A := \{x \in A \mid \nexists y \in A : x < y\}$

(b) Min $\overline{A} := \{x \in \overline{A} \mid \nexists y \in \overline{A} : y < x\}$

(c) $M(A) = \text{Max } A \cup \text{Min } \overline{A}$

(d) $(X;<)$ is D-continuous iff $\forall (A,\overline{A}) \in D(X;<): |M(A)| = 1$.

According to this definition $(\mathbb{Z};<)$ and $(\mathbb{Q};<)$ are not D-continuous, but $(\mathbb{R};<)$ is.

We would like to generalize the concept of D-continuity to posets. In order to do so we need to generalize - in the first place - the definition of a D-cut given in definition 3.11.

According to definition 3.11, a D-cut $(A,\overline{A})$ has two main properties:

(1) $(A,\overline{A})$ is a partition of $(X;<)$.

(2) Every element in A is less than every element in $\overline{A}$.

In a poset we can not have both properties since not every two elements are comparable. Following the main ideas introduced in [6] and [10] we would like to sacrifice the property (2) in favor of (1).
We start with the following definition.

Definition 3.13 Let $(X;<)$ be a poset, $A \subseteq X$ and $\overline{A} = X-A$. $(A,\overline{A})$ is a D-cut iff:

(1) $A \neq \emptyset \wedge \overline{A} \neq \emptyset$.

(2) $\forall x \in A \quad \forall y \in \overline{A} : \neg (y < x)$

In this definition we have respected the fact that $(A,\overline{A})$ must be a partition of X and we have sacrificed the fact that "Every element in A must be less than every element in $\overline{A}$". However we have replaced this property by the property (2) of definition 3.13 which in a sense says something very close to (2) of definition 3.11. Following the idea used for totally ordered sets, we would like to look closely the set M(A).

For a poset $(X;<)$ and for $(A,\bar{A}) \in D(X;<)$ we could define Max A, Min $\bar{A}$ and M(A) exactly as in definition 3.12. Now, we would like to say that a poset is D-continuous iff $|M(A)| = 1$. However, in a totally ordered set $|M(A)| \leq 2$, but in a poset M(A) could be - for instance - infinite. So, the condition $|M(A)| = 1$ must be respected not for the poset as a whole but for every line of the poset (In a totally ordered set there is only one line). So, one possibility is to say:

I $(X;<)$ is D-continuous iff $\forall l \in L \quad \forall (A,\bar{A}) \in D : |M(A) \cap l| = 1$.

However, if we assume this definition, then it is easy to prove (see for instance [3]) that if $(X;<)$ is D-continuous then $(X;<)$ must be dense. Since we are mainly interested in combinatorial posets we must change a little bit the definition of D-continuity. We would like to do so by refining the sets Max A and Min $\bar{A}$ to two new sets Obmax A and Obmin $\bar{A}$, i.e. we would like to define two new sets Obmax A and Obmin A such that:

$$\text{Obmax } A \subseteq \text{Max } A$$
$$\text{Obmin } \bar{A} \subseteq \text{Min } \bar{A}$$

Finally, we shall define $c(A) = \text{Obmax } A \cup \text{Obmin } \bar{A}$, i.e. $c(A) \subseteq M(A)$ and we shall use c(A) instead of M(A) in the formula I.

In order to see intuitively how to make this refinement we shall consider an example.

Let us consider the poset of figure 12 with the D-cut $(A,\bar{A})$ indicated in the figure.

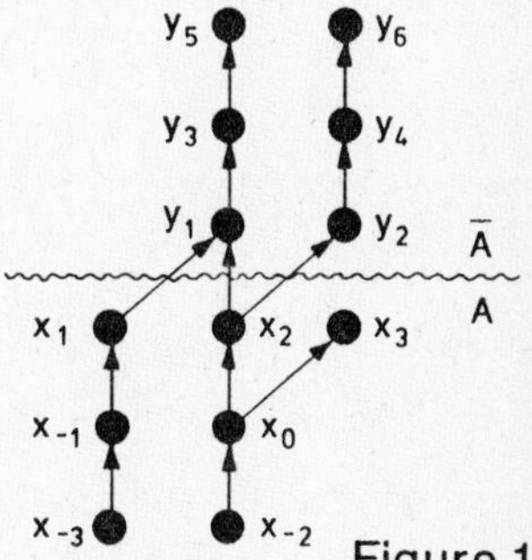

Figure 12

In this case, we have:
Max A = $\{x_1, x_2, x_3\}$
Min $\bar{A}$ = $\{y_1, y_2\}$

There is a difference between x_1, x_2 and x_3.

In fact if we want to go from one side of the D-cut (A) to the other side $(\bar{A})$, then starting from x_1 we can only do so in a unique way (we must go from x_1 to y_1). However starting from x_2 we can go to y_1 or to y_2, i.e. starting from x_2 there is no unique way to go from one side of the cut to the other side. Furthermore, starting from x_3 we can not go to $\bar{A}$.

We would like to consider only those points in Max A from which we can go to $\bar{A}$ in a unique way or from which we can not go to $\bar{A}$. Intuitively we would like to have the following refinement.

$$\text{Obmax } A = \{x_1, x_3\} \subset \text{Max } A = \{x_1, x_2, x_3\}.$$

In the same way, going from $\bar{A}$ to A; there is no unique way of doing so from y_1 (y_1 connects to x_1 or to x_2). From y_2, however, there is a unique way of doing so (it connects to x_2).

In this case we would like to have:

$$\text{Obmin } \bar{A} = \{y_2\} \subset \text{Min } \bar{A} = \{y_1, y_2\}.$$

Formally we have the following definition.

Definition 3.14 Let $(X;<)$ be a combinatorial poset and $(A,\bar{A}) \in D(X;<)$.

(a) $\text{Obmax } A := \{x \in \text{Max } A \mid |x^{\bullet}| \leq 1\}$

(b) $\text{Obmin } \bar{A} := \{x \in \text{Min } \bar{A} \mid |{}^{\bullet}x| \leq 1\}$

(c) $c(A) := \text{Obmax } A \cup \text{Obmin } \bar{A}$

(d) $(X;<)$ is D-continuous iff $\forall (A,\bar{A}) \in D \; \forall l \in L : |c(A) \cap l| = 1$.

In the example of figure 12, $x_2 \notin \text{Obmax } A$, $y_1 \notin \text{Obmin } \bar{A}$ $x_1, x_3 \in \text{Obmax } A$ and $y_2 \in \text{Obmin } \bar{A}$.

In figure 12, we have $c(A) = \{x_1, x_3, y_2\}$ and since $l \cap c(A) = \emptyset$ where $l = \{x_{-2}, x_o, x_2, y_1, y_3, y_5\}$ then $(X;<)$ is not D-continuous. The well known example of figure 5 is D-continuous.

It is not difficult to prove that the definition 3.14 is equivalent to the one given by C.A. Petri in [10]. (Remember we are considering only combinatorial posets).

Remark.

The way how we have generalized the concept of D-continuity from totally ordered set to posets is not unique.

One could sacrifice the fact that $(A,\bar{A})$ is a partition of X and give then the following definition of a D-cut.

Definition Let $(X;<)$ be a poset and $A,B \subseteq X$.

The pair (A,B) is a D-cut iff:

(a) $A \neq \emptyset \wedge B \neq \emptyset$

(b) $\forall x \in A \; \forall y \in B : x \leq y$

(c) $\forall z \in X$ if $\forall y \in A : z \geq y$ then $z \in B$.

(d) $\forall z \in X$ if $\forall y \in B : z \leq y$ then $z \in A$.

This definition respects the fact that "Every element in A is less or equal than every element in B". However, we do not have any more a partition of X. Properties (a), (c) and (d) try to make the D-cut (A,B) "close" to a partition of X. Properties (c) and (d) ensure that "between" A and B there "must be not too much space".

It is not difficult to see that postulating $A \cap B \neq \emptyset$ for all D-cuts (A,B), we eliminate "gaps". "Jumps" must be eliminated directly. A reader interested in this topic could consult the paper of C.A. Petri which appears in this volume.

4. Relations between the different properties of a poset

In this very short section we would like to say some words about the relations between the properties we have defined in section 3.

In figure 13 we have drawn in full lines the relations we have until now.

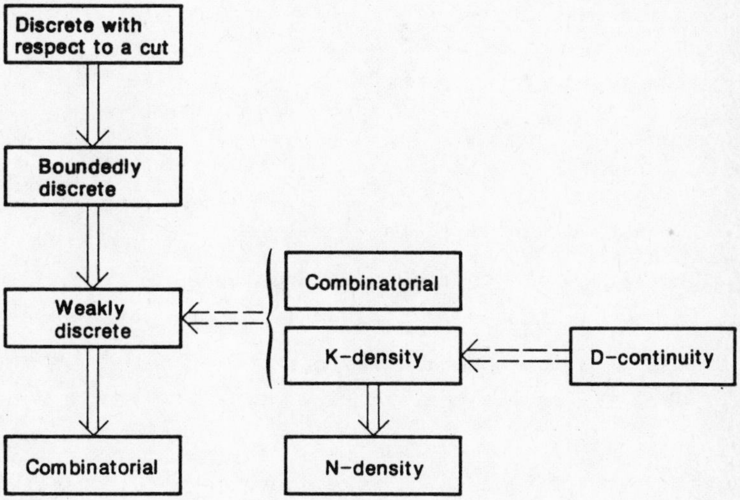

Figure 13

We would like to state the relations indicated with dotted lines.

Theorem 4.1 Let $(X;<)$ be a poset.
If $(X;<)$ is D-continuous then it is K-dense.

Proof. Let $l \in L$ and $c \in C$. We have to prove that $l \cap c \neq \emptyset$.
If $X = c$ then the result is trivially true.
We can assume $x \neq c$.

Define: $\downarrow c = \{x \in X \mid \exists y \in c : x \leq y\}$

$\uparrow c = \{x \in X \mid \exists y \in c : y \leq x\}$.

If $X \neq c$ then $\downarrow c \neq c$ or $\uparrow c \neq c$ or both. Assume $\uparrow c \neq c$ (the other case is similar) and define: $A = \downarrow c \quad \bar{A} = X - A$.

$(A,\overline{A})$ is clearly a D-cut with Max A = c, i.e. Obmax $A \subseteq c$. Since $(X;<)$ is D-continuous we have:

$$c(A) \cap l \neq \emptyset$$

Let $x_o \in c(A) \cap l$.

If $x_o \in$ Obmax $A \subseteq c$ then $x_o \in c$. But $x_o \in l$ and we are done.
Assume $x_o \in$ Obmin $\overline{A}$.
If $x_o \in c$ we are done. If $x_o \notin c$ then $\exists\, y_o \in c : y_o < x_o$.
Clearly $y_o \lessdot x_o$, because if $y_o < z < x_o$ then $z \notin A$ i.e. $z \in \overline{A}$ and $z < x_o$, a contradiction with the fact that $x_o \in$ Obmin $\overline{A}$.

But $x_o \in$ Obmin $\overline{A}$ implies $|{}^{\bullet}x_o| \leq 1$. But $y_o \lessdot x_o$ then ${}^{\bullet}x_o = \{y_o\}$ which means that $y_o \in l$. i.e. $y_o \in c \wedge y_o \in l$ and again we have $l \cap c \neq \emptyset$.

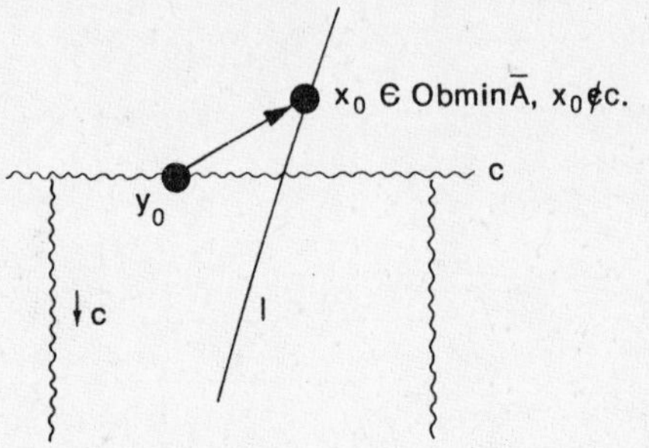

□

The other implication given by dotted lines is:

<u>Theorem 4.2</u> Let $(X;<)$ be a combinatorial poset.
If $(X;<)$ is K-dense then $(X;<)$ is weakly discrete.

<u>Proof.</u> The proof is a long one and we do not want to repeat it here. The interested reader may consult [2].

□

Finally we would like to remark that the converse of theorem 4.1 and 4.2 are in general not true.

5. <u>Conlusions</u>

In this paper we have tried to present some properties of a non-sequential process and study their relationships.

We have concentrated only on a few properties and we have tried to introduce a lot of examples in order to make them clear.

We have deleted - for sake of brevity - the "translation" of system properties to process properties and vice-versa. The interested reader may look the nice papers [8] and [4].

Using the property of discreteness with respect to a cut it is possible to give a general and formal definition of a process for C/E system. Many other properties of a poset (non-sequential process) are found in the literature ([10],[3],[2],[7], etc.).

References

[1] E. Best, C. Fernández and H. Plünnecke, Concurrent Systems and Processes, Final report of the foundational part of the project BEGRUND, GMD-Studien Nr. 104 (1985)

[2] E. Best and C. Fernández, A Petri Net Theory of Systems and Processes. Draft of a projected monograph. GMD, St. Augustin, Federal Republic of Germany (February 1986)

[3] E. Best and A. Merceron, Concurrency Axioms and D-Continuous Posets, Advances in Petri Nets 1984, Lecture Notes in Computer Science Nr. 188, pp. 32-47. (Springer-Verlag, 1985)

[4] E. Best and A. Merceron, Frozen Tokens and D-Continuity: A Study in Relating System Properties to Process Properties, Advances in Petri Nets 1984, Lecture Notes in Computer Science Nr. 188, pp. 48-61 (Springer-Verlag, 1985)

[5] R. Dedekind, Was sind und was sollen die Zahlen? Stetigkeit und Irrationale Zahlen (Vieweg, Braunschweig, 1969)

[6] C. Fernández and P.S. Thiagarajan, D-Continuous Causal Nets: A Model of Non-Sequential Processes, Theoretical Computer Science, 28, pp. 171-196 (1984)

[7] C. Fernández, M. Nielsen and P.S. Thiagarajan, Notions of Realizable Non-Sequential Processes, Report DAIMI PB-205, Aarhus University, Aarhus, Denmark (February 1986)

[8] U. Goltz and W. Reisig, The Non-Sequential Behaviour of Petri Nets, Information and Control 57, pp. 125-147 (1983)

[9] C.A. Petri, Non-Sequential Processes, Interner-Bericht ISF-77-5, Gesellschaft für Mathematik und Datenverarbeitung, St. Augustin, Federal Republic of Germany (1977)

[10] C.A. Petri, Concurrency, in: W. Brauer, ed., Net Theory and and Applications, Lecture Notes in Computer Science Nr. 84, pp. 251-260 (Springer-Verlag, 1981)

[11] G. Winskel, Events in Computation, Ph. D. Thesis, University of Edinburgh (1980)

SECTION 2

PLACE/TRANSITION SYSTEMS – FUNDAMENTALS

W. Reisig: *Place/Transition Systems*

K. Lautenbach: *Linear Algebraic Techniques for Place/Transition Nets*

E. Best: *Structure Theory of Petri Nets: the Free Choice Hiatus*

Place/Transition Systems

Wolfgang Reisig

Gesellschaft für Mathematik und Datenverarbeitung
D–5205 St. Augustin 1

ABSTRACT In the 1970ies, Place/Transition Systems were certainly the most common and the most extensively studied class of nets. Often they have just been called *Petri Nets*.

We introduce their basic concepts, viz. the idea of places that carry any number of (identical) tokens. This introduces a dimension of infinity that implies a lot of interesting theoretical problems such as liveness, boundedness and the reachability of markings.

We especially stress the viewpoint of General Net Theory, considering such nets as shorthand notation for elementary net systems. In this way the rich body of theory for c/e systems is applicable also for place/transition nets. Finally we will study net properties that can be derived from coverability trees.

Key Words place/transition systems, relationships to elementary net systems and to c/e-systems, occurrence sequences, causal dependencies, coverability tree, liveness

CONTENTS

Introduction

Introductory books and articles on Petri Nets quite extensively study the model of Place/ Transition Systems. They often have been taken as "the Petri Nets" or at least as the core calculus of Nets.

A revised judgement of this calculus came up during the recent years. For practical applications it turned out that Petri Net models with individual tokens are more suitable and handy. For fundamental studies of concurrency, the basic model of Condition/Event Systems is of greater relevance.

There exists however a widely developed and very sophisticated theory on Place/Transition Systems that was mainly developed during the 1970ies.

In this article we emphasize the indicated revised viewpoint of Place/Transition Nets and contrast it with the conventional approach.

The first Chapter explains two different views of relating Place/Transition Systems to Condition/Event Systems. To a certain extent, this causes two different views of what kind of behaviour is represented by such systems. Chapter 2 is to show the inherent complexity of Place/Transition Systems, that comes up with unlimited capacities and hence infinite state spaces. We concentrate on the set of "reachable markings", and the idea of obtaining at least some information on this – generally infinite – set by means of finite "coverability trees". Other topics in this area, including the set of (finite or infinite) execution sequences, or problems of algorithmic complexity, are left to the contributions [Valk 86], [Jantzen 86a] and [Jantzen 86b] in this volume.

We likewise will not discuss any analysis- or proof techniques (other than coverability trees) for Place/ Transition Systems. The fundamental linear algebraic techniques of S- and T-invariants will be discussed in the contributions [Lautenbach 86] and [Memmi 86] in this volume, further techniques for distinguished net classes will be considered in the contribution [Best 86].

With respect to notations and terminology we essentially follow the proposals of [Best, Fernandez 86].

1. FUNDAMENTAL CONCEPTS AND NOTATIONS OF PLACE/TRANSITION SYSTEMS

There are two main alternatives to introduce the issue of Place/Transition Systems (P/T-systems, for short) and to embed them into the general framework of Petri Net Theory: Both start with Elementary Net Systems (EN-systems, for short) as introduced by P.S. Thiagarajan in this volume. The first approach conceives P/T-systems as **generalized** EN-systems. Its core idea is to drop the limitation of having not more than one token (dot) on each circle in the net. The second approach conceives P/T-systems as **shorthands** and **abstractions** of EN-systems. Its core idea is to fold several conditions to one circle and several events to one box.

We shall discuss both these approaches in the following. Our starting point however is an intuitive introduction of the essentials of P/T-systems, based on a small example.

1.1 Intuitive Concepts of Place/Transition Systems

The issue of this section will be presented by a simple example.

An arrangement consisting of certain aspects of a producer and a consumer is shown in (1.1). It is represented as an EN-system. A buffer capacity of one item is assumed. Thus the essential property of the buffer is to be occupied or to be empty.

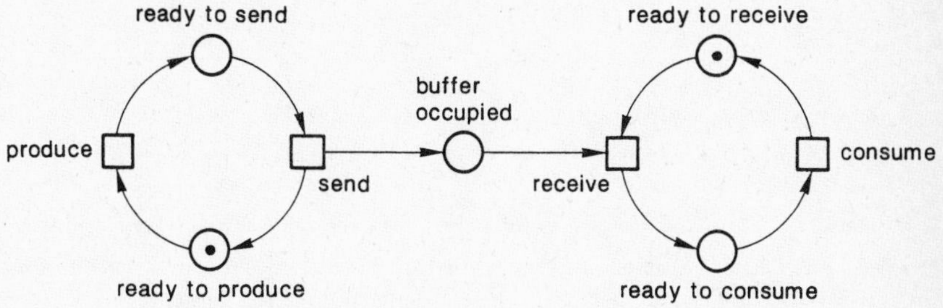

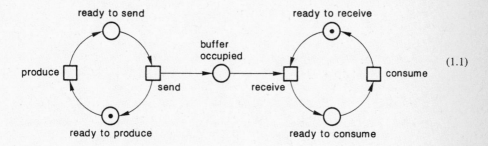

(1.1)

Now our task might be to extend the capacity of the buffer. A capacity of three items is specified in (1.2). The buffer is assumed to consist of three cells in sequential order. Each cell has a capacity of one item. (1.2) specifies a situation with altogether two items in the buffer.

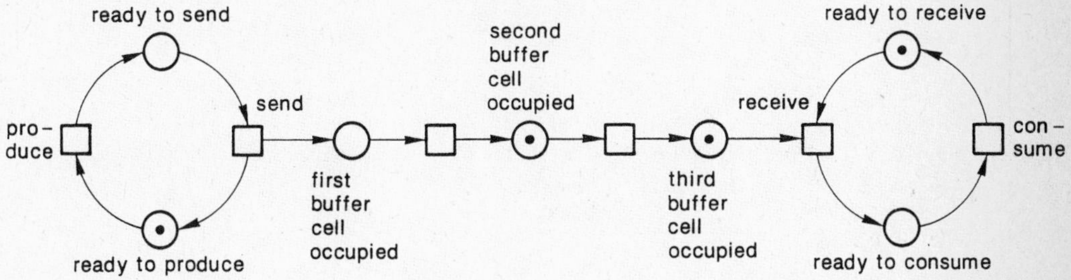

(1.2)

It should be clear by this example how buffers of any finite capacity can be specified as a sequence of cells. However this technique is clearly inacceptable for large capacities (at the order of 100 cells, say). One might furthermore not at all be interested in the internal structure of the buffer and in the details of how the items are distributed over the buffer cells. The only concern is the capacity of the buffer and the actual number of items in it.

In order to represent the producer/consumer system on this level one may come up with a representation as shown in (1.3). The buffer itself is represented here. The number of items in the buffer is given by a corresponding number of dots (called **tokens**) in the circle that represents the buffer.

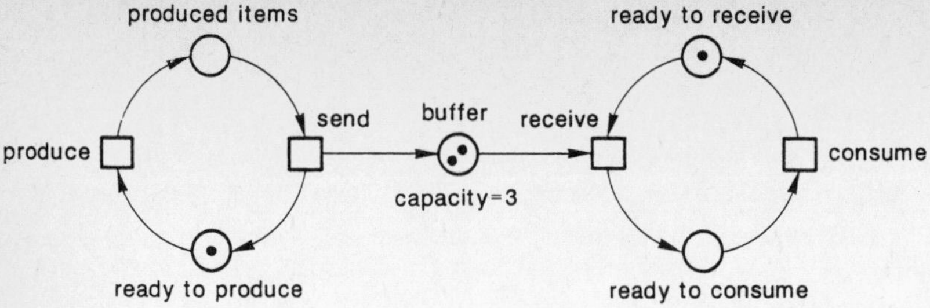

(1.3)

The number of tokens in that circle should not exceed the buffer capacity. The effect of "send" and of "receive" is to increase or to decrease, respectively, the number of tokens on the buffer circle by one.

The technique applied in (1.3) can also be used in other parts of the producer/consumer system. To give an example we assume two consumers, but we are not concerned in identifying them as distinguishable individuals. This is represented in (1.4) by just adding to (1.3) a second token to "ready to receive".

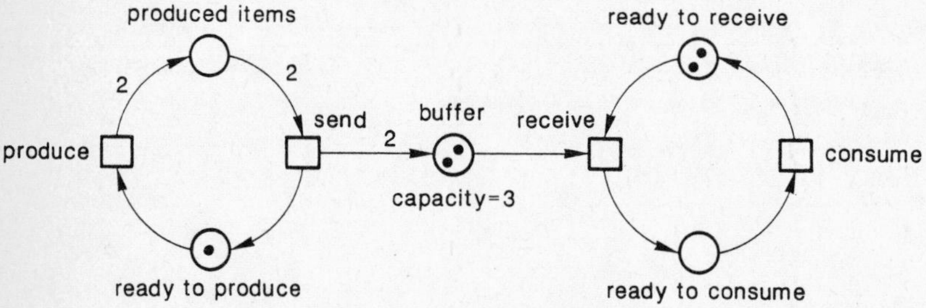

(1.4)

In addition, "arc weights" are specified in (1.4): Some arcs are inscribed by "2", thus specifying that two items are produced and sent in each round of the producer.

1.2 P/T-Systems Conceived as Generalized C/E-Systems

We shall give formal definitions for the fundamental notions of P/T-systems in this section. EN-systems will formally turn out as a special case in the framework of this calculus, assuming a slight reformulation of some concepts (roughly, subsets are represented by their characteristic functions).

The static aspects of P/T-systems are defined as follows:

Definition

A sixtuple $\Sigma = (S, T; F, K, W, M_0)$ is called a *place/transition system* (P/T-system) iff:

(a) $(S, T; F)$ is a net where the S-elements are called *places* and the T-elements are called *transitions*. (1.5)

(b) $K: S \to \mathbf{N}^+ \cup \{\infty\}$ is a *capacity* function.

(c) $W: F \to \mathbf{N}^+$ is a *weight* function.

(d) $M_0: S \to \mathbf{N}$ is an *initial marking* function which sat isfies $M_0(s) \leq K(s)$ for all $s \in S$.

This is the most general definition of place/transition systems. A special subclass of this model deserves special attention. It is defined by the constantly infinite capacity function $K(s) = \infty$ for all $s \in S$, and $W(x,y) = 1$ for all $(x,y) \in F$. In [Reisig 85a] this net model is called "Marked nets". Most publication on P/T-systems are based on this model.

It is often convenient to assume W cannonically extended to $(S \times T) \cup (T \times S)$ by $W(x,y) = 0$ iff $\neg (x,y) \in F$. This is e.g. done in Definition (1.7(b)) and (1.7(c)) below.

In graphical representations of P/T-systems, the arcs $f \in F$ are labelled by $W(f)$ whenever $W(f) > 1$. If the capacity of a place s is finite we may write "capacity = K(s)" or similar next to the circle representing s. The marking M_o is indicated by drawing $M_o(s)$ black dots on each place s. (1.6)

These graphical conventions have already been applied in the above Figures.

To each EN system $\Sigma = (B,E;F,c_{in})$ one associates a P/T-system $\Sigma' = (S,T;F,K,W,M_o)$ with $S = B$, $T = E$, $K(s) = 1$ for all $s \in S$, $W(x,y) = 1$ for all $(x,y) \in F$ and $M_o(s) = 1$ for $s \in c$, $M_o(s) = 0$ for $-(s \in c)$. A similarly smooth relationship of C/E-systems to P/T-systems can not be established, because C/E-systems include forward- and backward case classes which do not properly fit to initial markings of P/T-systems.

We now come to the dynamic aspects of P/T-systems:

Definition

Let $\Sigma = (S, T; F, K, W, M_0)$ be a P/T-system.

(a) A function $M: S \to \mathbf{N}$ is called a *marking* of Σ iff $M(s) \leq K(s)$ for all $s \in S$.

(b) A transition $t \in T$ is *enabled at M* (or *has concession at M*) iff $\forall s \in S: W(s,t) \leq M(s) \leq K(s) - W(t,s)$.

(c) If $t \in T$ is a transition which is enabled at a marking M then t may occur, yielding a new marking M' given by the equation: $M'(s) = M(s) - W(s,t) + W(t,s)$ for all $s \in S$. (1.7)

(d) The occurrence of t changes the marking M into the new marking M'; we may denote this fact by $M[t\rangle M'$ or by $M \xrightarrow{t} M'$.

(e) We denote by $[M_0\rangle$ the smallest set of markings of Σ such that:

(i) $M_0 \in [M_0\rangle$;

(ii) if $M_1 \in [M_0\rangle$ and $M_1[t\rangle M_2$ for some $t \in T$ then $M_2 \in [M_0\rangle$.

In the literature the occurrence of a transition is often denoted as "firing".

Let $\Sigma = (B,E;F,c_o)$ be an EN system and let $\Sigma' = (S,T;F,K,W,M_o)$ be an associated P/T-system, as defined above. Each case c of Σ corresponds to a marking c' of Σ', defined for all $s \in S$ by $c'(s) = 1$ iff $s \in c$ and $c'(s) = 0$, otherwise. Then we obtain for all cases $c_o, c_1 \in C$ and all $e \in E$:

$$c_o\,[e > c_1 \text{ in } \Sigma \text{ if and only if } c_o\,[e > c_1 \text{ in } \Sigma'.$$

The last relationship shows that EN systems indeed can be conceived as a sub-calculus of P/T-systems.

1.3 P/T-Systems Conceived as Shorthand and Abstractions of C/E-Systems

A rich body of concepts, notions, theorems and experience has been developed for C/E-systems and EN systems. The core aspects of concurrency have been formulated in this setting. All these insights are not applicable to P/T–systems if they are conceived as a generalization of EN systems. This is a severe drawback of the approach given in the previous section.

In the following we informally describe how to consider P/T-systems as shorthand for and abstraction of certain EN systems, thus conceiving P/T-systems as **special** EN systems. We shall remain on an informal level, mainly because otherwise the reader should be aware of Predicate/Transition Systems and of net morphisms in the framework of General Net Theory.

We again introduce the issues of this section by our running example of a producer/consumer system.

A buffer with a capacity of three items has been realized in (1.2) as a **sequence** of three cells. One may argue about the adequateness and usefulness of this idea: Sequences of this kind may lead to temporary jams, because the internal events may be "too slow".

So we suggest a more convenient solution that requires for the buffer no internal events at all. The idea is to give the producer and the consumer direct access to each buffer cell. This concept is realized in (1.8) in terms of a C/E-system for three cells. The freedom of access to the buffer has been increased in (1.8) in comparison with (1.2). Upon sending an item to the buffer, it is the sender's freedom and responsibility to select one out of all actually free cells. The consumer is likewise free to select an item from any of the occupied cells.

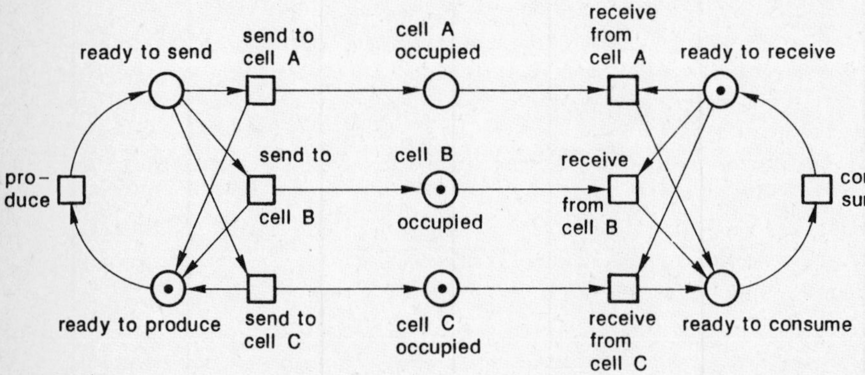

(1.8)

(1.8) is quite regularly structured. We now "condense" this structure: The three conditions "cell x occupied" (x ∈ { A,B,C }) are in (1.9) condensed to one circle. An index of each token denotes the cell it occupies. In (1.9) tokens are represented by their indices only. Arc inscriptions identify the correct token flow: The index x (x ∈ {A,B,C}) of an arc □—x→○ yields an x-indexed token on the place when the transition is fired. Similarly, a transition with an adjacend arc ○—x→□ is enabled only if the involved place holds an x-indexed token. This token is removed from the place upon firing the transition.

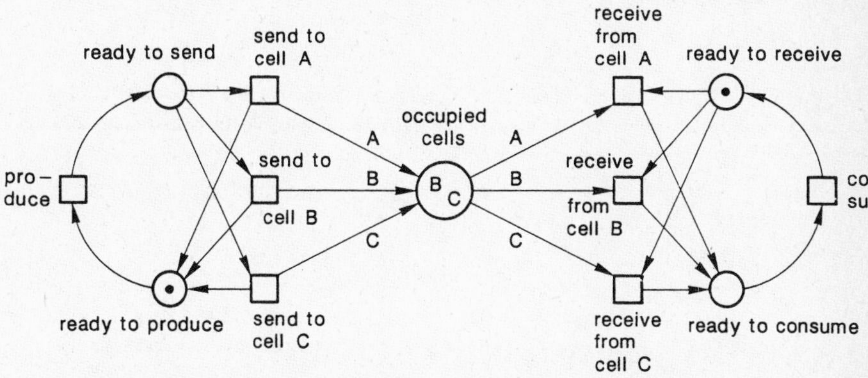

(1.9)

We further condense (1.9) and attain (1.10). This step includes the condensation of transitions. In order to fire a transition in (1.10), the variable x has to be valuated by one of the indexes A, B or C. This yields one of the transitions of (1.9), and one proceeds as described for (1.9).

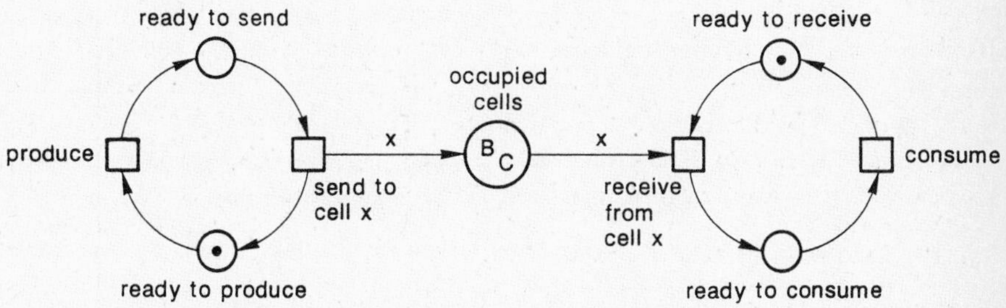

(1.10)

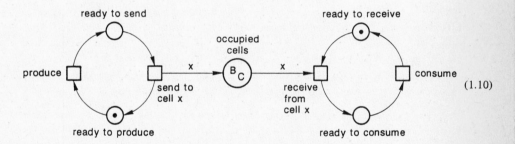

Systems such as shown in (1.10) are denoted as "Predicate/Transition Systems" (PrT-systems) and are discussed by H.J. Genrich in more detail elsewhere in this volume. PrT-systems serve for us only as an intermediate step towards the derivation of P/T-systems. The next (and final) step is now to abstract in (1.10) from the individuality of the tokens. This is simply achieved by just skipping token indices and arc inscriptions in (1.10). This procedure returns the system as already discussed in (1.3).

To sum up, starting from (1.8) we derived (1.9) and (1.10) by condensation and finally (1.3) by abstraction. We shall not derive the general principles for this procedure here, but refer to [Smith, Reisig 87]. Every EN system can in the outlined way be condensed to a P/T-system, and every P/T-system is a condensation of an EN system. As a consequence, one can "unfold" every P/T-system to an EN system. In this way we conceive P/T-systems as shorthands of certain C/E-systems.

The unfolding of a P/T-system to an EN system is however not unique. Several different EN systems may correspond to one P/T-system. This is caused by a loss of information during the abstraction step.

1.4 Occurrence Sequence Semantics of P/T-Systems

The literature on Petri Nets of the 1970ies concentrates to great extent on occurrence sequence semantics of P/T-systems. The concept of changing a marking M into a new marking M' by the occurrence of a transition t (in (1.6) denoted M[t > M') is repeatedly applied. We define by again quoting [Best, Fernandez]:

Definition

Let $\Sigma = (S,T;F,K,W,M_0)$ be a P/T-system.

(a) $\sigma = M_0 t_1 M_1 t_2 \dots t_n M_n$ is a *finite occurrence sequence* of Σ iff $\forall i, 1 \le i \le n\colon M_{i-1}[t_i\rangle M_i$; the *length* of σ is $|\sigma| = n$. (1.11)

(b) $\sigma = M_0 t_1 M_1 t_2 \dots$ is an *infinite occurrence sequence* of Σ iff $\forall i, 1 \le i\colon M_{i-1}[t_i\rangle M_i$.

(c) A sequence $t_1 t_2 \dots$ of transitions is a **transition sequence of** Σ, **iff there exists an occurrence sequence** of Σ, of the form $M_0 t_1 M_1 t_2 \dots$.

In the Literature, occurrence sequences or transition sequences are often denoted as "firing sequences". The change of terminology in this paper is oriented at other net models such as EN systems and PrT nets.

Two different views of P/T-systems have been discussed in this chapter: The conventional one (conceiving P/T-systems as generalised EN systems) and one that is orientated at the ideas of General Net Theory and Net Morphisms (conceiving P/T-systems as shorthand and abstraction of EN systems).

There exist likewise two different views of the behaviour of P/T-systems. The conventional one considers sequences of markings and of transition occurrences, and will in the following be denoted "occurrence sequence semantics".

Occurrence sequence semantics has its merits to cover a number of problems of P/T-systems. The core issue of Net Theory, viz. the adequate treatment of concurrency, is however not adequately settled in the framework of occurrence sequences. Those matters will be treated in the next section.

The semantics of P/T-systems has in the 1970ies usually been defined in the framework of occurrence sequences.

On a somewhat more abstract level it is adequate to denote this technique as "transition system oriented". This name is derived from [Keller 72], where it was used the first time, to argue on occurrence sequences. Transition systems have later been used to describe the operational semantics of several models for concurrency, including parallel programs, CCS, and CSP.

There are at first glace a lot of good reasons to define the semantics of P/T-systems in a transition system oriented style. First of all it fits properly to the standard technique of operational semantics for any kind of system model. There is furthermore a tight relationship to formal languages.

The **language** $L(\Sigma)$ of a P/T-system Σ is usually defined as the set of its transition sequences. Transitions are often labelled by a labelling function h such that sequences $h(t_1)h(t_2)...$ are taken as words in $L(\Sigma)$ instead of $t_1t_2...$.

The attempt was made to derive properties of P/T-systems from properties of their language, or to define two P/T-systems equivalent if their languages are equal. Petri Nets have been classified according to classifications of Petri Net languages. Such classifications then have been embedded into well known hierarchies of language classes, e.g. the Chomsky hierarchy. Decidability of properties of P/T-systems has been reduced to decidability questions of the corresponding languages. To give an example, a P/T-systems is deadlock prone iff its language is finite. This property is decidable. Details on Petri Net languages can be found in the contribution of [Jantzen 86a] in this volume.

1.5 Causal Precedence of Transition Occurrences

An occurrence sequence, as considered in the above section, states a total order on transition occurrences. This order is partly implied by the structure of the underlying system, and partly arbitrarily augmented.

In the following we endeavour to seperate these two aspects, and to concentrate on system based, causal precedence (order) of transition occurrences.

The intuitive idea of this procedure is as follows: Upon running a P/T-system Σ, each instance of transition occurrences of Σ is particularly identified and recorded. The entries in this record are partially ordered by the relation of "causal precedence": Two entries a,b are by definition ordered $a < b$ iff a is a prerequisite of b, i.e. iff b can not occur without a having occurred already. In graphical representations, $a \rightarrow b$ will express that a is a direct predecessor of b (i.e. $a < b$, and for no c, $a < c < b$ holds valid).

As an example, the occurrences of the transitions "produce" and " send" are expected to be totally ordered upon running the system (1.1):

$$p \longrightarrow s \longrightarrow p \longrightarrow s \longrightarrow \dots \qquad (1.12)$$

In this representation, the i-th appearanc (to be red from left to right) of "p" and of "s" represents the i-th occurrence of the transition "produce" and "send" in (1.1), respectively. The arcs in (1.12) indicate that the i-th occurrence of "produce" precedes directly the i-th occurrence of "send", and that the i-th occurrence of "send" directly precedes the i+1st occurrence of "produce".

The occurrences of "receive" and "consume" in (1.1) are likewise ordered:

$$r \longrightarrow c \longrightarrow r \longrightarrow c \longrightarrow \dots \qquad (1.13)$$

The appearances of "r" and "c" in (1.13) represent the corresponding occurrences of the transitions "receive" and "consume" in (1.1).

Both, (1.12) and (1.13) represent only parts of the behaviour of (1.1). It is clear that the reception of the i-th item must be preceded by its being sent. So we get the order

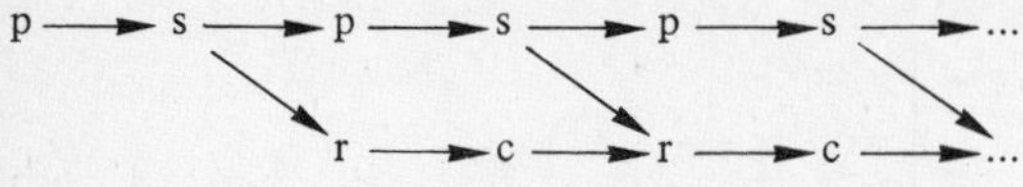

(1.14)

which unites the total orders (1.12) and (1.13) to a partial one.

The capacity of the buffer has in (1.1) been limited to one item. Sending the i+1st item must therefore be preceded by reception of the i-th item, and we end up with the following representation of the transition occurrences of (1.1):

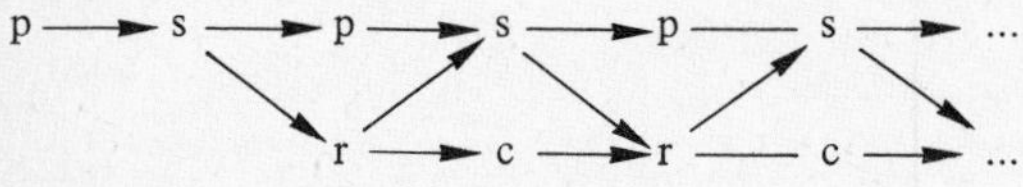

(1.15)

The difference between the systems in (1.1) and in (1.3) can now clearly be observed by the corresponding representation of the transition occurrences of the system in (1.3). On the base of (1.14), the limitation of the buffer capacity of (1.3) to three items implies that the sending of the i+3rd item must be preceded by the reception of the i-th item. This yields the following representation of the transition occurrences of (1.3):

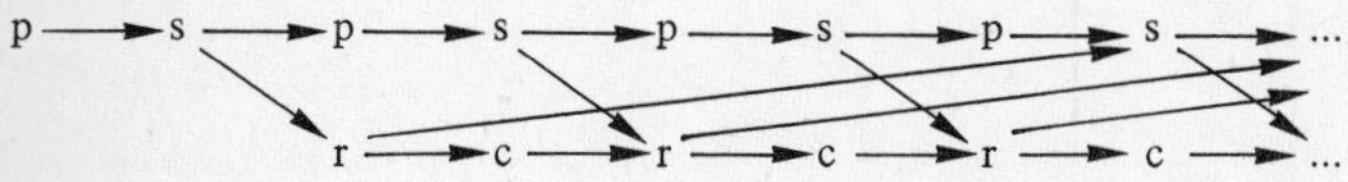

(1.16)

Notice that (1.15) and (1.16) include the same sets of transition occurrences. But in (1.16) they are less strictly ordered than in (1.15). This shows that increasing buffer capacities yield decreasing causal dependencies of event occurrences. If the buffer capacity is assumed to be unlimited, the causal dependencies of transition occurrences are already given by the order of (1.14).

We shall not go into details of this kind of semantics here. Instead we refer to the contribution [Rozenberg 86] in this volume, where formal definitions are discussed for the fundamental model of Elementary Net Systems. Further details can be gained from [Goltz, Reisig 83] and [Reisig 85b].

1.6 Particular Notions for P/T-systems

Some particular notions concerning P/T-systems Σ will be discussed here, including "contact", "loops", "concurrent enabling" and "conflict".

In case of contact, a transition is prevented from occurring by too narrow place capacities. Assuming a P/T-system as above, we define:

Definition

A transition t has **contact at a marking** M iff $s \in S$: $W(s,t) \leqslant M(s)$, (1.17)
but there exists a place $s_o \in S$ with $M(s_o) > K(s_o) - W(t,s)$.

As an example, consider the system shown in (1.4) after the occurrence of the transition "produce". This yields a marking at which the transition "send" has contact.

As a global property of P/T-systems we define:

Definition

A P/T-system is **contact-free** iff there exists no transition which has contact (1.18)
at any reachable marking.

In a contact-free system, the capacity function places no actual constraint and might as well be ommited.

Every P/T-system Σ can be transformed to a contact-free system Σ' by augmenting "complementary places" according to the following scheme:

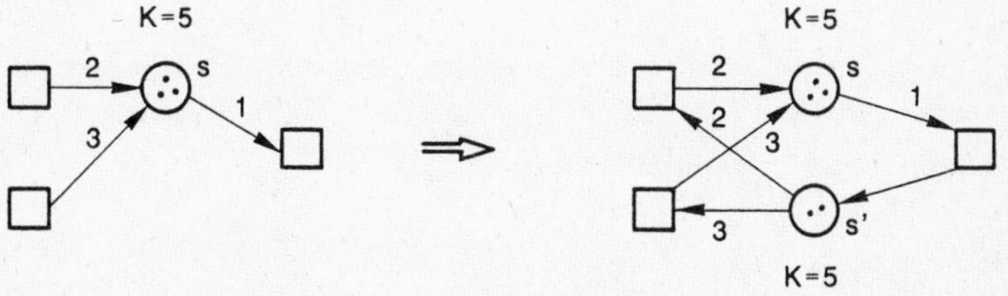

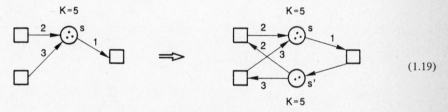

(1.19)

To be slightly more precise, to every place with limited capacity, a place s' is constructed with $F(s',t) = F(t,s')$ and $F(t,s') = F(s,t)$ for all transitions t. Additionally, $K(s') = K(s)$, and $M_o(s') = K(s) - M_o(s)$.

Then we get:

Theorem

(i) Σ' is contact-free. (1.20)

(ii) The set of transition sequences of Σ and of Σ' coincide.

Now a few words on **loops**: Definitions (1.5) and (1.6) include pairs of places and transitions, being linked in either direction,

(1.21)

i.e. $F(s,t) \geqslant 1$ and $F(t,s) \geqslant 1$. Then from Definition 1.7(b) follows immediatedly that for t to be enabled in any marking M, $K(s) \geqslant 2$ is mandatory. This properly fits with the conception of EN systems as special P/T-systems, as discussed in the text following (1.6): According to the definition of enabledness in EN systems (Def. 2.6 in [Thiagarajan 86]), transition can never be enabled if they are involved in loops.

One of the shortcomings of transition sequences as a semantic model for P/T-systems can drastically be exemplified by help of loops: Let Σ' be a P/T-system, obtained from a system Σ by an additional place s, initially marked by one token $M_0(s) = 1$, and let for all $t \in T$, $F(t,s) = F(s,t) = 1$. This means that s be linked to every transition by a loop.

Intuitively, all concurrent transition occurrences of Σ are prevented in Σ' but the sets of transition sequences of Σ and of Σ' coincide! Causal precedence semantics, as hinted to in 1.5, of course clearly shows up the difference between Σ and Σ', and indeed records totally ordered sets of event occurrences only. This difference is also reflected by the notion of "concurrently enabled" transitions: Assuming Σ as usual, we define

Definition

two transitions t_1 and t_2 are **concurrently enabled** at a marking M iff (1.22)
$\forall\, s \in S$: $W(s,t_1) + W(s,t_2) \leqslant M(s) \leqslant K(s) - W(t_1,s) - W(t_2,s)$.

As an example, in the net of (1.4), the transitions "produce" and "receive" are concurrently enabled at the indicated marking.

In this way, in a system Σ' with loops from all transitions to a distinguished place s, as described above, all pairs of transitions are prevented from concurrent occurrence. If two such transitions are both enabled at a marking M, they are in conflict. We generally define:

Definition

two transitions t_1 and t_2 are in **conflict** at a marking M, iff both are enabled at M, but not concurrently enabled. (1.23)

In the example considered so far, this situation did not occur. The reader may turn to (2.1), where a conflict between a and b occurs at the indicated marking.

1.7 Concluding Remarks on Chapter 1

Place/Transition systems are adequate for modelling those pieces and views of reality that involve items which all behave according to one scheme. Furthermore one should not be interested in the individuality of the items, but only in their quantity.

From a formal, purely mathematical point of view, P/T-systems introduce a new dimension of infinity into the net calculus.

The first dimension of infinity has been brought up by EN systems: A finite EN system characterizes in general an infinity of behaviours. But the state space as well as the degree of concurrency of finite C/E-systems is finite. Infinite behaviours are on this base necessarily quite "regular".

P/T-systems introduce with infinite place capacities the new dimension of infinite state spaces. If P/T-systems are considered as shorthands for EN systems, as discussed in Section 1.3, P/T-systems with infinite capacities correspond to infinite EN systems. In this way a class of "regularly structured" infinite EN systems is distinguished.

Increasing numbers of tokens intuitively denote increasing degrees of concurrency.

In the following Chapter we discuss mainly analysis techniques for P/T-systems that do not rely on place capacities.

2. REACHABLE MARKINGS

A "classical" concern in the theory of P/T-systems is the investigation of the set $[M_0\rangle$ of all reachable markings of a finite P/T-system. Hard problems belong to this area. The most prominent one is surely the "reachability problem", questioning for a given freely chosen marking $M : S \rightarrow N$ whether or not M is reachable (i.e. $M \in [M_0\rangle$). This problem was open for more than a decade, and eventually (positively) answered by [Kosaraju 82].

To mention a further problem, assume two finite P/T-systems Σ and Σ' with equal sets of places. If their sets $[M_0\rangle$ and $[M_0\rangle$ of reachable markings are infinite, the problem $[M_0\rangle = [M_0\rangle$ is undecidable. If both sets are finite, the problem is decidable, but not in primitive recursive time (or space)! For details of problems in this area we refer to the contribution [Jantzen 86b] in this volume.

2.1 The Concept of Coverability Trees

A P/T-system in general evolves an infinite set of reachable markings. A means will be developed to outline essential properties of this set. A node- and arc-labelled finite tree will be constructed for each P/T-system Σ such that every reachable marking of Σ either appears as a node label in that tree, or is "covered" by a node. Therefore such trees will be denoted "coverability trees".

The coverability tree is based on the tree $T'(\Sigma)$ of all reachable markings. The root of $T'(\Sigma)$ is labelled by the initial marking M_0 of Σ. The branches starting at a node n with label M are constructed as follows: If the occurrence of a transition t at M yields the marking M', the tree $T'(\Sigma)$ has a t-labeled arc that starts at n and ends at an M'-labeled node.

This construct yields of course in general infinite trees $T'(\Sigma)$. But we can derive from $T'(\Sigma)$ a finite tree $T(\Sigma)$ without loosing too much information about the reachable markings. The idea is to skip "regularly structured" paths and to indicate this regularity in the inscription of leafs.

Assume a path $M_0 \xrightarrow{t_1} M_1 \xrightarrow{t_2} M_2 \ldots$ of $T'(\Sigma)$ with two nodes M_i, M_j such that $i < j$ and for all $s \in S$ $M_i(s) \leq M_j(s)$. $T'(\Sigma)$ has in this case an infinite path which infinitely often repeats the transition sequence $t_{i+1} \ldots t_j$. This infinite sequence is in $T(\Sigma)$ replaced by a single leaf. Its label M is for $s \in S$ given by $M(s) = M_i(s)$ iff $M_i(s) = M_j(s)$, and $M(s) = \omega$ iff $M_i(s) < M_j(s)$. $M(s) = \omega$ describes that the value of s unboundedly increases within the replaced path.

As an example we consider the P/T-system Σ

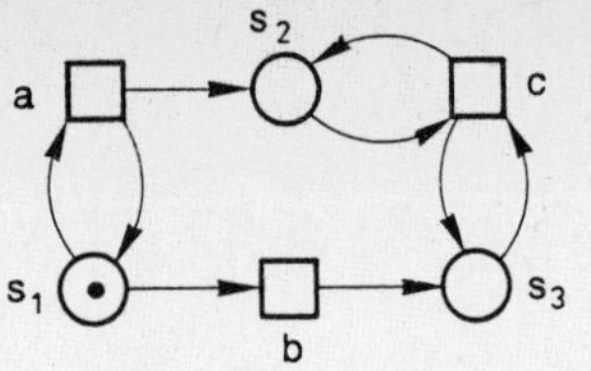

(2.1)

Markings M of this system will be represented by vectors $(M(s_1), M(s_2), M(s_3))$. Hence the initial marking is $(1, 0, 0)$.

The tree $T'(\Sigma)$ of all reachable markings of the system Σ in (2.1) is infinite. It starts as follows:

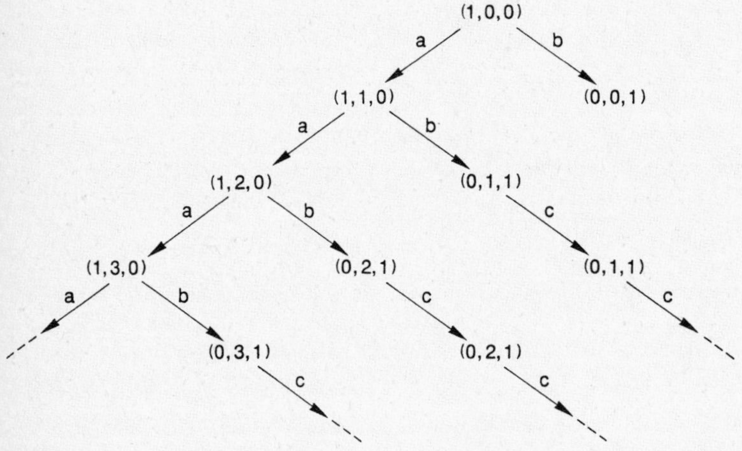

(2.2)

The coverability tree $T(\Sigma)$ is as follows:

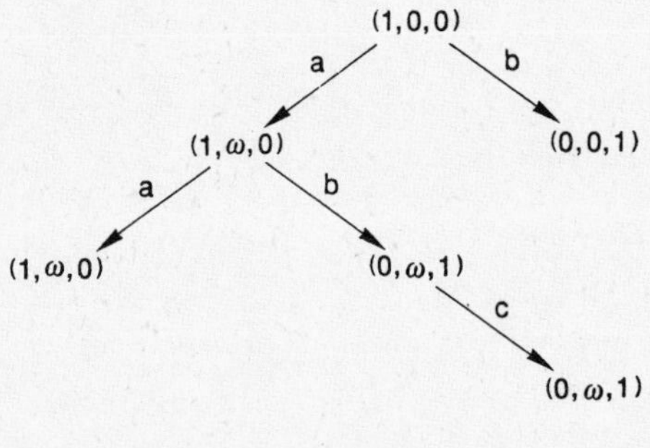

(2.3)

The following definition of coverability trees is a modification of the corresponding definition in [Best, Fernández 86] (where the name "reachability tree" has been used). The modification has been suggested by Horst Müller [Müller 86] in order to obtain a unique tree.

Definition

Let $\Sigma = (S,T;F,K,W,M_O)$ be a finite P/T-system.

The **coverability tree** of Σ is a tree whose nodes x are labelled by functions M_X from S to $N \cup \{\omega\}$ (where the rules for ω are given below) and whose arcs are labelled by elements of T. It is constructed inductively by the follwing algorithm.

(a) The root r is labelled by M_O, i.e. $M_r = M_O$.

(b) A node x is a leaf node iff either $\neg \exists t \in T : M_X$ enables t, or there is a node $y \neq x$ on the path from r to x which is also labelled by M_X, i.e. $M_y = M_X$. (2.4)

(c) If x is not a leaf node then for all $t \in T$ such that M_X enables t a new arc labelled t from x to a new node y is introduced. The label M_y is calculated by first defining M' as the successor of M under t (i.e. $M'(s) = M(s) + W(s,t) - W(t,s)$ for all $s \in S$) and then modifying M' as follows:

Let Z be the set of nodes on the path from the root r to the node y with labels $M_Z < M'$ for all $z \in Z$.
Then M_y is defined by

$$M_y(s) = \begin{cases} \omega \text{ iff } z \in \mathbf{Z} \text{ with } M_Z(s) < M'(s) \\ M'(s), \text{ otherwise.} \end{cases}$$

Certain information about the set of reachable markings can not be gained from coverability trees. To give an example, consider the following P/T-system Σ:

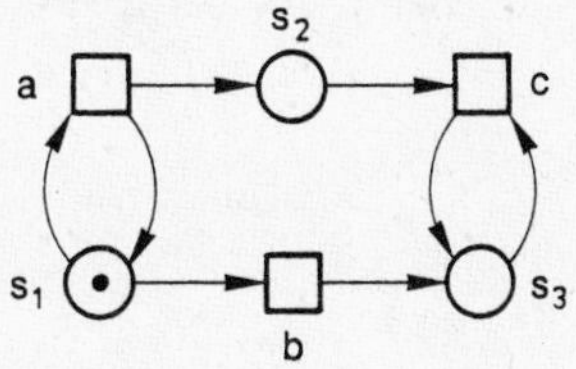

(2.5)

The infinite tree $T'(\Sigma)$ of the system in (2.5) starts as follows:

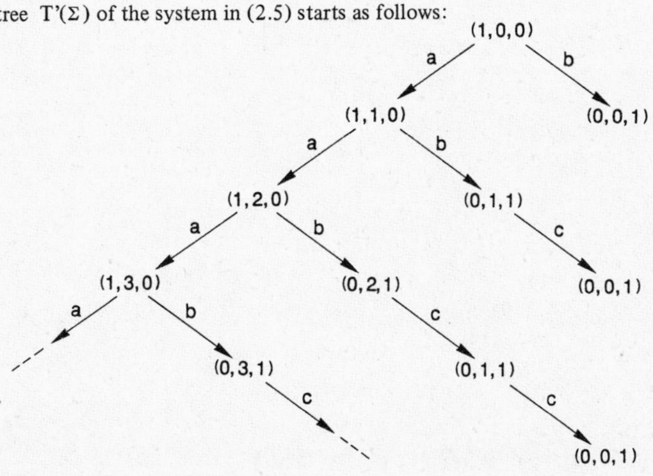

(2.6)

The systems in (2.1) and in (2.5) behave quite differently. They have different trees of reachable markings: After the occurrence of both the transitions a and b, in (2.1), c can occur more often than a did before. Therefore the tree of (2.2) has infinitely many infinite paths, whereas the tree of (2.6) has only one infinite path.

Both systems have nevertheless the same coverability tree. This tree is shown in (2.3).

The intuitive concept behind coverability trees, i.e. to "cover" the reachable markings, is properly met only for contact free P/T-systems. Their analytic power displays only for finite systems.

Assumption
in the rest of Chapter 2, let $\Sigma = (S,T;F,K,W,M_o)$ be a finite, contact free P/T-system, and let $T(\Sigma)$ be its covering tree. Additionally we assume for mappings $M, M' : S \rightarrow N \cup \{\omega\}$ a partial ordering, defined by $M \leqslant M'$ iff for all $s \in S$ $M(s) \leqslant M'(s)$, and $M < M'$ iff $M \leqslant M'$, and $M \neq M'$. (2.7)

2.2 Finiteness of Coverability Trees

We will show in this section that the coverability tree $T(\Sigma)$ is always finite.

We start with a merely technical lemma:

Lemma
Let S be a finite set and let $\tau = M_1, M_2, \ldots$ be an infinite sequence of mutually distinct mappings $M_i : S \rightarrow N$. Then there exists an infinite subsequence $\tau' = M_{i_1}, M_{i_2}, \ldots$ of τ such that for $j = 1,2,\ldots$, $M_{i_j} < M_{i_{j+1}}$. (2.8)

Proof by induction on $n = |S|$. $n = 1$ implies $M_i < M_j$ or $M_j < M_i$ for all $i \neq j$. In this case let $M_{i_1} = M_1$. Given M_{i_j}, let $M_{i_j}(s) = k$. There exist no more than k mappings $M : S \rightarrow N$ with $M < M_{i_j}$. Hence for some $m \leqslant k$, $M_{i_j} < M_{i_j+m}$.

For $S = \{s_1,\ldots,s_{n+1}\}$ there exists by induction hypothesis an infinite subsequence $\tau'' = M_{q_1}, M_{q_2}, \ldots$ of τ such that

$$(*) \quad M_{q_j}(s_k) < M_{q_{j+1}}(s_k) \quad \text{for all} \quad 1 \leqslant k \leqslant n \text{ and all } j \in \mathbb{N}.$$

We now construct the wanted sequence τ' as a subsequence of τ'' : Let $M_{i_1} = M_{q_1}$. Given M_{i_j}, there are only finitely many markings in τ'' such that $M(s_{n+1}) \leqslant M_{i_j}(s_{n+1})$. Hence there exists some index $i_{j+1} > i_j$ such that $M_{i_{j+1}}$ is in τ'' and $M_{i_{j+1}}(s_{n+1}) > M_{i_j}(s_n)$. With (*) we have $M_{i_{j+1}} > M_{i_j}$. □

Based on this Lemma we get that no path is infinite:

Lemma
Each path of $T(\Sigma)$ is finite. (2.9)

Proof Let $M_o \xrightarrow{t_1} M_1 \xrightarrow{t_2} \dots \rightarrow M_i \rightarrow \dots \rightarrow M_j \rightarrow \dots$ be a path in $T(\Sigma)$.

The construction of (2.4, 3.) implies: If $M_i < M_j$, then for all places $s \in S$ with $M_i(s) < M_j(s)$, it holds $M_j(s) = \omega$. Hence,

(*) any sequence $M_{i_1} < M_{i_2} < \dots$ has at most $|S|$ elements.

If $M_i = M_j$, (2.4, 2.) implies that M_j is a leaf, hence the path is finite. If we assume that all labels M_i are pairwise different, (*) and (2.8) imply the finiteness of the path. □

The finiteness of coverability trees is now obtained as follows:

Theorem
$T(\Sigma)$ is finite. (2.10)

Proof For each node n of $T(\Sigma)$, let tree (n) be the subtree of $T(\Sigma)$ with root n. Assuming $T(\Sigma)$ infinite, we inductively construct an infinite path $n_o \rightarrow n_1 \rightarrow n_2 \rightarrow \dots$ of $T(\Sigma)$ as follows: Let n_o be the root of $T(\Sigma)$. Let the node n_i be given and assume tree (n_i) infinite. n_i has at most finitely many daughter nodes $m_1,\dots,m_k$. As tree (n_i) is infinite, for at least one node m_j, tree (m_j) is infinite, too. Then let $n_{i+1} = m_j$.

According to (2.9), $T(\Sigma)$ can however not contain an infinite path.

□

2.3 Basic Properties of Coverability Trees

It will be shown in this section that the coverability tree of a P/T-system indeed "covers" the reachable markings of the system: First, to each reachable marking $M \in [M_o\rangle$ there exists a node M' in the tree such that $M \leqslant M'$. Secondly, the ω-components of nodes are taken up indeed, i.e. the corresponding places can obtain an unlimited number of tokens.

Theorem
Let $M \in [M_o\rangle$ be a reachable marking. Then $T(\Sigma)$ has a node labeled M'
such that $M \leqslant M'$. (2.11)

Proof by induction on the structure of $[M_o\rangle$ (cf. (1.7) (e)). For the initial marking M_o the proposition holds trivially, because M_o is the label of the root of $T(\Sigma)$.

By induction hypothesis assume the Theorem for $M_1 \in [M_o\rangle$. This means there exists a node in $T(\Sigma)$ with a label $M \geqslant M_1$. Of all nodes with this property, let x be a node (with label $M_x = M$), such that

(*) no node y from the root to x is labeled by M.

Let now $M_1 [t> M_2$. We have to show:

(**) $\quad T(\Sigma)$ has a node labeled M" such that $M_2 \leqslant M''$.

Because M_1 enables t and $M_1 \leqslant M$, M enables t, too. And if M' is the successor of M under t, i.e. $M[t>M'$, then

(***) $\quad M_2 \leqslant M'$.

By (*) and (2.4)(c) follows that $T(\Sigma)$ has an arc $x \xrightarrow{t} y$ with $M' \leqslant M_y$. With (***) we get $M_2 \leqslant M_y$, hence (**) and the Theorem. □

In order to show that all ω-components of coverability trees are indeed justified, we need the notion of covering sets:

Definition

Let S be any set, and let $M_1 : S \to N \cup \{\omega\}$ be a mapping. A set $\mathfrak{M}$ of mappings $M : S \to N$ is a **covering set of M_1** iff for all $i \in N$ there exists a mapping $M_i \in \mathfrak{M}$ such that for all $s \in S$ (2.12)

$$M_i(s) \begin{cases} = M(s) & \text{iff} \quad M(s) \in N \\ \geqslant i & \text{iff} \quad M(s) = \omega . \end{cases}$$

We can now show that each node of a coverability tree has a covering set of reachable markings:

Theorem

Let M be the label of a node of $T(\Sigma)$. Then there exists a covering set $\mathfrak{M} \subseteq [M_o>$ of M. (2.13)

Proof A covering set $\mathfrak{M}$ of a marking M will be called **reachable** iff $\mathfrak{M} \subseteq [M_o>$.

We start with a path

(a) $\quad x_o \xrightarrow{t_1} x_1 \xrightarrow{t_2} \ldots \rightarrow x_{k-1} \xrightarrow{t_k} x_k$

of $T(\Sigma)$, and for $0 \leqslant i \leqslant k$, let M_i be the label of x_i.

By induction on k we show:

(b) $\quad$ To each node x_i there exists a reachable covering set $\mathfrak{M}_i$.

For k = 0, with the initial marking M_o, $\mathfrak{M}_o = \{M_o\}$ is clearly a reachable covering set of the root x_o. By induction hypothesis we assume $\mathfrak{M}_o, \ldots, \mathfrak{M}_{k-1}$ exist.

Let now M' be given by $M_{k-1}[t_k> M'$, and let $\hat{M} \geqslant M'$.

We first show the following proposition:

(c) Let $\mathfrak{M}$ be a reachable covering set of $\hat{M}$, and for some $0 \leqslant q \leqslant k-1$ let $M_q < \hat{M}$. Then there exists a reachable covering set $\mathfrak{M}^q$ of $M + \omega \cdot (M' - M_q)$.

The occurrence of $t_{q+1},\ldots,t_k$ may decrease the token count on places s with $M_q(s) = \omega$ only. These decreases will be estimated by an integer $d \geqslant 0$ that is constructed as follows: For each $s \in S$ let $\bar{s} = \sum_{j=q}^{k} W((t_j,s) - W(s,t_j)$. Notice that $\bar{s}$ may be negative only in case $M_q(s) = \omega$. Now, let

$d = -\min(\{\bar{s} \mid s \in S\} \cup \{0\})$.

This construction guarantees:

(d) If $M_q \xrightarrow{t_{q+1}} \cdots \xrightarrow{t_k} M_k$ is an occurrence sequence, if $M_q(s) = \omega$, and if $M_q(s) \geqslant i+d$, then $M_k(s) \geqslant i$.

To show that the wanted covering set $\mathfrak{M}^q$ exists, it is sufficient to show that to each $i \in N$ exists a marking M which is reachable from a marking in $\mathfrak{M}_q$ such that

(e)
$$M(s) \begin{cases} = M_q(s) & \text{iff} \quad \neg(M_k(s) = \omega) \\ \geqslant i & \text{iff} \quad M_k(s) = \omega \end{cases}$$

This is done as follows:
To each $i \in N$, $\mathfrak{M}_q$ contains a marking $\overline{M}_q$ with $\overline{M}_q(s) \geqslant id + i$ for all s with $M_q(s) = \omega$.
Then an occurrence sequence $M_q \xrightarrow{t_{q+1}} \cdots \xrightarrow{t_k} M_k$ exists, and it holds with (d):

$$\overline{M}_k(s) \begin{cases} = M_q(s) & \text{iff} \quad \neg(M_k(s) = \omega) \\ \geqslant (i\text{-}1)d+i & \text{iff} \quad M_q(s) = \omega \\ > M_q(s) & \text{iff} \quad \neg(M_q(s) = \omega) \wedge M_k(s) = \omega. \end{cases}$$

So, it is possible to iterate the occurrences of $t_{q+1},\ldots,t_k$ i times and we end up by a marking M with

$$M(s) \begin{cases} = M_q(s) & \text{iff} \quad \neg(M_k(s) = \omega) \\ \geqslant i & \text{iff} \quad M_q(s) = \omega \\ = i\,(M_q(s) - M_k(s)) & \text{iff} \quad \neg(M_q(s) = \omega) \wedge M_k(s) = \omega \end{cases}$$

This marking clearly meets the requirements of (e) because $M_q(s) = \omega$ implies $M_k(s) = \omega$. By construction of (e), this completes the proof of (c).

We now can show the induction step of (b) as follows.
In accordance with (2.4)(c), let $Z = \{x_{i_1},\ldots,x_{i_n}\}$ be the set of nodes x_{i_j} in the path (a) with labels $M_{i_j} < M'$ $(j=1,\ldots,n)$.

For q = 0,...,n let $M^q = M' + \omega\,(\sum_{i=1}^{q} M'-M_q)$. Notice that for q = n, with (2.4)(c)

(f) M^n is the label of the node x_k in (a).

By induction on q = 0,...,n we inductively define reachable covering sets $\mathfrak{M}^q$ of M^q as follows:

Let $\mathfrak{M}^o = \{\tilde{M} \mid \exists\, M \in \mathfrak{M}_{k-1} \wedge M[t_k > \tilde{M}\}$. By the inductive assumption (b), $\mathfrak{M}_{k-1}$ is reachable. So $\mathfrak{M}^o$ is reachable, too, and $\mathfrak{M}^o$ is clearly a covering set of $M' = M^o$.

For $q \leqslant n$, by induction hypothesis let $\mathfrak{M}^{q-1}$ be a reachable covering set of M^{q-1}. By (c) then there exists a reachable covering set of $M^{q-1} + \omega(M'-M_q) = M^q$.

In this way we obtain a reachable covering set $\mathfrak{M}^n$ of M_n. As M_n is the label of x_k (according to (f)), with $\mathfrak{M}_k = \mathfrak{M}^n$ we have obtained the wanted covering set.

□

2.4 Decision Procedures Based on Coverability Trees

In the initial remarks to this Chapter we mentioned some "hard" problems, including the reachability problem, that can certainly not be solved by help of coverability trees. Some problems that concern coverability, boundedness and liveness can nevertheless be reduced to problems of coverability trees, and be solved in this framework.

To begin with, let $M : S \rightarrow N$ be an arbitrary marking. The problem " $\exists\, M' \in [M_o>$ with $M = M'$ " is the reachability problem and, as mentioned, very hard. The related problem " $\exists\, M' \in [M_o>$ with $M \leqslant M'$ " can however be reduced to coverability trees:

Theorem
Let M be a freely chosen marking of Σ. A marking $M' \in [M_o>$ with $M \leqslant M'$ exists iff a label M" of a node of $T(\Sigma)$ exists such that $M \leqslant M''$. (2.14)

Proof Let $M' \in [M_o>$ with $M \leqslant M'$. Using Theorem (2.11) there exists a node of $T(\Sigma)$ with a label M" such that $M' \leqslant M''$. $M \leqslant M''$ follows trivially.

Conversely, assume a node of $T(\Sigma)$ exists with a label M" and $M \leqslant M''$. Using Theorem (2.13) there exists a covering set $\mathfrak{M}$ of M". Clearly for some $M \in \mathfrak{M}$, $M \leqslant M'$ follows.

□

An interesting property of P/T-systems is the simultaneous unboundedness of subsets of places:

Definition

A subset $S' \subseteq S$ of the places of Σ is called **simultaneously unbounded** iff $\forall\, i \in N\ \exists M_i \in [M_o\rangle$ such that $\forall\, s \in S' : M_i(s) \geq i$. (2.15)

Theorem

Let S' be a subset of the places of Σ. S' is simultaneously unbounded iff a label M of a node of $T(\Sigma)$ exists such that $M(s) = \omega$ for all $s \in S'$. (2.16)

Proof Let $M_1, M_2, \ldots \in [M_o\rangle$ such that $\forall s \in S'\ \forall i \in N : M_i(s) \geq i$. Using Theorem (2.11) there exists, for each M_i, a node label M_i in $T(\Sigma)$ such that $M_i \leq M_i$. Since $T(\Sigma)$ is finite (Theorem 2.10), there exists a node label M such that for infinitely many $i_1, i_2, \ldots \in N$, $M_{i_j} \leq M$. Since for all $s \in S'$, $i_j \leq M_{i_j}(s) \leq M(s)$, $M(s) = \omega$ is inevitable.

The converse is Theorem (2.13). □

Theorem

The set $[M_o\rangle$ of the reachable markings of Σ is finite iff no node label of $T(\Sigma)$ has an ω-component. (2.17)

Proof $[M_o\rangle$ is infinite iff at least one place of Σ is unbounded. According to Theorem (2.14) this is true iff at least one node of $T(\Sigma)$ has an ω-component. □

The following (non-) liveness property will be reduced to covering graphs:

Definition

A transition t of Σ is called **dead** iff there exists no reachable marking $M \in [M_o\rangle$ that enables t. (2.18)

Theorem

Let t be a transition of Σ. t is dead iff there exists no arc of the form $M \xrightarrow{t} M'$ in $T(\Sigma)$. (2.19)

Proof Let $M \xrightarrow{t} M'$ be an arc in $T(\Sigma)$, and let $\mathcal{M} \subseteq [M_o\rangle$ be a covering set of M, in accordance with Theorem (2.13). $\mathcal{M}$ clearly contains a marking that enables t.

Conversely, if t is not dead, then there exists a marking $M_1 \in [M_o\rangle$ that enables t. From Theorem (2.11) follows the existence of a label M of a node of $T(\Sigma)$ with $M_1 \leq M$. M clearly enables t, too. □

2.5 Liveness Problems

A simple liveness problem has already been posed and satisfactorily solved in Definition 2.18 and Theorem 2.19. A rule of monotonity is valid for the notion of dead transitions, as introduced above:

Theorem

Let Σ' be a P/T-system that is obtained from Σ by replacing the initial marking M_o with a marking $M'_o < M_o$. If a transition t is dead in Σ, then t is also dead in Σ'. (2.20)

Proof Assume t is not dead in Σ'. Then there exists an execution sequence $M'_o\,[t_1> M'_1 ... M'_{n-1}[t_n> M'_n$ in Σ' such that M'_n enables t. Then however also exists an execution sequence $M_o[t_1> M_1 ... M_{n-1}[t_n > M_n$ in Σ such that M_n enables t. □

Other notions in the area of liveness are more involved. To give an example, we define:

Definition

Σ is a **live** P/T-system iff for all transition t of Σ and all reachable marking $M \in [M_o>$ there exist a marking $M' \in [M>$ reachable from M that enables t. (2.21)

This problem can not be solved by means of the covering tree $T(\Sigma)$. Even a rule of monotonicity like the one for dead transitions is not valid: The intuitively obvious conjecture that enlarging (adding tokens to) the initial marking of a live system yields again a live system turns out to be false. As a counterexample, Figure (2.22) shows a live P/T-system. If, additionally, the place s is initially marked, this yields a system which is no longer live.

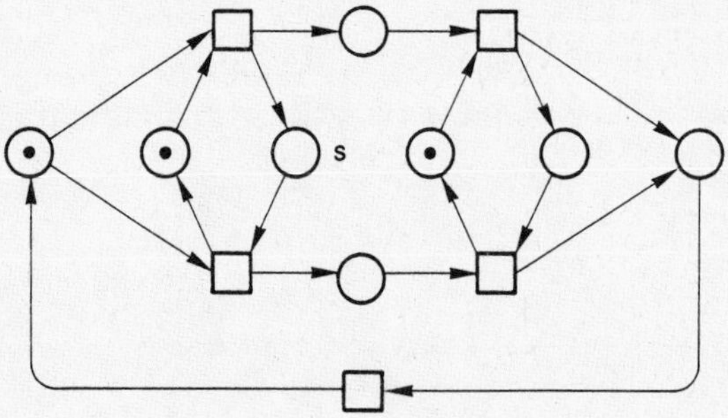

(2.22)

2.6 Concluding Remarks on Chapter 2

It has been shown that coverability trees support the analysis of Place/Transition Systems to a certain degree. Their applicability is however not only limited by the fact that they leave a lot of problems open. For the practical analysis of nets, algorithms for the construction of coverability trees are too complex. To outline these matters, we just mention that a sequence $\Sigma_1, \Sigma_2, ...$ of P/T-systems can be constructed that grows linear in size, whereas the corresponding coverability trees $T(\Sigma_1), T(\Sigma_2), ...$ grow quicker than any primitive recursive function.

The definition of coverability trees is not uniform in the literature. We quoted the definition as stated in [Best, Fernandez 86], that was adopted from [Brams 83]. Some authors suggest labeled graphs with properties similar to those of coverability trees. Such graphs may be obtained by identifying equally labeled nodes of the coverability tree. Additionally, backward directed arcs may lead to nodes with smaller labels. As an example we refer to Section 5.3 in [Reisig 85b]. Such graphs have the additional property that to each execution sequence $M_o[t_1> M_1[t_2>\ldots$ there exists a path $M_o \xrightarrow{t_1} M_1 \xrightarrow{t_2} \ldots$ in the graphs such that for all $i = 0,1,\ldots,$ $M_i \leq M_i$. Furthermore they are in general smaller than the corresponding coverability trees. This does however not imply that the algorithms for their construction were less complex.

The advantage of coverability trees (and the reason for us to introduce them here) is that the proofs of Lemmas and Theorems in Section 2.2 – 2.4 are less involved than the corresponding proofs for coverability graphs.

Some Remarks on the Development of P/T-systems

The work on P/T-systems started in the late 1960ies with some effort to discover properties of special net classes. Two institutions are to be named here: One is the "Institut für Informationssystemforschung" at GMD, where "synchronization graphs" (also called "marked graphs") were studied [Genrich 69] and [Genrich 71]. Nets with "regulation circuits" were investigated in [Lautenbach 73]. The other place to be mentioned is MIT with the "Information System Theory Project" (reported in [Holt et al 68]), that essentially worked in the area of what we now call "elementary net systems" [Thiagarajan 86]. On this background, "free choice nets" were studied in [Hack 72] (see [Best 86] in this volume). The general case of P/T-systems and their relationship to formal languages were investigated in [Hack 86]. This was the base for a lot of researach in language based analysis techniques.

The most important analysis methods for general P/T-systems are S- and T-invariants, introduced in [Lautenbach 73], in this volume presented in [Lautenbach 86]. Further techniques include transformation and decomposition [Berthelot 86], and stepwise refinement [Valette 79], [Suzuki, Murata 80]. An abstract version of P/T-systems with occurrence sequence semantics are vector replacement systems [Keller 72]. A lot of theoretical questions, including the reachability problem, are usually discussed in this setting.

Early applications of P/T-systems include the translation of Fortran programs into nets, showing precedence constraints between operations [Shapiro, Saint 70], and a model of the SCOPE 3.2 operating system [Noe 71]. P/T-nets have later on been applied in a wide range of areas in computer science in the 1970ies. With the introduction of Petri Net models with individual tokens (in this volume discussed in [Genrich 86] and [Jensen 86]), a lot of new applications have been and will be formulated in the framework of those models.

References

[Berthelot 86] G. Berthelot: Transformations and Decompostitions of Nets. this volume

[Best 84] Eike Best: Concurrent Behaviour: Sequences, Processes and Axioms. Arbeitspapiere der GMD 118, November 1984, also: Lecture Notes in Computer Science vol. 197 (1985)

[Best 86] Eike Best: Structure Theory of Petri Nets: The Free Choice Hiatus. This volume

[Best, Devillers 85] Eike Best, Raymond Devillers: Concurrent Behaviour: Sequences, Processes and Programming Languages. Studien der GMD No. 99 (1985)

[Best, Fernandez 86] Eike Best, Cesar Fernandez: Notations and Terminology of Petri Net Theory. Arbeitspapiere der GMD 195, Gesellschaft für Mathematik und Datenverarbeitung (1986)

[Brams 83] G.W. Brams (nom collectif): Reseaux de Petri: Theorie et Pratique; Tome 1 and 2, Masson publ. comp. Paris (1983)

[Genrich 69] H.J. Genrich: Das Zollstationenproblem. GMD internal report ISF/69–01–15 (1969), revised version: GMD internal report ISF/71–10–13 (1971).

[Genrich 71] H.J. Genrich: Einfache nicht-sequentielle Prozesse. GMD-Bericht 37 (1971)

[Genrich 86] H.J. Genrich: Predicate/Transition Nets. this volume

[Goltz, Reisig 83] Ursula Goltz, Wolfgang Reisig: The Non-Sequential Behaviour of Petri Nets. Information & Control 57, Nos. 2–3, pp. 125–147 (1983)

[Hack 72] M. Hack: Analysis of Production Schemata by Petri Nets. Cambridge, Mass.: MIT, Dept. of Electrical Engineering, MS Thesis (1972). also: MIT Project MAC, Computation Structures Note 17 (1974)

[Hack 75] M. Hack: Decidability Questions for Petri Nets. MIT, Dept. of Electrical Engineering (1975), also: MIT, Technical Report TR–159 (1976)

[Holt et al 68] A.W. Holt et al: Information System Theory Project, Final Report. Princeton, N.J.: Applied Data Research Inc., RADC–TR–68–305, N TIS AD 679972 (1986)

[Jantzen 86] Mathias Jantzen: Complexity of Place/Tansition Nets. This volume

[Jantzen 86a] Mathias Jantzen: Language Theory of Nets. This volume

[Jensen 86] K. Jensen: Coloured Petri Nets. this volume

[Keller 72] R.M. Keller: Vector Replacement Systems: A Formalism for Modelling Asynchronous Systems. TR 117, Computer Science Lab., Dept. of Electrical Engineering, Princeton University, December 1972 (revised Jan. 1974)

[Kosaraju 82] S.R. Kosaraju: Decidability of Reachability in Vector Addition Systems. Proceedings of the Fourteenth Annual ACM Symposium on Theory of Computing, San Francisco, California, pp. 267–281 (1982)

[Lautenbach 73] K. Lautenbach: Exakte Bedingungen der Lebendigkeit für eine Klasse von Petri-Netzen. GMD-Bericht 82 (1973)

[Lautenbach 86] Kurt Lautenbach: Linear Algebraic Techniques for Place/Transition Nets. This volume

[Memmi 86] Gerard Memmi: Advanced Algebraic Techniques of Nets. This volume

[Müller 86] Horst Müller: private communication

[Noe 71] J. Noe: A Petri Net Model for the CDC 6400. Proceedings of the ACM SIGOPS Workshop on System Performance Evaluation, New York, ACM, pp. 362–378 (1971)

[Reisig 85a] Wolfgang Reisig: Petri Nets. EATCS Monographs on Theoretical Computer Science, Springer Verlag (1985)

[Reisig 85b] Wolfgang Reisig: On the Semantics of Petri Nets. in: Neuhold, Chroust (eds.), Formal Models in Programming. North Holland Publ. Company, IFIP, (1985)

[Rozenberg 86] Grzegorz Rozenberg: Behaviour of Condition/Event Systems. This volume

[Rozenberg, Veraedt 83] G. Rozenberg, R. Verraedt: Subset Languages of Petri Nets. Theoretical Computer Science Vol. 26, pp. 301–326, and Vol. 27, pp. 85–108, (1983)

[Shapiro, Saint 70] R. Shapiro, H. Saint: A New Approach to Optimization of Sequencing Decisions. Annual Review in Automatic Programming. Vol. 6, Part 5, pp. 257–288 (1970)

[Smith, Reisig 87] Einar Smith, Wolfgang Reisig: The Semantics of a Net in a Net: A Exercise in General Net Theory. To appear in: K. Voss, H.J. Genrich, G. Rozenberg (eds.): Concurrency and Nets, Springer-Verlag (1987)

[Suzuki, Murata 80] I. Suzuki, T. Murata: A Method for Hierarchically Representing Large Scale Petri Nets. Proc. of the 1980 Int. Cof. on Circuits and Computers, pp. 620–623 (1980)

[Thiagarajan 86] P.S. Thiagarajan: Elementary Net Systems. This volume

[Valette 79] R. Valette: Analysis of Petri Nets by Stepwise Refinements. Journal of Computer and System Sciences, Vol. 18, pp. 35–46 (1979)

[Valk 86] Rüdiger Valk: Infinite Behaviour and Fairness of P/T-Systems. This volume

Linear Algebraic Techniques for Place/Transition Nets

Kurt Lautenbach

University of Bonn
Dept. of Computer Science
Wegeler Str. 6
D-5300 Bonn

and

GMD-F1P
Postfach 1240
D-5205 St. Augustin 1

ABSTRACT This paper is an introdurction into linear algebraic techniques for place/transition nets. Based on a linear representation of processes S- and T-invariants are introduced. S- and T-invariants are both, solutions of linear homogeneous equation systems and subnets with special properties.

Key words: S- and T-invariants, linear invariants, place/transition nets, Petri nets.

CONTENTS

1. Introduction

S- and T-invariants have turned out to be important means for analyzing Petri nets.

They are structural components of nets with important properties. They are calculated as solutions of linear homogeneous equation systems.

In this paper we introduce into the technique of linear invariants for place/transition nets.

The paper is organized as follows. In this introduction we show the linear representation of processes in place/transition nets. This representation is fundamental for the application of linear algebraic means.

In the second section we define S- and T-invariants for a restricted class of nets and interpret them by means of examples. Furthermore, we show some basic properties of invariants and how they can be applied.

In the third section we show how the concepts of section two can be applied to general place/transition nets.

In section four we show a further application of S-invariants and a certain kind of limitation of the linear algebraic techniques in place/transition nets.

Definition 1.1 (cf. [BF86])

A fivetuple $N = (S,T;F,K,W)$ is called a place/transition net (P/T-net) iff:

(1) (S,T;F) is a net where the S-elements are called places and the T-elements are called transitions

(2) $K : S \to \mathbb{N}^{+} \cup \{\infty\}$ is a capacity function

(3) $W : F \to \mathbb{N}^{+}$ is a weight function

(With respect to [BF 86] a P/T-net is nothing but a "P/T-system without marking").

Remark 1.2

As a tacit assumption for the sequel it is stated that all P/T-nets considered in this paper are finite, i.e. $|S| < \infty$ and $|T| < \infty$.

Under the following definition we will subsume some concepts which we need in the sequel. For all concepts which are used but not introduced in this paper we refer to [BF 86].

Definition 1.3

Let $N = (S,T;F,K,W)$ be a P/T-net.

(1) N is called pure iff $\forall (s,t) \in S \times T : (s,t) \in F \Rightarrow (t,s) \notin F$

(2) A function $M : S \to \mathbb{N}$ is called a marking of N

(3) A transition $t \in T$ is called enabled under a marking M of N iff $\forall s \in {}^{\bullet}t : M(s) \geq W(s) \wedge \forall s \in t^{\bullet} : M(s) + W(s) \leq K(s)$

(4) Let a transition $t \in T$ be enabled under a marking M of N. Then t may occur, yielding a new marking M' of N given by:

$M'(s) = M(s) - W(s,t)$ for all $s \in {}^{\bullet}t$

$M'(s) = M(s) + W(t,s)$ for all $s \in t^{\bullet}$

$M'(s) = M(s)$ for all $s \notin {}^{\bullet}t \cup t^{\bullet}$

This is denoted by M[t>M' and M' is called an immediate follower marking of M. By [M> we denote the set of (not necessary immediate) follower markings of M.

Example 1.4

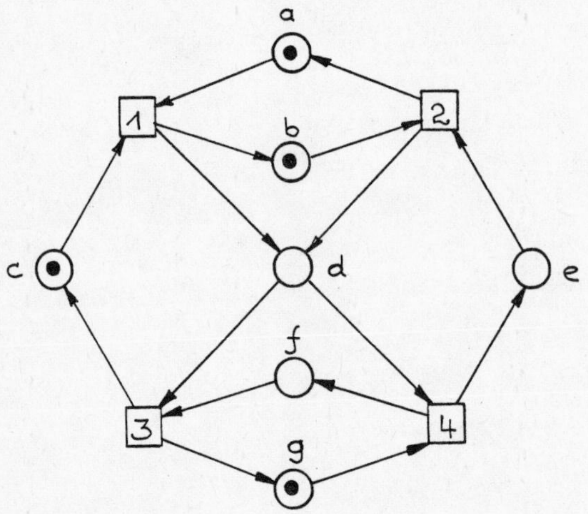

Figure 1.1

Let $N = (S,T;F,K,W)$ be the net of fig. 1.1. Then we have

$S = \{a,b,c,d,e,f,g\}$

$T = \{1,2,3,4\}$

$F = \{(a,1),(c,1),(1,b),(1,d),(b,2),(e,2),(2,a),(2,d),$
$(d,3),(f,3),(3,c),(3,g),(d,4),(g,4),(4,e),(4,f)\}$

and in addition

$K : S \to \{\infty\}$
$W : F \to \{1\}$.

Furthermore the net is pure.

Let M be the marking of N shown in fig. 1.1, then

$$M : \quad S \to \{0,1\} \quad \text{where}$$
$$\{a,b,c,g\} \to \{1\}$$
$$\{d,e,f\} \to \{0\}$$

The only enabled transition is $1 \in T$ and the immediate follower marking of M is

$$M' : \quad S \to \{0,1,2\} \quad \text{where}$$
$$\{b\} \to \{2\}$$
$$\{d,g\} \to \{1\}$$
$$\{a,c,e,f\} \to \{0\}$$

Under M' the only enabled transition is $4 \in T$. The immediate follower marking of M' is

$$M'' : \quad S \to \{0,1,2\} \quad \text{where}$$
$$\{b\} \to \{2\}$$
$$\{e,f\} \to \{1\}$$
$$\{a,c,d,g\} \to \{0\}$$

□

To conclude this introduction we want to show how the effects of transition occurrences can be represented by linear-algebraic means.

<u>Definition 1.5</u>

Let $N = (S,T;F,K,W)$ be a pure P/T-net. For the sets S and T an arbitrary but fixed order is assumed:

$$S : s_1 < s_2 < \ldots < s_m$$
$$T : t_1 < t_2 < \ldots < t_n$$

where $m = |S|$ and $n = |T|$.

(1) A column vector $v : S \to \mathbb{Z}$ indexed by S in called an <u>S-vector</u> of N.

(2) A column vector $w : T \to \mathbb{Z}$ indexed by T is called an <u>T-vector</u> of N.

(3) A matrix $N : S \times T \to \mathbb{Z}$ indexed by S and T such that

$$N(s_i,t_j) := W(t_j,s_i) - W(s_i,t_j)$$

is called the <u>incidence matrix</u> of N .

We usually denote a net and its incidence matrix by the same (capital) letter. The i-th row and the j-th column of N are denoted by $N(s_i,-)$ and $N(-,t_j)$, respectively.

Let us use these concepts to represent the transition occurrences of example 1.4.

<u>Example 1.6</u> (cf. example 1.4)
The net of example 1.4 has the following incidence matrix:

N	1	2	3	4
a	-1	1		
b	1	-1		
c	-1		1	
d	1	1	-1	-1
e		-1		1
f			-1	1
g			1	-1

Figure 1.2

(We usually omit 0-entries)

N(a,1) = -1 and N(b,1) = 1 indicate that when transition 1 occurs it <u>takes</u> one token from place a and it <u>puts</u> one token on b.

So, the entire effect of the occurrences of a transition is recorded in its column of the incidence matrix.

That is, what transforms the markings is represented by S-vectors.

Consequently, also the markings themselves will be represented by S-vectors.

	M	M'	M"
a	1		
b	1	2	2
c	1		
d		1	
e			1
f			1
g	1	1	

Now the transition occurrences of example 1.4 can be represented in the following way:

$$\begin{array}{c} \\ a\\ b\\ c\\ d\\ e\\ f\\ g \end{array} \quad \begin{array}{c} M \\ \begin{bmatrix} 1\\ 1\\ 1\\ \\ \\ \\ 1 \end{bmatrix} \end{array} + \begin{array}{c} N(-,1) \\ \begin{bmatrix} -1\\ 1\\ -1\\ 1\\ \\ \\ \ \end{bmatrix} \end{array} = \begin{array}{c} M' \\ \begin{bmatrix} \\ 2\\ \\ 1\\ \\ \\ 1 \end{bmatrix} \end{array}$$

$$\begin{array}{c} \\ a\\ b\\ c\\ d\\ e\\ f\\ g \end{array} \quad \begin{array}{c} M \\ \begin{bmatrix} 1\\ 1\\ 1\\ \\ \\ \\ 1 \end{bmatrix} \end{array} + \begin{array}{c} N(-,1) \\ \begin{bmatrix} -1\\ 1\\ -1\\ 1\\ \\ \\ \ \end{bmatrix} \end{array} + \begin{array}{c} N(-4) \\ \begin{bmatrix} \\ \\ \\ -1\\ 1\\ 1\\ -1 \end{bmatrix} \end{array} = \begin{array}{c} M'' \\ \begin{bmatrix} \\ 2\\ \\ \\ 1\\ 1\\ \ \end{bmatrix} \end{array}$$

That is, the current marking M" is the result of adding to the initial marking M the colums N(-,t) for all $t \in T$ as often as t occurred to reach M" from M.

A short form for this linear representation of transition occurrences is

$$M + N \cdot \begin{bmatrix} 1\\ 0\\ 0\\ 1 \end{bmatrix} = M'' ,$$

where the incidence matrix is multiplied by the corresponding T-vector of the transition occurrences.

□

<u>Remark 1.7</u>
Obviously every transformation of a marking M into a (not necessarily immediate) follower marking M' can be linearly represented as

$$M + N \cdot f = M'$$

where N is the incidence matrix and f is a T-vector indicating the transition occurrences.

The converse, however, is not true. That is, even if the above equation holds it is not true in general that M' can be reached from M with transition occurrences according to f.

<u>Example 1.8</u> (cf. example 1.6)
For the net N of figure 1.1 and its incidence matrix (figure 1.2) the following equation holds

$$O + N \cdot \begin{bmatrix} 1 \\ 1 \\ 1 \\ 1 \end{bmatrix} = O \ .$$

But this representation is not realistic since under the zero marking no transition of the net N is enabled.

□

2. S- and T-invariance

The dynamic behaviour of P/T-systems depends on the net structure and the initial marking. The influence of the net structure on the behaviour is of particular importance since it holds under every initial marking.

Moreover, the net structure can be investigated independently of any dynamic process.

So, in this section we want to identify net structures enforcing a certain behaviour which then is predictable.

Remark 2.1

All P/T-nets N = (S,T;F,K,W) in this section are pure and have unbounded capacities for all places, that is $K : S \to \{\infty\}$.

In the next section we will deal with P/T-nets without these restrictions.

□

For modeling dynamic systems by means of P/T-nets, it is very important to know whether it is guaranteed that tokens cannot be lost - at least not in an uncontrolled way - and whether it is possible to reproduce markings.

What we mean will be demonstrated by means of some examples.

Example 2.2

In the P/T-net of figure 2.1.a no token can be lost. But it is impossible to reproduce the marking of this net.

In the net of figure 2.1.b, however, all tokens can be lost, namely by two occurrences of the transitions 2,3,4.

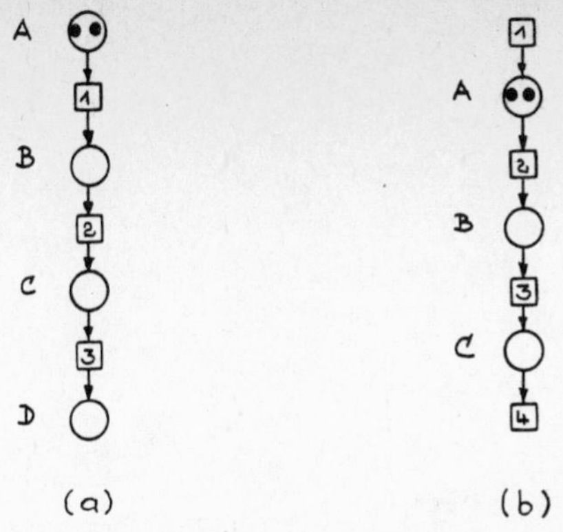

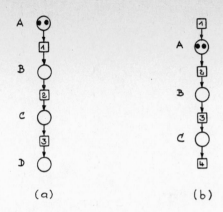

Figure 2.1

On the other hand, the marking of this net is reproduced if also the transition 1 occurs twice.

□

This example shows that the capabilities of not to lose tokens and to reproduce markings are different and that one can occur without the other one.

The next example shows a P/T-net with both properties and a P/T-net without any of both properties.

Example 2.3
In the P/T-net of figure 2.2.a no token can be lost. Moreover, the marking of this net will be reproduced if all transitions occur equally often.

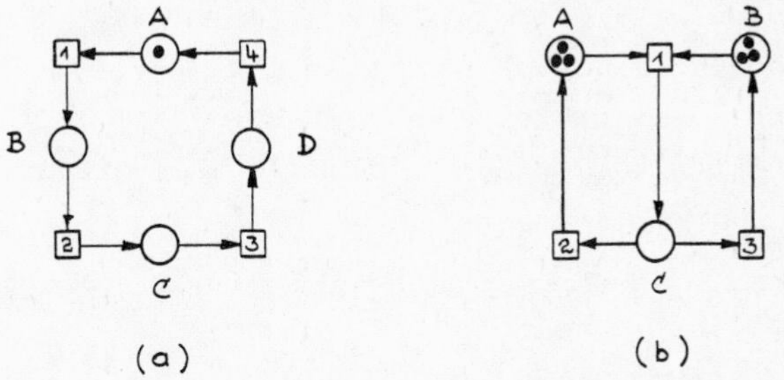

Figure 2.2

In figure 2.2.b a net is shwon in which by each occurrence of transition 1 one token is irretrievably lost. Thereby also the reproducibility of the marking is made impossible. Maximally all but one token can be lost.

□

The next example shows that there are also seeming losses of tokens.

Example 2.4

By every occurrence of the respective transition 1 in both P/T-nets of Figure 2.3 the number of tokens is reduced by one. But this loss of tokens is not irreparable. Since after the occurrence of the respective transition 2 the marking consists again of two tokens.

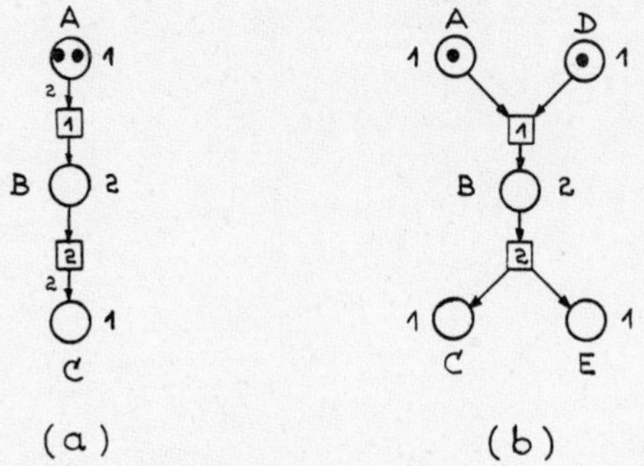

Figure 2.3

One could say that by transition 1 two tokens are glued together and that by transition 2 they are separated again.

But then we had two types of tokens ones which are glued and ones which are not.

To be able to compensate temporal losses using only one type of tokens we define a token weight. On place B a token has twice the weight or value it has on the other places.

So the weight of a token on a place is a property of that place and not of the token.

The numbers assigned to the places in figure 2.3 are the relative token weights.

The following yields for figure 2.3.a:

the weight of two tokens on A equals 2
the weight of one token on B equals 2
the weight of two tokens on C equals 2

For figure 2.3.b:

the weight of one token on A
and one token on D equals 2
the weight of one token on B equals 2
the weight of one token on C
and one token on E equals 2

□

Thus, the seeming loss of tokens is represented by the invariance of the weighted marking.

To represent this fact formally we again use S-vectors.

Example 2.5 (cf. example 2.4)
The net in figure 2.3.a has an initial marking M and two follower markings M' and M" where

$$\begin{matrix} A \\ B \\ C \end{matrix} \quad M = \begin{bmatrix} 2 \\ \ \\ \ \end{bmatrix}, \quad M' = \begin{bmatrix} \ \\ 1 \\ \ \end{bmatrix}, \quad M'' = \begin{bmatrix} \ \\ \ \\ 2 \end{bmatrix}.$$

The vector of the relative token weights is

$$\begin{matrix} A \\ B \\ C \end{matrix} \quad g = \begin{bmatrix} 1 \\ 2 \\ 1 \end{bmatrix}.$$

Then the observed invariance of the weighted markings is

$$g^T \cdot M = \begin{bmatrix} 1 & 2 & 1 \end{bmatrix} \begin{bmatrix} 2 \\ \ \\ \ \end{bmatrix} = 2$$

$$g^T \quad M' = \begin{bmatrix} 1 & 2 & 1 \end{bmatrix} \begin{bmatrix} \ \\ 1 \\ \ \end{bmatrix} = 2$$

$$g^T \quad M'' = \begin{bmatrix} 1 & 2 & 1 \end{bmatrix} \begin{bmatrix} \ \\ \ \\ 2 \end{bmatrix} = 2 \quad .$$

In order to show an elegant way to define (and calculate) the token weights we use the incidence matrix

$$N = \begin{array}{c|cc} & 1 & 2 \\ \hline A & -2 & \\ B & 1 & -1 \\ C & & 2 \end{array}$$

and we write

$$M + \begin{bmatrix} -2 \\ 1 \\ \ \end{bmatrix} = M + N(-,1) = M'$$

$$M' + \begin{bmatrix} \\ -1 \\ 2 \end{bmatrix} = M + N(-,2) = M''$$

$$g^T \cdot M = g^T \cdot M' = g^T \cdot M'' \quad \text{implies}$$

$$g^T \cdot N(-,1) = g^T \cdot N(-,2) = 0$$

and consequently

$$g^T \cdot N = 0 .$$

That is, g is a solution of the equation

$$x^T \cdot N = 0;$$

according to the next definition it is a non-negative S-invariant.

□

In order to formalize what we have observed so far we start introducing the calculus of invariants [La 73].

Definition 2.6

Let $N = (S,T;F,K,W)$ be a P/T-net and I and S-vector of N.

(1) I is called an S-invariant of N iff $I^T \cdot N = 0^T$

(2) $P_I \subseteq S$ is called the support of I iff $P_I = \{s \in S \mid I(s) \neq 0\}$

(3) An S-invariant I of N is called non-negative iff $I \geq 0$.

(4) A non-negative S-invariant $I \neq 0$ of N is called minimal iff there exists no non-negative S-invariant I' of N with $0 \lneqq I' \lneqq I$.

(5) A subnet $N_I = (S_I, T_I; F_I, K_I, W_I)$ or N is called the graphical representation of I iff

S_I is the support of I

$T_I := {}^\bullet S_I \cup S_I^\bullet$

$F_I := F \cap [(S_I \times T_I) \cup (T_I \times S_I)]$

$K_I(s) := K(s)$ for all $s \in S_I$

$W_I(f) := W(f)$ for all $f \in F_I$.

Corollary 2.7

Every integer linear combination of S-invariants is an S-invariant.

□

This corollary is, of course, of some importance. It enforces, however, tocall $I = 0$ an S-invariant, even though the support P_I is empty.

Consequently, every P/T-net has an S-invariant, at least the trivial (non-negative) S-invariant $I = 0$.

On the other hand, a net is usually said to have "no S-invariants" if $I = 0$ is the only one.

We will follow this diction and lay it down in the following remark.

<u>Remark 2.8</u>

If the only S-invariant of a P/T-net N is $I = 0$ we will say that N has no S-invariants.

<u>Example 2.9</u> (cf. examples 2.2, 2.3, 2.4, 2.5, 1.4, 1.6)

The P/T-nets of the figures 2.1.b and 2.2.b have no S-invariants.

$$\begin{matrix} A \\ B \\ C \\ D \end{matrix} \qquad I = \begin{bmatrix} 1 \\ 1 \\ 1 \\ 1 \end{bmatrix}$$

is the minimal S-invariant of the P/T-nets of the figures 2.1.a and 2.2.a.

The minimal S-invariant of the net in figure 2.3.a is

$$\begin{matrix} A \\ B \\ C \end{matrix} \qquad g = \begin{bmatrix} 1 \\ 2 \\ 1 \end{bmatrix} .$$

The net in figure 2.3.b has four minimal S-invariants

$$\begin{matrix} A \\ B \\ C \\ D \\ E \end{matrix} \quad I_1 = \begin{bmatrix} 1 \\ 1 \\ 1 \\ \\ \\ \end{bmatrix} , \quad I_2 = \begin{bmatrix} \\ 1 \\ \\ 1 \\ 1 \end{bmatrix} , \quad I_3 = \begin{bmatrix} 1 \\ 1 \\ \\ \\ 1 \end{bmatrix} , \quad I_4 = \begin{bmatrix} \\ 1 \\ 1 \\ 1 \\ \\ \end{bmatrix} .$$

The weights assigned to the places of figure 2.3.b are the entries of the S-invariant

$$\begin{matrix} A \\ B \\ C \\ D \\ E \end{matrix} \quad I = I_1 + I_2 = I_3 + I_4 = \begin{bmatrix} 1 \\ 2 \\ 1 \\ 1 \\ 1 \end{bmatrix}$$

Now we come to the P/T-net N in figure 1.1.

A collection of S-invariants of N is shown in the following table:

	I_1	I_2	I_3	I_4	I_5
a	1				
b	1			1	1
c			1	2	2
d			1	1	1
e			1		
f		1		1	
g		1			-1

Figure 2.4

The graphical representations of I_3 and I_5 are shown in fig. 2.5.

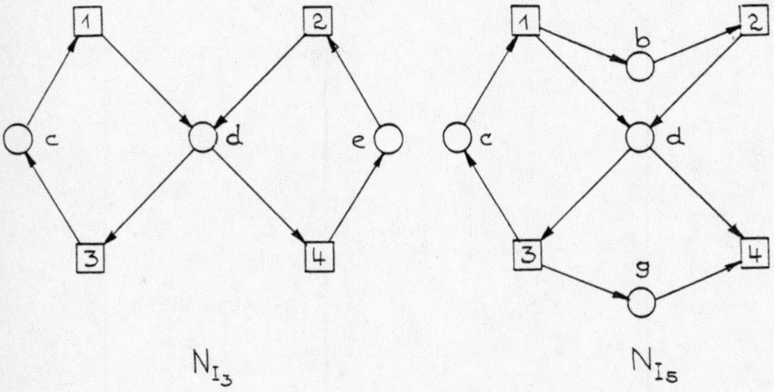

Figure 2.5

□

The following theorem summarizes what the S-invariance is about: The inner product of an S-invariant and the follower markings of some initial marking is an invariant quantity.

<u>Theorem 2.10</u>

Let $N = (S,T;F,K,W)$ be a P/T-net, M a marking of N, and I an S-invariant of N.

Then: $\forall M' \in [M] : I^T \cdot M' = I^T \cdot M$

<u>Proof</u>

Let $M' \in [M\rangle$ and $f' \geq 0$ be a T-vector whose entries $f'(t)$ indicate how often the transition $t \in T$ have occurred in order to reach M' from M.

Then $M' = M + N \cdot f'$ holds,

which implies
$$I^T \cdot M' = I^T \cdot M + I^T \cdot N \cdot f'$$
$$= I^T \cdot M + 0$$
$$= I^T \cdot M .$$

Now let $M'' \in \langle M']$. That is, M" is reached from M' by backward occurrences. Let $f'' \leq 0$ be the T-vector indicating which transitions have occured and how often to reach M" from M'.

Then $M'' = M' + N \cdot f''$ holds

which implies
$$I^T \cdot M'' = I^T \cdot M' + 0$$
$$= I^T \cdot M .$$

So, the invariance of the inner product between an S-invariant I and the follower markings of one initial marking holds independently of the direction of occurrences.

□

Usually this theorem is used in order to state propositions about follower markings (cf. [GLT 80], [MR 80]). If there exists an S-invariant I such that $I^T \cdot M' \neq I^T \cdot M$ then M' cannot be a follower marking of M. If, on the other hand, a marking M' is only partly known the equations $I^T \cdot M' = I^T \cdot M$ for S-invariants yield necessary conditions for completing M' as a follower marking of M.

Example 2.11 (cf. examples 1.4 and 2.9)

Let M and M' be markings of N where

$$\begin{matrix} a \\ b \\ c \\ d \\ e \\ f \\ g \end{matrix} \quad M = \begin{bmatrix} 1 \\ 1 \\ \\ 1 \\ \\ 1 \\ 1 \end{bmatrix} \qquad M' = \begin{bmatrix} \\ 2 \\ \\ 1 \\ \\ 1 \\ 1 \end{bmatrix} ; \qquad I_5 = \begin{bmatrix} \\ 1 \\ 2 \\ 1 \\ \\ \\ -1 \end{bmatrix}$$

Then $I_5^T \cdot M = 1$ and $I_5^T \cdot M' = 2$.

So $M' \notin [M\rangle$ can be stated without any simulation

□

Corollary 2.12

Let $N = (S,T;F,K,W)$ be a P/T-net, M a marking of N, and $I \gneq 0$ an S-invariant of N.

Let furthermore P_I be the support of I.

Then $I^T \cdot M = n \Rightarrow \forall p \in P_I : p$ n-safe

Proof

Let $M' \in [M>$ and $p \in P_I$.

$$M'(p) \leq I(p) \cdot M'(p) \leq \sum_{s \in S} I(s) \cdot M'(s) = I^T \cdot M' = I^T \cdot M = n$$

□

The converse of theorem 2.10 can be proved under the additional assumption that all transitions can occur with respect to the initial marking:

Theorem 2.13

Let $N = (S,T;F,K,W)$ be a P/T-net; let M be a marking of N such that

$$\forall t \in T \quad \exists M^{(t)} \in [M> : t \text{ is enabled under } M^{(t)}.$$

Let I be an S-vector of N such that

$$\forall M' \in [M> : I^T \cdot M' = I^T \cdot M .$$

Then I is an S-invariant of N.

Proof

Let $t \in T$ be an arbitrary transition and let $M^{(t)} \in [M>$ be a follower marking of M such that t is enabled under $M^{(t)}$.

If $M'^{(t)}$ is the marking after the occurrence of t, the following holds:

$$M'^{(t)} = M^{(t)} + N(-,t)$$

Since $\quad I^T \cdot M'^{(t)} = I^T \cdot M^{(t)} = I^T \cdot M$

we have $\quad I^T \cdot N(-,t) = 0$

and consequently $\quad I^T \cdot N = 0^T$

□

The same assumption leads to the fact that non-negative S-invariants $I \neq 0$ carry at least one token:

Theorem 2.14

Let $N = (S,T;F,K,W)$ be a P/T-net and M a marking of N such that

$$\forall t \in T \; \exists M^{(t)} \in [M> : t \text{ is enabled under } M^{(t)}.$$

Then for all S-invariants $I \gneq 0 \quad I^T \cdot M > 0$ holds.

Proof

Let $I \gneq 0$ be an S-invariant and $p \in S$ and place where $I(p) > 0$. p is either an input place of a transition or an output place of a transition or both.

If p is an input place of some transition t, then p is marked under any marking $M^{(t)} \in [M>$ for which t is enabled, i.e. $M^{(t)}(p) > 0$.

If p is an output place of some transition t, then p is marked under any marking $M^{(t)}$ where $M'^{(t)}[t> M^{(t)}$ and t enabled under $M'^{(t)}$, i.e. $M^{(t)}(p) > 0$.

Since $M^{(t)} \in [M>$ in both cases and I is an S-invariant, we have

$$I^T \cdot M = I^T \cdot M^{(t)} = \sum_{s \in S} I(s) \cdot M^{(t)}(s) > I(p) \cdot M^{(t)}(p) > 0$$

□

Remark 2.15

(1) The assumption of the last two theorems that all transitions can occur is particularly satisfied if M is a live marking of N (cf.[La 75]).

(2) The converse of theorem 2.14 that $I^T \cdot M > 0$ for all S-invariants $I \gneq 0$ implies the liveness of M is true only for very special classes of P/T-nets. It is true for example for marked graphs (cf. [CEHP 71], [GL 73]).

□

With respect to the two properties mentioned above, we have found subnets in which no tokens can be lost or gained in an uncontrolled way, namely the graphical representations of non-negative S-invariants I. Here $I^T \cdot M'$ is an invariant quantity for all follower markings M' of the initial marking M.

We now come to formalizing the second property, the reproducibility of markings.

We remember that every sequence of transition occurrences has a linear representation.

Example 2.16 (cf. example 2.4)

In the P/T-net of figure 2.6 the initial marking is reproduced by

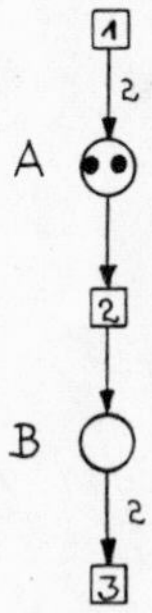

Figure 2.6

one occurrence of transitions 1 and 3 and two occurrences of transition 2.

The linear representation of this reproduction is

$$M + N \cdot \begin{bmatrix} 1 \\ 2 \\ 1 \end{bmatrix} = M .$$

That is, the occurrence vector is a solution of a linear homogeneous equation system

$$N \begin{bmatrix} 1 \\ 2 \\ 1 \end{bmatrix} = 0$$

With respect to the next definition we call this solution a T-invariant (cf. [La 73]).

Definition 2.17

Let $N = (S,T;F,K,W)$ be a P/T-net and J a T-vector of N.

(1) J is called a T-invariant of N iff $N \cdot J = 0$

(2) $P_J \subseteq T$ is called the support of J iff $P_J = \{t \in T \mid J(t) \neq 0\}$

(3) A T-invariant J of N is called non-negative iff $J \geq 0$.

(4) A non-negative T-invariant $J \neq 0$ of N is called minimal iff there exists no non-negative T-invariant J' of N with $0 \lneqq J' \lneqq J$.

(5) A subnet $N_J = (S_J,T_J;F_J,K_J,W_J)$ of N is called the graphical representation of J iff

T_J is the support of J

$S_J := {}^{\bullet}T_J \cup T_J^{\bullet}$

$F_J := F \cap [(S_J \times T_J) \cup (T_J \times S_J)]$

$K_J(s) := K(s)$ for all $s \in S_J$

$W_J(f) := W(f)$ for all $f \in F_J$

Corollary 2.18

Every integer linear combination of T-invariants is a T-invariant.

□

Remark 2.19 (cf. remark 2.8)

If the only T-invariant of a P/T-net N is $J = 0$ we will say that N has no T-invariants.

Example 2.20 (cf. 2.2, 2.3, 1.4)

The P/T-nets of the figures 2.1.a and 2.2.b have no T-invariance.

$$\begin{matrix}1\\2\\3\\4\end{matrix} \qquad J = \begin{bmatrix}1\\1\\1\\1\end{bmatrix}$$

is the minimal T-invariant of the P/T-nets in the figures 2.1.b, 2.2.a, and 1.1 .

□

<u>Corollary 2.21</u>

Let M be a reproducible marking of a P/T-net N = (S,T;F,K,W). Then the transitions occurring during the reproduction of M are the transitions of the graphical representation of a T-invariant.

□

<u>Theorem 2.22</u>

Let N = (S,T;F,K,W) be a P/T-net and $J \neq 0$ a T-invariant of N. Then there exists a marking M_J of N that is reproducible under J as occurrence vector.

<u>Proof</u>

We may assume that $J \neq 0$ is non-negative. Otherwise we simply change the directions of all arcs incidenting with transitions $t \in T$ where $j(t) < 0$. So all backward occurrences are replaced by forward ones.

Now, for all $p \in S$ we define $M_J(p) := \sum_{t \in p^\cdot} J(t) \cdot W(p,t)$.

Under this marking all transitions t can occur concurrently as often as indicated by J(t). So J can be realized and we have

$$M_J + N \cdot J = M_J + 0 = M_J$$

□

In other words, the graphical representation of a T-invariant can by sufficiently many tokens be marked in such a way that a reproduction fo this marking is realizable.

The graphical representations of S- and T-invariants are net structures with a predictable behaviour.

We have developed these concepts for nets which are restricted by remark 2.1.

In the next section we will recommend a technique to extend these concepts to finite P/T-nets without further restrictions.

3. Extension of the invariance concepts to non-pure P/T-nets with bounded place capacities.

We have defined the incidence matrix for pure P/T-nets.

Furthermore, we have tacitly used the fact that there is a 1-1-relationship between the net and its incidence matrix.

This is not true for non-pure P/T-nets.

Example 3.1
The P/T-nets of figure 3.1 have a different behaviour since in order to enable transition 1 one needs at least 1,2,...,n+1,... tokens on A.

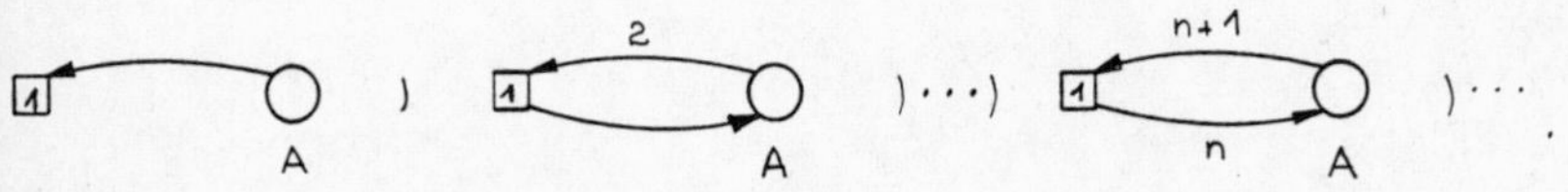

Figure 3.1

Extending the definition of the incidence matrix to the non-pure P/T-nets of figure 3.1 yields for all nets

$$N(A,1) = W(1,A) - W(A,1) = -1.$$

That is, nets with different behaviour can have the same incidence matrix and, consequently, the same S- and T-invariants.

□

To have the same incidence matrix for nets with different behaviour is of course unsatisfactory since it is impossible to include the differences into investigations based on S- or T-invariants.

So, we recommend a different approach where non-pure nets are transformed into pure ones with "the same" behaviour.

The non-pure P/T-nets of figure 3.1 will then be transformed into the pure ones of figure 3.2.

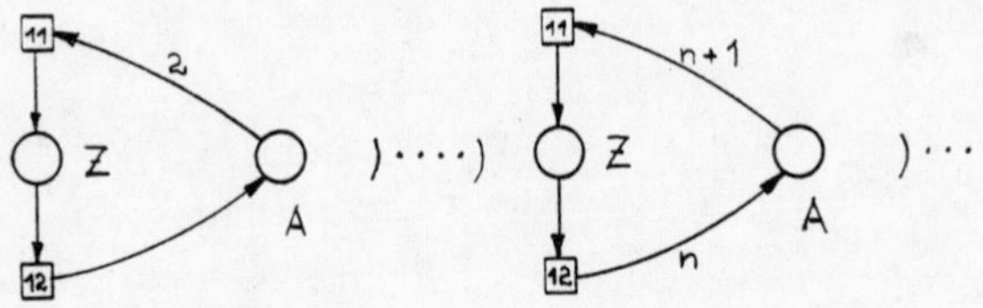

Figure 3.2

Instead of modeling an event by one transition we now use two transitions; one representing the beginning and one representing the end of that event.

Between both transitions there is a place with capacity 1 indicating whether the event is just occurring or not.

We now want to precisely define this transformation.

Definition 3.2

Let $N = (S,T;F,K,W)$ be an non-pure P/T-net and M its marking.

Let $t \in T$ be a transition and $p \in S$ be a place such that

$$(t,p) \in F \quad \text{and} \quad (p,t) \in F.$$

Then the P/T-net $N_t' = (S',T';F',K',W')$ is defined by

$$S' := S \cup \{z\} \qquad \text{where } z \notin S \cup T$$

$$T' := (T - \{t\}) \cup \{t_1,t_2\} \text{ where } t_1,t_2 \notin S' \cup T$$

$$F' := (F \cap ((S' \times T') \cup (T' \times S'))) \cup ({}^{\bullet}t \times \{t_1\}) \cup (\{t_2\} \times t^{\bullet}) \cup \{(t_1,z),(z,t_2)\}$$

$K'(s) := K(s)$ for all $s \in S$

$K'(z) := 1$

$W'(f) := W(f)$ for all $f \in F' \cap F$

$W'((s,t_1)) := W((s,t))$ for all $s \in {}^{\bullet}t$

$W'((t_2,s)) := W((t,s))$ for all $s \in t^{\bullet}$

$W'((t_1,z)) := 1$

$W'((z,t_2)) := 1$

$M'(s) := M(s)$ for all $s \in S$

$M'(z) := 0$

□

The P/T-net N_t' has less non-purities than N. That is, a finite number of transformations of this kind leads to a pure net N' which we then analyze instead of N.

So far, the assumption for the nets under consideration has been that the places have unbounded capacities.

In order to also be able to analyze nets with bounded capacities we will transform such nets into nets with unbounded capacities.

<u>Example 3.3</u>

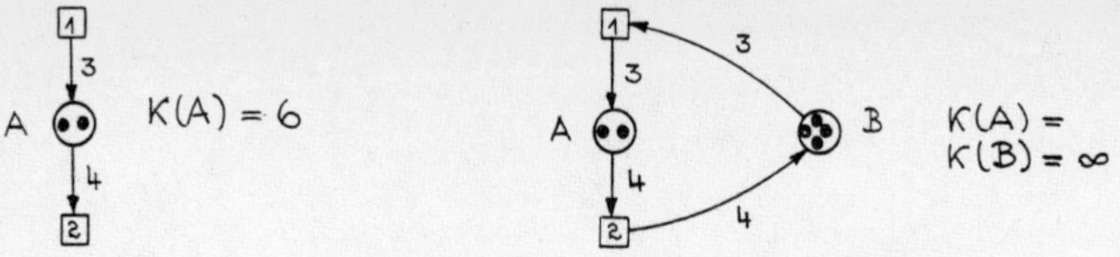

(a) (b)

Figure 3.3

The net in figure 3.3.a has the place capacity K(A) = 6.

The place capacities of the net in figure 3.3.b are unbounded. But here by construction $M'(A) \le 6$ holds for all follower markings M' of the initial marking M.

This has been achieved by a place B which is "conplementary" to A, that is

(1) B is connected to the same transitions as A by means of arcs with the same arc weights but opposite directions.

(2) $M'(B) = 6 - M'(A)$ for all markings.

The respective marking of B indicates exactly how many tokens can still be put on A without violating the capacity bound.

So, given M'(A) both transitions 1 are enabled or both are not.

□

The next definition precisely shows how the capacity bound of a place can be replaced by a complementary place.

<u>Definition 3.4</u>
Let $N = (S,T;F,K,W)$ be a P/T-net and M its marking.

Let $p \in S$ be a place with $K(p) < \infty$.

Then the P/T-net $N'_p = (S',T';F',K',W')$ is defined by

$S' := S \cup \{p'\}$ where $p' \notin S \cup T$

$T' := T$

$F' := F \cup (\{p'\} \times {}^{\bullet}p) \cup (p^{\bullet} \times \{p'\})$

$K'(s) := K(s)$ for all $s \in S' - \{p,p'\}$

$K'(p) := \infty$

$K'(p') := \infty$

$W'(f) := W(f)$ for all $f \in F$

$W'((p',t)) := W((t,p))$ for all $t \in {}^{\bullet}p$

$W'((t,p')) := W((p,t))$ for all $t \in p^{\bullet}$

$M'(s) := M(s)$ for all $s \in S$

$M'(p') := K(p) - M'(p)$

□

The P/T-net N'_p has less places with bounded capacities than N.

Thus, after a finite number of such transformations one finds a net N' with unbounded place capacities.

Altogether, one needs a finite number of transformations to transform a finite P/T-net such that it meets the restrictions of remark 2.1.

4. Applications and limitations

We have seen that the graphical representations of S-invariants are subnets in which tokens cannot be lost.

This is an important fact for the prediction of the future behaviour of a net. Theorem 10 tells about the details of applying this fact.

Another well known result with respect to S-invariants is the liveness condition for marked graphs.

Definition 4.1

Let $N = (S,T;F,K,W)$ be a pure P/T-net.

If $|{}^{\bullet}s| = |s^{\bullet}| = 1$ for all $s \in S$,

$K : S \to \{\infty\}$ and

$W : F \to \{1\}$ holds

then N is called a marked graph.

Theorem 4.2 (cf. [GL 73],[Re 85])

Let N be a marked graph and M its marking.

Then M is a live marking of N iff

$$I^T \cdot M \geq 1$$

for all minimal (non-negative) S-invariants of N.

□

This theorem says that all circuits of N have to be marked in order to get a live marking since the graphical representation of the minimal S-invariants are the simple circuits of N.

Unfortunately, theorem 4.2 is not true for more general net classes. It is, for example, not true for free choice nets (cf. [Ha 73]).

It is even not true for the following generalization of marked graphs.

Definition 4.3

Let N = (S,T;F,K,W) be a pure P/T-net.

If N is the graphical representation of a non-negative T-invariant and

if	$\lvert {}^{\bullet}s \rvert = \lvert s^{\bullet} \rvert = 1$	for all $s \in S$
and	$K : S \rightarrow \{\infty\}$	hold,

then N is called a generalized marked graph.

Remark 4.4

A marked graph N is the graphical representation of a non-negative T-invariant.

□

The difference between marked graphs and generalized marked graphs with respect to theorem 4.2 is the following.

The condition of theorem 4.2 says that circuits are marked which trivially implies that these circuits, taken as single nets, are lively marked.

One can prove that also generalized marked graphs are lively marked if and only if their circuits, taken as single nets, are lively marked.

The problem, however, is to find a necessary and sufficient liveness condition based on S-invariants for these circuits.

Example 4.5

The circuits of figure 4.1 are generalized marked graphs. The minimal

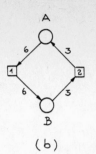

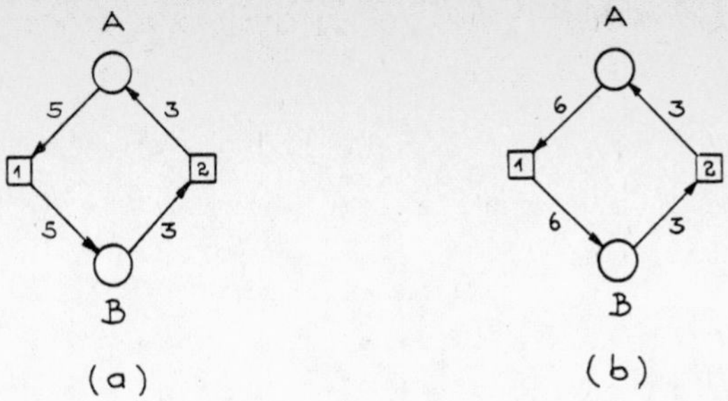

Figure 4.1

S-invariant of both nets is

$$\begin{matrix} A \\ B \end{matrix} \quad I = \begin{bmatrix} 1 \\ 1 \end{bmatrix} .$$

The net of figure 4.1.a is lively marked by a marking M <u>if and only if</u>

$$\begin{aligned} M(A) + M(B) &\geq W((A,1)) + W((B,2)) - 1 \\ &= 5 + 3 - 1 \\ &= 7 . \end{aligned}$$

The net of figure 4.1.b is lively marked by a marking M <u>if</u>

$$\begin{aligned} M(A) + M(B) &\geq W((A,1)) + W((B,2)) - 1 \\ &= 6 + 3 - 1 \\ &= 8 . \end{aligned}$$

Unfortunately here the condition is not necessary:

(1) Markings with 7 tokens:

$M = \begin{bmatrix} 7 \\ 0 \end{bmatrix}$ live

$M = \begin{bmatrix} 6 \\ 1 \end{bmatrix}$ live

$M = \begin{bmatrix} 5 \\ 2 \end{bmatrix}$ dead

etc.

(2) Markings with 6 tokens:

$M = \begin{bmatrix} 6 \\ 0 \end{bmatrix}$ live

M " $\begin{bmatrix} 5 \\ 1 \end{bmatrix}$ dead

etc.

□

This shows that the S-invariant structure is neither appropriate to express the differences between both nets nor to explain the differences between the markings of the second net with respect to liveness.

In a way, theorem 10 and example 4.5 describe the scope of the applicability of S-invariants.

For a lot of problems it is sufficient to know which subnets preserve their tokens. But this kind of "token counting" is by far not subtle enough to solve general liveness problems.

We did not deal with methods for the calculation of invariants itself. Here we refer to [AT 85], [Ja 85], [MS 82], and [Pa 85].

5. References

[AT 85] Alaiwan, H.; Toudic, J.M.:
Recherche des semi-flots, des verrous et des trappes dans le réseaux de Petri, Technique et Science Informatiques, Vol. 4, 103-112, 1985

[BF 86] Best, E.; Fernandez, C.:
Notations and Terminology on Petri Net Theory, Gesellschaft für Mathematik und Datenverarbeitung, Arbeitspapiere der GMD No. 195, 1986

[CEHP71] Commoner, F.; Holt, A.; Even, S.; Pnueli A.:
Marked Directed Graphs, JCSS, Vol. 5, 511-523, 1971

[Ga 60] Gale, D.:
The Theory of Linear Economic Models, Mc Graw-Hill, NY, Toronto, London, 1960

[GL 73] Genrich, H.J.; Lautenbach, K.:
Synchronisationsgraphen, Acta Informatica, Vol. 2, 143-161, 1973 (in German)

[GLT 80] Genrich, H.J.; Lautenbach, K.; Thiagarajan, P.S.:
Elements of Genral Net Theory, In: Net Theory and Applications, Brauer ed., Springer LNCS 84, 1980

[Ha 73] Hack, M.H.T.:
Analysis of Production Schemata by Petri Nets, MIT Project MAC, TR 94, 1973

[Ja 85] Jaxy, M.:
Analyse linearer diophantischer Ungleichungs- und Gleichungssysteme im Hinblick auf Anwendungen in der Theorie der Petri-Netze, Diplomarbeit, Universität Bonn, 1985, (in German)

[La 73] Lautenbach, K.:
Exakte Bedingungen der Lebendigkeit für eine Klasse von Petri-Netzen, Gesellschaft für Mathematik und Datenverarbeitung, GMD-Report No. 82, 1973, (in German)

[La 75] Lautenbach, K.:
Liveness in Petri Nets, Gesellschaft für Mathematik und Datenverarbeitung, GMD-ISF Internal Report 02.1/75-7-29, 1975

[MR 80] Memmi, G.; Roucairol, G.:
Linear Algebra in Net Theory, In: Net Theory and Applications, Brauer ed., Springer LNCS 84, 1980

[MS 82] Martinez, J.; Silva, M.:
A Simple and Fast Algorithm to Obtain All Invariants of a Generalized Petri Net, In: Application and Theory of Petri Nets, Girault, Reisig eds., Springer Informatik-Fachberichte No. 52, 1982

[Pa 85] Pascoletti, K.-H.:
Diopantische Systeme und Lösungsmethoden zur Bestimmung aller Invarianten in Petri Netzen, GMD-Bericht Nr. 160, Oldenbourg Verlag, München, Wien, 1986 (in German)

[Re 85] Reisig, W.:
Petri Nets, Springer-Verlag, Berlin, Heidelberg , New York, Tokyo, 1985

Structure Theory of Petri Nets: the Free Choice Hiatus

Eike Best

Institut für methodische Grundlagen
Gesellschaft für Mathematik und Datenverarbeitung
D-5205 St.Augustin

ABSTRACT

Structure theory asks whether a relationship can be found between the behaviour of a marked net and the structure of the underlying unmarked net. From the rich body of structure theoretical results that exists in Petri net theory, this paper selects a few examples which are deemed to be typical. The class of free choice nets, whose structure theory is particularly agreeable, is studied in some detail.

1 Introduction

By the 'structure' of a P/T-system we mean marking-independent properties depending on the way in which the places and the transitions of the underlying net are interconnected by the flow relation. By the 'behaviour' of a P/T-system we denote marking-dependent properties relating to the token flow effected by the transition rule, depending on the set of processes, the set of reachable markings, the reachability graph, and so on.

The behaviour of a marked net is, in general, less easily analysable than its structure. But it is the behavioural properties that are of foremost interest in the analysis of systems. They include, for example, the property of deadlock-freeness, the existence of invariant assertions, safeness properties, the validity of intermediate assertions, and others.

Structure theory asks whether a relationship can be found between the behaviour of a marked net and the structure of the underlying unmarked net. It asks questions such as: Can one deduce, from certain 'nice' structural properties of a net, that its behaviour will also be 'nice'? Or, conversely: Does certain 'bad' behaviour preordain some 'bad' structure? In any case one may hope that the (behavioural) properties which are of interest may be reduced to easier-to-investigate (structural) properties.

A rich body of structure theoretical results exists in net theory. From this body, we shall select some typical examples, neither too many in order not to let the paper grow out of size, nor too few let the reader get an idea of the kind of reasoning employed in structure theory (hopefully).

There is a class of nets which has an interesting motivation and allows for a very satisfactory structure theory. This class is called free choice nets. While being a non-trivial class of nets, their theory is so nice that it has sometimes jokingly been said that every conjecture is true for free choice nets and false for other nets. Although we will exhibit some 'counterexamples' to this statement, a good part of these notes will be dedicated to the study of free choice nets.

These notes are organised as follows. In section 2 we introduce and explain almost all notions we need, but we will rely on [39] for some definitions and explanations. We introduce some basic behavioural properties (liveness and safeness), and we show that they have an impact in terms of the connectedness of a system. Sometimes it is necessary to compare nets with each other and to state that one is 'similar' to another one. In section 3 we define a notion of simulation to capture this idea. In sections 4-6 we introduce various subclasses of nets (free choice nets, amongst others) and we investigate some basic properties of these classes. In sections 7 and 8 we deal almost exclusively with free choice nets, listing and explaining some more advanced results about their structure and behaviour.

Most of the results reported in this paper are drawn from published literature, and appropriate references will always be given. However, some proofs are not easily accessible and some belong to the 'folklore'. Because of the size of the material we have done a selection of the proofs. We give in detail only those proofs that cannot be retrieved easily from the literature. All other proofs will be given by outline only, or will even be omitted, and a reference will be supplied instead.

2 Basic definitions and general results

Our object of study are P/T-systems in the sense of [39]. However, we will restrict ourselves to P/T-systems without capacity constraints (that is, we will assume all capacities to be infinite) and with a trivial weight function (i.e. the weight equals 1 on every F-arrow). For the sake of simplicity and brevity, we will change the sixtuple notation of [39](1.5) into a fourtuple notation; thus, $\Sigma = (S, T; F, M_0)$ will henceforth denote a P/T-system (with infinite capacities and trivial weight function). As usual, S, T, F and M_0 are the set of places, the set of transitions, the flow relation and the initial marking, respectively. We mention that the relation $F \subseteq (S \times T) \cup (T \times S)$ could equivalently be viewed as a function

$$F\colon\ (S \times T) \cup (T \times S) \ \rightarrow\ \{0,1\}$$

such that $(x, y) \notin F$ or $(x, y) \in F$ (in the relational view) iff $F(x, y) = 0$ or $F(x, y) = 1$, respectively (in the functional view). We will sometimes make use of the functional view in order to shorten formulae.

Without repeating their definitions, we shall use the following concepts: the transition rule [39](1.7a-d), the set of occurrence sequences of Σ [39](1.11a,b), the set of transition sequences of Σ [39](1.11c), the set $[M_0\rangle$ of forward reachable markings of Σ [39](1.7e), the coverability graph (sometimes also called the reachability graph) of Σ [39](2.4), and the notion of a side condition being a place $s \in S$ with ${}^\bullet s \cap s^\bullet \neq \emptyset$ (called a 'loop' in [39](1.17)). As usual, ${}^\bullet x$ denotes the set of F-predecessors of $x \in X$ and $x^\bullet$ denotes the set of F-successors of $x \in X$. The reader may also consult [6] for the various formal definitions.

We will now introduce two restrictions, the purpose of which is to focus our scope of concern on such P/T-systems as are of primary interest.

Restriction 2.1 *Finiteness of* Σ

From now on, we will always assume Σ to be finite, that is, $S \cup T$ to be a finite set. ∎ 2.1

The reason for restricting ourselves to finite systems is simply a pragmatic one: they are the main cases of practical interest. Besides, a theory of infinite systems exists only in rudimentary form.

A (finite) system Σ may consist of two or more parts which are unconnected with each other in the sense that no (undirected) F-path leads from one part to the other. To all intents and purposes, it is then sufficient to study the two (or more) parts in isolation. The next definition and the restriction following it are intended to capture this property.

Definition 2.2 *Weak connectedness*

$\Sigma = (S, T; F, M_0)$ is weakly connected *iff* all $x, y \in S \cup T$ are in the relation $(F \cup F^{-1})^*$. ∎ 2.2

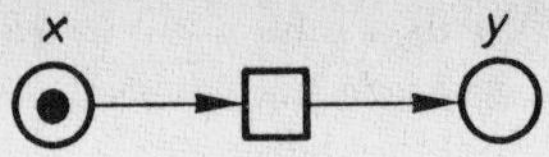

Figure 1: A system which is weakly connected but not strongly connected

Restriction 2.3

From now on, we will always assume Σ to be weakly connected. ■ 2.3

Weak connectedness means that one can always travel from x to y along some F-arcs, be it in forward or in backward direction. It does not mean that there is always a *directed* path from x to y. Consider the simple system shown in Figure 1. It is weakly connected and there is a directed F-path from x to y but not from y to x. The existence of directed paths is captured by the next definition.

Definition 2.4 *Strong connectedness*

$\Sigma = (S, T; F, M_0)$ is strongly connected *iff* all $x, y \in S \cup T$ are in the relation F^*. ■ 2.4

Weak connectedness is a much weaker property that strong connectedness. We will not require the latter universally because there are interesting non-strongly connected nets and because it is not easily possible to split such nets into strongly connected components without disrupting their behaviour.

The terms 'weak connectedness' and 'strong connectedness' are generally agreed upon in graph theory. The above definitions are applications of this general terminology. We will sometimes use the definitions in a more general sense, for example applying to the reachability graph which is (by definition) always weakly connected.

We will often be interested in the set $[M_0\rangle$ of forward reachable markings and its properties. After all, this set models the set of states the P/T-system Σ may be in. We assume the usual definition of $[M_0\rangle$ (as given in [6], for instance) which works, essentially, using occurrence sequences.

It is well known that in order to represent concurrency directly, one should replace occurrence sequences by processes [35,18,5]. It is possible to define the set $[M_0\rangle$ using processes instead of occurrence sequences. However, it is also known [5] that for finite P/T-systems, the two definitions coincide, so that the definition of $[M_0\rangle$ using occurrence sequences is sufficient.

On the other hand, we will then have to investigate concurrency indirectly via the notion of two transitions being concurrently enabled by some marking. We repeat this definition from [6], in a simplified form implied by the fact that all capacities are infinite.

Definition 2.5 *Concurrent enabling*

For $\Sigma = (S, T; F, M_0)$, let $M \in [M_0\rangle$ be a marking and $t_1, t_2 \in T$ two transitions.
t_1 and t_2 are concurrently enabled by M *iff* $\forall s \in S: F(s, t_1) + F(s, t_2) \leq M(s)$.
(Here F is viewed as a function to $\{0, 1\}$, as explained above.) ■ 2.5

For concurrently enabled transitions, the following simple fact is true:

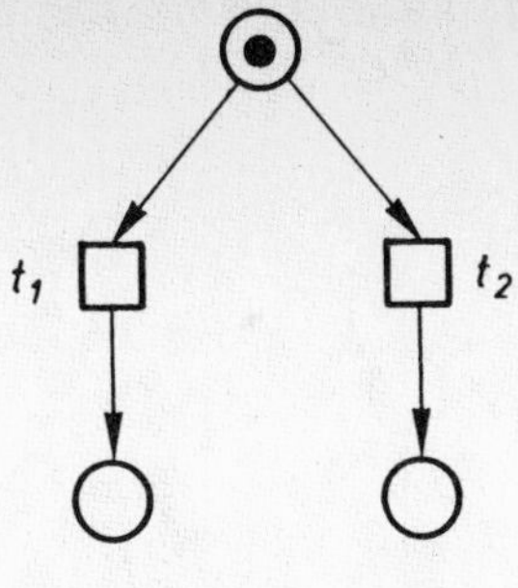

Figure 2: A conflict

Fact 2.6 *Exchanging concurrently enabled transitions in an occurrence sequence*

If t_1 and t_2 are concurrently enabled by M then both $Mt_1M't_2M''$ and $Mt_2\hat{M}t_1M''$ are occurrence sequences starting with M and ending with M'' (but not necessarily $M' = \hat{M}$).

Proof: From the transition rule and from $M(s) \geq F(s,t_1) + F(s,t_2)$ it follows immediately that $M'(s,t_2) \geq F(s,t_2)$ and $\hat{M}(s,t_1) \geq F(s,t_1)$. ■ 2.6

If M enables both t_1 and t_2 then it is by no means necessarily true that t_1 and t_2 are concurrently enabled by M; failing the latter, the situation is called a 'conflict' (see Figure 2).

Definition 2.7 *Conflict at a marking*

For $\Sigma = (S, T; F, M_0)$, let $M \in [M_0\rangle$ be a marking and t_1, t_2 two transitions.
Then t_1 and t_2 are in conflict at M *iff* M enables both t_1 and t_2 but does not concurrently enable t_1 and t_2. ■ 2.7

Fact 2.8 *Characterisation of conflict*

t_1 and t_2 are in conflict at M iff both are enabled at M and $M(p) = 1$ for some $p \in {}^\bullet t_1 \cap {}^\bullet t_2$.

Proof: Easy from the definitions.
This result depends on the facts that all capacities are infinite and that all arc weights equal 1; otherwise it becomes false. ■ 2.8

If t_1 and t_2 do not share an input place then their combined enabling implies their concurrent enabling, as shown by the next simple fact.

Fact 2.9 *Sufficient conditions for concurrent enabling*

(a) *If ${}^\bullet t_1 \cap {}^\bullet t_2 = \emptyset$ and M enables both t_1, t_2 then M concurrently enables t_1 and t_2.*

(b) *If $t_1^\bullet \cap {}^\bullet t_2 = \emptyset$ and $Mt_1M't_2M''$ is an occurrence sequence then M concurrently enables t_1 and t_2.*

Proof: (a) M enables both t_1 and t_2 implies $M(s) \geq F(s,t_1)$ and $M(s) \geq F(s,t_2)$ (for all $s \in S$). But

$$\left.\begin{array}{l} F(s,t_1) \neq 0 \;\Rightarrow\; F(s,t_2) = 0 \\ F(s,t_2) \neq 0 \;\Rightarrow\; F(s,t_1) = 0 \end{array}\right\} \text{ since } {}^\bullet t_1 \cap {}^\bullet t_2 = \emptyset.$$

Hence $M(s) \geq F(s,t_1) + F(s,t_2)$.

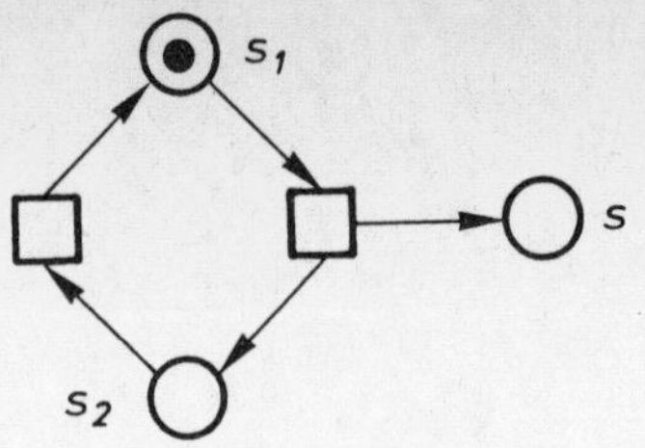

Figure 3: An unsafe system

(b) We have $\forall s \in S\colon M'(s) \geq F(s,t_2)$ and $M'(s) = M(s) - F(s,t_1) + F(t_1,s)$.
Hence $M(s) \geq F(s,t_2) - F(t_1,s) + F(s,t_1)$. But

$$\left.\begin{array}{l} F(s,t_2) \neq 0 \;\Rightarrow\; F(t_1,s) = 0 \\ F(t_1,s) \neq 0 \;\Rightarrow\; F(s,t_2) = 0 \end{array}\right\} \text{ since } t_1^\bullet \cap {}^\bullet t_2 = \emptyset.$$

Hence $M(s) \geq F(s,t_2) + F(s,t_1)$.

■ 2.9

Definition 2.5 and facts 2.6-2.9 provide a means of rearranging occurrence sequences. The typical argument is the following: if σ is an occurrence sequence in which some marking concurrently enables the two next transitions, then the latter can be switched around to give another occurrence sequence which agrees with σ except in the order of the two transitions and the marking between them.

We will now define two simple but important behavioural properties of Σ. One of them (safeness) is concerned with the places of Σ while the other (liveness) is concerned with the transitions of Σ. On a given place s of S (in Σ), more than one token may assemble in the course of a behaviour of Σ; indeed, s may have (finitely many but) more than one token already in the initial marking. There may not even be a bound on how many tokens may assemble on s. For example, in the system shown in Figure 3, for any given natural number $n \in \mathbf{N}$, s may receive more than n tokens; however, s_1 and s_2 may always carry at most one token each. Safeness introduced in the next definition, measures the amount of tokens that can assemble on a given place; in the literature, safeness is often also called 'boundedness'.

Definition 2.10 *Safeness*

Let $\Sigma = (S,T;F,M_0)$ be a place/transition system.

(a) $s \in S$ is n-safe ($n \in \mathbf{N}$) *iff* $\forall M \in [M_0\rangle\colon M(s) \leq n$.

(b) Σ is n-safe ($n \in \mathbf{N}$) *iff* $\forall s \in S\colon s$ is n-safe.

■ 2.10

The case that $n = 1$, that is 1-safeness, plays a particular rôle. Every place can then contain at most one token. A 1-safe place can be interpreted as a condition which either 'holds' (if $M(s) = 1$) or 'does not hold' (if $M(s) = 0$). 1-safeness is a very important property which holds in many practical situations (e.g.: a variable always has exactly one value; in a sequential program, control is always at exactly one location). We will focus our attention on 1-safe systems (and we will sometimes write 'safe' instead of '1-safe', but only when the '1' is unimportant, i.e. could be replaced by 'n').

A given transition t of T (in Σ) may be repeated infinitely often, or there may be bounds on the number of times it can be repeated (including zero, in which case it is called 'dead'). It may even be the case that a system has the choice of entering a state in which t is 'dead' or entering a state in which t can be repeated over and over again, never becoming 'dead'. Liveness measures whether or not it is possible to 'kill' a transition.

Definition 2.11 *Liveness*

Let $\Sigma = (S, T; F, M_0)$ be a place/transition system.

(a) $t \in T$ is live *iff* for all $M \in [M_0\rangle$ there is some $M' \in [M\rangle$ such that M' enables t.

(b) Σ is live *iff* $\forall t \in T: t$ is live.

■ 2.11

Notation 2.12 *LS systems*

If Σ is live and 1-safe then we shall call Σ an LS system, for short. ■ 2.12

The next result relates three interesting notions introduced so far, i.e. safeness, liveness and strong connectedness, to each other. We intend to show that a net which is not strongly connected cannot be live and 1-safe at the same time, i.e. that the (structural) property of strong connectedness is necessary for the existence of a live and 1-safe marking. The previous examples show that a system could be either live or 1-safe and non-strongly connected: The systems shown in Figures 1 and 2 are not strongly connected but 1-safe (but they are not live), while the system shown in Figure 3 is not strongly connected but live (but it is not safe).

Theorem 2.13 *Liveness and safeness implies strong connectedness*

Let $\Sigma = (S, T; F, M_0)$ be a (finite, weakly connected) P/T-system which is live and 1-safe. Then Σ is strongly connected.

Proof: For any arbitrarily chosen $x, y \in S \cup T$ we have to prove that $(x, y) \in F^*$, i.e. that there is a directed F-chain from x to y. Weak connectedness implies only that there is a $(F \cup F^{-1})$-chain from x to y, i.e. there is a sequence

$$x_0, \ldots, x_m \; (m \geq 0, x_i \in S \cup T)$$

such that $x = x_0$, $x_m = y$ and $(x_i, x_{i+1}) \in (F \cup F^{-1})$ for $0 \leq i < m$. Let us now try to construct an F-chain from x to y. We start with $x = x_0$. If $(x_0, x_1) \in F$ then we may pass on to x_1; if $(x_1, x_2) \in F$, we may then pass on to x_2, and so on. The bad case is that $(x_i, x_{i+1}) \in F^{-1}$ (rather than $\in F$) for some $0 \leq i < m$. But if we then have $(x_i, x_{i+1}) \in F^*$, we may still pass from x_i to x_{i+1} along an F-chain. So the really bad case is that $(x_i, x_{i+1}) \in F^{-1}$, but no F-chain leads from x_i to x_{i+1}.
So, we assume now that we have $(x_i, x_{i+1}) \in F^{-1}$, but $(x_i, x_{i+1}) \notin F^*$; the proof is done if we can derive a contradiction from this assumption. Because we will be concerned exclusively with deriving this contradiction, we may drop the index i from now on and re-use the letters x and y.
There are two cases:

<u>Case 1:</u> $(x, y) \in F \cap (S \times T)$ and $(y, x) \notin F^*$ (see Figure 4(i));

<u>Case 2:</u> $(y, x) \in F \cap (T \times S)$ and $(x, y) \notin F^*$ (see Figure 4(ii)).

If we succeed in obtaining a contradiction in both cases then the theorem is proved.

Let us consider Case 1 first. That is, we assume $(x, y) \in F \cap (S \times T)$, but no directed F-path leads from y to x. We consider the set of places and the set of transitions from which a directed path leads to x, calling them S_1 and T_1, respectively:

$$S_1 = \{s \in S \mid (s, x) \in F^*\}, \;\; T_1 = \{t \in T \mid (t, x) \in F^*\}.$$

and no directed path from y to x

Case 1

and no directed path from x to y

Case 2

Figure 4: Illustrating the case distinction in the proof

$$M_0[\ldots\rangle \underbrace{M_1}_{\text{enables } y} [y\rangle \underbrace{M_2}_{<M_1 \text{ on } S_1} [\quad \ldots\tau\ldots \quad \rangle \underbrace{M_3}_{\text{enables } y}$$

Figure 5: Illustrating Case 1: M_1, M_2, M_3

By this definition we have:

$$\begin{array}{l} x \in S_1 \\ y \notin T_1 \ \ (\text{since } (y,x) \notin F^*) \\ y^\bullet \cap S_1 = \emptyset \text{ and} \\ {}^\bullet T_1 \subseteq S_1. \end{array}$$

By the liveness of Σ, a reachable marking M_1 can be found which enables y, i.e.:

$$\exists M_1 \in [M_0\rangle : M_1 \text{ enables } y.$$

Let us fix such a marking M_1 and let us consider the successor marking M_2 under y, i.e. $M_1[y\rangle M_2$.
Because $y^\bullet \cap S_1 = \emptyset$, the token load on S_1 cannot be increased by the occurrence of y, that is:

$$\forall s \in S_1 : M_1(s) \geq M_2(s).$$

Furthermore, we have

$$1 = M_1(x) > M_2(x) = 0,$$

that is, there is a token on x under M_1 but not under M_2; abbreviating this, we may say that M_1 is 'strictly bigger' than M_2 on S_1.
Again by the liveness of Σ, there is a successor marking M_3 of M_2 which enables y; let τ be the transition sequence which leads from M_2 to M_3 (see Figure 5).

The sequence τ may contain transitions from T_1 and transitions from $T \setminus T_1$. We claim, however, that it is possible to rearrange the transitions in τ in such a way that all transitions in T_1 come first. To this end, assume that τ has the following form:

$$\tau = \ldots tt' \ldots$$

with $t \in T \setminus T_1$, $t' \in T_1$. We plan to show that $t^\bullet \cap {}^\bullet t' = \emptyset$; then facts 2.9(b) and 2.6 can be applied to show that t and t' can be exchanged in τ. But suppose that $s \in t^\bullet \cap {}^\bullet t'$; Then there is a directed path (of length 2) from t to t', and hence also from t' to x, contradicting the assumption that $t' \in T \setminus T_1$.
Hence $t^\bullet \cap {}^\bullet t' = \emptyset$ and t and t' may be exchanged in τ.
By repeating such exchanges exhaustively, τ can be rearranged into a transition sequence

$$M_0[\ldots\rangle \underbrace{M_1}_{\text{enables } y} [y\rangle \underbrace{M_2}_{\text{no token on } x} [\tau_1\rangle \underbrace{M'}_{\text{token on } x} [\tau_2\rangle \underbrace{M_3}_{\text{enables } y}$$

Figure 6: Illustrating Case 1: τ_1 and τ_2

$$M_0[\ldots\rangle \underbrace{M_1}_{\text{enables } y} [\tau_1\rangle \underbrace{M''}_{\text{2 tokens on } x!}$$

Figure 7: Illustrating Case 1: M''

τ' which also transforms M_2 into M_3 and which can be split as $\tau' = \tau_1\tau_2$ where τ_1 contains only transitions from T_1 while τ_2 contains only transitions from $T\backslash T_1$ (see Figure 6; it could happen that τ_2 is empty).

Now we consider the intermediate marking M' reached from M_2 after τ_1; is there a token on x in this marking or not? There is surely a token on x in M_3 because M_3 enables y; this token can have come there only through a transition in ${}^\bullet x$, i.e. in T_1, but since between M' and M_3 no such transition occurs, the token must have been on x already in M'. Hence $M'(x) = 1$.
On the other hand, the transitions in τ_1 (between M_2 and M') need only tokens from S_1, since ${}^\bullet T_1 \subseteq S_1$. But because M_1 is bigger than M_2 on S_1, this implies that τ_1 is also a transition sequence from M_1 rather than M_2; let M'' denote the marking reached from M_1 after τ_1 (see Figure 7).

Let us now count the number of tokens on x in the marking M''. In M_1, there is one token on x because M_1 enables y. But this token is not needed in the course of τ_1 because τ_1 is enabled in M_2 and we have $M_2(x) = 0$; hence we may consider it to remain unmoved on x during the sequence $M_1[\tau_1\rangle M''$. On the other hand, we have just seen that $M'(x) = 1$, hence τ_1 creates another token on x. Together, we have 2 tokens on x in M''. This contradicts 1-safeness. Hence the assumptions made in Case 1 are wrong, and we have $(x,y) \in F \cap (S \times T) \Rightarrow (y,x) \in F^*$.
It remains to consider Case 2. That is, we assume $(y,x) \in F \cap (T \times S)$ and $(x,y) \notin F^*$ (as in Figure 4(ii)).
It is tempting to think that this case can be reduced to Case 1, but this is not easy. However, the reasoning is quite similar and we therefore give a shortened account[1]. We define:

$$S_2 = \{s \in S \mid (x,s) \in F^*\} \text{ and } T_1 = \{t \in T \mid (t,y) \in F^*\}.$$

S_2 is the set of places to which a directed path leads from x; T_1 is the set of transitions from which a directed path leads to y.
By liveness, we find $M_1 \in [M_0\rangle$ such that M_1 enables y; define M_2 such that $M_1[y\rangle M_2$.
We have $M_2(s) \geq M_1(s)$ for all $s \in S_2$ and $1 = M_2(x) > M_1(x) = 0$; that is, M_2 is strictly bigger than M_1 on S_2.
By liveness, again, there is a transition sequence τ transforming M_2 into M_3 such that M_3 enables y (see Figure 8).

By an argument which is similar to that used above, τ can be rearranged to a sequence $\tau_1\tau_2$

[1]Recently, Wolfgang Reisig has produced a modification of the proof in which the two cases are treated more analogously.

$$M_0[\ldots\rangle M_1[y\rangle M_2\underbrace{[\ \ \tau\ \ \rangle}_{\tau_1 M' \tau_2}\underbrace{M_3}_{\text{enables } y}$$

Figure 8: Illustrating Case 2: τ_1, τ_2 and M'

such that τ_1 contains only transitions from T_1 and τ_2 contains only transitions from $T \setminus T_1$ (see Figure 8).
Let M' be the marking reached from M_2 by τ_1. In M', y must be enabled because otherwise, y could not be enabled in M_3. On the other hand, x carries a token in M' because the transitions in T_1 cannot take away that token. This contradicts 1-safeness, showing that Case 2 cannot arise and completing the proof. ■ 2.13

By iterating the argument in the proof, it is easy to see that the premise of 1-safeness in theorem 2.13 can be weakened to n-safeness (for any n).

3 A notion of simulation

The result 2.13 gives a necessary condition for liveness and safeness. It is general in the sense that it applies to all (finite, weakly connected) systems. Such results are rare. In particular, non-trivial sufficient conditions for liveness and safeness are not known. Most known results are more specialised. One may ask, for instance: what happens if we don't allow conflict? Or: what happens if there is no concurrency? This means that one focusses on particular classes of nets. In the main body of this paper we will investigate a range of classes of nets.

Quite often when arguing about net classes, one is led to say that a certain class of nets is 'essentially the same' as another (maybe simpler) class. Usually, one can give a construction which translates every net in the first class into a 'similar' net of the second (simpler) class. We will consider some such constructions. To accommodate these constructions, we will define a general concept which captures the idea that a P/T-system 'simulates' another P/T-system. If a system simulates another one then we may say that they are in some sense 'similar'.

In order to be able to state the definition of simulation we need have a preparatory look at functions on strings which are induced by functions on letters. Let $f\colon A \to A'$ be an injective function from an alphabet A into an alphabet A'. Then f may be extended to a function $f\colon A^* \to A'^*$ in the canonical way[2], i.e. $f(\epsilon_A) = \epsilon_{A'}$, $f(va) = f(v)f(a)$ $(v \in A^*, a \in A)$. Furthermore, f^{-1} is a relation in $A' \times A$ and can be extended to a *function* $f^{-1}\colon A'^* \to A^*$ in the following way:

$$f^{-1}(\epsilon_{A'}) = \epsilon_A,\ f^{-1}(wa) = \begin{cases} f^{-1}(w) & \text{if } a \notin f(A) \\ f^{-1}(w)f^{-1}(a) & \text{if } a \in f(A) \end{cases},\ w \in A'^*, a \in A'$$

(The injectivity of f is used in the last clause of this definition.) We are now ready to state the definition of simulation; we shall explain the definition after giving it.

Definition 3.1 Σ' *simulates* Σ

Let $\Sigma = (S,T;F,M_0)$ and $\Sigma' = (S',T';F',M_0')$ be two P/T-systems and $f\colon T \to T'$ an injection. We shall say that Σ' simulates Σ (with respect to f) *iff* there is a surjection $\beta\colon [M_0'\rangle \to [M_0\rangle$ such that the following holds:

(i) $M_0 = \beta(M_0')$.

[2] A^* is the set of strings over the alphabet A, including the empty string ϵ_A

(ii) Suppose $M_1 = \beta(M_1')$, $M_1' \in [M_0'\rangle$ and $M_1 \in [M_0\rangle$;

(a) whenever $M_1[t\rangle M_2$ with $t \in T$, $M_2 \in [M_0\rangle$ then $\exists M_2' \in \beta^{-1}(M_2)\ \exists w \in T'^{\star}: M_1'[w\rangle M_2' \wedge f^{-1}(w) = t$;

(b) whenever $M_1'[w\rangle M_2'$ with $w \in T'^{\star}$, $M_2' \in [M_0'\rangle$ then $M_1[f^{-1}(w)\rangle\beta(M_2')$.

(iii) $\forall M \in [M_0\rangle: |\beta^{-1}(M)| < \infty$.

■ 3.1

Because f is an injection, Σ' has at least as many transitions as Σ. The extra transitions of Σ' (i.e. those in $T' \setminus f(T)$) should be thought of as 'silent internal actions' of Σ'. The transitions in $f(T)$ simulate the transitions of Σ. A reachable marking M' of Σ' should be thought of as 'representing' the marking $\beta(M')$ of Σ. There may be more than one marking of Σ' representing the same marking of Σ, but every marking of Σ should be covered; hence the surjection requirement for β. Requirement 3.1(i) means that the initial marking of Σ' must represent the initial marking of Σ. Requirement 3.1(iia) states that any occurrence of the transition t in Σ must be simulatable in Σ' by a transition sequence w which involves $f(t)$ and (possibly) a few intermediate 'silent' occurrences. Moreover, the new marking M_2' of Σ' must represent M_2 (the requirement $M_2' \in \beta^{-1}(M_2)$ is important). 3.1(iib) requires that every occurrence sequence in Σ' corresponds, via f^{-1}, to an occurrence sequence in N which, moreover, respects the representation function β. Requirement 3.1(iii) simply implies that n-safe systems can only be simulated by n-safe systems; it is a somewhat arbitrary requirement that could be dropped if only n-safe systems are under consideration. Some examples are given by Figure 9. In the examples, we indicate the function f by labelling the transitions in $f(T)$ with the names of their counterparts in T, and the transitions in $T' \setminus f(T)$ by a 'τ'; this terminology is borrowed from R.Milner's CCS [31].

We will now show that the simulation relation preserves n-safeness and, essentially, also liveness.

Theorem 3.2 *Simulation preserves n-safeness*

Suppose $\Sigma = (S,T;F,M_0)$, $\Sigma' = (S',T';F',M_0')$, $f: T \to T'$ *injective and* Σ' *simulates* Σ *with respect to* f.
Then Σ *is n-safe* $\iff$ Σ' *is n'-safe.* (n need not be the same as n'.)

Proof: Σ is n-safe
$\Rightarrow [M_0\rangle$ is finite
$\Rightarrow \bigcup_{M \in [M_0\rangle} \beta^{-1}(M)$ is finite (with 3.1(iii))
$\Rightarrow |[M_0'\rangle|$ is finite (because $|[M_0'\rangle| \le \Sigma_{M \in [M_0\rangle} |\beta^{-1}(M)|$).
Conversely, Σ' is n'-safe
$\Rightarrow [M_0'\rangle$ is finite
$\Rightarrow [M_0\rangle$ is finite ($|[M_0\rangle| \le |[M_0'\rangle|$ because β is surjective). ■ 3.2

Theorem 3.3 *Simulation preserves liveness*

Suppose $\Sigma = (S,T;F,M_0)$, $\Sigma' = (S',T';F',M_0')$, $f: T \to T'$ *injective and* Σ' *simulates* Σ *with respect to* f.
Then Σ *is live* $\iff$ *for all* $t' \in f(T)$: t' *is live in* Σ'.

Proof: $\Rightarrow$: Assume that Σ is live.
Let $M_0'[w\rangle M_1'$, $w \in T'^{\star}$ and let $t' \in f(T)$, i.e. $t' = f(t)$ with $t \in T$.
By 3.1(i) and (iib), $M_0[f^{-1}(w)\rangle M_1$, where $M_1 = \beta(M_1')$.
Because Σ is live, $\exists v \in T^{\star}\ \exists M_2 \in [M_0\rangle: M_1[v\rangle M_2$ and t occurs in v.
By 3.1(iia) and because β is a surjection, there are a sequence $v' \in T'^{\star}$ and a marking $M_2' \in [M_0'\rangle$ such that $M_1'[v'\rangle M_2'$ and t' occurs in v'.
Hence all $t' \in f(T)$ are live in Σ'.

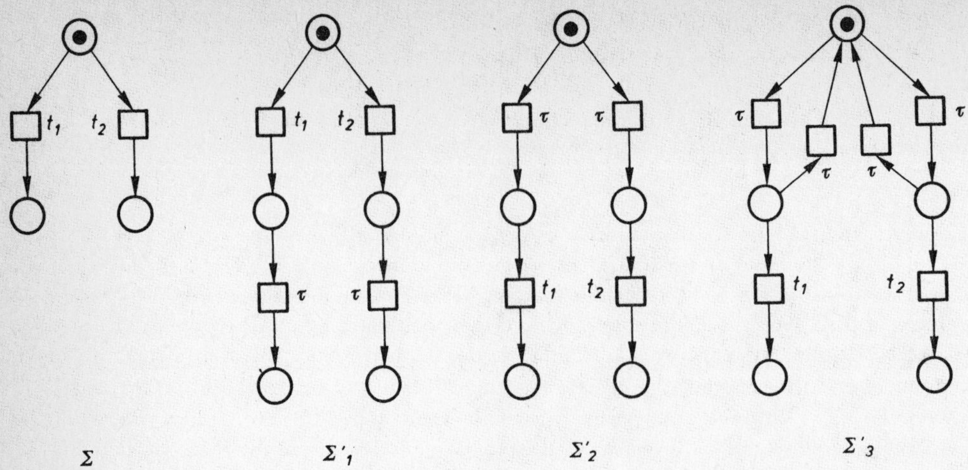

(i) Σ_2' does not simulate Σ: no β can be found which satisfies the requirements; however, Σ_1' and Σ_3' simulate Σ.

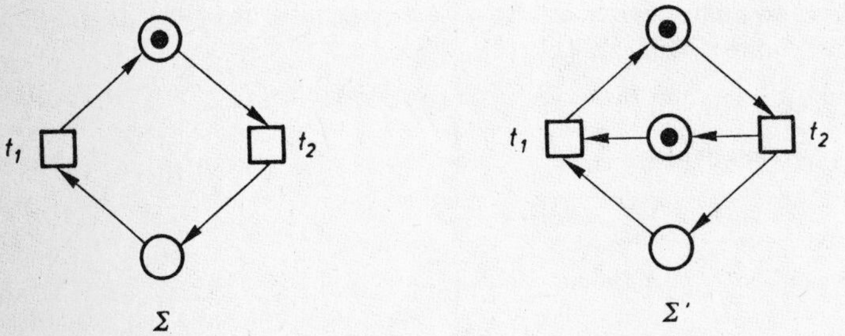

(ii) Σ' simulates Σ; a β can be found which is even a bijection.

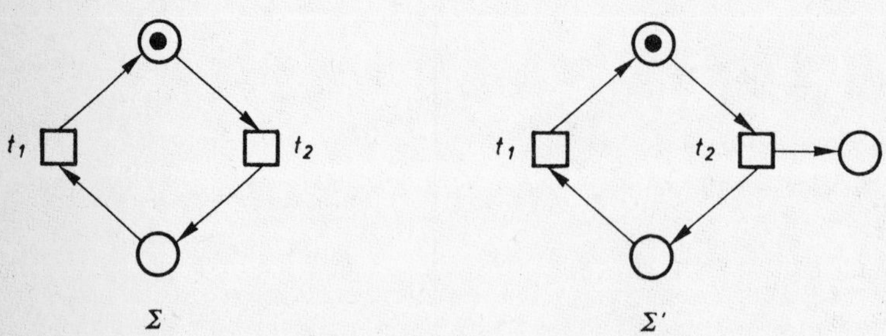

(iii) Σ' does not simulate Σ (only 3.1(iii) is violated).

Figure 9: Illustrating the notion of simulation

$\Leftarrow$: Assume that all $t' \in f(T)$ are live in Σ'.
Let $M_0[v\rangle M_1$, $v = t_1 \dots t_m \in T^*$ and let $t \in T$.
By 3.1(i) and (iia), $\exists w_1, \dots, w_m: M_0'[w_1 \dots w_m\rangle M_1'$ and $M_1 = \beta(M_1')$.
Since all $t' \in f(T)$ are live in Σ', there are a sequence $w' \in T'^*$ and a marking $M_2' \in [M_0'\rangle$ such that $M_1'[w'\rangle M_2'$ and $f(t)$ occurs in w'.
By 3.1(iib), $M_1[f^{-1}(w')\rangle M_2$ for $M_2 = \beta(M_2')$ and t occurs in $f^{-1}(w')$ by the definition of f^{-1}.
Hence Σ is live.

■ 3.3

Theorem 3.3 states that, while Σ' may contain non-live internal transitions, the liveness or otherwise of Σ' on the relevant sets of transitions, viz. on $f(T)$, coincides with the liveness or otherwise of Σ.

Remark 3.4 *Relationship to other literature*

The concept of simulation defined above is much related to the notion of bisimulation introduced by D.Park in [34], and applied to nets by M.Nielsen and P.S.Thiagarajan [33]. Bisimulation does not include the requirement 3.1(iii) and specifies β to be only a relation, rather than a surjective function, on the sets $[M_0\rangle$ and $[M_0'\rangle$. Bisimulation is known to be essentially equivalent to R.Milner's notion of observational equivalence [31], [10]. L.Pomello has shown that the latter is a comparatively strong notion of equivalence [36]. Hence we suggest that our notion of simulation is a comparatively strong one, but we shall not pursue these connections any further in these notes. More recently, K.Voss has investigated a notion of simulation which is similar to the above but is based on step sequences (i.e. sequences of concurrently enabled transitions) rather than transition sequences [42]. A related notion of simulation has also been defined by L.Priese [37]. Readers wishing to compare various definitions are referred to the paper [32] by H.Müller. ■ 3.4

4 T-systems

In the next three sections we introduce, and start to study, three important classes of nets of increasing generality. The first class, called T-nets (or T-systems if a marking is implied), admits concurrency and synchronisation, but no conflict. In the literature, T-systems are often known as 'marked graphs' or 'synchronisation graphs'.

Definition 4.1 *T-nets and T-systems*

$\Sigma = (S, T; F, M_0)$ is a T-system *iff*
its underlying net is a T-net, i.e. for all $s \in S$: $|{}^\bullet s| \leq 1 \wedge |s^\bullet| \leq 1$. ■ 4.1

In a T-system there is never any conflict, simply because there are no (forward) branched places. A token can be taken away from a place only by its unique (if existing) output transition. T-systems are very well understood. The basic references are [12,17], and [27,19] may be consulted for further reading.

The cycles of a T-system play an important rôle in its analysis.

Definition 4.2 *Cycles and paths*

A cycle of a net $(S,T;F)$ is a sequence $x_0,\ldots,x_m$ with $x_i \in S \cup T$ $(0 \le i \le m)$, $(x_i, x_{i+1}) \in F$ $(0 \le i < m)$ and $x_0 = x_m$. A cycle is called simple *iff* no element (except $x_0 = x_m$) appears twice in it, i.e. $\forall k,j$: $(0 \le k \le m \wedge 1 \le j \le m-1 \wedge k \ne j) \Rightarrow x_k \ne x_j$.
For later use, we define the (simple) paths of a net exactly as the (simple) cycles, except that the requirement $x_0 = x_m$ is omitted. ■ 4.2

We shall say that a net $(S,T;F)$ is covered by (simple) cycles *iff* every $x \in S \cup T$ lies on some (simple) cycle. The reader should be cautious with definition 4.2, because it may occur that an element of a cycle has more than one F-predecessors (or successors) on the same cycle, and similarly for paths. In cases of doubt, it may be advisable to include F-arrows that are meant to belong to the cycle or to the path explicitly in the definition.

Theorem 4.3 *Characterisation of the liveness of T-systems*

A T-system $\Sigma = (S,T;F,M_0)$ is live iff all of its simple cycles carry at least one token and for all places $s \in S$: $|{}^\bullet s| = 1$.

Proof: See [12], theorem 1 and [17], theorem (8S); but when looking up these references, the reader should be cautious because in both of them, $|{}^\bullet s| = 1 = |s^\bullet|$ is required in place of $|{}^\bullet s| \le 1 \ge |s^\bullet|$. ■ 4.3

Theorem 4.4 *Characterisation of the safeness of live T-systems*

A live T-system $\Sigma = (S,T;F,M_0)$ is 1-safe iff it is covered by simple cycles which carry at most one token.

Proof: See [12], theorem 2 and [17], theorem (28S). ■ 4.4

The last theorem can be generalised by dropping the liveness assumption; see [17], theorem (28S). Often one needs to use the fact that markings are 'reproducible'. In T-systems, reproducibility is very much related to liveness.

Definition 4.5 *Reproducibility*

A marking $M \in [M_0\rangle$ of $\Sigma = (S,T;F,M_0)$ is reproducible *iff* there is an occurrence sequence σ of non-zero length such that $M = first(\sigma)$ and $M = last(\sigma)$, that is, σ starts with M and ends with M. ■ 4.5

Theorem 4.6 *Link between reproducibility and liveness*

A strongly connected T-system $\Sigma = (S,T;F,M_0)$ is live iff its initial marking M_0 can be reproduced by σ in such a way that every transition occurs exactly once in σ.

Proof: For the direction ($\Rightarrow$) of this theorem, see [12], theorem 7 and [17], theorem (15S).
The direction ($\Leftarrow$) is easy to prove: the reproducing sequence necessitates at least one token on each cycle, and liveness follows with theorem 4.3. ■ 4.6

This theorem can be generalised by dropping the strong connectedness assumption (see [17], (14S) and (15S)). However, we will not bother to do so, since the chief interest is in strongly connected T-nets.

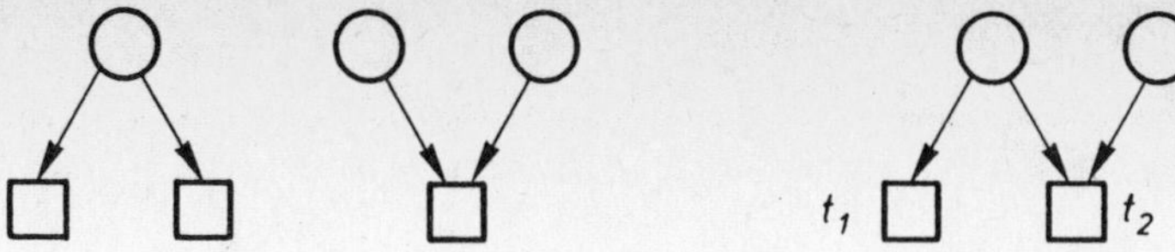

(i) included (ii) excluded

Figure 10: Illustrating the free choice structure

Corollary 4.7 *Characterisation of liveness in strongly connected T-systems*

In a strongly connected T-system Σ the following are equivalent:

(i) *Σ is live.*

(ii) *All simple cycles of Σ carry at least one token.*

(iii) *The initial marking is reproducible such that every transition occurs exactly once.*

■ 4.7

In fact, strong connectedness nicely characterises the existence of a live and safe marking:

Theorem 4.8 *Existence of live and 1-safe markings of T-nets*

A T-net N can be endowed with a live and 1-safe marking iff it is strongly connected.

Proof: See [12], theorem 4, and [17], theorem (32S). ■ 4.8

The class of nets which is dual to T-nets is called S-nets [6]; their characterising property is that $|{}^\bullet t| \leq 1$ and $|t^\bullet| \leq 1$ always holds for $t \in T$. S-nets allow conflict, but no synchronisation. The behavioural theory of S-nets is rather simpler than the theory of T-nets[3], unless one is interested in information flow: [25] have developed a nice and non-trivial theory of information flow in S-nets. S-nets play a particularly important rôle as substructures of larger nets, a topic which will not be studied here (but see [3]).

5 Free choice systems

Free choice nets have been invented as a common generalisation of S-nets and T-nets, with the aim of retaining as much as possible of the nice theory of these classes. They allow synchronisation (but only in the 'T-net way') and conflicts (but only in the 'S-net way'). The former is to say that if two places share a common output transition then they may not have any further output transitions, and the latter is to say that if two transitions share a common input place then they may not have any further input places. But these two properties are equivalent! They allow the structures shown in Figure 10(i) but exclude the structure shown in Figure 10(ii).

[3]The reader may check that a strongly connected S-net is live iff it carries at least one token and 1-safe iff it carries at most one token.

Definition 5.1 *Free choice nets and free choice systems*

$\Sigma = (S, T; F, M_0)$ is called a free choice system (abbreviated FC system) *iff* its underlying net is free choice, i.e. for all $t_1, t_2 \in T, t_1 \neq t_2$: ${}^\bullet t_1 \cap {}^\bullet t_2 \neq \emptyset \Rightarrow |{}^\bullet t_1| = 1 = |{}^\bullet t_2|$. ■ 5.1

It is clear that every T-net, as well as every S-net, is free choice; that is, free choice nets are indeed a common generalisation. F.Commoner and M.Hack have shown that there exist generalisations of the two theorems 4.3 and 4.4 about liveness and safeness of T-systems. These generalisations will be described below in sections 8.1 and 8.2, respectively.

An essential consequence of the free choice property is that if t_1 and t_2 share a common input place then it can never be the case that one of them is enabled while the other is not. That is, every marking enables either both of them or none of them. This may be contrasted with the (excluded) case of Figure 10(ii) where a marking can be found which enables t_1 but not t_2. The next result shows that, in the sense of the simulation notion defined in section 3, the property just explained is a characteristic one.

Definition 5.2 *Extended and behavioural free choice systems*

$\Sigma = (S, T; F, M_0)$ is

(a) extended free choice (EFC) *iff* $\forall t_1, t_2 \in T$: ${}^\bullet t_1 \cap {}^\bullet t_2 \neq \emptyset \Rightarrow {}^\bullet t_1 = {}^\bullet t_2$.

(b) behaviourally free choice (BFC) *iff*
$\forall t_1, t_2 \in T$: ${}^\bullet t_1 \cap {}^\bullet t_2 \neq \emptyset \Rightarrow \forall M \in [M_0\rangle$: M enables $t_1 \iff M$ enables t_2.

■ 5.2

It is immediate that every FC system is also EFC. Furthermore, every EFC system satisfies the BFC Property. Conversely:

Theorem 5.3 *Equivalence of FC, EFC and BFC systems w.r.t. simulation*

(i) *Every BFC system can be simulated by an EFC system.*

(ii) *Every EFC system can be simulated by an FC system.*

Proof: See [7]; the two easy constructions are sketched in Figure 11. ■ 5.3

Theorem 5.3 shows that the three classes of FC systems, EFC systems and BFC systems are 'the same modulo simulation'. In the sequel we shall consider FC nets only.

We will take a closer look at liveness in FC systems. Our aim is to relate liveness to a weaker, easier-to-check, property called deadlock-freeness.

Definition 5.4 *Deadlock-freeness*

$\Sigma = (S, T; F, M_0)$ is called deadlock-free *iff* $\forall M \in [M_0\rangle\ \exists t \in T$: M enables t. ■ 5.4

A system is deadlock-free if it may always go on working as a whole; no global system 'stop' is possible.

Liveness implies deadlock-freeness in general, simply because by definition, every net contains at least one transition. Conversely, Figure 12 shows a P/T-system (even a 1-safe free choice one) which is deadlock-free but not live.

However, it is possible to characterise those transitions whose liveness is guaranteed by deadlock-freeness:

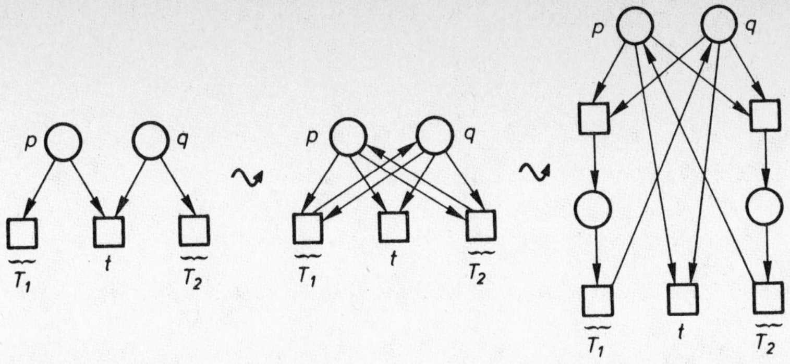

(i) BFC → EFC

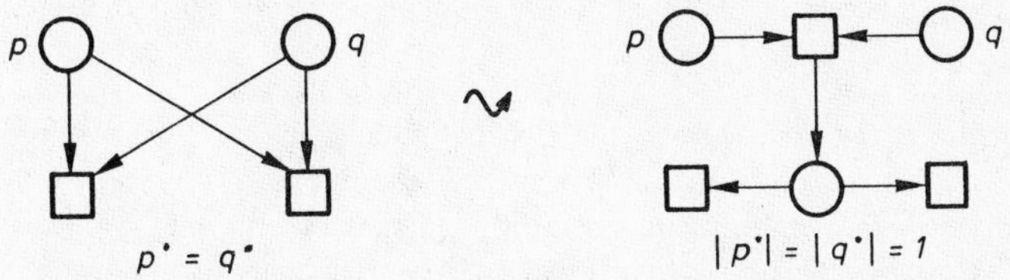

(ii) EFC → FC

Figure 11: Constructions reducing EFC and BFC systems to FC systems

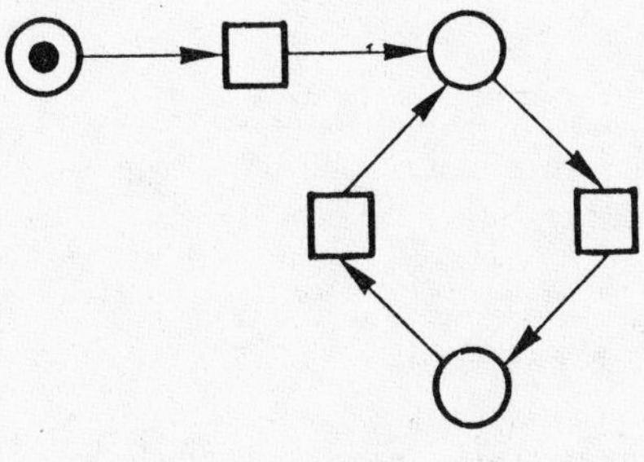

Figure 12: A 1-safe FC system which is deadlock-free but not live

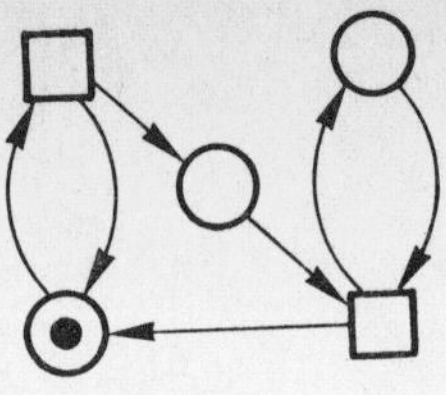

Figure 13: A strongly connected FC system which is deadlock-free but not live

Theorem 5.5 *Relationship between deadlock-freeness and liveness in FC systems*

Let $\Sigma = (S,T;F,M_0)$ be a 1-safe FC system which is deadlock-free and let $t \in T$ be such that $\forall t' \in T\colon (t',t) \in F^*$ (i.e. t can be reached from every other transition by a directed path). Then t is live.

Proof: The proof proceeds by contradiction. Assume that t is not live; then there exists a marking $M_1 \in [M_0\rangle$ at which t is dead, i.e. no successor marking of M_1 enables t.
Consider any $p \in {}^\bullet t$; then, by the free choice property, all $t' \in p^\bullet$ (not just t itself) are dead at M_1. But this implies that any token put on p after M_1 will remain there.
By 1-safeness, it follows that the transitions in ${}^\bullet p$ can occur at most once, i.e. there is a marking $M_2 \in [M_1\rangle$ at which all transitions in ${}^\bullet p$ are dead.
Since this holds for all $p \in {}^\bullet t$ (and since the net is finite), there is some $M_3 \in [M_1\rangle$ at which all transitions in ${}^\bullet({}^\bullet t)$ are dead.
Repeating this argument shows that every transition in the set $\{t' \in T \mid (t',t) \in F^*\}$ can be made dead; but since by assumption, the latter set equals T, this means that a deadlock can be reached. ■ 5.5

Corollary 5.6 *Liveness equals deadlock-freeness in strongly connected FC systems*

Let Σ be a 1-safe strongly connected FC system.
Then Σ is live iff Σ is deadlock-free. ■ 5.6

It is seen readily that the 1-safeness assumption in 5.5 and 5.6 can be weakened to n-safeness (for any n). However, Figure 13 shows that it cannot be omitted altogether; this observation, as well as the proof of 5.5/5.6 are due to D.Hillen [24].

6 Asymmetric choice systems

The EFC (extended free choice) property can be rewritten equivalently as follows:

$$\forall s_1, s_2 \in S\colon s_1^\bullet \cap s_2^\bullet \neq \emptyset \Rightarrow s_1^\bullet = s_2^\bullet.$$

It has turned out that some of the free choice results hold also if a weaker condition is assumed, namely $(s_1^\bullet \subseteq s_2^\bullet \vee s_2^\bullet \subseteq s_1^\bullet)$ instead of $s_1^\bullet = s_2^\bullet$ in the above formula. The resulting class of nets will be called asymmetric choice nets.

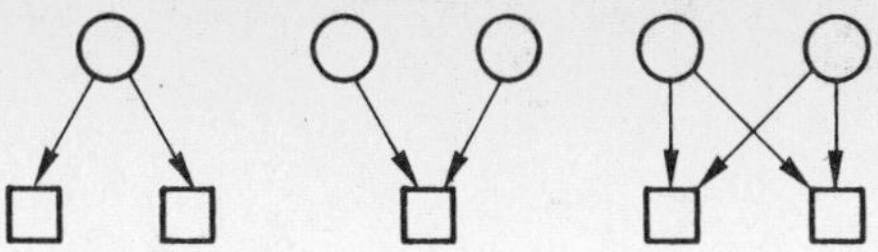

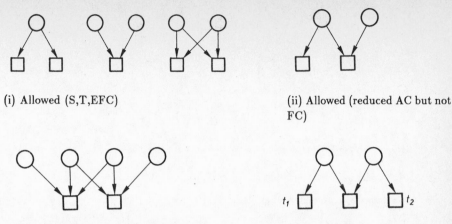

(i) Allowed (S,T,EFC)

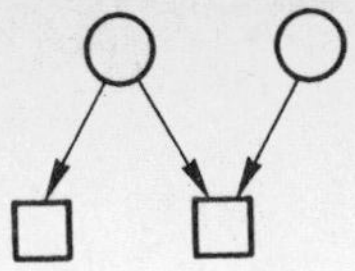

(ii) Allowed (reduced AC but not FC)

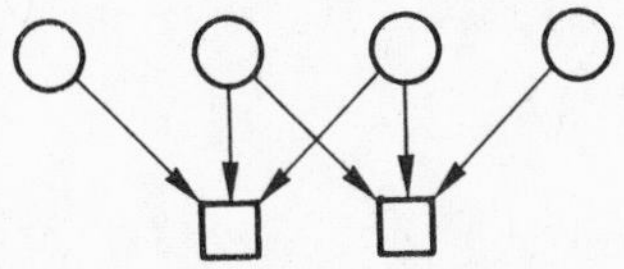

(iii) Allowed (AC but not EFC)

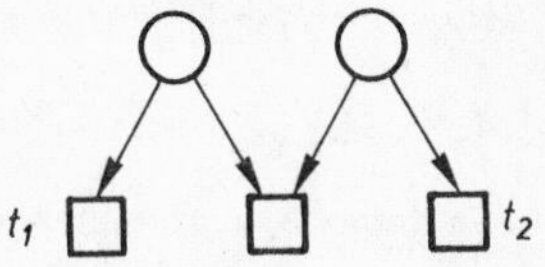

(iv) Excluded

Figure 14: Illustrating the AC structure

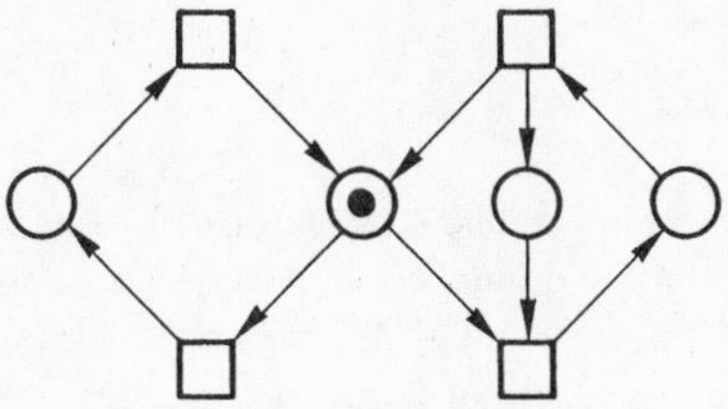

Figure 15: A simple AC system

Definition 6.1 *Asymmetric choice systems*

$\Sigma = (S, T; F, M_0)$ is called asymmetric choice (AC) system *iff*
$\forall s_1, s_2 \in S: s_1^\bullet \cap s_2^\bullet \neq \emptyset \Rightarrow (s_1^\bullet \subseteq s_2^\bullet \vee s_2^\bullet \subseteq s_1^\bullet)$. ■ 6.1

Figures 14(i)-(iii) show some allowed structures while Figure 14(iv) shows the typical structure which is excluded by the asymmetric choice property. It is immediate that every (extended) free choice net is also asymmetric choice.

There are many theorems which hold for FC systems but fail to hold for AC systems. An example is corollary 5.6: Figure 15 shows an AC system which is 1-safe, strongly connected and deadlock-free but not live.

Just as for FC systems, there is a property which explains AC systems in behavioural terms; but it is slightly more complicated. We introduce it by means of Figure 14(iv). In this Figure, a marking which enables t_1 but not t_2, as well as a marking which enables t_2 but not t_1, can be found. The behavioural correspondent of the asymmetric choice property excludes just this possibility. That is, if t_1 and t_2 are related to each other as in Figure 14(iv) (and this means: if there is some $t_0 \in ({}^\bullet t_1)^\bullet \cap ({}^\bullet t_2)^\bullet$) then either the enablement of t_1 must always imply the enablement of t_2, or the other way round (hence the name: 'asymmetric choice property'). This property is captured by part (i) of the next definition.

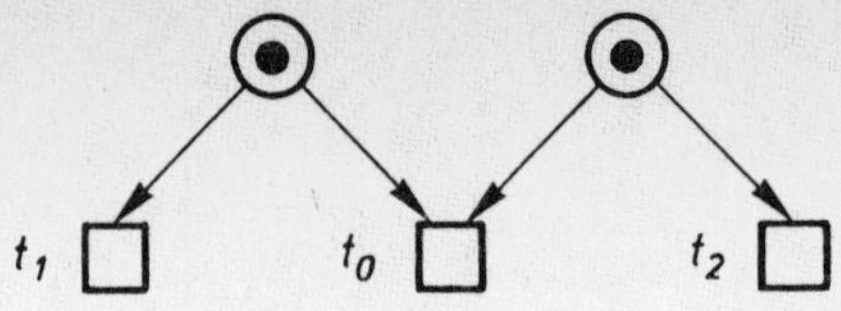

Figure 16: A non-transitive conflict situation

Definition 6.2 *Behavioural and reduced asymmetric choice property*

Let $\Sigma = (S, T; F, M_0)$ be a P/T-system.

(i) Σ is behaviourally asymmetric choice (BAC) *iff* for all $t_1, t_2 \in T$:

$$({}^\bullet t_1)^\bullet \cap ({}^\bullet t_2)^\bullet = \emptyset \;\vee\; (\forall M \in [M_0\rangle \colon M \text{ enables } t_1 \Rightarrow M \text{ enables } t_2) \\ \vee\; (\forall M \in [M_0\rangle \colon M \text{ enables } t_2 \Rightarrow M \text{ enables } t_1).$$

(ii) Σ is reducedly asymmetric choice (RAC) *iff* for all $p, q \in S$:

$$p^\bullet \cap q^\bullet = \emptyset \;\vee\; (|p^\bullet| = 1 \wedge |q^\bullet| \leq 2 \wedge {}^\bullet(q^\bullet) = \{p, q\}) \\ \vee\; (|q^\bullet| = 1 \wedge |p^\bullet| \leq 2 \wedge {}^\bullet(p^\bullet) = \{p, q\}).$$

■ 6.2

The reduced AC property allows all free choice structures having no more than two input places for each transitions, and only one type of non-FC structure, namely the very simplest AC structure shown in Figures 10(ii) and 14(ii). It excludes AC structures such as shown in Figure 14(iii) and even EFC structures such as the third net of Figure 14(i). Thus RAC systems seem to be a 'tiny' subclass of AC systems. However, there is the following:

Theorem 6.3 *Characterisation of asymmetric choice nets*

Let Σ be a P/T-system.

(a) *If Σ is RAC then Σ is BAC.*

(b) *If Σ is BAC then Σ can be simulated by Σ' such that Σ' is AC.*

(c) *If Σ is AC then Σ can be simulated by Σ' such that Σ' is RAC.*

Proof: (a) is obvious from the definitions.
For (b), see [7], theorem 3.4. For (c), see [7] and [2], theorem 4. ■ 6.3

Part (c) of this theorem means that all the complexity of AC nets is already hidden in reducedly AC nets. But notice that (unlike in the FC case) not all (structurally) AC systems are behaviourally AC.

A further useful fact about AC systems is that the conflict relation is transitive. To see that this need not always be true, consider the 'typical' non-AC net of Figure 14(iv) with the marking shown in Figure 16. In this marking, both t_1 and t_2 are in conflict with t_0, but they are concurrently enabled, i.e. not in conflict with each other.

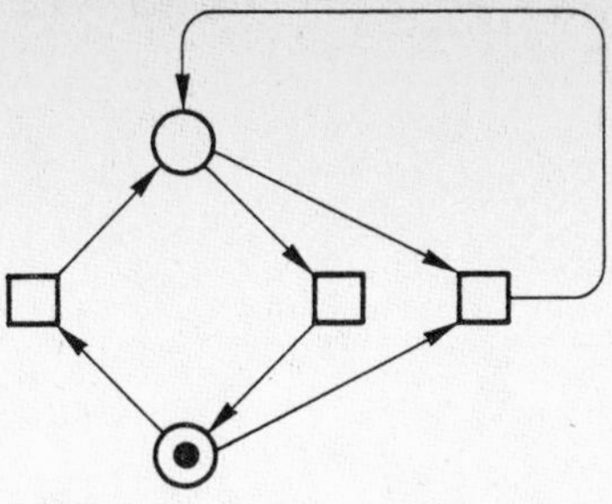

Figure 17: A system which is place-live but not live

Theorem 6.4 *Conflict is transitive in AC systems*

Let $\Sigma = (S,T;F,M_0)$ be an AC system, let $M \in [M_0\rangle$ be a marking and let t_0, t_1, t_2 in T be such that both t_1 and t_2 are in conflict with t_0 at M.
Then t_1 is in conflict with t_2 at M.

Proof: By lemma 2.8($\Rightarrow$), we may pick $p \in {}^\bullet t_1 \cap {}^\bullet t_0$ and $q \in {}^\bullet t_0 \cap {}^\bullet t_2$ such that $M(p) = 1$ and $M(q) = 1$. By the AC property, either $p^\bullet \subseteq q^\bullet$ or $q^\bullet \subseteq p^\bullet$. If $p^\bullet \subseteq q^\bullet$ then $q \in {}^\bullet t_1 \cap {}^\bullet t_2$ and hence, by lemma 2.8($\Leftarrow$), t_1 and t_2 are in conflict at M. If $q^\bullet \subseteq p^\bullet$ then $p \in {}^\bullet t_1 \cap {}^\bullet t_2$, yielding the same conclusion. ∎ 6.4

We will prove another typical property of AC nets. It yields a characterisation of liveness (which we will call 'place-liveness') which is easier to check. Place-liveness captures the idea that no place of a net can ever become empty and unable to receive a token again.

Definition 6.5 *Place-liveness*

$\Sigma = (S,T;F,M_0)$ is place-live *iff* $\forall M_1 \in [M_0\rangle\ \forall s \in S\ \exists M \in [M_1\rangle : M(s) > 0$. ∎ 6.5

Lemma 6.6 *Liveness implies place-liveness*

If $\Sigma = (S,T;F,M_0)$ is live then Σ is place-live.

Proof: If, for $s \in S$, ${}^\bullet s \neq \emptyset$ then whenever $t \in {}^\bullet s$ occurs, a token is put (or remains) on s.
If $s^\bullet \neq \emptyset$ then whenever $t \in s^\bullet$ occurs, a token must previously have been on s.
The case ${}^\bullet s = \emptyset = s^\bullet$ is excluded by the definition of a net. ∎ 6.6

Figure 17 shows the typical example of a (non-AC) system which is place-live but not live.

We intend to show next that such a case cannot occur in an AC net. For the purpose of proving this, the following small technical lemma is helpful.

Lemma 6.7 *A technical lemma*

Let $\Sigma = (S, T; F, M_0)$, $M \in [M_0\rangle$ *and* $t, t' \in T$ *such that:*

(i) ${}^\bullet t = \{s_1, \ldots, s_m\}$ *and* $s_1^\bullet \subseteq s_2^\bullet \subseteq \ldots \subseteq s_m^\bullet$;

(ii) *for some* i, $1 \leq i \leq m$, $s_1, \ldots, s_i$ *are marked under* M, *i.e.* $M(s_1), \ldots, M(s_i) > 0$;

(iii) ${}^\bullet t' \cap \{s_1, \ldots, s_i\} \neq \emptyset$;

(iv) M *enables* t'.

Then M *also enables* t.

Proof: Suppose not, then as a consequence of (ii), $\exists q \in \{s_{i+1}, \ldots, s_m\}: M(q) = 0$.
But by (iii), ${}^\bullet t' \cap \{s_1, \ldots, s_i\} \neq \emptyset$, say $p \in {}^\bullet t' \cap \{s_1, \ldots, s_i\}$.
By (i), $p^\bullet \subseteq q^\bullet$, which implies $t' \in q^\bullet$.
Hence M does not enable t', contradicting (iv). ∎ 6.7

Theorem 6.8 *Equivalence of liveness and place-liveness for AC systems*

Let $\Sigma = (S, T; F, M_0)$ *be an AC system. Then* Σ *is live iff* Σ *is place-live.*

Proof: ($\Rightarrow$) follows from 6.6.
To prove ($\Leftarrow$), let $M \in [M_0\rangle$, $t \in T$ and ${}^\bullet t = \{s_1, \ldots, s_m\}$; we have to prove that t can be enabled from M.
The AC property implies that the $s_1, \ldots, s_m$ can be linearly ordered as in 6.7(i), so without loss of generality we may assume $s_1^\bullet \subseteq \ldots \subseteq s_m^\bullet$.
We construct a reachable marking which enables t by putting tokens on $s_1, \ldots, s_m$, one after the other, in this order.
By place-liveness, there exists a marking $M_1 \in [M\rangle$ which marks s_1, i.e. $M_1(s_1) > 0$.
Suppose that a marking M_i has been reached which marks all of $s_1, \ldots, s_i$, i.e. satisfying 6.7(ii), for some $i, 1 \leq i < m$. Then by place-liveness, a marking M_{i+1} in $[M_i\rangle$ exists which marks s_{i+1}, i.e. $M_{i+1}(s_{i+1}) > 0$. Two cases are possible:

(1) In the transition from M_i to M_{i+1}, an output transition t' of $\{s_1, \ldots, s_i\}$ has occurred, removing a token from one of $s_1, \ldots, s_i$. In this case, lemma 6.7 can be applied to show that the marking which enables t' also enables t, and the proof is done.

(2) In the transition from M_i to M_{i+1}, all tokens have remained on $s_1, \ldots, s_i$. In this case, M_{i+1} marks $s_1, \ldots, s_{i+1}$, and the construction can be repeated; eventually, all $s_1, \ldots, s_m$ are marked and t is enabled.

∎ 6.8

A very similar result is lemma 4.3 of [26] which states that every dead transition in an AC system has an input place which remains unmarked. Theorem 6.8 holds even if the AC premise is changed to BAC. The proof is given in [7] (proposition 3.8); it is different from the above because it is not obvious that the construction which associates a simulating AC system to each BAC system preserves place-liveness.

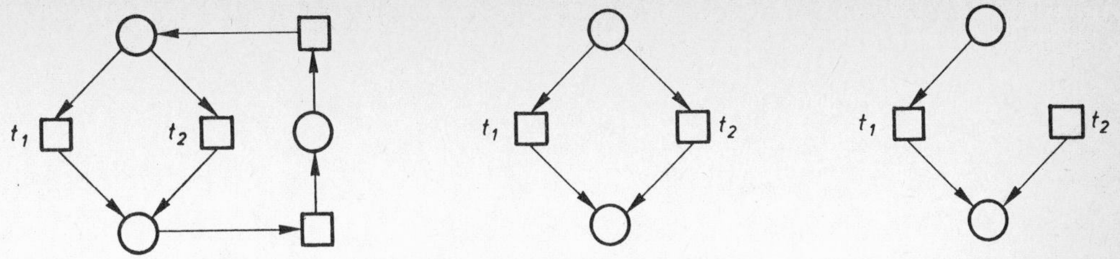

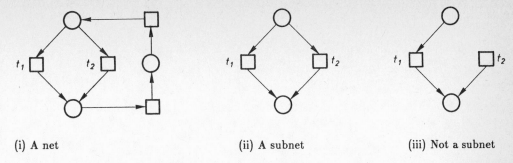

(i) A net (ii) A subnet (iii) Not a subnet

Figure 18: Illustrating the definition of a subnet

7 T-component covers of free choice systems

The small results presented so far hardly scratch the surface of the rich and elegant structure theory of free choice nets uncovered by F.Commoner [11] and M.Hack [21], and amplified (and made accessible to a wider audience) by other authors [41,40,15,9,38].

It is impossible to explain all of the results in detail in these notes. We shall concentrate on only one of them and explain its proof in full. This is M.Hack's theorem that a live and 1-safe FC system is covered by strongly connected T-components. It is the basis for many further results about free choice nets.

This theorem was chosen for two reasons. Firstly, its proof highlights some typical ways of arguing about free choice nets. Secondly, its proof is rather 'hidden' in the published literature. Hack's original proof in [21] is not very easily accessible. Besides, it is not exactly perspicuous and contains some serious mistakes which have been corrected in [22] and in [14]. Thus, at present, one would have to examine closely at least three papers in order to understand it.

To introduce T-components we first need the notion of a subnet.

Definition 7.1 *Subnet*

Let $N = (S, T; F)$ and $N_1 = (S_1, T_1; F_1)$ be two nets.
N_1 is a subnet of N *iff* $S_1 \subseteq S$, $T_1 \subseteq T$ and $F_1 = F \cap ((S_1 \times T_1) \cup (T_1 \times S_1))$. ■ 7.1

The restriction on F_1 in this definition deserves an explanation. It means that F_1 must contain not just some subset of the F-arrows between elements of $S_1 \cup T_1$, but even *all* such F-arrows. Figure 18 explains the difference.

T-components are special subnets which satisfy two further conditions. Firstly, if a T-component contains a transition then it must contain all of its bordering places as well. In this case we say that the subnet is 'generated' by its transitions:

Definition 7.2 *Transition generated subnets*

Let $N_1 = (S_1, T_1; F_1)$ be a subnet of $N = (S, T; F)$. N_1 is generated by T_1 *iff*
$S_1 = {}^\bullet T_1 \cup T_1^\bullet$ (where the presets and postsets are taken w.r.t. F). ■ 7.2

For any $T_1 \subseteq T$ there is always exactly one subnet generated by T_1, namely the net $N_1 = (S_1, T_1; F_1)$ with $S_1 = {}^\bullet T_1 \cup T_1^\bullet$ and $F_1 = F \cap ((S_1 \times T_1) \cup (T_1 \times S_1))$.

The second requirement to be satisfied by a T-component is that 'by itself' it must be a T-net. We capture this as follows:

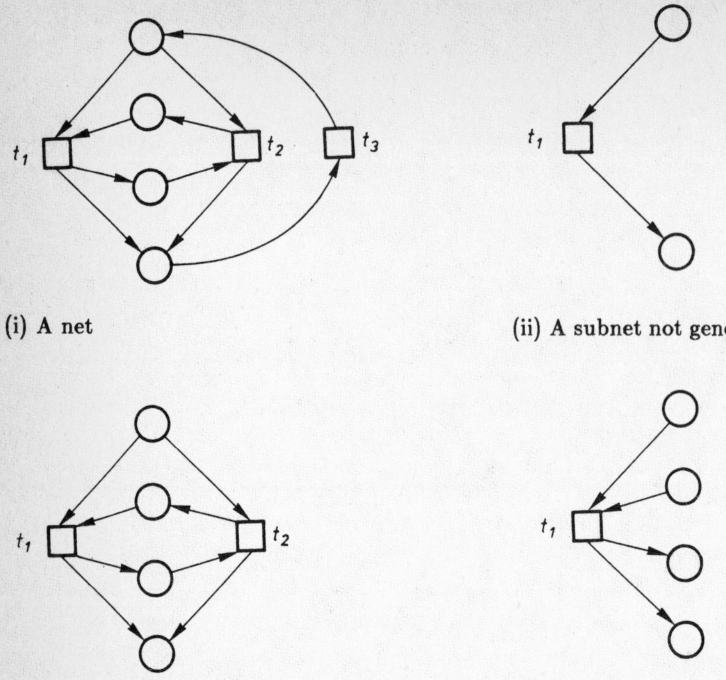

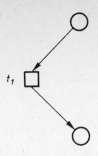

(i) A net

(ii) A subnet not generated by t_1

(iii) A subnet generated by $\{t_1, t_2\}$ which is not a T-component

(iv) A non-strongly connected T-component (generated by t_1)

Figure 19: Illustrating the definition of T-components

Definition 7.3 *T-components*

> $N_1 = (S_1, T_1; F_1)$ is called a T-component of $N = (S, T; F)$ *iff* N_1 is the subnet generated by T_1 and, in addition, $\forall s \in S_1: |{}^\bullet s \cap T_1| \leq 1 \wedge |s^\bullet \cap T_1| \leq 1$ (where the preset and the postset are taken w.r.t. F, but it would come to the same if they were taken w.r.t. F_1). ■ 7.3

A T-component N_1 will be called strongly connected iff it is strongly connected as a T-net 'by itself', that is, if there is a directed F_1-path between any two distinct elements of N_1. Definitions 7.1-7.3 are quite subtle and deserve careful study. Figure 19 explains them further. The net shown in Figure 19(i) has no strongly connected T-component. We will give examples of strongly connected T-components later in this section (Figure 21).

The reader should be cautioned that T-components are different from T-invariants [6]. While the set $\{t_1, t_2, t_3\}$ in Figure 19(i) defines a T-invariant (where one has to count t_3 twice), it does not define a T-component. On the other hand, every strongly connected T-component (and those are of chief interest) defines also a T-invariant. In this sense, T-invariants are more general. In the following, the notion of a T-invariant will play no further rôle, but see [28].

The objective of this section is to prove, by elementary means, Hack's result that every live and 1-safe free choice system Σ is covered by strongly connected T-components. That is to say: every place and every transition of a live and safe free choice system is contained in some strongly connected T-component. A moment's reflection reveals that the theorem need only be proved for transitions, since the covering of the places can be deduced immediately from that of the transitions (using the property that T-components are generated by their transitions). Hence the essential statement which we wish to prove is the following:

Every transition $\hat{t}$ of Σ lies on some strongly connected T-component $\hat{N}$ of Σ.

We solve this problem by defining an algorithm which constructs $\hat{N}$, given $\hat{t}$. Before defining this algorithm we give several examples. Figure 20 shows that the three preconditions (liveness, safeness and the free choice property) are necessary to establish the theorem.

The example in Figure 21 explains the construction of the T-component $\hat{N}$ covering $\hat{t}$. (In passing, the system shown in Figure 21(i) is live, 1-safe and FC, but its initial marking in not reproducible, so that corollary 4.7 fails to hold for FC nets.)

The task of the algorithm is to grow a T-component from a given single transition $\hat{t}$. Because the T-component is generated by its transitions, it stands to reason to extend the 'current' $\hat{N}$ at those transitions that have input places or output places *not* in $\hat{N}$. For instance, if $\hat{N}$ consists only of $\hat{t} = t_3$ initially (see Figure 21(i)), we might extend $\hat{N}$ by the output place s_5 of t_3 and hence include t_7 in it as well (to make $\hat{N}$ strongly connected). But one has to be careful because in the next step, $\hat{N}$ may not be further extended by t_2 (this being an output transition of an output place of t_7), since no T-component will result; we will have to choose t_1 rather than t_2.

To account for this, our algorithm extends $\hat{N}$ not in terms of single elements but in terms of certain 'nice' directed F-paths. The initial $\hat{N}$ (which equals $\hat{t}$) in Figure 21(i) will be extended, in the first iteration, by the cycle consisting of $\hat{t}$, t_7 and t_1 as a whole (see Figure 21(ii)). The next iteration detects that t_1 has an output place not yet in $\hat{N}$, and another path including t_4 will be added to $\hat{N}$. The construction then finishes because the subnet shown in Figure 21(iii) is already a T-component of the original net. Formally, the algorithm is defined as follows:

Algorithm 7.4 *Algorithm to construct T-components*

Let $\Sigma = (S, T; F, M_0)$ be a live and 1-safe free choice system and let $\hat{t} \in T$. We construct inductively a triple $\hat{N} = (\hat{S}, \hat{T}; \hat{F})$ which will turn out to be a strongly connected T-component containing $\hat{t}$.

Step 1: $\hat{S} := \emptyset$, $\hat{T} := \{\hat{t}\}$, $\hat{F} := \emptyset$ and $\hat{N} := (\hat{S}, \hat{T}; \hat{F})$.

Step 2: Repeat the following exhaustively: If there is $t \in \hat{T}$ with $t^\bullet \not\subseteq \hat{S}$ then choose $s \in t^\bullet \backslash \hat{S}$ arbitrarily and $t' \in s^\bullet$ in such a way that there is a nice path $p = \{t_0, s_1, t_1, \ldots, s_m, t_m\}$ from $t' = t_0$ to $\hat{N}$ (see below for what this means); then put

$$\hat{S} := \hat{S} \cup \{s\} \cup \{s_1, \ldots, s_m\}$$
$$\hat{T} := \hat{T} \cup \{t_0, \ldots, t_m\}$$
$$\hat{F} := \hat{F} \cup \{(t, s), (s, t')\} \cup \{(t_0, s_1), (s_1, t_1), \ldots, (s_m, t_m)\}$$

and $\hat{N} := (\hat{S}, \hat{T}; \hat{F})$.

■ 7.4

Notice that we immediately have $\hat{S} \subseteq S$, $\hat{T} \subseteq T$ and $\hat{F} \subseteq F$ always. However, it is not even clear that $\hat{N}$ is a subnet, leave alone a T-component, of Σ.

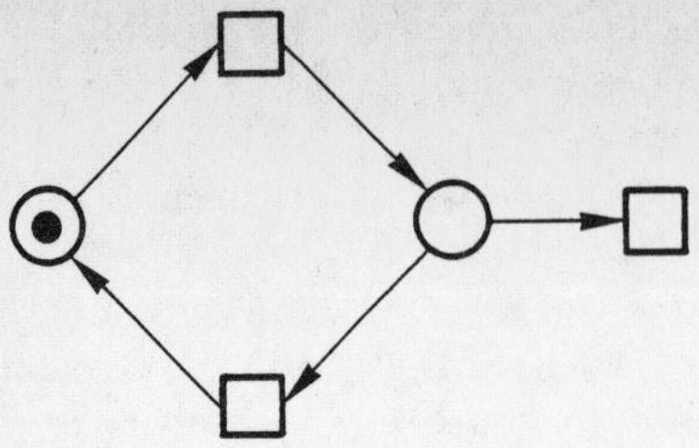

(i) 1-safe, FC and not covered by strongly connected T-components (but not live)

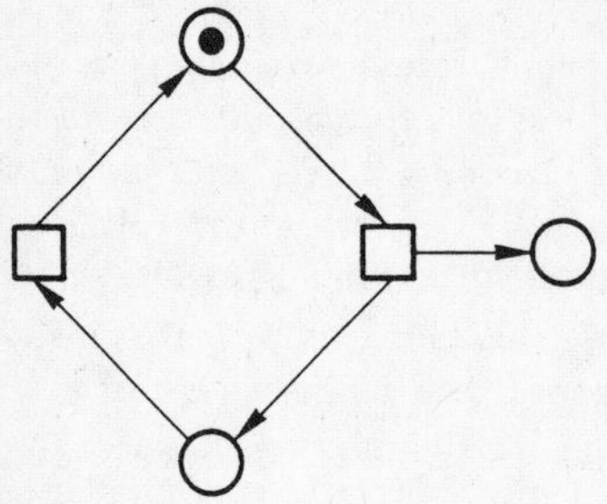

(ii) live, FC and not covered by strongly connected T-components (but not safe)

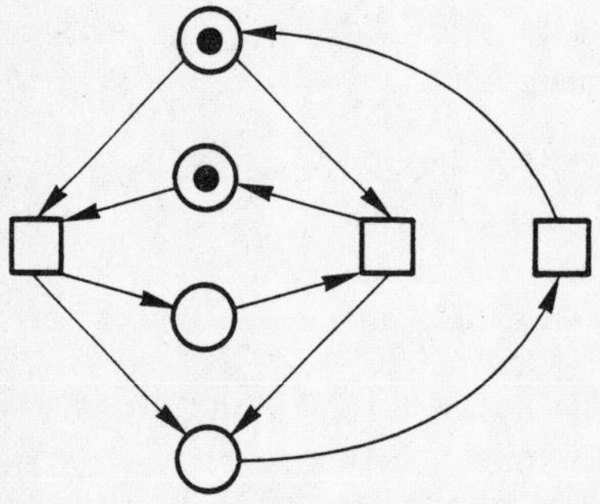

(iii) live, 1-safe and not covered by strongly connected T-components (AC but not FC)

Figure 20: Illustrating the preconditions of the main theorem

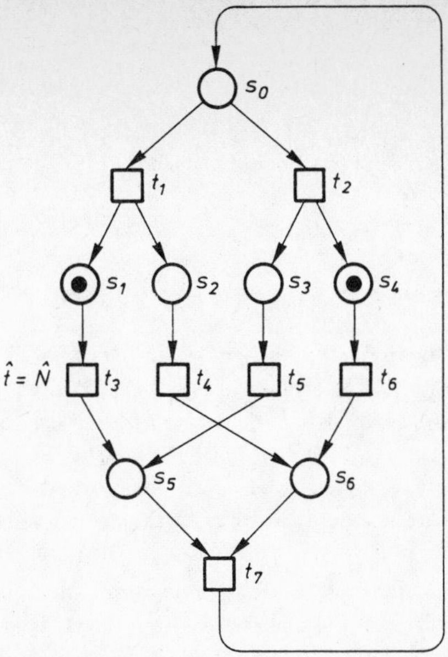

(i) An LSFC system; $\hat{t} = t_3$, and at the first step of the construction, $\hat{N}$ consists only of $\hat{t}$.

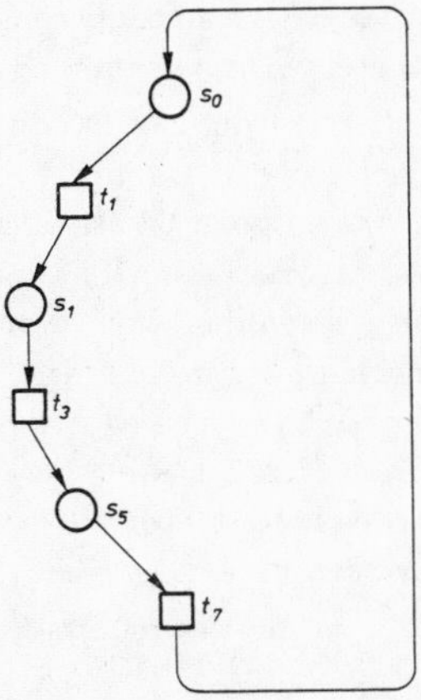

(ii) Second step of the construction: $\hat{N}$ is just a simple cycle.

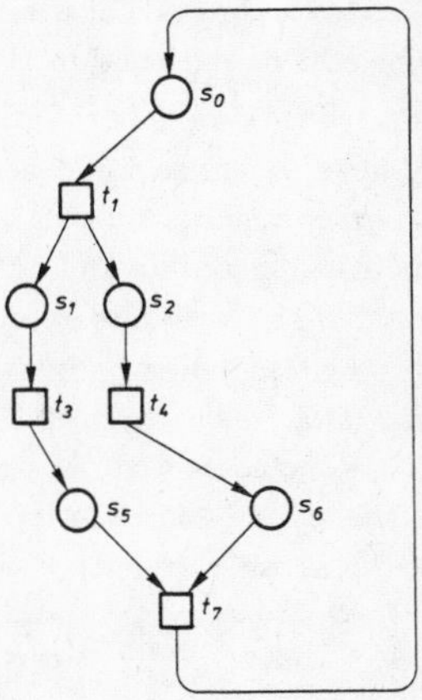

(iii) Third and last step of the construction: the final $\hat{N}$.

Figure 21: Illustrating the algorithm

Definition 7.5 *Nice paths*

With the notation as in 7.4, $p = \{t_0, s_1, \ldots, s_m, t_m\}$ is a nice path from t' to $\hat{N}$ *iff*

- $(t_{j-1}, s_j) \in F \wedge (s_j, t_j) \in F \; (1 \le j \le m)$ (p is a directed path)
- p is simple (i.e. no element occurs twice in it)
- $t' = t_0$ and $t_m \in \hat{T}$
- $s_j \notin \hat{S} \; (1 \le j \le m)$ and $t_j \notin \hat{T} \; (1 \le j < m)$.

The special case that $m = 0$ is allowed; we then have $t' = t_0 = t_m \in \hat{T}$. ■ 7.5

p being a 'nice path' simply means that p must start with t' and lead back into $\hat{N}$ at a *transition*; it is important that p may not directly lead to a place of $\hat{N}$. If $t' \in \hat{T}$ already, then p is the trivial path $\{t'\}$, and all that gets added to $\hat{N}$ by 7.4 is the place s. Otherwise, both s and the path p are included in the new $\hat{N}$. Hence what is added to $\hat{N}$ at each step of 7.4 is always a simple path which leaves $\hat{N}$ at a transition (namely at t) and re-enters $\hat{N}$ at another transition (namely at t_m, which might equal t'). It could even be the case that $t = t'$; then s is a side condition of t which will be included in the new $\hat{N}$.

The reader should carefully check this construction on the example of Figure 21(i) and convince himself that with $\hat{t} = t_3$ only the two iterations as shown in Figures 21(ii) and 21(iii) are possible. However, the construction need not be deterministic; to see this, the reader could try $\hat{t} = t_7$ in Figure 21(i). The reader may also wish to try the example of Figure 20(iii) to find out that the algorithm works as well, but may yield a triple $\hat{N}$ which is not a subnet.

It has to be shown that a transition $t' \in s^\bullet$ with the properties demanded in 7.4 always exists. Furthermore, it has to be shown that when the construction is completed, $\hat{N}$ is a strongly connected T-component. The rest of this section is devoted to the proofs of these two statements.

Let us first collect a few simple facts about the construction. First, every place is handled (i.e. added to $\hat{N}$) only once, either as some $s \in t^\bullet \backslash \hat{S}$ or as an s_j in some path p of construction 7.4. As a result, every place in $\hat{S}$ has exactly one incoming $\hat{F}$-arc and exactly one outgoing $\hat{F}$-arc (although it may have many other incoming and outgoing arcs). Moreover, every transition in $\hat{T}$ has at least one incoming $\hat{F}$-arc and at least one outgoing $\hat{F}$-arc, except at the very beginning when $\hat{N}$ consists only of $\hat{t}$. Also, at any stage of the construction, $\hat{N}$ is strongly connected in terms of $\hat{F}$ (i.e. every two distinct elements of $\hat{N}$ are connected by a directed $\hat{F}$-path), since at the very beginning, $\hat{N}$ is trivially strongly connected and adding directed paths emanating from $\hat{N}$ and leading back to $\hat{N}$ does not destroy the strong connectedness of $\hat{N}$. These four properties hold at every iteration of the algorithm (with the only exception that initially, $\hat{t}$ does not have any bordering $\hat{F}$-arcs).

Let us now turn to the proof that a transition $t' \in s^\bullet$ exists with the properties required in 7.4, provided $s \notin \hat{S}$ and $t \in \hat{T} \cap {}^\bullet s$ are as in 7.4. Figure 22 shows the setup.

In this proof we will encounter the same type of arguments that have been employed in the basic lemmata of [41]. In particular, we will use the notion of a maximal marking which plays an important rôle in lemmata 3.1 and 3.2 of [41]. Unfortunatley, it is not possible to apply these lemmata directly here, because their proofs in [41] make actual use of Hack's results, particularly the dual of the one we wish to prove here, and because the class of nets considered in [41] slightly differs from the class we are interested in. Hence we will have to do the proof 'from scratch'.

Now let us consider the initial setup of the problem shown in Figure 22. We know that $t \in \hat{T}$, $s \notin \hat{S}$ and $s \in {}^\bullet t$, and we wish to prove that there is some $t' \in s^\bullet$ from which a simple directed path re-enters $\hat{N}$ at a transition[4]. First, let us settle the case that s is also an input place of t, i.e.

[4] After reading the first version of this paper, P.S.Thiagarajan has noticed that, in fact, *every* transition $t' \in s^\bullet$ can be used to start some simple path which re-enters $\hat{N}$ at a transition. For a proof which yields this result, the reader is referred to a forthcoming paper [8]. Also, J.Desel has recently found a direct proof of this fact [13].

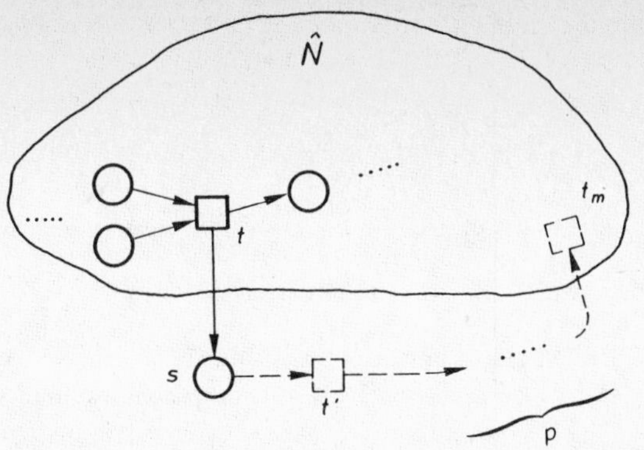

Figure 22: Knowing t and s, t' and p must be found

a side condition of t. Then the choice $t = t'$ already satisfies the requirements, so that we need not consider this case any further.

Since the system is live, the transition t can be enabled. After one occurrence of t, it can be re-enabled. But between two occurrences of t, some token must have disappeared from s because of 1-safeness, so that some $t' \in s^\bullet$ must have occurred between the two occurrences of t. The idea is that if the reproduction of the occurrence of t is properly chosen, then this t' might be a suitable transition which satisfies the requirements of the algorithm.

Let us make this argument more precise. We can find a sequence of the following form:

$$M_0 \dots M[t\rangle M'[\dots \tau \dots\rangle M''[t\rangle M''',$$

where τ is a transition sequence leading from M' to M'' which re-enables t. We have just seen that because of the 1-safeness of s (and because $s \notin {}^\bullet t$), τ must contain some $t' \in s^\bullet$. Let us, in order to discount 'unimportant' occurrences (of transitions that have nothing to do with the part of the net presently under consideration) assume that τ is a *minimal* sequence with the above properties; that is, τ cannot be made any shorter. Then define $t_0 \in s^\bullet$ such that t_0 occurs in τ and consider the *last* occurrence of t_0 in τ:

$$M'\tau M'' \quad = \quad M' \dots t_0 \underbrace{\dots}_{\text{no } t_0} M''$$

If t_0 is in $\hat{T}$ then there is nothing more to prove; we have found a path of the required kind, namely $\{t_0\}$. If t_0 is not in $\hat{T}$ then we must consider the set of output places of t_0, i.e. $t_0^\bullet$, in order to prolong the path. Let us suppose, for the moment, that *none* of the output places of t_0 are in $\hat{S}$, i.e. that $t_0^\bullet \cap \hat{S} = \emptyset$. Because τ is minimal, the output places of t_0 cannot remain all marked from (the last occurrence of) t_0 to M'' in τ (if so, the last occurrence of t_0 could be omitted from τ). Hence between (the last occurrence of) t_0 and M'' in τ, some $t_1 \in t_0^{\bullet\bullet}$ must have occurred; consider again the last such occurrence. If t_1 is in $\hat{T}$ then there is again nothing more to prove, because a nice path leads from t_0 to t_1. If t_1 is not in $\hat{T}$, however, then we have to consider the output places of t_1. Assume again that we can prove that $t_1^\bullet \cap \hat{S} = \emptyset$. Then the argument can be repeated, using the minimality of τ again, to show that between (the last occurrence of) t_1 and M'' in τ, some $t_2 \in t_1^{\bullet\bullet}$ must have occurred. However, this cannot go on forever, since τ is a finite sequence. Hence eventually, some nice path must result; the *last* occurrences were always taken in order to ensure that this path is simple.

The above argument depends on the assumption that we have $t_i^\bullet \cap \hat{S} = \emptyset$ whenever $t_i \notin \hat{T}$ in τ. We now turn to look how this assumption can be ensured. Apparently, we have to examine more closely the possible shape of the sequence τ. Let us first see what it would mean for a transition

t (we are now re-using the previously fixed name t for an arbitrary transition) to have an output place in $\hat{S}$ but not to be contained in $\hat{T}$: $t^{\bullet} \cap \hat{S} \neq \emptyset$ and $t \notin \hat{T}$. Then every occurrence of t puts at least one token on the set of places $\hat{S}$. We call t an 'input transition' of $\hat{N}$ and define

$$T^{in} \;=\; \{t \in T \mid t^{\bullet} \cap \hat{S} \neq \emptyset \wedge t \notin \hat{T}\}$$

(or shorter: $T^{in} = {}^{\bullet}\hat{S} \backslash \hat{T}$) as the set of input transitions of $\hat{N}$. Symmetrically,

$$T^{out} \;=\; \{t \in T \mid {}^{\bullet}t \cap \hat{S} \neq \emptyset \wedge t \notin \hat{T}\}$$

(or shorter: $T^{out} = \hat{S}^{\bullet} \backslash \hat{T}$) is defined to be the set of output transitions of $\hat{N}$. Notice that T^{in} and T^{out} are defined for every step of the construction 7.4; they depend on (and vary with) $\hat{N}$. It could well be true that $T^{in} \cap T^{out} \neq \emptyset$ (even for the final $\hat{N}$), but we have, by definition, $T^{in} \cap \hat{T} = \emptyset$ as well as $T^{out} \cap \hat{T} = \emptyset$.

In terms of these definitions, we may rephrase our assumption: we must find a transition sequence τ with the above properties which does not contain any T^{in}-transitions. Our aim now becomes to show that every transition in $\hat{T}$ can be enabled and re-enabled by some τ which does not contain any transitions from T^{in}.

Since $\hat{N}$ always likens a (strongly connected) T-net, we may examine corollary 4.7 to find that, at least, all the cycles of $\hat{N}$ should be filled with tokens if there is to be a chance of $\hat{T}$-transitions being reproduced without the occurrence of input transitions. In order to achieve this, we may try to put as many tokens as possible on $\hat{N}$. To this end, let us call a marking M (again, *any* marking, not just the one considered previously) to be $\hat{N}$-maximal iff, starting from M, no further tokens can be put on $\hat{N}$ without some tokens having to be taken away first. More precisely, we define a marking M to be $\hat{N}$-maximal *iff* :

> $\forall\tau$: if τ is a transition sequence from M and τ does not contain any transitions from T^{out}, then τ does not contain any transitions from T^{in} either.

This means that $\hat{N}$ is 'saturated' at the marking M. We may hope that from a 'saturating' marking of $\hat{N}$, the transitions of $\hat{N}$ may be reproduced without the use of transitions from T^{in}.

Hence, our next subtask becomes to show that for every $\hat{N}$ that may arise in construction 7.4, an $\hat{N}$-maximal marking exists and can be reached from the initial marking. We prove this statement by counting the number of tokens on the simple cycles of $\hat{N}$. First we recall that (except at the very beginning) $\hat{N}$ is covered by simple cycles since it is strongly connected. Now consider any marking M and the number $\hat{n}(M)$, defined as follows:

$$\hat{n}(M) \;=\; \sum_{\hat{c} \text{ a simple cycle of } \hat{N}} M(\hat{c}),$$

where $M(\hat{c}) = \sum_{s \in S \cap \hat{c}} M(s)$. This number is simply the count of the tokens on the simple cycles of $\hat{N}$, such that each token is counted as often as it is covered by a simple cycle. (Initially, when the sum is empty, we may put $\hat{n}(M) = 0$ by definition.) We will now classify the transitions of the system in accordance with whether their occurrence increases $\hat{n}(M)$, decreases $\hat{n}(M)$, or leaves $\hat{n}(M)$ invariant.

First consider the transitions that have nothing to do with $\hat{N}$, i.e. are neither in $\hat{T}$ nor in T^{in} nor in T^{out}: $t \in T \backslash (\hat{T} \cup T^{in} \cup T^{out})$. Then, clearly, ${}^{\bullet}t \cap \hat{S} = \emptyset = t^{\bullet} \cap \hat{S}$, and hence, the occurrence of t changes nothing on the marking of $\hat{S}$. In particular, $\hat{n}(M)$ is left untouched since it depends only on the tokens of $\hat{S}$.

Next, consider a transition t in $T^{in} \backslash T^{out}$. Such a transition could be called a 'proper' input of $\hat{N}$. Because $t \notin T^{out}$ and $t \notin \hat{T}$, we have ${}^{\bullet}t \cap \hat{S} = \emptyset$; that is, the occurrence of t cannot decrease the

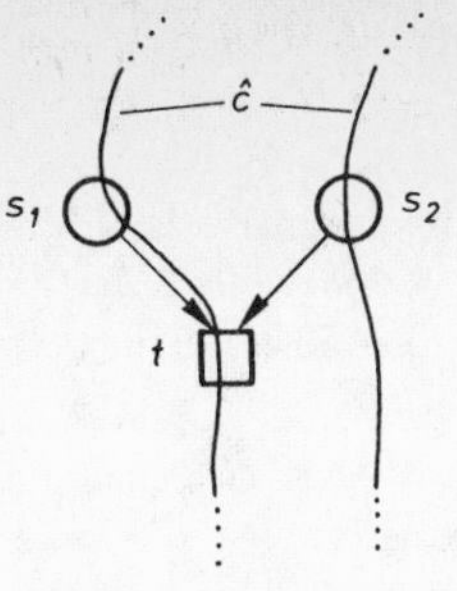

Figure 23: Illustrating the case that $|{}^\bullet t \cap \hat{c}| > 1$

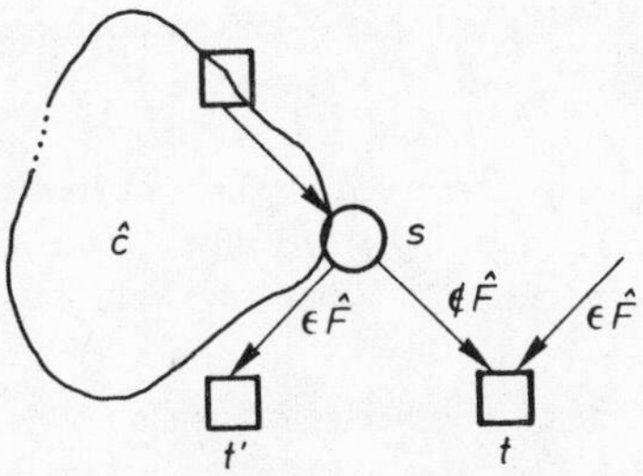

Figure 24: Illustrating the case that $|t^\bullet \cap \hat{c}| = 0$

number $\hat{n}(M)$. But can $\hat{n}(M)$ be left invariant, or is it always increased by the occurrence of t? $t \in T^{in}$ implies that for at least one $s \in S$ we have $s \in t^\bullet \cap \hat{S}$. But since $\hat{N}$ is strongly connected, there is some simple cycle $\hat{c}$ of $\hat{N}$ which contains s. The number of tokens on this cycle is increased by the occurrence of t. Hence the occurrence of $t \in T^{in} \backslash T^{out}$ always properly increases $\hat{n}(M)$.

Next, consider a transition $t \in \hat{T}$; this is the hardest case to analyse. The result we will eventually get is that the occurrence of t leaves the number $\hat{n}(M)$ invariant. First, however, we will only prove that the occurrence of t does not decrease $\hat{n}(M)$, which is sufficient for our present purposes. In order to prove this claim, we will have to examine what t can do to the cycles of $\hat{N}$.

Let $\hat{c}$ be any simple cycle of $\hat{N}$. We claim that $|{}^\bullet t \cap \hat{c}| \leq 1$ (where the preset is taken w.r.t. F). Suppose otherwise, i.e. $|{}^\bullet t \cap \hat{c}| > 1$, say $\{s_1, s_2\} \subseteq {}^\bullet t \cap \hat{c}$ (see Figure 23).

Then by the FC property, we have $s_1^\bullet = s_2^\bullet = \{t\}$, and hence $\hat{c}$ cannot be a *simple* cycle (t must occur at least twice in it); this holds even if s_1 or s_2 (or both) are side conditions of t. Hence, in general, $|{}^\bullet t \cap \hat{c}| \leq 1$. Thus, the only way that t could possibly reduce the number of tokens on $\hat{c}$ is if the following holds true:

$$|{}^\bullet t \cap \hat{c}| = 1 \text{ and } |t^\bullet \cap \hat{c}| = 0;$$

suppose this is true and $s \in {}^\bullet t \cap \hat{c}$. However, t cannot then be the output transition of s in $\hat{c}$, so there must be another one, say t' (see Figure 24).

We have $(s, t') \in \hat{F}$ since $\hat{c}$ is a cycle in $\hat{N}$, and hence $(s, t) \notin \hat{F}$ since, as we have seen previously, every place in $\hat{S}$ has exactly one $\hat{F}$-output arc. But since $t \in \hat{T}$, t must have at least one $\hat{F}$-input arc, a contradiction to the FC property. This finishes the proof that the occurrence of a transition $t \in \hat{T}$ cannot decrease the number $\hat{n}(M)$.

The last class of transitions to be considered is the set T^{out}. However, let us recall our current aim, which is to find an $\hat{N}$-maximal marking M of $\hat{N}$. The existence of such a marking can be shown even without considering the effect of the T^{out}-transitions on $\hat{n}(M)$. Because of 1-safeness, the number $\hat{n}(M)$ has a marking-independent upper bound (for instance, the number of simple cycles of $\hat{N}$ times the number of places on them). Hence there is some maximal number of times that transitions of $T^{in} \backslash T^{out}$ can occur without transitions of T^{out} necessarily having to occur, since the former properly increase the number $\hat{n}(M)$ while only the latter could possibly decrease it. To construct a $\hat{N}$-maximal marking, it is therefore sufficient to let $T^{in} \backslash T^{out}$-transitions (but not T^{out}-transitions) occur until no longer possible.

This ends our first subtask, namely to show that an $\hat{N}$-maximal marking exists. Our next task is to show that from an $\hat{N}$-maximal marking, any $t \in \hat{T}$ can be enabled and reproduced without any occurrences of T^{in}-transitions. In fact we will show that this can be done even without the occurrences of any T^{out}-transitions (which implies, by $\hat{N}$-maximality, that T^{in}-transitions do not occur either). Instead of the above, we will prove the following, even stronger, statement:

> Let $t \in \hat{T}$ be given. Every $\hat{N}$-maximal marking M can be transformed into another $\hat{N}$-maximal marking M' by $M[\tau\rangle M'$ such that τ does not contain any transitions from T^{out} (an hence also none from T^{in}), and M' enables t.

First of all, we show that $\hat{N}$-maximality is preserved by the occurrences of transitions not in T^{out}. Suppose that M is $\hat{N}$-maximal, $t \notin T^{out}$ and $M[t\rangle M'$; if τ were a transition sequence from M' which contains transitions from T^{in} but not T^{out}, then $t\tau$ would be a similar sequence from M. Hence M' must also be $\hat{N}$-maximal.

Next, we remark that every $t' \in T^{out}$ has a conflicting transition $t'' \in \hat{T}$, i.e. $t'' \in ({}^\bullet t')^\bullet \cap \hat{T}$. This simply follows because any place $s \in {}^\bullet t' \cap \hat{S}$ has (exactly) one $\hat{F}$-arc leading to $t'' \in \hat{T}$.

Now let t be an arbitrary transition in $\hat{T}$ and M be an arbitrary $\hat{N}$-maximal marking. We have to show that there is a transition sequence τ and a marking M' such that $M[\tau\rangle M'$, τ does not contain T^{out}-transitions and M' enables t. The idea is to construct τ in such a way that whenever some $t' \in T^{out}$ is in danger of occurring, we choose the conflicting $t'' \in \hat{T} \cap ({}^\bullet t')^\bullet$ instead. This can happen only a finite number of times before the given $t \in \hat{T}$ must of needs occur.

More precisely, we consider a first $t' \in T^{out}$ that can be enabled from M and let its corresponding $t'' \in \hat{T} \cap ({}^\bullet t')^\bullet$ occur; this is possible because of the (behavioural) free choice property. From the resulting marking, another $t' \in T^{out}$ can be chosen to be enabled, and so on. Thus we may construct a transition sequence which contains arbitrarily many $\hat{T}$-transitions but no T^{out}-transitions. However, there cannot be arbitrarily many $\hat{T} \setminus \{t\}$-occurrences! This follows as in theorem 5.5: any $t^1 \in \hat{T} \cap {}^{\bullet\bullet}t$ can occur at most once before t has to occur; any $t^2 \in \hat{T} \cap {}^{\bullet\bullet\bullet\bullet}t$ can occur at most twice before t has to occur, etc. The claim follows because $\hat{N}$ is strongly connected and finite.

This concludes the proof that at any stage of the construction 7.4, a transition $t' \in s^\bullet$ can be found which satisfies the requirements, i.e. from which a nice path leads back to a transition of $\hat{N}$. What remains to be done now is to show that the end result of construction 7.4 is indeed a T-component of $\hat{N}$ (that $\hat{N}$ is strongly connected has already been shown, and of course it contains $\hat{t}$).

From now on, let $\hat{N} = (\hat{S}, \hat{T}; \hat{F})$ denote the final result of construction 7.4. The proof that $\hat{N}$ is a T-component involves three steps:

(1) Show that $\hat{N}$ is a subnet.
(2) Show that $\hat{N}$ is generated by $\hat{T}$.
(3) Show that $\hat{N}$ satisfies 7.3.

(1) means that we have to show that whenever $x \in \hat{S} \cup \hat{T}$, $y \in \hat{T} \cup \hat{S}$ and $(x,y) \in F$ then $(x,y) \in \hat{F}$. For (2), we have to show that every $t \in \hat{T}$ satisfies $t^\bullet \subseteq \hat{S}$ and ${}^\bullet t \subseteq \hat{S}$. (3) means that $|{}^\bullet t \cap \hat{S}| = 1 = |t^\bullet \cap \hat{S}|$ (the equality can be taken rather than $\leq$ since $\hat{N}$ is strongly connected). But

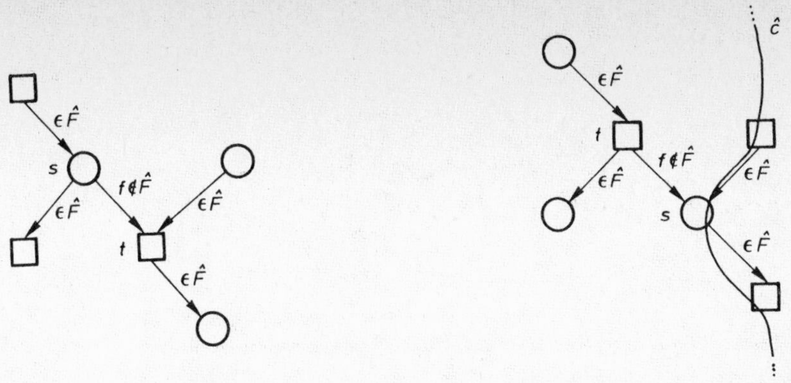

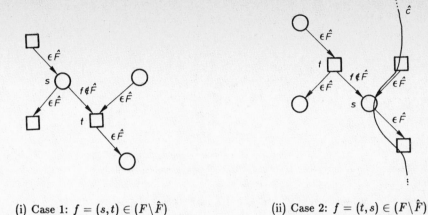

(i) Case 1: $f = (s,t) \in (F \backslash \hat{F})$ (ii) Case 2: $f = (t,s) \in (F \backslash \hat{F})$

Figure 25: Illustrating the proof that $\hat{N}$ is a subnet

(3) follows immediately from (1), together with the fact that each $s \in \hat{S}$ has exactly one incoming $\hat{F}$-arc and exactly one outgoing $\hat{F}$-arc. Thus, all that remains to be proved are the statements (1) and (2).

Let us deal with (1) first. (1) is wrong if there is an F-arc f between two elements of $\hat{N}$ which is not also an $\hat{F}$-arc. Two cases are possible: f leads from a place to a transition, or f leads from a transition to a place. Let us first consider the case that $f = (s,t)$ with $s \in \hat{S}$ and $t \in \hat{T}$. If $f \notin \hat{F}$ then there must be $\hat{F}$-arcs bordering on s and t in the way shown in Figure 25(i); but this is excluded by the FC property, whence f must be in $\hat{F}$.

Let us then consider the case that $f = (t,s)$ with $t \in \hat{T}$ and $s \in \hat{S}$. If $f \notin \hat{F}$ then there must be $\hat{F}$-arcs bordering on t and s as shown in Figure 25(ii). We claim that the occurrence of t properly increases the number $\hat{n}(M)$ defined above! To see this, consider any simple cycle $\hat{c}$ of $\hat{N}$ which contains s. There are two possibilities: if t is not included in $\hat{c}$ then $|{}^\bullet t \cap \hat{c}| = 0$ and $|t^\bullet \cap \hat{c}| = 1$; if t is included in $\hat{c}$ then $|{}^\bullet t \cap \hat{c}| = 1$ and $|t^\bullet \cap \hat{c}| = 2$; in both cases, $|{}^\bullet t \cap \hat{c}| < |t^\bullet \cap \hat{c}|$ and hence the occurrence of t increases the number of tokens on $\hat{c}$. On the other hand we have seen that t can occur arbitrarily often in some transition sequence which does not contain any T^{out}-transitions. This contradicts the fact that $\hat{n}(M)$ is bounded by a marking-independent constant number, and thus we must have $f \in \hat{F}$. This finishes the proof of (1), i.e. that $\hat{N}$ is a subnet. (In passing, the last argument also implies that $|t^\bullet \cap \hat{c}| \leq 1$ for any $t \in \hat{T}$ and simple cycle $\hat{c}$ of $\hat{N}$ and that, as has been claimed above, the occurrence of $t \in \hat{T}$ leaves the number $\hat{n}(M)$ invariant.)

The last step in the whole proof is to show (2), i.e. the fact that $\hat{N}$ is generated by $\hat{T}$. One half of this is trivial, because from construction 7.4 it follows immediately that $t^\bullet \subseteq \hat{S}$ for all $t \in \hat{T}$ (in fact, this is the termination condition of the algorithm). We have to exclude the case that $t \in \hat{T}$ but ${}^\bullet t \not\subseteq \hat{S}$; to do so, we shall assume $t \in \hat{T}$, $s \in {}^\bullet t \backslash \hat{S}$ (see Figure 26) and construct a contradiction.

We claim that from an $\hat{N}$-maximal marking which enables $t \in \hat{T}$, t can be reproduced by occurrences of $\hat{T}$-transitions only! Indeed, let

$$M_0 \ldots M[t\rangle M'[\ldots \tau \ldots\rangle M''[t\rangle M'''$$

be a sequence such that M is $\hat{N}$-maximal and τ contains no T^{out}-transitions (and consequently no T^{in}-transitions). Suppose that τ is of the form

$$\tau \quad = \quad \ldots t't'' \ldots$$

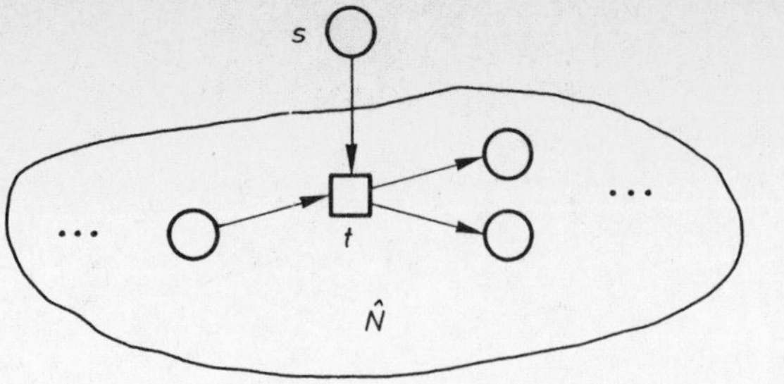

Figure 26: Illustrating the proof that $\hat{N}$ is generated by $\hat{T}$

where $t' \in \hat{T}$ and $t'' \in T \backslash \hat{T}$. We claim that $t'^{\bullet} \cap {}^{\bullet}t'' = \emptyset$. To see this, suppose $s' \in t'^{\bullet} \cap {}^{\bullet}t''$; by $t' \in \hat{T}$ and $t'^{\bullet} \subseteq \hat{S}$ we have $s \in \hat{S}$, but then by $t'' \notin \hat{T}$, we have $t'' \in T^{out}$, contradicting our assumption that τ contains no T^{out}-transitions. Hence $t'^{\bullet} \cap {}^{\bullet}t'' = \emptyset$, and lemmata 2.9(b) and 2.6 can be used to show that t' and t'' can be exchanged in τ. Repeating this, if necessary, the above sequence can be rearranged as follows:

$$M_0 \ldots M[\ldots \tau_1 \ldots \rangle M^1 [t\rangle M^2 [\ldots \tau_2 \ldots \rangle M'' [t\rangle M''',$$

such that τ_1 contains only transitions from $T \backslash \hat{T}$ (even from $T \backslash (\hat{T} \cup T^{in} \cup T^{out})$, i.e. transitions that have nothing to do with $\hat{N}$) and τ_2 contains only transitions from $\hat{T}$.

Now assume that $t \in \hat{T}$ has an input place s which is not in $\hat{S}$, as in Figure 26. Then $M^1(s) = 1$ since M^1 enables t, and $M^2(s) = 0$ since s cannot also be an output place of t (since $t^{\bullet} \subseteq \hat{S}$ and $s \notin \hat{S}$). But $M''(s) = 1$ again because M'' also enables t. Hence in τ_2 some transition $t' \in {}^{\bullet}s$ occurs, but t' cannot be in $\hat{T}$ since $\hat{T}^{\bullet} \subseteq \hat{S}$. This gives a contradiction to the fact that τ_2 contains only $\hat{T}$-transitions, showing that the assumption ${}^{\bullet}t \not\subseteq \hat{S}$ is false. Hence (2) is also proved.

This completes the proof of the main theorem. We may remark that on two occasions (namely in the proof of the fact that $\hat{T}$-transitions do not decrease $\hat{n}(M)$ and in the proof that $\hat{N}$ is a subnet) we have used the FC property in a strict way. That is to say, if only the EFC property is assumed in place of the FC property, then the proof does not go through. As a matter of fact, construction 7.4 does not always produce the desired results for EFC systems. The interested reader may wish to find a counterexample and a modification to the algorithm which works for EFC nets as well.

It should be mentioned that M.Hack also proves a dual of the above theorem, namely that an LSFC system can be covered by S-components which carry exactly one token each (see section 8.2 below). Furthermore, he shows that theorem 4.8, i.e. the necessary and sufficient condition for the existence of a live and 1-safe marking in a T-net, can be generalised. Also, he shows that an FC net N has a live and 1-safe marking if and only if its reverse-dual net (i.e. the net $(N^{-1})^d = (N^d)^{-1}$ [6]) has a live and 1-safe marking. For the proof of these additional results, the reader is referred to [21,22,14].

In [23], M.Hack shows how some of his constructions can be generalised to EFC nets and to ESMA nets, which are another generalised class of nets; for the latter class, [26] can also be consulted. Further generalisations are described by G.Memmi [29,30] and by W.Griese [20]. These generalisations illustrate various essential aspects of the free choice property.

Finally, we mention that the free choice property (or a close analogon thereof) has been translated into other formalisms of concurrent systems, notably to COSY by M.W.Shields [40] and to FIFO nets by A.Finkel [16].

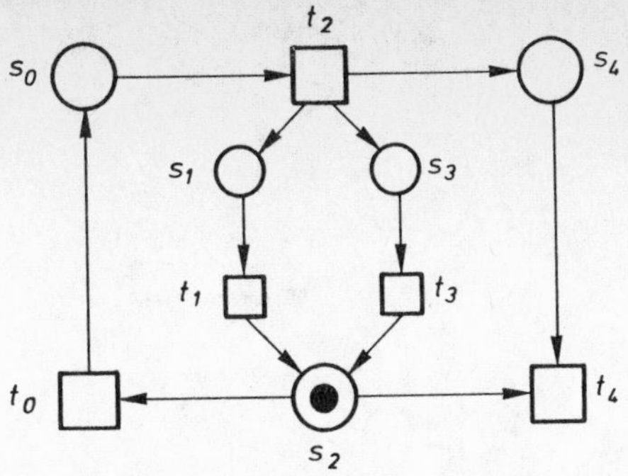

Figure 27: A live AC system which does not satisfy the dt-property

8 Some further results

The proof of section 7 was given in detail in order to explain the kind of reasoning employed in structure theory (of free choice nets). Once the reader is acquainted with this proof then, hopefully, he will find it easier to understand (the proofs of) the various other results that exist about free choice nets (and other net classes). We will give a selection of such other results in this section. They will only be explained briefly, and their proofs will be omitted.

8.1 A liveness criterion

An exact condition for the liveness of an FC system is due to F.Commoner and M.Hack [11,21]. A proof is also in [38] and, partly, in [26]. The theorem states that an FC system $\Sigma = (S,T;F,M_0)$ is live if, and only if it has the so-called dt-property, i.e., by definition, every 'deadlock' $S_0 \subseteq S$ contains a trap $S_1 \subseteq S$ which is marked under M_0, i.e. $M_0(S_1) > 0$. S_0 being a 'deadlock' means that ${}^\bullet S_0 \subseteq S_0^\bullet$; S_1 being a trap means that $S_1^\bullet \subseteq {}^\bullet S_1$. (We put 'deadlock' in quotes here since it is not a satisfactory term.)

F.Commoner has show in [11] that the dt-property is even a sufficient condition for the liveness of AC systems. However, conversely, it is not a necessary condition: Figure 27 shows an AC system which is live, even though the 'deadlock' $S_0 = \{s_0, s_1, s_2, s_3\}$ contains no marked trap (as the reader is invited to check). As an exercise, the reader may also wish to find out why the Commoner/Hack theorem reduces to theorem 4.3 for the special case of T-systems (a hint is that, according to the strict definition, no net may have isolated places).

8.2 A safeness criterion for live FC systems

In [21], M.Hack has proved a generalisation of theorem 4.4 as well. This states that a live FC system is 1-safe iff it is covered by S-components which carry exactly one token each. The concept of an S-component is defined dually to that of a T-component; for a definition, the reader is referred to [6]. In this safeness criterion, the S-components replace the simple cycles of theorem 4.4.

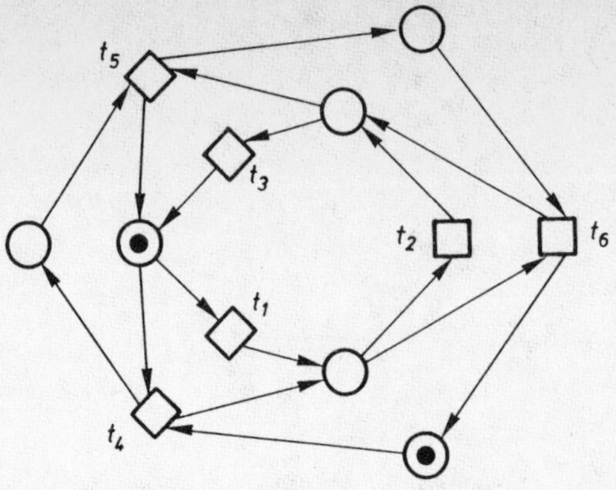

Figure 28: A live and 1-safe AC system violating the promptness theorem

8.3 A monotonicity result

In [15], K.Döpp has proved that a number of properties of an FC system $\Sigma = (S, T; F, M_0)$ do not change if its initial marking is increased by adding tokens to it, that is, by considering the new FC system $\Sigma' = (S, T; F, M_0')$ where $M_0' \geq M_0$. In particular, if Σ is live then so is Σ'. Also, if Σ is deadlock-free then so is Σ'. Furthermore, if Σ has certain reachability properties the so does Σ'. See [15] for the details. In general nets, this monotonicity property is false: adding a token to a live system may well 'kill' it; the reader may find examples by himself, or consult [38].

8.4 Promptness

Of the many nice results of [41], we shall mention only a few here. Promptness (of a system Σ with respect to a set of transitions T_0) means that the system may not go on working indefinitely without using transitions from T_0. T_0 may be thought of as a set of 'external' transitions of Σ; then Σ is prompt relative to T_0 if there is some maximal length of those behaviours that consist of 'internal' occurrences only.

Theorem 4.1 of [41] shows that an LSFC system Σ is prompt relative to T_0 iff T_0 has a non-empty intersection with every strongly connected T-component of Σ. This means that the behaviour of Σ is, in a sense, generated by its strongly connected T-components. Figure 28 shows that the theorem is not true for AC systems: with $T_0 = \{t_1, t_2, t_3\}$, no transition sequence can have two non-T_0-elements in succession, yet there is a T-component (namely that generated by $\{t_4, t_5, t_6\}$) which does not intersect with T_0.

The promptness theorem can be interesting when T_0 is interpreted as the 'interface' of the system to its environment.

8.5 A containment property

In section 5 of [41], it has been proved that every strongly connected subnet $N_1 = (S_1, T_1; F_1)$ of an LSFC system $\Sigma = (S, T; F, M_0)$ which is a T-net by itself (that is, N_1 satisfies $\forall s \in S_1 \colon |{}^{\bullet}s \cap T_1| \leq 1 \geq |s^{\bullet} \cap T_1|$) is contained in some strongly connected T-component of Σ. This result also follows directly from the arguments given in section 7 of these notes, since any strongly connected subnet which is also a T-net *could* be the result of an intermediate step of construction 7.4.

8.6 Home states

A marking $\hat{M}$ is a home state of a system $\Sigma = (S,T;F,M_0)$ if for all $M \in [M_0\rangle$: $\hat{M} \in [M\rangle$; that is, $\hat{M}$ always remains reachable. If the reachability graph of Σ is strongly connected then every marking is a home state. On the other hand, systems whose reachability graph is not strongly connected could still have home states; Figure 21(i) shows an example which is even an LSFC system.

[9] prove that an LSFC system always has at least one home state. The proof makes essential use of the T-component covering proved in section 7. It is a challenging exercise for the reader to prove that the theorem does not hold in general, i.e. to construct a live and 1-safe system which has no home states. K.Voss has even found an AC system with this property [9]. Home states may be useful in protocol validation [1].

8.7 Fairness

[41] and [4] show that in FC systems and in AC systems, fairness considerations are greatly simplified. Section 6 of [41] shows that global fairness of an LSFC system can be achieved locally, i.e. by taking care that every local conflict is resolved fairly. [4] shows that in AC systems (and a fortiori, in FC systems), there is no notion of 'proper conspiracy' (of, say, two processes against a third one), such as it may occur in the well-known 'five philosophers' example. The details of these results will be omitted here.

Acknowledgements

I wish to thank Ulrich Grude, Claudia Toussaint, P.S.Thiagarajan, K.Döpp and Wolfgang Reisig for giving me helpful comments on the structure and the contents of this manuscript. I am sincerely grateful to Frau Elisabeth Münch for producing the excellent drawings.

References

[1] G.Berthelot and R.Terrat: Petri Nets for the Correctness of Protocols. IEEE Trans. Comm. 30, 2497-2505 (1982).

[2] E.Best: Adequacy Properties of Path Programs. TCS Vol.18, 149-171 (1982).

[3] E.Best: COSY: its Relation to Nets and to CSP. These Notes.

[4] E.Best: Fairness and Conspiracies. IPL Vol.18, 215-220 (1984).

[5] E.Best and R.Devillers: Concurrent Behaviour: Sequences, Processes and Programming Languages. Studien der GMD No.99 (1985). A revised version of this report is due to appear in TCS (1987).

[6] E.Best and C.Fernández: Notations and Terminology on Petri Net Theory. Arbeitspapiere der GMD No.195 (1986). Also: Petri Net Newsletters No.23, 21-46 (April 1986).

[7] E.Best and M.W.Shields: Some Equivalence Results on Free Choice Nets and Simple Nets, and on the Periodicity of Live Free Choice Nets. Springer Lecture Notes in Computer Science Vol.159, 141-154 (1983).

[8] E.Best and P.S.Thiagarajan: (Forthcoming paper.)

[9] E.Best and K.Voss: Free Choice Systems have Home States. Acta Informatica 21, 89-100 (1984).

[10] S.D.Brookes and W.C.Rounds: Behavioural Equivalence Notions Induced by Programming Logic. Springer Lecture Notes in Computer Science Vol.154, 97-108 (1983).

[11] F.Commoner: Deadlocks in Petri Nets. Report, Applied Data Inc., CA-7206-2311 (1972).

[12] F.Commoner, A.W Holt, S.Even and A.Pnueli: Marked Directed Graphs. JCSS Vol.5, 511-523 (1971).

[13] J.Desel: (Forthcoming paper in Petri Net Newsletters.)

[14] K.Döpp: Zum Hack'schen Wohlformungssatz für Free-Choice-Petrinetze. EIK 19/1-2, 3-15 (1983).

[15] K.Döpp: Ein Satz über Free-Choice-Petrinetze. EIK 19/3, 107-113 (1983).

[16] A.Finkel: Boundedness and Liveness for Monogenous FIFO Nets and for Free Choice FIFO Nets — Applications to the Analysis of Protocols. Univ. Paris-Sud, L.R.I. Report No.205 (1985).

[17] H.J.Genrich and K.Lautenbach: Synchronisationsgraphen. Acta Informatica Vol.2, 143-161 (1973).

[18] H.J.Genrich, K.Lautenbach and P.S.Thiagarajan: Elements of General Net Theory. Springer Lecture Notes in Computer Science Vol.84, 21-163 (1981).

[19] H.J.Genrich and P.S.Thiagarajan: A Theory of Bipolar Synchronisation Schemes. TCS Vol.30, 241-318 (1984).

[20] W.Griese: Liveness in NSC Nets. In: Discrete Structures and Algorithms (ed. U.Pape), Carl Hanser Verlag, Munich, 256-264 (1980).

[21] M.Hack: Analysis of Production Schemata by Petri Nets. TR-94, MIT-MAC (1972).

[22] M.Hack: Corrections to MAC-TR-94. Computation Structure Notes 17, MIT-MAC (1974).

[23] M.Hack: Extended State-Machine Allocatable Nets, an Extension of Free Choice Petri Net Results. Computation Structures Group Memo 78-1, MIT-MAC (1974).

[24] D.Hillen: Relationship between Deadlock-freeness and Liveness in Free Choice Nets. Petri Net Newsletters No.19, 28-32 (1985).

[25] A.W.Holt: State Machines and Information. MIT-MAC Report (1970).

[26] M.Jantzen and R.Valk: Formal Properties of Place/Transition-Nets. Springer Lecture Notes in Computer Science Vol.84, 165-212 (1981).

[27] R.Johnsonbaugh and T.Murata: Additional Methods for Reduction and Expansion of Marked Graphs. IEEE Tr. on Circuits and Systems, Vol.28/10, 1009-1014 (1981).

[28] K.Lautenbach: Linear Algebraic Techniques for Place/transition Nets. These Notes.

[29] G.Memmi: Fuites et graphes à choix non imposé dans les réseaux de Petri. 3ème coll. int. sur la programmation, Dunod-Paris (1978).

[30] G.Memmi: Leakage Notion. Springer Informatik-Fachberichte No.52, 172-177 (1982).

[31] R.Milner: A Calculus of Communicating Systems. Springer Lecture Notes in Computer Science Vol.92 (1980).

[32] H.Müller: Prompt and hangup-free simulation of place/transition nets by pure nets without multiple arcs. Petri Net Newsletters No.15, 16-21 (October 1983).

[33] M.Nielsen and P.S.Thiagarajan: Degrees of Nondeterminism and Concurrency: A Petri Net View. DAIMI PB-180, University of Århus (1984). Also: 4th Conf. on Foundations of Software Technology and Theoretical Computer Science, Springer Lecture Notes in Computer Science, 89-117 (1984).

[34] D.Park: Concurrency and Automata on Finite Sequences. Computer Science Department, University of Warwick (1981).

[35] C.A.Petri: Nonsequential Processes. GMD-ISF Report 77.05 (1977).

[36] L.Pomello: Some Equivalence Notions for Concurrent Systems: An Overview. Arbeitspapiere der GMD No.103 (1984). Also: Springer Lecture Notes in Computer Science Vol.222, 381-400 (1985).

[37] L.Priese: Automata and Concurrency. TCS Vol.25(3), 221-265 (1982).

[38] W.Reisig: Petri Nets — An Introduction. Springer EATCS Monographs (1985).

[39] W.Reisig: Place/transition Systems. These Notes.

[40] M.W.Shields: On the Nonsequential Behaviour of Systems Possessing a Generalised Free Choice Property. Report CRS-92-81, Edinburgh University (1981).

[41] P.S.Thiagarajan and K.Voss: A Fresh Look at Free Choice Nets. Information and Control, Vol.61/2, 85-113 (1984).

[42] K.Voss: System Specification with Labelled Nets and the Notion of Interface Equivalence. Arbeitspapiere der GMD No.211 (June 1986).

SECTION 3

HIGH-LEVEL NETS – FUNDAMENTALS

PREDICATE/TRANSITION NETS

Hartmann J. Genrich
Institut für methodische Grundlagen
Gesellschaft für Mathematik und Datenverarbeitung
5205 St. Augustin 1, Fed. Rep. Germany

Abstract: The paper deals with conceptual, mathematical and practical aspects of developing a net theoretic system model. The model presented is based on common techniques of modelling static systems as structured sets of individuals (relational structures). These structures are 'dynamised' by allowing some relations between individuals to be changed by the processes of the modelled system.

Keywords: Predicate/transition nets (PrT-nets); higher-level Petri nets; variable relational structures; logical and linear-algebraic system invariants.

Contents

1 Introduction

Net theory is a systems theory that aims at an understanding of systems whose structure and behaviour are determined by the distributedness and combinatorial nature of their states and changes. It studies such systems at different conceptual levels, in various degrees of detail, and in many areas of application. One important branch of research in net theory is concerned with the conceptual and mathematical foundation of an adequate notion of *dynamic system* and its different ways of presentation (its *models*). The *basic* net theoretical system model is that of *condition/event systems (CE-systems)*. It was proposed by Petri as the common reference model of net theory [16]. Other models are considered theoretical in a strict sense if they are derived from or, can be translated into the basic model.

If a dynamic system has an adequate representation in a net theoretical model, we call it a *Petri system.* In this paper we give an example of introducing a net theoretical system model which is called *predicate/transition nets (PrT-nets)* and was first formulated by *Genrich&Lautenbach* [2]. There are various aspects concerned: syntactical and semantical, conceptual and analytical, theoretical and practical ones. The close relationships between these issues, the mutual effects they have on each other during the process of developing the model, constitutes one major difficulty of this presentation.

The central aim of developing PrT-nets has been to introduce, in a formal manner, the concept of *individuals with changing properties and relations* into net theory. The main ideas underlying the PrT-net model are so simple that we wish to demonstrate them at an introductory example before they are buried under all the formalism needed later.

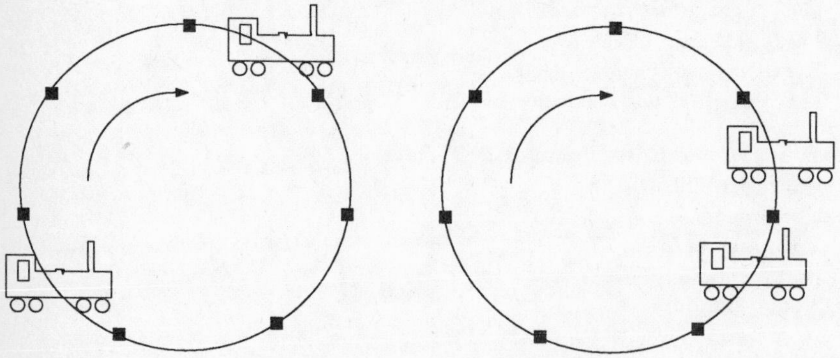

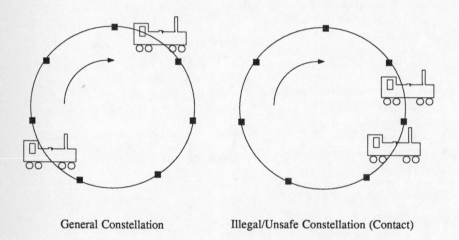

General Constellation   Illegal/Unsafe Constellation (Contact)

Figure 1: Contact-free Movements of Trains on a Circular Track

To this end we consider a small dynamic system sketched in figure 1. It consists of the one-directional movements of two trains on a circular track which is divided into seven sections. Safe operation requires that the movements are *contact-free*: two adjacent sections are never occupied by more than one train at a time.

Figure 2 shows a marked annotated net. It represents a CE-system that by virtue of the interpretation given in the legend is a model of the railway system shown in figure 1. Hence we have decided to view the railway system as a Petri system rather than, for example, a mechanical system.

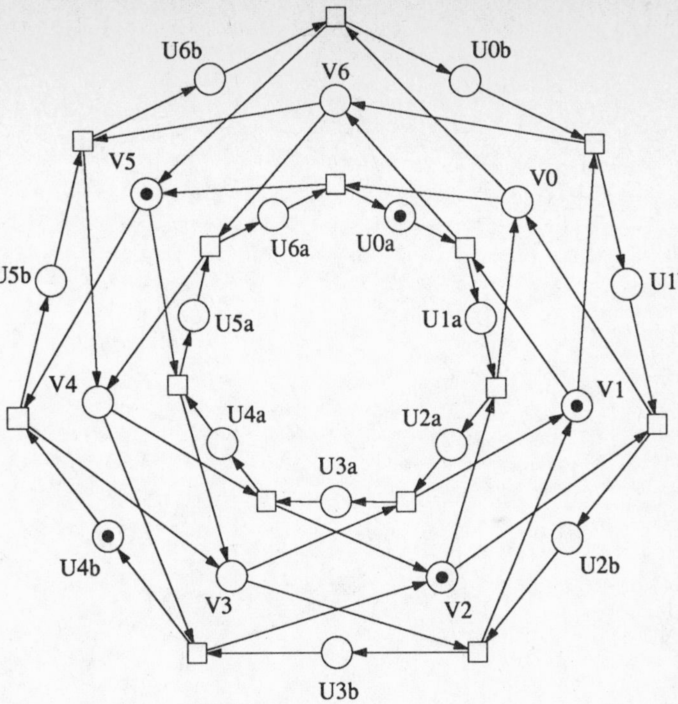

Legend: For $i = 0, \ldots, 6$ and $x = a, b$, Uix means that section i is occupied by train x, and Vi means that the sections i and $(i+1)\,mod\,7$ are vacant.

Figure 2: Railway System as a CE-system

The annotations of the conditions are expressions that serve as shorthands for affirmative sentences in natural language. They are built from two kinds of symbols. Letters a and b and digits 0 through 6 denote individuals, namely trains and sections, respectively. Letters U and V denote relations between individuals. (We treat properties as special, unary, relations.) These relations are *variable*, ie they are changed by the movements of the trains. In contrast, the cyclic order of the sections on the track is a *static* relation. It is depicted by the flow relation of the net.

The syntactical structure of the condition annotations is that of elementary propositions of first-order predicate logic. This is not by coincidence. Rather, we shall follow logic as a model for developing a net theoretic formalism dealing with individuals and their properties and relations.

As in logic, we call the symbols that are denoting individuals *(individual) constants* and we call the symbols that are denoting relations *predicates*. Using another class of symbols as (individual) *variables*, schemes of propositions can be formulated. Replacing in a proposition one or more occurrences of a constant by variables yields a propositional scheme called a *formula*. If we take, for example, proposition $U1a$ and replace the constant a by the variable x, we get the formula $U1x$ from which both $U1a$ and $U1b$ can be derived by means of the *substitutions* $\{x \leftarrow a\}$ and $\{x \leftarrow b\}$.

The same kind of abstraction is now used to simplify the annotated net representing the railway system considerably. Together with deriving a set of propositions from a formula we introduce schemes for the corresponding sets of conditions; they are called *places*. Figure 3 shows the result of merging, for each section i, conditions (annotated by) Uia and Uib into the place (annotated by) Uix. The events of the original net are now identified by annotating the arcs by constants. These

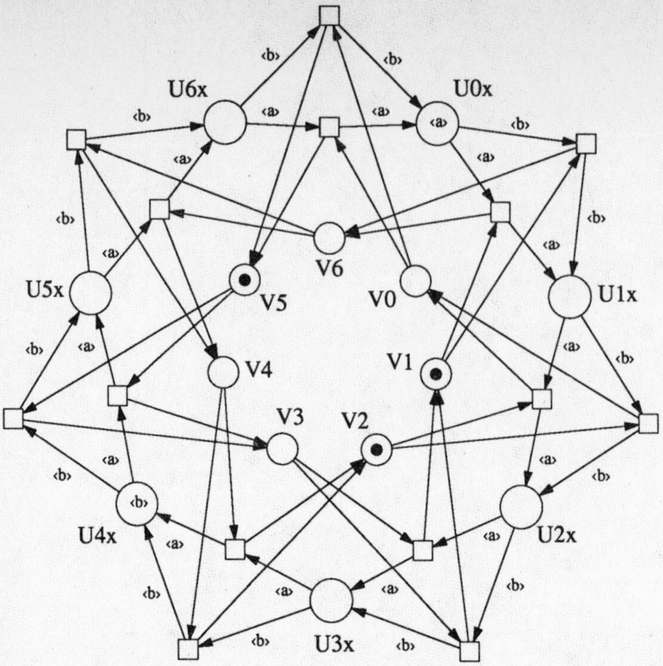

Legend: See figure 2.

Figure 3: Railway System with Sections as Places

are substituted for the variables at the places to get the corresponding condition. In the same way, some of the tokens indicating the current case of the system now carry individual constants.

Now observe how the token game translates. In the original net in figure 2, the event of train a moving from section 0 to section 1 takes a token from conditions $U0a$ and $V1$ and puts a token on conditions $U1a$ and $V6$. In the transformed net in figure 3, the same event takes an $\langle a \rangle$ from place $U0x$ and a plain token from place $V1$, and it puts an $\langle a \rangle$ on place $U1x$ and a plain token on place $V6$.

Looking closer at the net shown in figure 3 we recognise that there are pairs of events which are so similar that they can be viewed as *instances* of a single *event scheme*. For example, the event of train a moving from section 2 to section 3 is quite similar to the event of b moving from 2 to 3. Both events have the same set of input places and the same set of output places. They only differ in the annotations of the corresponding arcs. They can be represented by a single *transition* denoting *some* train moving from section 2 to 3. The result of merging pairs of similar events into transitions is shown in figure 4. The places and their markings are not affected by this transformation. For a transition to occur there must be a substitution of the train variable x at all surrounding arcs such that the resulting event has concession.

Note that this representation comes rather close to the informal presentation in figure 1. The sections are represented by the U places that may be occupied by (symbols for) trains. The borders between sections are represented by the transitions, and the direction of movements is represented by directed arcs connecting places and transitions. The control signals that avoid collisions and dangerous contacts are carried by the V places.

It now seems quite natural to try the same kind of abstraction again with respect to sections. The result of first merging places annotated by similar formulae and then merging similar transitions

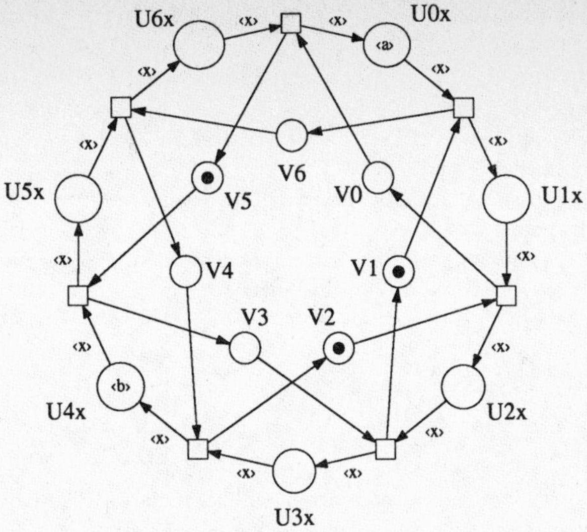

Legend: See figure 2.

Figure 4: Railway System with Places and Transitions

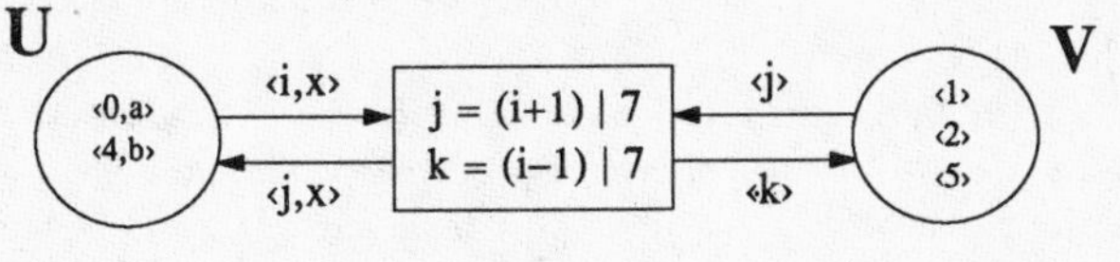

Legend: See figure 2.

Figure 5: Railway System with Variable Relations as Places

is shown in figure 5. The set of events denoted by the single transition in figure 5 cannot be determined any longer by just fixing the range of the variables. Rather, the set of substitutions generating these events is determined by the relation that exists between the sections annotating the arcs of similar transitions. Note that this relation is static; it is not dependent on the states of the system. It is expressed by the (first-order logical) formula annotating the new transition. Usually there are many ways of expressing such relations. We have expressed them in terms of the successor relation between sections in the form of addition of $1\, modulo\, 7$.

Note again how the token game is affected by the last transformation. For the transition to occur in some 'mode', the variables x, i, j, k must be replaced by constants in such a way that the formula at the transition holds and the tuples generated by that substitution at the arcs can be removed from respectively put on the corresponding places.

The two places of figure 5 represent the two variable relations of the railway system in a one-to-one fashion. To stress this fact, they are annotated by relation symbols, ie predicates, only. This is the reason why the annotated nets of which figures 2 through 5 are examples are called *predicate/transition nets (PrT-nets)*.

The rest of this paper is now organised as follows.

First we introduce in chapter 2 the basic form of predicate/transition nets as formal objects. This includes the exact definition of the language for annotating the nets, the semantics of PrT-nets as condition/event systems and the symbolic transition rule for the token game on PrT-nets that is compatible with the semantics.

In chapter 3 the basic form is refined and generalised in several respects to obtain the full modelling power and flexibility of PrT-nets.

The close affinity of Prt-nets to predicate logic that goes further than using logical formulae as annotations is demonstrated in 4.

Finally, we show in chapter 5 how linear algebraic analysis techniques known from the theory of ordinary Petri nets can be transferred to PrT-nets.

2 Predicate/Transition Nets

In the introduction we have sketched the presentation of a Petri system as an annotated net belonging to a class called *predicate/transition nets* (PrT-nets). In this chapter, PrT-nets will be defined as formal objects that can be interpreted and manipulated in a mathematical way that is comparable to working with logical formulae or algebraic expressions.

Our approach is to model a dynamic system in terms of a set of individuals that is structured by functions and relations. The structure is partially static and partially dynamic. (In the railway system of the introduction, for example, the cyclic order of the sections is static and the relation *is_occupied_by* between sections and trains is variable.

Intuitively we are going to dynamise the common notion of a relational structure. A structure is a tuple of objects, $\mathcal{R} = (D; f_1, \ldots, f_k; R_1, \ldots, R_n)$, where D is a non-empty set of *individuals* called the *domain* of $\mathcal{R}$, the f_i are *functions* in D and the R_j are *relations* in D. A *dynamic structure* will be characterised by the fact some relations are *variable* in the sense that their extensions may vary from state to state due to the occurrence of processes in the modelled system.

We shall separate the static and the variable part from each other. The static part will remain an ordinary relational structure. It is the *support* of the dynamic system. The dynamics will be represented as an annotated net, called *predicate/transition net (PrT-net)*, of the kind we have already met in the introduction. Here the variable relations appear as the places of the net. The functions and relations of the static part or more precisely, their names, ie operators respectively predicates, will appear in the annotations. In other words, the annotations of the net are interpreted in terms of a given static relational structure, the support. This will allow to derive from the annotated net the condition/event system that is the net theoretical expression for the dynamic structure. (For our introductory example this would mean to go from the PrT-net of figure 5 back to the CE-net in figure 2.)

2.1 The Language for Structures

We have chosen structured sets of individuals to support the modelling of dynamic systems. Operators (function symbols) and predicates (relation symbols) form the vocabulary of the language in which we will talk formally about structures, ie about properties and relations of individuals.

The language we use is that of *first-order predicate logic* plus a class of simple algebraic expressions for denoting linear combinations.

Definition 2.1 Let for each index $n \geq 0$, $\Omega^{(n)}$ be a set of n-ary operators and $\Pi^{(n)}$ a set of n-ary predicates and let $\Omega = \bigcup_{n \in \mathbf{N}} \Omega^{(n)}$ and $\Pi = \bigcup_{n \in \mathbf{N}} \Pi^{(n)}$. These operators and predicates form the *vocabulary* of the *first-order* language $\mathbf{L}$ that consists of two kinds of expressions, *terms* and *formulae*. In addition, there is a set of symbols, V, disjoint from Ω and Π whose elements serve as (individual) *variables*. Terms and formulae are built in the following way.

1. *Terms:*
   (a) A variable is a term.
   (b) If $f^{(n)}$ is a n-ary operator and $v_1, \ldots, v_n$ are terms then $f(v_1, \ldots, v_n)$ is a term. (Note that 0-ary operators are terms; they are used as proper names of distinct individuals.)
   (c) No other expression is a term.
2. *Formulae:*
   (a) If v_1 and v_2 are terms then $v_1 = v_2$ is an *atomic* formula.
   (b) If $P^{(n)}$ is a n-ary predicate and $v_1, \ldots, v_n$ are terms then $Pv_1 \ldots v_n$ is an atomic formula. (Note that 0-ary predicates are atomic formulae; they are unstructured propositions, the propositional variables of propositional logic.)
   (c) If p_1 and p_2 are formulae then $\neg p_1$ and $(p_1 \vee p_2)$ are formulae.
   (d) If x is a variable and p a formula then $(\exists x)p$ is a formula.
   (e) No other expression is a formula.

   Remark: The connectors $\wedge$, $\rightarrow$, $\leftrightarrow$ and $\forall$ are derived from $\neg$, $\vee$ and $\exists$ in the usual way.

An occurrence of a variable x in a formula E is called a *free occurrence* if it is not in the range of a $(\exists x)$ or $(\forall x)$. The occurrences of variables in a single term are free. The set of variables that occur freely in an expression (term or formula) is called the *index* of that expression. An expression is called *closed* iff its index is empty. Closed terms are compound names of individuals; closed formulae are propositions.

Free occurrences of a variable in an expression may be replaced by terms:

Definition 2.2 Let E be an expression (term or formula), $x_1, \ldots, x_n$ be variables and $v_1, \ldots, v_n$ terms. Then $\alpha = \{x_1 \leftarrow v_1, \ldots, x_n \leftarrow v_n\}$ is called a *substitution*, and $E{:}\alpha = E{:}\{x_1 \leftarrow v_1, \ldots, x_n \leftarrow v_n\}$ designates the result of simultaneously substituting v_i for each free occurrence of x_i for $1 \leq i \leq n$. $E{:}\alpha$ is called the *α-instance* of E. Note that $E{:}\alpha$ is a term or formula iff E is a term or formula, respectively.

We can use a first-order language **L** for talking about a relational structure $\mathcal{R}$ if we associate with each operator and each predicate in the vocabulary of **L** a function respectively a relation of $\mathcal{R}$.

Definition 2.3 Given a first-order language **L**, we call a structure $\mathcal{R}$ a *structure for* **L**, *or* **L**-*structure,* if every operator $f^{(m)}$ of **L** denotes a m-ary function of $\mathcal{R}$ designated by $f_\mathcal{R}$ and every predicate $P^{(n)}$ of **L** denotes a n-ary relation of $\mathcal{R}$ designated by $P_\mathcal{R}$. (A 0-ary relation is either $\emptyset$ or $\{\langle\rangle\} = \{\emptyset\}$.)

To ensure that each individual in the domain of $\mathcal{R}$ can be named in a sentence, we now add to the vocabulary of **L** a new set, $U_\mathcal{R}$, of *constants* denoting the individuals of $\mathcal{R}$ in a one-to-one fashion. The individual denoted by a constant d is designated as $d_\mathcal{R}$. Every constant is defined to be a term. The language derived from this augmented vocabulary is designated as $\mathbf{L}_\mathcal{R}$.

The structure $\mathcal{R}$ assigns to each closed term, v, of $\mathbf{L}_\mathcal{R}$ an individual of $\mathcal{R}$, designated by $\mathcal{R}(v)$, and to each closed formula (proposition), p, of $\mathbf{L}_\mathcal{R}$ the truthvalue $\top$ (*true*) or $\bot$ (*false*), designated by $\mathcal{R}(p)$.

Definition 2.4 Let v be a closed term and p a closed formula of the language $\mathbf{L}_\mathcal{R}$. Then $\mathcal{R}(v)$ and $\mathcal{R}(p)$ are defined recursively on their respective syntactic structure.

1. (a) If v is a constant d, $\mathcal{R}(v)$ is the individual denoted by d, $d_\mathcal{R}$.

(b) If v is $f^{(n)}(v_1, \ldots, v_n)$ then $\mathcal{R}(v) = f_{\mathcal{R}}(\mathcal{R}(v_1), \ldots, \mathcal{R}(v_n))$.

2. (a) If p is $v_1 = v_2$ then $\mathcal{R}(p) = \top$ iff $\mathcal{R}(v_1)$ and $\mathcal{R}(v_2)$ are the same individual.
   (b) If p is $P^{(n)}v_1 \ldots v_n$ then $\mathcal{R}(p) = \top$ iff $\langle \mathcal{R}(v_1), \ldots, \mathcal{R}(v_n) \rangle \in P_{\mathcal{R}}$.
   (c) If p is $\neg q$ then $\mathcal{R}(p) = \top$ iff $\mathcal{R}(q) = \bot$.
   (d) If p is $(p_1 \vee p_2)$ then $\mathcal{R}(p) = \top$ iff $\mathcal{R}(p_1) = \top$ or $\mathcal{R}(p_2) = \top$.
   (e) If p is $(\exists x)q$ then $\mathcal{R}(p) = \top$ iff there is a constant d such that $\mathcal{R}(q\{x = d\}) = \top$.

Definition 2.5 Let $\mathbf{L}$ be a first-order language, $\mathbf{A}$ a finite set of formulae of $\mathbf{L}$, p, q formulae of $\mathbf{L}$, $\mathcal{R}$ a $\mathbf{L}$-structure and r a formula of $\mathbf{L}_{\mathcal{R}}$. Then

1. r is said to be *valid* in $\mathcal{R}$ iff each closed instance of r is true in $\mathcal{R}$. Notation: $\mathcal{R} \models r$.
2. p is said to be *valid* iff it is valid in every $\mathbf{L}$-structure. Notation: $\models p$.
3. $\mathcal{R}$ is called a *model* of $\mathbf{A}$ iff each formula of $\mathbf{A}$ is valid in $\mathcal{R}$. Notation: $\mathcal{R} \models \mathbf{A}$
4. p implies q iff $(p \rightarrow q)$ is valid. Notation: $p \Rightarrow q$.
5. p is called a *logical consequence* of $\mathbf{A}$ iff p is valid in every model of $\mathbf{A}$. Notation: $\mathbf{A} \models p$

In an ordinary first-order structure $\mathcal{R}$, all functions and relations are static, as opposed to dynamic structures where some relations are variable. The presentation of dynamic structures requires that we distinguish between predicates denoting static relations and predicates denoting variable relations (we do not consider variable functions). Hence we divide the set of predicates, Π, into a set of static predicates, Π_s, and a set of variable predicates that will be designated by Π_v.

In the introduction we have demonstrated the principal ideas of simplifying the net representation of dynamic structures by means of merging conditions and events into places and transitions, respectively. Because of the simplicity of the example one particular effect did not show up during the abstraction process.

Look at the example of an annotated CE-net shown in figure 6(a). When merging conditions annotated by propositions built from the same predicate into a single place, multiple arcs will be created (see figure 6(b)). Arcs of a net representation, however, represent ordered pairs of net elements rather than being elements in their own right. Hence we want a notation for combining the annotations of multiple arcs into a single expression.

We propose to use symbolic sums indicating a linear combination of the constituent tuples (see figure 6(c)). What may look here as a mere notational convention will later prove very useful for exploiting the linear algebraic properties of dynamic structures.

In order to make the use of symbolic sums precise we introduce linear integer combinations and multi-sets.

Definition 2.6 Let D be a set. A *linear combination in D with integer coefficients* is a mapping $\lambda: D \rightarrow \mathbf{Z}$. The set of all linear combinations in D is denoted by $\mathcal{L}(D)$, $\mathcal{L}(D) = [D \rightarrow \mathbf{Z}]$.
Very often we shall work with linear combinations with *finite support*, ie with a finite number of coefficients only being non-zero. Their class will be designated by $\mathcal{L}_{fin}(D)$.
For $D = D_1 \times \cdots \times D_n$ we write $\mathcal{L}(D_1, \ldots, D_n)$. (Note that $\mathcal{L}() = \mathbf{Z}$.)
The set of non-negative linear combinations in D is denoted by $\mathcal{L}^+(D)$; its elements are *multi-sets* over D. (Note that for every subset of D, its characteristic function belongs to $\mathcal{L}^+(D)$).
The combinations whose coefficients are all 0 or all 1 are denoted by $\mathbf{0}$ and $\mathbf{1}$, respectively. ($\mathbf{0}$ corresponds to the empty set and $\mathbf{1}$ corresponds to D.)
Our notation for a single linear combination is such that for $D = \{a, b, c, d\}$, $2\langle a \rangle - 3\langle b \rangle + \langle d \rangle$ denotes $\{a \mapsto 2,\ b \mapsto -3,\ c \mapsto 0,\ d \mapsto 1\}$.

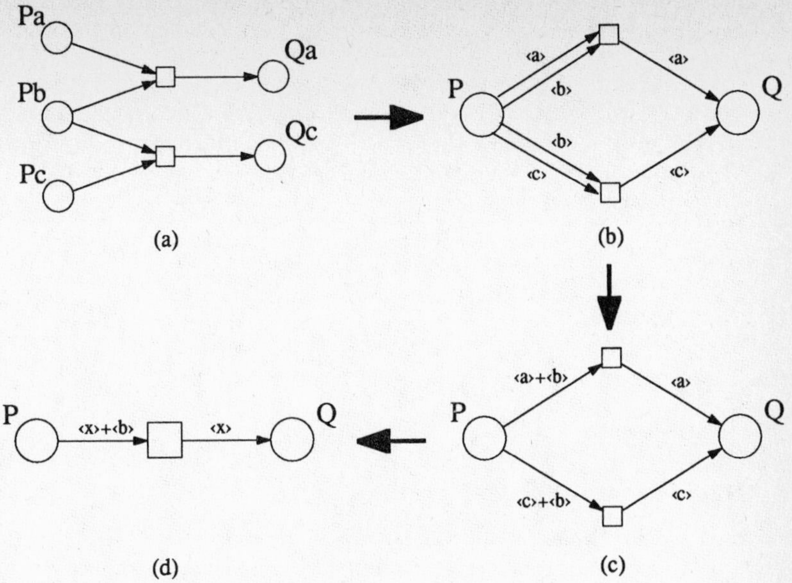

Figure 6: Notation for Multiple Arcs

In $\mathcal{L}(D)$, addition of two elements and multiplication of an element with an integer are defined in the straightforward way; additionally we define componentwise multiplication, as a generalisation of set intersection, and componentwise comparison.

Definition 2.7 Let $\lambda, \lambda_1, \lambda_2$ be in $\mathcal{L}(D)$ and z an integer. Then

1. $(\lambda_1 + \lambda_2) : x \mapsto \lambda_1(x) + \lambda_2(x) \quad (x \in D)$
2. $(z\lambda) : x \mapsto z\lambda(x) \quad (x \in D)$
3. $(\lambda_1 \sqcap \lambda_2) : x \mapsto \lambda_1(x) \cdot \lambda_2(x) \quad (x \in D)$
4. $\lambda_1 \leq \lambda_2 \iff \forall x \in X : \lambda_1(x) \leq \lambda_2(x)$

In chapter 5 where we look in detail at the linear algebraic properties of dynamic structures we shall see that by virtue of addition, multiplication and multiplication with a scalar, $\mathcal{L}(D)$ is a **Z**-linear algebra.

For annotating the arcs of PrT-nets we use symbolic sums denoting non-negative linear combinations.

Definition 2.8 Given a first-order language **L**, for each $n \geq 0$ a class $LC^{(n)}$ of *symbolic sums* of tuples of length n is defined in the following way.

1. The constant **0** is in $LC^{(n)}$.
2. If $v_1, \ldots, v_n$ are terms, then the n-tuple $\langle v_1, \ldots, v_n \rangle$ is in $LC^{(n)}$.
3. If l_1, l_2 are in $LC^{(n)}$, then $(l_1 + l_2)$ is in $LC^{(n)}$.
4. If l is in $LC^{(n)}$ and z is a non-negative integer, then zl is in $LC^{(n)}$.
5. No other expression is in $LC^{(n)}$.

The union of all classes $LC^{(n)}$ for $n \geq 0$ is designated by LC.

Each structure $\mathcal{R}$ assigns to a symbolic sum in $LC^{(n)}$ whose constituent tuples do not contain individual variables (that is closed) a linear combination in $\mathcal{L}^+(D^n)$ in the following way.

Definition 2.9 Given a structure $\mathcal{R}$ and a variable-free symbolic sum l in $LC^{(n)}$ for some $n \leq 0$, the value of l in $\mathcal{R}$ is an element of $\mathcal{L}(D^n)$, ie a linear combination of n-tuples of individuals, designated as $\mathcal{R}(l)$.

1. $\mathcal{R}(\mathbf{0})$ is $\mathbf{0}$.
2. If l is $\langle v_1, \ldots, v_n \rangle$ then for every $\langle d_1, \ldots, d_n \rangle \in D^n$, $\mathcal{R}(l)(d_1, \ldots, d_n) = 1$ iff $d_i = \mathcal{R}(v_i)$ for $1 \leq i \leq n$, and $\mathcal{R}(l)(d_1, \ldots, d_n) = 0$ otherwise.
3. If l is $(l_1 + l_2)$, $\mathcal{R}(l)$ is $\mathcal{R}(l_1) + \mathcal{R}(l_2)$.
4. If l is zl_1, $\mathcal{R}(l)$ is $z\mathcal{R}(l_1)$.

2.2 The Basic Form of PrT-Nets

We are now prepared to define, for a given first-order language $\mathbf{L}$, the class of *strict* predicate/transition nets with annotations in $\mathbf{L}$. It is that class of annotated nets that was used in the introduction for representing the railway system in its most abstract form (see figure 5). *Strict* means that we are not going to allow multiple occurrences of tuples on the places. The places represent variable relations, not multi-relations. Later we shall show how to weaken that restriction.

Definition 2.10 Let $\mathbf{L}$ be a first-order language and let $\mathbf{L}_s$ designate the sublanguage using only Π_s, the predicates denoting static relations. The class $PRT_{\mathbf{L}}$ consists of marked annotated nets, $MN = (N, A, M^0)$ where N is the underlying directed net, A is its *annotation* in $\mathbf{L}$, and M^0 is its *representative marking.*

1. N is a directed net, $N = (S, T; F)$.
2. A is the annotation of N, $A = (A_N, A_S, A_T, A_F)$ where
   (a) $A_N = \mathcal{R}$ is a first-order structure for $\mathbf{L}_s$ called the support of MN (it is the kind of legend that annotates the whole net rather than a particular element);
   (b) A_S is a bijection between the set of places, S, and the set of variable predicates, Π_v;
   (c) A_T is a mapping of the set of transitions, T, into the set of formulae (called transition *selectors*) that use only operators and static predicates (ie are in $\mathbf{L}_s$);
   (d) A_F is a mapping of the set of arcs, F, into the set of symbolic sums of tuples of terms of $\mathbf{L}$, LC, such that for an arc $(x, y) \in F$ leading into or out of a place s (ie $x = s$ or $y = s$) and n being the index of the predicate annotating s, $A_F(x, y)$ is in $LC^{(n)}$.
3. M^0 is a (*consistent*) marking of the places: it is a mapping that assigns to each place s in S a symbolic sum of tuples of constants such that if n is the index of the predicate annotating s, then $M^0(s)$ is in $LC^{(n)}$ and the value of $M^0(s)$, $\mathcal{R}(M^0(s))$, is a linear combination with coefficients being either 0 or 1, ie it is the characteristic function of a set.

Example 2.11 Figure 7 shows the representation of a simple resource management scheme for a group of $N \geq 2$ *agents* regulating the access to a common commodity. There are two access *modes*, either $\mathbf{s}$ = *shared* in which up to L agents may have access simultaneously, or $\mathbf{e}$ = *exclusive* in which only one agent at a time may have access.

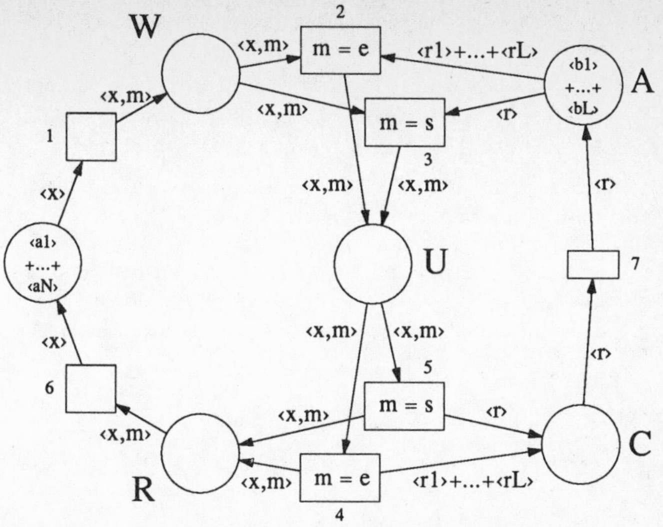

Legend: The support is $\mathcal{R} = (D; \mathbf{e}, \mathbf{s}; Ag, Tc, Md)$ where $D = Ag \cup Tc \cup Md$ with $Ag = \{a_1, \ldots, a_N\}$ being the agents, $Tc = \{b_1, \ldots, b_L\}$ being access tickets, and and $Md = \{\mathbf{e}, \mathbf{s}\}$ being the access modes.
The variable relations are:
Ix = agent x being idle, Wxm = agent x waiting for access in mode m, Uxm = agent x having access in mode m, Rxm = agent x having returned from access in mode m, Cr = access right r being closed, Ar = access right r being available.

Figure 7: Simple Resource Management Scheme as a PrT-net

2.3 The CE-Semantics of PrT-Nets

We now determine the denotation of a PrT-net $PN = (N, A, M^0)$ with $N = (S, T; F)$ and D designating the domain of the structure $A_N = \mathcal{R}$. It is a condition/event system $\Sigma(PN) = (B, E; F', [c^0])$ that is derived from PN in two steps. First, PN is unfolded into an *elementary net system* (see [21]), $\widehat{PN} = (\widehat{S}, \widehat{T}; \widehat{F}, \widehat{c}^0)$ (which corresponds to a place/transition system with all arc multiplicities and all place capacities being 1). The S-elements (conditions) of $\widehat{PN}$ are closed atomic formulae derived from the variable predicates annotating the places of PN. The T-elements (events) of $\widehat{PN}$ are 'feasible' instances of the transitions of PN. In the second step, $\widehat{PN}$ is first restricted to the subset of those events that have an occurrence in the full reachability class of $\widehat{PN}$; then it is simplified by abstracting from different elements with the same presets and postsets. The result is the CE-system $\Sigma(PN)$.

Definition 2.12 Let $t \in T$ be a transition of the PrT-net PN and $p = A_T(t)$ the formula annotating t (the selector of t). The set of all variables that occur in the tuples annotating the incident arcs, is called the *index* of t. Note that the set of variables that occur freely in p is not necessarily contained in the index of t. Those free variables of p that do not belong to the index of t will be called *dangling* variables in the sequel. They can be bound by existential quantifiers without changing the meaning of the annotation.
The index of a place s is defined to be the index of the annotating predicate, $A_S(s)$.

Definition 2.13 Let t, p be as above and let α be a substitution that replaces all variables in the index of t by constants. α is called *feasible* iff

1. α satisfies p, ie there is a substitution β replacing the dangling variables of p by constants such that $\mathcal{R}((p{:}\alpha){:}\beta) = \top$
2. α creates a set on every incident arc; for every place s and arc annotation $l = A_F(s,t)$ or $l = A_F(t,s)$, $\mathbf{0} \leq \mathcal{R}(l{:}\alpha) \leq \mathbf{1}$, ie $\mathcal{R}(l{:}\alpha)$ is a linear combination with coefficients being either 0 or 1, it is the characteristic function of a subset of D^n where n is the index of s.
3. α does not generate an impurity; for no s with both $(s,t) \in F$ and $(t,s) \in F$, there is a resulting tuple that occurs at both arcs: $\mathcal{R}(A_F(s,t){:}\alpha) \sqcap \mathcal{R}(A_F(t,s){:}\alpha) = \mathbf{0}$.

Definition 2.14 Let t, p be as above, and let α be a feasible substitution for t. Then the α-*instance* of t, designated by $t{:}\alpha$ is a pair of sets $({}^\bullet(t{:}\alpha), (t{:}\alpha)^\bullet)$ of closed atomic formulae.
A formula $Pd_1 \dots d_n$ is in ${}^\bullet(t{:}\alpha)$ iff there is a place s of PN such that $(s,t) \in F$ and

- s is annotated by P, $P = A_S(s)$;
- The coefficient of $\mathcal{R}(d_1 \dots d_n)$ in $\mathcal{R}(A_F(s,t){:}\alpha)$ equals 1.

A formula $Pd_1 \dots d_n$ is in $(t{:}\alpha)^\bullet$ iff there is a place s of PN such that $(t,s) \in F$ and

- s is annotated by P, $P = A_S(s)$;
- The coefficient of $\mathcal{R}(d_1 \dots d_n)$ in $\mathcal{R}(A_F(t,s){:}\alpha)$ equals 1.

The feasible instances of the transitions of PN are now put together to form an elementary net system $\widehat{PN} = (\widehat{S}, \widehat{T}; \widehat{F}, \widehat{c}^0)$ such that

- $\widehat{T}$ is the set of feasible instances of transitions of PN;
- $\widehat{S}$ is the set of all formulae belonging to the pre-set or post-set of a feasible instance, $\widehat{S} = \bigcup_{\widehat{t} \in \widehat{T}} ({}^\bullet\widehat{t} \cup \widehat{t}^\bullet)$;
- $\widehat{F}$ is derived from the pre/post-relation, $\widehat{F} = \bigcup_{\widehat{t} \in \widehat{T}} ({}^\bullet\widehat{t} \times \{\widehat{t}\} \cup \{\widehat{t}\} \times \widehat{t}^\bullet)$
- the representative case of $\widehat{PN}$, $\widehat{c}^0 \subseteq \widehat{S}$ is induced by the representative marking of PN, M^0: a condition of $\widehat{PN}$, $\widehat{s} = Pd_1 \dots d_n$, belongs to $\widehat{c}^0$ iff there is a place $s \in S$ annotated by $A_S(s) = P^{(n)}$ and the coefficient of $\mathcal{R}(\langle d_1, \dots, d_n \rangle)$ in $\mathcal{R}(M^0(s))$ equals 1.

The elementary net system $\widehat{PN}$ we have derived so far is almost a CE-system; however, there may be dead transitions that have no occurrence in any reachable case, and there may be several elements with same presets and postsets. The CE-system $\Sigma(PN)$ that we define as the denotation of the PrT-net PN is now the result of simplifying the restriction of $\widehat{PN}$ to the set of transitions that have an occurrence.

Definition 2.15 The denotation of the strict predicate/transition net PN is the condition/event system $\Sigma(PN) = (B, E; F', [c^0])$ which is derived from the EN system $\widehat{PN} = (\widehat{S}, \widehat{T}; \widehat{F}, \widehat{c}^0)$ in the following way.

1. Let $\widehat{T}'$ be set of transitions that have concession at some case in the full reachability class $[\widehat{c}^0]$.
2. Let $\widehat{PN}' = (\widehat{S}', \widehat{T}'; \widehat{F}', \widehat{c}'^0)$ be the restriction of $\widehat{PN}$ to $\widehat{T}'$.
3. Let two elements $\widehat{x}, \widehat{y}$ in $\widehat{X}' = \widehat{S}' \cup \widehat{T}'$ be equivalent – $\widehat{x} \sim \widehat{y}$ – iff ${}^\bullet\widehat{x} = {}^\bullet\widehat{y}$ and $\widehat{x}^\bullet = \widehat{y}^\bullet$.
Note that $\sim$ is a congruence relation with respect to $\widehat{F}'$ and $\widehat{c}'^0$; for $\widehat{x}_1 \sim \widehat{x}_2$ and $\widehat{y}_1 \sim \widehat{y}_2$ we have $(\widehat{x}_1, \widehat{y}_1) \in \widehat{F}' \iff (\widehat{x}_2, \widehat{y}_2) \in \widehat{F}'$ (by definition) and $\widehat{x}_1 \in \widehat{c}'^0 \iff \widehat{x}_2 \in \widehat{c}'^0$ (because dead transitions have been removed).
4. Let $\Sigma(PN) = (B, E; F', [c^0])$ be the quotient of $(\widehat{S}', \widehat{T}'; \widehat{F}', [\widehat{c}'^0])$ by $\sim$.

2.4 The Symbolic Transition Rule

The unfolding of PrT-nets defines their semantics as CE-systems. The purpose of PrT-nets, however, is not alone the more concise representation of CE-systems. Rather, structural and behavioural properties shall be studied, as much as possible, based on the PrT-net representation. A first step to this end is to introduce the 'symbolic token game' for PrT-nets such that unfolding procedure and token game commute.

Definition 2.16 Let $PN = (N, A, M^0) \in PRT_{\mathbf{L}}$ be a strict PrT-net with $A_N = \mathcal{R}$ being the supporting structure. Let M and M' be markings of PN (consistent with the arities of the annotating predicates and such that for all places s, $\mathcal{R}(M(s)) \leq \mathbf{1}$ and $\mathcal{R}(M'(s)) \leq \mathbf{1}$), let t be a transition and α a substitution replacing the variables of the index of t by constants. Then the *α-occurrence* of t at M leading to M' is designated as $M[t{:}\alpha\rangle_{\mathcal{R}}M'$ and defined by the following requirements.

1. α is a feasible substitution for t.
2. For all arcs (s,t) entering t, $\mathcal{R}(A_F(s,t){:}\alpha) \leq \mathcal{R}(M(s))$.
3. For all arcs (t,s) leaving t, $\mathcal{R}(A_F(t,s){:}\alpha) \sqcap \mathcal{R}(M(s)) = \mathbf{0}$.
4. For all places s, $\mathcal{R}(M'(s)) = (\mathcal{R}(M(s)) - \mathcal{R}(A_F(s,t){:}\alpha)) + \mathcal{R}(A_F(t,s){:}\alpha)$.

Two transitions t and t' may occur concurrently, in one *step*, for substitutions α respectively α' ($t = t'$ or $\alpha = \alpha'$ included) iff they both may occur and the instances $t{:}\alpha$ and $t'{:}\alpha'$ are independent (have disjoint pre-sets and post-sets).

The symbolic transition rule is consistent with the CE-semantics, ie the unfolding procedure and the occurrences of transitions commute. More precisely,

Lemma 2.17 Let $M[t{:}\alpha\rangle_{\mathcal{R}}M'$ as defined above. Then the unfolding of *PN* at M can be followed by an occurrence of an event with the same pre-set and same post-set as $t{:}\alpha$, and the result is the same as unfolding PN at M'.
Proof: Follows immediately from the definition of the unfolding procedure and the symbolic transition rule.

The formulation of the symbolic transition rule gives us an opportunity to end this chapter with a remark that might have come already at other occasions. One may view the variable relations as the magnitudes of a system whose current values determine the actual state of the system. Not only is the state of a Petri system a *distributed* state whose magnitudes may change independently; the magnitudes are 'distributed' as well. The current extension of a variable relation may be changed *concurrently* by several events.

3 Extensions of the Basic Form of PrT-nets

The basic form of predicate/transition nets was defined as a direct formal expression for the intuitive notion of dynamic structures. We will now provide PrT-nets with several generalisations to increase their modelling flexibility, power and conciseness in modelling systems as dynamic structures. The extensions are based upon different ideas which we try to keep clearly separated. The user of PrT-nets must decide very carefully which of the proposed generalisations he wants to adopt.

3.1 Many-sorted Structures

A first, obvious generalisation is the use of *many-sorted* structures. If we distinguish for a structure different sorts of individuals, the signature has to assign as indices not just numbers but strings of sort symbols to predicates and strings paired with a single sort symbol to operators indicating the distribution of domains. If A, B, C, D are sort symbols, for example, then $P^{(A,B,D)}$ denotes a relation in $(A{\times}B){\times}D$, and $F^{(A,C:B)}$ denotes a function from $A{\times}C$ into B.

In order not to overburden the formalism we continue using single-sorted structures. When desirable, static unary predicates will classify the individuals as we did in the example of the resource management scheme 2.11. In the next section, we shall see how to do this also for variable predicates.

3.2 More General Places

A considerable gain in flexibility of the PrT-net model can be achieved if we allow places to be merged or split in small portions. When folding the railway system in the introduction, there were intermediate stages at which the places represented only parts of the variable relation *is_occupied_by*. And the resource management scheme, figure 7, is much better to analyse by the linear algebraic technics developed in chapter 5 if the place U is split into two places Uxs and Uxe according to the mode of usage.

Splitting and merging places requires that any partition of a variable relation into disjoint places should be possible. To this end we allow a place to be annotated in a slightly more complicated way than in the basic form.

Notation 3.1 The generic annotation of a place s is $\pi|p$ where

- π is an atomic formula built from a variable predicate and constants and variables only (no compound terms); it is called the *predication* of the place s.
- p is a first-order formula in which no variable predicates occur; it is called the *selector* of s.

A place s annotated by $Pv_1 \dots v_n|p$ denotes that subset of the variable relation P that is contained in $\{\mathcal{R}(\langle v_1, \dots, v_n\rangle{:}\alpha) \mid \mathcal{R}(p{:}\alpha) = \top\}$.

In this way a variable relation may be partitioned arbitrarily into subsets each of which is represented by an extra place. For example, the relation U in the resource management scheme 2.11 may be split into two places $Uxm|m{=}\mathbf{s}$ and $Uxm|m{=}\mathbf{e}$. If the selector is trivial, ie valid in all structures, it may be dropped (see, for example, figure 4).

The consistency of the model requires that different places represent *disjoint* subsets of variable relations. This may be violated if the predications of two different places are derived from the same predicate. For example, $Pay|y{\neq}a$ and $Pxb|x{\neq}b$ are not disjoint but $Pay|\top$ and $Pby|\top$ are (a, b being constants).

Some care is needed concerning the arity (the index) of a place as in contrast with the index of the annotating variable predicate. The index of a place is defined as the set of variables occurring in the annotating predication, *ordered* by their first occurrences. For example, the index of $Pxayx$ is $\langle x, y\rangle$. The tuples in the marking of a place and at the incident arcs refer to this ordered index. Note the difference between $Pxayx|\top$ and $Pxzyx|z{=}a$ whose index is $\langle x, z, y\rangle$. The index is empty iff the place is annotated by a closed atomic formula (an elementary proposition).

The original form of annotating places by predicates only is considered as a shorthand for the common case where the whole variable relation is represented by a single place. For example, $P^{(3)}$ is a shorthand for $Px_1x_2x_3|\top$.

Tuples marking a place may not satisfy the selector. A pair $\langle a, \mathbf{e}\rangle$ put on a place annotated by $Uxm|m{=}\mathbf{s}$ is void. Putting it on a place annotated by $Ux\mathbf{s}|\top$, however, would be syntactically incorrect since the index is $\langle x\rangle$.

The more general way of annotating the places allows an alternative form of specifying the representative marking marking. Rather than writing down the set tuples explicitly as a symbolic sum, a formula in $\mathbf{L}_s$ (containing no variable predicates) may be used instead. Then the problem of void or syntactically incorrect tuples cannot occur. Let the marking of a place s be a formula m. If $\langle x_1, \ldots, x_n \rangle$ is the (ordered) index of place s, the actual marking of s is the set of all $\langle x_1, \ldots, x_n \rangle{:}\alpha$ where $\mathcal{R}((p \wedge m){:}\alpha) = \top$. The explicit listing of tuples is then a notational substitute for a corresponding formula.

The use of more general places requires a slight revision of the procedure that determines the CE-system being the denotation of a PrT-net. It concerns the way the pre- and post-sets of a feasible instance $t{:}\alpha$ are derived from the annotation of arcs. Some of the tuples given by the sum at an arc may be removed by the selector of the incident place.

Assume that l is annotating an arc (s,t) and the annotation of s is $P^{(n)}v_1 \ldots v_n | p$ with $\langle x_1, \ldots, x_k \rangle$ being the index. Then for some substitution β, $Pv_1 \ldots v_n{:}\beta$ belongs to $^{\bullet}t{:}\alpha$ iff both $p{:}\beta$ holds in $\mathcal{R}$ and the coefficient of $\mathcal{R}(\langle x_1, \ldots, x_k \rangle{:}\beta)$ in $\mathcal{R}(l{:}\alpha)$ equals 1.

One consequence of this is that the transitions of the PrT-net may no longer be *uniform* in the sense that all feasible instances of a transition have for every predicate the same number of state elements in their pre-sets and their post-sets. For example, some instances of an arc annotation $\langle x, y \rangle$ are void if the adjacent place is annotated by $Pxy | x \neq y$.

3.3 More General Arcs

The next extension is to increase the possibilities for merging events into transitions. In figure 7, the transitions 2 and 3 on top of place U have the same presets and same postsets of places. Furthermore they are intentionally closely related since they both represent ways of getting access to the commodity. They cannot be merged, however, because not all pairs of corresponding arcs are annotated by the same number of tuples.

The property that for a given arc of the PrT-net all instances of the respective transition yield the *same number* of conditions is called *uniformity*. It should not be given up easily. Rather there are good reasons to keep it. In particular, ordinary P/T-nets can be viewed as a special kind of uniform PrT-nets where the transitions ignore all differences between individuals.

To allow greater flexibility in merging transitions, we introduce arc selectors that work similarly to transition and place selectors. In the symbolic sums they appear as symbolic scalars, ie coefficients whose values depend on the truth value of a formula (1 for $\top$, 0 for $\bot$). Transition selectors can then be viewed as arc selectors that are common to all arcs around the transition.

Using such *conditional sums* we can equivalently transform the annotation of the arcs of transition 2 and 3 in figure 8(a) in a way that corresponding arcs are annotated identically; the transitions are *unified* (see figure 8(b)). The unified transitions can be merged into a single one whose selector is just the adjunction of the two original selectors (see figure 8(c)).

First we extend the class of expressions denoting linear combinations (definitions 2.8 and 2.9) by

- If l is in $LC^{(n)}$ and p is a formula, then $[p]l$ is in $LC^{(n)}$.
- If l is $[p]l_1$, $\mathcal{R}(l)$ is $\mathcal{R}(l_1)$ if $\mathcal{R}(p) = \top$ and $\mathbf{0}$ otherwise.

The symbolic coefficients derived from formulae are a kind of generalised *Kronecker* symbols: $\delta_{ij} \simeq [i{=}j]$. To stress their role as scalars, we treat them independently of the symbolic sums.

Definition 3.2 Let p be a closed formula. Then the value of $[p]$ in $\mathcal{R}$ is designated by $\mathcal{R}[p]$; it is defined such that $\mathcal{R}[p] = 1$ iff $\mathcal{R}(p){=}\top$ and $\mathcal{R}[p] = 0$ otherwise.
For two arbitrary formulae p, q, we call two symbolic scalars $[p]$ and $[q]$ equivalent – $[p] = [q]$ – if for all structures $\mathcal{R}$ and for all substitutions α such that $p{:}\alpha$ and $q{:}\alpha$ are closed, $\mathcal{R}[p{:}\alpha] = \mathcal{R}[q{:}\alpha]$.

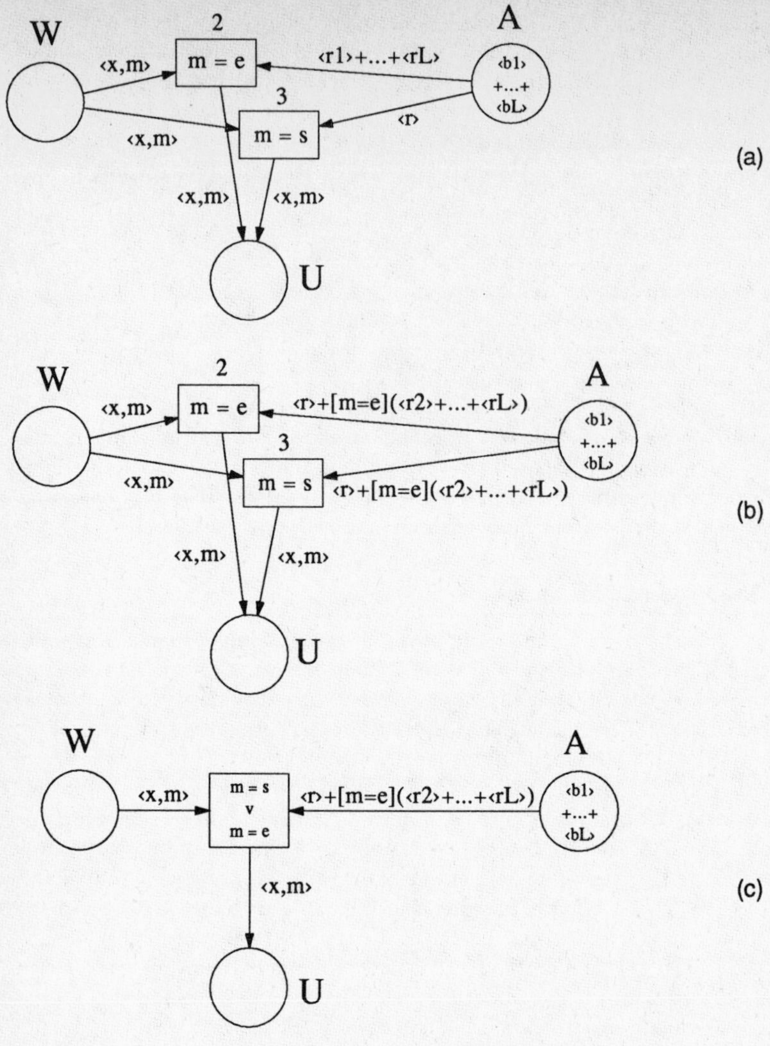

Figure 8: Unifying and Merging Non-uniform Transitions

From these definitions we get immediately some obvious rules for symbolic scalars and conditional sums.

Lemma 3.3 Let p, q be formulae. Then

1. $[\top] = 1$, $[\bot] = 0$
2. $[p] = [q]$ iff $p \Leftrightarrow q$
3. $[\neg p] = 1 - [p]$
4. $[p \wedge q] = [p][q]$
5. $[p \vee q] = [p] + [q] - [p][q]$
6. $[p]l_1 + [p]l_2 = [p](l_1 + l_2)$

7. $[p]l + [q]l = ([p] + [q])l$

Proof: The verification of these laws is straightforward.

3.4 Multi-Sets and the Weak Transition Rule

An object may belong to several sets at the same time but the notion *set* excludes that it occurs more than once in the same set. ($\{a,b\} \triangleq \{a\} \cup \{b\}$, hence $\{a,a\} = \{a\}$.) Therefore the feasibility constraint 2.13 for transition occurrences had to exclude those substitutions from being applicable that would put or take the same tuple more than once to respectively from a place.

The usual way of allowing multiple occurrences of an object at a place is to generalise the marking of places from sets to *multi-sets* (also called *bags*). Given a set D, a multi-set in D (or, more precisely, a multi-subset of D) is a function $B : D \to \mathbf{N}$, ie an element of $\mathcal{L}^+(D)$ as defined in 2.6.

The whole formalism of PrT-nets can be generalised easily from places representing sets to places representing multi-sets. The items 2 and 3 of 2.13 (feasibility) may be dropped, and the *strict* symbolic transition rule 2.16 is changed into the *weak* transition rule by dropping requirement 3 thus allowing arbitrarily many copies of a tuple on the same place.

Later we shall make extensive use of multi-sets when studying linear algebraic techniques for analysing PrT-nets. At this stage of the development, however, we take an alternative approach. We shall sketch an approach that treats PrT-nets marked by multi-sets as a *special* case, and not as a generalisation, of *strict* PrT-nets.

There are two reasons for doing so. Firstly, we want to demonstrate that *conceptually* there is no need for using multi-sets and the complication of the formalism that follows from it. Secondly, we have to show that multiple occurrences of an object on a place and the weak transition rule still allow a reduction to CE-systems and hence, do not lead us out of the realm of Petri systems.

Rather than counting the number of occurrences of an object in a multi-set we distinguish different copies of an object by attaching to it a *tag* that functions like the serial number of a bank-note. Tags are a special sort of individuals that have no structure and do not appear in formulae. We take the tags from the set of natural numbers, $\mathbf{N}$, and call, for example, the tagged object $\langle a,b\rangle.3$ the third copy of the object $\langle a,b\rangle$. ($\langle a,b\rangle.0$ may be called the original.)

Formally there is no difference between $\langle a,b\rangle.3$ and $\langle a,b,3\rangle$. Hence the use of tags means that a sort *tag* is appended to the index of each variable predicate.

In the same way, to each tuple occurring at an arc another variable has to be appended whose occurrence there is unique for the adjacent transition. Hence the transition occurrences will totally ignore the value of the tag that is assigned to it.

To stress this *don't-care* property of the tag variables, and to avoid using too many variables, their occurrences are indicated by a special *don't-care symbol* $\sim$. Each occurrence of $\sim$ represents an occurrence of a variable that occurs nowhere else at the respective transition. (This usage of $\sim$ is not restricted to tag variables.)

By appending tags, an arc annotation like $\langle x\rangle + \langle x\rangle$, or $2\langle x\rangle$ for short, that would not allow any feasible substitution becomes $\langle x,\sim\rangle + \langle x,\sim\rangle$, or equivalently, $2\langle x,\sim\rangle$. Any substitution that assigns different tags to the two different variables represented by the two occurrences of $\sim$ could be feasible, eg $\langle a,0\rangle + \langle a,7\rangle$.

In most cases of actual system modelling, the set of tags doesn't have to be $\mathbf{N}$ but some rather small number $n = \{0,\ldots,n-1\}$. One may even assign to each variable predicate a different number as tag sort indicating the upper bound for the number of copies of the same object that may occur on places annotated by that predicate. In this way we get a generalisation of the strict transition rule allowing more than one copy but restricting the number of copies to an upper bound.

The use of tags and don't-care symbols reduces PrT-nets with multi-sets as markings to strict PrT-nets. We don't have to leave ordinary set theory and logic. What is more important, PrT-nets with multi-sets have a denotation as CE-systems. They are standard models of net theory.

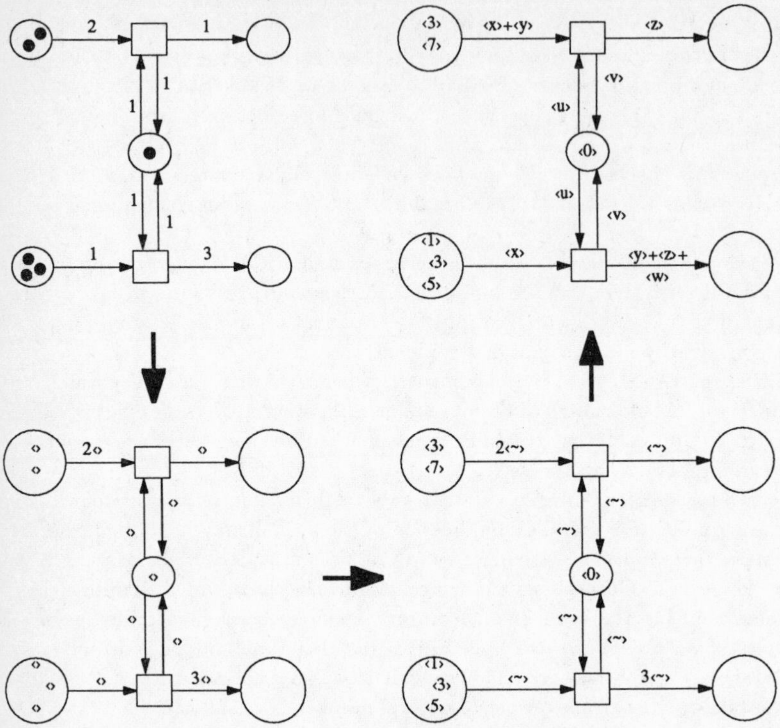

Figure 9: Semantics of PT-nets as CE-systems

Ordinary PT-nets in particular can be seen as a special class of PrT-nets with multi-sets where all places are 0-ary, ie the annotations of arcs and the marking the places are multiples of the zero-tuple $\langle\rangle$. By using tags, there are multiples of $\langle\sim\rangle$ at the arcs and sets of tags on the places. A place capacity n turns into the sort $n = \{0, \ldots, n-1\}$ of tags for that place.

An example of this transformation is shown in figure 9. In the first step, tokens are turned into 0-tuples; places become 0-ary multi-relations. In the next step, the 0-tuples at the places are distinguished by appending arbitrary but different tags and at the arcs, don't-care-symbols are introduced. Finally, the don't-care-symbols are replaced consistently by unique occurrences of variables. As in the original PT-net, the transitions of the PrT-net depend only the presence of tokens but not on their identity.

3.5 Place Projections

In this section we wish to reverse the operation of introducing tags and don't-care-symbols. Let $R = \{\langle a,b\rangle, \langle a,c\rangle, \langle b,c\rangle\}$ be a binary relation in the set $D = \{a,b,c\}$. If we are not interested in knowing which individuals occur at the second position of R, we may describe R as follows: R contains two pairs of the form $\langle a, \mathit{something}\rangle$ and one pair of the form $\langle b, \mathit{something}\rangle$. Using the don't-care symbol $\sim$ we write $R \in \{2\langle a,\sim\rangle, \langle b,\sim\rangle\}$ indicating that $\{2\langle a,\sim\rangle, \langle b,\sim\rangle\}$ denotes a whole family of relations of that form. More formally we have $R \in \{2\langle a,\sim\rangle, \langle b,\sim\rangle\}$ iff there are x_1, x_2, y such that $x_1 \neq x_2$ and $R = \{\langle a, x_1\rangle, \langle a, x_2\rangle, \langle b, y\rangle\}$. The affinity to cardinal numbers is obvious: $2 = |\{x \mid \langle a, x\rangle \in R\}|$ and $R \in \{|R|\langle\sim,\sim\rangle\}$.

If we are not interested in the details of the second position of R, we may eliminate this position as well. The idea is to introduce a kind of partial cardinal numbers that do not abstract totally from the identity of the elements of a set but only partially. We do so by means of an operation called *projection along the i-th position* and denoted by $|\ |_i$. As a result, we shall get $|R|_2 = \{2\langle a\rangle, \langle b\rangle\}$ and $||R|_2|_1 = \{3\langle\rangle\} \cong 3$.

Multi-sets and multi-relations may always be viewed as the result of projecting a relation along some position. For our purposes we define projections formally for linear combinations as defined in 2.6. It is important, however, to have finite supports only in order to avoid infinite multiplicities.

Definition 3.4 For $\mathcal{L}_{fin}(D_1, \ldots, D_n)$ $(n \geq 1)$, the *projection* of its elements *along the i-th position* $(1 \leq i \leq n)$ is defined such that for $\lambda \in \mathcal{L}_{fin}(D_1, \ldots, D_n)$,

$$|\lambda|_i \colon (x_1, \ldots, x_{i-1}, x_{i+1}, \ldots, x_n) \mapsto \sum_{y \in D_i} \lambda(x_1, \ldots, x_{i-1}, y, x_{i+1}, \ldots, x_n)$$

The *total projection* is denoted by $|\lambda|$: $|\lambda| = \sum_{D_1 \times \cdots \times D_n} \lambda(x_1, \ldots, x_n)$

It is easy to verify that $|\lambda|_i \in \mathcal{L}_{fin}(D_1, \ldots, D_{i-1}, D_{i+1}, \ldots, D_n)$, that $|\ |_i$, $|\ |$ are linear, and $||\lambda|_j|_i = ||\lambda|_i|_{j-1}$ for $n \geq 2$ and $1 \leq i < j \leq n$.

Example 3.5 For $\lambda = 2\langle a,b\rangle - 3\langle a,c\rangle + \langle b,c\rangle$,

$$\begin{aligned} |\lambda|_1 &= 2\langle b\rangle - 3\langle c\rangle + \langle c\rangle = 2\langle b\rangle - 2\langle c\rangle \\ |\lambda|_2 &= 2\langle a\rangle - 3\langle a\rangle + \langle b\rangle = -\langle a\rangle + \langle c\rangle \\ |\lambda| &= ||\lambda|_2|_1 = ||\lambda|_1|_1 = \mathbf{0} \end{aligned}$$

We will use the projection of linear combinations as a general means for abstracting from unnecessary or inconvenient details in a PrT-net. The idea is to project a place in order to introduce a partially quantitative view of the system. Tuples on a place that differ only at their *i–th* position are no longer distinguished but their occurrences are counted if $|\ |_i$ is applied to the place.

Projecting a place s means to eliminate the *i–th* position from its index. It is done in the following way.

1. Delete the *i–th* position in all tuples of the marking of s.

2. Delete the *i–th* position in all tuples annotating the arcs adjacent to s.

3. Prefix $|\ |_i$ to the annotation of s to indicate that the projection was applied.

As example, project the places A and C of the resource management scheme 7 along its first (and only) position. The tickets turn into tokens, the arc annotations become arc multiplicities, 1 or L. If projections are applied to a PrT-net it is assumed that the weak transition rule will be used such that projections commute with the occurrence of transitions. The result of totally projecting all places yields the merely quantitative presentation of a dynamic structure. If the PrT-net is uniform, its total projection is an ordinary PT-net. We have seen in the previous section that conversely, every PT-net can be viewed as the total projection of a strict PrT-net.

3.6 Structures as Parameters

The extensions to the PrT-net model introduced so far did not leave the concept of presenting a single dynamic structure as a PrT-net supported by a specific first-order structure $\mathcal{R}$. The last generalisation of the PrT-net model introduces a new layer of the presentation of dynamic structures. The idea is to use the structure $\mathcal{R}$ as a parameter of a family of similar dynamic structures.

To this end, we change the annotation A_N. Instead of a particular structure $\mathcal{R}$, it may carry a finite set of formulae, $\mathbf{A} \subseteq \mathbf{L}$, that specifies a whole class of $\mathbf{L}$-structures. For a given $\mathbf{L}$-structure $\mathcal{R}$ to be a feasible support, it must be a model of $\mathbf{A}$ (see 2.5).

Replacing a particular structure $\mathcal{R}$ by a set of formulae, however, does not yet accomplish the full job of parameterising a PrT-net. While the generic annotation of places introduced in section 3.2 in connection with marking formulae takes care of parameterised markings, the parameter L and the ellipsis "..." in figure 7 show that we may have to generate variables and certain expressions dependent on the domain of the actual structure $\mathcal{R}$. For example, the sum $\langle r_1 \rangle + \cdots + \langle r_L \rangle$ of ticket variables in figure 7 must be generated dependent on the number of tickets.

The use of indices for generating variables and of "..." for generating symbolic sums can be made formal by using the generalised +-operator $\sum_i^p E$ such that i is the variable bound by $\sum$, p is a formula specifying the range of i, and E is the argument expression. Then $\langle r_1 \rangle + \cdots + \langle r_L \rangle$ becomes $\sum_r^{\top} \langle r \rangle$. Furthermore, $\sum_r^{\top}([r \neq s]\langle s, r \rangle)$ is a *macro* operator (not an operator in the language $\mathbf{L}$) that assigns to every individual s the sum of all pairs $\langle s, r \rangle$ where $r \neq s$. Note that when this macro appears at the arc of a PrT-net (as in figure 16), it can be expanded once the domain of individuals has been fixed (at 'compile time') while $\sum_r^{r \neq s} \langle s, r \rangle$ could be expanded only after s has been fixed as well for the occurrence of the corresponding transition (at 'run time').

3.7 Other Formalisms for Structures

Rather than the formalism of first-order logical formulae and their structures, related ways of specifying the supporting structure and formulating annotations may be used. Examples could be a formalism for abstract data types or a data base description language.

4 Logical Invariants of PrT-Nets

When we chose first-order predicate logic as a model for introducing structured sets of individuals into net theoretical system modelling, it was not only a matter of taste. Rather, there is a kind of canonical relationship between net theory and logic which suggests to look for something of the kind of PrT-nets. It was first discovered by *Petri* when he set out to study net theoretical systems in terms of their *invariants* [16].

Petri defines the *enlogic structure* of a CE-system as the classification of all conceivable event-like elements in relation to the set of cases and the *synchronic structure* as the classification of all conceivable condition-like elements in relation to the set of processes. One such class of event-like elements is called *facts* and defined as those elements that at no reachable case would have concession (that are *dead*). Facts correspond to *invariant* propositions that hold at all cases although their constituents (the atoms are the conditions) may vary from case to case. And conversely, every such proposition corresponds to a set of facts.

The net representation of propositions yields a graphical calculus for propositional logic which was lifted to first-order predicate logic before the PrT-net model was found.[1,4,22] We shall now see that PrT-nets are those transition nets whose dead transitions have the power to express all first-order logical invariant assertions. The language of PrT-nets allows to formulate both the dynamic and the static properties of dynamical relational structures.

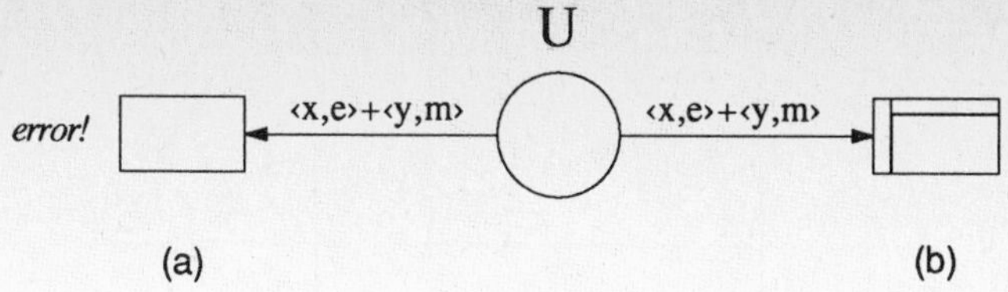

Figure 10: Mutual Exclusion Property Specified as a Dead Transition

4.1 Dead Transitions and Universal Invariants

Let us take the resource management scheme 2.11 as an example. The main restriction to the un-coordinated behaviour of the set of agents is the requirement that when one agent has exclusive access to the common commodity, no other agent may have access in either mode at the same time. We can formulate this requirement as a logical formula that must hold at all reachable markings.

◰ $(\forall x)[Ux\mathbf{e} \rightarrow \neg(\exists y)(\exists m)((y\neq x \vee m\neq\mathbf{e}) \wedge Uy\,m)]$

By prefixing the ◰ symbol we indicate that the formula is to hold at all reachable markings. It is the symbol for facts introduced by *Petri* and an instance of the necessity operator of modal logic (see eg [8]) which is often written as □. Here it is a shorthand for the universal quantifier $(\forall M\in[M^0])$ (which is *not* part of the first-order language **L**). An expression of the form ◰p where p is a formula of the first-order language **L** is called a *logical invariant* or, in the context of this chapter where no other invariants will be considered, just *invariant*.

Now assume that we want to add to the resource management scheme an error check that would issue a message whenever it detects a violation of the mutual exclusion requirement. In the PrT-net model of the scheme we could represent this check by a transition labelled by *error!* as shown in part (a) of figure 10. Obviously, this transition is not supposed to have concession at any reachable marking. Rather, if, and only if, the error transition is dead, the design of the system will be called correct with respect to the requirement.

In the sequel we shall indicate dead transitions by the ◰ symbol as in part (b) of figure 10. Normally we will not indicate, however, whether the ◰ transition is actually dead with respect to the class of reachable markings or not. All elements of a net theoretical model are to specify certain properties, and we do not demand that the elements of a specification are independent of each other.

If we add part (b) of figure 10 to the net in figure 2.11, we can easily derive from the control mechanism using access tickets that the transition is dead. As a specification, the ◰ transition would be redundant. If the ◰ transition replaces the control mechanism, however, it represents the mutual exclusion property without specifying a particular control mechanism. It tells that the class of system states is the class of those markings reachable by the transition rule at which the ◰ transition has no concession. In this sense, the ◰ transition and the ◰ formula have exactly the same meaning. They both represent the mutual exclusion property.

In chapter 5 we will study one particular technique of verifying such specifications. In this chapter, however, we are concerned with the expressive power of dead transitions.

To start with, we give a precise formulation to our observation that dead transitions are invariants.

Theorem 4.1 Every dead transition of a PrT-net *MN* represents a formula that holds at all reachable markings of *MN*; it is a logical invariant of *MN*.

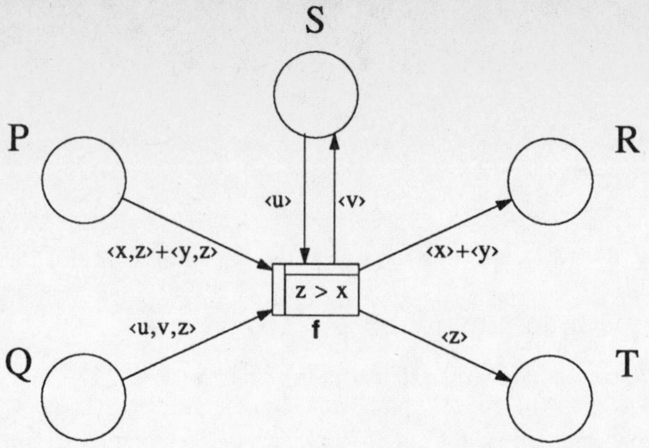

Figure 11: Universal Invariant Expressed by a Dead Transition

Proof: To avoid too complicated a formalism, let us consider a (totally meaningless) example that is general enough to show us all relevant aspects. It is shown in figure 11. The places are assumed to belong to a PrT-net *MN* with the marking class $[M^0]$. From the (strict) transition rule for PrT-nets (see 2.16) follows immediately that transition f is dead iff at all $M \in [M^0]$ and for all substitutions $\alpha = \{u \leftarrow u_0, v \leftarrow v_0, x \leftarrow x_0, y \leftarrow y_0, z \leftarrow z_0\}$, at least one of the following criteria applies.

1. α is not feasible (see 2.13);
2. there is at some incoming arc (s, f) a resulting tuple that does not belong to $M(s)$;
3. there is at some outgoing arc (s, f) a resulting tuple that belongs already to $M(s)$.

Consequently, the dead transition f represents the invariant

$$\Box(\forall u, v, x, y, z)[\underbrace{\neg(z{>}x \wedge x{\neq}y \wedge u{\neq}v)}_{1.} \vee \underbrace{(\neg Pxz \vee \neg Pyz \vee \neg Quvz \vee \neg Su)}_{2.} \vee \underbrace{(Sv \vee Rx \vee Ry \vee Tz)}_{3.}]$$

To study the consequences of this result we first collect some material known from logic.

A formula is said to be *open* if it contains no quantifiers. A formula p is said to be in *prenex form* if it has the form $(Q_1x_1)\ldots(Q_nx_n)q$ where the (Q_ix_i) are quantifiers and q is open. The part $(Q_1x_1)\ldots(Q_nx_n)$ is called the *prefix* and q the *matrix* of p.

Proposition 4.2 For every formula p exists a logically equivalent formula p' in prenex form.

For example, the formula $(\forall x)(\forall y)(\forall m)(\neg Ux\mathbf{e} \vee \neg Uym \vee (y{=}x \wedge m{=}\mathbf{e}))$ is a prenex form of the mutual exclusion property. Although the original formula contains an existential quantifier, the prefix of the prenex form contains only universal quantifiers.

If a formula in prenex form contains only universal quantifiers, it is called *universal.* We call an invariant $\Box p$ universal if p is universal.

An (open) formula q is said to be in *conjunctive form* if it has the form $q_1 \wedge \ldots \wedge q_m$ where each q_j is a disjunction of *literals.* (A literal is an atomic or negated atomic formula.)

Proposition 4.3 For every open formula q exists a logically equivalent formula q' in conjunctive form.

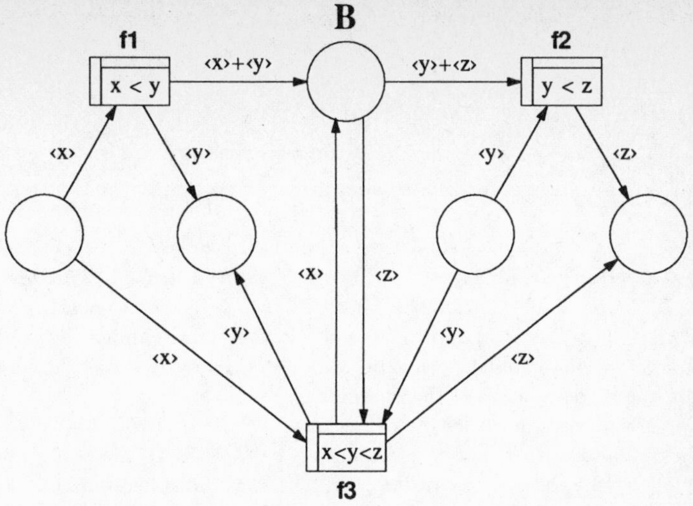

Figure 12: Mechanical Derivation of a Dead Transition

To begin our study of invariants, we state two obvious laws that show that the rules of first-order logic for inferring formulae from given ones can be also applied to invariants.

Proposition 4.4 For every PrT-net *MN* and two formulae p, q we have

1. If $\Box p$ holds for *MN* and p implies q, $\Box q$ holds for *MN*.
2. If both $\Box p$ and $\Box q$ hold for *MN*, $\Box(p \wedge q)$ holds for *MN*. (The converse follows from 1.)

This simple fact allows to derive new dead transitions from given ones in a mechanical manner. An example of applying the *cut* rule (resolution) is shown in figure 12. The places are assumed to belong to some PrT-net. Whenever transitions f_1 and f_2 are dead, transition f_3 will be dead as well. f_3 is the ***resolvent*** of f_1 and f_2. It is the result of merging f_1 and f_2 where the 'bridge' By is eliminated. The selector of f_3 is the conjunction of the selectors of f_1 and f_2 (in contrast with the merging of similar transitions where the selectors have to be $\vee$–ed; see figure 8).

It is now not difficult to see that universal invariants are of particular importance for us.

Theorem 4.5 Every universal invariant $\Box p$ of a PrT-net *MN* can be expressed by a finite set of dead transitions in *MN*.
Proof: Since p is universal, $\Box p$ has a form $\Box \mathcal{Q}(q_1 \wedge \ldots \wedge q_m)$ where $\mathcal{Q}$ is the prefix containing only universal quantifiers and the q_j are disjunctive clauses. Hence it follows from proposition 4.4 that $\Box p$ is logically equivalent to the set of invariants $\{\Box \mathcal{Q}q_1, \ldots, \Box \mathcal{Q}q_m\}$.

For each $\Box \mathcal{Q}q_j$ we add to the net *MN* a transition f_j in the following way: q_j is divided into two parts, $q_j \Leftrightarrow (c_j \vee v_j)$ where c_j is the disjunction of all literals in q_j that are built from static predicates and v_j is the disjunction of all literals in q_j that are built from variable predicates. The negation of the constant part, $\neg(c_j)$, becomes the selector annotating f_j. For each negated literal in v_j of the form $P^{(n)}u_1 \ldots u_n$, an arc is inserted leading from the place P to f_j and annotated by $\langle u_1, \ldots, u_n \rangle$. For each non-negated literal in v_j of the form $P^{(n)}u_1 \ldots u_n$, an arc is inserted leading from f_j to the place P and annotated by the tuple $\langle u_1, \ldots, u_n \rangle$. Multiple arcs are merged using symbolic sums.

From theorem 4.1 we know that f_j is dead in *MN* iff q_j holds at all reachable markings. Hence $\Box p$ and the set of dead transitions $f_1, \ldots, f_m$ are equivalent.

With this result at hand, what remains to do is to study the general case where for an invariant $\Box p$, the prefix of p (in prenex form) contains an existential quantifier.

4.2 Existential Invariants and Skolem Places

In ordinary predicate logic where we don't have variable predicates, every formula p in prenex form can be translated into a universal formula by eliminating, step by step, the existential quantifiers in the following way.

Let p be $(\forall x_1)\ldots(\forall x_n)(\exists y)\mathcal{Q}'q$. Let $\tilde{y}^{(n)}$ be a new n-ary operator (called *Skolem* operator) that is added to the given vocabulary of $\mathbf{L}$. Then p is valid in some $\mathbf{L}$-structure $\mathcal{R}$ iff there is an extension of $\mathcal{R}$, $\mathcal{R}'$ by a function interpreting the *Skolem* operator $\tilde{y}$ such that the formula $(\forall x_1)\ldots(\forall x_n)\mathcal{Q}'q{:}\{y{\leftarrow}\tilde{y}(x_1,\ldots,x_n)\}$ is valid there. (Rather than eliminating $(\exists y)$, it would be more correct to say that the explicit occurrence of $(\exists y)$ is removed and replaced by an implicit occurrence within the interpretation of the operator $\tilde{y}$).

Unfortunately, this procedure no longer works once we prefix a formula containing variable predicates by the modal operator $\Box$. Since $\Box$ stands for $(\forall M{\in}[M^0])$, the Skolem operator $\tilde{y}$ had to be $(n+1)$-ary depending at its first position on markings. In other words, it would denote a *variable* function. However, we do not consider dynamic structures with variable functions. The global constraint to the occurrence of transitions needed for maintaining variable functions would be inconsistent with the whole PrT-net approach.

There may be systems where some variable relation has the invariant property of being a function. However, then we are back again at the same question. How to express in net theoretical terms that, for example, Z denotes the graph of a variable binary function, ie how to express the invariant $\Box(\forall x)(\forall y)(\exists z)(\forall z')(Z x\, y\, z \wedge (Z x\, y\, z' \rightarrow z{=}z'))$.

The second part of this requirement, the uniqueness of the value for every pair of arguments, is a universal invariant $\Box(\forall x)(\forall y)(\forall z)(\forall z')((Z x\, y\, z \wedge Z x\, y\, z') \rightarrow z{=}z')$. It can be expressed by a dead transition.

For the first, existential, part we remember that the existential quantifier $\exists$ is a generalisation of the logical $\vee$. For a finite domain of individuals, $D = \{d_1,\ldots,d_n\}$, the formula $(\forall x)(\forall y)(\exists z)Z x\, y\, z$ is equivalent to the universal formula $(\forall x)(\forall y)(Z x\, y\, d_1 \vee \ldots \vee Z x\, y\, d_n)$ which may be written as $(\forall x)(\forall y)(\bigvee_{i=1,\ldots,n} Z x\, y\, d_i)$. It can be expressed by the dead transition shown in figure 13(a). In the same way as $\vee$ is generalised to $\exists$ (another notation is $\bigvee$), the symbolic $+$ can be generalised to $\sum$ as we suggested already in section 3.6. This is shown in parts (b) and (c) of figure 13.

This way of expressing $\exists$ by $\sum$, however, does still not enable us to express existential invariants in general. The *Skolem* operators allow one to separate the different disjunctive clauses of the conjunctive form of the matrix. While for example, $(\forall x)(\exists y)(P x\, y \wedge Q x\, y)$ is not equivalent to $((\forall x)(\exists y)P x\, y) \wedge (\forall x)(\exists y)Q x\, y)$, the formula $(\forall x)(P x\, \tilde{y}(x) \wedge Q x\, \tilde{y}(x))$ can be equivalently split into $(\forall x)(P x\, \tilde{y}(x)$ and $(\forall x)(Q x\, \tilde{y}(x)$.

However, there is a way of revising the procedure of eliminating $\exists$ quantifiers by using additional predicates rather than operators. Again, the $\exists$'s are not really eliminated; rather, they are brought into a special form such that we can express them by $\sum$ and separate several disjunctive subformulae.

Proposition 4.6 Let p be $(\forall x_1)\ldots(\forall x_n)(\exists y)\mathcal{Q}'q$. Let $Y^{(n+1)}$ be a new $(n+1)$-ary predicate that we call *Skolem* predicate and add to the given vocabulary. Then p is valid in some $\mathbf{L}$-structure $\mathcal{R}$ iff there is an extension of $\mathcal{R}$, $\mathcal{R}'$, by a relation interpreting the *Skolem* predicate Y such that the formulae $(\forall x_1)\ldots(\forall x_n)(\exists y)Y x_1 \ldots x_n\, y$ and $(\forall x_1)\ldots(\forall x_n)(\forall y)\mathcal{Q}'(Y x_1 \ldots x_n\, y \rightarrow q)$ are both valid in $\mathcal{R}'$.

If the matrix q has the form $q_1 \wedge \ldots \wedge q_m$, the transformed matrix, $(Y x_1 \ldots x_n\, y \rightarrow q)$, is logically equivalent to $(\neg Y x_1 \ldots x_n\, y \vee q_1) \wedge \ldots \wedge (\neg Y x_1 \ldots x_n\, y \vee q_m)$.

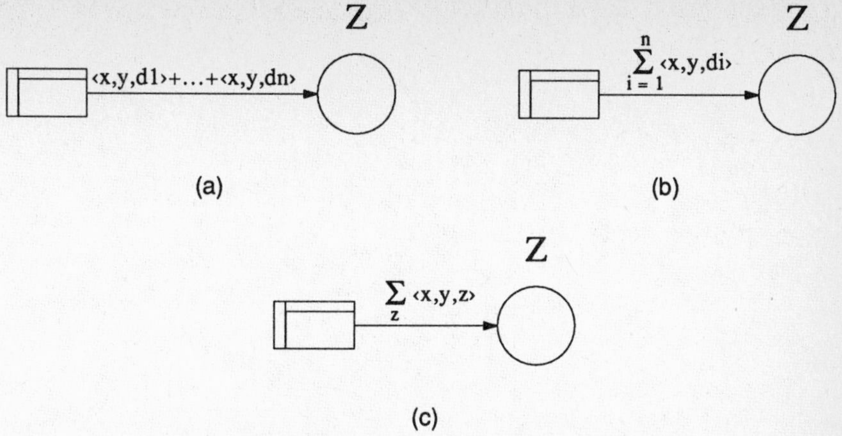

Figure 13: Generalised + for Existential Invariants

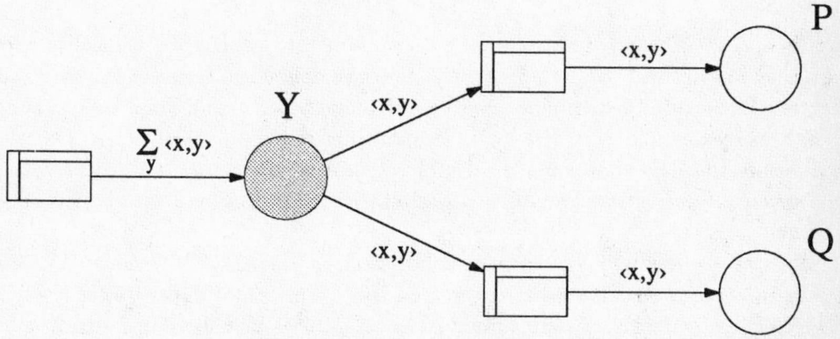

Figure 14: Existential Invariant Expressed by a Set of Dead Transitions

The revised procedure solves both our problems. It can be applied to the invariant $\Box p$ in like manner if we only require that the *Skolem* predicate Y denotes a *variable* relation. And it yields the two invariants $\Box(\forall x_1)\ldots(\forall x_n)(\exists y)Y x_1 \ldots x_n\, y$ and $\Box(\forall x_1)\ldots(\forall x_n)(\forall y)Q'(Y x_1 \ldots x_n\, y \rightarrow q)$ such that the existential invariant concerning Y can be expressed by a dead transition.

For example, the invariant $\Box(\forall x)(\exists y)(P x\, y \wedge Q x\, y)$ is translated into the set of three invariants, $\Box(\forall x)(\exists y)Y x\, y$, $\Box(\forall x)(\forall y)(\neg Y x\, y \vee P x\, y)$, and $\Box(\forall x)(\forall y)(\neg Y x\, y \vee Q x\, y)$. They are shown as dead transitions in figure 14 where the places P and Q are assumed to belong to a PrT-net but the place Y is added.

To summarise, we have arrived at the main result of this chapter.

Theorem 4.7 Every first-order logical invariant $\Box p$ can be expressed by a finite set of dead transitions using a finite number of *Skolem* places.

There is still one open question, however. We have to introduce new predicates Y that have no interpretation as variable relations in the original dynamic structure and do not appear as places in the PrT-net *MN*. They are added to *MN* together with the dead transitions expressing the invariant. What is their marking?

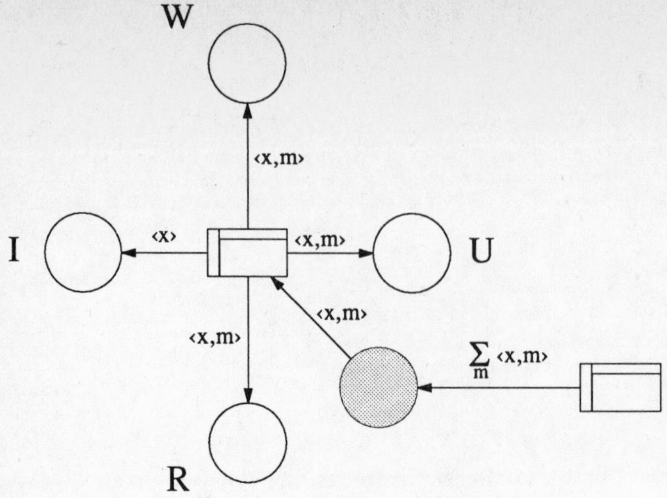

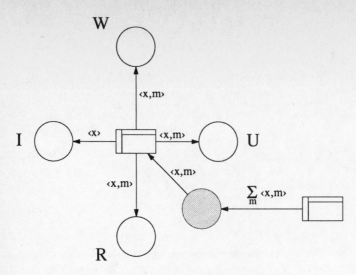

Figure 15: Example of an Existential Invariant

The answer is that the *Skolem* predicates are not *independent* variable predicates like the original ones. Rather, they are derived, virtual, predicates that are defined in terms of the given (independent) predicates. The kind of dependency can be left unspecified in the same way as the identity of individuals whose existence is stated by an $\exists$ quantifier is left unspecified. However, we may also specify it using the device of a place selector introduced in section 3.2 – but with a twist. The selector may contain not only operators and static predicates but variable (independent!) predicates as well.

As an example, take the obvious property of the resource management scheme 2.11 that every agent is always in some state. It can be expressed by the invariant $\Box(\forall x)(Ix \vee (\exists m)(Wxm \vee Uxm \vee Rxm))$ or, equivalently, by the subnet of dead transitions shown in figure 15. To verify the claim that the transitions are actually dead, define the *Skolem* place by annotating it with the selector $((Ix \wedge m{=}\mathbf{e}) \vee Wxm \vee Uxm \vee Rxm)$.

To end this chapter with, let us discuss what we have achieved. We have shown that the expressive power of dead transitions of a PrT-net is as strong as it could be. We are able to express every first-order logical invariant of a dynamic structure by a finite set of dead transitions. (Note that this power does not depend on annotating the transitions with first-order logical selectors. Rather, by representing the static relations of the supporting structure $\mathcal{R}$ of a PrT-net by places with constant markings, the selectors can be translated into net structure as well. This was done in [4]. It then follows that an invariant is contradictory iff from its representation as a set of selector-free dead transitions, the isolated transition can be derived.)

We do not suggest, however, to always translate invariants into dead transitions. Our main reason for assigning a net theoretic interpretation to every formula prefixed by the modal symbol $\Box$ was to make sure that it can be used safely, beyond any doubt about its meaning, for expressing an invariant property of a PrT-net. In addition, the translation into dead transition yields a decomposition of an arbitrary logical invariant into a set of elementary net theoretic system invariants.

5 Linear Algebraic Analysis of PrT-nets

The transition rules for ordinary PT-nets as well as for PrT-nets show that the occurrences of transitions have the following linearity property.

- The effects of the occurrences of a transition on markings are *independent* of the markings at which the transition occurs:
  $M_1[t\rangle M_2$ and $M_1'[t\rangle M_2'$ imply $M_2 - M_1 = M_2' - M_1'$ (where t is a (feasible instance of a) transition and $-$ denotes componentwise subtraction).

Let for the moment C^t denote this effect of a transition t. Then we get immediately:

- The total effect of several transition occurrences in a process is the *sum* of the individual effects; $M_1[t_1\rangle M_2[t_2\rangle M_3$ implies $M_3 - M_1 = (M_2 - M_1) + (M_3 - M_2) = C^{t_1} + C^{t_2}$.

In this chapter we want to exploit this linearity property for the analysis of PrT-nets. We will try to unify several approaches taken by *Genrich&Lautenbach* [2,3], *Jensen* [9], *Reisig* [18], and *Lautenbach&Pagnoni* [14].

5.1 Some Basic Mathematics

Before we start developing linear algebraic methods for analysing Petri systems modelled by PrT-nets we collect some basic notions and results we shall use throughout this chapter. Details can be found, for example, in [12].

Notation 5.1 For two sets A, B we designate the set of all functions of A into B as $[A \rightarrow B]$. For $B = \mathbf{N}$ or $B = \mathbf{Z}$, $[A \rightarrow B]_{fin}$ designates the set of all functions of A into B with *finite support*, ie with only finitely many elements of A having an image different from 0. (See also definition 2.6.)

There are two kinds of mathematical structures that are central to this chapter: rings and modules.

Definition 5.2 A *ring* is a set R provided with *addition* $(x, y) \mapsto x+y$, *multiplication* $(x, y) \mapsto x\,y$, and two constants 0,1 satisfying the following conditions:

1. Under addition, R is an abelian group with unit element 0. For all $x, y, z \in R$ we have
   - $(x + y) + z = x + (y + z)$ (*associativity*)
   - $x + y = y + x$ (*commutativity*)
   - $x + 0 = 0 + x = x$ (*unit element*)
   - There is an element x', usually designated as $-x$ such that $x + x' = 0$ (*inverse*)
2. Under multiplication, R is a momoid with unit element 1. For all $x, y, z \in R$ we have
   - $(xy)z = x(yz)$ (*associativity*)
   - $x1 = 1x = x$ (*unit element*)
3. For all $x, y, z \in R$ we have
   - $(x + y)z = xz + yz$ and $x(y + z) = xy + xz$ (*distributivity*)

R is called a *commutative* if multiplication is commutative.

Examples of rings are:

1. The integers $\mathbf{Z}$ (commutative).

2. For $n \geq 1$, the integer n, n-matrices.

3. The set of polynomials in several formal parameters $x_1, \ldots, x_n$ with integer coefficients (commutative).

Definition 5.3 Let R be a ring. A *(left) module over* R, or R-module, is a set M with addition $(v, w) \mapsto v{+}w$ and (left) multiplication by elements of R (called *scalars*), $(i, v) \mapsto i\,v$, satisfying the following conditions ($i, j \in R$ and $v, w \in M$).

1. Under addition, M is an abelian group.
2. $(ij)v = i(jv)$
3. For 1 being the unit element of multiplication in R, $1\,v = v$.
4. $(i + j)v = iv + jv$ and $i(v + w) = iv + iw$.

Definition 5.4 Let R be a commutative ring. A *R-linear algebra*, also called just R-algebra or algebra over R, is a R-module A which is provided with *multiplication* $(v, w) \mapsto v\,w$ satisfying the following conditions:

1. Under addition and multiplication, A is a ring.
2. For all $v, w \in A$ and $i \in R$, $i\,(v\,w) = (i\,v)\,w = v\,(i\,w)$.

Note that a ring R can be viewed as a R-module and a commutative ring can be viewed as a R-algebra. Another example of a R-algebra, for $R = \mathbf{Z}$, is $\mathcal{L}(D)$ with multiplication $\sqcap$ (see definition 2.7).

The modules in this chapter are all built according to the following scheme. We start with the ring of integers, $\mathbf{Z}$, and construct 'higher-order' $\mathbf{Z}$-modules by using the elements of a given $\mathbf{Z}$-module as entries for *vectors* and *matrices*.

Definition 5.5 Let R be ring, let M be a R-module, and let X, Y be arbitrary sets.

· A mapping $v{:}X \to M$ is called a *X-vector* over M.

· A mapping $F{:}X{\times}Y \to M$ is called a *X, Y-matrix* over M.

For vectors and matrices we define addition and multiplication by scalars as componentwise addition and multiplication by scalars in M. For $v, w{:}X \to M$, $F, G{:}X{\times}Y \to M$ and $i \in R$ we have

· $(v{+}w){:}x \mapsto v(x){+}w(x)$ and $(i\,v){:}x \mapsto i\,v(x)$ for $x \in X$,

· $(F{+}G){:}(x, y) \mapsto F(x, y){+}G(x, y)$ and $(i\,F){:}(x, y) \mapsto i\,F(x, y)$ for $x \in X, y \in Y$.

Note that in the special case that $M = R = \mathbf{Z}$, the set of X-vectors over M is the same as $\mathcal{L}(X)$ and the set of X, Y-matrices is $\mathcal{L}(X, Y)$ (linear combinations with integer coefficients as defined in 2.6).

Proposition 5.6 Let R be ring, let M be a R-module, and let X, Y be arbitrary sets. Under addition and multiplication by scalars, the set of X-vectors over M and the set of X, Y-matrices over M are R-modules.

Notation 5.7 For X-vectors and X, Y-matrices over a R-module M we use the following notations (vector v, matrix F, $x \in X, y \in Y$).

· 0 denotes the unit element of addition in M.

- $\mathbf{0}$ is the constant vector, $\mathbf{0}{:}X{\rightarrow}\{0\}$, respectively the constant matrix, $\mathbf{0}{:}X{\times}Y{\rightarrow}\{0\}$.
- $v_x = v(x)$ denotes the x-th entry of the vector v.
- F_x denotes the x-th *row* of the matrix F (when considered in the usual way as an rectangular array); it is a single-row matrix.
- F^y denotes the y-th *column* of F; it is a single-column matrix. A vector may always be viewed as a single-column matrix, and vice versa. Note that the X,Y-matrices can also be viewed as Y-vectors over the R-module of X-vectors, $[X{\times}Y{\rightarrow}M] \simeq [Y{\rightarrow}[X{\rightarrow}M]]$.
- $F_x^y = (F^y)_x$ denotes x,y-th entry of F.
- $F^\top{:}Y{\times}X{\rightarrow}M$ with $(F^\top)_y^x = F_x^y$ is the *transpose* of F.

If M is also a R-algebra with 1 denoting its unit under multiplication, we have:

- $\mathbf{1}$ denotes the constant vector, $\mathbf{1}{:}X{\rightarrow}\{1\}$.
- $\mathbf{e}^{(u)}$ is the u-th unit vector, $\mathbf{e}^{(u)}{:}x \mapsto [x{=}u]$ $(x \in X)$. (Hence $v = \sum_x v_x \mathbf{e}^{(x)}$.)

Normally the use of vectors and matrices implies that M is a R-algebra and X, Y and Z are *finite* sets. We then have:

- For two X-vectors v and w, the *scalar product* of v and w is defined as $v{\cdot}w = \sum_{x\in X} v_x\, w_x$.
- For two matrices $F{:}X{\times}Y{\rightarrow}M$ and $G{:}Y{\times}Z{\rightarrow}M$, the *(matrix) product* of F and G is the matrix $F\,G{:}X{\times}Z{\rightarrow}M$ defined by $(F\,G)_x^z = \sum_y F_x^y G_y^z$ (the scalar product of $(F_x)^\top$ and G^z). Note that $v{\cdot}w = v^\top\, w$ (vector v being viewed as a single-column matrix).

The main role of matrices is to serve as representations of *linear mappings* between modules.

Definition 5.8 Let R be a ring and M, M' be two R-modules. A function $f{:}M{\rightarrow}M'$ is called *R-linear* – designated as $f{:}M \overset{lin}{\rightarrow} M'$ – iff for all $i \in R$ and $v,w \in M$,
$f(v{+}w) = f(v){+}f(w)$ and $f(iv) = if(v)$.
If in particular $M' = R$, f is called a *linear form*.

Proposition 5.9 Let R be a ring, M, M' be two R-modules, and $f{:}M \overset{lin}{\rightarrow} M'$. The set of elements $v \in M$ for which $f(v) = 0$ (the *kernel* of f) is a submodule of M.

Proposition 5.10 If M is a the module of X-vectors over a ring R, a linear mapping $f{:}M \overset{lin}{\rightarrow} M'$ is uniquely determined by the values it takes on the unit vectors of M. For every vector $v \in M$, $f(v) = f(\sum_x v_x \mathbf{e}^{(x)}) = \sum_x v_x f(\mathbf{e}^{(x)})$.

Definition 5.11 For a mapping $g{:}X{\rightarrow}M'$, the R-linear mapping $f{:}[X{\rightarrow}R] \overset{lin}{\rightarrow} M'$ with $f(\mathbf{e}^{(x)}) = g(x)$ is called the *linear extension* of g.

Proposition 5.12 Let R be a ring and X,Y be finite sets. A R-linear mapping f of the module of X-vectors into the module of Y-vectors, $f{:}[X{\rightarrow}R] \overset{lin}{\rightarrow} [Y{\rightarrow}R]$, can be represented, in a unique manner, by a matrix $F{:}Y{\times}X{\rightarrow}R$ such that for all $v \in [X{\rightarrow}R]$, $f(v) = F\,v$.
Conversely, every matrix $F{:}Y{\times}X{\rightarrow}R$ represents a R-linear mapping $f{:}[X{\rightarrow}R] \overset{lin}{\rightarrow} [Y{\rightarrow}R]$ by virtue of $f(v) = F\,v$.
Proof: Take F such that for all $x \in X$, $F^x = f(\mathbf{e}^{(x)})$. Then we get from the linearity of f, $f(v) = f(\sum_x v_x \mathbf{e}^{(x)}) = \sum_x v_x f(\mathbf{e}^{(x)}) = \sum_x v_x\, F^x = F\,v$. Uniqueness follows from proposition 5.10. The converse is obvious.

Corollary 5.13 For a linear form $f{:}[X{\rightarrow}R] \stackrel{lin}{\rightarrow} R$, the matrix representation of f reduces to a vector (single-column matrix) $\tilde{f}{:}X{\rightarrow}R$ such that for all $v \in [X{\rightarrow}R]$, $f(v) = v{\cdot}\tilde{f}$.

Proposition 5.14 For a finite set X, the set of square matrices $[X{\times}X{\rightarrow}R]$ under addition and (matrix) multiplication is a ring and, if R is commutative, a R-algebra. The unit element under multiplication is the diagonal matrix $\mathbf{D}{:}x, y \mapsto [x{=}y] \quad (x, y \in X)$.

Let for $X = \{a, b, c\}$, $v = 2a - b$ and $w = -3a + 2b - c$ be two elements of $\mathcal{L}(X)$. While the scalar product $v{\cdot}w$ is an integer, $v{\cdot}w = -6 - 2 + 0 = -8$, we now wish to extend $\mathcal{L}(X)$ to the ring of formal polynomials in X such that the *ring product* of v and w is the polynomial $v\,w = -6a^2 + 7ab - 2ac - 2b^2 + bc$.

Definition 5.15 Let X be a finite set, $X = \{x_1, \ldots, x_n\}$. The set of polynomials in X over $\mathbf{Z}$ is designated as $\mathcal{A}(X)$ ($\mathcal{A}$ because we get a linear algebra over X). It is defined as $\mathcal{A}(X) = [[X{\rightarrow}\mathbf{N}]{\rightarrow}\mathbf{Z}]_{fin}$.
The elements of $[X{\rightarrow}\mathbf{N}]$ are called the *monomials*. The monomials form a commutative monoid which we write with multiplication. A monomial $v{:}X{\rightarrow}\mathbf{N}$ is written as $v = x_1^{v_{x_1}} \ldots x_n^{v_{x_n}}$. Hence the product of two monomials is $vw = x_1^{(v+w)_{x_1}} \ldots x_n^{(v+w)_{x_n}}$.
$\mathcal{A}(X)$ is provided with addition $(p, q) \mapsto p + q$ and (ring) multiplication $(p, q) \mapsto p\,q$ defined by $(p + q)_v = p_v{+}q_v$ and $(p\,q)_u = \sum_{u=vw} p_v q_w$ for $u, v, w \in [X{\rightarrow}\mathbf{N}]$.

Proposition 5.16 Let X be a finite set and $\mathcal{A}(X)$ the set of formal polynomials in X over $\mathbf{Z}$. Under addition, multiplication and multiplication by scalars, $\mathcal{A}(X)$ is a $\mathbf{Z}$-algebra.
Proof: All properties (see defintiton 5.4) are very easy to verify. The unit element of multiplication is $x_1^0 \ldots x_n^0$. The finite support property is preserved by addition and multiplication. It allows to define for each polynomial p its *degree* $\delta(p)$ which is the largest sum of powers in a monomial $v \in [X{\rightarrow}\mathbf{N}]$ with non-zero coefficient in p. Hence for each number $d \geq 0$, a polynomial p of degree d can be written as $\sum_{i_1+\ldots+i_n \leq d} c_{(i_1,\ldots,i_n)} x_1^{i_1} \ldots x_n^{i_n}$.

Note that $\mathcal{A}(X)$ is an extension of $\mathcal{L}(X)$; $\mathcal{L}(X)$ is the set of all elements of $\mathcal{A}(X)$ of degree 1 where the unit monomial $x_1^0 \ldots x_n^0$ has the coefficient 0.

5.2 The Representation of Linear Transformations

At the beginning of this chapter we have mentioned that the important role that linear algebra plays in net theory is due to fact that the transition rule of ordinary Petri nets has a linear-algebraic representation.

Definition 5.17 Let $N = (S, T; F)$ is a net of places S and transitions T. The *incidence matrix* of N is a matrix $C{:}S{\times}T{\rightarrow}\mathbf{Z}$ such that for $s \in S$, $t \in T$, $C(s,t) = \begin{cases} -1 & \text{if } (s,t) \in F \setminus F^{-1} \\ 1 & \text{if } (s,t) \in F^{-1} \setminus F \\ 0 & \text{otherwise} \end{cases}$.

Proposition 5.18 Let $N = (S, T; F)$ is a net and C the incidence matrix of N. Then for two markings $M, M'{:}S{\rightarrow}\mathbf{N}$ the following holds.

- If M' is reachable from M, there exists a vector $p{:}T{\rightarrow}\mathbf{Z}$ such that $M' = M + Cp$

To concentrate on the linear algebraic aspects we abstract from Petri nets for a while and consider what we call $\mathbf{Z}$-linear systems.

Definition 5.19 A $\mathbf{Z}$-linear system is a tuple $\mathcal{S} = (S, T; C, [m^0])$ where

- S is a finite, non-empty set of integer variables called *places*; a vector $m{:}S \to \mathbf{Z}$ is called a *state* of $\mathcal{S}$.
- T is a finite, non-empty set, disjoint from S, of integer variables called *transitions*; a vector $p{:}T \to \mathbf{Z}$ is called an *process* of $\mathcal{S}$.
- C is a matrix $C{:}S \times T \to \mathbf{Z}$ called *the transformation matrix* of $\mathcal{S}$.
- m^0 is the *representative* state of $\mathcal{S}$. $[m^0]$ is the set of all states that can be reached from m^0: $m \in [m^0]$ iff there is a process $p{:}T \to \mathbf{Z}$ such that $m = m^0 + C\,p$.

The power of linear algebra for the analysis of Petri systems is based above all on the possibility to compute an important class of system invariants.

Definition 5.20 Let $\mathcal{S} = (S, T; C, [m^0])$ be a $\mathbf{Z}$-linear system. A linear form on the integer S-vectors,, $l{:}\mathcal{L}(S) \overset{lin}{\to} \mathbf{Z}$, is called a (linear) S*-invariant* of $\mathcal{S}$ iff for every state $m \in [m^0]$, $l(m) = l(m^0)$.

Linear algebra tells us that the S-invariants of $\mathcal{S}$ can be found by solving a homogeneous system of linear equations whose coefficient matrix is transpose of the transformation matrix C.

Theorem 5.21 Let $\mathcal{S} = (S, T; C, [m^0])$ be a $\mathbf{Z}$-linear system. A linear form $l{:}\mathcal{L}(S) \to \mathbf{Z}$ is a S-invariant of $\mathcal{S}$ iff there is an integer S-vector $i \in \mathcal{L}(S)$ such that

1. i is a solution of the homogeneous system of linear equations $C^\top i = \mathbf{0}$,
2. for all $m \in \mathcal{L}(S)$, $l(m) = m{\cdot}i$.

Proof: (a) Let l be a S-invariant. Let i be the vector representing l according to corollary 5.13. Then $l(m) = m{\cdot}i$ for all S-vectors m. For every transition t there is a state m such that $m = m^0 + C\mathbf{e}^{(t)}$. Since $l(m) = l(m^0)$, $0 = l(m) - l(m^0) = l(C^t) = C^t{\cdot}i = (C^\top i)_t$.
(b) Let i be a solution of $C^\top i = \mathbf{0}$. Let $l{:}\mathcal{L}(S) \to \mathbf{Z}$ be defined by $l(m) = m{\cdot}i$ for all S-vectors $m \in \mathcal{L}(S)$. For all states $m \in [m^0]$ there is a process $p \in \mathcal{L}(T)$ such that $m = m^0 + C\,p$. Hence $l(m) = l(m^0 + C\,p) = l(m) + l(C\,p)$, and $l(Cp) = (Cp){\cdot}i = (Cp)^\top i = (p^\top C^\top)i = p^\top(C^\top i) = \mathbf{0}$.

Corollary 5.22 The S-invariants do not depend on the representative state $[m^0]$.

Corollary 5.23 The S-invariants form a submodule of (S).
Proof: $C^\top$ represents a linear mapping of $\mathcal{L}(S)$ into $\mathcal{L}(T)$ (see 5.12). The kernel of a linear mapping between modules is a submodul of the domain (see 5.9).

Because of their close relationship to S-invariants, the solutions of $C^\top i = \mathbf{0}$ will be called S-invariants, too.

The rest of this chapter will be concerned with three questions: How to compress the matrix representation of the system $\mathcal{S}$ in a way that is comparable to folding a CE-net into a PrT-net; how to compute S-invariants of $\mathcal{S}$ based on the compressed representation; how to apply the results to the analysis of PrT-nets.

5.3 The Compression of Matrices

Given a $\mathbf{Z}$-linear system $\mathcal{S} = (S, T; C, [m^0])$ we wish to compress its transformation matrix C in such a way that

- the number of rows and columns can be decreased;
- the original representation can be reproduced;

· there are techniques for computing $\mathcal{S}$-invariants of $\mathcal{S}$ using the compressed representation.

The basic idea is to partition the rows and columns of C and to merge the elements of every block to form a *coarse* matrix $\mathbf{C}$. To be able to identify the original constituents of a new row or column, they are 'painted' in different colours.

Definition 5.24 Let $C{:}S{\times}T{\to}\mathbf{Z}$ be an integer matrix, and let A and B be two sets of identifiers, not necessarily disjoint, serving as place colours and transition colours, respectively. Let $\mathbf{S} \subseteq \mathcal{P}(S)$ and $\mathbf{T} \subseteq \mathcal{P}(T)$ be partitions (into disjoint non-empty *blocks*) of S respectively T. A *colouring* of C is a pair of mappings $p_S{:}S{\to}A$ and $p_T{:}T{\to}B$. It is said to be *consistent* with the partitions of S and T if any two different elements of the same block are coloured differently.

Given a matrix C with partitions $\mathbf{S}$ and $\mathbf{T}$ and a consistent colouring (p_S, p_T) in colours A and B, we now construct the quotient matrix $\mathbf{C}$ by first merging rows and then merging columns.

The result of merging for each block $\mathbf{s} \in \mathbf{S}$ all rows of $\mathbf{s}$ into a single row associated with $\mathbf{s}$ is a matrix $\tilde{C}{:}\mathbf{S}{\times}T{\to}\mathcal{L}(A)$. Every entry $\tilde{C}^t_{\mathbf{s}}$ is the linear combination of the colours used for $\mathbf{s}$ with the corresponding entries in C^t as coefficients. $\tilde{C}^t_{\mathbf{s}}{:}A{\to}\mathbf{Z}$ is defined such that for every $a \in A$, $\tilde{C}^t_{\mathbf{s}}(a) = C^t_s$ if $s \in \mathbf{s}$ and $\tilde{C}^t_{\mathbf{s}}(a) = 0$ otherwise.
(Note that $\tilde{C}^t_{\mathbf{s}}$ is really a function since p_S is consistent with $\mathbf{S}$.)

In the second step, the columns of $\tilde{C}$ are merged according to the partition $\mathbf{T}$ in very much the same way the rows were merged. The difference is that the entries of $\tilde{C}$ are no longer integers but linear combinations of place colours. Hence the entries of $\mathbf{C}$ are functions that assign to transition colours linear combinations of place colours. We get $\mathbf{C}{:}\mathbf{S}{\times}\mathbf{T}{\to}[B{\to}\mathcal{L}(A)]$ defined such that for $b \in B$, $\mathbf{C}^{\mathbf{t}}_{\mathbf{s}}(b) = \tilde{C}^t_{\mathbf{s}}$ if $t \in \mathbf{t}$ and $\mathbf{C}^{\mathbf{t}}_{\mathbf{s}}(b) = 0$ otherwise.

Example 5.25 An example of compressing an integer matrix is shown in table 1. Places $s_1, \ldots, s_6$ and transitions $t_1, \ldots, t_4$ are given with their partitioning into $\mathbf{S} = \{L, R\}$ and $\mathbf{T} = \{O, E\}$ and their painting with colours $A = \{r, b, g, y\}$ and $B = \{l, h\}$. First the rows of the upper left matrix are compressed. The result is the lower left matrix. Its columns are then compressed to form the 2x2-matrix in the lower right part of the scheme. Its entries are functions that are defined separately below the scheme.

The method of compressing an integer matrix just described is, except for some technical details, the one used by *Jensen* in his model of *Coloured Petri nets (CP-nets)* [9,10]. As arc annotations and hence as entries of the incidence matrix of a coloured Petri net, he uses simple linear combinations of names for functions that map transition colours into integer vectors of place colours. An he develops a technique for finding S-invariants based on this representation.

5.4 Structured Colours and Individual Variables

So far we have used plain colours for compressing the transformation matrices of linear systems. Next we present a method that is strongly influenced by the PrT-nets. In the first step of compression, it uses tuples of individual constants as place colours. This leads to quite a different way of proceeding in the second step.

Definition 5.26 Let as before $C{:}S{\times}T{\to}\mathbf{Z}$ be the transformation matrix of a $\mathbf{Z}$-linear system $\mathcal{S} = (S, T; C, [m^0])$. Let U be a finite set of identifiers (individual constants), and let for a given $n \geq 0$, the colour set A be the set of tuples of elements of U of length $\leq n$: $A = \bigcup_{0 \leq m \leq n} U^m$. Let $\mathbf{S} \subseteq \mathcal{P}(S)$ be a partition of the places, and let $p_S{:}S{\to}A$ be a place colouring. p_S is called *consistent* with $\mathbf{S}$ if for each block $\mathbf{s}$,

		t_1 O,l	t_2 E,l	t_3 O,h	t_4 E,h	O	E
s_1	L,r	-1			1		
s_2	R,r	1	-1				
s_3	L,b		1	-1			
s_4	R,b			1	-1		
s_5	L,y	1			-1		
s_6	L,g		-1	1			
	L	$-\langle r\rangle+\langle y\rangle$	$\langle b\rangle-\langle g\rangle$	$-\langle b\rangle+\langle g\rangle$	$\langle r\rangle-\langle y\rangle$	$-G$	$\tilde{G}$
	R	$\langle r\rangle$	$-\langle r\rangle$	$\langle b\rangle$	$-\langle b\rangle$	F	$-F$

$F = \{l \mapsto \langle r\rangle, h \mapsto \langle b\rangle\}$
$G = \{l \mapsto \langle r\rangle - \langle y\rangle, h \mapsto \langle b\rangle - \langle g\rangle\}$
$\tilde{G} = \{h \mapsto \langle r\rangle - \langle y\rangle, l \mapsto \langle b\rangle - \langle g\rangle\}$

Table 1: Compression of an Integer Matrix

1. different places in **s** are coloured differently,
2. all places of **s** are coloured by tuples of the same length (the *arity* of **s**).

Let $\tilde{C}{:}\mathbf{S}\times T \to \mathcal{L}(A)$ be the result of merging the rows of each block of **S** into a single coarse place **s**, as described above. The second step of merging columns of $\tilde{C}$ will now differ essentially from the previous method (the 'Jensen method'). We no longer take an arbitrary partition **T** of T with some consistent colouring to compress $\tilde{C}$. Rather, we shall employ the general technique of abstracting from a set of similar expressions to a *scheme* from which the expressions can be derived by means of substitutions.

Definition 5.27 Two elements $v, w \in \mathcal{L}(A)$ are called *similar* if

1. all tuples with non-zero coefficients in v or w have the same length,
2. the sum of coefficients is the same for v and w, $v{\cdot}\mathbf{1} = w{\cdot}\mathbf{1}$ (*uniformity*).

Definition 5.28 Let $\tilde{C}{:}\mathbf{S}\times T \to \mathcal{L}(A)$ be the result of merging the rows of C as described above. Let **T** be a partition of T. $\tilde{C}$ is called *uniform* with respect to **T** if for each block $\mathbf{t} \in \mathbf{T}$ and any two transitions $t, t' \in \mathbf{t}$, the columns $\tilde{C}^t$ and $\tilde{C}^{t'}$ are similar, ie $\tilde{C}^t_{\mathbf{s}}$ and $\tilde{C}^{t'}_{\mathbf{s}}$ are similar for all **s**.

The uniformity of $\tilde{C}$ is the key to merging its columns according to **T**.

Theorem 5.29 Let V be a set of individual variables disjoint from U (and large enough as specified in the proof) and let $W = U \cup V$. Let $L \subseteq \mathcal{L}(A)$ be a set of linear combinations of tuples that are pairwise similar. Then there exists a scheme λ for L being a linear combination of tuples of individual variables such that for each element $v \in L$ there is a substitution $\beta{:}V \to U$ such that $v = \lambda{:}\beta$.

Proof: Let m be the length of tuples and k the sum of coefficients that are common to L due to similarity. Let l be the maximal 'length' of the elements of L, namely $l = max_{v \in L} \sum_x |v_x|$. Note that $l \geq |k|$. We split l into $l^+ = max_v \sum_{v_x > 0} v_x$ and $l^- = max_v \sum_{v_x < 0} -v_x$. Then $l = l^+ + l^-$ and $k = l^+ - l^-$.

To form the scheme λ, we take a set of l m-tuples of individual variables such that all variables are different. (Hence V must contain at least $l\,m$ variables.) We assign to l^+ tuples the coefficient $+1$ and to the remaining l^- tuples the coefficient -1. Then each member of L can be derived from λ by means of a substitution. If not all tuples of λ are needed for some element of L because its length is less than l, the same number of tuples with positive coefficients and with negative coefficients are left since the sum of coefficients $k = l^+ - l^-$ is the same for all elements of L. These remaining tuples can be made to sum up to zero if all their variables are replaced, for example, by the same constant.

This result now helps to construct from $\tilde{C}:\mathbf{S}\times T\to\mathcal{L}(A)$ the compressed representation $\mathbf{C}:\mathbf{S}\times \mathbf{T}\to\mathcal{L}(\tilde{A})$ where $\tilde{A}$ is built from W in the same way as A was built from U. Formally, every element λ of $\mathcal{L}(\tilde{A})$ denotes a function $\lambda:B\to[A\to\mathbf{Z}]]$ where the set of transition colours, B is the set of all substitutions of variables by constants, $B = [V\to U]$. (The representation of these functions forming the entries of the compressed matrix $\mathbf{C}$, however, differs essentially from those used by the other methods described previously (which are all tabular, ie in some matrix form). The advantage, as we shall see a little later, of this method is that algorithms for computing S-invariants will exploit the information about the function present in its representation as a scheme.

For every coarse transition $\mathbf{t}$, we have a subset $B_\mathbf{t} \subseteq B$ of transition colours (substitutions) that is one-to-one related to the elements of $\mathbf{t}$; for every $t \in \mathbf{t}$ we take exactly one element $\beta_t \in B_\mathbf{t}$ with $\tilde{C}^t_\mathbf{s} = \lambda{:}\beta_t$. In the PrT-net model, these 'firing modes' of the transitions are determined by the formulae annotating the transitions.

Note that like place colours, also the transition colours may be viewed as tuples of individual constants. Assume that the variables are alphabetically ordered and list for a transition $\mathbf{t}$, the variables that occur in its entries. Then a substitution can be represented by the tuple resulting from applying it to the tuple of variables.

To form the entries of a column $\mathbf{C}^\mathbf{t}$, the construction of theorem 5.29 requires disjoint sets of variables for different coarse places $\mathbf{s}$. What may look here as a terrible waste of variables leading to unnecessarily large substitution vectors, isn't that bad in practice where constants and shared variables are used.

5.5 Computing S-invariants

Let for the rest of this chapter, $\mathcal{S}/_{\mathbf{S},\mathbf{T}} = (\mathbf{S},\mathbf{T},\mathbf{C})$ be the compressed representation of the linear system $\mathcal{S} = (S,T;C,[m^0])$ constructed according to the 'PrT-method' described in the previous section. The ingredients of $\mathcal{S}/_{\mathbf{S},\mathbf{T}}$ are as follows:

- $\mathbf{S}$: the set of (coarse) places
- $\mathbf{T}$: the set of (coarse) transitions
- U: the set of (individual) constants
- V: the set of (individual) variables
- $W = U \cup V$: the set of (individual) names
- A: the set of place colours; for a given maximal arity of places, n, $A = \bigcup_{0\leq m\leq n} U^m$ with $U^0 = \{\langle\rangle\}$
- $\tilde{A}$: the set of place colour schemes; $\tilde{A}$ is built from W as A is built from U
- B: the set of transition colours; B is the set of substitutions, $B = [V\to U]$
- $B_\mathbf{t}$: the colour set of transition $\mathbf{t}$, ie the set of substitutions ('firing modes') of $\mathbf{t}$
- m: the generic state vector, $m{:}\mathbf{S}\to\mathcal{L}(A)$
- p: the generic process, $p{:}\mathbf{T}\to\mathcal{L}(B)$, with $p_\mathbf{t}(\beta) = 0$ if $\beta \notin B_\mathbf{t}$

- $\mathbf{C}$:$\mathbf{S}\times\mathbf{T}\rightarrow\mathcal{L}(\tilde{A})$: the compressed transformation matrix
- $m = m^0 + \mathbf{C}*p$: the system equation in terms of $\mathbf{C}$ where $\mathbf{C}*p = \sum_{\mathbf{t},\beta} p_{\mathbf{t},\beta}\mathbf{C}^{\mathbf{t}}{:}\beta$
- l: a linear form on states, l:$[\mathbf{S}\rightarrow\mathcal{L}(A)]\rightarrow\mathbf{Z}$; l is a S-invariant if $l(m) = l(m^0)$ for all m such that $m = m^0 + \mathbf{C}*p$ for some process p

We are now going to present a method for deriving S-invariants for the linear system $\mathcal{S}$ from its PrT-matrix $\mathbf{C}$. It is based on the ring extension of $\mathcal{L}(\tilde{A})$. For a second method that is based on a generalisation of the scalar product in $\mathcal{L}(A)$ to schemes, the reader is referred to [3,14].

Let $\mathcal{A}(\tilde{A})$ be the linear algebra based on the ring extension of $\mathcal{L}(\tilde{A})$, as defined in definition 5.15. In $\mathcal{A}(\tilde{A})$ we can solve the homogeneous equation system $\mathbf{C}^\top i = \mathbf{0}$, for example by a generalisation of the Gaussian algorithm (see [11,15]). If such a solution is variable-free, ie if its coefficients are in $\mathcal{A}(A)$ (the subring of $\mathcal{A}(\tilde{A})$ generated by $A \subseteq \tilde{A}$), it can be used as a S-invariant in the same way as the integer solutions of the ordinary integer equation system $C^\top i = \mathbf{0}$ for the uncompressed system (see theorem 5.21).

Theorem 5.30 [5] Let i:$\mathbf{S}\rightarrow\mathcal{A}(A)$ be a *variable-free* solution of the equation system $\mathbf{C}^\top i = \mathbf{0}$, ie for all $\mathbf{t}$, $\sum_\mathbf{s} \mathbf{C}^\mathbf{t}_\mathbf{s} i_\mathbf{s} = 0$. Then for all processes p:$\mathbf{T}\rightarrow\mathcal{L}(B)$, the scalar product of $\mathbf{C}*p$ and i (in the $\mathcal{A}(A)$-module $[\mathbf{S}\rightarrow\mathcal{A}(A)]$ is $\mathbf{0}$.

Proof:

$$\begin{aligned}
(\mathbf{C}*p)\cdot i &= \textstyle\sum_\mathbf{s}(\mathbf{C}*p)_\mathbf{s} i_\mathbf{s} \\
&= \textstyle\sum_\mathbf{s}(\sum_{\mathbf{t},\beta} p_{\mathbf{t},\beta}\mathbf{C}^\mathbf{t}{:}\beta)_\mathbf{s} i_\mathbf{s} \\
&= \textstyle\sum_{\mathbf{t},\beta} p_{\mathbf{t},\beta}\sum_\mathbf{s}(\mathbf{C}^\mathbf{t}_\mathbf{s}{:}\beta) i_\mathbf{s} && \text{(linearity)} \\
&= \textstyle\sum_{\mathbf{t},\beta} p_{\mathbf{t},\beta}\sum_\mathbf{s}(\mathbf{C}^\mathbf{t}_\mathbf{s} i_\mathbf{s}){:}\beta && (i_\mathbf{s}\text{ is variable–free}) \\
&= \textstyle\sum_{\mathbf{t},\beta} p_{\mathbf{t},\beta}\underbrace{(\sum_\mathbf{s}\mathbf{C}^\mathbf{t}_\mathbf{s} i_\mathbf{s})}{:}\beta && (\mathbf{C}^\top i) \\
&= \textstyle\sum_{\mathbf{t},\beta} p_{\mathbf{t},\beta}(\mathbf{0}{:}\beta) \\
&= \mathbf{0}
\end{aligned}$$

As a consequence every solution of $\mathbf{C}^\top\, i = \mathbf{0}$ whose entries do not contain individual variables determines a family of S-invariants.

Lemma 5.31 Let i:$\mathbf{S}\rightarrow\mathcal{A}(A)$ be a variable-free solution of $\mathbf{C}^\top\, i = \mathbf{0}$. Then for all monomials $v \in [A\rightarrow\mathbf{N}]$ the linear form l_v:$[\mathbf{S}\rightarrow\mathcal{L}(A)]\rightarrow\mathbf{Z}$, defined by $l_v(m) = (m^\top i)\cdot\mathbf{e}^{(v)}$ is a S-invariant. ($l_v(m)$ is the coefficient of v in $m^\top i \in \mathcal{A}(A)$. Of course, l_v is trivial (constantly 0) for most monomials v.)

Proof: Let m,m', p be such that $m' = m + \mathbf{C}*p$. By definition of l_v we have

$$\begin{aligned}
l_v(m') &= (m'^\top i)\cdot\mathbf{e}^{(v)} \\
&= ((m + \mathbf{C}*p)^\top i)\cdot\mathbf{e}^{(v)} \\
&= (m^\top i + \underbrace{(\mathbf{C}*p)^\top i})\cdot\mathbf{e}^{(v)} \\
&= (m^\top i + \mathbf{0})\cdot\mathbf{e}^{(v)} \\
&= l_v(m)
\end{aligned}$$

Very often, not enough variable-free solutions of $\mathbf{C}^\top i = \mathbf{0}$ will exist. The partial projection of places as defined in section 3.5 may then help to transform $\mathbf{C}$ in such a way that the variables are eliminated.

Theorem 5.32 Let $\mathbf{C}$ be a PrT-matrix and let $\mathbf{s}$ be a place whose arity is $m \geq 1$ (each entry of $\mathbf{C}^\mathbf{t}_\mathbf{s}$ is an element of $\mathcal{L}(U^m)$). Let for some k with $1 \leq k \leq m$, $\tilde{\mathbf{C}} = |\mathbf{C}|^{(\mathbf{s})}_k$ designate the result of projecting in $\mathbf{C}$ all entries of row $\mathbf{C}_\mathbf{s}$ along the k-th position. Let $\tilde{i}$:$\mathbf{S}\rightarrow\mathcal{L}(A)$ be a variable-free solution of $\tilde{\mathbf{C}}^\top\tilde{i} = \mathbf{0}$. Then for every monomial v:$A\rightarrow\mathbf{N}$, the linear form $\tilde{l}_v$ defined by

$\tilde{l}_v(m) = |m^\top|_k^{(\mathbf{s})}\,\tilde{i}$ is a S-invariant.
Proof: The result follows easily from the fact that projections are $\mathbf{Z}$-linear operations on $\mathcal{L}_{fin}(A)$ and commute with substitution. Due to uniformity we have
$|(m + \mathbf{C}{*}p)|_k^{(\mathbf{s})} = |m|_k^{(\mathbf{s})} + |\mathbf{C}{*}p|_k^{(\mathbf{s})} = |m|_k^{(\mathbf{s})} + |\mathbf{C}|_k^{(\mathbf{s})}{*}p = |m|_k^{(\mathbf{s})} + \tilde{\mathbf{C}}{*}p$
Hence the above proofs work also for $\tilde{\mathbf{C}}$ instead of $\mathbf{C}$.

Lemma 5.33 The total projection of $\mathbf{C}$, $|\mathbf{C}|$, is the transformation matrix of an ordinary linear system $|\mathcal{S}/_{\mathbf{S},\mathbf{T}}|$ that represents the mere quantitative aspect of $\mathcal{S}/_{\mathbf{S},\mathbf{T}}$. The total projection $|i|$ of every solution of $\mathbf{C}^\top i = \mathbf{0}$ is an S-invariant of $|\mathcal{S}/_{\mathbf{S},\mathbf{T}}|$.
Proof: From the theorem above follows immediately that $\mathbf{C}^\top i = \mathbf{0}$ implies $|\mathbf{C}|^\top |i| = \mathbf{0}$.

5.6 Two Examples

We are now going to demonstrate the S-invariant method for PrT-nets at two examples. The first one is to get us a little familiar with the practical aspects of finding invariants. We shall see how to combine solving linear symbolic equations with projections and other transformations of the net representation. The other example is to show how to use S-invariants in a mathematical proof of system propertries.

For our first example we return to the simple resource management scheme 2.11. The goal is to derive from its net representation, in a strictly formal manner, the validity of the two logical invariants (1) and (2) that we have already looked at in chapter 4 from a different point of view.

$$\Box\,(\forall x)[U x \mathbf{e} \rightarrow \neg(\exists y)(\exists m)((y{\neq}x \vee m{\neq}\mathbf{e}) \wedge U y\, m)] \tag{1}$$

$$\Box(\forall x)(I x \vee (\exists m)(W x\, m \vee U x\, m \vee R x\, m)) \tag{2}$$

Table 2 shows the matrix form of the net representation where the tickets of the control mechanism have been replaced by plain tokens (places A and C are totally projected). L is an integer parameter denoting the number of tickets (access rights).

The rows belong to the places. The columns, as place vectors, correspond to the transitions 1 through 7, the representative marking M^0, two 'quasi' invariants q_1, q_2 and a proper S-invariant i_1. 0 entries are omitted.

	1	2 $m{=}\mathbf{e}$	3 $m{=}\mathbf{s}$	4 $m{=}\mathbf{e}$	5 $m{=}\mathbf{s}$	6	7	M^0	q_1	i_1	q_2 $L{=}1$	
I	$-\langle x\rangle$					$\langle x\rangle$		$\sum_x^{Agx}\langle x\rangle$	$\langle x,m\rangle$	1		I
W	$\langle x,m\rangle$	$-\langle x,m\rangle$	$-\langle x,m\rangle$						$\langle x\rangle$	$1\|\ \|_2$		W
U		$\langle x,m\rangle$	$\langle x,m\rangle$	$-\langle x,m\rangle$	$-\langle x,m\rangle$				$\langle x\rangle$	$1\|\ \|_2$	L	U
R				$\langle x,m\rangle$	$\langle x,m\rangle$	$-\langle x,m\rangle$			$\langle x\rangle$	$1\|\ \|_2$		R
$\|A\|$		$-L$	-1				1	L			$\langle x,m\rangle$	$\|A\|$
$\|C\|$				L	1		-1				$\langle x,m\rangle$	$\|C\|$

Table 2: The Resource Management Scheme in Matrix Form

The left part of the scheme is the incidence matrix $\mathbf{C}$ of the PrT-net. The vector q_1 is a solution of the symbolic equation system $\mathbf{C}^\top i = \mathbf{0}$ in the ring $\mathcal{R}(\tilde{A})$. This is easy to check by multiplying the rows of $\mathbf{C}$ by the corresponding entries of q_1 and adding them up; the result is the 0-row.

Not so easy to verify is that q_1 is the only relevant solution provided that L is different from 1. All solutions are multiples of it. The programs, however, that compute a basis for the module of solutions (cf [11,15]) deliver only one element. Another system [20] (developed for other purposes than net theory) gives also q_2 for the special case $L = 1$.

q_1 is not variable-free, hence it does not satify the premises of theorem 5.30. However, if we could eliminate the second position of the I entry, $\langle x, m\rangle$, it would become a multiple of the vector that has 1's as entries for I, W, U, and R. The origin of the I entry, $\langle x, m\rangle$, is in the rows W, U, and R. If we project these rows along the second position, the four rows add up to the 0-row.

This result is given in the column i_1 which represents a *proper* S-invariant of the system. It states the following invariant equation that we split into two inequalities.

$$I + |W|_2 + |U|_2 + |R|_2 \;=\; I^0 = \sum_x^{Agx} \langle x\rangle \tag{3}$$

$$I + |W|_2 + |U|_2 + |R|_2 \;\geq\; I^0 = \sum_x^{Agx} \langle x\rangle \tag{4}$$

$$I + |W|_2 + |U|_2 + |R|_2 \;\leq\; I^0 = \sum_x^{Agx} \langle x\rangle \tag{5}$$

From inequality (4) follows immediately the validity of the logical invariant (1). In fact, (1) and (4) are equivalent. Inequality (5) states that no agent is ever in more than one state (knowing that the magnitudes I, W, U, R – the markings of the places I, W, U, R – are non-negative).

Since the case $L = 1$ is not of interest to us, the other solution q_2 does not allow us to come to conclusions about the control mechanism. However, it tells us what to do. If we use the values for m given on top of columns 2 through 5 (by the transition selectors) for splitting the place U into two places, $U x\mathbf{e}$ and $U x\mathbf{s}$, (cf section 3.2) we get the slightly more detailed yet equivalent representation of the system shown in table 3.

	1	2 T	3 T	4 T	5 T	6	7	M^0	q_1	i_1	q_2	i_2	
I	$-\langle x\rangle$					$\langle x\rangle$		$\sum_x^{Agx}\langle x\rangle$	$\langle x,m\rangle$	1			I
W	$\langle x,m\rangle$	$-\langle x,\mathbf{e}\rangle$	$-\langle x,\mathbf{s}\rangle$						$\langle x\rangle$	$1\vert\,\vert_2$			W
$Ux\mathbf{e}$		$\langle x\rangle$		$-\langle x\rangle$					$\langle x,\mathbf{e}\rangle$	1	L	$L\vert\,\vert$	$Ux\mathbf{e}$
$Ux\mathbf{s}$			$\langle x\rangle$		$-\langle x\rangle$				$\langle x,\mathbf{s}\rangle$	1	1	$1\vert\,\vert$	$Ux\mathbf{s}$
R				$\langle x,\mathbf{e}\rangle$	$\langle x,\mathbf{s}\rangle$	$-\langle x,m\rangle$			$\langle x\rangle$	$1\vert\,\vert_2$			R
$\vert A\vert$		$-L$	-1				1	L			$\langle x\rangle$	1	$\vert A\vert$
$\vert C\vert$				L	1		-1				$\langle x\rangle$	1	$\vert C\vert$

Table 3: The Transformed Resource Management Scheme

Here the solution q_2 exists in general. It yields, without difficulties, the (proper) S-invariant i_2 which represents the invariant integer equation

$$L|Ux\mathbf{e}| + |Ux\mathbf{s}| + |A| + |C| = |A^0| = L \tag{6}$$

Since all magnitudes are non-negative, this equation implies the logical invariant (2). (Assume indirectly that there is an agent x_0 using the resource in exclusive mode and simultaneously, another agent x_1 using it in any mode. Then $|Ux\mathbf{e}| \geq 1$ and $(|Ux\mathbf{e}|{\geq}2 \vee |Ux\mathbf{s}|{\geq}1)$. Hence $L|Ux\mathbf{e}| + |Ux\mathbf{s}| + |A| + |C| > L$, violating (6).)

The other example we look at is the (toy) scheme for maintaining multiple copies of a database taken from Reisig's book [17] (p.117). Figure 16 shows the PrT-net and table 4 shows its incidence matrix $\mathbf{C}$, the initial marking M^0, and eight solutions of the symbolic equation system $\mathbf{C}^\top i = \mathbf{0}$.

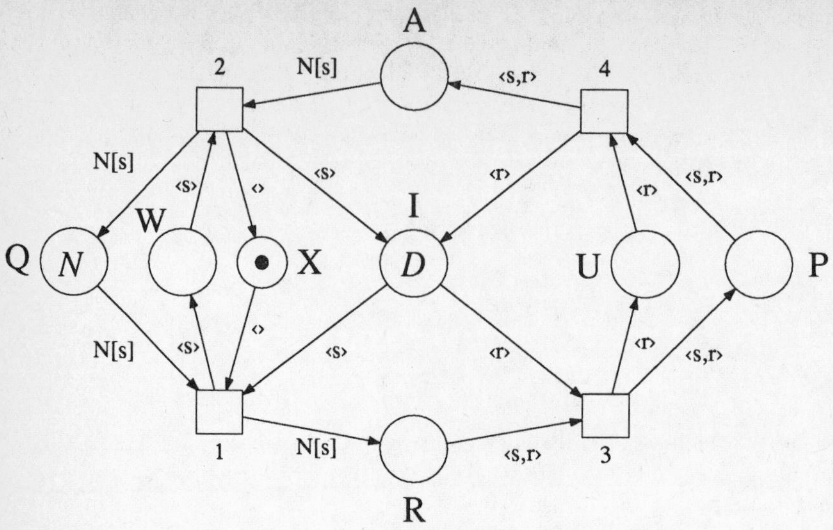

$$D = a_1 + \ldots + a_n; \quad N = \sum_{r,s}([r{\neq}s]\langle s,r\rangle); \quad N[s] = \sum_{r}([r{\neq}s]\langle s,r\rangle)$$

Figure 16: Protocol for Maintaining Multiple Copies of a Database

	1	2	3	4	M^0	i_1	i_2	q_3	q_4	q_5	q_6	q_7	q_8	
X	$-\langle\rangle$	$\langle\rangle$			$\langle\rangle$			$\langle s\rangle$			$-N[s]$	$\langle r\rangle N[s]$		X
I	$-\langle s\rangle$	$\langle s\rangle$	$-\langle r\rangle$	$\langle r\rangle$	D	1								I
W	$\langle s\rangle$	$-\langle s\rangle$				1		$\langle\rangle$		$N[s]$			$N[s]$	W
U			$\langle r\rangle$	$-\langle r\rangle$		1			$\langle s,r\rangle$			$\langle s,r\rangle$		U
Q	$-N[s]$	$N[s]$			N		1			$\langle s\rangle$	$\langle\rangle$			Q
R	$N[s]$		$-\langle s,r\rangle$				1					$\langle r\rangle$	$-\langle s\rangle$	R
P			$\langle s,r\rangle$	$-\langle s,r\rangle$			1		$-\langle r\rangle$				$-\langle s\rangle$	P
A		$-N[s]$		$\langle s,r\rangle$			1					$\langle r\rangle$	$-\langle s\rangle$	A

Table 4: The Database Example in Matrix Form

At most five solutions are linear independent; i_1, i_2, q_3, q_4, q_5, for example, form a basis. Only two solutions are free of individual variables, however, namely i_1 and i_2. They are *proper* S-invariants for which the equation $M{\cdot}i = M^0{\cdot}i$ holds for all markings M reachable from M^0 (see lemma 5.31).

The vectors q_3 through q_8 are 'quasi invariants'; they contain individual variables in some coefficients. To get rid of these variables we project those places from which they originate. For example, the coefficient $\langle s,r\rangle$ of row U in solution q_4 has its origin in row P. So we project row P such that the s disappears.

The result is shown in table 5. In some cases we cannot do better than projecting totally. In other cases, however, we can save a rest of the qualitative information given by the model. The vectors i_1 through i_8 yield the following eight system equations.

$$I + W + U = D \tag{7}$$
$$Q + R + P + A = N \tag{8}$$

	i_1	i_2	i_3	i_4	i_5	i_6	i_7	i_8	
X			1			$n-1$	$n-1$		X
I	1								I
W	1		$1\vert\vert$		$n-1$			$n-1$	W
U	1			1			$1\vert\vert$		U
Q		1			$1\vert\vert_2$	$-1\vert\vert$			Q
R		1					$1\vert\vert$	$-1\vert\vert_2$	R
P		1		$-1\vert\vert_1$				$-1\vert\vert_2$	P
A		1					$1\vert\vert$	$-1\vert\vert_2$	A

Table 5: Proper S-Invariants of the Database Scheme

$$
\begin{aligned}
X + |W| &= 1 && (9)\\
U - |P|_1 &= 0 && (10)\\
(n-1)W + |Q|_2 &= (n-1)D && (11)\\
|Q| - (n-1)X &= (n-1)^2 && (12)\\
|U| + |R| + |A| &= (n-1)(1-X) && (13)\\
|R|_2 + |P|_2 + |A|_2 &= (n-1)W && (14)
\end{aligned}
$$

These equations can now be used to verify system properties in an ordinary mathematical way.

Theorem 5.34 The scheme shown in figure 16 is deadlock-free (live) and contact-free (safe).

Proof: Contact-freeness means that even under the weak transition rule allowing multi-sets on places there is no marking reachable that puts the same tuple on a place more than once. This follows immediately from equations (7) and (8) since D and N are characteristic vectors of sets and markings are non-negative. Hence in the following, we only have to look at the input places of a transition to determine whether it is enabled.

Deadlock-freeness means that there is no forward reachable marking at which no transition is enabled. Let M be any marking that is reachable from M^0. Assume that neither t_4 nor t_3 nor t_1 is enabled. *Claim*: Then t_2 is enabled.

(a) t_4 not enabled implies that there is no s, r such that $\langle r \rangle$ is on U and $\langle s, r \rangle$ is on P. Hence because of equation (10), $U = P = \mathbf{0}$.

(b) t_3 not enabled implies that there is no s, r such that $\langle r \rangle$ is on I and $\langle s, r \rangle$ on R. Claim: $R = \mathbf{0}$. Assume that some $\langle s, r \rangle$ is on R. Then $\langle r \rangle$ is not on I, hence $\langle r \rangle$ on W (equ. (7) and $U = \mathbf{0}$), and $W = \langle r \rangle$ due to (9). So (14) and (8) give $R \leq N_r = \sum_{t \neq r} \langle r, t \rangle$ which contradicts $\langle s, r \rangle$ on R. Hence $R = \mathbf{0}$.

(c) t_1 not enabled implies that there is no s such that $\langle s \rangle$ is on I, $\langle\rangle$ is on X, and for all $r \neq s$, $\langle s, r \rangle$ is on Q. *Claim*: $W \neq \mathbf{0}$. Assume that $W = \mathbf{0}$. Then $X = \langle\rangle$ (9), $R = P = A = \mathbf{0}$ (14), so $Q = N$ (8). So t_1 would be enabled. Hence $W \neq \mathbf{0}$, and in fact $W = \langle s \rangle$ for some s (9). Then $A = N[s]$ (14) because $R = P = \mathbf{0}$ and $A \leq N$ (8).
Consequently, t_2 is enabled since $X = \mathbf{0}$ (9).

Conclusion

We have sketched the process of introducing a net theoretic system model called predicate/transition nets. Although the considerations leading to the model seem quite simple, there is a large amount of formalism needed to allow mathematical reasoning. Any improvement or simplification of the presentation would be most welcome.

Acknowledgement: Part of the material presented in this paper is based on course given by the author at the University of Nijmegen, The Netherlands. Many thanks to students and colleagues, in particular to Wil Dekkers for fruitful discussions and many improvements. Thanks also to the unknown referee of the preliminary version of this report. His criticisms and suggestions were of great help when preparing the final version.

References

[1] Darlington, J.L.: *A Net Based Theorem Prover for Program Verification and Synthesis.* Gesellschaft für Mathematik und Datenverarbeitung, GMD-IST Internal Report 3/79 (1979)

[2] Genrich, H.J.; Lautenbach, K.: *System Modelling with High-Level Petri Nets.* Theor. Comp. Science 13 (1981) 109-136

[3] Genrich, H.J.; Lautenbach, K.: *S-Invariance in Predicate/Transition Nets.* Informatik-Fachberichte 66: Application and Theory of Petri Nets. — Selected Papers from the Third European Workshop on Application and Theory of Petri Nets, Varenna, Italy, September 27–30, 1982 / Pagnoni, A.; Rozenberg, G. (eds.) — Springer-Verlag, pp. 98–111 (1983)

[4] Genrich, H.J.; Thieler-Mevissen, G.: *The Calculus of Facts.* Mathematical Foundations of Computer Science 1976 / Mazurkiewicz, A. (ed.) — Berlin, Heidelberg, New York: Springer-Verlag, pp. 588–595 (1976)

[5] Gerhards, B.: *S-Invarianten in Prädikat/Transitionsnetzen.* Diplomarbeit, Universität Bonn (1982) (in German)

[6] Halmos, P.R.: *Naive Set Theory.* Springer-Verlag (1974)

[7] Holt, A.W.; Commoner, F.; Even, S.; Pnueli, A.: *Marked Directed Graphs.* J. Comp. Sys. Sc. 5 (1971) 511-523

[8] Hughes, G.E.; Cresswell, M.J.: *An Introduction to Modal Logic.* Methuen (1982)

[9] Jensen, K.: *Coloured Petri Nets and the Invariant Method.* Theor. Comp. Science 14 (1981) 317-336

[10] Jensen, K.: *Coloured Petri Nets.* In this volume.

[11] Kujansuu, R.; Lindqvist, M.: *Efficient Algorithms for Computing S-invariants for Predicate/Transition Nets.* Proceedings of the 5th European Workshop on Applications and Theory of Petri Nets. — Aarhus University (1984) pp. 156–173

[12] Lang, S.: *Algebra.* Addison-Wesley Publ. Comp. (1965)

[13] Lautenbach, K.: *Linear Algebraic Techniques for Place/Transition Nets.* In this volume.

[14] Lautenbach, K.; Pagnoni, A.: *Invariance and Duality in Predicate/Transition Nets and in Coloured Nets.* Gesellschaft für Math. und Datenverarbeitung mbH Bonn, Arbeitspapiere der GMD Nr. 132 (Feb., 1985)

[15] Mevissen, H.: *Algebraische Bestimmung von S-Invarianten in Prädikat/Transitions-Netzen.* Gesellschaft für Math. und Datenverarbeitung mbH Bonn, ISF-Report 81.02 (März, 1985) (In German)

[16] Petri, C.A.: *Interpretations of Net Theory.* Gesellschaft für Math. und Datenverarbeitung mbH Bonn, Technical Report ISF 75–07, 2nd ed. (Dec., 1976)

[17] Reisig, W.: *Petri Nets.* Springer-Verlag (1985)

[18] Reisig, W.: *Petri Nets with Individual Tokens.* Theor. Comp. Science 41 (1985) 185–213

[19] Schoenfield, J.R.: *Mathematical Logic.* Addison-Wesley Publ. Comp. (1967)

[20] Schwarz, F.: *A* REDUCE *Package for Determining First Integrals of Autonomous Systems of Ordinary Differential Equations.* Computer Physics Communications 39,2 (1986) 285–296

[21] Thiagarajan, P.S.: *Elementary Net Systems.* In this volume.

[22] Thieler-Mevissen, G.: *The Petri Net Calculus of Predicate Logic.* Gesellschaft für Math. und Datenverarbeitung mbH Bonn, Technical Report ISF 76–09, 2nd ed. (May, 1977)

COLOURED PETRI NETS

KURT JENSEN
Computer Science Department
Aarhus University, Denmark

ABSTRACT: This paper describes a Petri net model, called Coloured Petri nets (CP-nets), where information is attached to each token. The information can be inspected and modified when a transition fires. For most applications, this generalization of ordinary Petri nets allows the user to make more manageable descriptions, due to the fact that equal subnets can be folded into each other, yielding a much smaller net. The paper investigates how to analyse Coloured Petri nets. It turns out that place-invariants and reachability trees, two of the most important methods for ordinary Petri nets, can be generalized to apply for Coloured Petri nets.

Coloured Petri nets and Predicate/transition-nets are very closely related to each other, in the sense that Coloured Petri nets have been developed as a modification of Predicate/transition-nets, in order to avoid some technical problems which arise when the method of place-invariants is generalized to apply for Predicate/transition-nets.

KEYWORDS: High-level Petri nets, analysis methods, place-invariants and reachability trees.

CONTENTS:

1. Informal introduction to CP-nets

This paper describes Coloured Petri nets and some of the analysis methods developed for Coloured Petri nets. Most of the material is taken from [3, 4, 5, 6].

The practical use of Petri nets to describe concurrent systems has shown a demand for more powerful net types, to describe complex systems in a manageable way. In Place/transition-nets (PT-nets) it is often necessary to have several identical subnets, because a folding into a single subnet would destroy the possibility to distinguish between different processes.

The development of **Predicate/transition-nets** (PrT-nets) was in this respect a significant improvement [1]. In PrT-nets, information can be attached to each token as a **token-colour** and each transition can occur in several ways represented by different **occurrence-colours**. When a transition occurs, the relation between the occurrence-colour and the involved token-colours is defined by **expressions** attached to the arcs. Restrictions on the possible occurrence-colours can be defined by a predicate attached to the transition. By the colours it is now possible to distinguish between different processes, even though their subnets have been folded into a single subnet. It should be emphasized that the "colour" attached to a token or to the occurrence of a transition can be a complex information unit, such as the entire state of a process or the contents of a buffer area. New colours can be created by transition occurrences and there may be an infinite number of them.

Although PrT-nets turned out to be very useful in the description of systems, they have a serious drawback concerning formal analysis. One of the most important analysis methods for PT-nets is the calculation of linear **place-invariants** (also called S-invariants) by means of homogeneous matrix equations [8, 9]. This method is generalized to PrT-nets in [1], but the place-invariants there contain **free variables** (over sets of colours). To interpret the place-invariants it seems necessary to bind the free variables via a substitution, where at least partial knowledge about the transition sequence leading to the marking in question must be used. Until now no satisfactory solution to the problem has been published, although some substitution rules are sketched in [1] without a proof of their soundness.

To overcome this problem, **Coloured Petri nets** (CP-nets) were defined in [4]. The main ideas of CP-nets are directly inspired by PrT-nets, but the relation between an occurrence-colour and the token-colours involved in the occurrence of the transition is now defined by **functions** attached to the arcs and not by expressions. This removes the free variables, and place-invariants can now be interpreted without problems as demonstrated in [4, 6]. Moreover CP-nets **explicitly** attach a set of possible token-colours to each place and a set of possible occurrence-colours to each transition. Compared to PrT-nets, where the colour sets are only implicitly defined, this often gives a more comprehensible net. On the other hand the functions attached to arcs in CP-nets sometimes seem to be more difficult to understand than the corresponding expressions of PrT-nets.

As indicated above there is a strong relation between PrT-nets (as defined in [1]) and CP-nets (as defined in [4]). From the very beginning it was clear that most descrip - tions in one of the net models could be informally translated to the other model and vice versa. In [6] it was shown how to combine the qualities of PrT-nets and CP-nets into a single net model, which was then called High-level Petri nets. Unfortunately this name has given rise to some confusion since the term "High-level nets" is also used as a generic name of Pr/T-nets, CP-nets, Relation nets [12], etc. Thus I shall in this paper - and in my future work - use the term **Coloured Petri nets (CP-nets)** to denote the net model defined in [6]. The few times it will be necessary to speak about the net model defined in [4] I shall use the term "old version of CP-nets".

A CP-net can be represented in two different forms: by drawing a directed bipartite graph with inscriptions attached to nodes and arcs, or by defining a 6-tuple containing sets and functions. The first form uses mainly the notation known from PrT-nets, i.e. expressions and predicates containing free variables. It is appropriate for the description and informal explanation of a system. The second form uses mainly the notation known from the old version of CP-nets, i.e. functions and colour-sets. It is appropriate for the formal analysis of a system, e.g. by place-invariants. The two forms are equivalent in the sense that a formal translation between them exists.

CP-nets differ from PrT-nets (as defined in [1]) in the following ways:

- The set of possible token-colours at a place is explicitly defined.
- The number of tokens added or removed at a given place may be different for two occurrence-colours of the same transition.
- The set of allowable expressions and predicates is not explicitly defined (but if desired this can be done by means of a many-sorted algebra, from which the allowable expressions, predicates, functions and sets can be built up).

CP-nets differ from the old version of CP-nets (as defined in [4]) in the following way:

- The incidence-function is split into a negative and a positive part (which allows us to handle side-conditions).

Place-invariants can be interpreted without problems in CP-nets, but they may be difficult to find. The problem is that the elements of the incidence-matrix are no longer integers (contained in a field), but functions (this means that we cannot be sure that the inverse of an element always exists). For this situation no general algorithm is known to solve homogeneous matrix equations. To overcome this problem, four **transformation rules** were defined in [5]†. They can be used to reduce the incidence-matrix of a CP-net without changing the set of place-invariants. It is often possible to reduce the original incidence-matrix to such a degree that a number of place invariants immediately can be found by inspection of the simplified matrix.

† They were defined in terms of the old version of CP-nets, but it is trivial to translate them to the notation of (the new version of) CP-nets.

In [3] it has been shown how to generalize the method of reachability trees to apply for CP-nets. The central idea is the observation, that CP-nets often possess classes of equivalent markings. As an example the CP-net describing the five dining philosophers (see section 11) has an equivalence-class consisting of those five markings in which exactly one philosopher is eating. These five markings are interchangeable, in the sense that their subtrees represent equivalent behaviours, where the only difference is the identity of the involved philosophers and forks. If we analyze one of these subtrees, we also understand the behaviour of the others.

This paper describes a net model and two analysis methods which are aimed directly towards practical applications of Petri nets. It is, however, also possible to apply the model of CP-nets for work which is more aimed towards theory. Most of the concepts known from PT-nets (e.g. conflict, concurrency, boundedness, liveness, home states, facts and net morphisms) and from PrT-nets (e.g. the close relationsship to first order predicate logic) can be immediately translated and applied also for CP-nets.

The rest of this paper is organized as follows: Section 2-3 defines CP-nets. Section 4-10 deals with the analysis method called place-invariants, while section 11-14 deals with reachability trees. Finally section 15 is a brief summary.

2. First example: Traffic lights described by PT-nets and CP-nets

This section contains a very small example which illustrates some of the basic ideas of CP-nets. The behaviour of a normal (danish) traffic light with three coloured lamps can be described by the PT-net in the following Figure 1.

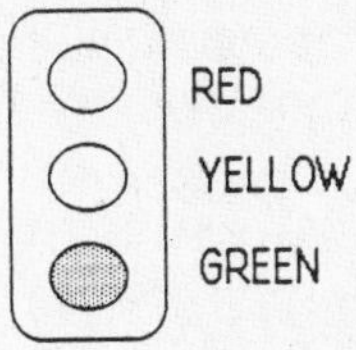

Since the traffic light has a state in which two lamps are lit simultanously, we shall give the net two tokens. These two tokens can either be on the same place (one lamp is lit) or on two different places (two lamps are lit). Initially both tokens reside on GREEN. Then the PT-net has only one possible marking sequence which is shown immediately below Figure 1†.

† Because of the lacking non-determinism and concurrency, this example is not typical for Petri nets. The behaviour of the traffic light could just as well be described by a simple state graph. However, the traffic light example is - due to its small size - well-suited to explain the relationship between PT-nets and CP-nets.

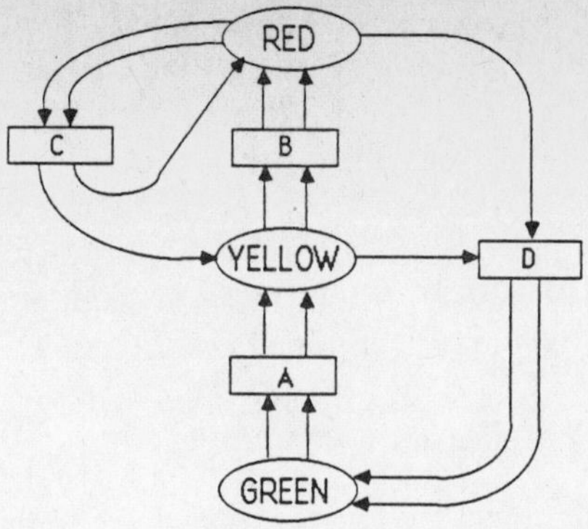

Fig. 1. PT-graph describing a single traffic light.

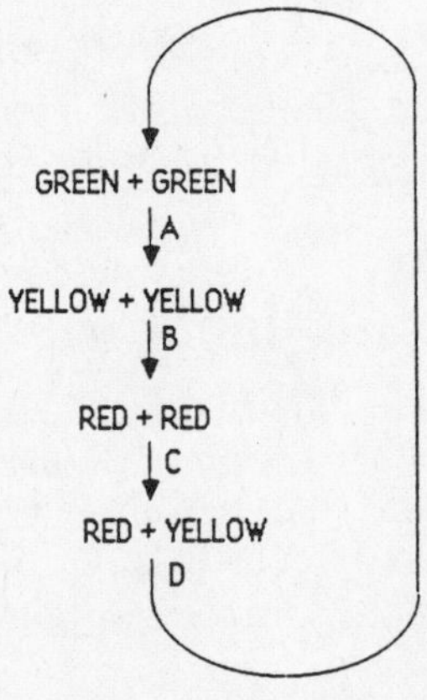

Until now we have only considered a single traffic light. Now let us consider a set of traffic lights synchronizing the traffic on two intersecting roads:

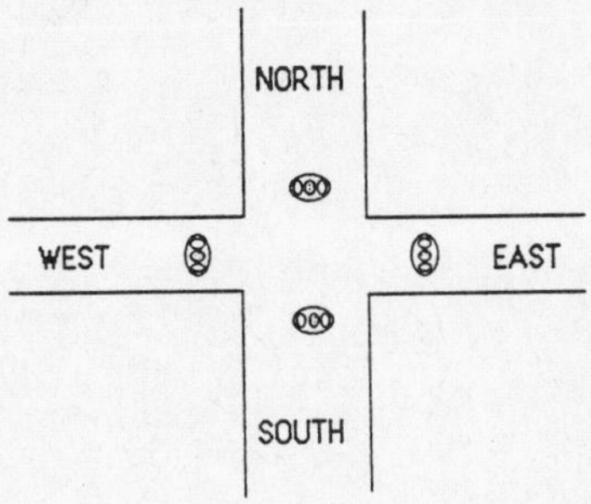

The system can be described by the CP-net in Figure 2 which has exactly the same net-structure as the PT-net in Figure 1 describing a single traffic light:

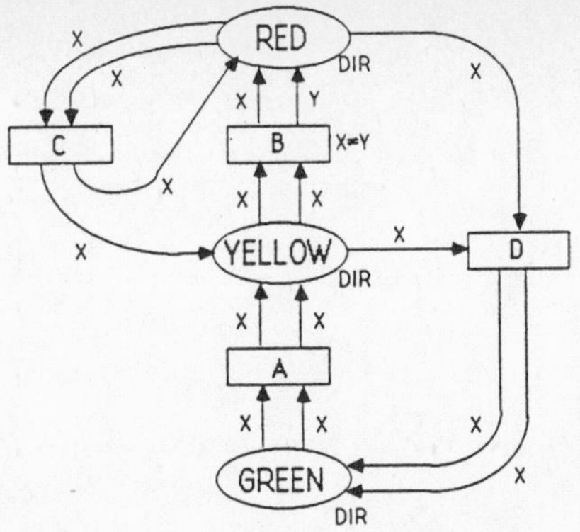

Fig. 2. CP-graph describing a set of synchronized traffic lights.

Each place has attached a set of possible **token-colours**, DIR={NS,EW}, containing two elements, where NS represents the traffic lights in the North/South direction, while EW represents the traffic lights in the East/West direction. This means that each place can have two different kinds of tokens: NS-tokens and EW-tokens. In other words, the information attached to tokens represents, in this net, the two different directions of roads.

Each arc has attached an **expression**, consisting of a single variable, x or y. These variables can take the values in the set of token-colours, attached to the place of the arc, i.e. the values NS or EW. When a transition occurs all its x-variables must take identical values, i.e. x is either NS for all x-variables surrounding the transition, or it is EW for all. This means that the transitions A, C and D always involve four tokens, which have identical colours. In some occurrences the colour may be NS. In other occurrences it may be EW.

The **predicate**, $x \neq y$, attached to transition B, specifies that when this transition occurs, x and y must take different values, i.e. one of them must be NS, while the other must be EW.

We define the initial marking of the CP-net to have two NS-tokens on GREEN and one EW-token on RED, while YELLOW is unmarked. Then the CP-net has only one possible marking sequence which is shown on the next page. This marking sequence describes the "standard" behaviour of a set of synchronized traffic lights. In all system states there are two tokens of one direction and a single token of the other direction. The next change will happen in the direction which currently has two tokens. The traffic lights of one direction "handles over" the control to the other direction by "converting" one of its tokens to become a token of the other direction.

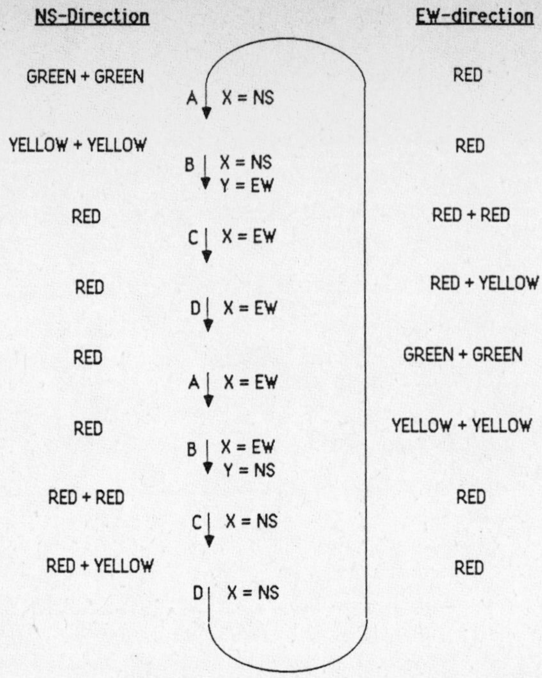

3. Formal definition of Coloured Petri nets

In this section we define the two different representations of CP-nets and we show how to translate between them. But first we need to introduce multi-sets:

A **multi-set** (also called a bag), over a non-empty set S, is a function $b \in [S \to \mathbf{N}]$ where $\mathbf{N}$ is the set of all non-negative integers.

Intuitively, a multi-set is a set which can contain multiple occurences of the same element. In this paper we shall only deal with finite multi-sets, and each multi-set b over S is represented as a formal sum:

$$b = \sum b(s)\, s$$

where the non-negative integer b(s) denotes the number of occurrences of the element s in the multi-set b. All summations in this section are over $s \in S$ unless anything else is explicitly mentioned. The formal sum is convergent since b is finite, i.e.:

$$\sum b(s) < \omega$$

where ω denotes infinity. The set of all **finite multi-sets** over the non-empty set S will be denoted by S_{MS}.

As an example, {a, b, d, b} is a finite multi-set over the set {a, b, c, d}, and it is represented by the formal sum a+2b+d.

Summation, scalar-multiplication, comparison, and multiplicity of multi-sets are defined in the following way, where $b, b_1, b_2 \in S_{MS}$ and $n \in \mathcal{N}$:

$$b_1+b_2 = \sum (b_1(s) + b_2(s)) s$$

$$n \times b = \sum (n\, b(s)) s$$

$$b_1 \le b_2 \Leftrightarrow \forall s \in S: b_1(s) \le b_2(s)$$

$$|b| = \sum b(s) .$$

When $b_1 \le b_2$, we also define subtraction:

$$b_2 - b_1 = \sum (b_2(s) - b_1(s)) s .$$

A function $F \in [S \rightarrow R_{MS}]$, where S and R are non-empty sets, can be **extended** uniquely to a **linear** function $\widehat{F} \in [S_{MS} \rightarrow R_{MS}]$ called the **multi-set extension** of F:

$$\forall b \in S_{MS} : \widehat{F}(b) = \sum b(s) \times F(s) .$$

Functions F and $\widehat{F}$ defined as above are said to be **uniform** with **multiplicity** $n \in \mathcal{N}$, iff:

$$\forall s \in S : |F(s)| = n$$

which is equvalent to:

$$\forall b \in S_{MS} : |\widehat{F}(b)| = n\, |b| .$$

When F and $\widehat{F}$ are uniform, their multiplicity is denoted by $|F|$ and $|\widehat{F}|$. It can be shown that F and $\widehat{F}$ are uniform iff there exists a multi-set of functions $b \in [S \rightarrow R]_{MS}$ such that:

$$F = \sum_{f \in [S \rightarrow R]} b(f)\, f$$

where the sum and product denote the normal sum and scalar-multiplication of functions. If $|F| = |\hat{F}| = 0$ the functions are said to be **zero-functions**, which will also be written as $F = \hat{F} = 0$. We shall use $[.....]_L$ to denote the set of all linear functions.

Definition A **CP-matrix**† is a 6-tuple $N = (P, T, C, I_-, I_+, M_0)$, where

(1) P is a set of **places.**

(2) T is a set of **transitions.**

(3) $P \cap T = \emptyset$ and $P \cup T \neq \emptyset$.

(4) C is the **colour-function** defined from $P \cup T$ into non-empty sets. It attaches to each place a set of possible **token-colours** and to each transition a set of possible **occurrence-colours.**

(5) I_- and I_+ are the **negative** and **positive incidence-function** defined on $P \times T$, such that $I_-(p,t), I_+(p,t) \in [\, C(t)_{MS} \to C(p)_{MS} \,]_L$ for all $(p,t) \in P \times T$.

(6) $\forall p \in P \; \exists t \in T\colon\; I_-(p,t) \neq 0 \;\vee\; I_+(p,t) \neq 0$ and
$\forall t \in T \; \exists p \in P\colon\; I_-(p,t) \neq 0 \;\vee\; I_+(p,t) \neq 0$.

(7) M_0 the **initial marking** is a function defined on P, such that $M_0(p) \in C(p)_{MS}$ for all $p \in P$.

Technical remark: The requirement (6) is not essential for the theory presented in this paper. It has been added in order to make the definition of CP-nets consistent with the standard definition of Petri nets, which do not allow isolated places or transitions.

◊

† The name CP-matrix is used because the 6-tuple can be represented as a two-dimensional table - traditionally called an incidence-matrix. How to do this will be shown later in this section.

Definition: A **CP-graph** is a graph with two disjoint sets of nodes called **places** and **transitions**. Any pair of a place and a transition may be connected with a **set of directed arcs** (which may go in both directions). Moreover the following is demanded:

(1) There exists a set V of **typed variables**. Each typed variable, v:D, has a **name** v and a **type** D. It is assumed that all variable names in V are distinct.

(2) Each place p has attached to it a non-empty set of **token-colours** C(p) and an **initial marking** $M_0(p) \in C(p)_{MS}$.

(3) Each arc has attached to it an **arc-expression**, EXP, containing a set of free variables $\{v_1{:}D_1, v_2{:}D_2, \ldots, v_n{:}D_n\}$ which is a subset of V. Moreover it is required that the lambda-expression:

$$\lambda\ (v_1, v_2, \ldots, v_n)\ .\ EXP$$

defines a function mapping from $D_1 \times D_2 \times \ldots \times D_n$ into $C(p)_{MS}$, where the place p is source/destination of the arc.

(4) Each transition has attached to it a predicate called the **guard**. The guard can only contain those variables which are already in the immediate surrounding arc-expressions. To avoid degenerate transitions with no occurrence-colours the guard must differ from the constant predicate FALSE.

(5) The graph has no isolated places or transitions.

As usual, places are drawn as ellipses, transitions as rectangles, and arcs as arrows.

If desired the allowable expressions and guards can be defined by means of a many-sorted algebra, from which the allowable expressions, functions and sets can be built up. This will not be done in this paper. Instead we shall assume that we work with a finite set of non-empty sets (which can be used as colour sets) and a finite set of function symbols (which are used in expressions and guards of the graph-form and incidence-functions of the matrix-form). Each function symbol denotes an abstract function mapping between colour sets (or cartesian products of colour sets). These functions normally include the identity functions (such as $\lambda\, x\, .\, x$ and $\lambda\, (x,y)\, .\, (x,y)$), the projection functions (such as $\lambda\, (x,y)\, .\, x$), the pairing-functions (such as $\lambda\, x,y\, .\, (x,y)$) and the sum-functions (such as $\lambda\, x,y\, .\, x+y$ where the "+" denotes the sum of two multi-sets). In practical applications of CP-nets it nearly always turns out, that only very few different functions are used, and most of these functions are of one of the forms mentioned above.

Next we show how to translate CP-graphs into CP-matrices:

(1) P, T, M_0, and C's restriction to P, are immediately defined by the places, transitions, initial-markings and token-colours of the CP-graph.

(2) For each $t \in T$ we define:
$C(t)=\{(d_1,d_2,\ldots,d_n) \in D_1 \times D_2 \times \ldots \times D_n \mid (\lambda\,(v_1,v_2,\ldots,v_n)\,.\,\mathrm{PRED})(d_1,d_2,\ldots,d_n)\}$
where PRED is the predicate attached to t and $V(t) = \{v_1{:}D_1, v_2{:}D_2, \ldots, v_n{:}D_n\}$ is the set of all variables appearing free in the immediate surrounding arc-expressions.

(3) Let $(p,t) \in P \times T$ be given and let C(t) and V(t) be defined as above. If a single arc from p to t exists, with expression EXP, we define $I_-(p,t)$ to be the multi-set extension of the following function (mapping C(t) into $C(p)_{MS}$):

$$\lambda\,(v_1,v_2,\ldots,v_n)\,.\,\mathrm{EXP}$$

If several arcs from p to t exist, $I_-(p,t)$ is the sum of the corresponding multi-set extensions constructed above. If no arc from p to t exists $I_-(p,t)$ is the zero-function.

(4) I_+ is defined in the same way as I_-, but by means of the arcs from transitions to places.

◊

Next we show how to translate CP-matrices into CP-graphs:

We only use a single variable, $x : \bigcup\{C(t) \mid t \in T\}$, typed with the union of all occurrence-colours:

(1) Places, transitions, initial-markings and token-colours are immediately defined by P, T, M_0, and C's restriction to P.

(2) Each transition t gets the predicate $x \in C(t)$ as guard.

(3) There is an arc from place p to transition t iff $I_-(p,t) \neq 0$. The arc-expression attached to the arc is $I_-(p,t)\,(x)$.

(4) There is an arc from transition t to place p iff $I_+(p,t) \neq 0$. The arc-expression attached to the arc is $I_+(p,t)\,(x)$.

◊

The definition of the two translations may seem a bit complicated - when they are given in their general form presented above. However, after a few times of exercise the translations can be done very fast and nearly "without thinking".

Let GRAPH and MATRIX be the set of all CP-graphs and CP-matrices respectively, and let:

$$T_{GM} \in [\text{GRAPH} \rightarrow \text{MATRIX}]$$

$$T_{MG} \in [\text{MATRIX} \rightarrow \text{GRAPH}]$$

be the two translations defined above.

Theorem 1

T_{GM} is surjective, but **not** injective.

T_{MG} is injective, but **not** surjective.

Proof: From the definition of T_{GM} and T_{MG} it can be checked, that $T_{GM} \circ T_{MG}$ is the identity-function on MATRIX. This implies surjectivity of T_{GM} and injectivity of T_{MG}. Proof of the two negative properties is trivial.

◊

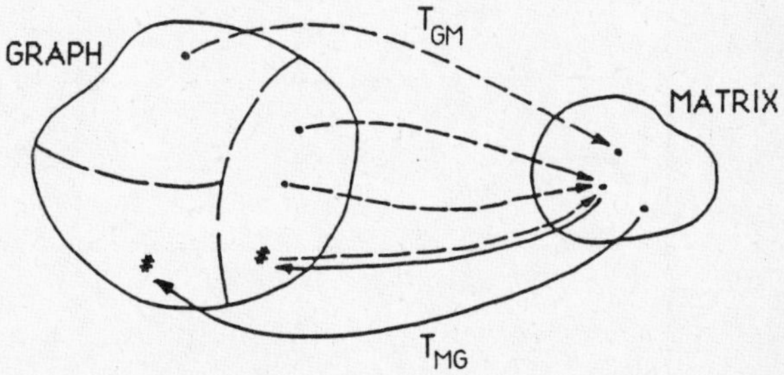

Fig. 3. Translations between CP-graphs and CP-matrices. Normal forms are shown by # .

T_{GM} induces, by its preimages, an equivalence relation $\approx$ on GRAPH, defined by:

$$g_1 \approx g_2 \quad \Leftrightarrow \quad T_{GM}(g_1) = T_{GM}(g_2) .$$

For each equivalence class there exists exactly one element, which is contained in T_{MG}(MATRIX), and this element is said to be in **normal form.** The translation $T_{MG} \circ T_{GM}$ maps each CP-graph into an equivalent CP-graph in normal form. The normal form is, except for minor differences, identical to the graph-form used for the old version of CP-nets in [4].

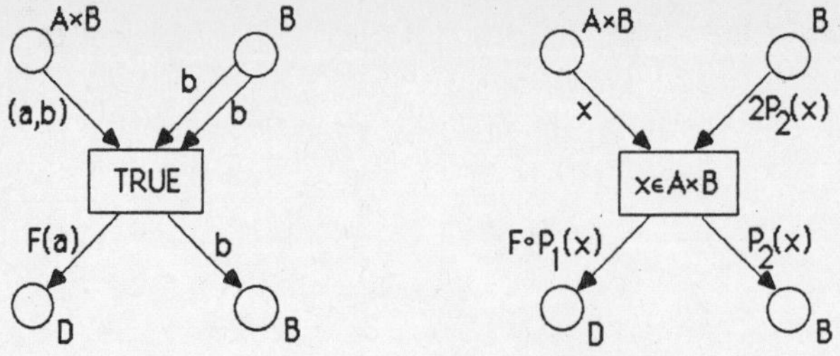

Fig. 4. Two equivalent CP-graphs. The right-most one is in normal form.

Example of a CP-matrix:

The CP-graph of the synchronized traffic lights was presented in Figure 2. It is by T_{GM} translated into a CP-matrix $N = (P, T, C, I_-, I_+, M_0)$, which can be represented by the following two-dimensional table, which is traditionally called an incidence-matrix (see explanation below).

TRAFFIC LIGHTS		A	B	C	D	M_0
		DIR	DIR⁺	DIR	DIR	
GREEN	DIR	-2ID			2ID	2 NS
YELLOW	DIR	2ID	$-2P_1$	ID	-ID	
RED	DIR		P_1+P_2	-2ID+ID	-ID	EW

Fig. 5. CP-matrix describing a set of synchronized traffic lights.

The leftmost column of Figure 5 represents the set of places:

$P = \{GREEN, YELLOW, RED\}$

while the uppermost row represents the set of transitions:

$T = \{A, B, C, D\}$.

The next column and the next row represent the colour-function:

C(GREEN) = C(YELLOW) = C(RED) = DIR

C(A) = C(C) = C(D) = DIR and C(B) = DIR⁺ (see explanation below).

The rightmost column represents the initial marking:

$$M_0(\text{GREEN}) = 2\ \text{NS}, \quad M_0(\text{YELLOW}) = 0, \quad M_0(\text{RED}) = \text{EW}.$$

Finally the rest of Figure 5 is a matrix $(I_{pt})_{p\in P, t\in T}$, containing a row for each place and a column for each transition. This matrix represents the incidence-functions I_- and I_+. Negative elements belong to I_-, while positive elements belong to I_+:

$$\begin{array}{ll} I_-(\text{GREEN,A}) = 2\ \text{ID} & I_+(\text{YELLOW,A}) = 2\ \text{ID} \\ I_-(\text{YELLOW,B}) = 2\ P_1 & I_+(\text{RED,B}) = P_1+P_2 \\ I_-(\text{RED,C}) = 2\ \text{ID} & I_+(\text{YELLOW,C}) = \text{ID} \\ I_-(\text{YELLOW,D}) = \text{ID} & I_+(\text{RED,C}) = \text{ID} \\ I_-(\text{RED,D}) = \text{ID} & I_+(\text{GREEN,D}) = 2\ \text{ID} \end{array}$$

All other elements in I_- and I_+ are zero-functions.

ID represents the identity-function on DIR, while P_1 and P_2 are the two projections with functionality $\text{DIR}^2 \to \text{DIR}$, restricted to the set:

$$\text{DIR}^+ = \{(d_1,d_2) \in \text{DIR}^2 \mid d_1 \neq d_2\} = \{(\text{NS,EW}), (\text{EW,NS})\}.$$

It should be noted that the colour sets, immediately below the transition names and immediately to the right of place names, define the domains and ranges of the functions in the matrix. As an example all functions in column B have DIR^+ as their domain, while all functions in the row YELLOW have DIR as their range.

The CP-matrix constructed above can be simplified considerably by the observation that the set:

$$\text{DIR}^+ = \{(\text{NS,EW}), (\text{EW,NS})\}$$

is isomorphic with the set:

$$\text{DIR} = \{\text{NS}, \text{EW}\}$$

via the isomorphism $P1 = \lambda\,(d_1,d_2)\,.\,d_1$

When we exploit this, we get the CP-matrix in Figure 6, which is isomorphic to the CP-matrix in Figure 5†. The function $\text{SHIFT} \in [\,\text{DIR}_{MS} \to \text{DIR}_{MS}\,]_L$ maps NS into EW, and vice versa.

† An experienced user of CP-nets would immediately construct the CP-matrix in Figure 6, without having to construct the CP-matrix in Figure 5.

TRAFFIC LIGHTS		A	B	C	D	M_0
		DIR	DIR	DIR	DIR	
GREEN	DIR	-2ID			2ID	2 NS
YELLOW	DIR	2ID	-2ID	ID	-ID	
RED	DIR		ID+SHIFT	-2ID+ID	-ID	EW

Fig. 6. Simplified CP-matrix describing a set of synchronized traffic lights.

The relationship between PrT-nets and the two versions of CP-nets are illustrated by Figure 7. CP-nets combine the virtues of the graph-form of PrT-nets and the matrix-form of the old version of CP-nets. CP-nets use expressions in the graph-form and functions in the matrix-form. The graph-form is normally applied for system description and informal explanation, while the matrix-form is applied for formal analysis.

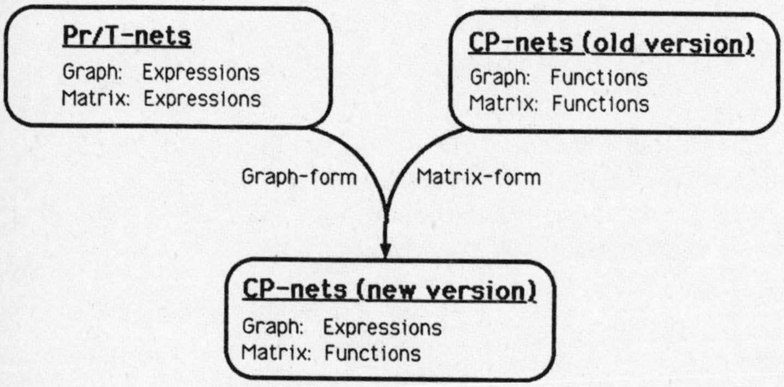

Fig. 7. Relationship between CP-nets and PrT-nets.

The dynamic properties of CP-nets will be defined in section 6 together with the analysis method of place-invariants.

4. Dynamic properties and the invariant-method for PT-nets

In this section we give a brief summary of the dynamic properties of PT-nets, and we define place-invariants for PT-nets. The latter was originally done by Lautenbach in [8]. The main purpose of this survey is to make it easier to understand the later generalization of the invariant method to CP-nets. We give the definitions in terms of the matrix-form.

Definition: A **PT-matrix** is a 5-tuple $N = (P, T, I_-, I_+, M_0)$, where

(1) P is a set of **places.**

(2) T is a set of **transitions.**

(3) $P \cap T = \emptyset$ and $P \cup T \neq \emptyset$.

(4) $I_-, I_+ \in [P \times T \rightarrow \mathcal{N}]$ are the **negative** and **positive incidence-function**†.

(5) $\forall p \in P \; \exists t \in T: \; I_-(p,t) \neq 0 \vee I_+(p,t) \neq 0$ and
$\forall t \in T \; \exists p \in P: \; I_-(p,t) \neq 0 \vee I_+(p,t) \neq 0.$

(6) $M_0 \in [P \rightarrow \mathcal{N}]$ is the **initial marking.**

Let a PT-net $N = (P, T, I_-, I_+, M_0)$ be given. For convenience we shall assume P and T to be finite.

A **marking** of N is a function $M \in [P \rightarrow \mathcal{N}]$. A **step** of N is a function $X \in [T \rightarrow \mathcal{N}]$. The step X is **enabled** at the marking M iff:

$$\forall p \in P: \sum_{t \in T} I_-(p,t)\, X(t) \leq M(p)$$

which can also be written:

$$I_- * X \leq M$$

† Our definition of PT-nets replaces the usual F-relation and W-function by I_- and I_+. This is, however, only a trivial change of notation. Traditionally PT-nets also have a K-function defining the capacity of places. In this paper we shall assume all places to have infinite capacity, and thus we omit the K-function. It would, however, be easy to augment our definition of PT-nets and CP-nets with the capacity-concept.

where I_-, X, and M are viewed as matrices (of size $|P|\times|T|$, $|T|\times 1$, $|P|\times 1$, respecti - vely), $*$ denotes matrix-multiplication and $\leq$ denotes element-wise comparison of matrix-elements.

When X is enabled at M_1 it may **occur** and thus transform M_1 into a **directly-reachable** marking M_2 defined by:

$$M_2 = (M_1 - I_- * X) + I_+ * X$$

Reachability is the reflexive, symmetric, and transitive closure of direct-reachability. M is **reachable** if it is reachable from M_0.

A **weight-function** of the PT-net N is a function $W \in [P \rightarrow \mathbf{Z}]$, where **Z** is the set of all integers.

Theorem 2 (Lautenbach)

If a weight-function satisfies $W * I_- = W * I_+$, then we have $W * M_1 = W * M_2$ for all markings M_1 and M_2 where one of them is reachable from the other.

Proof: If M_2 is directly-reachable from M_1 by the occurrence of step X we get, due to distributivity and associativity of the matrix-multiplication:

$$\begin{aligned} W * M_2 &= W * (M_1 - I_- * X + I_+ * X) \\ &= W * M_1 - W * I_- * X + W * I_+ * X) \\ &= W * M_1 - (W * I_- - W * I_+) * X \\ &= W * M_1. \end{aligned}$$

Thus the desired property is satisfied when M_2 is directly-reachable from M_1, and the proof is finished by induction over the number of steps between M_1 and M_2.

◊

Corollary 2

If $W * I_- = W * I_+$, the equation $W * M = W * M_0$ is satisfied for all reachable markings M, and it is called the linear **place-invariant** induced by W.

5. Second example: Readers/Writers system analysed by PT-invariants

To illustrate the use of the invariant-method we analyse the PT-net in Figure 8. It can be interpreted as a model of a system, consisting of n processes, n>0, which may read and write in a shared memory. Several processes may be reading concurrently, but when a process is writing, no other process can be reading or writing. No priority is assumed between the read and write operations. Each process can be in five different states: LP (local processing, where the shared memory is not used), WR (waiting to read), WW (waiting to write), R (reading), and W (writing). The place S (synchroni - zation) enforces the mutual exclusion of writers. Intuitively tokens on LP, WR, WW , R and W represent processes, while tokens on S represent the state of the shared memory. Initially, there are n tokens on place LP and n tokens on place S, while all other places are unmarked:

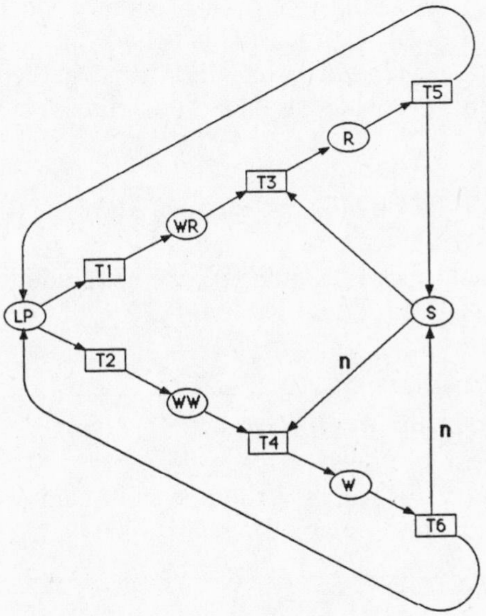

Fig. 8. PT-graph describing the Readers/Writers system.

From the CP-matrix in Figure 9 we find three place-invariants, i1, i2 and i3, induced by the weight-functions w1, w2 and w3 respectively.

From

$$\text{(i1)} \qquad M(LP) + M(WR) + M(WW) + M(R) + M(W) = n$$

we conclude that the number of processes is constant.

	T1	T2	T3	T4	T5	T6	M_0	Invariants w1	w2	w3
LP	-1	-1			1	1	n	1		-1
WR	1		-1					1		-1
WW		1		-1				1		-1
R			1		-1			1	1	
W				1		-1		1	n	n-1
S			-1	-n	1	n	n		1	1

Fig. 9. PT-matrix for the Readers/Writers system.

From

(i2) $\quad M(R) + n\,M(W) + M(S) = n$

we conclude that when a process is WRITING, no other process can be READING or WRITING. The number of READING processes is between zero and n. Moreover, if no process is READING or WRITING, $M(S) = n$. Thus T3 is enabled if at least one process is WAITING TO READ and T4 is enabled if at least one process is WAITING TO WRITE.

From

(i3) $\quad M(LP) + M(WR) + M(WW) = (n-1)\,M(W) + M(S)$

(which is a linear combination of (i1) and (i2)), we conclude that when no process is WRITING, $M(WR) \leq M(S)$. Thus T3 is enabled if at least one process is WAITING TO READ.

Analysis 1 (Absence of deadlock)

The PT-net describing the Readers/Writers system cannot deadlock (reach a marking where no transition is enabled).

Proof:

Case a: If $M(LP) + M(R) + M(W) > 0$, it follows from the net that T1, T2, T5 or T6 is enabled.

Case b: If $M(LP) + M(R) + M(W) = 0$, it follows from (i1) and (i2) that

$M(WR) + M(WW) = n$
$M(S) = n$

and thus T3 and T4 are enabled. ◊

6. Dynamic properties and the invariant-method for CP-nets

In this section we define the dynamic properties of CP-nets and we define place-invariants for CP-nets. We do this in terms of the matrix-form.

Let a CP-net $N = (P, T, C, I_-, I_+, M_0)$ be given. For convenience we shall assume P and T to be finite.

A **marking** of N is a function M defined on P, such that $M(p) \in C(p)_{MS}$ for all $p \in P$. A **step** of N is a function X defined on T, such that $X(t) \in C(t)_{MS}$ for all $t \in T$. The step X is **enabled** at the marking M iff:

$$\forall p \in P : \sum_{t \in T} I_-(p,t)\,(X(t)) \leq M(p)$$

which also can be written:

$$I_- * X \leq M$$

where I_-, X, and M are viewed as matrices (of size: $|P| \times |T|$, $|T| \times 1$, $|P| \times 1$, respec - tively), $*$ denotes generalized matrix-multiplication (to be defined below), and $\leq$ denotes element-wise comparison of matrix-elements (which are multi-sets).

Let $A = (a_{ij})_{1 \leq i \leq r, 1 \leq j \leq s}$ be a matrix with elements, which are linear functions mapping multi-sets into multi-sets, and let $B = (b_{jk})_{1 \leq j \leq s, 1 \leq k \leq t}$ be a matrix with elements which are multi-sets <u>or</u> linear functions mapping multi-sets into multi-sets. Then we define the **generalized matrix-multiplication** such that $A * B = (c_{ik})_{1 \leq i \leq r, 1 \leq k \leq t}$, where:

$$\forall i \in 1..r \;\; \forall k \in 1..t : \;\; c_{ik} = \sum_{j=1}^{s} a_{ij}\, b_{jk} \,.$$

The juxtaposition $a_{ij}\, b_{jk}$ means **function composition** (when b_{jk} is a function) or **function application** (when b_{jk} is a multi-set). We shall only use the generalized matrix-multiplication in situations where the matrix-elements fit together, in the sense that the function compositions/applications and sums are possible. The generalised matrix-multiplication was already introduced in [4]. It is a standard construction in mathematics to generalize matrix multiplication in this way, so that it also becomes applicable to matrices containing more general kinds of elements.

When X is enabled at M_1 it may **occur** and thus transform M_1 into a **directly-reachable** marking M_2 defined by:

$$M_2 = (M_1 - I_- * X) + I_+ * X$$

Reachability is the reflexive, symmetric, and transitive closure of direct-reachability. M is **reachable** if it is reachable from M_0.

A **weight-function** of the CP-net N, with respect to a non-empty set A† , is a function W, defined on P, such that $W(p) = W_+(p) - W_-(p)$, where $W_+(p), W_-(p) \in [C(p)_{MS} \to A_{MS}]_L$ for all $p \in P$.

Theorem 3

If a weight-function satisfies $W * I_- = W * I_+$, then we have $W * M_1 = W * M_2$ for all markings M_1 and M_2 where one of them is reachable from the other.

Proof: It is straightforward to prove that the generalized matrix-product is distributive and associative. Then the proof of Theorem 3 is identical to the proof of Theorem 2 given in section 4.

Corollary 3

If $W * I_- = W * I_+$, the equation $W * M = W * M_0$ is satisfied for all reachable markings M, and it is called the linear **place-invariant** induced by W.

7. Third example: Data base system analysed by CP-invariants

This section contains a small example, which illustrates the invariant-method used on CP-nets. The example was originally presented by Genrich and Lautenbach.

A set of data base managers, $DBM = \{d_1, d_2, ..., d_n\}$, where $n > 0$, communicate with each other. Each manager can make an update to his own data base. At the same time he must send a message to each of the other managers thereby informing them about the update. Having sent this set of messages, the sending manager waits until all other managers have received his message, performed an update and sent an acknowledg - ment. When all acknowledgments are present, the sending manager returns to be

† The set A can be chosen arbitrarily, but in practice it is normally one of the colour sets which is already used in N.

inactive. At that time (but not before) another manager may perform an update and send messages.

Each manager can be in three states: INACTIVE, WAITING (for acknowledgments) and PERFORMING (an update on request of another manager). The managers communicate via a fixed set of message buffers, $MB = \{(s,r) \mid s,r \in DBM \wedge s \neq r\}$, where s represents the sender and r represents the receiver. Each message buffer may be in four different states: UNUSED, SENT, RECEIVED, and ACKNOWLEDGED.

The system can be described by the CP-net in Figure 10, where E is a set containing a single element ε, while the function $MINE \in [DBM \rightarrow MB_{MS}]$ is defined by:

$$MINE(s) = \sum_{r \neq s} (s,r) \qquad \text{for all } s \in DBM.$$

The initial marking is defined by $M_0(inactive) = \sum DBM$ (the multi-set which has exactly one occurrence of each element in DBM), $M_0(unused) = \sum MB$, and $M_0(exclusion) = \varepsilon$, while all other places are unmarked.

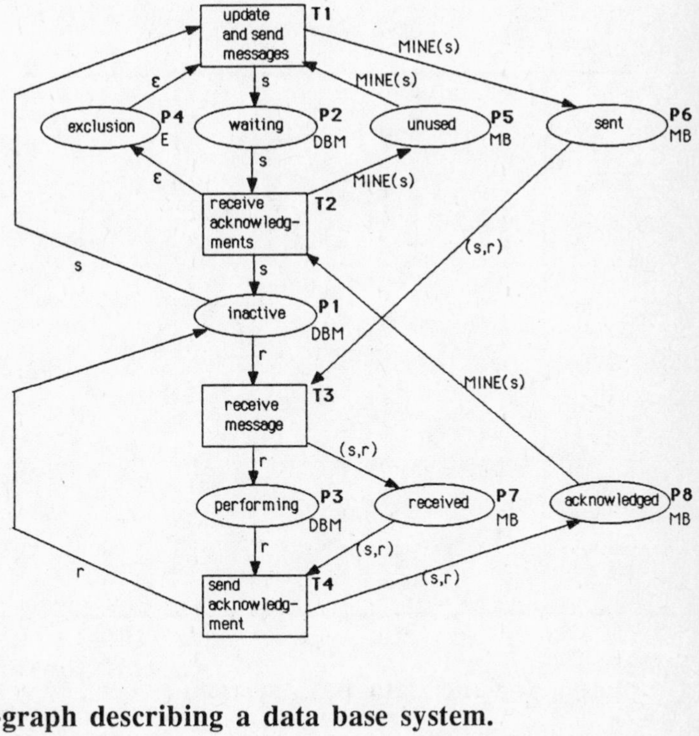

Fig. 10. CP-graph describing a data base system.

Defining the functions:

$$\begin{aligned}
ID &\in [DBM_{MS} \rightarrow DBM_{MS}]_L \\
ABS &\in [DBM_{MS} \rightarrow E_{MS}]_L \\
ID &\in [MB_{MS} \rightarrow MB_{MS}]_L \\
REC &\in [MB_{MS} \rightarrow DBM_{MS}]_L \\
MINE &\in [DBM_{MS} \rightarrow MB_{MS}]_L
\end{aligned}$$

by:

$$\begin{aligned}
ID(s) &= s && \text{for all } s \in DBM \\
ABS(s) &= \varepsilon && \text{for all } s \in DBM \\
ID((s,r)) &= (s,r) && \text{for all } (s,r) \in MB \\
REC((s,r)) &= r && \text{for all } (s,r) \in MB \\
MINE(s) &= \sum_{r \neq s} (s,r) && \text{for all } s \in DBM.
\end{aligned}$$

we obtain the CP-matrix shown in Figure 11.

DATA BASE SYSTEM		update and send message	receive acknowledgments	receive message	send acknowledgment	M_0	Invariants w1	w2	w3	w4	w5
		DBM	DBM	MB	MB		DBM	MB	E	DBM	MB
inactive	DBM	-ID	ID	-REC	REC	Σ DBM	ID				
waiting	DBM	ID	-ID				ID		ABS		MINE
performing	DBM			REC	-REC		ID			ID	
exclusion	E	-ABS	ABS			ε			ID		
unused	MB	-MINE	MINE			Σ MB		ID			
sent	MB	MINE		-ID				ID			-ID
received	MB			ID	-ID			ID		-REC	-ID
acknowledged	MB		-MINE		ID			ID			-ID

Fig. 11. CP-matrix for the data base system.

From

(i1) $M(\text{inactive}) + M(\text{waiting}) + M(\text{performing}) = \sum \text{DBM}$

we conclude that each data base manager is in exactly one of its three states.

From

(i2) $M(\text{unused}) + M(\text{sent}) + M(\text{received}) + M(\text{acknowledged}) = \sum \text{MB}$

we conclude that each message buffer is in exactly one of its four states.

From

(i3) $\text{ABS}(\ M(\text{waiting})\ ) + M(\text{exclusion}) = \varepsilon$

we conclude that at most one manager can be WAITING.

From

(i4) $M(\text{performing}) = \text{REC}(\ M(\text{received})\ )$

we conclude that a manager is PERFORMING iff there is a message buffer addressed to him on RECEIVED.

From

(i5) $\text{MINE}(\ M(\text{waiting})\ ) = M(\text{sent}) + M(\text{received}) + M(\text{acknowledged})$

we conclude that when a manager is WAITING, all his message buffers are either SENT, RECEIVED or ACKNOWLEDGED (and thus none of them are UNUSED). Moreover when he is not WAITING none of his message buffers are SENT, RECEIVED or ACKNOW - LEDGED (and thus they are all UNUSED).

Analysis 2 (Completing a marking)

Let M be a marking which is reachable from the initial marking with $M(\text{performing}) = u_1+u_2+u_3$ (where $u_1, u_2, u_3 \in \text{DBM}$).

Then $M(\text{received}) = (q,u_1) + (q,u_2) + (q,u_3)$ for some $q \in \text{DBM}$ and $q \neq u_i$ for all $i \in 1..3$.

Proof: From (i4) we conclude that $M(\text{received}) = (q_1,u_1) + (q_2,u_2) + (q_3,u_3)$ for some $q_i \in \text{DBM}$ and $q_i \neq u_i$ for all $i \in 1..3$.

From (i5) we conclude that $q_i \in M(\text{waiting})$ for all $i \in 1..3$, and then it follows from (i3) that $q_1 = q_2 = q_3$. ◊

Analysis 3 (Absence of deadlock)

The CP-net describing the data base system cannot deadlock (reach a marking where no transition is enabled).

Proof: Assume that a marking M is reachable from the initial marking.

Case a: If at least one manager $d \in$ DBM is WAITING in M, it follows from (i5) that his message buffers are either SENT, RECEIVED or ACKNOWLEDGED.

If at least one buffer $(d,r) \in$ MB is RECEIVED, it follows from (i4) that r is PERFORMING and then SEND ACKNOWLEDGMENT is enabled (with colour (d,r)).

If at least one buffer $(d,r) \in$ MB is SENT, it follows from (i3) and $d \neq r$ that r cannot be WAITING. If r is PERFORMING, we conclude from (i4) that there is a buffer $(d^+,r) \in$ MB which is RECEIVED and from (i5) d^+ is WAITING but then $d^+ = d$ from (i3). We then have that (d,r) is both SENT and RECEIVED in contradiction with (i2). Thus it follows from (i1) that r must be INACTIVE, and then RECEIVE MESSAGE is enabled (with colour (d,r)).

If all d's buffers are ACKNOWLEDGED, RECEIVE ACKNOWLEDGMENTS is enabled (with colour d).

Case b: If at least one manager $d \in$ DBM is PERFORMING in M, it follows from (i4) that there is a buffer (s,d) which is RECEIVED and thus SEND ACKNOWLEDGMENT is enabled (with colour (s,d)).

Case c: If no manager is WAITING or PERFORMING in M, it follows from (i1) that all managers are INACTIVE, from (i3) that EXCLUSION is marked and from (i2) and (i5) that all message buffers are UNUSED. Thus UPDATE AND SEND MESSAGES is enabled (with any colour in DBM).

◊

8. Fourth example: Telephone system analysed by CP-invariants

In this section we describe a telephone system, as it may be viewed by users. The status of a phone may change from INACTIVE to the situation where the receiver has been LIFTed and you hear a CONTINUOUS tone. Next a number may be DIALled and you hear NO TONE, until you either hear a tone with SHORT intervals (indicating that the dialled phone is ENGAGED) or a tone with LONG intervals (indicating that the dialled phone is RINGING). In the latter situation the receiver may be LIFTed at the called phone and the two phones are CONNECTED until one of the two receivers are REPLACEd. When a number is DIALled, a REQUEST is set up at the telephone exchange.

If the dialled phone is INACTIVE, the REQUEST may be transformed to a CALL, and next to a CONNEXION, if the receiver is LIFTed at the called phone.

A CP-graph for the telephone system is shown in Figure 12. There are two different colour sets: the set of all phone numbers, U, and the set of all pairs U×U, where the first component represents the calling phone, while the second component represents the called phone. REQUEST, CALL and CONNEXION have V = U×U as the set of token-colours, while all other places have U as the set of token-colours. ENGAGED is the complement of INACTIVE. This means that ENGAGED is marked with a colour u∈U iff INACTIVE is not. In Figure 12 we have omitted the arcs which update ENGAGED.

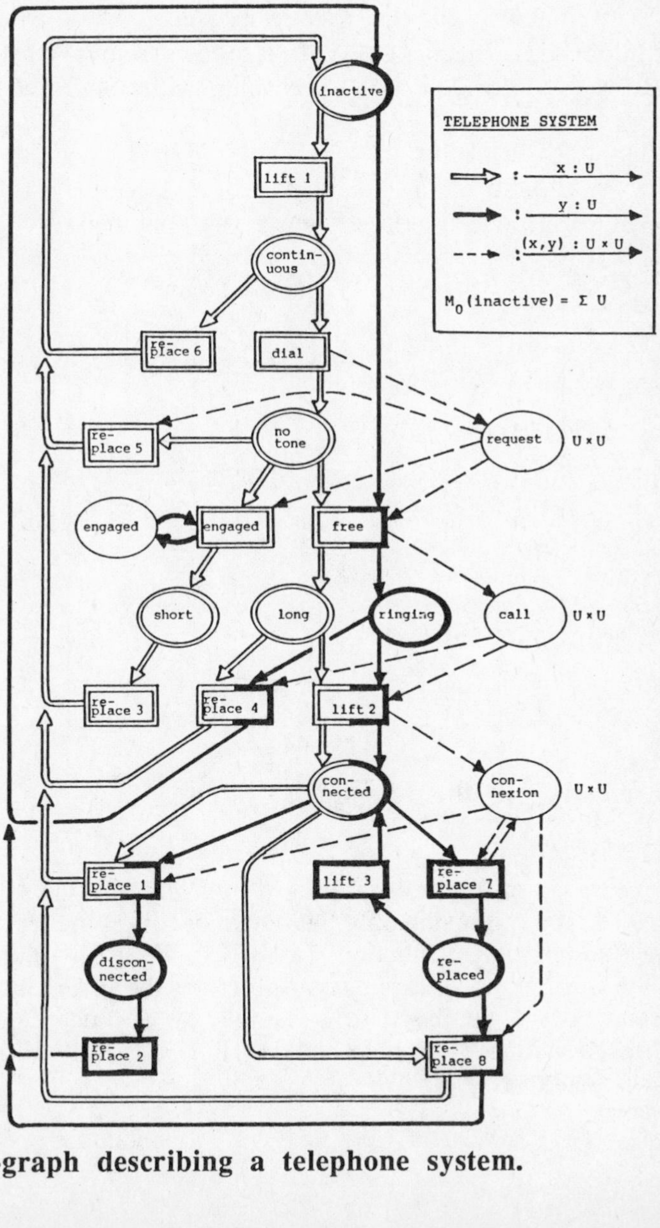

Fig. 12. CP-graph describing a telephone system.

Inspired by [10] three different kinds of arcs are used to indicate the three possible expressions: x:U, y:U, and (x,y):U×U . This visually splits the graph into three superposed parts, which describe the actions of a calling phone, a called phone, and the telephone exchange, respectively. Initially M_0(inactive) = $\sum$ U while all other places are unmarked.

The CP-graph in Figure 12 and its corresponding CP-matrix shown in Figure 13 constitute a formal model, which allows us to determine even the more subtle properties of the specified telephone system. As an example, we can investigate what happens when a phone is calling itself; and it can be seen that a CONNEXION can be removed only by the calling phone and not by the called phone. If only an informal description was given, it would be easy to overlook some of these special cases.

TELEPHONE SYSTEM		lift 1	dial	free	engaged	lift 2	replace 1	replace 2	replace 3	replace 4	replace 5	replace 6	replace 7	lift 3	replace 8	M_0
		U	V	V	V	V	V	U	U	V	V	U	V	U	V	
inactive	U	-ID		$-P_2$			P_1	ID	ID	P_1+P_2	P_1	ID			P_1+P_2	Σ u
continuous	U	ID	$-P_1$									-ID				
no tone	U		P_1	$-P_1$	$-P_1$						$-P_1$					
long	U			P_1		$-P_1$				$-P_1$						
short	U				P_1				-ID							
ringing	U			P_2		$-P_2$				$-P_2$						
connected	U					P_1+P_2	$-P_1-P_2$						$-P_2$	ID	$-P_1$	
disconnected	U						P_2	-ID								
replaced	U												P_2	-ID	$-P_2$	
engaged	U	ID		P_2	$-P_2+P_2$		$-P_1$	-ID	-ID	$-P_1-P_2$	$-P_1$	-ID			$-P_1-P_2$	
request	V		ID	-ID	-ID						-ID					
call	V			ID		-ID				-ID						
connexion	V					ID	-ID						-ID+ID		-ID	

Fig. 13. CP-matrix for the telephone system.

By means of the transformation rules from [5] (to be described in section 10) we can obtain a reduced matrix containing only four columns (c1-c4 in Figure 14). By simple inspection we find six weight-functions (w1-w6 in Figure 14) inducing six place-invariants (i1-i6 in Figure 15). It is easy to interpret the invariants in terms of the described system. As an example, i6 says that the RINGING phones are exactly those for which a CALL is waiting; i4 says that a phone is CONNECTED or REPLACED iff it is contained in a CONNEXION.

TELEPHONE SYSTEM		c1	c2	c3	c4	M_0	w1	w2	w3	w4	w5	w6
		U	V	V	V		U	U	U	U	U	U
inactive	U	-ID				Σ u	ID	ID				
cont, short, disc	U	ID	P_1	P_1+P_2	P_1+P_2		ID					
no tone	U		$-P_1$				ID		-ID			
long	U				$-P_1$		ID				-ID	
ringing	U				$-P_2$		ID					-ID
connec, replaced	U			$-P_1-P_2$			ID			-ID		
engaged	U	ID						ID				
request	V		-ID						P_1			
call	V				-ID						P_1	P_2
connexion	V			-ID						P_1+P_2		

Fig. 14. Reduced matrix and weight-functions for the telephone system.

Telephone system

(i1) M(inactive) + M(continuous) + M(short) + M(disconnected) + M(no tone) + M(long) + M(ringing) + M(connected) + M(replaced) = $\sum$ U

(i2) M(inactive) + M(engaged) = $\sum$ U

(i3) M(no tone) = $P_1 \circ$ M(request)

(i4) M(connected) + M(replaced) = $(P_1 + P_2) \circ$ M(connexion)

(i5) M(long) = $P_1 \circ$ M(call)

(i6) M(ringing) = $P_2 \circ$ M(call).

Fig. 15. Place-invariants for the telephone system.

9. Uniform CP-nets and uniform place-invariants

In this section we investigate the subclass of CP-nets, where all functions in I_- and I_+ are demanded to be uniform (see definition in section 3).

When A is a matrix, of multi-sets or uniform linear functions, we shall use $|A|$ to denote the matrix obtained from A by replacing each matrix-element by its multiplicity.

Lemma

$|A_1 * A_2| = |A_1| * |A_2|$ whenever $A_1 * A_2$ is defined.

Proof: The composition of two uniform linear functions $F_1 \circ F_2$ is a uniform function with multiplicity $|F_1 \circ F_2| = |F_1| |F_2|$, and the application $F(b^*)$ of a uniform linear function F to a multi-set b^* is a new multi-set with multiplicity $|F(b^*)| = |F| |b^*|$.

◊

A CP-net $N = (P, T, C, I_-, I_+, M_0)$ is **uniform** iff $I_-(p,t)$ and $I_+(p,t)$ are uniform for all $(p,t) \in P \times T$, and we then define its **underlying PT-net** as follows $N^* = (P, T, |I_-|, |I_+|, |M_0|)$. A weight-function W of N is **uniform** iff $W_+(p)$ and $W_-(p)$ are uniform for all $p \in P$, and we then define its **underlying weight-function** by $|W| = |W_+| - |W_-|$, which is a weight-function of N^*.

Theorem 4

If a uniform weight-function W induces a linear place-invariant of a uniform CP-net N, then its underlying weight-function $|W|$ induces a linear place-invariant of the underlying PT-net N^*.

Proof: $|W| * |I_-| = |W * I_-| = |W * I_+| = |W| * |I_+|$. ◊

The above theorem shows us where to look for uniform place-invariants in a uniform CP-net N. First we calculate a maximal set of linear independent weight-functions inducing place-invariants of the underlying PT-net N^*, e.g. by means of Gauss-elimination. Then, for each of these weight-functions W^*, we try to construct an overlying uniform weight-function W inducing a place-invariant of N; and to do this, we know that each element of W must be a uniform function with a multiplicity which equals the corresponding element of W^*. There may in some cases be several "independent" weight-functions of N overlying the same weight-function of N^*.

Given a weight-function W^* which induces a place-invariant of N^*, there is always at least one overlying weight-function $W°$ which induces a place-invariant of N. For each place $p \in P$ the weight $W°(p) = W°_+(p) - W°_-(p)$ is obtained from $W^*(p) = W^*_+(p) - W^*_-(p)$ by replacing the two non-negative integers $W^*_\pm(p)$ by the two functions $W°_\pm(p) \in [C(p)_{MS} \to E_{MS}]_L$ which are defined by:

$$W°_\pm(p)(c) = W^*_\pm(p) \times \varepsilon \qquad \text{for all } c \in C(p)$$

where $E = \{\varepsilon\}$. This means that in $W°$ we ignore all colour-information and thus it is $W°$ - of the weight-functions overlying W^* - which provides us with the least information.

10. How to find place-invariants for CP-nets

In sections 7 and 8 it was shown, by two examples, how to **use** place-invariants to prove properties of CP-nets. This section shows how to **find** place-invariants by a sequence of transformations, which reduces the CP-matrix into gradually simpler matrices without changing the set of place-invariants. The transformation rules are inspired by the method of Gauss-elimination, which is used for matrices, where all elements belong to a field. We prove that the transformation rules are **sound**, i.e. they do not change the set of place-invariants.

The matrix-elements for CP-nets are not contained in a field (this means that we cannot be sure that the inverse of an element always exists). For this situation no general algorithm is known to solve homogeneous matrix equations - without unfolding the CP-net into an equivalent (and normally very large) PT-net†. Thus we cannot expect our set of transformation rules to be **complete,** i.e. it is in general not possible to find all invariants only by means of the transformation rules.

Although our set of transformation rules is not complete, it often allows us to transform the CP-matrix to such a degree, that a number of place-invariants can be found immediately by inspection of the reduced matrix. In [5] this is demonstrated for the data base system (of section 7), the telephone system (of section 8), and a more complicated data base system (taken from [1]). In all three cases the reduced matrix is considerably smaller than the original CP-matrix, as shown by the table in Figure 16.

The telephone system analysed in [5] differs slightly from the telephone system presented in this paper. The statistics in Figure 16 apply to the version presented in this paper.

† If this unfolding is done, place-invariants for the PT-net can be calculated by means of Gauss-elimination. This normally yiels a large number of PT-invariants, which we want to fold into a few CP-invariants. However, to do this, no general method is known.

	Rows		Columns		Elements		Non-zero elements	
	Before	After	Before	After	Before	After	Before	After
Small data base system	8	7	4	2	32	14	18	9
Telephone system	13	10	14	4	182	40	55	13
Large data base system	14	6	18	2	252	12	47	8

Fig. 16. Size of the matrices before and after application of the transformation rules.

Definition of well-formedness and pseudo-surjectivity

A CP-matrix normally has the following properties:

- it is a sparse matrix
- there is a high degree of dependency between the individual columns
- there are several solutions for the homogeneous matrix equation
- many of the matrix-elements are simple commutative functions, e.g. identity-functions
- it is not a square-matrix.

Our transformation rules are designed to benefit from these properties, and they will not be adequate for other more general kinds of matrices.

It should be remembered that we consider homogeneous matrix equations of the form $W * I = 0$, where the unknown vector W has an element W(r) for each row r in the matrix I . In particular this means that our generalisation of Gauss-elimination operates on columns instead of rows.

In a CP-matrix each row corresponds to a single place. We shall, however, define our transformation rules on a more general form of matrices, where each row may have a **set** of places attached. Each place is attached to at most one row, and it carries a **weight-factor** indicating how to translate solutions for the homogeneous matrix equation into place-invariants (details will be defined later).

A matrix (with places and weight-factors attached) is **well-formed** (over the set of places P) iff it has the following properties:

(1) Each matrix element I_{cr} is of the form $I_{cr} = -(I_-)_{cr} + (I_+)_{cr}$ where $(I_-)_{cr}$ and $(I_+)_{cr}$ are linear functions.

(2) Each column c has attached a non-empty set C(c) called the **domain** of that column. All functions in the column has $C(c)_{MS}$ as their domain.

(3) Each row r has attached a non-empty set C(r) called the **range** of that row. All functions in the row has $C(r)_{MS}$ as their range.

(4) All places attached to rows are elements of P, and each element of P is attached to at most one row.

(5) When a place p with colour set C(p) is attached to a row with range C(r), it has a weight-factor $F(p) \in [\, C(p)_{MS} \rightarrow C(r)_{MS} \,]_L$.

For each CP-net $N = (P, T, C, I_-, I_+, M_0)$ the CP-matrix is well-formed over P. In each step of our transformations we shall assume the current matrix to be well-formed, and it can be proved that our transformation rules preserve this property.

We now show how to translate a solution U of the homogeneous matrix-equation of a well-formed matrix over P, into a weight-function W:

$$\forall p \in P: \quad W(p) = \begin{cases} U(r) \circ F(p) & \underline{\text{if}}\ p \text{ is attached to row } r \\ & \text{with weight-factor } F(p) \\ 0 & \underline{\text{if}}\ p \text{ is not attached to any row} \end{cases}$$

A weight-function W is said to **contain** a place p iff $W(p) \neq 0$.

To define our transformation rules we need the following definition, which may be motivated by a careful inspection of the proof for our soundness-theorem. A function of the form $Z \in [\, A_{MS} \rightarrow B_{MS} \,]_L$ is said to be **pseudo-surjective** iff:

$$\forall\, b \in B \;\exists\, a^* \in A_{MS} \;\exists\, n > 0: \; Z(a^*) = n\, b\,.$$

Surjectivity implies pseudo-surjectivity, but not vice versa. As an example the function 2 ID is pseudo-surjective, but not surjective. It can be proved that the product n Z is pseudo-surjective for all $n \in \mathcal{N} \setminus \{0\}$ and all linear functions $Z \in [\, A_{MS} \rightarrow B_{MS} \,]_L$.

Definition of the transformation rules

Before each transformation step we assume the current matrix to be well-formed and of the form $I = (I_{ij})_{1 \leq i \leq n, 1 \leq j \leq m}$, where $1 \leq n,m < \omega$.

Transformation 1: When a column j (i.e. the functions $(I_{ij})_{1 \leq i \leq n}$) has domain C(j), and there exists a pseudo-surjective function $Z \in [D_{MS} \rightarrow C(j))\,]_L$ for some non-empty set D, *replace* column j by $(I_{ij} \circ Z)_{1 \leq i \leq n}$ and *replace* the domain C(j) by D.

Transformation 2: When two columns j and k have domains C(j) and C(k), and there exists a function $Z \in [\ C(j)_{MS} \rightarrow C(k)_{MS}\ ]_L$, *replace* column j by $(I_{ij} + I_{ik} \circ Z)_{1 \leq i \leq n}$.

Transformation 3: When all elements in a column j are zero-functions, *remove* column j.

Transformation 4: When all elements in a column j are zero-functions, except two different elements $I_{ij} = Z$ and $I_{kj} = -Y \circ Z$, where Z is a pseudo-surjective linear function and Y is a linear function, *replace* row k by $(Y \circ I_{ij} + I_{kj})_{1 \leq j \leq m}$. For each place p attached to row i with weight-factor F(p), *replace* F(p) by $Y \circ F(p)$, and attach p to row k iff $Y \circ F(p) \neq 0$. *Remove* row i and column j.

◊

Transformations 1 and 2 are generalisations of the rules for Gauss-elimination. They can be used to simplify the matrix-elements, but do not change the size of the matrix. Columns and rows can be removed by transformation 3 and by transformation 4.

We say that a column j is a **linear combination** of a set of columns A iff there exists a family of linear functions $\{ G_a \mid a \in A \}$ such that:

$$\forall i \in 1..n: \quad I_{ij} = \sum_{a \in A} I_{ia} \circ G_a.$$

From transformations 2 and 3 we can derive a fifth transformation rule. It allows us to remove any column, which is a linear combination of a set of other columns. It should be noted that a column j may be a linear combination of a column k, without k being a linear combination of j.

Transformation 4 may seem complicated, but in most applications Y will be a very simple function. The two subcases where Y is either the identity-function or the zero-function are particularly important.

If Y is the identity-function we have a column with two non-zero elements which satisfy $I_{ij} = -I_{kj}$. Then column j corresponds to an equation, where any solution W must satisfy W(i) = W(k). Transformation 4 allows us to add row i and row k. The set of places attached to the new row is the union of those attached to the old. All weight-factors are unaltered.

If Y is the zero-function we have a column with only one non-zero element I_{ij}. Then column j corresponds to an equation, where any solution W must satisfy W(i) = 0. Transformation 4 allows us to remove row i, together with the places attached to it.

A matrix I^* (with domains, ranges, places, and weight-factors attached) is **obtainable** from a CP-matrix I iff there exists a sequence of transformations of types 1-4, which transforms I into I^*.

The four transformation rules are **independent**, i.e. omission of any of them would decrease the set of obtainable matrices.

Lemma

Any matrix obtainable from a CP-matrix with places P is well-formed over P.

Proof: Check that each transformation rule preserves well-formedness.

◊

Theorem 5 (Soundness of the transformation rules)

Let I^* be a matrix obtainable from the CP-matrix I. Then I^* and I have exactly the same set of place-invariants.

Proof: For each type of transformation rule we prove that a single application does not change the set of place-invariants. Then a simple induction argument finishes the proof. All summations are over $i \in 1..n$.

Transformation 1: We shall prove:

$$\sum W_i \circ I_{ij} = 0 \quad \Leftrightarrow \quad \sum W_i \circ (I_{ij} \circ Z) = 0 .$$

By linearity of the involved functions we get:

$$(\sum W_i \circ (I_{ij} \circ Z))(d^*) = (\sum W_i \circ I_{ij})(Z(d^*))$$

for all $d^* \in D$. It is thus enough to prove the following biimplication:

$$\forall c^* \in C(j)_{MS}: (\sum W_i \circ I_{ij})(c^*) = 0 \quad \Leftrightarrow \quad \forall d^* \in D_{MS}: (\sum W_i \circ I_{ij})(Z(d^*)) = 0.$$

$\Rightarrow$ follows directly from the functionality of Z, while $\Leftarrow$ follows from pseudo-surjectivity of Z and from linearity of the involved functions.

Transformation 2: By linearity of the involved functions we get the following biimplication:

$$\sum W_i \circ I_{ij} = 0 \quad \wedge \quad \sum W_i \circ I_{ik} = 0$$

$$\Updownarrow$$

$$\sum W_i \circ (I_{ij} + I_{ik} \circ Z) = 0 \quad \wedge \quad \sum W_i \circ I_{ik} = 0$$

Transformation 3: Column j corresponds to an equation which is always satisfied, and can thus be removed without changing the set of place-invariants. By transformation 3 we may obtain a matrix with no columns. Such a matrix has as solutions all vectors W which have the correct size and functionality.

Transformation 4: Column j corresponds to an equation, where any solution W must satisfy $W_i = W_k \circ Y$. When this is the case, linearity of the involved functions allow us to combine the two rows without changing the set of equations, and column j can be omitted since the corresponding equation is always satisfied (by the modification of the weight-factors). ◊

11. Informal introduction to reachability trees for CP-nets

The central idea behind reachability trees for CP-nets is the observation that CP-nets often possess classes of equivalent markings. As an example a CP-net describing "the five dining philosophers" (see later in this section) has an equivalence-class consisting of those five markings in which exactly one philosopher is eating. These five markings are interchangeable, in the sense that their subtrees represent equivalent behaviours, where the only difference is the identity of the involved philosophers and forks. If we analyse one of these subtrees, we also understand the behaviour of the others.

This paper shows how to define reachability trees for CP-nets (CP-trees). For PT-nets the reachability trees in [2, 7, 11] are kept finite by means of **covering** markings (introducing ω-symbols) and by means of **duplicate** markings (cutting away their subtrees). For CP-trees we reduce by means of **covering** markings and by means of **equivalent** markings (for each equivalence-class we only develop the subtree of one node, while the other equivalent nodes become leaves of the tree). Reduction by equivalent markings is a generalization of reduction by duplicate markings. We describe an algorithm which constructs the CP-tree. The algorithm can easily be automated and we will soon start the work on an implementation. The constructed CP-trees turn out to be considerably smaller than the corresponding PT-trees (reachability trees for the equivalent PT-nets, obtained from the CP-nets by the method described in [4]).

Definition of multi-sets containing infinity-symbols

All summations in this section are over $s \in S$ unless anything else is explicitly mentioned.

An **ω-multi-set** over a non-empty set S is a function $b \in [S \rightarrow \mathbb{N} \cup \{\omega\}]$ and it is represented as a formal sum, where $b(s) \in \mathbb{N} \cup \{\omega\}$ (all non-negative integers augmented with ω):

$$b = \sum b(s)\, s$$

$b(s)$ represents the number of occurrences of the element s. If $b(s) = \omega$ the exact value is unknown and may be arbitrarily large. An **ω-multi-set** b over the set S is **finite** iff its support $\{s \in S \mid b(s) \neq 0\}$ is finite. The set of all finite ω-multi-sets over the non-empty set S will be denoted by $S_{\omega MS}$. Summation, scalar-multiplication, comparison, and multiplicity of ω-multi-sets are defined in the following way, where $b, b_1, b_2 \in S_{\omega MS}$, $n \in \boldsymbol{N}$ and $m \in \boldsymbol{N} \cup \{\omega\}$:

$$\omega + m = \omega \qquad \omega > n \qquad m\,\omega = \begin{cases} \omega & \underline{\text{if}}\ m \neq 0 \\ 0 & \underline{\text{if}}\ m = 0 \end{cases}$$

$$\omega - m = \omega \qquad \omega \geq m$$

$$b_1 + b_2 = \sum (b_1(s) + b_2(s))\, s$$

$$m \times b = \sum (m\, b(s))\, s$$

$$b_1 \leq b_2 \Leftrightarrow \forall s \in S:\ b_1(s) \leq b_2(s)$$

$$b_1 < b_2 \Leftrightarrow (b_1 \leq b_2 \ \wedge\ b_1 \neq b_2).$$

When $b_1 \leq b_2$, we also define subtraction:

$$b_2 - b_1 = \sum (b_2(s) - b_1(s))\, s.$$

As shown in section 3, a function $F \in [S \rightarrow R_{MS}]$, where S and R are non-empty sets, can be extended uniquely to a linear function $\widehat{F} \in [S_{MS} \rightarrow R_{MS}]_L$ called the **multi-set extension** of F:

$$\forall b \in S_{MS}:\ \widehat{F}(b) = \sum b(s) \times F(s)\,.$$

Analogously, we define the **ω-multi-set extension** of a function $F \in [S \rightarrow S_{\omega MS}]$ to be $\overline{F} \in [S_{\omega MS} \rightarrow R_{\omega MS}]_L$ where:

$$\forall b \in S_{\omega MS}:\ \overline{F}(b) = \sum b(s) \times F(s)\,.$$

An **ω-marking** of a CP-net $N = (P, T, C, I_-, I_+, M_0)$ is a function M defined on P such that $M(p) \in C(p)_{\omega MS}$ for all $p \in P$. Th concepts of step, enabled, and reachability are generalized from markings to ω-markings by replacing the word "marking" by "ω-marking". An ω-marking M_1 **covers** another ω-marking M_2 which is written, $M_1 \geq M_2$, iff:

$$\forall p \in P:\ M_1(p) \geq M_2(p)$$

and it **strictly covers**, written $M_1 > M_2$, iff $M_1 \geq M_2 \wedge M_1 \neq M_2$.

The basic ideas behind reachability trees for CP-nets

In this subsection we give, by means of an example, an informal introduction to our notion of reachability trees for CP-nets. The basic idea of a reachability tree is to organize all reachable markings in a tree-structure where each node has attached a reachable marking, while each arc has attached a transition and an occurrence-colour (which transforms the marking of its source-node into the marking of its destination-node). Such a tree contains all reachable markings and all possible transition sequences. By inspection of the tree it is possible to answer a large number of questions about the system. However, in general the reachability tree described above will be infinite. For practical use it is necessary to reduce it to finite size. This is done by **covering** markings and by **equivalent** markings which is a generalization of **duplicate** markings. Reduction by covering markings and duplicate markings are well-known from PT-trees. Reduction by equivalent markings is, however, a new concept suitable for CP-trees.

Covering markings. When a node has a marking M_2, which strictly covers the marking M_1 of a predecessor, the transition sequence transforming M_1 into M_2 can be repeated several times starting from M_2†. Thus it is possible to get an arbitrarily large value for each coefficient which has increased from M_1 to M_2. In the tree we indicate this by substituting in M_2, the ω-symbol for each such coefficient. The situation is analogous to the idea behind the "pumping lemma" of automata theory and it means that some of the places can obtain an arbitrarily large number of tokens of certain colours.

This kind of reduction results in a loss of information. In [11] it is shown that if ω occurs in a PT-tree, it is not always possible to determine from the tree whether the net has a dead marking or not.

Duplicate markings. If there are several nodes with identical markings, only one of them is developed further, while the others are marked as "duplicate". This reduction will not result in a loss of information because we can construct the missing subtrees from the one developed. Due to reduction by covering markings, two such subtrees may not be completely identical, but they will represent the same set of markings and transition sequences.

Equivalent markings. In order to introduce our notion of equivalent markings we will look at a small example describing "five dining philosophers". The philosophers, $PH = \{ ph_1, ph_2, \ldots, ph_5 \}$, are sitting around a circular table with only five forks, $F = \{ f_1, f_2, \ldots, f_5 \}$, positioned between them:

† If M_2 already contains ω, the situation is more complicated, and it may be necessary to involve some extra occurrences, c.f. [3].

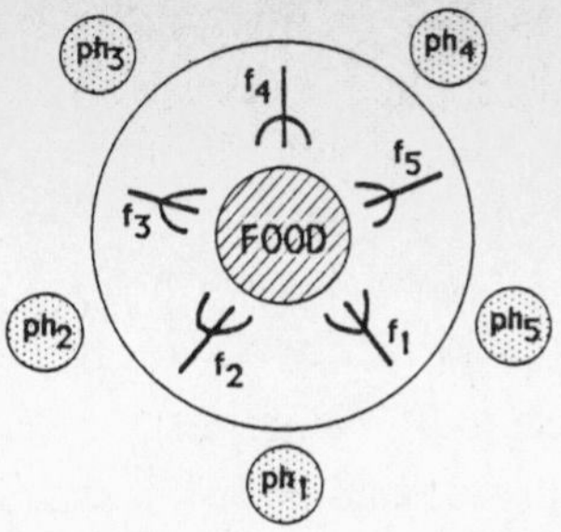

Each philosopher alternates between EATING and THINKING. To eat, a philosopher ph_i needs to take **both** of the two forks next to him. These forks can be found by the functions right, left $\in$ [$PH_{MS}) \rightarrow F_{MS}$ $]_L$ defined by $right(ph_i) = f_i$ and $left(ph_i) = f_{i \oplus 1}$ for all $i \in 1..5$ (where $i \oplus 1$ means: $i+1 \bmod 5$).

The philosopher system can be described by the following CP-net:

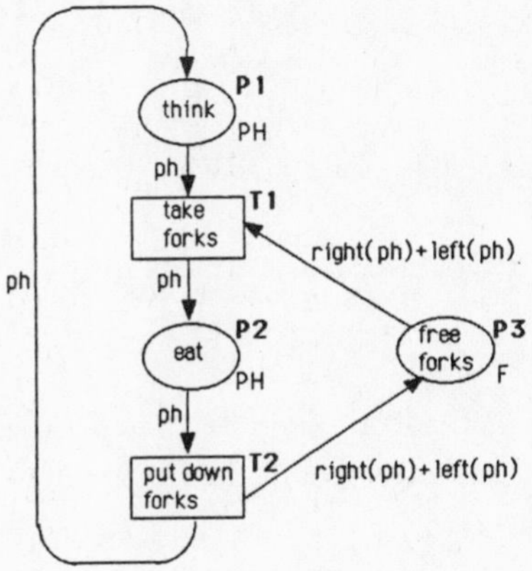

PHILOSOPHER SYSTEM		T1	T2	M_0
		PH	PH	
THINK	PH	-ID	ID	Σ PH
EAT	PH	ID	-ID	
FREE FORKS	F	-RIGHT -LEFT	RIGHT +LEFT	Σ F

Fig. 17. CP-graph and CP-matrix for the philosopher system.

We will analyse the following markings:

$$
\begin{aligned}
M_1 &= (ph_2+ph_3+ph_4+ph_5 , ph_1, \quad , f_3+f_4+f_5) \\
M_2 &= (ph_1+ph_3+ph_4+ph_5 , ph_2 \quad , f_1+f_4+f_5) \\
M_3 &= (ph_2+ph_4+ph_5 , ph_1+ph_3 , f_5) \\
M_4 &= (ph_2+ph_3+ph_4+ph_5 , ph_1, \quad , f_2+f_4+f_5) \\
M_5 &= (ph_3+ph_4+ph_5 , ph_1+ph_2 , f_5).
\end{aligned}
$$

By intuition we want M_1 and M_2 to be **equivalent**. The point is that we do not need to know the identity of eating philosophers, because all philosophers "behave in the same way". The marking M_3 contains a different number of eating philosophers and thus it is not equivalent to M_1 or M_2. However, two markings may be non-equivalent even though they have the same number of eating philosophers and the same number of free forks. In M_1 and M_2 the non-free forks are those belonging to the eating philosopher. This is not the case in M_4, and thus M_4 is not equivalent to M_1 or M_2. In M_5 the two eating philosophers are neighbours. This is not the case in M_3, and so these markings are not equivalent either. To obtain equivalent markings we must demand that the identity of all philosophers and forks are changed by the same **rotation**. As an example, M_1 is obtained from M_2 by the rotation which adds 4 (in a cyclic way) to the index of each philosopher and fork.

To formalize the notion of equivalent markings we associate to the colour set PH the symmetry type "rotation" and we define a bijective correspondence between F and PH by a function $r \in [F \to PH]$, where $r(f_i) = ph_i$ for all $i \in 1..5$. Two markings M and M^+ are equivalent iff there exists a rotation φ_{PH} of PH such that:

$$(*) \qquad M^+(p) = \overline{\varphi_{PH}}\,(M(p)) \qquad \text{for } p = \text{THINK, EAT}$$

$$M^+(p) = \overline{(r^{-1} \circ \varphi_{PH} \circ r)}\,(M(p)) \qquad \text{for } p = \text{FREE FORKS}$$

In our example the markings M_1 and M_2 are equivalent because the rotation:

$$\varphi_{PH} \in [PH \to PH] \text{ defined by } \varphi_{PH}(ph_i) = ph_{i \oplus 4}$$

satisfies (*). On the other hand M_2 and M_4 are not equivalent. From place EAT it is demanded that that:

$$ph_2 = \varphi_{PH}(ph_1)\text{ , i.e. } \varphi_{PH}(ph_i) = ph_{i \oplus 1}$$

but this does not work at place FREE FORKS:

$$M_2(\text{free forks}) = f_1+f_4+f_5 \neq f_1+f_3+f_5 = \overline{(r^{-1} \circ \varphi_{PH} \circ r)}\,(M_4(\text{free forks}))\,.$$

As a generalization of reduction by duplicate markings we will now reduce the reachability tree by equivalent markings: Only one element of each class of equivalent markings is developed further, and when a marking has several direct successors which are equivalent, only one of them is included in the tree.

Figure 18 shows a CP-tree obtained for the philosopher system. In the initial marking transition T1 can occur in all colours of PH producing five equivalent markings of which only one is included in the tree, while the existence of the others is indicated by the label attached to the corresponding arc. If we only reduced by covering markings and duplicate markings, the tree would have had 31 nodes (and exactly the same tree structure as the PT-tree corresponding to the equivalent PT-net).

The relation of equivalent markings is determined by the persons who analyse the system, and it must respect the inherent nature of the system. In the philosopher system, rotation is the suitable symmetry type. But in the telephone system of section 8, arbitrary permutation would be the suitable symmetry type (since there is no special relation between a phone number and its nearest neighbours). In general, several symmetry types (rotation, permutation or identity-function) may be involved in the same system (for different colour sets).

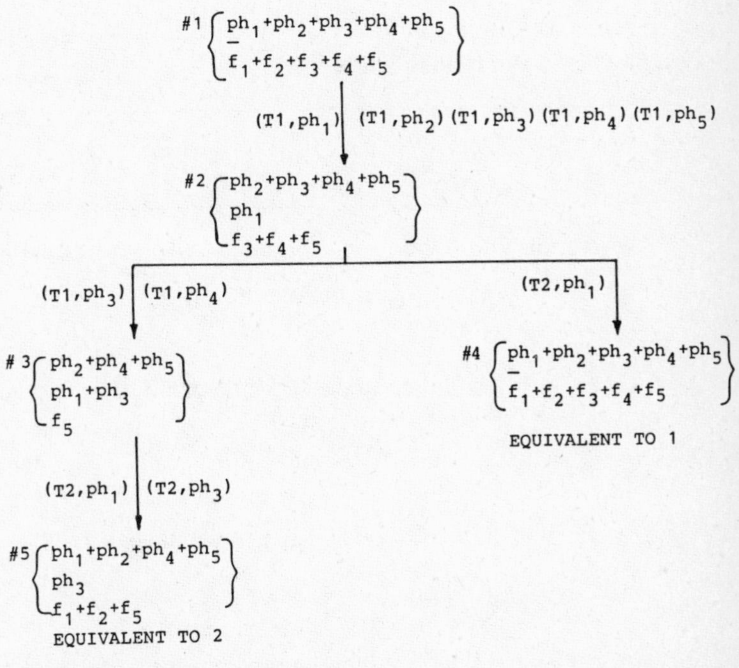

Fig. 18. CP-tree for the philosopher system. It is reduced by covering markings (none in this tree) and by equivalent markings.

When the relation of equivalent markings is defined in a sound way (to be formalized in section 13), the reduction by means of covering markings and equivalent markings does not result in a loss of more information than reduction by covering markings and duplicate markings only. This means that all net properties which can be proved by means of the PT-tree of the equivalent PT-net can also be proved by means of our (much smaller) CP-tree.

12. Formal definition of reachability trees for CP-nets

In this and the following section we consider a fixed CP-net $N = (P, T, C, I_-, I_+, M_0)$. We shall assume P, T, C(p), and C(t) to be finite for all $p \in P$ and $t \in T$.

Definition: The set of colour sets $\{C(x) \mid x \in P \cup T\}$ is **partitioned** into three pairwise disjoint classes:

(1) A is the set of **atomic** colour sets, where each $Ca \in A$ has attached a symmetry type: $sym(Ca) \in$ {permutation, rotation†, identity}.

(2) R is the set of **related** colour sets, where each $Cr \in R$ is related to an atomic colour set Ca by a bijective function $r \in [Cr \to Ca]$.

(3) Π is the set of **product** colour sets, where each $C\pi \in \Pi$ is the cartesian product of atomic and related colour sets.

Definition: A **symmetry** (allowed by the given partition) is a set of bijective functions $\varphi = \{\varphi_C\}_{C \in A \cup R \cup \Pi}$ where $\varphi_C \in [C \to C]$ for all C, and:

(1) For all $Ca \in A$, φ_{Ca} is a function of the kind specified by sym(Ca).

(2) For all $Cr \in R$, with $r \in [Cr \to Ca]$ we have $\varphi_{Cr} = r^{-1} \circ \varphi_{Ca} \circ r$.

(3) For all $C\pi \in \Pi$, with $C\pi = C1 \times C2 \times .... \times Cn$ we have
$\varphi_{C\pi} = \varphi_{C1} \times \varphi_{C2} \times .... \times \varphi_{Cn}$.

The **set of symmetries** (allowed by the given partition) is denoted by Φ. It is finite since P, T, C(p) and C(t) are assumed to be finite for all $p \in P$ and $t \in T$.

† When an atomic colour set has rotation as symmetry type, it must be a finite set and indexed by 1, 2,..., n where n is the cardinality.

The definition of φ_{Cr} can be visualized by the following commutative diagram:

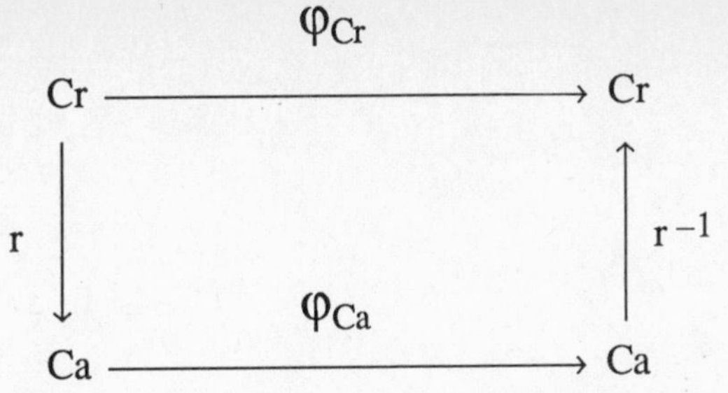

Since r is a bijection it follows that φ_{Cr} is a function of the kind specified by sym(Ca).

Technical remark: The definition of partition is here presented in its simplest form. In some cases (e.g. the data base system of section 7) it may be convenient/ necessary to allow P to contain **subsets** of cartesian products.

If $C\pi = C^n \setminus \{(a,a,...,a) \mid a \in C\}$ we define $\varphi_{C\pi} = (\varphi_C \times \varphi_C \times ... \times \varphi_C)|_{C\pi}$ (where the vertical bar means "restriction to"), yielding a bijection on $C\pi$ as requested Secondly in special cases, there can be sets in use to construct products in P which are not themselves ordinary colour sets in the CP-net. These sets have to be included as atomic or related sets.

◊

We shall use the notation $M [X > M^+$ to denote that the step X is enabled in M, and transforms M to M^+. In this section we will only consider steps which map a single transition into a single occurrence-colour $c \in C(t)$, while all other transitions are mapped into the empty multi-set. Such a step is denoted by (t,c) , where we sometimes omit the brackets. When, for $n \geq 0$:

$$M [t_1,c_1 > M_1 [t_2,c_2 > M_2 ...... M_{n-1} [t_n ,c_n > M^+$$

the sequence $\sigma = (t_1,c_1) (t_2,c_2) ...... (t_n,c_n)$ is a **transition sequence** at M, and M^+ is reachable from M, which we shall denote by $M [\sigma > M^+$.

By R(M) we denote the set of all markings which are reachable from M. A marking is **dead** iff only the empty step is enabled in it. A CP-net is **bounded at place $p \in P$ and colour $c \in C(p)$** iff:

$$\exists\, k \in N\ \forall M \in R(M_0) :\ M(p)\,(c) \leq k$$

and it is **bounded** iff it is bounded at all places and all colours.

Given an ω-marking M, a transition sequence $\sigma = (t_1,c_1)\ (t_2,c_2)\ldots\ldots(t_n,c_n)$ and a symmetry $\varphi \in \Phi$, we define an **equivalent** ω-marking $\varphi(M)$ by:

$$\varphi\,(M)\,(p) = \overline{\varphi_{C(p)}}\,(M(p)) \qquad \text{for all } p \in P$$

and an **equivalent** transition sequence $\varphi(\sigma)$ by:

$$\varphi(\sigma) = (t_1,\varphi_{C(t_1)}(c_1))\ (t_2,\varphi_{C(t_2)}(c_2))\ \ldots\ldots(t_n,\varphi_{C(t_n)}(c_n))\ .$$

Definition

Two ω-markings M_1 and M_2, of a CP-net are **equivalent**, which is written as $M_1 \approx M_2$, iff there exists a symmetry $\varphi \in \Phi$ such that $M_1 = \varphi(M_2)$. It is easy to verify that $\approx$ is an equivalence relation.

Definition: A reachability tree, **CP-tree** , for a CP-net with an equivalence relation $\approx$ (specified by a partition) is the full reachability tree† reduced with respect to covering markings and equivalent markings:

(1) If a node y strictly covers one of its predecessors z then we assign $M_y(p)(c) := \omega$ for all $p \in P$ and all $c \in C(p)$ satisfying $M_y(p)(c) > M_z(p)(c)$.

(2) Only one node in each (reachable) equivalence class of $\approx$ is developed further. Only one node in a set of equivalent brothers is included in the tree. The other nodes are removed, but the arc to the included brother node contains information of their existence.

(3) Associated to each node is an **ω-marking** and a **node-label**. The node-label is a (possibly empty) sequence of status information, which may indicate that the marking is **equivalent** to the marking of an earlier processed node, **covering** the marking of a predecessor node, or **dead**.

(4) Associated to each arc from node n_1 to n_2 is an arc-label which is a list of occurrence information. Each element is a pair (t,c) where $t \in T$ and $c \in C(t)$. Each pair in the list is enabled in the marking of n_1. An occurrence of the first pair in the list results in the marking of n_2, whereas occurrences of the other pairs result in markings which are equivalent to the marking of n_2.

† The full reachability tree contains all reachable markings and all transition sequences starting from the initial marking.

We will draw attention to the fact that, given a net there are often several meaningful ways to define a partition. The user decides the partition and this choice determines the possible symmetries, and thus the relation of equivalent markings. In section 13 we define two soundness criteria for partitions and we establish four proof rules, which for sound partitions allow us to deduce properties of CP-nets from properties of the corresponding CP-trees.

Now we will describe our algorithm to produce the CP-trees. To create a node we use the operation "NEWNODE(M,L)" where M and L are the ω-marking and the node-label of the node. A new arc is created by "NEWARC(n_1,n_2,L)" where n_1, n_2 and L are the source-node, destination-node and arc-label. It is possible to append new information to an existing label, L, by the operation "APPEND(L,new-inf)". The ω-marking and the node-label of a node x are denoted by M_x and L_x, respectively. The arc-label of the arc from node x to node y is denoted by L_{xy}. By "NEXT(M,t,c)" we denote the ω-marking which is obtained from the ω-marking M by an occurrence of transition t with occurrence-colour $c \in C(t)$.

```
ALGORITHM TO PRODUCE HL-TREES

UNPROCESSED := {NEWNODE(M_0,empty)}; PROCESSED := Ø
REPEAT
   SELECT some node x∈UNPROCESSED
   IF M_x≈M_y for some node y∈PROCESSED
   THEN APPEND(L_x,"equivalent to y")
   ELSE IF no pair (t,c) has concession in M_x
        THEN APPEND(L_x,"dead")
        ELSE BEGIN {x is non-equivalent and non-dead}
                   FOR ALL (t,c) having concession in M_x DO
                   BEGIN
                       M := NEXT(M_x,t,c); L:=empty
                       FOR ALL ancestors z with M>M_z DO
                       BEGIN
                           FOR ALL p∈P,c∈C(p) where M(p)(c)>M_z(p)(c) DO
                               M(p)(c) := ω
                           APPEND(L,"covering of z")
                       END
                       IF M≈M_u for some node u being a son of x
                       THEN APPEND(L_xu,"(t,c)")
                       ELSE BEGIN
                                 v := NEWNODE(M,L)
                                 UNPROCESSED := UNPROCESSED ∪ {v}
                                 NEWARC(x,v,"(t,c)")
                            END
                   END
             END
   UNPROCESSED := UNPROCESSED\{x}; PROCESSED := PROCESSED ∪ {x}
UNTIL UNPROCESSED = Ø
```

Fig. 19. Algorithm to produce CP-trees.

The algorithm works in the following way: as long as there are more unprocessed nodes, one is selected and processed. The processing of a node starts with a check for equivalence with an already processed node, i.e. only the first processed node in each equivalence class of $\approx$ is developed further. If no equivalent node is found, the node is checked for being dead. If it is not dead, for each pair (t,c) being enabled, a son is produced and included in the tree (unless it is an equivalent brother). Each CP-tree is a subtree of a PT-tree for the equivalent PT-net, obtained from the CP-net by the method described in [4]. In [2, 7, 11] it is shown that each PT-tree is finite. Thus each CP-tree is finite and our algorithm always halts.

Technical remark: The constructed CP-tree normally depends on the order in which the nodes are processed. This means that each CP-net may have several corresponding CP-trees. Normally, an implementation enforces an ordering-rule for the processing of nodes, and this rule then determines the actual CP-tree, constructed for the CP-net by that implementation.

◊

Technical remark: In an implementation of the algorithm it is crucial to minimize the time spent by testing for equivalence. Our implementation will have a fairly effective algorithm to test two ω-markings for equivalence. Moreover our implementation will use hash coding to divide markings into subclasses in such a way, that equivalent markings always belong to the same subclass. This hash coding drastically decreases the number of pairs to be tested for equivalence.

◊

13. What can be proved by means of CP-trees?

In this section we discuss how CP-trees can be used to prove properties of the corresponding CP-nets.

A **proof rule** is a theorem by which properties of CP-nets can be deduced from properties of CP-trees (or vice versa). For PT-trees, [2, 11] describe a number of such proof rules, from which it is possible to deduce information concerning: boundedness, coverability, reachability, liveness, etc. Some of the proof rules are total, in the sense that the question concerning presence or absence of the particular net property can always be answered by means of the proof rule. Other proof rules are partial, in the sense that the question can only sometimes be answered.

For CP-trees the situation is a bit more complicated, since the observed tree properties in a crucial way may depend on the chosen partition which determines the relation of equivalent markings. Hence it is necessary to introduce the notion of a **sound** partition, which intuitively means that the partition respects the inherent symmetry properties of the CP-net. If we allowed arbitrary permutation for the philosopher system, instead of just rotation, this would be a typical example of a non-sound partition, since it neglects the fact that in this system there is another relationship between neighbours than between non-neighbours. Analogously, it would be non-sound to have both PH and F as atomic colour sets, since this would neglect the fact that there is another relationship between a philosopher and the two nearest forks than between the philosopher and the three remote forks.

Definition: A partition is **sound** iff it satisfies the following:

(SC1) $\forall p\in P\ \forall t\in T\ \forall \varphi\in\Phi:\ \widehat{\varphi_{C(p)}} \circ I_{\pm}(p,t) = I_{\pm}(p,t) \circ \widehat{\varphi_{C(t)}}$

(SC2) $\forall \varphi\in\Phi:\ M_0 = \varphi(M_0)$.

SC1 can be visualized by the following commutative diagram:

$$\begin{array}{ccc} C(t)_{MS} & \xrightarrow{\widehat{\varphi_{C(t)}}} & C(t)_{MS} \\ I_{\pm}(p,t)\ \downarrow & & \downarrow\ I_{\pm}(p,t) \\ C(p)_{MS} & \xrightarrow{\widehat{\varphi_{C(p)}}} & C(p)_{MS} \end{array}$$

SC1 demands that the chosen partition for the CP-net and hence the set of allowed symmetries must agree with the occurrences of transitions in the sense that equivalent colours have to be treated in the "same way". SC2 demands that the initial marking has to be symmetric. In practice it is often nearly trivial to verify the soundness criteria by means of the following rules:

(R1) Due to the linearity of the functions, SC1 can be verified by checking only steps of the form (t,c).

(R2) When $I_{\pm}(p,t)$ is an identity-function or a zero-function, SC1 is always satisfied.

(R3) When $I_{\pm}(p,t)$ is a sum of several functions, SC1 can be verified for each of them, separately.

(R4) When a function appears in $I_{\pm}(p,t)$ for several places/transitions it needs only to be considered once to verify SC1.

(R5) When the symmetry types of C(t) and C(p) both are identity, SC1 is always satisfied.

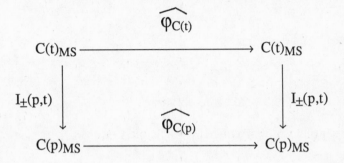

(R6) When the symmetry type of C(t) is rotation, it is enough to consider the "one step forward" rotation to verify SC1.

(R7) When the symmetry type of C(t) is permutation, it is enough to consider transpositions (interchanging of two elements) to verify SC1.

(R8) SC2 is satisfied iff:

$$\forall p \in P : [\, \mathrm{sym}(C(p)) \neq \mathrm{identity} \;\Rightarrow\; \exists\, k \in \mathbf{N} : M_0(p) = k \times \Sigma\, C(p) \,].$$

As an example, soundness of the partition used in section 11 for the philosopher system, can easily be verified. We only have to prove the following properties, where r is the function relating F to PH, while φ_{PH} is the "one step forward" rotation on PH:

$$(r^{-1} \circ \varphi_{PH} \circ r) \circ \mathrm{right} = \mathrm{right} \circ \varphi_{PH}$$

$$(r^{-1} \circ \varphi_{PH} \circ r) \circ \mathrm{left} = \mathrm{left} \circ \varphi_{PH} .$$

To formulate our proof rules we need some notation:

$R(M_0)$ is the set of markings which are reachable from M_0.

$R(M_0)(p) = \{M(p)(c) \mid M \in R(M_0) \wedge c \in C(p)\}$
is the coefficients appearing at place p.

$R(M_0)(p)(c) = \{M(p)(c) \mid M \in R(M_0)\}$
is the coefficients appearing at place p for colour c.

$T(M_0)$ is the set of nodes in the CP-tree having M_0 as root. $T(M_0)(p)$ and $T(M_0)(p)(c)$ are defined analogous to $R(M_0)(p)$ and $R(M_0)(p)(c)$, respectively.

Furthermore we define the function $\mathrm{map}_{C(p)}$ from C(p) into subsets of C(p) by:

$$\mathrm{map}_{C(p)}(c) = \{\, c^+ \in C(p) \mid \exists\, \varphi \in \Phi : \varphi_{C(p)}(c^+) = c \,\} .$$

Observation:

(O1) $$\mathrm{map}_{C(p)}(c) = \begin{cases} \{c\} & \underline{\text{if}}\ \mathrm{sym}(C(p)) = \mathrm{identity} \\ C(p) & \underline{\text{if}}\ \mathrm{sym}(C(p)) \in \{\mathrm{rotation}, \mathrm{permutation}\}. \end{cases}$$

We now formulate our proof rules for CP-trees. They are generalizations of the proof rules given in [11]. Some of the proof rules have SC1 and/or SC2 as prerequisite (i.e. the proof rule is only valid when the prerequisite is satisfied).

Theorem 6 (Proof rules for CP-trees)

proof rule:		**prerequisite:**
(PR1)	N is bounded $\Leftrightarrow \forall p \in P : \omega \notin T(M_0)(p)$	**SC1**
(PR2)	$\sup R(M_0)(p)(c)^{\dagger} = \max \bigcup_{c^+ \in map_{C(p)}(c)} T(M_0)(p)(c^+)$	**SC1, SC2**
(PR3)	$\exists\, \alpha \in T(M_0)$: "dead"$\in L_\alpha \Rightarrow \exists\, M \in R(M_0)$: M is dead	**none**
(PR4)	$\exists\, M \in R(M_0)$: M is dead $\Rightarrow ((\exists\, \alpha \in T(M_0)$: "dead"$\in L_\alpha) \vee (\exists\, p \in P : \omega \in T(M_0)(p)))$	**SC1**

The correctness of our proof rules is established by a sequence of lemmas. The proofs are rather complicated and lengthy. They can be found in [3].

14. Fifth example: Data base system analysed by CP-trees

In this section we show how to analyse the data base system from section 7 by means of CP-trees. We also give some statistics about the sizes of CP-trees, compared to the corresponding PT-trees.

For the data base system described by the CP-net in Figure 10 we define the following partition:

atomic: DBM : permutation; E : identity
product: MB : subset of DBM $\times$ DBM

Soundness criterion SC1 is verified by means of rules R1-R7. By R1, R2 and R4 it is sufficient to check that the incidence-functions ABS, MINE and REC satisfy:

$$\widehat{\varphi_{C(p)}} \circ I_{\pm}(p,t)(c) = I_{\pm}(p,t) \circ \varphi_{C(t)}(c)$$

for each $\varphi \in \Phi$ and $c \in C(t)$.

† By convention $\sup A = \omega$, for $A \subseteq N$, when $\forall k \in N\, \exists\, a \in A : a \geq k$.

ABS: Let $\varphi \in \Phi$ and $s \in DBM$. Then:

$$\varphi_E(\ ABS(s)\ ) = \varphi_E(\varepsilon) = \varepsilon = ABS(\ \varphi_{DBM}(s)\ )$$

MINE: Let $\varphi \in \Phi$ and $s \in DBM$. Then:

$$\widehat{\varphi_{MB}}\ (\ MINE(s)\ ) = \widehat{\varphi_{MB}}\ (\ \sum_{x \neq s} (s,x)\ ) = \sum_{x \neq s} (\ \varphi_{DBM}(s)\ ,\ \varphi_{DBM}(x)\ )$$

$$= \sum_{y \neq \varphi_{DBM}(s)} (\ \varphi_{DBM}(s)\ ,\ y\ ) = MINE(\ \varphi_{DBM}(s)\ )$$

In this particular case we do not use rule R7, since it is just as easy to prove the property for arbitrary permutations.

REC: Let $\varphi \in \Phi$ and $(s,r) \in MB$. Then:

$$\varphi_{DBM}(\ REC((s,r))\ ) = \varphi_{DBM}(\ r\ ) = REC((\ \varphi_{DBM}(s)\ ,\ \varphi_{DBM}(r)\ ))$$
$$= REC(\ \varphi_{MB}((s,r))\ )\ .$$

Soundness criterion SC2 follows immediately from rule R8.

Having verified soundness for the chosen partition, we can now construct the CP-tree shown in Figure 20, and from this we deduce the following properties of the CP-net for the data base system:

Analysis 4 (Boundedness and absence of deadlock)

(PR1) The CP-net is bounded.

(PR2) All places and all colours in the CP-net have 1 as a uniform bound.

(PR3) Cannot be applied.

(PR4) The CP-net has no reachable marking which is dead.

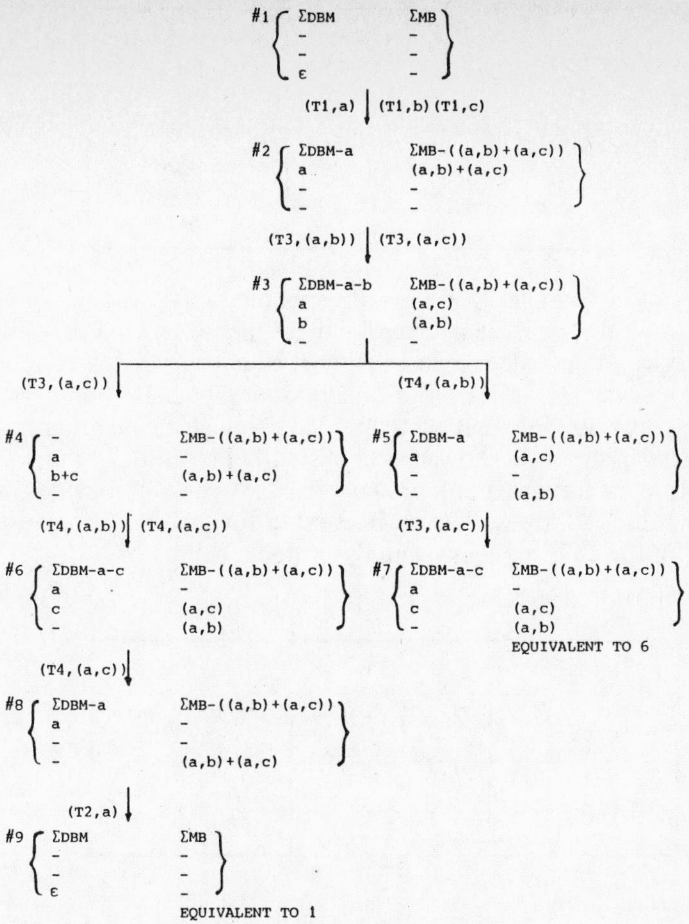

Fig. 20. CP-tree for the data base system with three data base managers (DBM = {a,b,c}).

The two leaves, #7 and #9, of the CP-tree in Figure 20 are not only equivalent, but in fact identical with #6 and #1, respectively. This is, however, a coincidence and it changes if the nodes are processed in another order.

As mentioned earlier, an alternative to the CP-tree is to construct the PT-tree for the equivalent PT-net. In the following table we compare the size of the CP-tree with the size of the PT-tree (for different sizes of DBM):

DATA BASE SYSTEM		
number of data base managers	number of nodes in the HL-tree	number of nodes in the PT-tree
2	5	9
3	9	43
4	14	225
5	23	> 1400

The CP-trees are not just smaller than the corresponding PT-trees, but they also seem to grow slower when the sizes of the involved colour sets increase. It is, however, normally not necessary to consider colour sets, which have more than a few elements: If you know how a system with five philosophers works, you also know how a system with six or more works. Analogously, you only have to investigate a system with three data base managers in order to know how a system with arbitrarily many managers would work. But, even for small colour sets, the CP-trees are considerably smaller than the corresponding PT-trees. This is illustrated for the data base system by the table above, and for the philosopher system by the table below:

PHILOSOPHER SYSTEM		
number of philosophers	number of nodes in the HL-tree	number of nodes in the PT-tree
3	3	7
4	5	17
5	5	31

It should be mentioned that the data base system and the philosopher system do not introduce covering markings (i.e. there is no ω in the trees). An example with covering markings can be found in [3]. It has the following statistics:

PORDUCER / CONSUMER SYSTEM		
number of producers	number of nodes in the HL-tree	number of nodes in the PT-tree
2	30	93

15. Summary

In this paper we have defined Coloured Petri nets and showed how they can be analysed by means of place-invariants and reachability trees.

CP-nets combines the virtues of the graph-form of PrT-nets and the matrix-form of the old version of CP-nets. CP-nets uses expressions in the graph-form and functions in the matrix-form. The graph-form is normally applied for system description and informal explanation, while the matrix-form is applied for formal analysis.

References

[1] H.J. Genrich and K. Lautenbach: **System modelling with high-level Petri nets.** Theoretical Computer Science 13 (1981), 109-136.

[2] M. Hack: **Decidability questions for Petri nets**. TR 161, MIT, 1976.

[3] P. Huber, A.M. Jensen, L.O. Jepsen and K. Jensen: **Reachability trees for high-level Petri nets**. Theoretical Computer Science 45 (1986).

[4] K. Jensen: **Coloured Petri nets and the invariant-method**. Theoretical Computer Science 14 (1981), 317-336.

[5] K. Jensen: **How to find invariants for coloured Petri nets**. In: J. Gruska, M. Chytill (eds.): Mathematical Foundations of Computer Science 1981, Lecture Notes in Computer Science vol. 118, Springer-Verlag, 1981, 327-338.

[6] K. Jensen: **High-level Petri nets**. In: A. Pagnoni and G. Rozenberg (eds.): Applications and Theory of Petri Nets, Informatik-Fachberichte vol. 66, Springer-Verlag, 1983, 166-180.

[7] R.M. Karp and R.E. Miller: **Parallel program schemata**. Journal of Computer and System Sciences, vol. 3, 1969, 147-195.

[8] K. Lautenbach: **Liveness in Petri nets**, Interner Bericht ISF-75-02.1, GDM Bonn, 1975.

[9] G. Memmi and G. Roucairol: **Linear algebra in net theory**. In: W. Brauer (ed.), Net theory and applications, Lecture Notes in Computer Science vol. 84, Springer-Verlag, 1980, 213-223.

[10] H. Oberquelle: **Communication by graphic net representations**, Bericht Nr. 75, Fachbereich Informatik, Universität Hamburg, 1981.

[11] J.L. Peterson: **Petri net theory and the modeling of systems**. Prentice-Hall, 1981.

[12] W. Reisig: **Petri nets with individual tokens.** Theoretical Computer Science 41 (1985), 185-213.

ANALYSING NETS BY THE INVARIANT METHOD[1]

G. MEMMI

BULL - C.R.G. - 68 Route de Versailles. 78430 LOUVECIENNES - FRANCE

J. VAUTHERIN

L.R.I. - UA 410 CNRS - Université Paris Sud. 91405 ORSAY Cedex - FRANCE

CONTENTS

I. INTRODUCTION

Methods for analysing P/T-systems can be roughly divided into several categories : study of the reachability set, transformation by homomorphism, and invariants. Each of these methods have advantages and disadvantages.

Here we will focus on the methods based upon the computation and the analysis of invariants. The invariant method [Lautenbach... 74], [Jensen 81], [Memmi 83] is well known for at least two advantages : on the one hand, analysis can be performed on local subnets while ignoring how the whole system behaves ; on the other hand, this method still holds, even when the P/T-system is enriched with parameters - i.e. even when considering Pr/T-systems or other high level nets.

In this paper, three theoretical results about linear invariants and semi-flows computation are presented (we call *semi-flows* the weighting vectors f - solutions of the linear system $f^T.C = 0$ - which generate the linear invariants) :

- The first one deals with the computation of a smallest set of generators of the positive semi-flows of a P/T-system. An algorithm - the Farkas algorithm - is presented and proved.

- The second result is about the computation of semi-flows of unary Pr/T-systems : it states that the set of semi-flows of such a system can be generated by a finite number of integers vectors which are computable

1 A part of this work was granted by the Esprit project FOR-ME-TOO.

directly from the incidence matrix of the system ; thus without unfolding and independently of the colors which are not effectively present in the incidence matrix.

- The third one shows how to characterize all the minimal supports of the set of positive semi-flows while the net contains some parameters but with special connection constraints.

These results are illustrated by the modelling and analysis of a parallel system - namely the "general channel" of the L language. Other important issues of this study are

- to show how different kinds of nets (P/T-systems, unary Pr/T-systems, fifo nets) can be used at different steps of an analysis, depending on the aspects of the system that we want to study.

- to outline an analysis methodology of nets based on the proof of invariants. For that purpose, we introduce the notion of home space (a set of markings that we are always sure to reach after any evolution of the system).

- to introduce and show the interest of a combined use of nets and algebraic specifications.

The paper is organized as follows :

The general channel is described in section II and modelled by a P/T-system in section III, omitting some details voluntarily. In this first model, we describe the Farkas algorithm (III.1) and the notion of home space (III.2). We show how to use these results in order to obtain informations on the length of some data and the behaviour of the system. We show that the P/T-system can reach a deadlock.

This is due to a lack of precision in the description of the data structures ; thus we make the model evolve from a P/T-system to a unary Pr/T-system [Vautherin... 85] where some aspects of the system can be detailed. Then the invariants also bring more information (IV.2). In this model, we describe the computation of a set of generators of semi-flows, and we characterize all the minimal supports of the set of positive semi-flows (IV.3 and IV.4).

Then we change the model again and choose the fifo nets model [Memmi... 85] (see also the lecture of G. Roucairol in this course) for taking into account the fifo mechanism of the main data structure of the system (V.I). Here, by stepwise refinements of home spaces, also with the help of non linear invariants, we prove that the initial marking is a home state, and then that the system is live (V.2).

Next we try to find the most general data structure such that the system remains live. at the same time, we want this data structure to impose the least synchronization constraints, so that the whole system runs as fast as possible. This structure is specified by an algebraic abstract data type associated with a Pr/T-system [Vautherin 85] (VI.1). Here again the invariant method is transposed : the liveness question is studied for different data structure with the same sketch of proof (VI.2).

We must warn the reader that we had to homogenize some notations between the different nets models. However, we tried to remain unchanged the most standard ones though it may induce some slight ambiguities (such as C for the incidence matrix and for a set of colors). Our belief is that they are context-sensitive.

II. THE GENERAL CHANNEL EXAMPLE

The general channel is a central element in the L language [Boussinot 83] for processes to communicate. It has been analysed first in [Memmi 81]. Mainly it is a bounded fifo ; one can put into or get messages from it. Its functioning is formally described in the Boussinot-Kahn model [Boussinot 81] ; here, we simplify the original description a little and consider the schema of figure 1.

Sequential processes (represented by rectangles) communicate via infinite fifo channels :

- *put (c, e)* put into the channel c the value e,

- *get (c, v)* get from the channel c some value assigned to the variable v. If c is empty, the process is locked until some process puts a value into c. Only one process can get from a given channel c.

The general channel is a bounded fifo Fileval managed by a sequential process G. Its length is max. ip producers can put information into it ; ic consumers can get information from it.

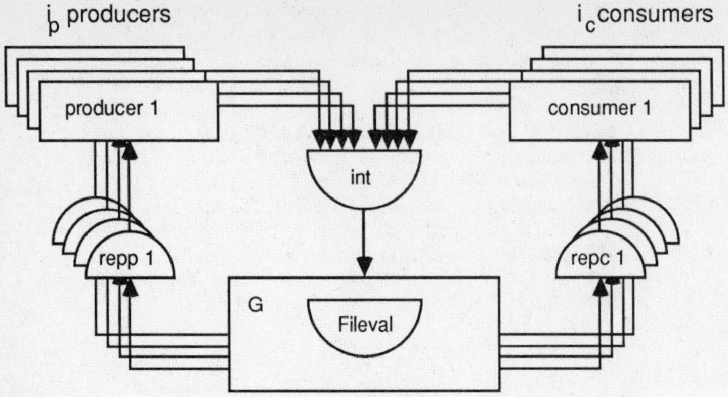

Figure 1

Before putting some value e into Fileval, a producer pr_k must send its identity in order to get from the channel $repp_k$ an acknowledgement from G. Then its code is :

<u>loop</u> put (int, pr_k) ; get ($repp_k$, v) ; put (int, e) <u>end loop</u>

Let us point out that the variable v is used in order to store the acknowledgment from G which is only a way to synchronize the two processes. A consumer c_k will ask G some value and will store it in z by :

<u>loop</u> put (int, c_k) ; get ($repc_k$, z) <u>end loop</u>

G uses auxiliary queues :

- Depos, of length ip, contains the identities of producers which sent a request while Fileval was full.

- Prise, of length ic, contains the identities of consumers which sent a request while Fileval was empty.

Moreover, G controls Fileval via a variable Per which indicates the number of acknowlegments G can deliver. In its loop, G begins to get a message in its input channel int :

In case of a request from producer pr_k, G executes

<u>If</u> Per = 0 <u>then</u> put (Depos, pr_k) <u>else</u> {Per $\leftarrow$ Per - 1; put ($repp_k$, ok)} <u>end if</u>.

In case of a request from consumer c_k, G executes :

<u>If</u> Fileval is empty <u>then</u> put (Prise, c_k)
<u>else</u> {get (Fileval, x) ; put ($repp_k$, x) ;
<u>if</u> Depos is empty <u>then</u> Per $\leftarrow$ Per + 1
<u>else</u> {get (Depos, pr_h) ; put ($repp_h$, ok)}
<u>end if</u>
<u>end if</u>.

In case of a value e sent by a producer, G executes :

<u>If</u> Prise is empty <u>then</u> put (Fileval, e)
<u>else</u> {get (Prise, c_h) ; put ($repc_h$, e) ; Per ← Per + 1}
<u>endif</u>.

At the initial state, processes are idle ; all the fifos are empty ; the value of Per is max.

III. THE P/T-SYSTEM MODEL

With this first net, int is unstructured and modelled by three places intp, intc, inte receiving the three different types of messages which can be sent to int. The channels $repp_i$ are folded in one place repp, the channels $repc_i$ in the place repc. All the messages are merged and modelled by a mere token. The initial marking m° is given by :

$$m°(p1) = ip,\quad m°(p8) = ic,\quad m°(p3) = 1,\quad m°(Per) = max,\quad m°(p) = 0 \text{ otherwise.}$$

In the figure 2, we have duplicated the place p3, and used inhibitor arcs (between Fileval and t7 for example) for readability.

The places p1 and p2 represents the states of producers ; p8 and p9 the states of consumers ; p3 and p7 the states of G :

When m(p3) = 1, G is idle and waits for a message in int.
When m(p4) = 1, G treats a request from a producer and tests Per.
When m(p5) = 1, G treats a request from a consumer and tests Fileval.
When m(p6) = 1, G treats a value and tests Prise.
When m(p7) = 1, G sent a value into repc and tests Depos.

A first approach to analyze the net should be to construct the reachability set for ip = ic = max = 1 and to invoke some induction step or to developp a kind of high-level reachability tree like in [Hubert 85] ; but it is still open to investigation. Thus, let us apply the invariant method. First, we have to find a family of semi-flows to generate our invariants.

It is well known that the set of semi-flows, over Z or Q, of a given P/T-system admits a basis which can be computed by using Hermite's or Gauss algorithms for instance. In the following we are interested in the computation of of *positive* semi-flows. A reason for doing that is given below ; others can be found in [Memmi 83].

III.1. The Farkas algorithm

This algorithm which we delicate to Farkas has been rediscovered at the same time by several authors [Martinez 82], [Alaiwan... 85], [Memmi 83], with slight variations. In fact, a first attempt to solve a system of linear equations with solutions in the natural numbers is found in the Farkas works [Farkas 02]. In [Alaiwan 85] a program of this algorithm is presented. Here, we give only the proof that this algorithm provides a smallest set of generator of the set of the semi-flows of a given system over Q^+, i.e. a set of generators of minimal support (see [Memmi... 80]).

Let us recall that the support of a vector v, denoted by ||v||, is defined by :

$$||v|| = \{i \mid v_i \neq 0\}.$$

As usual, S and T denote the sets of places and transitions of the P/T-system. We take n = | S | ; then I_n denotes the (n×n) identity matrix.

For each k, e_i in Z^k is defined by $e_i(i) = 1$, $e_i(j) = 0$ otherwise.

C(.,i) denotes the column indexed by i of the incidence matrix C.

Figure 1

The P/T-system model

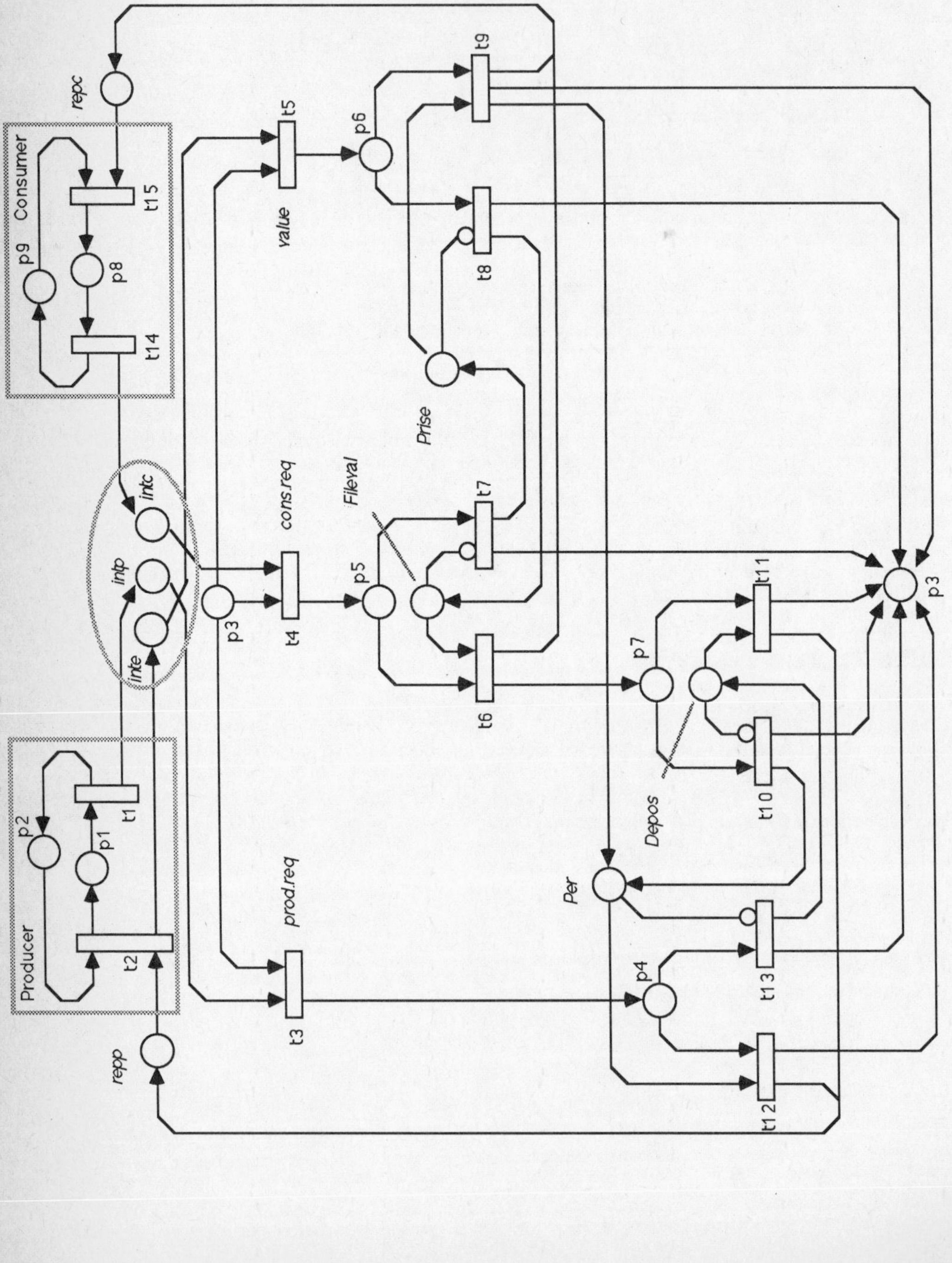

Algorithm :

Initialisation : Let $F_0^* = I_n$; $m_0 = | T |$, $T_0 = \emptyset$

Step i : choose a transition t_i not in T_{i-1}

Let $x = (F_{i-1}^*)^T.C(.,i)$
$E = \{e_k \in Z^{m_{i-1}} \mid x_k = 0\}$
$P = \{i \mid x_i > 0\}$, $Q = \{j \mid x_j < 0\}$
$F = \{f_{ij} \in N^{m_{i-1}} \mid \forall i \in P, \forall j \in Q, f_{ij}(i) = -x_j, f_{ij}(j) = x_i, f_{ij}(k) = 0 \text{ otherwise}\}$
$F_i = F_{i-1}^*.[F \mid E]$,

where [F | E] is the matrix obtained by the justaposition of the vectors of F with the vectors of E considered as columns.

F_i^* is obtained from F_i by canceling all columns of non minimal support and such that there is not two columns with the same support. m_i is the number of columns in F_i.

$T_i = T_{i-1} \cup \{t_i\}$.

Termination : when $(F_k^*)^T.C = 0$.

Theorem 1. *This algorithm does terminate at some step $k < n_0$ where F_k is a smallest set of generators of the set of semi-flows over Q^+.*

Proof. By induction on step i: at this step, F_i^* is a smallest set of generators of the set of semi-flows of the system generated by the treated transitions.
i) At step 0, each place p_j is isolated, so e_j is a semi-flow, and the result is straigtforward.
ii) Let us assume it holds until step i-1. At step i we have to solve $u^T.C(.,k) = 0$ for each k such that t_k is in T_i ; in particular, $u = F_{i-1}^*.w$ by induction and, $u^T.C(.,i) = 0$. With $u = F_{i-1}^*.w$, we get $w^T.(F_{i-1}^*)^T.C(.,i) = 0$. But $w = [F \mid E].v$, so $u = F_{i-1}^*.[F \mid E].v$, and the columns of $F_{i-1}^*.[F \mid E]$ are a family of generators for the set of semi-flows of the P/T-system generated by T_i. []

This algorithm is complex ; some heuristics based upon the choice one can make on the transition t_i are described in [Memmi 83]. In [Martinez... 82], a proposition is made for not comparing the supports of every columns when transforming F_i in F_i^*. In [Graubmann 85] an interesting calculation of semi-flows by composition is presented.

When the P/T-system is a marked graph, a circuit can be associated with any semi-flow ; and algorithms for finding circuits in a graph [Mateti... 76] are in many cases more efficient than the Farkas algorithm.

Applying this algorithm to our P/T-system we get six semi-flows generating the six following invariants : three of them are related to the three kinds of processes :

IPP : $\forall m \in [m°>, m(p1) + m(p2) = ip$
IPC : $\forall m \in [m°>, m(p8) + m(p9) = ic$
IPG : $\forall m \in [m°>, \Sigma_{i=3,\dots,7}\, m(p_i) = 1$

while the three others are related to the three kinds of messages :

IP : $\forall m \in [m°>$, m(p1) + m(intp) + m(p4) + m(Depos) + m(repp) = ip

IC : $\forall m \in [m°>$, m(p8) + m(intc) + m(p5) + m(Prise) + m(repc) = ic

IV : $\forall m \in [m°>$, m(repp) + m(inte) + m(p6) + m(Fileval) + m(p7) + m(Per) = max

We know ([Memmi... 80]) that all linear invariants with positive coefficients can be generated with these six ones: they contain all the information that any linear invariant can bring.

With IP, IC, IV, we already can conclude that all the channels are bounded with :

$$m(repp) \leq ip \; ; \; m(repc) \leq ic \; ; \; m(int) \leq max + ic + ip.$$

Moreover, from IV we directly have : m(Fileval) $\leq$ max for any behaviour of the net. Thus, when a producer sends a value for Fileval we are sure that there exists a place for it in Fileval : Per controls Fileval efficiently.

In fact, we could not conclude such properties so straightforwardly if coefficients of the semi-flows were not positive. This justifies to investigating the set of positive semi-flows.

To go further in our study, we need to introduce the notion of home space.

III.2. The notion of home space

Home states are well known in protocol analysis ; the notion of home space generalizes this idea. A home space is a set of markings such that after any sequence of transistions there always exists a possibility to reach one element of this set. This notion is closely related to the notion of liveness.

Definition 1. *$E \in N^S$ is a <u>home space</u> if and only if ,*

$\forall m \in [m°>, \exists e \in E \cap [m>$

If E = {m}, m is said to be a home state.

The equivalence of the three following properties can easily be stated:

i) The initial marking m° is a home state.
ii) Each marking m of [m°> is a home state.
iii) The reachability graph is strongly connected.

The set of markings at which a given transition t is enabled is a home space if and only if t is live. But, if there exists a home space for a given P/T-system, this one is not necessarily live. Let us point out that N^S is a home space for any marked P/T-system.

If m is a home state then each transition enabled at m is live. Our method of analysis will consist in finding some home space and trying to reach a home state by successive refinements.

In our example, let us prove that E3 = $\{m \in N^S \mid m(p3) = 1\}$ is a home space. Let M be a marking of [m°>. From IPG, there exists a token among p3 to p7 :

- if M(p4) = 1, either t12 or t13 is enabled, then we reach a marking of E3

- if M(p7) = 1, either t10 or t11 is enabled, then we reach E3

- if M(p5) = 1, either t6 is enabled then we reach m' with m'(p7) = 1 or t7 is enabled and we reach E3.

- if M(p6) = 1, either t8 or t9 is enabled and allows to reach E3.

Thus E3 is a home space. It means that the process G can always return to its idle state (p3) after any occurrence sequence of the system.

Moreover, we have proved that we always can reach E3 without t1, t2 or t14 occurring (and these transitions are the only ones that put messages in int). This means that we can easily refine E3 by :

$$E3int = \{m \in E3 \mid m(intp) = m(intc) = m(inte) = 0\}.$$

E3int is a home space, meaning that G can always return to its idle state while int is empty.

Even though E3int exists, there exists a deadlock for this P/T-system : the producers send max values in inte, then they are all put in Depos ; the ic consumers are then put in Prise. At this state, the sequence : t5, t9, t15, t14, t4, t5 may occur max times (Fileval is always empty) ; and then the P/T-system is dead.

Let us point out that the dead markings are necessarily in E3int.

We can refine E3int again by :

$$E3R = \{m \in E3int \mid m(repp) = m(repc) = 0\}.$$

Indeed, let us consider $m \in E3int$ with m(repp) = xp, m(repc) = xc. From IP and IPP, we have

$$m(p2) = m(repp) + m(Depos) + m(p4) + m(intp).$$

So m(p2) > xp and t2 may occur xp times yielding m' with m'(inte) = xp. Then the sequences t5, t8 or t5, t9 may occur xp times reaching m'' of E3int m''(repp) = 0 and m''(repc) > xc. From IC and IPC, we have :

$$m''(p9) = m''(repc) + m''(Prise) + m''(intc) + m''(p5).$$

So t15 may occur as many times as necessary to empty repc. Hence we reach a marking of E3R.

Thus a message sent by G can always be consumed by some process but we are not at all sure that a message sent for pr_i has been be consumed by itself.

IV. COLOURED P/T-SYSTEMS AND UNARY Pr/T-SYSTEMS

This analysis can be made more precise by distinguishing the processes from each other. For this purpose, we use a P/T-system with individual tokens. More precisely, we use a system in a particular class of coloured P/T-systems (or coloured Petri nets [Jensen 81]) : unary Predicate/Transition-systems ([Vautherin... 85]).

IV.1. Definitions

In a P/T-system with individual tokens, the marking of a place is a multiset instead of a positive integer. Before recalling the definitions of coloured P/T-systems, we precise some notations about multisets and neighbouring concepts.

In the following, K denotes either N or Z or Q^+ or Q. Let A be any set, we denote by K^A the set of functions from A into K provided with the usual "pointwise" operations :

$$(w + w')(x) = w(x) + w'(x), \qquad (n.w)(x) = n.w(x) \qquad \forall x \in A,$$

for every w and w' in K^A and every n in K. We write δ for the null function of K^A (i.e. $\delta(x) = 0$ for every x in A). The set K^A is ordered by defining $w \geq w'$ iff

$$\forall x \in A, \qquad w(x) \geq w'(x).$$

For each x in A, we write e_x the element of K^A such that $e_x(x) = 1$ and $e_x(y) = 0$ when $y \neq x$.

We denote by $K^{(A)}$ the subset of K^A containing the functions whose support is finite (remember that the support of w is defined by $\| w \| = \{x \mid w(x) \neq 0\}$). An element of $N^{(A)}$ is called a *multiset* over A. Obviously we have:

$$w = \Sigma_{x \in A}\, w(x).e_x$$

for every w in $K^{(A)}$. Notice that this summation is well defined because there is only a finite number of non null terms.

When no confusion is possible, we only write $<x>$ for e_x. So, for instance, with $A = \{a,b\}$, $2<a> + <b>$ denotes the multiset w over A such that $w(a) = 2$ and $w(b) = 1$.

Now let us consider a finite set X of variables. We can represent by multisets over $A \cup X$ some functions into $N^{(A)}$: let w be a multiset over $A \cup X$ and let A^X be the set of all variables assignment $\sigma : X \rightarrow A$; w determines a function $[[w]]$ from A^X into $N^{(A)}$ by :

$$[[w]](\sigma) = \Sigma_{a \in A}\, w(a).<a> + \Sigma_{x \in X}\, w(x).<\sigma(x)>$$

For instance, with $X = \{x\}$ and $\sigma : x \rightarrow a$, $[[a + b + x]](\sigma) = 2<a> + <b>$.

The set of functions from A^X into $N^{(A)}$ that can be represented in this way by elements of $N^{(A \cup X)}$ is denoted by $[[N^{(A \cup X)}]]$.

Finally, for every w in $K^{(A)}$, we write $| w |$ for $\Sigma_{a \in A}\, w(x)$. When w is a multiset, $| w |$ is the length of w. Notice that for all σ in A^X, $| [[w]](\sigma) | = | w |$.

Definition 2. *A* <u>*coloured P/T-system*</u> *is a 5-tuple $R = <S, T, C, W, M°>$ where :*
i) $S = \{p1, \ldots, pn\}$ and T are the finite sets of places and transitions.
ii) C is a $(S \cup T)$-indexed family of non empty sets (possibly infinite) C(x). For each place p, elements of C(p) are called colours.
iii) W is a $(S{\times}T \cup T{\times}S)$-indexed family of functions, such that, for each p in S and each t in T, W(p,t) and W(t,p) have C(t) for domain and $N^{(C(p))}$ for codomain.
iv) M° is a marking of R, i.e. an element of the product set $N^{(C(p1))} \times \ldots \times N^{(C(pn))}$; M° is called the initial marking of R.

The behaviour of a coloured P/T-system is defined just as for a P/T-system : a transition t may occur at the marking M, yielding to the marking M', if and only if :

$$\exists \sigma \in C(t),\ \forall p \in S, \quad M(p) \geq W(p,t)(\sigma) \text{ and, } \quad M'(p) + W(p,t)(\sigma) = M(p) + W(t,p)(\sigma).$$

This is denoted by : $M[t > M'$.

A unary Predicate/Transition-system is a coloured P/T-system whose functions valuating the arcs can be represented by multisets over $A \cup X$, where A is a set of colours and X a set of variables.

Definition 3. *A (free) unary Predicate/Transition-system (UPr/T-system for short), is a coloured P/T-system $R = < S, T, C, W, M° >$ such that :*

i) all places are associated with the same set of colours A : $\forall p \in S$, $C(p) = A$

ii) there is a set X such that for every t in T, $C(t) = A^X$

iii) for every p and t, the functions W(p,t) and W(t,p) can be represented by multisets over $A \cup X$:

$W(p,t), W(t,p) \in [[N^{(A \cup X)}]]$.

Notice that, since all the places have the same set of colors, a marking of an UPr/T-system can be seen as a function from S into $N^{(A)}$.

Remark. The original definition of UPr/T-systems ([Vautherin... 85]) differs slightly from this one on the sets C(t) which may be proper subsets of A^X. This is the reason why we call these systems "free" UPr/T-systems.

According to the definition of $[[N^{(A \cup X)}]]$, a UPr/T-system is totally described by a 6-tuple <S, T, A, X, w, M°> where :

i) S, T, A, X and M° are defined as previously,

ii) w is an $(S \times T \cup T \times S)$-indexed family of multisets over $A \cup X$.

Notice that we use the lower case form w when the valuations of the arcs are multisets and we use the capital form W when these valuations are functions. The relation between the two notations is $W(x,y) = [[w(x,y)]]$ for every arc (x,y).

It is well known that each coloured P/T-system R whose sets C(x) (for $x \in S \cup T$) are finite, admits an equivalent P/T-system which is obtained by unfolding R (one unfolds p in | C(p) | places, t in | C(t) | transitions). Then, we define the semi-flows of a coloured P/T-system R in such a way that they coincide with those of the equivalent P/T-system, when it is defined.

Definition 4. *Let $R = <S, T, C, W, M°>$ be a coloured P/T-system with $S = \{p1,...,pn\}$, a K-semi-flow of R is an element $f = (f_{p1},..., f_{pn})$ of $K^{C(p1)} \times ... \times K^{C(pn)}$ such that*

$$\forall t \in T,\ \forall \sigma \in C(t),\ \sum_{p \in S, a \in C(p)} f_p(a).W(p,t)(\sigma)(a) = \sum_{p \in S, a \in C(p)} f_p(a).W(t,p)(\sigma)(a)$$

The set of K-semi-flows of R is denoted by $F_K(R)$.

Notice that f_p may have an infinite support. However, since $W(p,t)(\sigma)$ and $W(t,p)(\sigma)$ have a finite support, the summations in this definition are always defined. Let us also mention that in [Jensen 81] and [Silva... 85], any set Z(U) can be used instead of K ; but in that case, each semi-flow with respect to U thus defined, can be viewed as a family of Z-semi-flows as we defined them here.

Finally notice that for a UPr/T-system, since all the places have the same set of colors A, a semi-flow is a vector $f = (f_p)_{p \in S}$ with $f_p \in K^A$.

Proposition 1. (Lautenbach) *If f is a K-semi-flow of R, then*

$$\forall M \in [M°>,\ \sum_{p \in S, a \in C(p)} f_p(a).M(p)(a) = \sum_{p \in S, a \in C(p)} f_p(a).M°(p)(a)$$

When satisfied, this formula is called a linear invariant of R.

With the usual componentwise operations $(f_1,..., f_n) + (g_1,..., g_n) = (f_1 + g_1,..., f_n + g_n)$ and $k.(f_1,..., f_n) = (k.f_1,..., k.f_n)$, it is easy to see that $F_K(R)$ is closed under addition and product by a scalar ; hence $F_Z(R)$ has a Z-module structure.

IV.2. The channel modelling

A unary Pr/T-system representing the channel is drawn in figure 3. Here we have : $A = Cp \cup Cc \cup \{*\}$ where

$Cp = \{pr_i \mid i \in [1,..., ip]\}$ represents the set of producers,
$Cc = \{c_i \mid i \in [1,..., ic]\}$ the set of consumers,

and * is used to denote a produced value in inte and Fileval, as well as the usual token marking Per, p3, p6 and p7. We have $X = \{x,y\}$.

The initial marking M° is such that :

$M°(p1) = \Sigma_i <pr_i>$, $M°(p8) = \Sigma_i <c_i>$, $M°(Per) = \max <*>$,
$M°(p3) = <*>$ and $M°(p) = \delta$ otherwise

This coloured system has the same deadlock as the P/T-system of figure 2, but its behaviour is more precise : for each marking, we know in which state the different processe are and the position of their request, if any.

By considering the invariants of the P/T-system, one can foresee that the coloured system admits the following ones :

$\forall i \in [1,..., ip]$,
IPPi : $\forall M \in [M°>, M(p1)(pr_i) + M(p2)(pr_i) = 1$
IPi : $\forall M \in [M°>, M(p1)(pr_i) + M(intp)(pr_i) + M(p4)(pr_i) + M(Depos)(pr_i) + M(repp)(pr_i) = 1$

$\forall i \in [1,..., ic]$,
IPCi : $\forall M \in [M°>, M(p8)(c_i) + M(p9)(c_i) = 1$
ICi : $\forall M \in [M°>, M(p8)(c_i) + M(intc)(c_i) + M(p5)(c_i) + M(Prise)(c_i) + M(repc)(c_i) = 1$

IPG : $\forall M \in [M°>, \Sigma_{i=3,...,7} \mid M(p_i) \mid = 1$
IV : $\forall M \in [M°>, \mid M(repp) \mid + \mid M(inte) \mid + \mid M(p6) \mid + \mid M(Fileval) \mid + \mid M(p7) \mid + \mid M(Per) \mid = \max$

From the two families of invariants IPi and ICi, we can conclude that each channel $repp_i$ and each channel $repc_i$ has length 1. Also from IPi and IPPi we can deduce :

$M(p2)(pr_i) = M(intp)(pr_i) + M(p4)(pr_i) + M(Depos)(pr_i) + M(repp)(pr_i)$,
and $M(p2)(pr_i) \leq 1$.

Hence any message sent by G to a producer pr_i is well consumed by pr_i. That could not be deduced from the ordinary P/T-system.

Now, some questions arise :

- How are these invariants really connected to those of the P/T-system of figure 1 ?
- Do they constitute an exhaustive list of "basic" invariants of the Pr/T-system ?
- Was it possible to generate them by a computation over the Pr/T-system ?

The following two paragraphs answer these questions.

Figure 3

The Unary Pr/T-system model

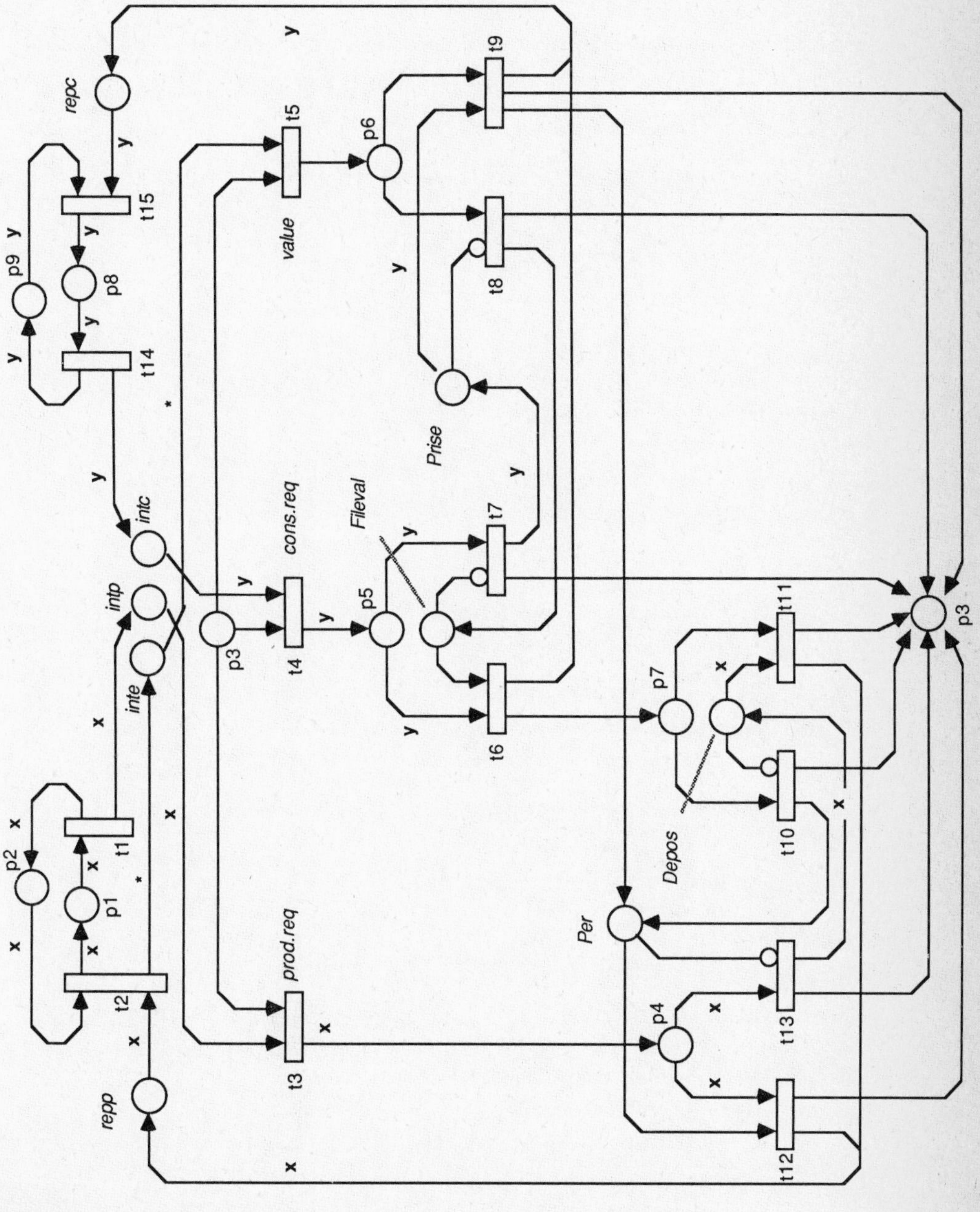

IV.3. Computation of invariants for unary Pr/T-systems

At first we describe more precisely the structure of $F_Z(R)$ when R is a unary Pr/T-system.

Let R = < S, T, A, X, w, M°> be a unary Pr/T-system ; we denote by $(c_{p,t})_{p\in S, t\in T}$ the incidence matrix of R; so for every p and t, $c_{p,t}$ = w(p,t) - w(t,p). We write E for the subset of colors which are effectively present in the incidence matrix (i.e., a∈E <=> $\exists$p,t / $c_{p,t}(a) \neq 0$). The complementary of E in A is denoted by NE. Notice that E is always finite, but NE is infinite as soon as A is infinite.

Now we choose an arbitrary element a° in A. We denote by ¶ the element of Z^A such that ¶(a) = 1 for all a in A ; remember that e_a is such that $e_a(a) = 1$ and $e_a(a') = 0$ for a' ≠ a.

Proposition 2. *Let* $u = ((X_p)_{p\in S}, (Y_{p,a})_{p\in S, a\in E\setminus\{a°\}})$ *be a solution of*

$$(\mathrm{I})\begin{cases} \forall t\in T, \ \sum_{p\in S}\left(X_p\,/\,c_{p,t}\,/ + \sum_{a\in E\setminus\{a°\}} Y_{p,a}\, c_{p,t}(a)\right) = 0 \\ \forall a\in E\setminus\{a°\},\ \forall x\in X,\ \sum_{p\in S} Y_{p,a}\, c_{p,t}(x) = 0 \end{cases}$$

then the vector $f = (f_p)_{p\in S}$ *such that*

$$\forall p\in S,\ f_p = X_p.¶ + \sum_{a\in E\setminus\{a°\}} Y_{p,a}.e_a$$

is a semi-flow of R. The corresponding invariant is

$$\forall M\in[M°>,\ \sum_{p\in S}\left(X_p\,/\,M_p\,/ + \sum_{a\in E\setminus\{a°\}} Y_{p,a}\, M_p(a)\right) = C^{te}$$

Proof. Cf. [Vautherin 86b].

Proposition 3. *Let* $w = ((Z_p)_{p\in S})$ *be a solution of*

$$(\mathrm{II})\left\{ \forall x\in X,\ \forall t\in T,\ \sum_{p\in S} Z_p\, c_{p,t}(x) = 0 \right.$$

then for each color α *in* $NE\setminus\{a°\}$*, the vector* $f^\alpha = (f^\alpha{}_p)_{p\in S}$ *such that*

$$\forall p\in S,\ f_p^\alpha = Z_p.e_\alpha$$

is a semi-flow of R. The corresponding invariant is

$$\forall \alpha\in NE\setminus\{a°\},\ \forall M\in[M°>,\ \sum_{p\in S} Z_p\, M_p(\alpha) = C^{te}$$

Proof. Cf. [Vautherin 86b].

Theorem 2. *Let* $B_I = (u^1,\ldots, u^i,\ldots, u^n)$ *be a basis of solutions to (I) and* $B_{II} = (w^1,\ldots, w^j,\ldots, w^m)$ *be a basis of solutions to (II). Denoting by* f^i *the semi-flow constructed from* u^i *as indicated by proposition 2, and by* $f^{j\alpha}$*, for* α *in* $E\setminus\{a°\}$*, the semi-flows constructed from* w^j *as indicated by proposition 3, then the two following propositions are equivalent:*

i) *f is a semi-flow of R*

ii) *there is a family of integers* $((\lambda_i)_{i=1..n}, (\mu_{j\alpha})_{j=1..m,\alpha\in NE\setminus\{a^\circ\}})$ *such that*

$$f = \sum_{i=1}^{n} \lambda_i f^i + \sum_{\alpha\in NE\setminus\{a^\circ\}} \sum_{j=1}^{m} \mu_{j\alpha} f^{j\alpha}$$

When ii) is satisfied, the family $((\lambda_i)_{i=1..n}, (\mu_{j\alpha})_{j=1..m,\alpha\in E\setminus\{a^\circ\}})$ *is unique.*

Proof. Cf. [Vautherin 86b].

Thus, even in the case where A is infinite, one can compute a finite number of integer vectors which generates all the Z-semi-flows of R. The computation of these vectors does not depend on the set NE of colors which are not effectively present in the incidence matrix of the system. Especially that allows parametrization of the set of colors.

For instance, in the channel example, the computation is done independently of the parameters ip and ic :

Let us take $a^\circ = *$; so NE = $\{pr_1,..., pr_{ip}\}\cup\{c_1,..., c_{ic}\}$. From proposition 2, we deduce the following invariants :

IPG : $\forall M\in [M^\circ>, \Sigma_{i=3,...,7} \mid M(p_i) \mid = 1$

IV : $\forall M\in [M^\circ>, \mid M(repp) \mid + \mid M(inte) \mid + \mid M(p6) \mid + \mid M(Fileval) \mid + \mid M(p7) \mid + \mid M(Per) \mid = max$

I1 : $\forall M\in [M^\circ>, \mid M(p1) \mid + \mid M(p2) \mid = 1$

I2 : $\forall M\in [M^\circ>, \mid M(p8) \mid + \mid M(p9) \mid = 1$

I3 : $\forall M\in [M^\circ>, \mid M(p1) \mid + \mid M(intp) \mid + \mid M(p4) \mid + \mid M(Depos) \mid + \mid M(repp) \mid = ip$

I4 : $\forall M\in [M^\circ>, \mid M(p8) \mid + \mid M(intc) \mid + \mid M(p5) \mid + \mid M(Prise) \mid + \mid M(repc) \mid = ic$

and from proposition 3 we deduce

$\forall i\in [1,..., ip]$,

IPPi : $\forall M\in [M^\circ>, M(p1)(pr_i) + M(p2)(pr_i) = 1$

IPi : $\forall M\in [M^\circ>, M(p1)(pr_i) + M(intp)(pr_i) + M(p4)(pr_i) + M(Depos)(pr_i) + M(repp)(pr_i) = 1$

I5i : $\forall p\in \{inte, p3, p6, Fileval, p7, Per\}, \forall M\in [M^\circ>, M(p)(pr_i) = 0$

I6i : $\forall M\in [M^\circ>, M(p8)(pr_i) + M(p9)(pr_i) = 0$

I7i : $\forall M\in [M^\circ>, M(p8)(pr_i) + M(intc)(pr_i) + M(p5)(pr_i) + M(Prise)(pr_i) + M(repc)(pr_i) = 0$

$\forall i\in [1,..., ic]$,

IPCi : $\forall M\in [M^\circ>, M(p8)(c_i) + M(p9)(c_i) = 1$

ICi : $\forall M\in [M^\circ>, M(p8)(c_i) + M(intc)(c_i) + M(p5)(c_i) + M(Prise)(c_i) + M(repc)(c_i) = 1$

I8i : $\forall p\in \{inte, p3, p6, Fileval, p7, Per\}, \forall M\in [M^\circ>, M(p)(c_i) = 0$

I9i : $\forall M\in [M^\circ>, M(p1)(c_i) + M(p2)(c_i) = 0$

I10i : $\forall M\in [M^\circ>, M(p1)(c_i) + M(intp)(c_i) + M(p4)(c_i) + M(Depos)(c_i) + M(repp)(c_i) = 0$

Following theorem 2 all linear invariants can be generated with these ones.

Notice that the additional invariants (I1-I10i) are trivial ones : invariants I5i-I7i means that there is never any token marked by pr_i in the places inte, intc, Fileval, Prise, Per, repc, p3, p5, p6, p7 ; invariants I8i-I10i means that there is never any token marked by c_i in the places inte, intp, Fileval, Depos, Per, repp, p3, p4, p6, p7 ; invariants I1-I4, according to IPPi, IPi, IPCi, ICi can be rewritten

$$I'1 : \forall M \in [M°>, M(p1)(*) + M(p2)(*) = 0$$

$$I'2 : \forall M \in [M°>, M(p8)(*) + M(p9)(*) = 0$$

$$I'3 : \forall M \in [M°>, M(p1)(*) + M(intp)(*) + M(p4)(*) + M(Depos)(*) + M(repp)(*) = 0$$

$$I'4 : \forall M \in [M°>, M(p8)(*) + M(intc)(*) + M(p5)(*) + M(Prise)(*) + M(repc)(*) = 0$$

which means that there is never any token marked by * in the places intp, intc, p1, p2, p8, p9, Prise, Depos, repp, repc, p4, p5.

Also notice that in this example, system (I) is equivalent to the system of equations which gives the semi-flows of the P/T-system considered in section III.

More generally, when R = <S, T, A, X, w, M°> is a UPr/T-system, we define an ordinary P/T-system | R |, called the *skeleton* of R, by | R | = <S,T, | w |, | M° |> with :

$$| w |(x,y) = | w(x,y) | \quad \forall (x,y) \in S \times T \cup T \times S$$

$$| M° |(p) = | M°(p) | \quad \forall p \in S$$

Roughly speaking, | R | is obtained from R by "forgetting the colours of the tokens". The following proposition is a corollary of proposition 2 ; it expresses a connection between the semi-flows of R and those of | R |.

Proposition 4. *Let $g \in K^S$ be a semi-flow of | R |, then the vector f of $K^{S \times A}$ defined by :*

$$f(p,a) = g(p) \quad \forall p \in S,\ \forall a \in A$$

is a semi-flow of R (such a vector g is called a type-1 semi-flow of R in [Vautherin... 85]).

Now, notice that all the semi-flows that we have found here are positive. Thus one can ask whether they constitue also a smallest set of generators of positive linear invariants. We answer this question in the following paragraph.

IV.4. Parameter reduction

Often, subsets of transitions are folded in the same manner for a subset of colours ; unfolding them gives birth to isomorphic incidence submatrices. A general study about this fact can be found in [Memmi 83] for fifo nets.

Here, we consider a family of unary Pr/T-systems defined with the help of a parameter $d \in N$.

We set R_d = <P∪Q, TP∪TQ, A∪Ad, X, w, M°> with | A_d | = d

R_d is a unary Pr/T-system with the following constraints :

i) $\forall p \in P, \forall t \in TP, \forall x \in X, w(p,t) \in [[N^{(\{x\})}]]$ and $w(t,p) \in [[N^{(\{x\})}]]$
ii) $\forall p \in P, \forall t \in TQ, w(p,t) = w(t,p) = \delta$
iii) $\forall t \in TP, \forall p \in Q, w(p,t) \in [[N^{(A)}]]$ and $w(t,p) \in [[N^{(A)}]]$

iv) $\forall t\in TP$, $C(t) = A_d{}^X$; $\forall t\in TQ$, $C(t) = A^X$

We want to characterize $F(R_d)$ from $F(R_1)$ and to be able to compute a set of generators for R_d from a set of generators for R_1. Let us point out that R_1 is defined with $| A_1 | = 1$, it is to say that R_1 behaves like a P/T-system over P and TP.

Let us set $A_1 = \{a_1\}$ and $A_d = \{a_1,..., a_d\}$, and let us define a set of projections :

$$\mathrm{proj}_i : N^{P\times A_d\cup Q\times A} \rightarrow N^{P\times A_1\cup Q\times A}$$
$$g \rightarrow \mathrm{proj}_i(g)$$

such that

$$\mathrm{proj}_i(g)(p,a_1) = g(p,a_i) \text{ if } p\in P$$
$$\mathrm{proj}_i(g)(q,a) = g(q,a) \text{ if } q\in Q \text{ and } a\in A$$

We need the followling equivalence relation $\equiv^Q$ over $N^{P\times A_1\cup Q\times A}$:

$$g \equiv^Q g' \text{ if and only if } \forall a\in A, \forall g\in Q, g(q,a) = g'(q,a)$$

i.e., g and g' have the same projection on Q. Then we define a fonction ext from $(N^{(P\times A_1\cup Q\times A)})^d$ into $N^{P\times A_d\cup Q\times A}$ with

$$\mathrm{dom(ext)} = \{v = (v_1,..., v_d) \in (N^{(P\times A_1\cup Q\times A)})^d \mid \forall i, j\in [1,..., d], v_i \equiv^Q v_j\}$$

and

$$\mathrm{ext}(v)(p,a_i) = v_i(p,a_1) \text{ if } p\in P$$
$$\mathrm{ext}(v)(q,a) = v_1(q,a) \text{ if } g\in Q \text{ and } a\in A$$

When $| A | = 1$, R_1 is clearly the skeleton of R_d ; proposition 4 says that if g is a semi-flow of R_1 then ext(g,..., g) is a semi-flow of R_d. With the constraints set on R_d, we can be more precise :

Theorem 3.
i) If $g\in F(R_d)$ then $\forall i\in[1,..., d]$, $proj_i(g)\in F(R_1)$
ii) If $(g_1,..., g_d)\in(F(R_1))^d\cap dom(ext)$ then $ext(g_1,..., g_d)\in F(R_d)$
Moreover, $F(R_d)$ is isomorphic to $(F(R_1))^d\cap dom(ext)$.

The proof is somewhat tedious and is given in [Memmi 83]. Now, we still need to characterize when a given semi-flow v of $F(R_d)$ has minimal support.

First, let us point out that if $e\in F(R_1)$ and $\| e \|$ is minimal then :

If $\| e \|\cap Q\times A \neq \emptyset$ then $\| ext(e,..., e) \|$ is minimal else $\| ext(0,..., e,..., 0) \|$ is minimal (where e appears one times in any position).

If $\| e_1 \|$ and $\| e_2 \|$ are minimal in R_1, with $e_1 \equiv^Q e_2$ then $\| ext(e_{Y(1)},..., e_{Y(d)}) \|$ where $Y\in \{1, 2\}^{[1,..., d]}$, is minimal.

But these two remarks are not sufficient to characterize any minimal support of $F(R_d)$, and examples of minimal supports of $F(R_d)$ not captured by these two cases can be constructed : consider for instance the following system.

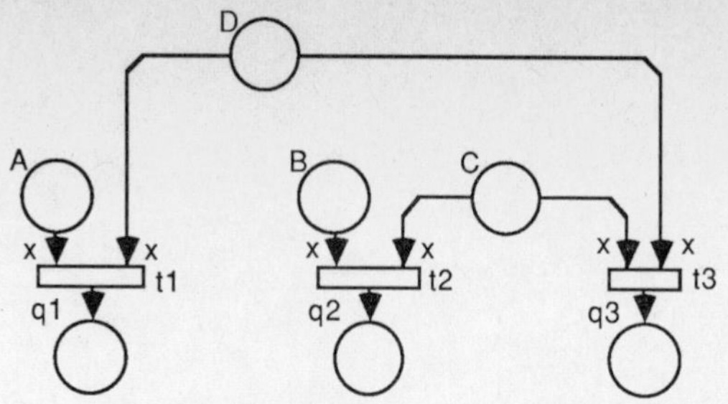

Figure 4

with A = {*}, A2 = {al, a2}, X = {x}, P = {A, B, C, D}, Q = {q1, q2, q3}, TP = {t1, t2, t3}, TQ = ∅.

Neither v1 = (0,1,0,1,1,1,1) nor v2 = (1,0,1,0,1,1,1) have a minimal support in R_1. However ext((v1,v2)) = ((0,1,0,1), (1,0,1,0), (1,1,1)) is such that || ext ((v1,v2)) || = {(B,a1), (D,a1), (A,a2), (C,a2), (q1,*), (q2,*), (q3,*)} is minimal.

Now, let v be a semi-flow of R_1. We denote by Comp(v) = $\{e \in F(R_1) \mid \| e \| \text{ is minimal and } \| e \| \subseteq \| v \| \}$.
Let B = $\{b_1, \ldots, b_k\}$ be a family of semi-flows,

$$[B] = \{v \mid \exists\, \mu_1, \ldots, \mu_k \in Q^+,\ v = \Sigma_{i=1,\ldots,k}\, \mu_i . b_i\}$$

Then, the following result characterizes when v has minimal support in R_d by considering its projections $proj_i(v)$ in R_1. In many cases it will allow to compute a set of generators in a unary Pr/T-system by partial unfoldings.

Theorem 4. *Let v be a semi-flow in R_d, || v || is minimal if and only if :*
i) either there exists a unique i such that $\forall j \neq i$, $proj_j(v) = 0$, || $proj_i(v)$ || is minimal in R_1 and is included in $P \times A_l$.
ii) or *i) $\forall i \in [1,\ldots, d]$, $\forall u \in [Comp(proj_i(v))]$,*
if $\exists k \in N$, $u \equiv^{Q} k.proj_i(v)$ then $u = k.proj_i(v)$
ii) if $u_1, \ldots, u_d$ are such that $u_i \in [Comp(proj_i(v))] \setminus [\{proj_i(v)\}]$
then there exist k and j such that $u_k \equiv^{Q} u_j$.

The proof uses theorem 3 and the decomposition theorem given in [Memmi... 80] for the set of positive semi-flows. Let us point out that this result only depends on the definition of $proj_i$, ext and $\equiv^Q$; it gives us an important insight on $F(R_d)$.

Now, we can go back to our example. We define P with the help of all the arcs valuated by x and all the arcs valuated by y. Then R_1 corresponds to the P/T-system defined in III ; and $F(R_1)$ contains the six semi-flows of minimal support associated with the three kinds of processes :

f_{IPP} is such that $f_{IPP}(pl) = f_{IPP}(p2) = 1$, $f_{IPP}(x) = 0$ otherwise
f_{IPC} is such that $f_{IPC}(p8) = f_{IPC}(p9) = 1$, $f_{IPC}(x) = 0$ otherwise
f_{IPG} is such that $f_{IPG}(p3) = f_{IPG}(p4) = f_{IPG}(p5) = f_{IPG}(p6) = f_{IPG}(p7) = 1$, $f_{IPG}(x) = 0$ otherwise

and with the kinds of data :

$f_{IP}(pl) = f_{IP}(p4) = f_{IP}(intp) = f_{IP}(p4) = f_{IP}(Depos) = f_{IP}(repp) = 1$, $f_{IP}(x) = 0$ otherwise
$f_{IC}(p8) = f_{IC}(intc) = f_{IC}(p5) = f_{IC}(Prise) = f_{IC}(repc) = 1$, $f_{IC}(x) = 0$ otherwise
$f_{IV}(repp) = f_{IV}(intc) = f_{IV}(p6) = f_{IV}(Fileval) = f_{IV}(p7) = f_{IV}(Per) = 1$, $f_{IV}(x) = 0$ otherwise

Now let v be a semi-flow of $F(R_d)$ (here d = ip + ic + 1) such that $\| v \|$ is minimal. The application of theorem 4 is straightforward. Either there exists a unique i such that :

$$proj_i(v) \in \{f_{IPP}, f_{IPC}, f_{IP}, f_{IC}\} \text{ or } Comp(proj_i(v)) \subseteq \{f_{IPG}, f_{IV}\}.$$

We then point out that p3 of Q appears uniquely in f_G and Fileval of Q uniquely in f_{IV}. So

$$\text{either } v = ext(f_{IPG},..., f_{IPG}) \text{ or } v = ext(f_{IV},..., f_{IV}).$$

In conclusion, a set of generators for $F(R_d)$ is given by :

$ext(f_{IPG},..., f_{IPG})$ and $ext(f_{IV},..., f_{IV})$;
$ext(0,..., 0, f, 0,..., 0)$ where $f \in \{f_{IPP}, f_{IPC}, f_{IP}, f_{IC}\}$ is in the ith position, for i in [1,..., d].

And the associated invariants are

IPG, IV
IPPi, I9i and I'1 ; IPCi, I6i and I'2 ; IPi, I10i and I'3 ; ICi, I7i and I'4.

Notice that we do not find the invariants I5 and I8, because here, we have not suppose that the places inte, p3, p6… , which constitute the set Q, are colored.

V. THE FIFO NET MODEL

For our P/T-system model as for our Pr/T-system model, we have not structured the channel int. In fact, in the L-language, int has been designed as an infinite queue. Fifo nets are particularly fitted for that king of modelling. Examples and some theoretical results about this kind of nets are presented in the lecture of G. Roucairol in this course.

On a historical point of view, the code of the general channel has been automatically translated into a fifo net by a software tool named Rafael. The six linear invariants were also computed via Rafael [Behm… 84], [Memmi 83].

Here, we just recall the basic definition of fifo nets, then extend their descriptive power by changing the transition rule again so that one can pass from coloured P/T-systems to fifo nets in a continuous manner. At last, we prove the liveness of the general channel.

V.1. Definitions

Let A be a set, we denote by A* the set of finite words over A. We write λ for the empty word.

Definition 5. *A <u>fifo net</u> is a 5-tuple* $R = <F, T, A, W, M°>$ *where :*
i) F is the finite set of fifos, T the finite set of transitions ($F \cap T = \emptyset$) *;*
ii) A is a finite alphabet. Each letter is called a message.
iii) W is a function from $(F \times T) \cup (T \times F)$ *into A*.*
iv) $M°$ *is a marking of R, i.e. a function from F into A* ;* $M°$ *is called the initial marking.*

A transition t is enabled at the marking M if and only if :

$$\forall f \in F,\ W(f,t) \leq M(f) \ \ (\text{i.e. } \exists x \in A^*, M(f) = W(f,t).x \text{ ; thus } W(f,t) \text{ is a prefix of } M(f)).$$

Then, we reach M' from M by removing the prefix W(f,t) and appending W(f,t) as a suffix to the marking of each fifo f :

$$\forall f \in F,\ W(f,t)\ .M'(f) = M(f)\ .W(t,f).$$

As for coloured P/T-systems, we can generalize fifo nets by folding sets of transitions (i.e. extending the transition rule). Then we can add a set X of variables to A and introduce the unary fifo nets.

Definition 6. *A <u>general fifo net</u> is a 6-tuple $R = \langle F, T, A, C, W, M° \rangle$ where :*
i) F and T are the finite sets of fifos and transitions respectively.
ii) A is a finite alphabet, C is a T-indexed family of non empty sets C(t) (possibly infinite).
iii) W is a ($F{\times}T \cup T{\times}F$)-indexed family of functions such that, for each f in F and each t in T, W(f,t) and W(t,f) are from C(t) into A.*
iv) M° is a marking of R, i.e. a function from F to A ; M° is called the initial marking.*

A transition t is enabled at the marking M and yields to the marking M' if and only if :

$$\exists \sigma \in C(t),\ \forall p \in F, \qquad W(f,t)(\sigma) \le M(f) \text{ and,}$$
$$W(f,t)(\sigma)\ .\ M'(f) = M(f)\ .W(t,f)(\sigma)$$

We can see a word w of A* as a function from N into $A \cup \{\lambda\}$ with :

$w(0) = \lambda$
w(i) is the ith letter in w if $i \le |w|$
$w(i) = \lambda$ if $i > |w|$

thus, w = w(1)w(2)...w(| w |). Then let X be a set of variables, a word w over $(A \cup X)^*$ determines a function [[w]] from A^X into A* with

$[[w]](\sigma)(i) = w(i)$ if $w(i) \in A$
$[[w]](\sigma)(i) = \sigma(w(i))$ if $w(i) \in X$

for each $i \le |w|$. For $L \subseteq (A \cup X)^*$, [[L]] will denote $\{[[w]] \mid w \in L\}$.

Definition 7. *A <u>unary fifo net</u> is a general fifo net $R = \langle F, T, A, A^X, [[w]], M° \rangle$ where :*
i) X is a set of variables,
ii) for every transition t, $C(t) = A^X$,
iii) w is a ($F{\times}T \cup T{\times}F$)-indexed family of words over $A \cup X$.

It is easy to deduce a multiset w~ from a word w over A with w~(a) = #(a,w), where #(a,w) denotes the number of occurrences of a in w. Then, each fifo net R can be associated with a coloured P/T-system R~.

The semi-flows of a fifo net are defined as being exactly those of R~. This definition implies that for a fifo net, linear invariants bring information on the number of occurrences of messages in fifos but never on their order.

V.2. The general channel is live

For our example, we obtain the unary fifo net of the figure 5 by merging the places intp, intc, inte into a fifo int. Notice that p1, p2, p8, p9, repp and repc remain "coloured" : i.e. messages have to be considered merged in these elements. This functioning can easily be simulated with fifos (see [Memmi 83]).

It is easy to see that all the invariants and the home spaces established for the coloured system of figure 2 remain true (the initial marking is the same as for the UPr/T-system).

Figure 5

The fifo net model

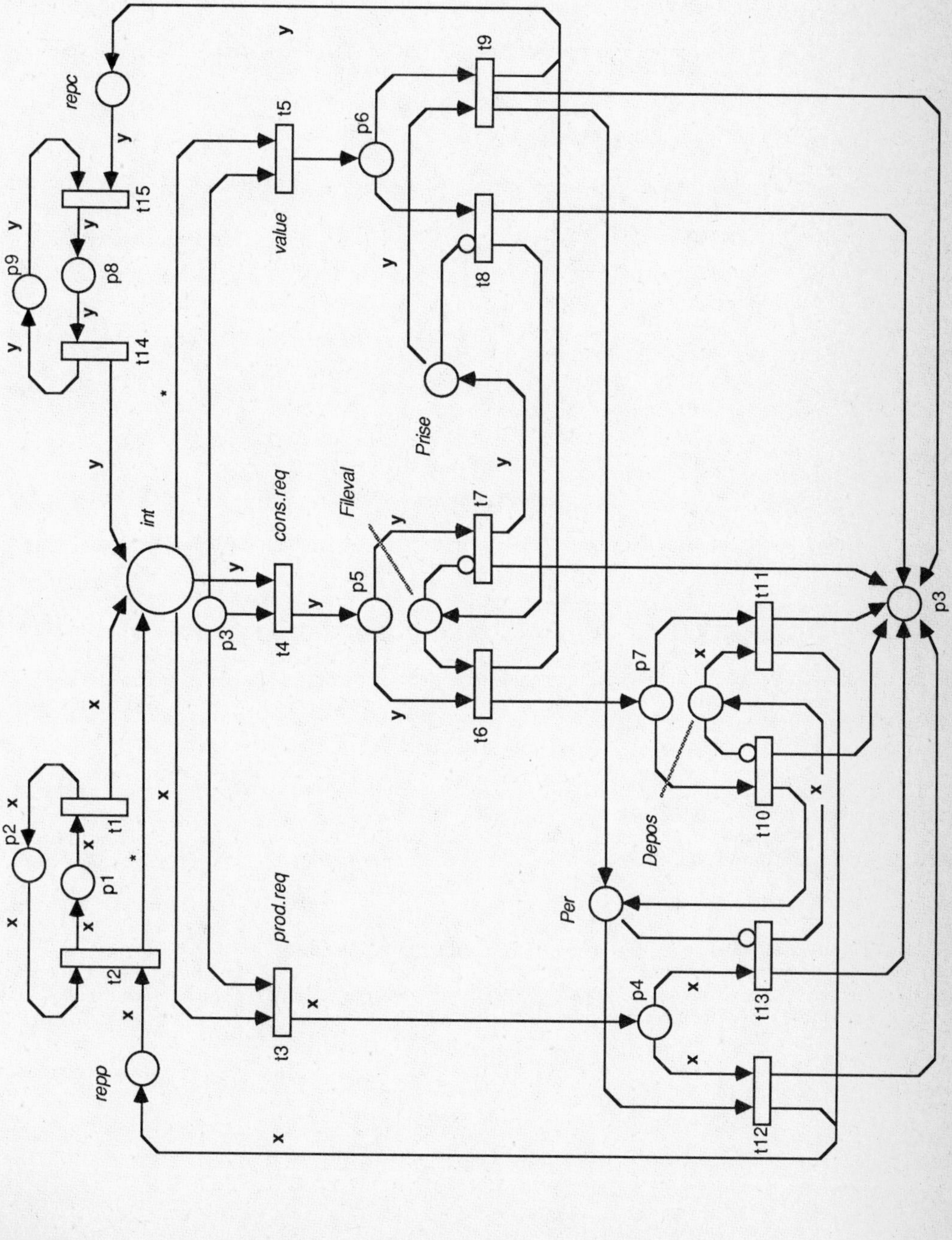

Now, two additional (non linear) invariants can be proved :

IPF : $\forall M \in [M°>$, | M(Fileval) | . | M(Prise) | = 0

This is true at M°. We can put a message in Fileval only by t8, i.e., if and only if |M(Prise) | = 0. Similarly, we can put a message in Prise only by t7, i.e., if and only if | M(Fileval) | = 0. Let us point out that this first non linear invariant can be proved in the initial P/T-system.

IDP : $\forall M \in [M°>$, | M(Per) | + | M(Depos) | < max + ip.

For proving IDP, we need to consider the fifo mechanism in int : a value produced for Fileval can always be followed by a production request. Hence t9 cannot be enabled with | M(Depos) | = ip. This is the main difficulty for proving IDP.

Now, we can show that the initial marking M° is a home state :

Let M be a reachable marking of E3R (it is not empty since M° belongs to this set). According to IV, M verifies | M(Fileval) | + | M(Per) | = max.
a) If M(Fileval) = λ, then M(Per) = $*^{max}$ and | M(Depos) | < ip (from IDP) ; then from IP, M(p1) $\neq \lambda$. If |M(Prise)| = k with k > 0, then we empty Prise with the sequence $(t1, t3, t12, t2, t5, t9, t15)^k$. Then we reach a marking M' such that (according to IC), M(p8) $\neq \lambda$. Now if | M'(Depos) | = k' with k' > 0, we empty Depos with the sequence t1, t3, t12, t2, t5, t8, t14, t4, $(t6, t15, t11, t2, t5, t8)^{k'}$. Finally we empty Fileval by t14, t4, t6, t15, t10 as many times as needed, and we reach M°.
b) If M(Fileval) $\neq \lambda$, then from IPF, M(Prise) = λ and | M(p8) | = ic according to IC. Then we empty Depos and Fileval successively as in the previous case, and we reach M°.

From that, we easily conclude that

The general channel is live.

Now, one can ask whether there exists some buffer structures which are both less compelling than the fifo queue structure and such that the system remains live. It is the purpose of the following section.

VI. ALGEBRAIC ABSTRACT DATA TYPES AND COLOURED SYSTEMS

In order to answer, this question, we need to be able to define what a buffer is in an abstract way ; that is to say, without precisely specifying its implementation. Then we need a specification method for the whole system which respects this abstraction.

VI.1. The model

Such a method is described in [Vautherin 86a] and, applied to the channel example, gives the specification presented in figures 6 and 7.

In this method a specification has two parts. In the first one (fig. 6), the data structure of the system that we consider is specified by an *algebraic specification of abstract data type* ([ADJ 78], [Gaudel 79],[Ehrig... 85]) ; that is to say, a triplet $<\underline{S}, \Sigma, E>$ where $\underline{S}$ is a set of sorts names, Σ a set of symbols with their corresponding arity in $\underline{S}$ (the names of domains and codomains) and E a set of axioms. These axioms are equations between terms composed of operations symbols and free variables. The variables are implicitly universally quantified over their corresponding sort.

We denote by $F : s_1 \times .. \times s_n \rightarrow s$ the arity of F. A function without any specified domain ($F : \rightarrow s$) is a constant.

Here we consider four non-constant functions : repp(-) and repc(-) associate each process with its corresponding request, unit(-) associates a message with the buffer containing only this message and app(-,-) (for "append") constructs a buffer from two others ; this function is used in the following with the function unit(-) to express the fact that messages go into or out of the buffer.

($\underline{S}°$) <u>Sorts</u> : Producer, Consumer, Message, Buffer ;
($\Sigma°$) <u>Operations</u> : $pr_1, \ldots, pr_{ip} : \to$ Producer,
$c_1, \ldots, c_{ic} : \to$ Consumer,
$* : \to$ Message
repp(-) : Producer $\to$ Message
repc(-) : Consumer $\to$ Message
unit(-) : Message $\to$ Buffer
empty : $\to$ Buffer
app(-,-) : Buffer, Buffer $\to$ Buffer
(E°) <u>Equations</u> : app(empty, f) == f
app(f, empty) == f
app(app(f, f'), f'') == app(f, app(f', f''))

Figure 6

The couple $<\underline{S},\Sigma>$ is called a *signature*. It characterizes some many-sorted algebras called Σ-algebras : more precisely, a Σ-algebra is a many-sorted algebra A such that for each name of sort s there corresponds a carrier A_s ; and for each operation symbol F there corresponds an operation F_A of A.

The algebras which satisfy the axioms of E are called the *models* of the specification $<\underline{S},\Sigma,E>$. Each model is intended to represent a possible implementation of the specified data structure.

For instance, we give below two models of the specification given in figure 6. The first algebra, A°, represents the implementation where the buffer is structured as a fifo queue ; while the second algebra, B°, represents the implementation where the buffer is managed as a multiset.

$A°_{Producer} = B°_{Producer} = \{pr_1, \ldots, pr_{ip}\}$
$A°_{Consumer} = B°_{Consumer} = \{c_1, \ldots, c_{ic}\}$
$A°_{Message} = B°_{Message} = \{*\} \cup \{pr_1, \ldots, pr_{ip}\} \cup \{c_1, \ldots, c_{ic})$

$repp_{A°}(x) = repp_{B°}(x) = x$ (we identify a request from a
$repc_{A°}(y) = repc_{B°}(y) = y$ process and the process itself).

$A°_{Buffer} = (A°_{Message})^*$ (the set of words over $A°_{Message}$)

$Unit_{A°}(m) = m$ ($Unit_{A°}(m)$ is the word of containing only the letter m)

$empty_{A°} = \lambda$ (the empty word)
$app_{A°}(w, w') = w.w'$ (the concatenation of w and w')

$B°_{Buffer} = N^{(B°_{Message})}$ (the set of multisets over B° Message)

$Unit_{B°}(m) = <m>$ (unitB(m) is the multiset which contains only m)

$empty_{B°} = \delta$ (the empty multiset)
$app_{B°}(w, w') = w + w'$ (the union of multisets)

The second part of the channel specification (figure 7) is a Pr/T-system like schema $\Omega°$, which is intended to specify how the data structure can evolve in the system.

Figure 7

The algebraic specification

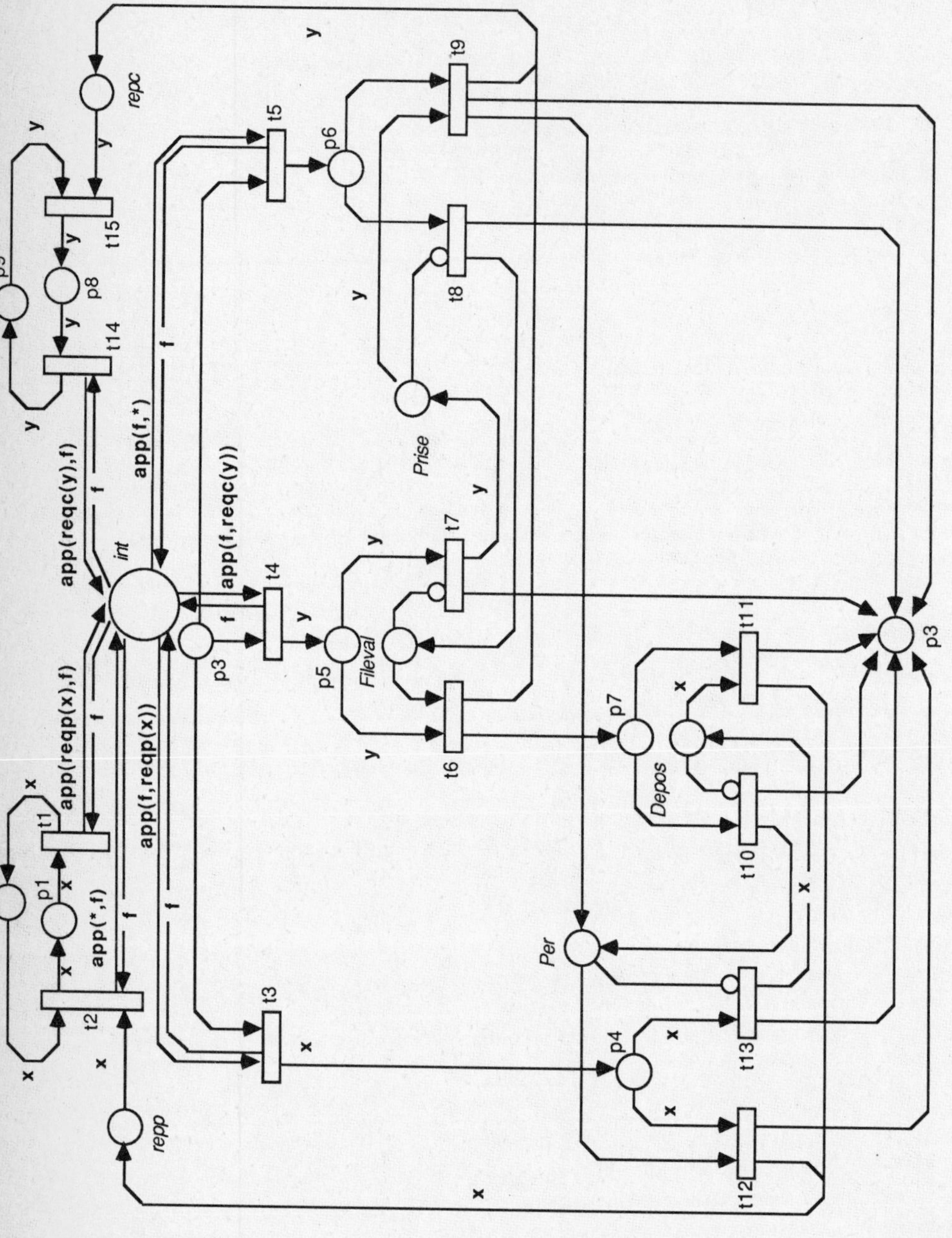

The arcs of $\Omega°$ are valuated by terms composed of variables and symbols of $\Sigma°$: let X be a set of $\underline{S}$-sorted variables ; we write X_s the subset of X which contains the variables whose sort is s. We denote by $T(\Sigma \cup X)$ the set of well-formed terms that one can write using symbols of Σ and variables of X. These terms are called Σ-terms. The subset of Σ-terms without variables (closed Σ-terms) is denoted by $T(\Sigma)$ and $T(\Sigma \cup X)_s$ denotes the subset of Σ-terms whose sort is s.

Definition 8. *A (free)*[1] *Σ-schema is a 5-tuple $\Omega = \langle S, T, X, w, M° \rangle$ where :*
i) S and T are two finite sets of places and transitions respectively. The places are $\underline{S}$-sorted ; i.e. we also suppose an application $z : S \rightarrow \underline{S}$.
ii) X is a finite set of variables.
iii) w is a $(S{\times}T \cup T{\times}S)$-indexed family of multisets of Σ-terms which is coherent with the places sorts ; i.e. such that for every (p,t) in $S{\times}T$, w(p,t) and w(t,p) are in $N^{(T(\Sigma \cup X)_{z(p)})}$.
iv) $M°$ is a terms-marhing, i.e., an S-indexed family of multisets of closed terms, coherent with the places sorts ; i.e. such that for every place p, $M°(p) \in N^{((T(\Sigma)_{z(p)}))}$.

[1] Cf. [Vautherin 85a]

Notice that, in order to simplify the notations, the operation symbol unit is omitted in the valuations of $\Omega°$ (figure 7).

For each algebra A specified by the first part of the specification, the schema is interpreted as a coloured P/T-system $[[\Omega]]_A$ whose sets of colours are domains of A. The behaviour of this system is intended to represent the behaviour of the real system (here, the channel) for the implementation of the data structure coresponding to A.

The interpretation of the valuation w(p,t) and w(t,p) as functions is done as follows : let $X = \{x_1,..., x_n\}$ and denote by s_i the sort of x_i ; the product set $A_{s1} \times ... \times A_{sn}$ is denoted by A^X.

Each Σ-term θ of sort s can be interpreted as a function $[[\theta]]_A$ from A^X into A_s by defining inductively :

$$[[x_i]]_A(a_1,..., a_n) = a_i, \quad \forall (a_1,..., a_n) \in A^X, \forall x_i \in X$$
$$[[F]]_A(a_1,..., a_n) = F_A, \quad \forall (a_1,..., a_n) \in A^X \text{ and for every constant F of } \Sigma.$$
$$[[F(\theta_1,..., \theta_m)]]_A = F_A([[\theta_1]]_A,..., [[\theta_m]]_A) \quad \text{otherwise}$$

(the right member of the last equation is a composition of operations).

Next, by considering A_s as a subset of $N^{(A_s)}$ (by the injection $a \rightarrow e_a$), $[[\theta]]_A$ can also be considered as a function from A^X into $N^{(A_s)}$. And then, for every multiset of terms $w \in N^{(T(\Sigma \cup X)_s)}$, we can define a function $[[w]]_A$ from A^X into $N^{(A_s)}$ by :

$$[[w]]_A = \Sigma\, w(\theta).[[\theta]]_A \quad \text{if } w = \Sigma\, w(\theta).\langle\theta\rangle \qquad (6.1)$$

Though this interpretation of multisets of terms a functions seems to be complicated, it is often obvious in practice. An example is given below. Notice that, when all the terms of w are closed, i.e. $w \in N^{(T(\Sigma)_s)}$, $[[w]]_A$ is a constant function into $N^{(A_s)}$ and so can be viewed as a multiset over A_s. Notice also that for every assignment σ A^X,

$$|\, [[w]]_A(\sigma)\, | = |\, w\, |. \qquad (6.2)$$

Definition 9. *Let $\Omega = \langle S, T, X, w, m^{\circ} \rangle$ be a Σ-schema and A be a Σ-algebra, the* <u>*interpretation of Ω*</u> *in A is the coloured P/T-system $[[\Omega]]_A = \langle S, T, C_A, w_A, M^{\circ}_A \rangle$ where*
i) for every transition t, $C_A(t) = A^X$
ii) for every place p, $C_A(p) = A_{z(p)}$
iii) for every (x,y) in $(S{\times}T \cup T{\times}S)$, $W_A(x,y) = [[w(x,y)]]_A$
iv) for every p in S, $M^{\circ}_A(p) = [[m^{\circ}(p)]]$.

Then we call *system specification* a 4-tuple $\langle S, \Sigma, E, \Omega \rangle$ where $\langle S, \Sigma, E \rangle$ is an algebraic specification of an abstract data type and Ω a Σ-schema. The *models* of such a specification are the interpretations of Ω in the models of $\langle S,\Sigma,E \rangle$.

Hence, from now on, we are working on a class of coloured systems instead of a single one.

Let us by example consider the following schema Ω^1 :

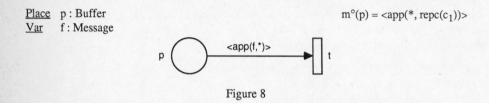

<u>Place</u> p : Buffer $\qquad$ $m^{\circ}(p) = \langle app(*, repc(c_1)) \rangle$
<u>Var</u> f : Message

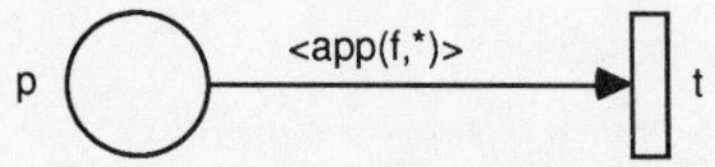

Figure 8

(here again, we omit the symbol "unit")

When it is interpreted in the algebra $A = A^{\circ}$ defines above, this schema gives a coloured system $[[\Omega^1]]_A$ such that $M^{\circ}_A(p) = \langle *.c_1 \rangle$ and $W_A(p,t)$ is the function from $A^X \approx A_{Message}$ which associates each message m with $\langle m.* \rangle$.

When it is interpreted in $B = B^{\circ}$, it gives a coloured system $[[\Omega^1]]_B$ such that $M^{\circ}_B(p) = \langle\langle * \rangle + \langle c_1 \rangle\rangle$ and $W_B(p,t)$ is the function from $B^X \approx B_{Message}$ into B_{Buffer} which associates each message m with $\langle\langle m \rangle + \langle * \rangle\rangle$.

Notice that in both interpretations, there is only *one* token in p at the initial marking. In the first system, this token is "colored" by the word $*.c_1$ and in the second one, it is "colored" by the multiset $\langle * \rangle + \langle c_1 \rangle$ which is *one* value of B_{Buffer}.

Likewise, we show below (IB) that for every interpretation of the schema Ω° (figure 7) there is always one and only one token in the place int ; but this token can be "colored" by a word, or a multiset or something else, depending on the choosen interpretation.

Notice also that the transition t of Ω^1 may occur at the initial marking in the system $[[\Omega^1]]_B$, but not in the system $[[\Omega^1]]_A$, because the addition of multiset is commutative, but the concatenation of words is not. So, different interpretations of a schema may have different behaviours. The following proposition gives more details about the relationship between two interpretations of a schema.

Let A and B be two Σ-algebras ; a *Σ-morphism* from A into B is an $\underline{S}$-indexed family of functions $h = (h_s)_{s \in \underline{S}}$ which preserves the operations of Σ (i.e. such that $h(F_A(x)) = F_B(h(x))$).

Proposition 5. *If A and B are two Σ-algebras such that there is a Σ-morphism h from A into B, then the behaviour of $[[\Omega]]_A$ is included in the behaviour of $[[\Omega]]_B$. More precisely, $M°_B = h(M°_A)$ and h(M) (t > h(M') in $[[\Omega]]_B$ whenever M(t >M' in $[[\Omega]]_A$ (here h(M) denotes the marking of $[[\ \Omega\ ]]_B$ such that for every place p, $h(M)(p) = <h(c_1)> + ... + <h(c_k)>$ when $M(p) = <c_1> + ... + <c_k>$).*

Proof. Cf. [Vautherin 86a]. Intuitively, B satisfies more properties than A and thus, the synchronization imposed by Ω is less compelling in the system $[[\Omega]]_B$ than in $[[\Omega]]_A$.

Each operation F of Σ naturally defines an operation between terms which associates the term $F(\theta_1,..., \theta_n)$ to $\theta_1,...,\theta_n$. Then, $T(\Sigma \cup X)$ is naturally provided with a Σ-algebra structure. We denote by $T(\Sigma,E)$ the quotient algebra of $T(\Sigma)$ by the smallest congruence $\equiv_E$ which contains the equations of E. Roughly speaking, this congruence $\equiv_E$ is defined by $\theta \equiv_E \theta'$ if and only if the equation $\theta == \theta'$ is a consequence of E by substitutions and replacements of equal terms. The algebra $T(\Sigma,E)$ is initial in the class $Alg(\Sigma,E)$ of all Σ-algebras satisfying E ; i.e. there is a unique Σ-morphism from $T(\Sigma,E)$ into every algebra A of $Alg(\Sigma,E)$.

An other particular Σ-algebra is the trivial algebra $\perp(\Sigma)$ where all carriers are reduced to singletons : $\perp(\Sigma)_s = \{¢_s\}$. This algebra is terminal in the class of all Σ-algebra ; i.e. there is a unique Σ-morphism from every Σ-algebras (and especially those of $Alg(\Sigma,E)$) into $\perp(\Sigma)$.

Thus, we represent $Alg(\Sigma,E)$ by the diagram of figure 9.a, denoting Σ-morphisms by arrows. And then, from the previous proposition, we deduce the diagram of figure 9.b which represents the class of all models of a specification <S, Σ, E, Ω>, where arrows denote behaviour inclusion.

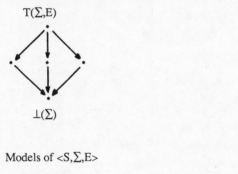

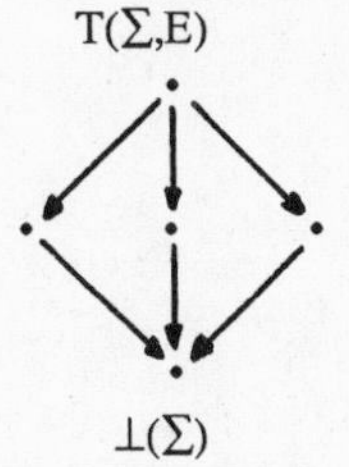

Models of <S,Σ,E>

Figure 9.a

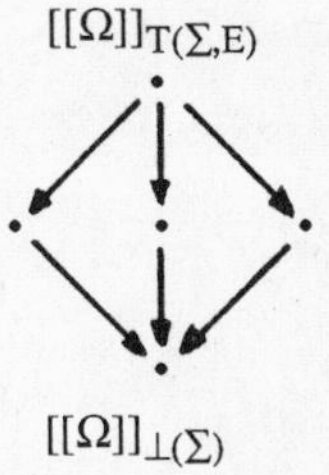

Models of <S,Σ,E,Ω>

Figure 9.b

As far as the channel is concerned, it is not very difficult to see that the algebra A° is isomorphic to the initial algebra of <S°, Σ°, E°> (figure 6). Also, we claim that the coloured system $[[\Omega°]]_{A°}$ has the same behaviour as our fifo-net (figure 5), that the coloured system $[[\Omega°]]_{B°}$ has the same behaviour as the UPr/T-system of figure 3 and that the P/T-system of figure 2 also is equivalent to a model of the specification <S°, Σ°, E°, Ω°>. Hence, we have the diagram of figure 10.

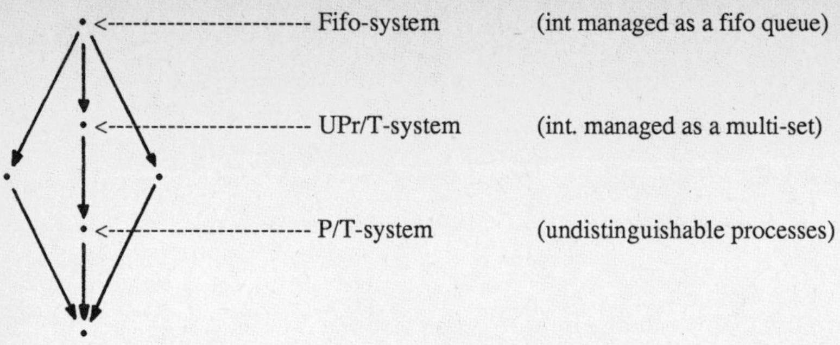

Figure 10

The following proposition gives light on the terminal model. At first, we define the skeleton of a schema, just as for UPr/T-systems : let $\Omega = <S, T, X, W, M°>$; the *skeleton* of Ω is the (ordinary) P/T-system $|\ \Omega\ | = <S, T, |\ w\ |, |\ M°\ |>$ with :

$$|\ w\ |(x,y) = |\ w(x,y)\ | \quad \forall (x,y) \in S\times T \cup T\times S \tag{6.3}$$

$$|\ M°\ |(p) = |\ M°(p)\ | \quad \forall p \in S \tag{6.4}$$

Remember that w(x,y) and M°(p) are multisets over $T(\Sigma \cup X)$ and that $|\ w\ |$ denotes the length of the multiset w.

Proposition 6. *The interpretation of a Σ-schema in the terminal algebra $\perp(\Sigma)$ is (equivalent to) the skeleton of Ω ; and for every Σ-algebra A,*

$$|\ M°_A\ | = M°_{\perp(\Sigma)} \text{ and, if } M(t > M' \text{ in } [[\Omega]]_A \text{, then } |\ M\ |\ (t > |\ M'\ | \text{ in } |\ \Omega\ |.$$

Proof. The equivalence between $[[\Omega]]_{\perp(\Sigma)}$ and $|\ \Omega\ |$ results from the isomorphism |.| from $N^{(\{¢\})}$ into N which associates w with | w |. The second part of the proposition results from (6.2). []

Thus the terminal model of $<S°, \Sigma°, E°, \Omega°>$ is the P/T-system obtained by erasing the arcs valuations of the figure 7.

VI.2. Proof of liveness

Now let us study the liveness of the different models of the channel specification.

At first, we consider the set of equations

$$E^1 = \{ \begin{array}{lll} app(repp(x),*) & == & app(*, repp(x)) \\ app(repc(y),*) & == & app(*, repc(y)) \} \end{array}$$

The sequence which leads to a deadlock in the P/T-system of figure 2 also can occur in $R = [[\Omega°]]_{T(\Sigma°,E°\cup E1)}$. Let M be the marking of R reached by this sequence. It satisfies

$$|\ M(Depos)\ | = ip, \ |\ M(Prise)\ | = ic, \ |\ M(p3)\ | = 1 \text{ and } |\ M(p)\ | = 0 \text{ otherwise.}$$

Hence | M | is a deadlock in $|\ \Omega°\ | = [[\Omega°]]_{\perp(\Sigma°)}$. Now, let A be an algebra of $Alg(\Sigma°,E°)$ which also satisfies E^1. There is a morphism $h : T(\Sigma°,E°\cup E^1) \rightarrow A$ and thus, according to the proposition 5, h(M) can be reached in $[[\Omega°]]_A$. Moreover, by the definition of h(M), | h(M) | = | M |. Then, according to the proposition 6, since |M| is a deadlock in | Ω° | , also h(M) is a deadlock in $[[\Omega°]]_A$. we can summarize that by :

If the buffer structure allows the commutation of values and production requests, and the commutation of values and consummation requests, then the channel can reach a deadlock.

Next, we try to see for which conditions over the algebra A the liveness proof given above for the fifo net can also be applied to $[[\Omega°]]_A$.

The first step of this proof consists in establishing that it is always possible to empty the buffer int and to put the manager back in its initial state. In both the P/T-system and the fifo-net this property can be deduced from the fact that there is always one and only one token in the set of places {p3,..., p7}. The following proposition shows that for the interpretations of a schema such invariants over the number of tokens can also be computed by way of the skeleton.

Proposition 7. *Let f be a semi-flow of | Ω |, then for every interpretation* $[[\Omega]]_A$,

$$\forall M \in [M°_A>,\ \sum_{p\in S} f_p\,|M(p)| = \sum_{p\in S} f_p\,|M°(p)| \tag{6.5}$$

Proof. It is a consequence of the proposition 6 by also using the fact that $|M°_A| = |M_°(p)|$ (cf (6.2)).

Applying that to the schema Ω°, we deduce that for every Σ°-algebra A, the interpretation $[[\Omega°]]_A$ satisfies

$$\text{IPG} : \forall M \in [M°_A>,\ \Sigma_{i=3..7}\,|M(p_i)| = 1$$

$$\text{IB} : \forall M \in [M°_A>,\ |M(int)| = 1$$

Then we deduce that for every algebra A of Alg(Σ°,E°), the set

$$E3int = \{M \mid M(int) = [[empty]]_A \text{ and } |M(p3)| = 1\}$$

is a home space of $[[\Omega°]]_A$.

Indeed, let A be an algebra of Alg(Σ°,E°).

a) At first, we notice that since for each transition of Ω°, every variable on an incoming arc is also on an incoming arc, then :

$$\forall M \in [M°_A>,\ \forall p \in S,\ M(p) \in N^{([[T(\Sigma°)]]_A)} \tag{6.6}$$

where $[[T(\Sigma°)]]_A$ is the subset of A whose elements can be obtained by interpreting a closed Σ°-term.

b) Then, according to (IB),

$$\forall M \in [M°_A>,\ \exists b \in T(\Sigma°)_{Buffer},\ M(int) = [[b]]$$

Let suppose that b ≠ empty and denote by n the size of b. Since n ≠ 1, either $b \equiv_{E°} app(b', repp(x))$ or $b \equiv_{E°} app(b, repc(y))$ or $b \equiv_{E°} app(b',*)$. In any case, there is a transition t (t = t3, t4 or t5) such that M(t >M' with $M'(int) = [[b']]_A$. The size of b' is then smaller than n. Thus, by induction on n, we show that $\{M \mid M(int) = [[empty]]_A\}$ is a home space of $[[\Omega°]]_A$.

c) Finally, by IPG, this home space can be refined in E3int, just as for the P/T-system of figure 2.

According to (6.6), in any $\Sigma°$-algebra A , the only useful part for $[[\Omega°]]_A$ is the finitely generated part of A, $[[T(\Sigma°)]]_A$. Thus, from now on, *we consider only finitely generated algebras* ; i.e., algebras such that $[[T(\Sigma°)]]_A = A$. The class of finitely generated algebras satisfying E is denoted by Gen(Σ,E).

The remainder of the liveness proof given for the fifo-net requires invariants about the number of messages of each kind in the buffer int (IPi, ICi, IV). Of course, such invariants may exist only for implementations such that the number of messages in a buffer can be defined. For instance, it is not the case when the algebra satisfies an equation like : app(repp(x), repp(x)) == repp(x). Indeed, in such an implementation, a buffer can create or destroy some messages. In order to formalize that, we enrich the specification <S°, Σ°, E°> with observers which count the number of messages of each kind in the buffer :

(S^i) Sorts : Integer, Boolean.

(Σ^i) Operations :
- Occ_* : Buffer → Integer
- Occ_p : Producer, Buffer → Integer
- Occ_c : Consumer, Buffer → Integer

(E^i) Equations :

Occ_*(app(f,f')) == Occ_*(f) + Occ_*(f')
Occ_*(unit(*)) == 1
Occ_*(unit(repp(x))) == 0
Occ_*(unit(repc(y))) == 0
Occ_p(x,app(f,f')) == Occ_p(x,f) + Occ_p(x,f')
Occ_p(x,unit(*)) == 0
Occ_p(x,unit(repp(x')) == if x = x' then 1 else 0
Occ_p(x,unit(repc(y)) == 0
Occ_c(y,app(f,f')) == Occ_c(y,f) + Occ_c(y,f')
Occ_c(y,unit(*)) == 0
Occ_c(y,unit(repp(x))) == 0
Occ_c(y,unit(repc(y'))) == if y = y' then 1 else 0

Figure 11

Remark. We assume that the sort integer is provided with the operations 0, 1, + and =. For simplicity, these operations are not specified here. Similarly, the specification of booleans and equalities in the sorts Producer and Consumer are omitted.

Now, let us denote by $\mathfrak{I}(A)$ the free algebra over A generated by this enrichment. A formal construction of $\mathfrak{I}(A)$ is given in the appendix. Roughly speaking, denoting by Σ^i and E^i the sets of new operations symbols and equations that we are considering, $\mathfrak{I}(A)$ is the $\Sigma° \cup \Sigma^i$ - algebra which just satisfies the same equations as A and the equations of E^i. Then we have :

(R1) : for each algebra A of Gen($\Sigma°$,E°) such that $\mathfrak{I}(A)$ is consistent, i.e. does not satisfy true == false, the interpretation $[[\Omega°]]_A$ satisfies :

For every reachable marking M and every terms marking m ($\forall p,\ m(p) \in N^{(T(\Sigma))}$) which represents M, i.e. such that $M(p) = [[m(p)]]_A,\ \forall p$,

$\forall i \in [1,..., ip]$,
IPP'i : $\#(pr_i, m(repp)) + \#(pr_i, m(int)) + \#(pr_i, m(p4)) + \#(pr_i, m(Depos)) = \#(pr_i, m(p2))$

$\forall j \in [1,..., ic]$,

$IPC'j : \#(c_j, m(repc)) + \#(c_j, m(int)) + \#(c_j, m(p5)) + \#(c_j, m(Prise)) = \#(c_j, m(p9))$

$IP' : | m(repp) | + | m(p1) | + \#(repp, m(int)) + | m(p4) | + | m(Depos) | = ip$

$IC' : |m(repc) | + | m(p8) | + \#(repc, m(int)) + | m(p5) | + | m(Prise) | = ic$

$IV' : | m(repp) | + \#(*, m(int)) + | m(p6) | + | m(Fileval) | + | m(p7) | + | m(Per) | = max$

where #(F,w), with $F \in \Sigma$ and $w \in N^{(T(\Sigma))}$, denotes the number of occurrences of F in the multiset of terms w.

The proof of this result is given in the appendix. From IPP'i and IPC'j, we deduce that

For every algebra A in Gen(Ω°,E°) such that $\Im(A)$ *is consistent,* $E3R = \{M \in E3int \;|\; |M(repp)| = |M(repc)| = 0\}$ *is a home space of* $[[\Omega°]]_A$.

Indeed, let M be a marking in E3int and let m be a marking with terms which represents M. Assume that $|M(repp)| \neq 0$; then there is a multiset of terms, $w \in N^{(T(\Sigma°))}$ and $i \in [1,..., ip]$ such that m(repp) = $<pr_i>$ + w (otherwise, 0 = | m(repp) | = | M(repp) | by (6.2)). Then, according to IPP'i, m(p2) = $<pr_i>$ + w' and thus, m(t2 >m' in the initial model $[[\Omega°]]_{T(\Sigma°,E°)}$ with m'(repp) = w. Then, M(t2 >M' in $[[\Omega°]]_A$ with M'(repp) = $[[w]]_A$; and so | M'(repp) | = | m'(repp) | < | m(repp) | = | M(repp) |. Hence, by induction over | M(repp) |, we conclude that E3int $\cap$\{M | | M(repp) | = 0\} is a home space of $[[\Omega°]]_A$; and, by similar arguments with repc, that E3R is a home space.

Intuitively, as far as $\Im(A)$ is consistent, the buffer int cannot generate arbitratry messages and thus, no unexpected requests are sent by the manager.

The remainder of the liveness proof of the fifo net, is based on the fact that each time there is a value in the buffer int, then either a producer is in its initial state, or has sent a request in the buffer that will *necessarily* go out of the buffer *after* the considered value.

As above, in order to formalize this intuition, we enrich the abstract data type specification with some observers :

(Σ^{ii}) Operations : in?p(-), in ?*(-) : Buffer → Boolean
P?(-) : Buffer → Boolean

(E^{ii}) Equations :

in?p(empty) == false
in?p(app(f,*)) == in?p(f)
in?p(app(f, repp(x))) == true
in?p(app(f, repc(x))) == in?p(f)
in?*(empty) == false
in?*(app(f,*)) == true
in?*(app(f, repp(x))) == in?*(f)
in?*(app(f, repc(y))) == in?*(f)
P?(empty) == false
P?(app(f,*)) == (in?p(f) and non in?*(f)) or P?(f)
P?(app(f, repp(x))) == P?(f)
P?(app(f, repc(y))) == P?(f)

Figure 12

The predicate P? indicates if there is in the considered buffer a production request which came in after the last value entered. Let us denote by $\mathfrak{I}'(A)$ the free algebra over A generated by the enrichment $<\Sigma^{i} \cup \Sigma^{ii}, E^{i} \cup E^{ii}>$. We have

(R2) : for every algebra A in $Alg(\Sigma°,E°)$ and every reachable marking M in $[[\Omega]]_A$, $M(int) = a$ with $a \in A_{Buffer}$ and :

if $in?^*(a) \equiv true$ in $\mathfrak{I}'(A)$, then either $| M(p_1) | > 1$ or $P?(a) \equiv true$ in $\mathfrak{I}'(A)$.

And from that, we can deduce :

(R3) : for every algebra A in $Gen(\Sigma°,E°)$ such that $\mathfrak{I}'(A)$ is consistent, $[[\Omega°]]_A$ satisfies :

$$IDP : \forall M \in [M°_A>, \ | M(Per) | + | M(Depos) | < max + ip$$

The proof of these two results is given in the appendix. Finally, in order to establish that the initial marking of $[[\Omega]]_A$ is a home state, we need the following invariant :

$$IPF : \forall M \in [M°_A>, \ | M(Prise) | \,.\, | M(Fileval) | = 0$$

which is satisfied by every interpretation $[[\Omega°]]_A$ since it is satisfied by the skeleton $| \Omega° |$ (cf proposition 6). Then, from IP', IC', IV', IDP and IPF, we conclude, just like for the fifo net that for every algebra A in $Gen(\Sigma,E°)$ such that $\mathfrak{I}'(A)$ is consistent, $M°_A$ is a home state ; and thus $[[\Omega°]]_A$ is deadlock free.

Moreover, we already know that the initial model $[[\Omega°]]_{T(\Sigma°,E°)}$, which is equivalent to the fifo net of figure 5, is live. Thus for this model, for every transition t, there is a reachable marking M' such that M'[t >. According to proposition 5, this property is also satisfied by any model $[[\Omega°]]_A$ ($A \in Alg(\Sigma°,E°)$) ; and thus , from the previous result, we conclude that

For every algebra A in $Gen(\Sigma°,E°)$, such that $\mathfrak{I}'(A)$ is consistent, $[[\Omega°]]_A$ is live.

Now, let us take an example. We consider the set of equations

PERM = {app(repc(y),*) == app(*,repc(y))
app(repc(y), repp(x)) == app(repp(x), repc(y))
app(repc(y), repc(y')) == app(repc(y'), repc(y))
app(repp(x), repp(x')) == app(repp(x'), repp(x)) }

The algebra $C° = T(\Sigma°,E° \cup PERM)$ is such that $\mathfrak{I}'(C°)$ is consistent. Thus $[[\Omega°]]_{C°}$ is live, and so one can allow the commutation of consummation requests and values, and the commutation of consummation and production requests among themselves.

The following implementation is equivalent to C°, but more concrete :

- A buffer is implemented by three (multi-) sets S_p, S_c, S_v and a fifo queue over the two symbols p and v.
- The entry of a production request (resp. a value) in the buffer is done by adding this request to S_p (resp. this value to S_v) and pushing a symbol p (resp. v) in q.
- The entry of a consummation request is done by adding this request to S_c.
- Any consummation request in S_c can always be taken out of the buffer.
- Any production request in S_p (resp. any value in S_v) can be taken out of the buffer provided that the head of q is a sysmbol p (resp. a symbol v). When a message is taken out, the corresponding symbol is pulled out of q.

The results of this section are summarized in the following diagram, where the models corresponding to A°, B° and C° are respectively denoted by FIFO, SET and FIFO/PERM.

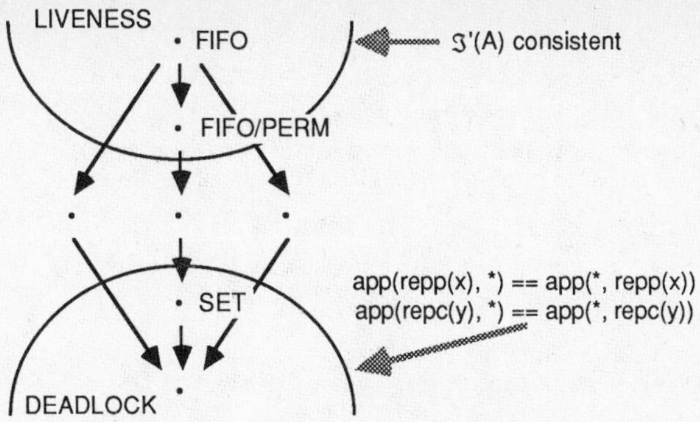

Figure 10

Let $E^2 = \{app(repp(x),*) == app\ (*, repp(x))\}$. The algebra $D° = T(\Sigma°, E° \cup E^2)$ is such that $\mathfrak{I}'(D°)$ is not consistent. So, when we just assume the commutation of production requests and values we cannot conclude anything from the previous analysis, about the liveness of the corresponding model. This model is just between the two areas "LIVENESS" and "DEALOCK" of the previous diagram. In fact, *for this model*, the liveness depends on the parameters i_c and max of the channel : we claim that

The system corresponding to D° is live if and only if $i_c < max$.

On the other hand, for the models which are on the areas "LIVENESS" or "DEADLOCK", the liveness or the presence of deadlock does not depend on the parameter values of the system.

VII. CONCLUSION

At each step of the analysis we have changed the model in order to describe elements of our example more and more precisely. But in no case, we had to make a translation from one model into another one: the changes have been done rather continuously, adding each time some descriptive power, leading to more and more acute results, verifying how the invariant method holds and showing how complementary the models are.

The study of our example can be pursued by making precise again which data structures of int lead to a deadlock, which ones do not, and for which values of max, ip and ic.

We think we have shown how the invariant notion is fundamental in programming. Though the calculus of semi-flows defined for the P/T-systems has been somewhat extended to high level systems, it should be extended again towards other models of parallel computation and completed. Also, we think it would be interesting to unify the results of section IV.3 (computation of invariants for UPr/T-systems) with the results in [Haddad 86] where the invariants of another subclass of coloured P/T-systems (namely the regular coloured nets) are investigated.

From a theoretical point of view, the Farkas algorithm has to be optilized. Some transformations on a P/T-system preserving the set of invariants are under study. We are also studying a polynomial algorithm giving one linear invariant if it exists.

The notion of home space is a nice extension of the home state notion. Nevertheless, we do not know whether it is decidable if a given set is a home space or not. The stepwise refinement of home spaces method seems to be a helpful guideline for reasoning about systems. Today, we do not know of another way to prove the liveness of the general channel.

ACKNOWLEGMENT

We would like to thank L. Meima for many improvements of the english version of this paper. Also many thanks to the two referees of this paper for their careful reading of a rough preliminary version.

VIII. BIBLIOGRAPHY

[ADJ 78] : Groupe ADJ : J.A. Goguen, J.W. Thatcher and E.G. Wagner
"An initial algebra approach to the specification, correctness and implementation of abstract data types". Current Trends in Programming Methodology, Vol. IV, R.T. Yeh (Ed.), Prentice Hall, New Jersey (1978).

[Alaiwan... 85] : H. Alaiwan and J.M. Toudic
"Recherche des semi-flows, des verrous et des trappes dans les réseaux de Petri". T.S.I., Vol.4, N°1 - Numero spécial réseaux de Petri, G. Memmi (Ed.), pp 103 - 112 (1985).

[Behm... 84] : P. Behm and G. Memmi
"Rafael : Un outil d'analyse de systèmes temps réel". 2ème Colloque de Génie Logiciel AFCET, Nice, pp 13-32 (1984).

[Boussinot 81] : F. Boussinot
"Réseaux de processus avec mélange équitable : une approche du temps réél". Thèse d'état, Université Paris VII (1981).

[Boussinot... 83] : F. Boussinot, R. Martin, G. Memmi, G. Ruggiu and J. Vapné
"A language for formal descriptions of real time systems". Proc. of SAFECOMP'83 - 3rd IFAC/IFIP Workshop, J.A. Baylis (Ed.), Pergamon Press, Cambridge UK. (1983).

[Brams 82] : G. W. Brams
"Réseaux de Petri : théorie et pratique". Tome 1, Edition Masson, Paris (1982).

[Ehrig... 85] : H. Ehrig and B. Mahr
"Fundamentals of Algebraic Specification 1 : Equations and Initial Semantics". EATCS Monographs on Theoretical Computer Science, Vol. 6, W. Brauer, G. Rozenberg, A. Salomaa (Eds.), Springer Verlag (1985)

[Farkas 02] : J. Farkas
"Theorie der einfachen Ungleichungen". Journal für reine und angew. Mathematik 124, pp 1-27 (1902).

[Gaudel 79] : M.C. Gaudel
"Algebraic Specification of Abstract Data Type". R.R. N° 360, INRIA, Le Chesnay (1979).

[Graubmann 85] : P. Graubmann
"Composition of place transition nets using additional places (or transitions) and the calculation of their invariants". Internal Report of the Esprit project n° 283 FO-ME-TOO, september 1985 (1985).

[Haddad... 86] : S. Haddad and C. Girault
"Algebraic structure of flows of a regular coloured net". 7th European Workshop on Application and Theory of Petri Nets, Oxford, June 1986 (1986).

[Huber... 85] : P. Huber, A.M. Jensen, L.O. Jepsen and K. Jensen
"Towards reachability trees for high-level Petri nets". in "Advances in Petri Nets 1984", L.N.C.S. 188, G.Rozenberg (Ed.), Springer Verlag, pp 215-233. (1985).

[Lautenbach... 74] : K. Lautenbach and H. Schmid
"Use of Petri nets for proving correctness of concurrent process systems". Information Processing 1974 - North Holland Pub. Co., pp 187-191 (1974).

[Jensen 81] : K. Jensen
"Coloured Petri nets and the invariant method". T.C.S. 14, pp 317-336 (1981).

[Martinez... 82] : J. Martinez and M. Silva
"A simple and fast algorithm to abtain all invariants of a generalized Petri Net". Informatik - Fachbrichte 52, C. Girault and W. Reisig (Eds.), Springer Verlag, pp 301-310, (1982).

[Mateti... 76] : P. Mateti and D. Nardingh
"On algorithms for enumerating all circuits of a graph". SIAM J. Comput., Vol.5, N°1, pp 90-99 (1976).

[Memmi... 80] : G. Memmi and G. Roucairol
"Linear algebra in net theory". Proc. of "Advanced Course on genral Net Theory of Processes and Systems" Hambourg 1979, L.N.C.S. 84, W. Brauer (Ed.), Springer Verlag (1980).

[Memmi 81] : G. Memmi
"Contrôle du parallèlisme et détection des blocages". Journée de Synthèse "Quelques outils d'aideà la conception et à la réalisation de systèmes informfatiques". AFCET - Informatique Gif/s/Yvette, pp 35-69, (1981).

[Memmi 83] : G. Memmi
"Methode d'analyse de réseaux de Petri, réseaux à files, et applications aux systèmes temps réel". Thèse de Doctorat d'Etat, Université Pierre et Marie Curie, Juin 1983 (1983)

[Memmi... 85] : G. Memmi and A. Finkel
"An introduction to fifo nets - monogeneous nets : a subclass of fifo nets". T.C.S. 35, pp 191-214, (1985).

[Silva... 85] : M. Silva, J. Martinez, P. Ladet and H. Alla
"Generalized inverses and the calculation of symbolic invariants for coloured Petri nets". T.S.I., Vol.4, N°1 - Numéro spécial Réseaux de Petri, G. Memmi (Ed.), pp 113-126, (1985).

[Toudic 81] : J.M. Toudic
"Algorithmes d'analyse structurelle des réseaux Petri". Thèse de 3ème cycle, Université Pierre et Marie Curie, Octobre 1981 (1981).

[Vautherin 85] : J. Vautherin
"Un modèle algebrique, basé sur les réseaux de Petri, pour l'étude des systèmes parallèles". Thèse de Docteur-Ingénieur, Université Paris-Sud, Juin 1985 (1985).

[Vautherin 85] : J. Vautherin and G. Memmi
"Computation of flows for unary Predicates/Transitions nets". in "Advances in Petri Nets 1984", L.N.C.S. 188, G.Rozenberg (Ed.), Springer Verlag, pp 307-327 (1985).

[Vautherin 86a] : J. Vautherin
"Parallel systems specifications with coloured Petri nets and algebraic abstract data types". 7th European Workshop on Application and Theory of Petri Nets, Oxford, June 1986 (1986).

[Vautherin 86b] : J. Vautherin
"Calculation of semi-flows of Pr/T-systems". Research Report L.R.I., N° 130, Université Paris Sud, Octobre 1986 (1986).

IX. APPENDIX

IX.1. Construction of $\mathfrak{T}(A)$

Let $<S', \Sigma', E'> = <S \cup S^i, \Sigma \cup \Sigma^i, E \cup E^i>$. The free algebra over A, $\mathfrak{T}(A)$, generated by the enrichment $<S^i, \Sigma^i, E^i>$ is constructed as follows:

Let us denote by $T(\Sigma'\cup A)$ (resp. $T(\Sigma\cup A)$) the algebra of terms constructed with operations symbols of Σ' (resp. Σ) and values of A considered as constants. $T(\Sigma\cup A)$ is a Σ-algebra and there is a unique Σ-morphism $eval_A$ from $T(\Sigma\cup A)$ into A which extends the identity of A.

We define in $T(\Sigma'\cup A)$ a relation |--| by θ|--|θ' iff

either there is an equation g == d or d == g in E', an occurrence u and a substitution σ such that $\theta|_u = g\sigma$ and $\theta' = \theta[u \leftarrow d\sigma]$

or there is an occurrence u and a term θ_1 in $T(\Sigma\cup A)$ such that $\theta|_u \in T(\Sigma\cup A)$, $eval_A(\theta|_u) = eval_A(\theta_1)$ and $\theta' = \theta[u \leftarrow \theta_1]$

Now, let $\equiv$ be the reflexive and transitive closure of |--|. It is a Σ'-congruence and $\mathfrak{I}(A)$ is the quotient algebra $T(\Sigma'\cup A)/\equiv$.

Notice that $\mathfrak{I}(A)$ satisfies E' and, if A is a finitely generated algebra, $\mathfrak{I}(A)$ is also finitely generated. Indeed, if A is finitely generated, then for every a in A, there is a term $\underline{a}$ in $T(\Sigma)$ such that $eval_A(\underline{a}) = a$. Then, let θ be a term of $T(\Sigma'\cup A)$; by substituting each value $a \in A$ occuring in θ by the term $\underline{a}$, we get a term θ' of $T(\Sigma')$ such that $\theta' \equiv \theta$. So the unique Σ'-morphism from $T(\Sigma')$ into $\mathfrak{I}(A)$ which associates a term with its $\equiv$-class ($T(\Sigma') \subseteq T(\Sigma'\cup A)$) is surjective and thus $\mathfrak{I}(A) \in Gen(\Sigma',E')$.

IX.2. Proof of (R1), a notion of semi-flows for schemas

Let $X = \{x^1,\ldots, x^n\}$; we associate with each variable x^i and each symbol F a new variable x^i_F. Then we denote by $Z[\{x^i_F\}]$ the set of integer polynoms over these new variables.

For every F in Σ, we define a function Q_F from $T(\Sigma\cup X)$ into $Z[\{x^i_F\}]$ by

$$Q_F(\theta) = \#(F, \theta) + \sum_{i=1..n} \#(x^i, \theta).\ x^i_F.$$

(remember that $\#(F, \theta)$ denotes the number of occurrence of F in θ). Then this function is extended to $N^{(\Sigma\cup X)}$ by

$$Q_F(\sum w(\theta).\theta) = \sum w(\theta).Q_F(\theta)$$

Thus Q_F associates with each multiset of terms an integer polynom, and, for instance, with X = {f, x},

$$Q_*(app(f,*) + app(repp(x), f)) = 1 + 2\ f_* + x_*$$

When all the terms of w are closed, then $Q_F(w)$ is constant and equals to the number of occurrence of F in w. When w contains non closed terms, for each substitution σ: $X \to T(\Sigma)$, $Q_F(w\sigma)$ can be obtained by substituting in the polynom $Q_F(w)$ each variable x^i_F by the number of occurrences of F in $\sigma(x^i)$.

Now, let Ω = <S, T, X, w, m°> be a Σ-schema ; f be a vector of integers in $Z^S \times Z^{\Sigma\times S}$: $f = ((f_p), (f_{F,p}))$; and let A be a finitely generated algebra. Assume that

(A1) for every F in Σ such that $f_{F,p} \neq 0$ for one p at least,

$$\forall w, w' \in T(\Sigma), \quad ([[w]]_A = [[w']]_A) \Rightarrow (\#(F,w) = \#(F,w'))$$

(A2) for every transition t,

$$\sum_p \left[f_p . | c_{p,t} | + \sum_F f_{F,p} . Q_F(c_{p,t}) \right] = 0$$

where $c_{p,t} = w(p,t) - w(t,p)$ and $Q_F(c_{p,t}) = Q_F(w(p,t)) - Q_F(w(t,p))$.

Then for every reachable marking M of $[[\Omega]]_A$ and every terms-marking m which represents M (i.e., for each place p, $m(p) \in N^{(T(\Sigma))}$ and $[[m(p)]]_A = M(p)$),

$$\sum_p \left[f_p . | m(p) | + \sum_F f_{F,p} . \#(F, m(p)) \right] = \sum_p \left[f_p . | m^\circ(p) | + \sum_F f_{F,p} . \#(F, m^\circ(p)) \right] \quad \text{(B1)}$$

Indeed, let suppose that M(t >M' in $[[\Omega]]_A$; since A is finitely generated, there is a substitution $\sigma : X \rightarrow T(\Sigma)$ and, for each place p, there is w(p) in $N^{(T(\Sigma))}$ such that $M(p) = [[w(p,t) + w(p)]]_A$ and $M'(p) = [[w(t,p) + w(p)]]_A$. Let $m(p) = w(p,t) + w(p)$ and $m'(p) = w(t,p) + w(p)$;

$$\sum_p \left[f_p . | m(p) | + \sum_F f_{F,p} . \#(F, m(p)) \right] - \sum_p \left[f_p . | m'(p) | + \sum_F f_{F,p} . \#(F, m'(p)) \right]$$

$$= \sum_p \left[f_p . | c_{p,t} | + \sum_F f_{F,p} . Q_F(c_{p,t}) \right] = 0$$

according to (A2). According to (A1), this is right also for every terms-markings representing M and M'. Then, by induction on the set of reachable markings, we deduce the expected result.

Vectors f satisfying (A2) are called *general semi-flows* of the schema Ω. Hence, the general semi-flows of a schema give invariants assertions (B1) over the markings *for every algebra satisfying (A1).*

Notice that a basis of general semi-flows can be computed from (A2).

Now, let us come back to the channel example. One can easily prove that the vector f such that :

$f_{repp} = f_{p6} = f_{Fileval} = f_{p7} = f_{Per} = 1$, $f_p = 0$ otherwise,
$f_{*,int} = 1$ and $f_{p,F} = 0$ otherwise,

is a general semi-flow of Ω°. In order to conclude from (B1) that the invariant IV' is satisfied, we need to establish that $[[w]]_A = [[w']]_A$ implies $\#(*,w) = \#(*,w')$ whenever $\mathfrak{I}(A)$ is consistent:

Let suppose that $[[w]]_A = [[w']]_A$ and $\#(*,w) \neq \#(*,w')$. Since (x = x) == true is a theorem of $T(\Sigma',E')$, it is satisfied by $\mathfrak{I}(A)$. Hence true $\equiv$ (Occ$_*$(w) = Occ$_*$(w)). Moreover, since $[[w]]_A = [[w']]_A$, (Occ$_*$(w) = Occ$_*$(w)) $\equiv$ (Occ$_*$(w) = Occ$_*$(w')) in $\mathfrak{I}(A)$; thus true $\equiv$ (Occ$_*$(w) = Occ$_*$(w')). But one can prove by induction on the size of w and w' that $\#(*,w) \neq \#(*,w')$ implies that (Occ$_*$(w) = Occ$_*$(w')) $\equiv_{E'}$ false. Then (Occ$_*$(w) = Occ$_*$(w')) $\equiv$ false in $\mathfrak{I}(A)$. Thus true $\equiv$ false in $\mathfrak{I}(A)$.

The other invariants of (R1) are proved in the same way.

IX.3. Proof of (R2)

At first the proof requires to establish the following theorems in $T(\Sigma',E')$:

$$\begin{array}{ll} In?^*(app(repp(x), f) == In?^*(f) & (th1) \\ P?(app(repp(x), f)) == In?^*(f) & (th2) \\ In?^*(app(*, f)) == true & (th3) \\ P?(app(repc(y), f)) == P?(f) & (th4) \\ [(In?^*(f) \text{ and } P?(app(f, *)) => P?(f)] == true & (th5) \end{array}$$

which can be proved by structural induction over f. Since $\mathfrak{I}'(A)$ is finitely generated, then these theorems are also satisfied by $\mathfrak{I}'(A)$. Then we show (R2) by induction over the sequence leading to M :

a) For $M = M°$, $a = [[empty]]_A$ thus $In?^*(a) \equiv In?(empty) \equiv false$ in $\mathfrak{I}'(A)$. Then either $false \not\equiv true$ in $\mathfrak{I}'(A)$ and thus $In?^*(a) \not\equiv true$ or $false \equiv true$ in $\mathfrak{I}'(A)$ and then $P?(a) \equiv true$ anyway.

b) Assume that M(t >M' and that the property is satisfied by M. Then M'(int) = a' with $a' \in A_{Buffer}$.

1) <u>If t = t1</u>, then $a' = app_A(repp_A(x), a)$ with $x \in A_{Producer}$. If $In?^*(a) \not\equiv true$, then $In?^*(a') \equiv In?^*(app(repp(x), a)) \equiv_{(th1)} In?^*(a) \not\equiv true$. Similarly, if $In?^*(a) \equiv true$, then $In?^*(a') \equiv true$ and then, $P?(a') \equiv P?(app(repp(x), a)) \equiv_{(th2)} In?^*(a) \equiv true$.

2) <u>If t = t2</u>, then $a' = app_A(*_A, a)$ and thus $In?(a') \equiv In?^*(app(*, a)) \equiv_{(th3)} true$. Moreover $|M'(p1)| \geq 1$.

3) <u>If t = t14</u>, then $a' = app_A(repc_A(y), a)$ with y in $A_{Consumer}$ and so, $In?^*(a') \equiv In?^*(a)$ (by the same theorem as th2 for repc(y)) and $P?(a') \equiv P?(a)$ by th5.

4) <u>If t = t3</u>, then $a' = app_A(repp_A(x), a)$ with x in $A_{Producer}$ and so, $In?^*(a') \equiv In?^*(a)$ and $P?(a') \equiv P?(a)$.

5) <u>If t = t4</u>, idem.

6) <u>If t = t5</u>, then $a = app_A(a', *_A)$ and thus $In?^*(a) \equiv true$. Now, assume that $In?^*(a') \equiv true$. If $|M(p1)| \geq 1$ then also $|M'(p1)| \geq 1$. Otherwise, $P?(a) \equiv true$ and then $P?(a') \equiv (true => P?(a')) \equiv [(In?^*(a') \text{ and } P?(a)) => P?(a')] \equiv [(In?^*(app(a', *)) \text{ and } P?(a)) => P?(a')] \equiv_{(th5)} true$.

7) For every other transition the property is obvious.

IX.4. Proof of (R3)

From IV' and IP', we already know that $|M(Per)| = |m(Per)| \leq max$ and $|M(Depos)| \leq ip$.

If $|M(per)| = max$, then no transition can occur and increase M(Depos).

If $|M(Depos)| = ip$, then a marking M' has necessarily been reached before M such that $|M'(Depos)| = ip$, and M'(t5 >. Let us put M'(int) = a with $a \in A_{Buffer}$; $a = app_A(a', *_A)$ and thus $In?^*(a) \equiv true$ in $\mathfrak{I}'(A)$. But, according to IP', since $|M'(Depos)| = ip$, then $|M(p1)| = 0$; and so, according to (R2), $P?(a) \equiv true$ in $\mathfrak{I}'(A)$. In addition, by structural induction, one can establish the following theorem in $T(\Sigma',E')$: $[P?(f) => In?p(f)] == true$. Thus $In?p(a) \equiv [true => In?p(a)] \equiv [P?(a) => In?p(a)] \equiv true$ in $\mathfrak{I}'(A)$.

On the other hand, let m be a terms marking which represents M'. According to IP', #(repp, m(int)) = 0. Let m(int) = x with x in $T(\Sigma)$; $a = [[x]]_A$. By induction over the size of x, one can prove that #(repp, x) = 0 implies $In?p(x) \equiv_{E'} false$ and thus $In?p(x) \equiv false$ in $\mathfrak{I}'(A)$. Hence we get a contradiction with the consistency of $\mathfrak{I}'(A)$.

SECTION 4

SPECIAL TOPICS

U. Goltz:	*Synchronic Distance*
G. Berthelot:	*Transformations and Decompositions of Nets*
R. Valk:	*Infinite Behaviour and Fairness*
M. Jantzen:	*Language Theory of Petri Nets*
M. Jantzen:	*Complexity of Place/Transition Nets*

Synchronic Distance

Ursula Goltz
Gesellschaft für Mathematik und Datenverarbeitung
D-5205 St. Augustin 1

ABSTRACT The concept of synchronic distance is introduced and motivated by S-completion. A definition based on processes of C/E-systems is given and several properties are proved. Weighted synchronic distances are shortly discussed.

Key words: Petri nets, condition/event systems, processes, synchronic distance

CONTENTS

1. Overview

Mutual dependency or independency of events is an important issue in the design and analysis of systems. The concept of synchronic distance serves as a measure allowing not only qualification but also quantification in this respect.

For introducing synchronic distances and investigating their properties, C.A. Petri started with an operation called S-completion and applied it to condition/event-systems. We will follow his approach here and introduce the concept of synchronic distance by S-completion in section 2.

The problem then was to define synchronic distance using only concepts of the condition/event level (or below), since S-completion yields places carrying more than one token. We will present the result of these attempts in section 3. However, we will also discuss difficulties with currently existing definitions.

Section 4 is devoted to properties of synchronic distances. In particular it is shown how synchronic distances reflect mutual dependencies in a system and how synchronic distances may actually be computed. in section 5, we give an idea how weights may be used for measuring event dependencies more precisely. We conclude by showing some application oriented examples in section 6.

2. S-completion and synchronic structure

We start by considering a simple example. The system shown in Fig. 1 consists of two cyclic parts which act independently of each other. More precisely, with $E_1 = \{a,b\}$, $E_2 = \{c,d\}$, we may say: E_1 and E_2 are not synchronised in any way.

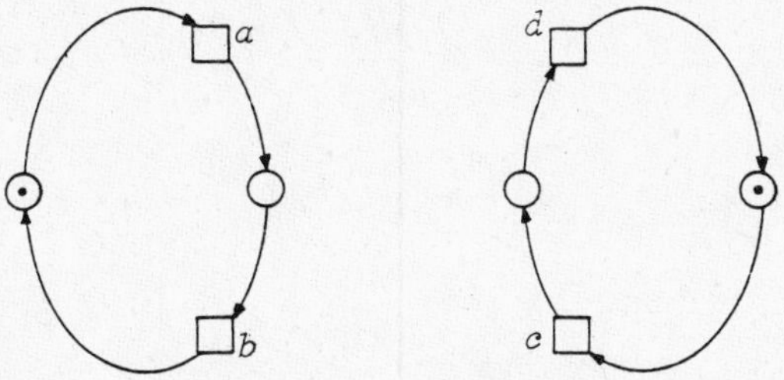

Fig. 1 A condition/event-system

We may now add some structure for coupling E_1 and E_2. Fig. 2 shows a rather strict organisation.

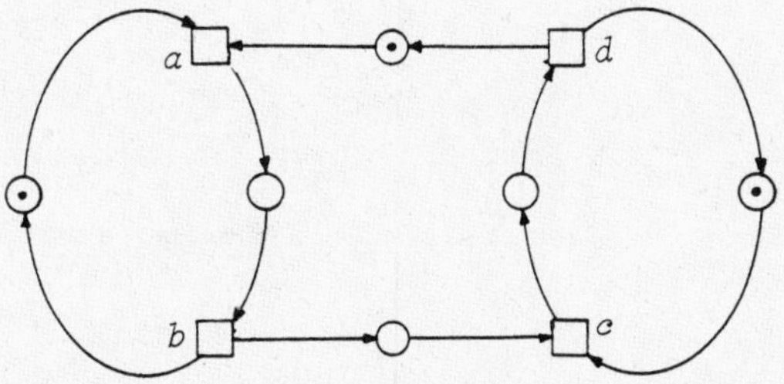

Fig. 2 $\{a,b\}$ and $\{c,d\}$ are now synchronised to occur alternatingly. First a and b occur, then c and d, and so on.

For measuring the degree of synchronisation between E_1 and E_2, we add a new S-element, s, with ${}^{\bullet}s = E_1$ and $s^{\bullet} = E_2$ in Fig. 3. It does not belong to the original condition/event-system, and it has been added with the intention not to influence its behaviour. Every occurrence of some event in E_1 will add a token to s, every occurrence of some event in E_2 will remove a token from s. Consequently, we need to allow it to carry two tokens, otherwise the system would deadlock after the first occurrence of *a*. However we see that s will never carry more than two tokens. s could be interpreted as a buffer between E_1 and E_2, and the necessary capacity of this buffer depends on the degree of synchronisation of E_1 and E_2.

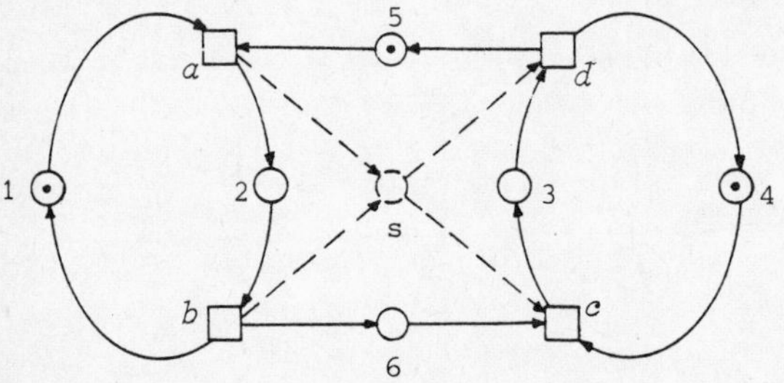

<u>Fig. 3</u> The system of Fig. 2, augmented by an additional S-element, s. The smallest possible capacity of s which does not restrict the behaviour of the original system is 2.

To represent all mutual dependencies between sets of events in a system, we must have, for every pair (E_1,E_2) of sets of events with $E_1 \cup E_2 \neq \emptyset$, an S-element s with ${}^{\bullet}s = E_1$ and $s^{\bullet} = E_2$. A net where this is the case is called <u>S-complete</u>. Any net may be transformed into an S-complete net by adding the necessary S-elements. When considering the possible token number on all these S-elements, we call this the <u>synchronic structure</u> of the system.

<u>Definition</u> Let $N = (B,E;F)$ be a net. Then the S-completion of N is the net $N' = (S',E;F')$ where

1. $S' = B \cup S$,
   $S = \mathcal{P}(E) \times \mathcal{P}(E) \setminus (\{({}^{\bullet}b, b^{\bullet}) \mid b \in B\} \cup \{(\emptyset,\emptyset)\})$
2. $F' = F \cup \bigcup_{(E_1,E_2) \in S} (E_1 \times \{(E_1,E_2)\} \cup \{E_1,E_2)\} \times E_2)$

When considering a particular case (specifying the case class of the system) it is sometimes necessary to assume that the additional S-elements carry tokens in order not to obstruct event occurrences. For example, considering the case {1,4,6} instead of {1,4,5} in Fig. 3, we need two tokens on s to allow *c* and *d* to occur. In this example, we know that these two tokens are definitely used. However, it is also possible that we do not know whether this kind of extra tokens are really used in an execution. In the system shown in Fig. 4, a case may be reached where both *a* and *b* are enabled and may occur concurrently, independent of each other. If *a* would occur before *b*, then the token on s would not be used. However, as *a* and *b* are independent, we need the token on s to be sure that *b* is not obstructed.

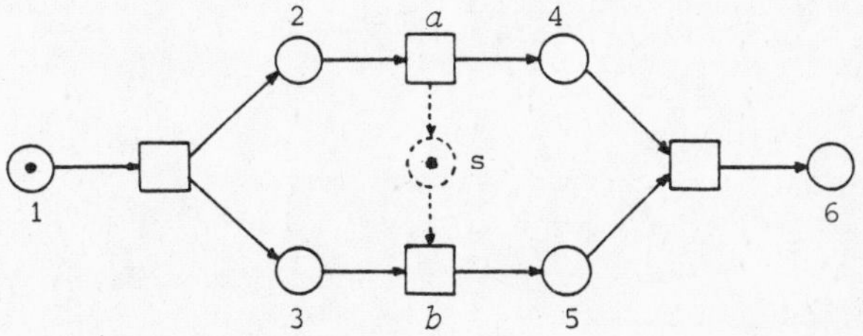

Fig. 4 The token on s is necessary in order not to disable *b*.

We could try to define the synchronic distance $\sigma(E_1,E_2)$ of two sets E_1 and E_2 as the smallest possible capacity of an S-element s with $^{\bullet}s = E_1$ and $s^{\bullet} = E_2$ such that the behaviour of the original system is not restricted. In particular, we need to consider necessary extra tokens for this as discussed above. Then $\sigma(\{a,b\}, \{c,d\}) = 2$ in Fig. 3, $\sigma(\{a\},\{b\}) = 2$ in Fig. 4.

However, when E_1 and E_2 are not disjoint, we need to modify our considerations as shown by the next example. Consider $E_1 = E_2 = \{a\}$ as shown in Fig. 5.

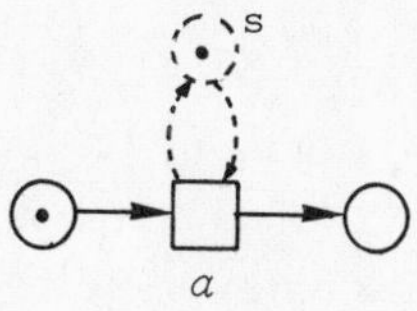

Fig. 5 The token on s is necessary, otherwise *a* would never be able to occur.

An event certainly depends on itself in the strongest sense we could ever imagine, hence $\sigma(\{a\},\{a\})$ should be zero. This is reflected on s, in no case of the system the token number on s will be changed.

Hence we could try to define synchronic distance as the variance of the number of tokens on S-elements as added by S-completion.

However, another example will show that the interpretation of S-completion contains some vagueness. Consider the example in Fig. 6.

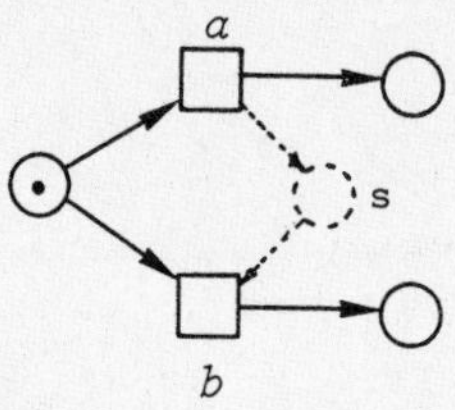

Fig. 6 An example where currently existing definitions of synchronic distance might fail.

If we put a token on s in the represented case in order not to obstruct b then the smallest necessary capacity of s is 2. However, when considering single executions of this system it is possible that this extra token will definitely not be used (when only a occurs). It could be argued that when solving the conflict between a and b, we have to make sure that s contains the smallest possible number of tokens initially. By this we could argue that capacity 1 is sufficient. However, when considering the full behaviour of the system, the variance of the number of tokens on s is certainly 2.

The reason for this discussion is the following. The procedure of S-completion bears some problems when considered as a formal definition of synchronic distance, not only because its interpretation needs some clarification but also for technical reasons. Considering again Fig. 1, we find that the S-completion for $E_1 = \{a,b\}$ and $E_2 = \{c,d\}$ yields an S-element where no finite number of "initial" tokens is sufficient in order not to prevent event occurrences. The synchronic distance is infinite in this case. If we do not want to consider infinite markings, this would have to be handled as a special case. More severely, S-completion leads from the well-understood class of condition/event-systems into a more high-level class, to place/transition-systems, because the new S-elements may carry more than one token. To avoid this, there have been several attempts to define synchronic distance with techniques available on the level of C/E-systems. However, currently existing definitions yield $\sigma(\{a\},\{b\}) = 1$ for the example of Fig. 6. This may be interpreted as discussed above, however it perhaps disagrees with the interpretation of S-completion by C.A. Petri.

We conclude this section with some historical remarks. The concept of S-completion and synchronic distance was introduced by C.A. Petri (see e.g. [P]). The first attempt for a definition based on processes of C/E-systems has been presented at the first advanced course on Petri nets in 1979 [GLT]. Two alternative definitions using the same concepts and both equivalent to this first one (but formally simpler) have been suggested in [GRT]. One of these last ones will be presented and discussed in the following sections.

3. Processes of C/E-systems and synchronic distance

For the definition of C/E-system, we refer to [Th] for the concepts and basic notions. $\Sigma = (B,E;F,C)$ denotes a C/E-system with full reachability class C.

We also presuppose the concept of processes of C/E-systems as explained in [Ro], however the formalisation of processes we use is slightly different (following [Re], see also [BF]).

Definition Let $\Sigma = (B,E;F,C)$ be a contact-free, finite C/E-system and let $N = (S,T;F)$ be an occurrence net. $p : S \cup T \to B \cup E$ is called a process of Σ iff

(a) $\forall t \in T : p({}^{\bullet}t) = {}^{\bullet}p(t) \wedge p(t^{\bullet}) = p(t)^{\bullet}$,

(b) $\forall$ slices S of N : $p|_S$ is injective,

(c) $\exists$ slice S_o of N, with $p(S_o) \in C$.

A process p is called finite iff $S \cup T$ is finite.

Note that a slice is a maximal set of mutually independent S-elements (see [Ro]).

The main difference to the process notion of [Ro] is that we require in (c) that a full case (not only a subset of a case) is contained in the process. Consequently we need to allow isolated places in occurrence nets.

For synchronic distance, we will only consider finite processes (for infinite systems, we would consider possibly infinite processes with only finite lines). It is not necessary to distinguish isomorphic processes, the definitions are independent of the names of the elements of the underlying occurrence nets. Note that, if $p : N \rightarrow \Sigma$ is a finite process, then the maximal and the minimal elements of N both constitute slices, denoted by ${}^{o}p$ and p^{o}.

We will restrict ourselves to contact-free, finite C/E-systems in the sequel, so we may use this process definition. Contact-freeness may be obtained by S-complementation (see [Re]). By modifying the process definition, we could consider infinite C/E-systems. Most of the definitions and results stated here may be transfered to infinite systems.

After these preliminaries, we start introducing the definition of synchronic distance by showing that a straightforward approach fails with respect to the intuition given in section 2. We will later show that in fact it coincides with the definition we will give for a restricted class of C/E-systems.

For two sets of events, E_1, E_2, of some C/E-system Σ and the S-element s with ${}^{\bullet}s = E_1$ and $s^{\bullet} = E_2$, it seems natural to estimate the token variance on s by counting the number of occurrences of E_1-type events against occurrences of E_2-type events in all possible (finite) processes of Σ.

<u>Definition</u> Let $\Sigma = (B,E;F,C)$, $E_1, E_2 \subseteq E$.

$$\sigma'(E_1,E_2) = \sup\{\,||p^{-1}(E_1)| - |p^{-1}(E_2)||\mid p \text{ is a finite process of } \Sigma\}.$$

As a process p is a mapping from the occurrence net, N, to the C/E-system, Σ, $p^{-1}(E_i)$ denotes the set of T-elements which are mapped to elements of E_i, hence $|p^{-1}(E_i)|$ is the number of occurrences of events of E_i in p.

It turns out that this definition fails with respect to our considerations in section 2. Whenever two events may occur concurrently then this should result in a synchronic distance ≥ 2. However, for the example in Fig. 4, no process will ever contain more than one occurrence of each a and b, hence $\sigma'(\{a\},\{b\}) = 1$.

Obviously, it is necessary to extract some information about concurrency from the considered processes. To explain how this is done, we consider a process of the system of Fig. 4, shown in Fig. 7 (the mapping is indicated by node labels).

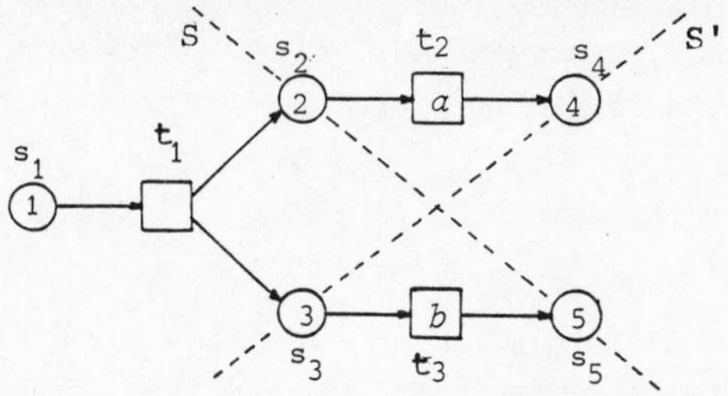

Fig. 7 A process, p, of the system Σ of Fig. 4.
$S=\{s_2,s_5\}$, $S'=\{s_3,s_4\}$ are slices.

In processes, cases of the system are represented by slices (see [Ro]). Two slices, S, S', are indicated in Fig. 7 which have a special property. It is not possible to put S and S' into any order derivable from the flow relation of the occurrence net. This represents the fact that there is no ordering between the two cases {2,5} and {3,4}. This absence of ordering characterises the concurrency of *a* and *b*. Let us consider more closely what the two cases {2,5} and {3,4} mean for the token number on s in Fig. 4. When moving from case {2,5} to the case {3,4} then *a* adds 1 token to s. However, with respect to *b*, the token number on s is also increased by 1 between the cases {2,5} and {3,4}, since the token number in {3,4} would be bigger considering only the effect of *b*. This may be seen by assuming that *b* may occur "backwards" (reversing all arrows). Since we do not consider backward occurrences in processes, we will capture this by reversing the order of the considered cases and count effects between these reversed cases negatively. Formally, this is achieved by the following definitions.

Definition Let $N=(S,T;F)$ be an occurrence net.

(i) Let S_1,S_2 be slices of N. We define $[S_1,S_2]=\{z\in S\cup T \mid \exists x\in S_1\ \exists y\in S_2 : x\le z\le y\}$ (hence $[S_1,S_2]$ is the set of elements "between" S_1 and S_2).

(ii) Let $T'\subseteq T$, let S_1,S_2 be slices of N. We count T' with respect to S_1 and S_2 by counting elements of T' positive if they are between S_1 and S_2 and negative if they are between S_2 and S_1: $\mu(T',S_1,S_2)=|T'\cap[S_1,S_2]|-|T'\cap[S_2,S_1]|$.

For the process of Fig. 7 we have $\mu(p^{-1}(a),S,S')=1$ and $\mu(p^{-1}(b),S,S')=-1$. Now the maximal variance between a and b is obtained by $\mu(p^{-1}(a),S,S') - \mu(p^{-1}(b),S,S') = 2$ (there is no pair of slices yielding more than 2). The synchronic distance between two sets of events is obtained as the supremum of the maximal variances in all finite processes of the system, hence $\sigma(\{a\}, \{b\}) = 2$ for Fig. 4 (there is no process with a variance greater than 2).

<u>Definition</u> Let $\Sigma = (B,E;F,C)$ be a (contact-free, finite) C/E-system, $E_1, E_2 \subseteq E$.

(i) For any (finite) process p of Σ,

$$\nu(p,E_1,E_2) = \max \{\mu(p^{-1}(E_1),S_1,S_2) - \mu(p^{-1}(E_2),S_1,S_2) \mid S_1,S_2 \text{ slices of } p\}$$

(<u>variance of E_1 and E_2 in p</u>).

(ii) The <u>synchronic distance of E_1 and E_2</u> is defined by $\sigma(E_1,E_2) = \sup \{\nu(p,E_1,E_2) \mid p \text{ a finite process of } \Sigma\}$.

Note that $\nu(p,E_1,E_2) \in \mathbb{N}$ since $\mu(p^{-1}(E_i),S_1,S_2) = -\mu(p^{-1}(E_i),S_2,S_1)$, $i=1,2$.

In the next section, we will use this definition to investigate some important properties of synchronic distance. Even though we rely in the proofs on the definition as given above, the presented properties should hold for any reasonable definition of synchronic distance.

4. Properties of synchronic distance

We have already discussed one property which is implied by the basic idea of S-completion: Whenever there are concurrent occurrences of events from E_1 with events from E_2 then $\sigma(E_1,E_2) \geq 2$. However, the converse is not true (see Fig. 8).

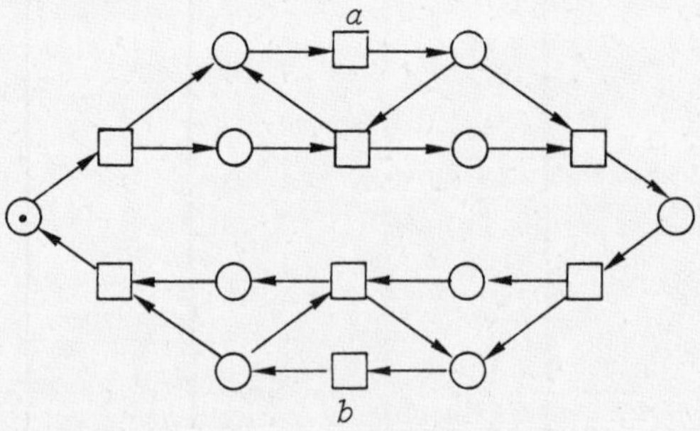

<u>Fig. 8</u> This system is purely sequential, and $\sigma(a,b) = 2$.

Using σ, we can collect the S-elements of the S-completion of a system Σ into equivalence classes. $s = (E_1, E_2)$ is equivalent to $s' = (E_1', E_2')$ iff $\sigma(E_1, E_2) = \sigma(E_1', E_2')$. An important class giving precise information about behaviour aspects is that for synchronic distance 1. We have $\sigma(E_1, E_2) = 1$ iff occurrences of events in E_1 strictly alternate with occurrences of events in E_2.

The facts discussed above support our statement that synchronic distances give a quantitative criterion for event dependencies. Furthermore, the following theorem shows that synchronic distances satisfy the metric properties.

Theorem Let $\Sigma = (B,E;F,C)$ be a C/E-system, $E_1, E_2, E_3 \subseteq E$.

1. $\sigma(E_1, E_2) = 0 \Leftrightarrow E_1 = E_2$,
2. $\sigma(E_1, E_2) = \sigma(E_2, E_1)$
3. $\sigma(E_1, E_2) \leq \sigma(E_1, E_3) + \sigma(E_3, E_2)$,

i.e. σ is a metric on $P(E)$.

Proof straightforward.
For "$\Rightarrow$" in 1. we use that every event has concession in some case of Σ.
□

It would be a step towards the design of systems by means of synchronic distances and similar methods, if it would be possible to find a set of equations (including the metric properties) which allow to decide whether a mapping from $P(E) \times P(E)$ into $\mathbb{N} \cup \{\omega\}$ specifies a possible synchronic structure. Two equations of this kind are suggested in the next theorem. However, the full characterisation is still an open problem.

Theorem The synchronic distance function $\sigma : P(E) \times P(E) \to \mathbb{N} \cup \{\omega\}$ satisfies the following laws:

1. $E_1, E_2, E_3, E_4 \subseteq E \Rightarrow \sigma(E_1 \cup E_2, E_3 \cup E_4) \leq \sigma(E_1, E_3) + \sigma(E_2, E_4) + \sigma(E_1 \cap E_2, E_3 \cap E_4)$
2. $\sigma(E_1, E_2) = \sigma(E_1 \setminus E_2, E_2 \setminus E_1)$

Proof straightforward calculations.
□

After having established that synchronic distance really constitutes a measure, we may now ask in which way, or how precisely, synchronic dependencies in a system are reflected by this measure. The following theorem shows that synchronic distances give an upper bound for mutual independencies of events (or sets of events).

Theorem If $\sigma(E_1,E_2)=n$ in a C/E-system Σ, then there is no process p of Σ with
$|p^{-1}(E_1)|>n$ and $|p^{-1}(E_2)|=0$, or $|p^{-1}(E_2)|>n$ and $|p^{-1}(E_1)|=0$.

Proof straightforward.

□

However, the converse of this theorem is not true (see for example the system in Fig. 4). In particular, $\sigma(E_1,E_2)=\omega$ does not imply that the events in E_1 and E_2 may occur fully independent of each other, even if weights are associated with events (see section 5).

When introducing the definition of synchronic distance in the previous section, we started with a straightforward attempt (by defining σ'). We have shown that this definition fails for an example with concurrency with respect to the considerations in section 2. We will now show that we may use σ' as a much simpler definition of synchronic distance when concurrent occurrences may be repeated. This is certainly the case in systems where every case is forward reachable from any other case.

Definition A C/E-system $\Sigma = (B,E;F,C)$ is called cyclic iff
$\forall c_1,c_2 \in C : c_1(r^*)c_2$ (where r is the forward reachability relation.

Theorem [Re] Let $\Sigma=(B,E;F,C)$ be a cyclic C/E-system.
For all $E_1,E_2 \subseteq E$, $\sigma(E_1,E_2) = \sigma'(E_1,E_2)$.

Proof
Let $E_1,E_2 \subseteq E$. Obviously, $\sigma'(E_1,E_2) \le \sigma(E_1,E_2)$. We show $\sigma(E_1,E_2) \le \sigma'(E_1,E_2)$ by constructing, for each process p, a process p' with $\nu(p,E_1,E_2) \le \big|\,|p'^{-1}(E_1)|-|p'^{-1}(E_2)|\,\big|$.

Let p be a process and let S_1,S_2 be slices such that $\nu(p,E_1,E_2)=\mu(p^{-1}(E_1),S_1,S_2)-\mu(p^{-1}(E_2),S_1,S_2)$. Since Σ is cyclic, the case $p(S_2)$ may be reproduced by forward steps after executing p. Let p" be the process which is obtained by extending p such that $p(S_2)$ is reproduced. p" contains a subprocess p_o which starts and ends with $p(S_2)$ (see Fig. 9).

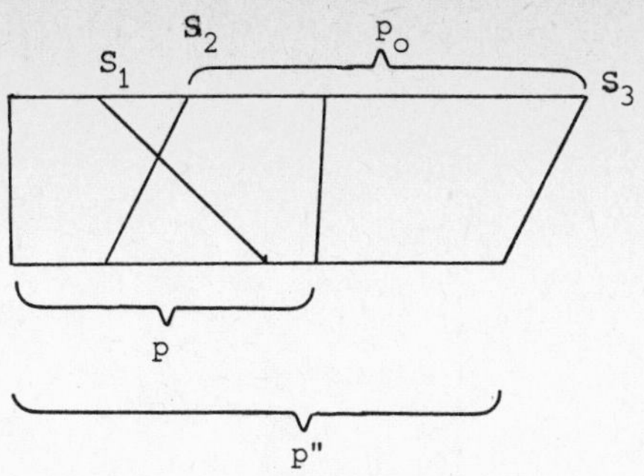

Fig. 9   p is extended such that $p(S_2) = p(S_3)$.

If $|p_o^{-1}(E_1)| - |p_o^{-1}(E_2)| \neq 0$, the required process p' is obtained by iterating p_o $\nu(p,E_1,E_2)$ times.

Otherwise, let p' be the process which is obtained as the part of p" between S_1 and S_3. Then $||p'^{-1}(E_1)| - |p'^{-1}(E_2)||$

$$= ||p_o^{-1}(E_1)| + |p^{-1}(E_1) \cap [S_1,S_2]| - |p^{-1}(E_1) \cap [S_2,S_1]|$$
$$- |p_o^{-1}(E_2)| - |p^{-1}(E_2) \cap [S_1,S_2]| + |p^{-1}(E_2) \cap [S_2,S_1]|| = \nu(p,E_1,E_2).$$

□

When considering the definition of σ', we see that it is not even necessary to consider processes if a system is cyclic. For simply counting the number of event occurrences without taking concurrency aspects into account, it is sufficient to use occurrence sequences.

The final part of this section is devoted to the problem whether synchronic distances can actually be computed. Following the definition, it would be necessary to consider all (finite) processes of the system. In general, a system will have infinitely many processes. Fortunately we are able to show that it is sufficient to consider only finitely many processes up to a limited length.

It will turn out that it is sufficient to consider only processes which do not contain proper cyclic subprocesses (no case is repeated inside the process).

Definition

(i) A process p is called cyclic iff $^{o}p \neq p^{o}$ and $p(^{o}p) = p(p^{o})$ (p is not trivial and the initial and final slice of p are mapped to the same case).

(ii) A process p is called simple iff, for all slices, S,S' of p, $S \neq S' \Rightarrow p(S) \neq p(S')$.

(iii) A process p is called a reproduction process iff p is cyclic and every proper subprocess of p is simple.

As an example consider Fig. 10.

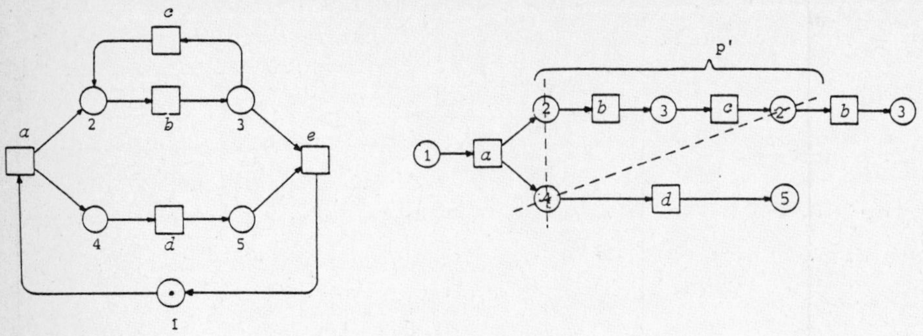

Fig. 10 A system and a process, p, of this system which contains a cyclic subprocess p'. Hence p is not simple, but p' is a reproduction process.

The following lemma shows that the size of simple processes and reproduction processes is bounded by the number of cases of the considered system.

Lemma Let $\Sigma = (B,E;F,C)$, let p be a process of Σ, let size(p) be the number of slices of p. If p is simple then size(p) $\leq |C|$; if p is a reproduction process then size(p) $\leq |C| + 1$.

Proof obvious from the definition of simple and reproduction processes. □

The following theorem guarantees that only simple processes and reproduction processes need to be considered for the computation of synchronic distances.

Theorem Let $\Sigma = (B,E;F,C)$ be a C/E-system and $E_1, E_2 \subseteq E$. Then

$$\sigma(E_1,E_2) = \begin{cases} \omega & \text{iff there exists a reproduction process } p \text{ with } |p^{-1}(E_1)| - |p^{-1}(E_2)| \neq 0, \\ \max\{\nu(p,E_1,E_2) \mid p \text{ a simple process of } \Sigma\} & \text{otherwise.} \end{cases}$$

Proof

If there exists a reproduction process p with $|p^{-1}(E_1)| - |p^{-1}(E_2)| \neq 0$ then, by iterating p, we find $\sigma(E_1,E_2) = \omega$.

We now assume $|p^{-1}(E_1)| - |p^{-1}(E_2)| = 0$ for all reproduction processes p.

We will show that, for an arbitrary process p, we find a simple process p' with $\nu(p',E_1,E_2) \geq \nu(p,E_1,E_2)$. In particular, this implies that $\sigma(E_1,E_2)$ is finite since there are only finitely many simple processes of Σ.

Let p be a process, let S_1,S_2 be slices with

$$\nu(p,E_1,E_2) = \mu(p^{-1}(E_1),S_1,S_2) - \mu(p^{-1}(E_2),S_1,S_2).$$

If p is not simple, there exist two slices S_3,S_4 with $S_3 \neq S_4$ and $p(S_3) = p(S_4)$, and no case is repeated between S_3 and S_4. Then it can be shown that there are slices S_3',S_4' with the same properties and furthermore, for all $x \in S_3'$, $y \in S_4'$, $\neg (y \leq x)$. Hence, the part of p between S_3' and S_4' is a reproduction process (see Fig. 11).

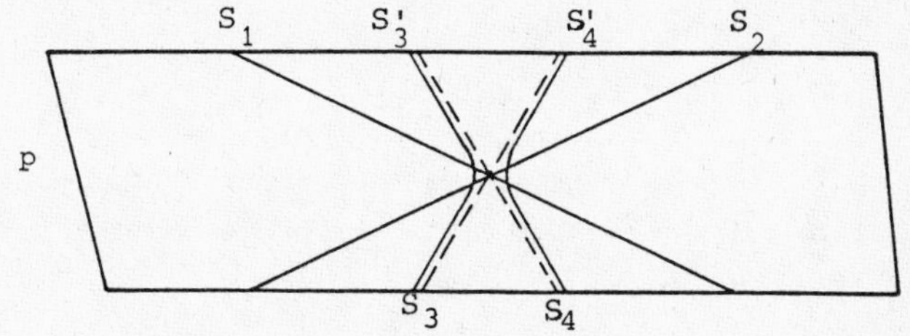

Fig. 11 The part between S_3' and S_4' is a reproduction process.

Let p' be the process which is obtained from p by cutting out the part between S_3' and S_4'. We will show that $\nu(p',E_1,E_2) \geq \nu(p,E_1,E_2)$. For this we consider the processes p_{12} and p_{21} as shown in Fig. 12.

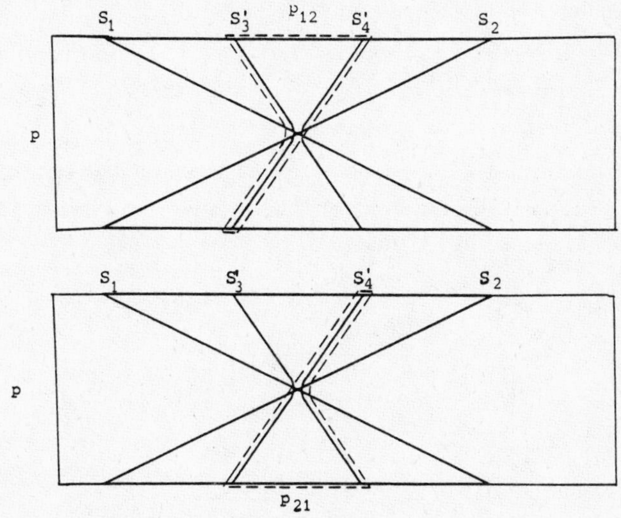

Fig. 12 The processes p_{12} and p_{21}.

p_{12} and p_{21} are either reproduction processes or empty (consist only of a slice). This implies

$$|p_{12}^{-1}(E_1)| - |p_{12}^{-1}(E_2)| = 0,$$
$$|p_{21}^{-1}(E_1)| - |p_{21}^{-1}(E_2)| = 0.$$

Furthermore, S_1 and S_2 are slices of p' (this is somewhat tedious to show), and we have

$$\begin{aligned}\nu(p,E_1,E_2) &= |p^{-1}(E_1) \cap [S_1,S_2]| - |p^{-1}(E_1) \cap [S_2,S_1]| \\ &\quad - |p^{-1}(E_2) \cap [S_1,S_2]| + |p^{-1}(E_2) \cap [S_2,S_1]| \\ &= |p'^{-1}(E_1)\cap[S_1,S_2]|+|p_{12}^{-1}(E_1)|-|p'^{-1}(E_1)\cap[S_2,S_1]|-|p_{21}^{-1}(E_1)| \\ &\quad - |p'^{-1}(E_2)\cap[S_1,S_2]|-|p_{12}^{-1}(E_2)|+|p'^{-1}(E_2)\cap[S_2,S_1]|+|p_{21}^{-1}(E_2)| \\ &= \mu(p'^{-1}(E_1),S_1,S_2) - \mu(p'^{-1}(E_2),S_1,S_2) \\ &\le \nu(p',E_1,E_2).\end{aligned}$$

If p' is not simple the whole procedure may be repeated. However, since we always cut out a non-trivial piece, we find a simple process satisfying the requirements after finitely many steps.

□

As an example how to apply this result, we consider the system of Fig. 10. We may conclude that $\sigma(b,d) = \omega$ because $|p'^{-1}(b)| - |p'^{-1}(d)| = 1$. However, $|p^{-1}(a)| - |p^{-1}(d)| = 0$ for all reproduction processes p. Hence $\sigma(a,d) = 1$, the maximal variance is for example assumed for the simple process consisting of a single occurrence of a.

5. Weighted synchronic distance

We have seen that synchronic distance is an upper bound for the mutual independence of events in a system. For discussing which kind of dependencies are captured, we consider the system shown in Fig. 13.

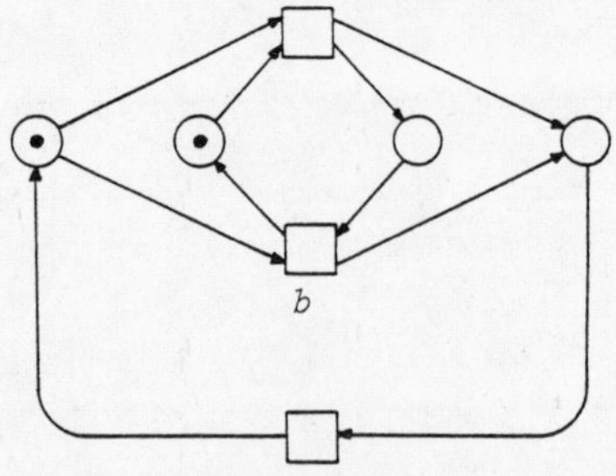

Fig. 13 The synchronic distance $\sigma(a,b)$ is infinite.

The events *a* and *b* occur in a strictly organised way. Two occurrences of *a* in sequence alternate with single occurrences of *b*. Since the difference between the number of occurrences of *a* and *b* may grow unlimited, we have $\sigma(a,b) = \omega$. However, these two events are tightly coupled; we may have at most two occurrences of one event without the other event occurring. This is not captured by the definitions of section 2.

We will now discuss how to improve our measure for event dependencies by weighting the number of occurrences of events. By the last theorem of the previous section we know that the synchronic distance between two sets of events is finite iff the variance of occurrences in each reproduction process is zero. We may now try to weight each event of the C/E-system to achieve this. If we succeed, we get finite synchronic distances in some cases where the original definition yields ω. In the above example, we might associate weight 2 with event *b*, so every occurrence of *b* will be counted twice, this obviously yields synchronic distance 2.

To formalise this idea, we introduce weight functions which associate weights ($\neq 0$) with events and then modify the definition of variance by weighting the number of occurrences of each event. For a C/E-system $\Sigma = (B,E;F,C)$, a function $g : E \to \mathbb{N} \setminus \{0\}$ is called a <u>weight function</u>.

<u>Definition</u> Let $\Sigma = (B,E;F,C)$ be a C/E-system, g a weight function, and $E_1, E_2 \subseteq E$.

1. Let p be a process of Σ. The <u>g-weighted variance</u> of E_1 and E_2 is defined by

$$\nu_g(p,E_1,E_2) = \max \{ \sum_{e \in E_1} g(e) \cdot \mu(p^{-1}(e),S_1,S_2) - \sum_{e \in E_2} g(e) \cdot \mu(p^{-1}(e),S_1,S_2) \mid S_1,S_2 \text{ slices of p} \}.$$

2. The <u>g-weigthed synchronic distance</u> of E_1 and E_2 is defined by $\sigma_g(E_1,E_2) = \sup\{\nu_g(p,E_1,E_2) \mid p \text{ a finite process of } \Sigma\}$.

When exhibiting the concept by S-completion, then weighted synchronic distances correspond to S-elements with appropriate arc-weights as illustrated for the system of Fig. 13 in Fig. 14.

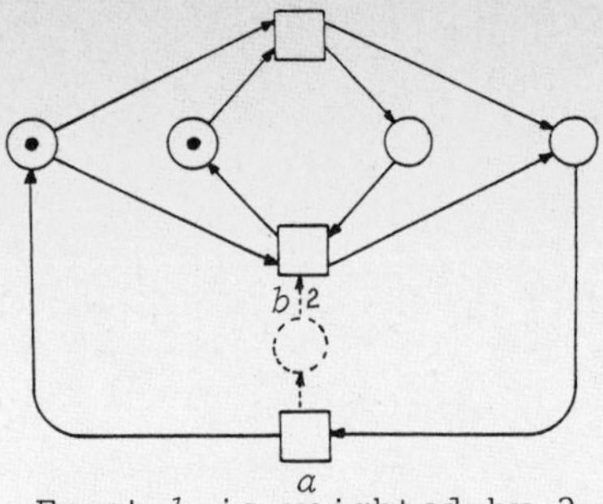

Fig. 14 Event b is weighted by 2.

For a fixed weight function g, all theorems given in the previous section are still true when changing ν and σ to ν_g and σ_g, respectively.

Now the question arises how to decide whether or not a weight function exists such that a finite synchronic distance may be obtained between two sets of events and how to find such a weight function. As said before, we may use the theorem on computation of synchronic distance and consider only reproduction processes. These determine a linear equation system such that its solutions are weight functions which yield a finite synchronic distance. Interested readers are referred to [GR] where this procedure is described.

However, we do not always find weights for a finite synchronic distance in cases where two sets of events are synchronised in some way. Consider the system shown in Fig. 15.

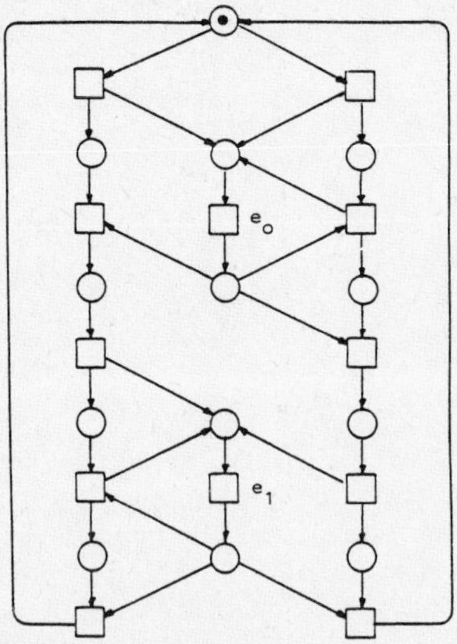

Fig. 15 In this system e_i, occurs at most twice, then e_{1-i} must occur. Nevertheless, for all weight functions g, $\sigma_g(e_o,e_1) = \omega$.

In this system we have two reproduction processes. In the one operating in the left part of the system, one occurrence of e_o is followed by two occurrences of e_1. Conversely, we have two occurrences of e_o and one occurrence of e_1 in the other reproduction process. Hence there is no way to weight e_o and e_1 to obtain a finite synchronic distance, even though we never have more than two occurrences of any event in sequence.

To understand in which respect the two systems of Fig. 13 and Fig. 15 differ, we consider the global possibilities for the number of event occurrences as shown in Fig. 16.

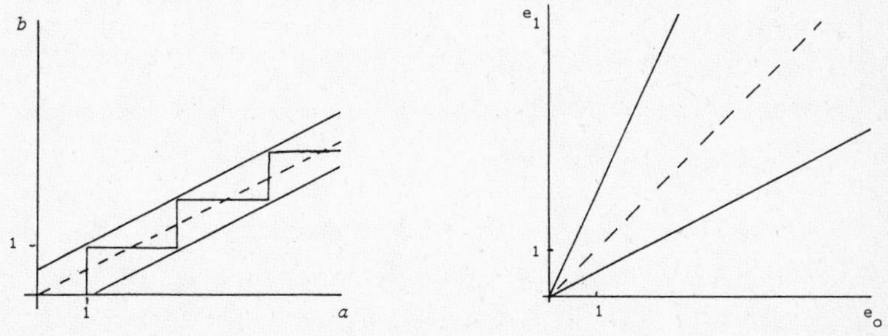

Fig. 16 The relationship between the total number of event occurrences of *a* and *b* and of e_o and e_1 in processes of the systems of Fig. 13 and Fig. 14, respectively.

We see that, in the system of Fig. 13, the overall variance between *a* and *b* is bounded, whereas e_o and e_1 behave in a less disciplined way in the system of Fig. 15. Weighting yields finite synchronic distances in exactly these cases where such a bound for the global independency exists.

6. Application of synchronic distance for system design

In the final section of this paper, we want to illustrate the use of synchronic distance as a design tool. Rather than computing synchronic distances for a given system, we may specify the intended behaviour of a system by requiring certain synchronic distance values.

The following example exhibits one aspect of system behaviour which may be specified with synchronic distances.

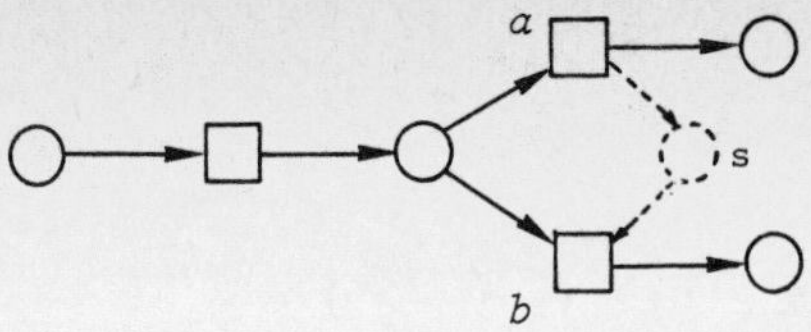

Fig. 17 Part of a system to be designed.

The structure shown in Fig. 17 is assumed to be part of a system. The events a and b will be in conflict whenever both of them are enabled in a case. It is not yet specified how these two events are connected to the rest of the system. In the system design phase, the relative behaviour of a and b, or in other words, how a and b are synchronised, can be specified by assigning a synchronic distance to them (represented by s). The resolution of a conflict in a system will always require some information from the environment of the system (for example, from a human user). By this, the environment gains control over the system. By assigning a value to $\sigma(a,b)$, we specify which degree of control is desired. Since $a \neq b$, $\sigma(a,b)$ can not be zero. $\sigma(a,b) = 2$ forces a and b to occur alternatingly, the only choice left to the environment is: Which one should occur first. $\sigma(a,b) = 2$ allows more control. After the decision which one occurs inially, there will be in any case again a real conflict when a and b are enabled the second time. Whenever one event has occurred twice consecutively, then $\sigma(a,b) = 2$ forces the other one to occur. Otherwise, the environment has control. In this way we can allow as much control as we want by enlarging synchronic distances.

The final example (due to Lautenbach, see [Lau],[GLT]) is devoted to an important issue in the design of concurrent systems. Let us assume that two parts of a system are supposed to work concurrently, however both contain a critical region. These critical regions may only be executed in a mutual exclusive fashion, for example because both partners compete for a resource which may only be used by one of them at a time (see Fig. 18).

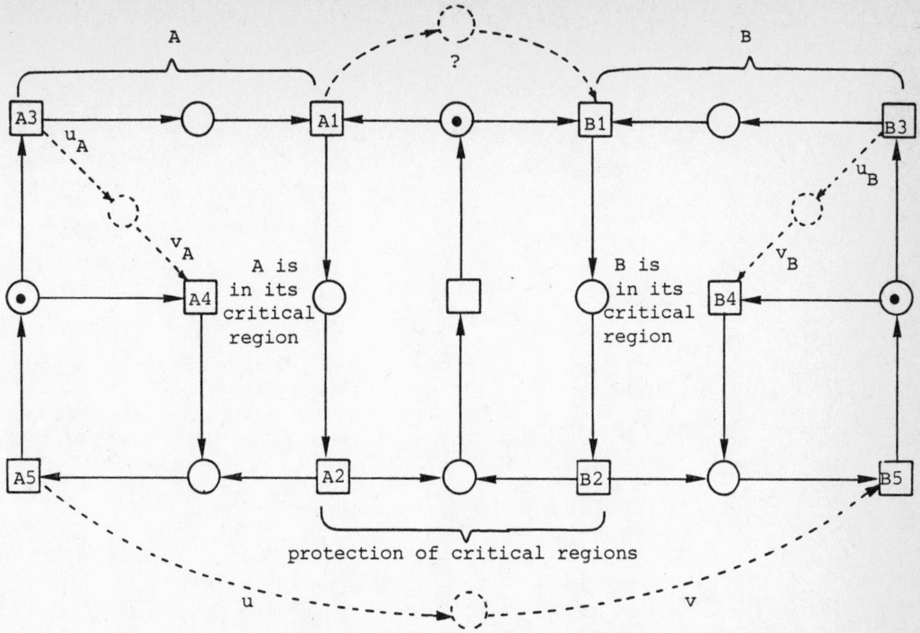

Fig. 18 Two partners, A and B, with critical regions. Arc-weights at additional S-elements denote weights for the corresponding synchronic distances.

It is now important to make sure that each partner can not block the other one from entering its critical region in an "unfair" way. A usual definition of fairness is the following: If a partner is infinitely often ready to enter its critical region it should also infinitely often excecute it. However, this is not very useful for practical applications: We may still have arbitrary long executions of the system where one partner blocks the other one in an unfair way. What we look for is a way to limit the deviations from an average relative frequency of the two partners being in their critical regions.

First we note that the events A3 and B3 denote that A or B, respectively, wishes to enter its critical region, whereas A4 and B4 correspond to activities of A and B outside of their critical regions. A5 and B5 may be considered as local clocks for each A and B. Every activity inside or outside the critical region is followed by a "tick" of the clock. The relative frequency of A3 and A4 expresses how frequently A wishes to enter its critical region, this may be expressed by specifying a weighted synchronic distance for A3 and A4. In Fig. 18, the weights u_A and v_A specify a relative frequency for A3 and A4. Symmetrically this is done for B. Furthermore, the clocks of A and B are made comparable by associating weights u and v to A5 and B5 and specifying their synchronic distance. From these three synchronic distance values, we may now compute a synchronic distance for A1 and B1 which has to be implemented by some mechanism to ensure fairness (for details, see [Lau],[GLT]).

References

For a more complete discussion of the work on synchronic distances and corresponding references, see [GY].

[BF] E. Best, C. Fernandez: "Notation and Terminology on Petri Net Theory", Arbeitspapiere der GMD 195, January 1986

[GLT] H.J. Genrich, K. Lautenbach, P.S. Thiagarajan: "Elements of General Net Theory", in: Net Theory and Applications, Lecture Notes in Computer Science 84, Springer-Verlag, 1980

[GR] U. Goltz, W. Reisig: "Weighted Synchronic Distance", in: Application and Theory of Petri Nets, Informatik Fachberichte 52, Springer-Verlag, 1982

[GRT] U. Goltz, W. Reisig, P.S. Thiagarajan: "Two Alternative Definitions of Synchronic Distance", in: Application and Theory of Petri Nets, Informatik Fachberichte 52, Springer-Verlag 1982

[GY] U. Goltz, Yuan Chong-Yi: "Synchronic Structure", in: Advances in Petri Nets 1985, Lecture Notes in Computer Science 222, Springer-Verlag, 1986

[Lau] K. Lautenbach: "Ein kombinatorischer Ansatz zur Beschreibung und Erreichung von Fairness in Scheduling-Problemen", in: Applied Computer Science, Vol. 8, Verlag Carl Hanser, 1977

[P] C.A. Petri: "Interpretations of Net Theory", internal report GMD-ISF 75-07, revised version, Bonn 1976

[Re] W. Reisig: "Petri Nets", Springer-Verlag, 1985

[Ro] G. Rozenberg: "Behaviour of Elementary Net Systems", in this volume

[Th] P.S. Thiagarajan: "Elementary Net Systems", in this volume

TRANSFORMATIONS AND DECOMPOSITIONS OF NETS

G.BERTHELOT

CNAM-IIE
18 allée J.Rostand
B.P. 77
91002 EVRY CEDEX
FRANCE

and

LRI
Bat 490
Université PARIS 11
91405 ORSAY
FRANCE

Abstract We present a set of transformations of place/transition systems which preserve several classical properties of nets namely boundedness, deadlock freeness, liveness and covering by S-invariants. These transformations may simplify or refine a system and allow either to simplify a place/transition system before analysing it or to introduce more details in a given system having some propreties without changing them. We also present a decomposition technique to split a system into subsytems which can be analysed separatly.

Key words transformations of P/T Nets, decompositions of P/T nets, equivalence of P/T Nets

CONTENTS

1. Introduction

The verification of concurrent systems described by nets very often implies the analysis of the set of all reachable markings. Such a set may be huge and its analysis cumbersome or even physically impossible if it contains millions of elements. To avoid a complete enumeration of all the states, we present here tools that allow transformations or decompositions of systems. Transformations modify a net without affecting some of its interesting properties. In this sense the main properties concern occurrence sequences : deadlock freeness, 1-liveness, liveness and equivalence of behaviour .

Another technique consists in the decomposition of a system into subsystems in order to study every component separately. This is a new application of the well known "divide and conquer" principle which has been applied numerous times in sequential programming. With concurrency, however, a new problem arises : every component may seem to work perfectly when isolated, but the whole system itself may fail due to a synchronization error. So the composition of net must follow some rules both at the structure level and behaviour level. At the structure level valuable results can be obtained only if the composition is done either by fusion of places or by fusion of transitions, but not both simultaneously. At the behaviour level, rules can be termed as observational equivalences between components. Moreover, since composition must be usable in conjunction with stepwise refinements then equivalence must be also congruent w.r.t. to composition.

2.Transformations

A transformation may be applied only if some conditions are satisfied. These conditions called application conditions, may concern either the structure of the net (these are the conditions on structure), or their verification may need partial knowledge of its dynamic behaviour (those are conditions on evolution).
Obviously conditions on structure are easier to verify but they lead to the specification of a lot of details, although conditions on evolution allow the most general cases to be treated elegantly. Moreover, conditions on evolution provide a general framework which may be adapted to various situations. By the way, it is often quite easy to find a set of specific conditions on structure which fulfill the requirements of conditions on evolution. Hence, we now present transformations specified with conditions on evolution and some examples of corresponding structural versions taken from [Be2].

The goal of a transformation being either to simplify, or on the contrary to refine a net, every transformation presented is associated with the converse transformation.

Notations : in the following we assume a P/T system $\Sigma = (S,T;F,K,W,M_0)$ with infinite capacities so K will be ommitted and C(p,t) denotes its incidence matrix in accordance with [BeF].

Definition : 1-liveness.

Let Σ be a system. A transition t is 1-live iff there exists a reachable marking M belonging to $[M_0>$ such that M[t>. The system Σ is 1-live iff every transition of T is 1-live.
1-liveness of a system means that every transition may occur at least one time and hence is not **dead** according to [Rei]. This notion is weaker than deadlock freeness and liveness from [BeF] .

Transformations may be classified in two categories, according to objects concerned : places or transitions.

2.1.Transformation on places

Transformations of this kind do not modify the functioning of a net, but the enabling conditions of transitions are expressed in another way.

2.1.1.Redundant places

A redundant place contains, for every reachable marking, enough tokens so as not to prevent transitions connected to it from occurring.

Definition 2.1.1.1 : redundant place

Given a system Σ, a place p of S is a **redundant place** iff there exists a subset I (named reference set of p, and possibly empty) of S not containing p and a "weight function" $V : I \cup \{p\} \rightarrow \mathcal{N} - \{0\}$ ($\mathcal{N}$ denotes naturals) such that the two following conditions are true (the role of V may be intuitively seen as corresponding to the role of weight functions in the context of S-invariants) :

i). $\forall\ M \in [M_0>\quad V(p)\,M(p) \geq \sum_{I} V(q)\,M(q)$

(i.e. the weighted sum of tokens is greater for p than for the places of I)

ii). $\forall\ t \in T \quad V(p)\ W(p,t) \leq \sum_{I} V(q)\ W(q,t)$

(the occurrence of every transition demands more (weighted) tokens from I than from p)

The corresponding transformation consists in eliminating the redundant place, contained tokens and related arcs. The rest of the system is left unchanged and the resulting system is denoted by Σ'.

We shall claim that this transformation does not change the language of the net so deadlock-freeness, 1-liveness , liveness and behaviour condition (see section 3.2) are not changed.

Theorem 2.1.1.2 : $L(\Sigma) = L(\Sigma')$.
idea of the proof : from the conditions of definition2.1.1.1 it is easy to derive that when every place of I contains enough tokens to allow occurrence of any transition, the same holds for place p.

Corollary 2.1.1.3 : Σ is deadlock-free (1-live, live, satisfying the behavioural condition on a subset of distinguished transitions T_D) iff Σ' is deadlock-free (1-live, live , satisfying the behavioural condition on a subset of distinguished transitions T_D)

The conditions on evolution used in this general definition of redundant places may be characterized purely in terms of conditions on the structure of a system Σ in order to define a structurally redundant place .

Definition 2.1.1.4 : structurally redundant place
Given a system Σ , a place p of S is a **structurally redundant place** iff there exists a subset I (possibly empty) of S and a valuation function $V : I \cup \{p\} \to \mathcal{N} - \{0\}$ such that the three following conditions are satisfied :

i) $\exists\ b_{M0} \in \mathcal{N} : V(p)\ M_0(p) - \sum_{I} V(q)\ M_0(q) = b_{M0}$

(for the initial marking M_0, p has a weighted marking greater than the sum of weighted marking of places belonging to I)

ii) $\forall\ t \in T : V(p)\ W(p,t) - \sum_{I} V(q)\ W(q,t) \leq b_{M0}$

(the difference between the weighted marking of p and those of places belonging to I necessary to give concession to t must be less than or equal to this difference in the initial marking)

iii) $\forall t \in T\ \exists c_t \in \mathcal{N} : \quad V(p)\ C(p,t) - \sum_{I} V(q)\ C(q,t) = c_t$

(when a transition t occurs, the growth of the weighted marking of p is greater than that one of I)

Example : Places p_1 of figure 1 is a structurally redundant place with $I = \{p_3, p_4\}$, $V(p_1) = 1$, $V(p_3)= 1$ and $V(p_4) = 1$. Place p_2 is also a structurally redundant with $I = \varnothing$

Theorem 2.1.1.5
A structurally redundant place is a redundant place.

idea of the proof : from condition i of definition 2.1.1.4 the condition i of definition 2.1.1.1holds for the initial marking and, from condition iii, its remains true when any transition occurs. Last , condition ii of definition 2.1.1.4. implies condition ii of definition 2.1.1.1.

Since the definition of a structurally redundant place requires stronger conditions than the definition of a redundant place, it is possible to preserve more properties (see [Be1] or Be2]), namely safeness and S-invariant covering, if place p is kept as output of transitions such that $c_t > 0$ instead of being removed.

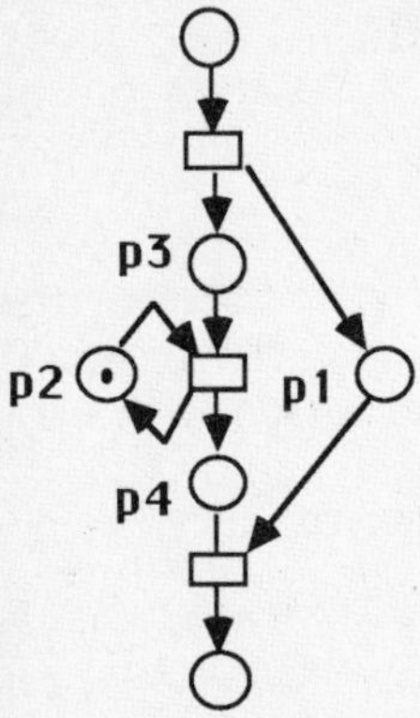

figure 1

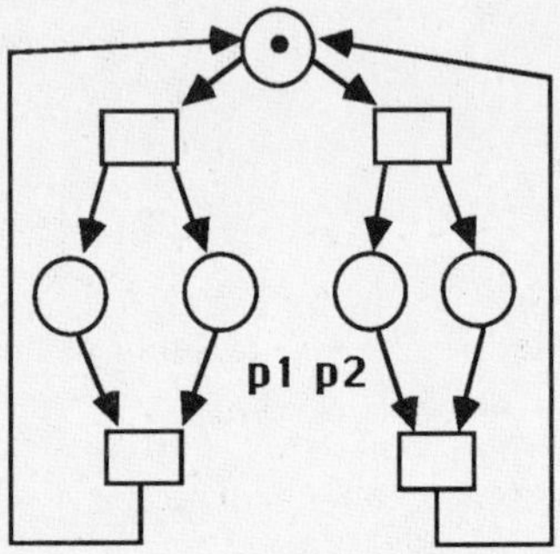

figure 2

2.1.2. Doubled places

Two doubled places can be fused when, for every reachable marking, tokens of one of these places can never be confused with the tokens of the other and conversely.

Definition 2.1.2.1 : doubled places
Given a system Σ. Two places p_1 and p_2 of Σ are **doubled places** iff
i) $\forall t \in T : |{}^{\bullet}t \cap \{p_1,p_2\}| \leq 1$ (no transition simultaneously has p_1 and p_2 as inputs)
ii) $\forall t \in T,\ \forall i \in \{1,2\} :\ [{}^{\bullet}t \neq \{p_i\}]$ or
$[{}^{\bullet}t = \{p_i\} \Rightarrow\ \exists t' \in T, \exists j \in \{1,2\}, i \neq j$ such that ${}^{\bullet}t' = \{p_j\}$ and $\forall p \in S,\ W(t,p) = W(t',p)]$.
(either every transition which has p_i ($i \in \{1,2\}$) as input has also at least another input, or there exist two transitions (t,t'), t whose only input is p_1 and t' whose only input is p_2 such that W(t',p) = W(t,p) for every p belonging to S)
iii) $\forall M \in [M_0>, \forall\ t \in p_1{}^{\bullet},\ [\forall s \in S\text{-}\{p_1\}\ M(s) \geq W(s,t)] \Rightarrow\ M(p_2) = 0$ and conversely.
(For every reachable marking, when all places except p_1 contain enough tokens to enable a transition with p_1 as input, then p_2 is empty and conversely)

Remark : according to the condition iii) if a transition having p_i ($i \in \{1,2\}$) as input may occur then p_j ($j \in \{1,2\}, i \neq j$) is empty.

The transformation consists in the fusion of p_1 and p_2 into a place p_{12} and addition of their tokens . Let us denotes Σ' the resulting system.

Note :A subset of doubled places may be defined using some conditions on structure (see [Be1] or [Be2]).

Example : places p_1 and p_2 of figure 2 are doubled.

This transformation does not change the language of the system so properties bound to occurrence sequences are not affected.

Theorem 2.1.2.2 : $L(\Sigma) = L(\Sigma')$
idea of the proof : when some transition t_1 with p_1 as input is enabled in the initial system, no transition t_2 with p_2 as input is enabled and the same applies in the modified system.

Corollary 2.1.2.3 : Σ is deadlock-free (1-live, live , satisfying the Behavioural condition on on a subset of distinguished transitions T_D) iff Σ' is deadlock-free (1-live, live , satisfying the Behavioural condition on a subset of distinguished transitions T_D)

2.1.3. Equivalent places

Two places are equivalent when, for every reachable marking, the tokens they contain allow, after the occurrence of only one transition , the same set of markings to be reached.

Definition 2.1.3.1 : equivalent places
Given a system Σ. Two places p_1 and p_2 are **equivalent** if and only if
i) $\forall\, t_1 : p_1 \in \bullet t_1 \;\Rightarrow\; \exists\, t_2$ such that [($p_2 \in \bullet t_2$) and ($\forall\, p \in S\;\; W(t_2,p) = W(t_1,p)$) and
($\forall\, p \notin \{p_1,p_2\}\; W(p,t_1) = W(p,t_2)$)] .
ii) $\forall\, t_1 : p_1 \in \bullet t_1 \;\Rightarrow\; W(p_1,t_1) = 1$.
iii) $|\bullet p_1| > 0$ and $|\bullet p_2| > 0$ (both p_1 and p_2 are output of at least one transition).

If condition ii) is not satisfied then deadlock freeness is not preserved.

Remark this definition, although quite general, uses only conditions on structure.

The transformation consists in the fusion of p_1 and p_2 into a place p_{12} which contains the sum of token of places of p_1 and p_2. This results in a system Σ'.

Example : places p_1 and p_2 of figure 3 are equivalent places.

The language of the system is slightly changed this time since in the transformed system, transitions which had p_1 as input and transitions which had p_2 as input are identical. Let us denote T_{12} (resp. T_{12}') this subset of T (resp. T') and Proj(X / Y) the projection of a language X over a subset Y of its alphabet where the symbols which do not belong to Y are erased from words of X.

Theorem 2.1.3.2 : $Proj(L(\Sigma)/T_{12}) = Proj(L(\Sigma')/T_{12}')$.
idea of the proof :
1. Obviously every occurrence sequence of Σ is also an occurrence sequence of Σ'.
2. For every occurrence sequence s' of Σ' there exists an occurrence sequence s of Σ containing the same transitions and which differs only for transitions which have p_1 and p_2 as input.

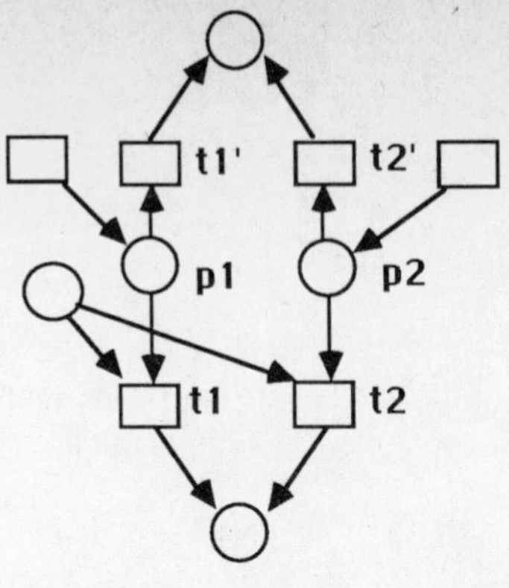

figure 3

Nevertheless all properties concerning occurrence sequences are preserved except 1-liveness . The Behavioural condition may be not preserved if it relies on transitions which have p_1 and p_2 as input.

2.2.Fusions of transitions

Transformations of this kind have been defined in order to make indivisible some occurrence sequences representing elementary actions which logically may occur more or less at the same time. They are based on the fact that it is not mandatory for a transition to occur as soon as it may occur. Hence, it is sometimes possible to postpone the occurrence of a transition until the occurrence of another transition in order to have simultaneous occurrences. There are three possible configurations which lead to three different definitions : post-fusion, pre-fusion and asymmetric fusion. The transformation is unique and is defined in section 2.2.4

2.2.1. Post-fusion

This transformation fuses two sets of transitions T_u and T_v, when it is always possible to have an occurrence of one transition of T_v immediately after any occurrence of a transition of T_u or conversely.

Notations :

In the following we denote by || the shuffle operator on languages i.e. $(X \| Y) = \{ xy \mid x \in X, y \in Y\} \cup \{ yx \mid y \in Y, x \in X\}$.

$[M_0>^=$ is the set of reachable markings reached from M_0 using the same number of occurrences of whatever elements of T_u and T_v.

Definition 2.2.1.1 post-fusable transitions

Given a system Σ , a set of transitions T_v can be **post-fused** with a set of transitions T_u iff one of these two sets contains only one transtion and the three following conditions are satisfied :

i) **synchrony** : $\forall s \in L(\Sigma)$ $Proj(s/T_u \cup T_v)$ is prefix of $(T_u \| T_v)^*$

(i.e. the synchronic distance of T_u and T_v is 2 or in other words : in any occurrence sequence s the difference between the number of occurrences of T_u and the number of occurrences of T_v cannot exceed 1).

ii) **continuity** : $\forall M_1 \in [M_0>^=, \forall s,s' \in T_0^*, \forall t_u \in T_u : M_1[st_us'>M_2 \Rightarrow \exists t_v \in T_v$ such that $M_2[t_v>M_3$ and $M_3 \in [M_0>^=$ and conversely.

(i.e. it is always possible to continue an occurrence sequence containing an occurrence of T_u with an occurrence of a transition of T_v and conversely)

iii) **1-dependency** : $\forall M_1, M_2 \in [M_0>^=, \forall s,s' \in T_0^* : M_1[st_us't_v>M_2 \Rightarrow M_1[st_ut_vs'> M_2$ and conversely.

(i.e. in any occurrence sequence containing an occurrence of T_u and an occurrence of T_v it is always possible to place the occurrence of t_v immediately after the occurrence of t_u and conversely).

A consequence of the transformation 2.2.4.1 is to enforce simultaneous occurrences of transitions of T_u and T_v which are in one occurrence sequence in the initial system. Apart from that, the language of the system is not changed.

Theorem 2.2.1.2 :

1) $[M_0'>' = [M_0>^=$ where $[M_0'>'$ is the set of reachable markings in Σ.

2) $\forall s \in T^*, \forall M_1,M_2 \in [M_0>^=: M_1[s> M_2$ iff $M_1[s_r>' M_2$ where s_r is the sequence s reordered to have simultaneous occurrences of couples of transitions (t_u,t_v).

idea of the proof : from continuity and 1-dependency, it can be shown that every occurrence sequence of Σ may be continued and reordered to become an occurrence sequence of Σ'. Conversely, an occurrence sequence of Σ' is obviously an occurrence sequence of Σ since a transition of Σ' is either a transition of Σ or can be decomposed in two transitions of Σ.

Theorem .2.2.1.3 :

Σ is deadlock-free (1-live, live , satisfying Behavioural condition on a subset T_D such that $T' \cap (T_u \cup T_v) = \varnothing$) iff Σ' is deadlock-free (1-live, live , satisfying Behavioural condition on the subset T_D)

idea of the proof : from theorem 2.2.1.2 for every occurrence sequence of Σ there is a corresponding occurrence sequence in Σ' and conversely.

The same idea of post-fusion may be expressed only structurally by requiring a place p which is an ouptut of transitions of T_u and the only input of transitions of T_v. Moreover the place p must not be connected to any other transition. This leads to the following definition.

Definition 2.2.1.4 : structurally post-fusable transitions

Let Σ be a system. A non empty subset T_{post} of transitions is structurally post-fusable with a subset of transitions T_{pre}, if and only if there exists a 1-safe place p such that the four following conditions are satisfied :

i) $\forall t_{post} \in T_{post} : W(q,t_{post}) =$ if (q = p) then 1 else 0 and (the only input of t_{post} is p)
$p \notin t_{post}^\bullet$ (p is not output of t_{post})

ii) $\forall t_{pre} \in T_{pre} : p \notin t_{pre}^\bullet$ and (p is not an input of t_{pre})
$W(t_{pre},p) = 1$ (p is an output of t_{pre})

iii) $\forall t \notin (T_{post} \cup T_{pre})\ W(p,t) = W(t,p) = 0$

(except those of $(T_{post} \cup T_{pre})$, no transition is connected to p)

Example : $T_{pre} = \{ h \}$ and $T_{post} = \{ f_1, f_2 \}$ are post-fusable in figures 4 and 5, and structurally post-fusable in figure 4 when the redundant place p' is eliminated.

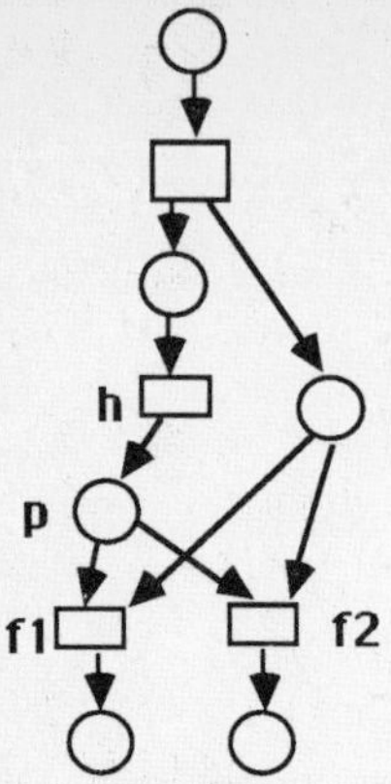

figure 4

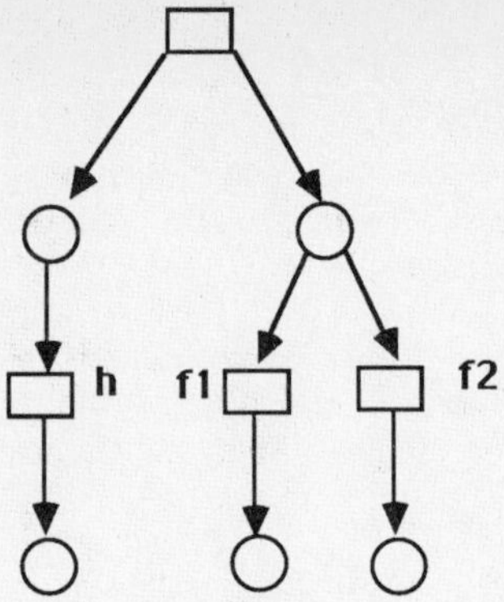

figure 5

Note : with the conditions on structure of definition 2.2.1.4, neither the requirement of definition 2.2.1.1 to have at least T_b reduced to one element, nor synchrony condition of definition 2.2.1.1 are necessary. Consequently definition of fusion (2.2.4.1) must be extended in order to associate , in Σ', a transition to every possible combination of transitions of T_{pre} and T_{post} . With this new definition theorem 2.2.1.2 and corollary 2.2.1.3 remain valid and moreover, under some additional constraints, this transformation may preserve safeness , S-invariant covering and home states (see [Be1] for details).

2.2.2. Pre-fusion

This transformation fuses two sets of transitions T_u and T_v if the occurrence of any transition of T_u does not give concession to any transition until the occurrence of one transition of T_v or conversely.

Definition 2.2.2.1 pre-fusable transitions

Given a system Σ, a set of transitions T_v may be pre-fused on a set of transition T_u iff the three following condition are satisfied :

i) **synchrony** : $\forall s \in L(\Sigma)$ proj($s/T_u \cup T_v$) is prefix of $(T_u \parallel T_v)^*$
(i.e. in any occurrence sequence s the difference between the number of occurrences of T_u and the number of occurrences of T_v cannot exceed 1)

ii) **persitency** : $\forall t_u \in T_u, \forall s \in T_0^*, \forall M_1 \in [M_0> : (M_1[t_u> \wedge M_1[s>) \Rightarrow (\exists M_2 \in [M_0> : M_1[st_u>M_2 \wedge M_1[t_us>M_2$) and the same holds for T_v.

iii) **transparency** : $\forall t_u \in T_u, \forall M \in [M_0>^=, \forall s \in T_0^* : M[t_us> \Rightarrow M[s>$ and the same holds for T_v

Remark : from transparency and persistency, any occurrence of T_u (or T_v) can be postponed until just before the next occurrence of T_v (or T_u)

The theorem 2.2.1.2 and the corollary 2.2.1.3 obtained for post-fusion also hold for pre-fusion.

Idea of the proof : since no transition receives concession from occurrences of t_u, the fusion of t_v and t_u does not prevent any occurrence sequence. Consequently, every occurrence sequence containing the same number of occurrences of T_v and T_u in Σ can be reordered to become an occurrence sequence of Σ'. The unique difference with post-fusion is that there is no garantee of having an occurrence of t_v after an occurrence of t_u.

Again this behavioural definition can be translated into a structural one(see [Be2]). In comparison with structural post-fusion, 1-safety of place p is necessary, but with some additional conditions it is again possible to preserve more properties (see [Be1] for details).

Examples : T_{pre} = {h } and T_{post}= { f_1, f_2 } are prefusable in figures 6 and 7 and structurally pre-fusable in figure 6.

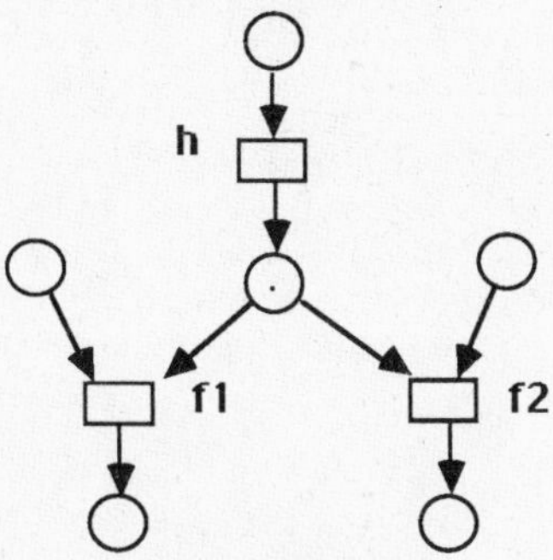

figure 6

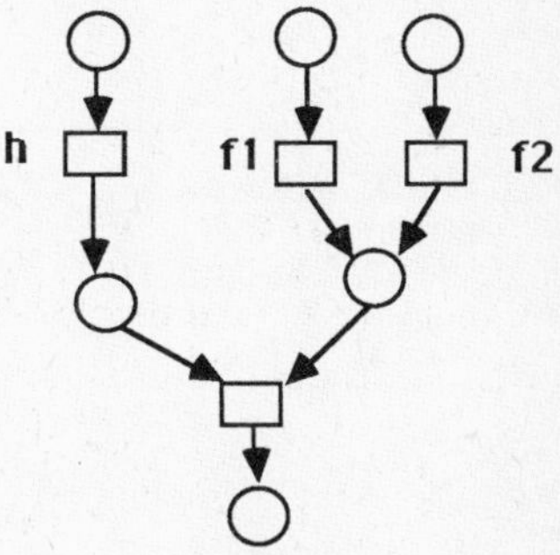

figure 7

2.2.3. Asymmetric-fusable transitions

This transformation may be used when T_u and T_v do not play the same role as they do in pre-fusion and post-fusion. For instance, if t_v does not give concession to any transition until the occurrence of t_u (transparency) but may always occur after an occurrence of t_u (continuity) then t_v and t_u are asymmetric-fusable .

Definition 2.2.3.1 : asymmetric fusion

Given a system Σ, two set of transitions T_u and T_v are **asymmetricaly fusable** iff the four following conditions are satisfied :

i) **synchrony** : $\forall s \in L(\Sigma)$ proj(s/ $T_u \cup T_v$) is prefix of $(T_u \,||\, T_v)^*$

ii) **persistency** : $\forall s \in T_0^*$, $\forall M_1,M_2 \in [M_0>$: $M_1[t_v>$ and $M_1[s> \Rightarrow M_1[st_v>M_2$ and $M_1[t_vs>M_2$.

iii) **transparency** : $\forall M \in [M_0>^=$,$\forall s \in T_0^*$ $M[t_vs> \Rightarrow M[s>$

iv) **continuity** : $\forall M_1 \in [M_0>^=$,$\forall s,s' \in T_0^*$: $M_1[st_us'>M_2 \Rightarrow \exists t_v \in T_v$ such that $M_2[t_v> M_3$ and $M_3 \in [M_0>^=$

v) **1-dependency** : $\forall M_1,M_2 \in [M_0>^=$ $\forall s,s' \in T_0^*$: $M_1[st_us't_v>M_2 \Rightarrow M_1[st_ut_vs'>M_2$

Examples : T_u = {h } and T_v = { f } are asymmetricaly fusable in figures 8 and 9.

The theorem 2.2.1.2 and the corollary 2.2.1.3 obtained for post-fusion and pre-fusion can also be proved for asymmetric-fusion. These proofs combine proofs of pre- and post-fusion. Finally this behavioural definition can also be translated into a structural one.

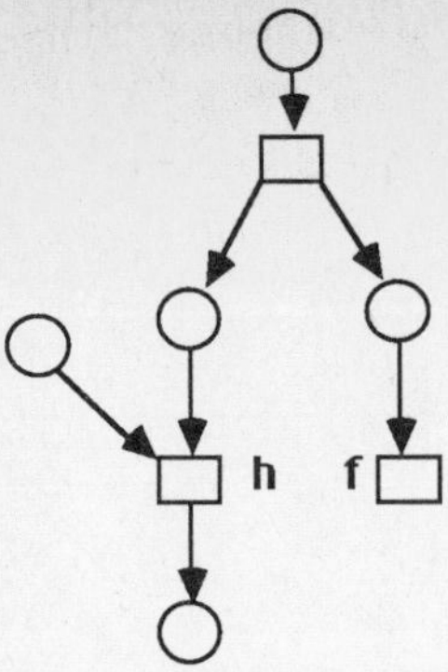

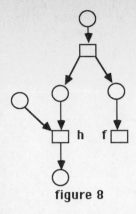

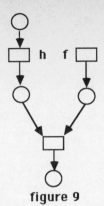

figure 8

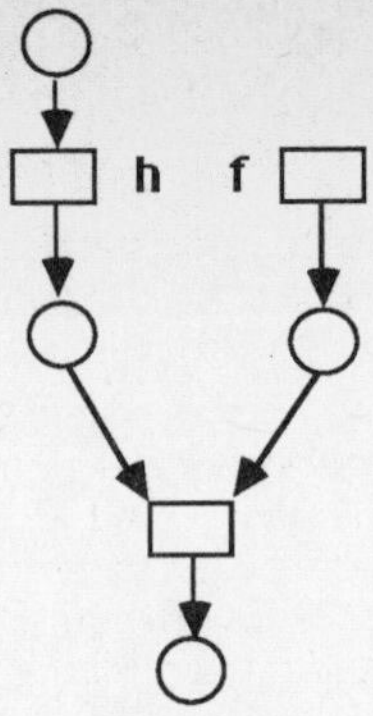

figure 9

2.2.4. System resulting from the fusion of transitions

First, we define a transformation which will be the same for the three configurations of fusion. This transformation consists in the fusion of a transition with each transition of a subset of transitions. The result of the fusion of two transitions is a new transition and its occurrence is equivalent for the change of marking to the occurences of the two transitions fused.

Definition 2.2.4.1: fusion of sets of transitions

Let $\Sigma = (S,T; F,W, M_0)$ with $T=T_0 \cup T_a \cup T_b$. If $(T_b = \{ t_b \})$ and $(\{ t_b \} \cap T_a = \varnothing)$ and $(t_b{}^\bullet \cap {}^\bullet T_a = \varnothing$ or ${}^\bullet t_b \cap T_a{}^\bullet = \varnothing)$ and one of the three definitions 2.2.1.1, 2.2.2.1 or 2.2.3.1 above applies then T_b can be fused with T_a. The system resulting from the fusion of T_b and T_a will be $\Sigma' = (P',T';F',W',M_0')$ with

a) $P' = P$

b) $T' = T_0' \cup T_a'$ where T_0' and T_a' are defined as follows :

.to each transition t of T_0 is associated one transition t' in T_0' such that for each $p \in S$: $W'(p,t') = W(p,t)$ and $W'(t',p)=W(t,p)$

.to each transition t_a of T_a is associated one transition t_a' in T_a' such that :

-If($t_b{}^\bullet \cap {}^\bullet T_a = \varnothing$ and ${}^\bullet t_b \cap T_a{}^\bullet = \varnothing$) then

$.W'(p,t_a') = W(p,t_b) + W(p,t_a)$ and $W'(t_a',p) = W(t_a,p) + W(t_b,p)$

-If ($t_b{}^\bullet \cap {}^\bullet T_a \neq \varnothing$) then for each $p \in S$:

$.W'(p,t_a') = W(p,t_b) + \sup(0, W(p,t_a)-W(t_b,p))$ and

$.W'(t_a',p) = W(t_a,p) + \sup(0, W(t_b,p)-W(p,t_a))$

-If (${}^\bullet t_b \cap T_a{}^\bullet \neq \varnothing$) then for each $p \in S$:

$.W'(p,t_a') = W(p,t_a) + \sup(0, W(p,t_b)-W(t_a,p))$ and

$.W'(t_a',p) = W(t_b,p) + \sup(0, W(t_a,p)-W(p,t_b))$

c) $M_0' = M_0$

Remark : An occurrence sequence of Σ' is obviously an occurrence sequence of Σ.

3.Decomposition

Decompositions, in combination or not with transformations, can be used to split a system into subsystems which will be studied separately.

The first and quite simple method is to refine a node (place or transition) into a system. Corresponding results can be found in [SuM] and [Val].

The decomposition into interacting components is more difficult due to the possibilities of interactions.The main problems of this approach are composition/decomposition methods and equivalence notions.
By the way, the composition of subsystems may always be defined in terms fo fusion of (common) places and fusion of (common) transitions. Fusion of places corresponds to synchronization by means of communication channels or common variables while fusion of transitions represents synchronization by the "rendez-vous" technique. It turns out that composition both by fusion of places and fusion of transitions is semantically and theoretically very difficult to handle. Moreover, a synchronization mixing "rendez-vous" and common variables or communication channels may always be avoided and consequently practical problems may be solved, at a given level of detail, using only fusion of places or fusion of transitions. So it will not be necessary to perform, in a single step of composition, fusion of places and fusion of transitions even if further refinements may use the converse technique.
Equivalence relations are related to composition/decomposition methods since an equivalence is defined either for place composition of for transition composition.

3.1S-decomposition

A S-decomposition is a partition of the set of places of one net, while transitions are split.

Definition 3.1.1 [BeF] : Let $N_1 = (S_1,T_1,F_1)$ and $N = (S,T,F)$. N_1 is an S-component of N iff N_1 is a subnet of N and furthermore : $T_1 = {}^\bullet S_1 \cup S_1{}^\bullet \;\wedge\; \forall\; t \in T_1 : |\,{}^\bullet t \cap S_1| \leq 1 \;\wedge\; |t^\bullet \cap S_1| \leq 1$.
i.e. one S-component is defined by its set of places and has some transitions shared with other S-components.

S-composition of several S-component is the converse operation : common transitions are fused.

S-composition corresponds to "rendez-vous" synchronization and has led to several interesting results.

3.1.1 SMD decomposition(hack)

The first attempt to decompose a net was carried out by M.Hack in [Hac] in order to extend results about liveness of so called "free choice Petri Nets". His S-components are S-Nets i.e. nets in which every transition has at most one output place and at most one input place.

Defintion 3.1.1.1 : A net N = (S,T,F) is called **state machine net** iff $\forall\; t \in T \;\; |{}^\bullet t| = |t^\bullet| = 1$.

Definition 3.1.1.2 : A net N = (S,T,F) is called **state machine decomposable** (or SMD-net) iff there are n strongly connected state machine nets $N_1,\ldots,N_n$ such that :

$$S = \bigcup S_i \;\wedge\; T = \bigcup T_i \;\wedge\; \forall\, i,j\; (1 \leq i, j \leq n \;\wedge\; i \neq j) \;\Rightarrow\; S_i \cap S_j = \varnothing .$$

State-machine nets are in fact finite automata and hence are live if they strongly connected and contain at least one token. But does a composition on live state-machine nets produce a live net ?

Both nets N_1 and N_2 in figure 10 and 11 are strongly connected state-machines (SCSM for short) and therefore live for every marking. If we suppose that these nets reprensent two sequential processes, which identical events t_1, t_6 and t_7, the composed system is represented by the net N_3 of figure 12, where these transitions are identified. We now compare the behaviour of N_3 with the expected behaviour of N_1 and N_2. For $M_{01}[t_1t_2t_6>$ in N_1 and $M_{02}[t_1t_4t_6>$ in N_2 we have $M_{03}[t_1t_2t_4t_6>$ in N_3. But $M_{01}[t_1t_2t_6>$ in N_1 and $M_{02}[t_1t_5t_7>$ in N_2 results in a deadlock in N_3. Furthermore , N_3

has no live initial marking . This example shows that liveness of SCSM components does not imply liveness of the composed net. Therefore a stronger property is required.

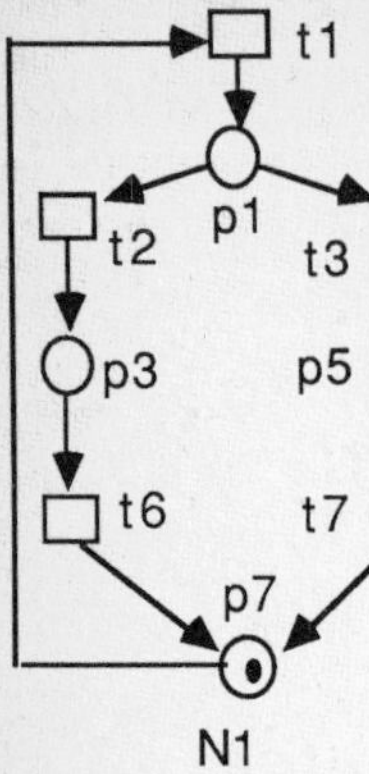

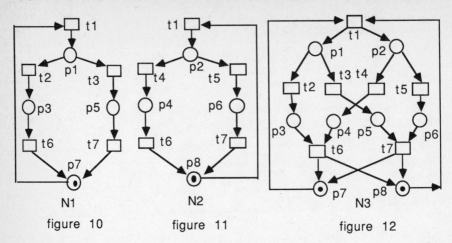

figure 10

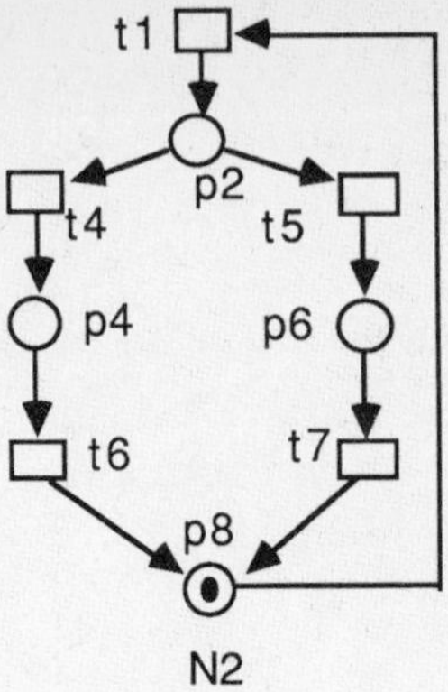

figure 11

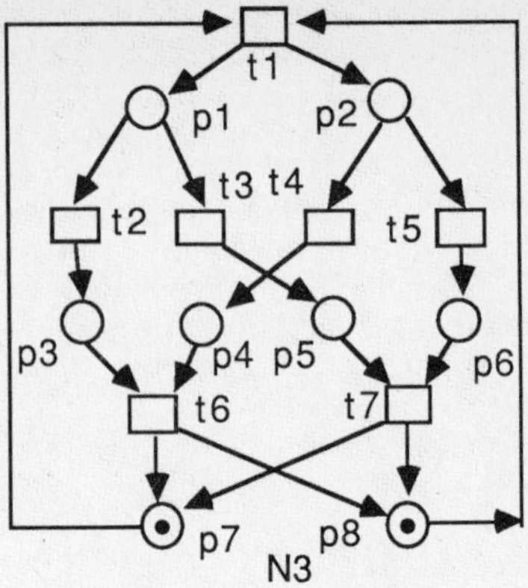

figure 12

An **allocation** of a directed net N is a function **al** $:T \rightarrow {}^{\bullet}T$ such that $\forall\, t \in T\ al(t) \in {}^{\bullet}t$. A subnet N' is said to **agree with al**, if $\forall\, t \in S'^{\bullet}\ al(t) \in S'$. A SMD-net N is called a **state machine allocatable net** if for every allocation al at least one SCSM component agrees with al.

For the net N_3, a non-trivial choice of an allocation is possible only for transition t_6 and t_7 . If $al_1(t_6)= p_3$ and $al_1(t_7) = p_5$, the net N_1 agrees with al, but there is no SCSM component which agrees with $al_2(t_6) = p_3$ and $al_2(t_7) = p_6$. Therefore N_3 is not a state machine allocatable net.

3.1.2 behavioural equivalence (André [An1] [An2])

To generalize the composition by fusion of transitions we must regard one net as a "black box" interacting with its environment through common transitions named "distinguished transitions" while the others are internal. The problem is to decide whether or not distinguished transitions report a good summary of the behaviour of the net

This is precisely the goal of the notion of Behaviour of André . The Behaviour condition implies that every conflict resolution that has some influence on the future behaviour of the net must be done at a visible level, i.e. that these transitions must be distinguished transitions.

First we need a labelling function h to hide internal transitions.

Definition 3.1.2.1:hiding function (T' denotes the set of distinguished transitions)

Let Σ be a P/T system .We denote by $h : T \rightarrow T' \cup \{\lambda\}$ a function such that :

$h(t)$ = if $t \in T'$ then t else λ .

This mapping is then extended to an homomorphism $h : T^* \rightarrow T'^*$.

To obtain suitable properties, h must agree with the following requirement.

Definition 3.1.2.2 : Behaviour condition :

A system Σ satisfies the **Behaviour condition** on a distinguished subset T' of T iff

$\forall\ s_1,s_2 \in L(\Sigma),\ \forall\, s_1' \in (T-T')^*,\ \forall\, a \in T',\ h(s_1) = h(s_2)$ and $M_0[s_1s_1'a\rangle \Rightarrow$

$\exists\ s_2' \in (T-T')^*$ such that $M0[s_2s_2'a\rangle$

i.e. equivalent sequences (i.e. sequence with the same trace by h) must be continued by equivalent sequences.

Definition 3.1.2.3 : Behaviour
If the Behaviour condition is satisfied the behaviour of the system Σ is $B(\Sigma/T') = h(L(\Sigma))$

Definition 3.1.2.4 : Behaviour equivalence (B-equivalence).
Two systems Σ_1 and Σ_2 such that $S_1 \cap S_2 = \emptyset$ and $T_1 \cap T_2 = T'$ are **Behaviour equivalent** iff
i) each of them satisfies the Behaviour condition
ii) $B(\Sigma_1/T') = B(\Sigma_2/T')$

Example : the net in figure 13 satisfies the Behaviour condition but the net of figure 14 does not satisfy the Behaviour condition on the set of all transitions t with $h(t) \neq \lambda$.

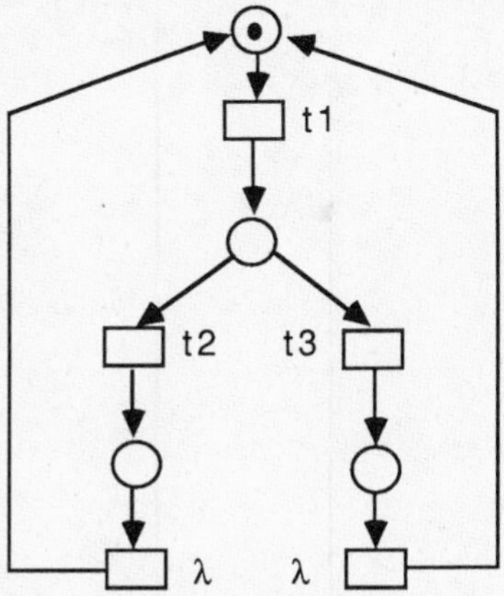

figure 13

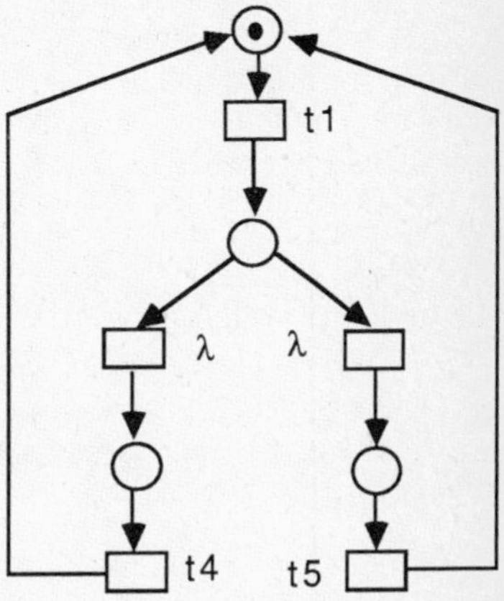

figure 14

Theorem 3.1.2.5 : fusion of systems [An1]
Let two systems Σ_1 and Σ_2 be given such that $S_1 \cap S_2 = \emptyset$ and $T_1 \cap T_2 = T'$. If the Behaviour condition is satisfied for Σ_1 and Σ_2 on T' then the Behaviour condition for the system Σ_{12} resulting of the fusion of common transitions of Σ_1 and Σ_2 is satisfied and $B(\Sigma_{12}/T') = B(\Sigma_1/T') \cap B(\Sigma_2/T')$.

The following theorem shows that Behavioural equivalence is a congruence w.r.t. to fusion of nets.

Theorem 3.1.2.6 : substitution of systems [An1]
Let Σ be the system resulting of the fusion of common transitions of Σ_1 and Σ_2 such that $S_1 \cap S_2 = \emptyset, T_1 \cap T_2 \neq \emptyset$.
Let us denote $T_F = T_1 \cap T_2$ and $T' \subset T_1$ any subset of T_1.
Let Σ_2' be a system such that :
$S_2' \cap S = \emptyset$ and $T_2' \cap T = T_F$. If $B(\Sigma_2/T_F) = B(\Sigma_2'/T_F)$
and let Σ' be the system resulting of the fusion of common transitions of Σ_1 and Σ_2' then
i) $(L(\Sigma)/T_1) = (L(\Sigma'))/T_1)$.
ii) Behaviour condition holds for Σ on T' $\Leftrightarrow$ Behaviour condition holds for Σ' on T'.

iii) $B(\Sigma_1/T') = B(\Sigma'/T')$

The drawback of definition 3.1.2.2 is that it cannot help to handle systems with non injective labelling where several distinguished transitions may have the same label. However, this definition may be extended under some restrictions to do so ([Pla]).

Another equivalence notion defined for a restricted class of P/T systems is the Exhibited Behaviour equivalence (EB-equivalence) which can be found in [DDP].

For both of these two equivalences, structural transformations of nets which preserve equivalences have been defined (in [An3] for B-equivalence and in [DDP] for EB-equivalence).

A notion similar to these equivalences has been developed for CCS by Milner in [Mil] with Observational equivalence on a set of observable transitions. This equivalence and several related equivalences (Failure equivalence, Testing-equivalence and Bisimulation) have been expressed in net formalism and compared with B-equivalence and EB-equivalence in [Pom]. In comparison with the one presented here all these notion allow several observable transitions to have the same label but only on 1-safe systems.

3.2. T-decomposition

T-decomposition is the dual operation of S-decomposition. A T-decomposition is a partition of the set of transition of one net while places are split.

Definition 3.2.1[BeF] : Let $N_1 = (S_1,T_1,F_1)$ and $N = (S,T,F)$. N_1 is an T-component of N iff N_1 is a subnet of N and furthermore : $S_1 = {}^\bullet T_1 \cup T_1{}^\bullet \wedge \forall s \in S_1 : |{}^\bullet s \cap T_1| \leq 1 \wedge |s^\bullet \cap T_1| \leq 1$.

This means that one T-component is defined by its set of transitions and has some places shared with other T-components.

T-composition of several T-components is the converse operation : common places are fused. There are also several results available for this method.

3.2.1 1-safe Superposed Automata decomposition

De Cindio and al([DDS])have defined both equivalences for S-composition and T-composition. These equivalences were defined in the framework of 1-safe Superposed Automata Nets.

1-safe Superposed Automata nets are state machine decomposable nets carrying exactly one token per component and satisfying the further condition that all the transitions have the same number of inputs and outputs. Only needed definitions are reported below.

Definition 3.2.1.1.: observable markings

Let R be a 1-safe Superposed Automata net and $OS \subset S$ be the set of observable places of R.

A marking $M \in [M_0>$ of R is **observable** if only places belonging to OS are marked for M.

Let OM denote the set of observable markings of R.

Definition 3.2.1.2.: S-observable net

A 1-safe Superposed Automata net R is **S-observable** iff $M_0 \in OM$ and $\forall w \in T^*$ such that $M_0[w>M$, $\exists\, w' \in T^*$ such that $M[w'>M'$ and $M' \in OM$

Definition 3.2.1.3: elementary observable path

A $w \in T^*$ is an **elementary observable path** of R iff $\exists$ $M, M' \in [M_0>$ such that the following conditions hold:

1) $M[w>M'$ and $\{M, M'\} \subset OM$;
2) the subnet $R_w = (S_w, T_w, F_w)$ generated by the transitions occurring in w, with $M \cap S_w$ as initial marking and $OS_w = OS \cap S_w$ as the set of observable places, is such that $OM_w = \{M \cap S_w, M' \cap S_w\}$.

Let $M[(w>>M'$ denote the firing sequence when w is an elementary observable path.

Definition 3.2.1.4.: EF-equivalence

Two S-observable nets R_1 and R_2, such that:

1) $S_1 \cap S_2 \neq \emptyset$;
2) $OS_1 = OS_2 = S_1 \cap S_2$;
3) $M_{01} = M_{01}$

are **EF-equivalent** (equivalent w.r.t. Exhibited Functionality, $R_1 \approx^{EF} R_2$) iff for each sequence $M_{01}[(w_1>>M_1[(w_2>>...M_{n-1}[(w_n>>M_n$, with $w_i \in T_1^*$ $(1 \le i \le n)$ there is a sequence $M_{02}[(v_1>>M_1[(v_2>> ...M_{n-1}[(v_n>>M_n$, with $v_i \in T_2^*$ $(1 \le i \le n)$, and vice versa.

Remarks:

-Conditions 1, 2 and 3 in the above definition could be expressed in terms of a suitable place labelling function.

-It can be proved that EF-equivalence is a congruence w.r.t. S-observable net composition, obtained via a superposition of observable places. This makes the S-observable net class closed under this operation.

Example: the nets of Fig. 15 and Fig. 16 with {A,B,C,D} as observable places are EF-equivalent.

Definition 3.2.1.5.: part

Let R be a S-observable net, $W_{M,M'} = \{w \in T^* | M[(w>>M'\}$ and $R_{M,M'}$ the subnet of R generated by all the transitions occurring in any $w \in W_{M,M'}$ with set of observable places $OS_{M,M'} = (M \cup M') \cap S_{M,M'}$.

$R_{M,M'}$ is a **part** of R1 with initial marking $M_{0,M,M'} = M \cap S_{M,M'}$ iff the following conditions hold:

1) $\forall$ $w \in W_{M,M'}$, $\forall$ $u \in T^+$: $w=uv$, not $\exists$ $z \in T^*$ and not $\exists$ $M'' \in OM$ such that $M[(uz>>M''$ and $M'' \neq M'$;
2) $\forall$ $w \in W_{M,M'}$, $\forall$ $u \in T^+$: $w=uv$, not $\exists$ $z \in T^*$ and not $\exists$ $M''' \in OM$ such that $M'''[(zu>>M'$

(i.e.: first, all the firing sequences of $R_{M,M'}$ starting from M and having a not-empty prefix in common with some element of $W_{M,M'}$ must reach M'; secondly, M' cannot be reached through a firing sequence starting from outside $R_{M,M'}$ and having a not-empty postfix in common with some element of $W_{M,M'}$).

Remark Parts of S-observable nets are S-observable nets.

Definition 3.2.1.6.: functional refinement

A **functional refinement** of a S-observable net R over a set of n parts $R'_i = (S'_i, T'_i, F'_i)$ such that $\forall$ h,k $(1 \le h,k \le n)$: $T'_h \cap T'_k = \emptyset$, is a net Q obtained via a substitution for each R'_i of a S-observable net $Q''_i = (S''_i, T''_i, F''_i)$, such that:

1) $\forall$ $i{:}1 \le i \le n$: Q''_i is a part of Q
2) $\forall$ $i{:}1 \le i \le n$: $R'_i \approx^{EF} Q''_i$

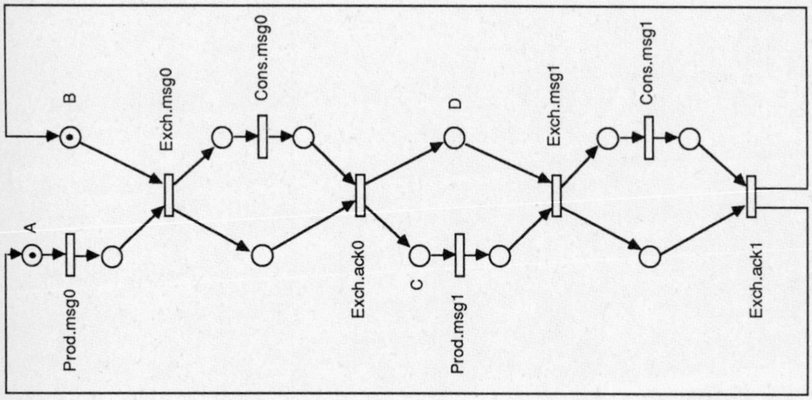

Figure 15

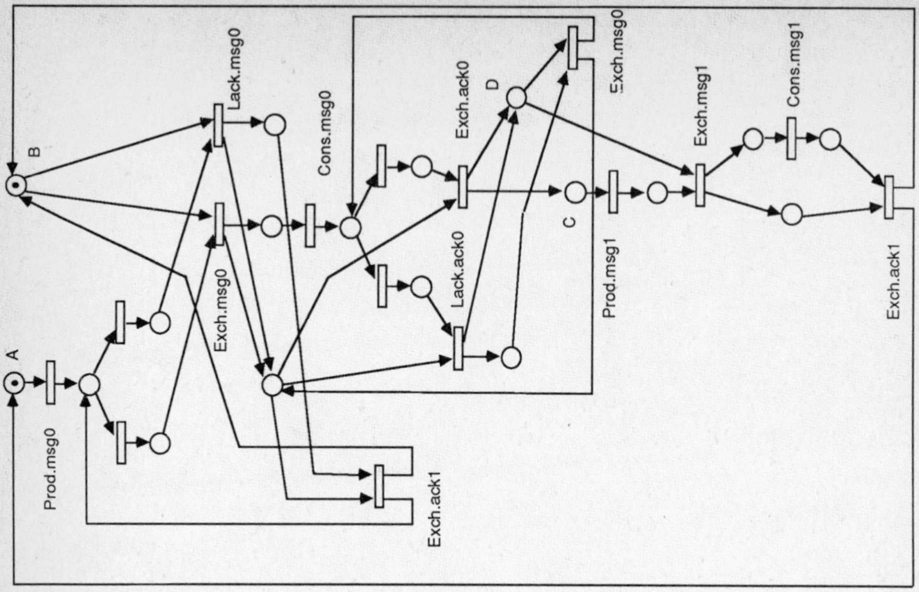

Figure 16

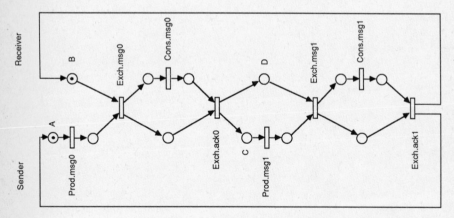

Remark: The substitution of a net for another net can be expressed componentwise in terms of set union and complementation. In addition, it can be proved that nets R and Q of the above definition are EF-equivalent by using the fact that EF-equivalence is a congruence (see an above remark).

Example [DDS] **:** The net of Fig. 16 which has been taken from [DDS] is a functional refinement of the net of Fig. 15 over the part $R_{M,M'}$, where M = {A,B} and M' = {C,D}.

Since this notion is defined for 1-safe Superposed Automata net it normally only works on this type of net. Nevertheless the principle is quite general and the required conditions are very similar to the conditions needed for the application of the transformation called "addition of a derivative net" defined in [Be2] and which can be applied on Place/Transition systems.

4 Strategies

From a general point of view, transformations and compositions /decompositions of nets may be used for checking the properties of a given system, according to two strategies : reduction if a model has been constructed and refinement otherwise . Reduction means to start from a given model and to reduce it using a sequence of transformations and decompositions until subsystems are obtained which are so simple that they can be easily analysed. Reduction can be compared with the bottom-up approach since one starts from the lowest level of details in order to derive global properties of the whole system.

The refinement strategy is the analogon for nets of the top-down strategy . It uses the opposite approach : starting from a collection of systems specifying the abstract properties of some phenomenon to be analysed, we must refine and compose them in order to obtain a detailed model of this phenomenon. This strategy allows us to take advantage of the knowledge of the goal we want to achieve.

5.Concluding remarks

Transformations and decompositions are the keystone of analysis and specifications of complex systems and those we have presented here have proved their adequacy on real problems such as various communication protocols [Be2] or spooling system [DDS].
Due to lack of space, we have focused our attention on place/transition systems because they are probably the most widely studied and used class of nets, but numerous results exist for other levels, namely for conditions/events systems ([Vos]) and Bipolar synchronization systems [GLT].
However, transformations and decomposition must be computer aided and also extended to high level nets to provide an efficient toolbox to their users .

Acknowledgments

I am grateful to S.Haddad from whom came the first definitions of fusion of transitions with conditions on evolution only (in [Had] and [Bel]). This gave me concepts to achieve a large generalization of previously defined transformations.

References

[An1] C.André "systèmes à évolutions parallèles : modèlisation par réseaux de Petri à capacités et analyse par abstraction" thèse d'état, Université de Nice, France, February 1981.

[An2] C.André "behaviour of a place/transition Net on a subset of transitions" IFB 52 Springer Verlag 1982.

[An3] C.André " Structural transformations giving B-equivalent PT-nets" IFB 66, Springer-Verlag 1983.

[Be1] G.Berthelot "Transformations et analyse de Réseaux de Petri.Application aux protocoles" Thése d'état, Université P. et M. Curie, Paris France, June 1983.

[Be2] G.Berthelot "Checking properties of Nets using transformations" LNCS 222 Advances in Petri Nets 85, G. Rozenberg ed , Springer-Verlag 1986 .

[Bel] N.H.Beldiceanu " Vérification de propriétés de réseaux de Petri à l'aide de règles de production" Rapport de recherche MASI n°154 , Université P. et M. Curie, Paris, France, October 1986

[BeF] E.Best, C.Fernandez "Notations and terminology on Petri Nets theory" Arbeitspapiere der GMD n° 195, January 1986.

[DDP] F.De Cindio , G.De Michelis, L.Pomello, C.Simone " Exhibited-Behaviour equivalence and Organizational abstraction in concurrent system design" The 5th Int. Conf on Distributed Computing Systems, Denver, Colorado , May 13-17, 1985, IEEE, pp 486-495.

[DDS] F. De Cindio, G. De Michelis, C. Simone "Giving back some freedom to system designer" ,System Research , n°2.4, 1985.

[GLT] Genrich, Lautenbach, Thiagarajan "Elements of general Net theory", LNCS 84, Springer-Verlag 1980.

[Hac] M.Hack "Extended State-Machine allocatable Nets, an extension of Free Choice Petri Nets results" Cambridge, Massachussets, MIT Project MAC, CSG-Memo 78-1, 1974

[Had] S.Haddad .Private conversation, lecture notes and thèse de 3ième cycle Université P. et M. Curie, Paris France, to appear in March1987.

[Lau] K.Lautenbach "Linear algebraic techniques for Place/Transitions Nets". Proceedings of the Advanced Course on Petri Nets, Bad Honnef , Germany , September 8-19, 1986.

[Mem] G.Memmi "Advanced algebraic techniques". Proceedings of the Advanced Course on Petri Nets, Bad Honnef , Germany ,September 8-19, 1986.

[Mil] R.Milner "A calculus for communicating systems", LNCS 92, Springer-Verlag 1980.

[Pom] L.Pomello "Some equivalence notions for concurrent systems : An overview" , LNCS 222 Advances in Petri Nets 85, G.Rozenberg ed. Springer-Verlag 1986.

[Pla] M.Placide "Transformations de réseaux de Petri préservant des propriétés significatives. Définition des homomorphismes associés" Thése de 3ième cycle, Université de Nice, France, December 1982.

[Rei] W.Reisig " Place / Transition Systems" Proceedings of the Advanced Course on Petri Nets, Bad Honnef , Germany ,September 8-19, 1986.

[SuM] I.Suzuki, T.Murata "Stepwise refinements of transitions and places" IFB 52, Springer-Verlag 1982.

[Val] R.Valette "Analysis of Petri Nets by stepwise refinement" J. Compt. System Sci., vol 18, n°1, pp 35-46, February 1979.

[Vos] K.Voss "On the notion of interface in condition/event-systems" IFB 66, Springer-Verlag 1983.

INFINITE BEHAVIOUR AND FAIRNESS

Rüdiger Valk
Fachbereich Informatik, Universität Hamburg
Rothenbaumchaussee 67-69, D-2000 Hamburg 13

ABSTRACT Specification techniques for the infinite behaviour of a P/T-system are introduced and their expressive power is compared. In particular, fair behaviour is related to the wellknown liveness problem. Finally, the problem is studied how to implement fair behaviour using a fair occurrence rule for transitions.

Key words: infinite behaviour, Landweber-hierarchy, fairness, liveness, resource allocation, fair and productive occurrence rule, finite delay property.

CONTENTS

1. Introduction

Petri nets are frequently used to model systems performing infinite processes like operating systems, real time control devices, communication protocols or information systems. Properties and problems concerning their behaviour should therefore be studied by a propriate model of infinite processes. Serial process models (transition sequences) have many advantages over partial order processes, which is in particular true for notions of fairness.

Liveness and fairness are important properties of systems. We will study their differences as well as their interconnections. While liveness is a commonly accepted notion - at least in net theory -, fairness has been studied less frequently. Nevertheless, many properties of real systems are based on elementary notions of fairness. In many cases, however, such fairness properties are either not mentioned explicitly or identified by completely different notions.

The classical example for a system where liveness and fairness properties are introduced are the celebrated Five Dining Philosophers [Dijkstra 71] (a formulation of the problem can be found in [Valk 83, p. 322]). Fig. 1.1 without dashed lines gives a P/T-system called FDPh1, modelling some interpretation of the Five Dining Philosophers' system. This net is not live: a deadlock occurs if all philosophers take their right-hand side fork (e.g. after the occurrence of $a_1a_2a_3a_4a_5$). The net becomes live if picking up both forks is implemented as an atomic action. This is represented by replacing a_i and a_i' by the dashed transition $pick_i$ for all $i \in \{1,\ldots,5\}$. The resulting P/T-system will be referenced by FDPh2 . An alternative way to avoid deadlocks consists in supplementing FDPh1 by a common reading room where all philosophers are in their

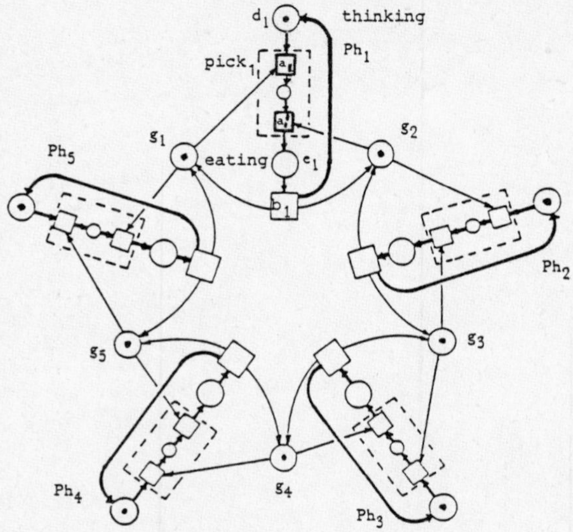

Fig. 1.1: Five philosophers P/T-system: FDPh1 , abstraction: FDPh2

initial state. A door-keeper allows at most four philosophers to be in the dining room at the same time. This extension, which is not given here, will be referenced by PDPh3 .

The behaviour of a P/T-system can be defined either as the set of <u>all</u> infinite occurrence sequences (*section 2*) or as some particular subset of this set. For instance, one might be interested in the behaviour, where philosopher 1 never eats for the last time. Such specification techniques are described in *section 3*.

In FDPh2 two philosophers can behave unfair against a third one (e.g. Ph_1 and Ph_3 against Ph_2) by picking up their forks in such a way that the latter never sees both forks simultaneously on the table (e.g. g_2 and g_3 are never marked at the same time). As a consequence transition $pick_2$ of FDPh2 cannot occur. Motivated by this example, the problem of achieving fair behaviour is also called the "problem of starvation". Using the definitions of *section 3* the fair behaviour of this system could be defined as the set of all infinite occurrence sequences, where all places d_i ("thinking") and e_i ("eating") for $1 \leq i \leq 5$ infinitely often contain a token.

Such a globally fair behaviour cannot be implemented without assuming a particular ("local") occurrence rule for transitions. By the "fair occurrence rule" (f-rule) no transition can be enabled infinitely often without occurring. The problem of implementing the fair behaviour of P/T-systems under the f-rule will be studied in *section 5*. Assuming this occurrence rule, we obtain for our example:

a) FDPh1 behaves fair but is not live

b) FDPh2 is live but behaves unfair

c) FDPh3 behaves fair and is live.

The tight relationship of the liveness and fairness problem shown by this example will be discussed in *section 4*.

2. Infinite behaviour of P/T-systems

Let $\Sigma=(S,T,F,W,m_o)$ be a Place/Transitions system (P/T-system), where (S,T,F) is a net, $W:F \to \mathbb{N}^+$ is a weight function and $m_o:S \to \mathbb{N}$ is an initial marking. (Throughout this paper we do not use finite capacities.)

By $F(\Sigma):=\{w \in T^* \mid \exists m: m_o \overset{w}{\to} m\}$ we denote the set of (finite) occurrence sequences or free Petri net language. If M_E is a finite set of (terminal) markings, then $F(\Sigma,M_E):=\{w \in T^* \mid \exists m \in M_E: m_o \overset{w}{\to} m\}$ is the free terminal Petri net language of (Σ,M_E). Assuming a labelling function $h:T \to X \cup \{\lambda\}$, then $L(\Sigma,h):=\{h(w) \mid w \in F(\Sigma)\}$ is the language of (Σ,h) and $L(\Sigma,M_E,h):=\{h(w) \mid w \in F(\Sigma,M_E)\}$ denotes the terminal language of (Σ,M_E,h). $L_{cyc}(\Sigma,h):=L(\Sigma,\{m_o\},h)$ is the cyclic language of Σ. A language is λ-free, if $h(t) \neq \lambda$ for all $t \in T$. Finally, by $\mathcal{L}^\lambda$, $\mathcal{L}$, $\mathcal{L}_o^\lambda$, $\mathcal{L}_o$ we denote the families of languages, λ-free languages, terminal languages and λ-free terminal languages of Petri nets.

We now come to the corresponding definitions for infinite occurrence sequences. To this end we first recall some definitions on infinite words. An infinite sequence or ω-word over an alphabet X is a mapping $w:\mathbb{N}^+ \to X$. For $i \in \mathbb{N}$ let $w(i)$ denote the i-th letter and $w[i]:=w(1)w(2)\dots w(i)$ the prefix of length $i \geq 1$ and $w[o]:=\lambda$ the empty word. $\tau_i(w):=w(i+1)w(i+2)\dots$ is the i-th truncation of w. As usual in literature, X^ω denotes the set of all ω-words and $X^\infty:=X^* \cup X^\omega$. A set $L \subset X^\omega$ is said to be an ω-language.

The concatenation on finite words is extended to words $u \in X^*$ and $v \in X^\omega$ by $uv:=w$ with $w[i]=u, \tau_i(w)=v$ and $i=lg(u)$. Also the finite product $v_1v_2\dots v_n = \prod_{i=1}^{n} v_i$ is extended to the infinite case by $w = \prod_{i=1}^{\infty} v_i$ iff $w[i] = v_1 \ldots v_j$ with $i = lg(v_1) + \ldots + lg(v_j)$.

There are three classical operators that allow to define sets of infinite words from finite words:

a) for a language $L \subset X^*$ the <u>closure</u> or <u>ω-closure</u> is defined by $L^{\omega} := \{w \in X^{\omega} \mid w = \prod_{i=1}^{\infty} w_i$ and $\forall i \in \mathbb{N}^+ : w_i \in L\}$

examples: $\{a\}^{\omega} = a^{\omega} = aaa..$, $ba^{\omega} = baa...$

b) for a language $L \subset X^*$ the <u>limit</u> of L [Eilenberg 74] is defined by $\lim(L) := \{w \in X^{\omega} \mid \exists_{\infty} i : w[i] \in L\}$ ($\exists_{\infty} i$ denotes: "there are infinitely many $i \in \mathbb{N}$ such that")

examples: $L_1 = ba^*$ and $\lim(L_1) = ba^{\omega}$; $L_2 = a^*b$ and $\lim(L_2) = \emptyset$

c) for a language $L \subset X^*$ the <u>adherence</u> of L [Boasson/Nivat 80] is defined by $Adh(L) := \{w \in X^{\omega} \mid \forall i \in \mathbb{N}^+ \, \exists v \in X^* : w[i]v \in L\}$

examples: $Adh(L_1) = ba^{\omega}$, $Adh(L_2) = a^{\omega}$

All these operators are interrelated. Define for $L \subset X^{\infty}$ the <u>prefix language</u> $Pref(L) := \{v \in X^* \mid \exists w \in X^{\infty} : vw \in L\}$. Then we have for arbitrary languages $L \subset X^*$: $Adh(L) = \lim(Pref(L))$, $L^{\omega} \subset \lim(L^*)$ and if L is prefixfree then $L^{\omega} = \lim(L^*)$. A particular subbehaviour is the <u>center</u> of a language $L \subset X^*$ [Boasson/Nivat 80] defined by $ctr(L) := Pref(Adh(L))$, which is the subset of those occurrence sequences of L that have an infinite continuation. In order to avoid deadlocks a system control has to allow only those occurrence sequences that belong to the center of L . For instance consider the P/T-system Σ of

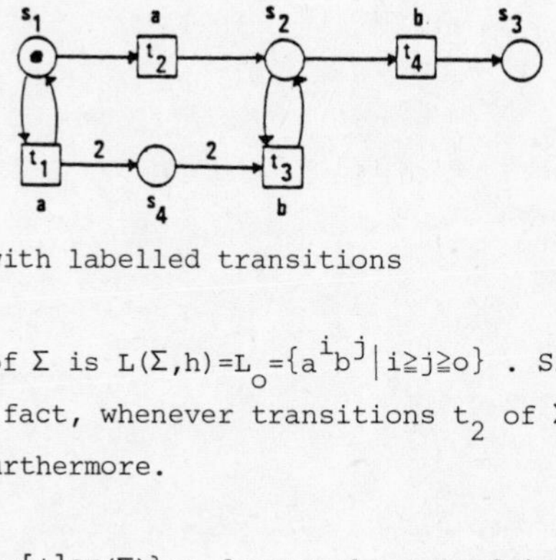

Fig. 2.1: A P/T-system with labelled transitions

Fig. 2.1 . The language of Σ is $L(\Sigma,h) = L_o = \{a^i b^j \mid i \geq j \geq o\}$. Since $Adh(L_o) = a^{\omega}$ the center of L_o is $ctr(L_o) = a^*$. In fact, whenever transitions t_2 of Σ occurs, a deadlock situation cannot be avoided furthermore.

By $F_{\omega}(\Sigma) := \{w \in T^{\omega} \mid \forall i : w[i] \in F(\Sigma)\}$ we denote the set of <u>infinite occurrence sequences</u> or <u>free ω-net-language</u> of Σ . $L_{\omega}(\Sigma,h) := \{h(w) \mid w \in F_{\omega}(\Sigma)\}$ is the <u>ω-language</u> or <u>ω-behaviour</u> of (Σ,h) . If $h(t) \neq \lambda$ for all $t \in T$ then the ω-language is <u>λ-free</u>. By $\mathcal{F}_{\omega}$, $\mathcal{L}_{\omega}$ and $\mathcal{L}_{\omega}^{\lambda}$ we denote the <u>families</u> of infinite occurrence sequences, λ-free ω-languages and ω-languages of P/T-systems, respectively.

To give an example for the P/T-system Σ of Fig. 2.1 we have $F_{\omega}(\Sigma) = t_1^{\omega}$ and $L_{\omega}(\Sigma,h) = a^{\omega}$.

<u>Lemma 2.1</u>

Let (Σ,h) be a P/T-system.

a) $F_\omega(\Sigma)=\lim(F(\Sigma))=Adh(F(\Sigma))$

b) If h is λ-free then: $L_\omega(\Sigma,h)=\lim(L(\Sigma,h))=Adh(L(\Sigma,h))$.

c) There are P/T-systems (Σ,h) with $L_\omega(\Sigma,h) \subsetneq \lim(L(\Sigma,h))$

For the (easy) proofs (a) and (b) we refer to [Valk 83], but give a system satisfying (c). We redefine h of (Σ,h) in Fig. 2.1 by $h(t_1)=h(t_2)=\lambda$ and then obtain: $L_\omega(\Sigma,h)=\emptyset$ and $\lim(L(\Sigma,h))=b^\omega$.

We conclude this section by the following hierarchy of ω-behaviours, which is an analogon to the corresponding hierarchy of Petri net languages (see [Jantzen 86]).

Theorem 2.2

$$\mathcal{F}_\omega \subsetneq \mathcal{L}_\omega \subsetneq \mathcal{L}^\lambda_\omega \subsetneq \mathrm{TYPEO}_\omega$$

(where TYPEO_ω is a family of ω-languages accepted by Turing machines).

In the proof of $\mathcal{L}_\omega \neq \mathcal{L}^\lambda_\omega$ we again use the system $(\Sigma,h)$of Fig. 2.1 . First we add a new transition t_5 with $W(s_3,t_5)=W(t_5,s_3)=1$ and redefine h by $h'(t_1)=h'(t_2)=h'(t_4)=\lambda, h'(t_3)=a$ and $h'(t_5)=b$. Then we obtain a P/T-system (Σ',h') with $L:=L_\omega(\Sigma',h')=a^*b^\omega$. Since $a^\omega \in Adh(L)-L$ the ω-language L has not property (b) of Lemma 2.1 and therefore does not belong to $\mathcal{L}_\omega$. To prove $\mathcal{L}^\lambda_\omega \neq \mathrm{TYPEO}_\omega$ we define $L:=\{a^ib^ic \mid i\geq 1\}$. Then any reasonable definition of TYPEO_ω contains L^ω . With $v_i:=a^ib^ic$ the ω-word $v:=\prod_{i=1}^{\infty} v_i$ belongs to L^ω . Assume $v\in L_\omega(\Sigma,h)$ for some P/T-system (Σ,h) . Then the sequence of markings $m_o,m_1,m_2,\ldots$ where m_j is reached after the occurrence of $(\prod_{i=1}^{j} v_i)a^{j+1}$ contains two elements $m_r \leq m_s$ with $r<s$. But then also the ω-word $v':=(\prod_{i=1}^{s} v_i)(a^{s+1}b^{r+1})cu$ with $u=\prod_{i=r+2}^{\infty} v_i$ is in L^ω , which is impossible since $r\neq s$. This last proof can be illustrated by showing the reader/writer-problem with unbounded numbers of readers to be not solvable by P/T-systems.

3. Specification of infinite behaviour

As mentioned in the introduction the fair behaviour of the five philosophers' P/T-system FDPh1 in Fig. 1.1 is a proper subset of the ω-behaviour, e.g. $(a_1a_1'b_1)^\omega \in F_\omega(\mathrm{FDPh1})$ is not fair. In order to specify this subset we could say that a sequence is fair if each of the places $e_1,\ldots,e_5$ infinitely often contains a token. The following definition will allow to specify such behaviour formally.

Let be $m=m(1)m(2)\ldots\in M^\omega$ be an infinite sequence. (You can imagine that m is a sequence of 'states'). Then the infinity set $In(m):=\{m_1 \mid \exists_\infty i:m(i)=m_1$ is the set of elements of m occurring infinitely often.

Now we assume a finite set $\mathcal{A}=\{A_1,\ldots,A_k\}$ of finite, nonempty subsets $A_i \subset M$ $(1 \leq i \leq k)$ to be given. The m is called

a) <u>1-successful</u> or <u>touching</u> for $\mathcal{A}$, iff $\exists A \in \mathcal{A}\ \exists i \in \mathbb{N}^+ : m(i) \in A$

b) <u>1'-successful</u> or <u>completely enclosed</u> for $\mathcal{A}$, iff $\exists A \in \mathcal{A}\ \forall i \in \mathbb{N}^+ : m(i) \in A$

c) <u>2-successful</u> or <u>repeatedly successful</u> for $\mathcal{A}$, iff $\exists A \in \mathcal{A} : In(m) \cap A \neq \emptyset$

d) <u>2'-successful</u> or <u>eventually enclosed</u> for $\mathcal{A}$, iff $\exists A \in \mathcal{A} : \emptyset \neq In(m) \subset A$

e) <u>3-successful</u> or <u>eventually terminal</u> for $\mathcal{A}$, iff $\exists A \in \mathcal{A} : In(m) = A$

f) <u>4-successful</u> or <u>eventually containing</u> for $\mathcal{A}$, iff $\exists A \in \mathcal{A} : A \subset In(m)$

The sets $A_i \in \mathcal{A}$ are called <u>anchor sets</u> since the sequence m is attached in some sense to them. The definitions of "i-successful sequences" come from [Landweber 69] for $i \in \{1,1',2,2',3\}$. For practical reasons we add the case $i=4$. For given anchor sets we have the following implications [Carstensen 86]:

m is 4-successful ⇒ m is 2-successful ⇒ m is 1-successful

⇑ ⇑ ⇕

m is 3-successful ⇒ m is 2'-successful ⇒ m is 1'-successful

We will apply the notion of successful sequence in three different ways. First, for a given P/T-system Σ we take $m=m_o m(1) m(2)\ldots$ as infinite sequence of markings occurring with an infinite sequence $w \in F_\omega(\Sigma)$ of transitions. Here the anchor sets are finite sets of markings. Hence, given such a set $\mathcal{A}$ we define for $i \in \{1,1',2,2',3,4\}$

$L^i_w(\Sigma,h,\mathcal{A}) := \{h(v) \in X^\omega \mid v \in F_\omega(\Sigma)$ and v occurs with a corresponding sequence of markings that is i-successful for $\mathcal{A}\}$. h is omitted if h=id is the identity map on X=T .

The <u>families</u> of these i-behaviours are denoted by $\mathcal{L}^i_\omega$. i-behaviours $\mathcal{R}^i_\omega$ for $i \in \{1,1',2,2',3\}$ of finite automata (or bounded P/T-systems) were shown in [Landweber 69] to correspond to the Borel hierarchy for a topology on X^ω.

As an exercise we specify the fair behaviour of the P/T-system FDPh1 in Fig. 1.1 as 3-behaviour. To find an appropriate set of anchor set we first define for arbitrary places p_i the following subset of reachable markings $R(\Sigma)$:

$A(p_1,\ldots,p_k) := \{A \subset R(\Sigma) \mid \forall i \in \{1,\ldots,k\} \exists m \in A : m(p_i) > o\}$.

To specify that no philosopher ever eats for the last time (i.e. $e_1,\ldots,e_5$ are infinitely often marked), we define $\mathcal{A} := A(e_1\ldots,e_5)$. Now the corresponding 'fair' behaviour is given by $L^3_\omega(\text{FDPh1},\mathcal{A})$.

Let $\mathcal{L}_1$, $\mathcal{L}_2$, $\mathcal{L}_3$ be families of languages. $\mathcal{L}_3$ can also be a family of ω-languages. Then we define:

$$\mathcal{L}_1 \circ \mathcal{L}_3 := \{\bigcup_{i=1}^{k} A_i B_i \mid A_i \in \mathcal{L}_1, B_i \in \mathcal{L}_3, k \in \mathbb{N}^+\}$$

$$\mathcal{L}_1 \circ_\omega \mathcal{L}_2 := \{\bigcup_{i=1}^{k} A_i B_i^\omega \mid A_i \in \mathcal{L}_1, B_i \in \mathcal{L}_2, k \in \mathbb{N}^+\}$$

Using this notation we are able to characterize i-behaviours by the following theorem, where $\mathcal{L}_{cyc}$ denotes the family of cyclic languages of P/T-systems.

Theorem 3.1

The families of i-behaviours with $i \in 1,1',2,2',3,4$ are closed under finite union and

(a) $\mathcal{L}^1_\omega = \mathcal{L}_o \circ \mathcal{L}_\omega$

(b) $\mathcal{L}^{1'}_\omega = \mathcal{R}^{1'}_\omega$

(c) $\mathcal{L}^2_\omega = \mathcal{L}_o \circ_\omega \mathcal{L}_{cyc}$

(d) $\mathcal{L}^{2'}_\omega = \mathcal{L}_o \circ \mathcal{R}^{1'}_\omega$

(e) $\mathcal{L}^3_\omega = \mathcal{L}_o \circ \mathcal{R}^3_\omega$

The characterization of $\mathcal{L}^2_\omega$ in (c) expresses that the 2-behaviour of a P/T-system is the finite union of terminal languages of P/T-systems followed by an iteration of a cyclic language. In (d) and (e) the cyclic language is replaced by ω-behaviours of finite automata. Besides such intuitive interpretation the characterization was shown to be useful for proving the following hierarchy [Valk 83]. It was also used in [Pelz 86] for deriving a characterization of $\mathcal{L}^3_\omega$ by logical formulas.

Theorem 3.2

The hierarchy of i-behaviours $\mathcal{L}^i_\omega$ in Fig. 3.1 is strict and complete, i.e. there are no other inclusions.

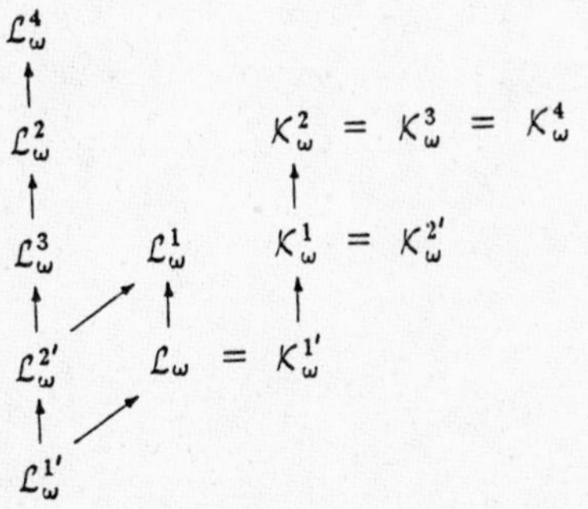

Fig. 3.1: The hierarchy of i-behaviours

To give some idea of the proof for theorem 3.2, the reader is invited to show that $L_1 := L^2(\Sigma, \{\underline{O}\}) \notin \mathcal{L}^3_{\omega_3}$, where Σ_1 is the P/T-system of Fig. 3.2(a) and $\underline{O}$ the zero-marking, hence $\mathcal{L}^2_\omega \not\subseteq \mathcal{L}^3_\omega$. For Σ_2 in Fig. 3.2(b) we have $L_2 := L_\omega(\Sigma_2) \notin \mathcal{L}^2_\omega$, from which $\mathcal{L}_\omega \not\subseteq \mathcal{L}^2_\omega$ [Valk 83]. The results concerning $\mathcal{L}^4_\omega$ are from [Carstensen 86].

Assume now that one philosopher, say philosopher 1, has priority over philosopher 2, i.e. at any time the number of occurrences of the event "start eating" (tran-

a)

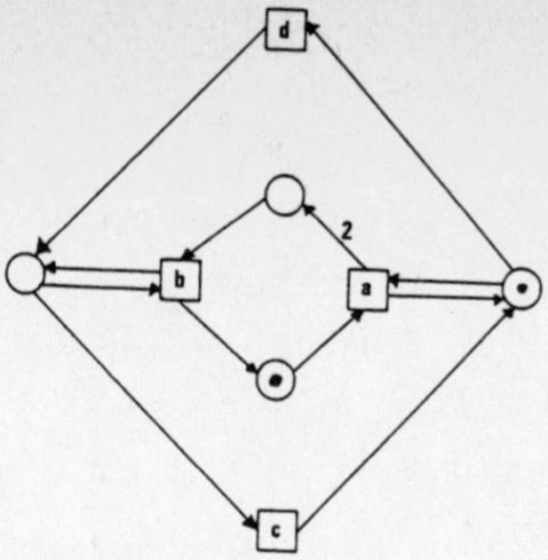

b)

Fig. 3.2: Two counterexample P/T-systems

sition a_2') of philosopher 2 does not exceed the corresponding number for philosopher 1 (transition a_1'). To model this extension we add a new place p_{12} and arcs (a_1',p_{12}) and (p_{12},a_2'). Since this new place is unbounded, the anchor set $\mathcal{A}$, just defined before, becomes infinite.

Therefore we introduce a new class of i-behaviours, where anchor sets only refer to bounded places and do not care on tokens in unbounded places. For the exact definition we refer to [Valk 83]. For a given set $\mathcal{A}$ the so-called <u>bounded i-behaviour</u> of a P/T-system Σ is denoted by $B^i_\omega(\Sigma,h,\mathcal{A})$ and the corresponding class by $\mathcal{B}^i_\omega$. A similar notion is used in [Merceron 86]. The hierarchy of bounded i-behaviours is different from the hierarchy of i-behaviours, but similar to the corresponding hierarchy for nondeterministic pushdown automata [Cohen/Gold 77]. In fact, bounded places correspond to states in the finite control of pushdown automata, whereas unbounded places are weak counters.

In applications, in particular when dealing with fairness, it may be profitable to base the specification of i-behaviour on <u>events</u> instead of markings. For instance, in a fair occurrence sequence of FDPh1 each <u>transition</u> of $\{a_1',\ldots,a_5'\}$ must appear infinitely often. For a given set $\mathcal{A}$ of sets $A_i \subset T$, a P/T-system $\Sigma=(S,T,F,W,m_o)$ and a map $h:T\to X$ for $i\in\{1,1',2,2',3,4\}$ the <u>transitional i-behaviour</u> of Σ is defined by $K^i_\omega(\Sigma,h,\mathcal{A}):=\{h(v)\in X^\omega \mid v\in F_\omega(\Sigma)$ and v is i-successful for $\mathcal{A}\}$. The corresponding <u>classes of transitional i-behaviour</u> are denoted by $\mathcal{K}^i_\omega$.

It is remarkable that the classes $\mathcal{K}^i_\omega$ and $\mathcal{B}^i_\omega$ are identical for all i [Carstensen/Valk 85]! Their relative power and relationship to the classes $\mathcal{L}^i_\omega$ is shown in Fig. 3.1 .

<u>Theorem 3.3</u>
$\mathcal{K}^i_\omega = \mathcal{B}^i_\omega$ for all $i\in\{1,1',2,2',3,4\}$.

4. Live and fair behaviour

All of the classes of i-behaviour, introduced in section 3, may specify the fair behaviour of a P/T-system under a suitable interpretation. We now considerably simplify the situation and concentrate on the behaviour $K^4_\omega(\Sigma,h,\mathcal{A})$ of a P/T-system where $\mathcal{A}$ = $\{E\}$ with $E \subset T$, i.e. the set of all infinite occurrence sequences where all transitions from E appear infinitely often (among others).

Given a P/T-system $\Sigma=(S,T,F,W,m_o)$ and a subset $E \subset T$, then the E-fair behaviour of Σ is defined by $Fair_E(\Sigma)=K^4_\omega(\Sigma,h,\{E\})=\{w \in F_\omega(\Sigma) \mid E \subset In(w)\}$. For $E=\emptyset$ we have $Fair_E(\Sigma)$ $=F_\omega(\Sigma)$ and if E=T , we obtain the fair behaviour of Σ : $Fair(\Sigma):=Fair_T(\Sigma)$. Σ is called E-fair and fair , if $F_\omega(\Sigma)=Fair_E(\Sigma)$ and $F_\omega(\Sigma)=Fair(\Sigma)$, respectively. Σ is fair, if there are no infinite occurrence sequences with finite occurrence numbers of some transitions.

If Σ is E-fair, then the initial marking m_o has the following property to be "E-continual". A marking m of a P/T-system $\Sigma=(S,T,F,W,m_o)$ is E-continual, if there is an infinite occurrence sequence $v \in T^\omega$ starting in m with $E \subset In(v)$. m is said to be continual if m is $\emptyset$-continual, i.e. if there is at least one infinite occurrence sequence in $\Sigma_m:=(S,T,F,W,m)$, hence $F_\omega(\Sigma_m) \neq \emptyset$.

Since we have no finite capacities (or represent them with the aid of complementary places), the set CONTINUAL(E) is right-closed. A set $K \subset \mathbb{N}^S$ of vectors is right-closed if $m \in K$ and $m' \geq m$ ($\geq$ componentwise) implies $m' \in K$. The sets NOTDEAD of nondead markings and UNBOUNDED of unbounded markings are other examples of right-closed sets. The set of minimal elements of a right-closed set K is called the residue set $res(K):=$ $\{m \in K \mid (m' \in K \wedge m' \leq m) \Rightarrow m'=m\}$ of K . As shown in [Valk/Jantzen 85] res(K) is finite for all right-closed sets K and effectively computable for $K \in \{$CONTINUAL(E), NOTDEAD, UNBOUNDED$\}$.

This implies that for given P/T-system Σ and marking m it can be decided whether there is some infinite occurrence sequence $v \in T^\omega$ such that all $t \in E$ appear infinitely often. Furthermore from $\Sigma=(S,T,F,W,m_o)$ with $m_o \in K$ a system $\Sigma_K=(S,T',F',W',m_o)$ can be effectively constructed such that in Σ_K exactly those markings are reachable that are reachable in Σ when Σ does not leave K . Furthermore, the occurrence sequences of Σ_K are essentially those of Σ when restricted to K [Valk/Jantzen, Theorem 4.2]. Therefore Σ_K is called the K-restricted P/T-system.

To give an example, if K=CONTINUAL:=CONTINUAL($\emptyset$) , then Σ_K is deadlock-free and has exactly the deadlock-free subbehaviour of Σ . Hence, the K-restriction Σ_K of Σ can be seen as supplementing Σ with a control unit to implement a desired behaviour (here deadlock freeness). Consider for instance the P/T-system Σ in Fig. 4.1 representing the wellknown banker's problem of Dijkstra as given in [Brinch Hansen 73].

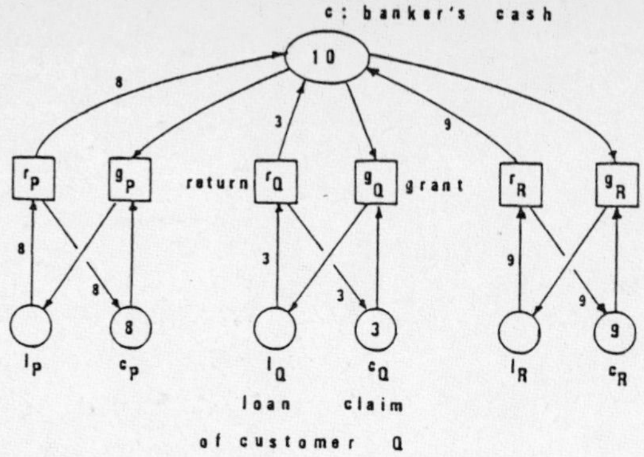

Fig. 4.1: The banker's system

The banker's problem was given in [Dijkstra 68] as an example of a resource sharing problem. A banker wishes to share a fixed capital c among a fixed number of n customers. The maximal claim of customer i is c_i . The banker will accept a customer if his claim does not exceed his initial capital, i.e. $c_i \leq c$. The customers borrow the money unit by unit and return all the loan money some time after the maximal claim c_i was reached. Sometimes it may be necessary for a customer to wait before he can borrow another unit of money, but the banker guarantees that the customer will get the money after some finite time.

The problem for the banker is to avoid deadlock situations, i.e. states where neither the banker has any money himself nor any customer has get enough money to return his credit. There may be situations which are not deadlocks themselves, but unavoidably lead to a deadlock. Therefore to avoid deadlocks, it is not sufficient to look whether the next step leads to a deadlock directly. Dijkstra introduced the notion of 'safe' states. A state is safe if there is at least one continuation of actions from this state leading to a proper termination of all credit transactions. For the banker it is therefore important to know the safe states.

For the P/T-system of the banker's problem in Fig. 4.1 safe states are identical with T-continual markings. By the following four S-invariant equations of this P/T-system,

$$i_1: m(c) + m(l_P) + m(l_Q) + m(l_R) = 10$$
$$i_2: m(l_P) + m(c_P) = 8$$
$$i_3: m(l_Q) + m(c_Q) = 3$$
$$i_4: m(l_R) + m(c_R) = 9 ,$$

the knowledge of $(m(c_P), m(c_Q), m(c_R))$ is sufficient to uniquely describe any reachable marking m . Fig. 4.2 shows the set of reachable markings in this 3-dimensional representation. For instance, the initial marking is represented by the point (8,3,9). 24

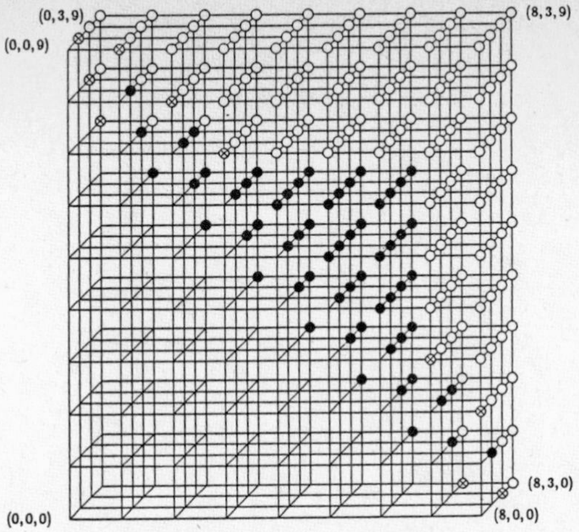

Fig. 4.2: T-continual markings of the banker's system

of these markings are deadlocks. The 137 T-continual markings are represented as white circles, which contain a cross if they are minimal. These ten minimal markings represent the residue res(K) of K=CONTINUAL(T) intersected with the reachability set. As shown in [Hauschildt/Valk 86] these 10 vectors can be obtained from only three vectors (0,1,9), (0,2,8), (0,3,7).

Hence the knowledge of three vectors is sufficient for the banker to avoid deadlocks by granting money in the wrong time. (Remember that T-continual markings are the 'safe' states of [Dijkstra 68]!) From this example we learn another aspect of fairness. The banker behaves fair against the customers by granting resources in such a way that every customer is able to perform his task!

In the introduction we saw that the properties of fairness and liveness are not independent for P/T-systems. We therefore will now have a closer look at these properties.

For any P/T-system $\Sigma=(S,T,F,W,m_o)$ and a marking m the <u>set of markings reachable from m</u> is denoted by $R(m):=\{m' \mid \exists w\in T^* \; m \xrightarrow{w} m'\}$. $R(\Sigma):=R(m_o)$ is the <u>reachability set</u> of Σ .A marking m of Σ is <u>live</u> if for any $t\in T$ and $m_1\in R(m)$ there is some $m_2\in R(m_1)$ such that t is enabled at m_2 . Σ is <u>live</u> if the initial marking m_o is live.

To compare this property of Σ with the property of fairness we also give a different but equivalent definition for liveness where $m \xrightarrow{w}$ denotes that w can occur from m :

(I) <u>Σ is live</u> or <u>behaves live</u> iff $\forall t\in T \forall m\in R(\Sigma) \exists w\in T^{\omega}: m \xrightarrow{w} \wedge t\in In(w)$

(II) <u>Σ is fair</u> or <u>behaves fair</u> iff $\forall t\in T \forall m\in R(\Sigma) \forall w\in T^{\omega}: m \xrightarrow{w} \Rightarrow t\in In(w)$

The difference between these notions becomes clear if you recognize that liveness means the "potential occurrence" of all transitions, whereas fairness denotes the "actual occurrence" of all transitions. To apply the construction of a K-restricted P/T-system it would be necessary that the set LIVE of all live markings is right-closed. This is, however, not the case as the P/T-system of Fig. 4.3(b) shows. The indicated initial marking m_o is live, but by adding a token to s_4 we obtain a marking m_1 that is not live such that $m_1 \geq m$!

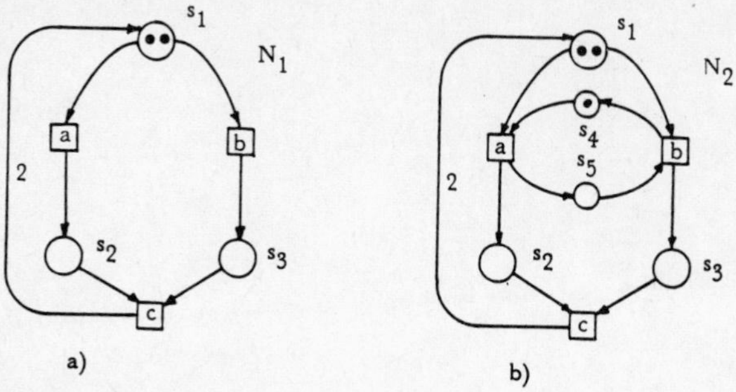

Fig. 4.3: Two P/T-systems

Obviously the system N_1 of Fig. 4.3(a) is not live, but there is a subset of $F(\Sigma)$ which is live (i.e. forbid two successive occurrences of a or b). Therefore it would be important to have a general procedure to construct a control for a P/T-system such that the system becomes live. To this end we mention the following relation between live and T-continual markings.

Theorem 4.1

For a P/T-system Σ a marking m is live if and only if all markings of R(m) are T-continual.

By this theorem we obtain the maximal live subbehaviour (see [Valk/Jantzen 85]) of a P/T-system, if we construct a control unit that disallows all occurrences of transitions that would transform a marking $m \in$ CONTINUAL(T) into a marking outside of this set! Hence for any P/T-system Σ with initial marking $m_o \in K=$CONTINUAL , the K-restricted system Σ_K is automatically live and has the "maximal live" subbehaviour of Σ . To be more precise, Σ_K is not live in the strict sense, since we introduce 'copies' of transitions. But if we define the same label h(t) for these copies, we can use the following variant of definition (I):

(III) a labelled P/T-system (Σ,h) where $h:T\rightarrow X$ is live, iff
$\forall x \in X \forall m \in R(\Sigma) \exists w \in T^{\omega}: m \overset{w}{\rightarrow} \wedge x \in In(h(w))$

Using this definition and the result on K-restricted P/T-systems, we can formulate:

Theorem 4.2

For any P/T-system $\Sigma=(S,T,F,W,m_o)$ with $F_{\omega}(\Sigma)\neq\emptyset$ a live and labelled P/T-system (Σ',h) can be constructed such that $L(\Sigma',h) \subset F(\Sigma)$ is maximal with respect to the

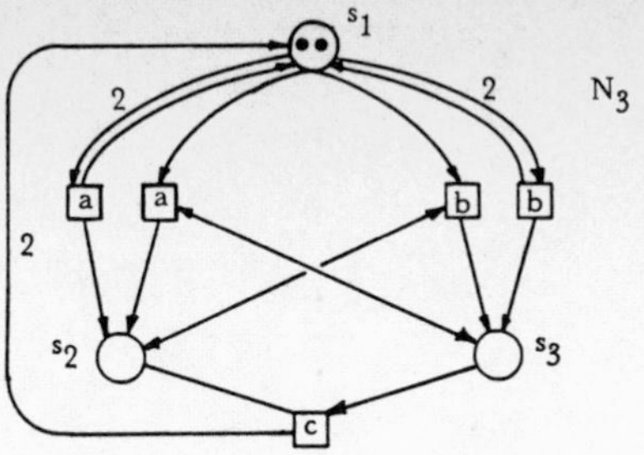

Fig. 4.4: A live labelled P/T-system

property of liveness.

Applying to the non-live P/T-system $\Sigma=N_1$ of Fig. 4.3(a), this construction gives the live labelled P/T-system $\Sigma'=N_3$ of Fig. 4.4 . Note that Σ' has the maximal live subbehaviour of Σ . This is not the case for Σ_1 in Fig. 4.3(b), since bac $\in L(\Sigma')$ but bac $\notin F(\Sigma_1)$.

5. Fair occurrence rules

In the preceeding sections we have studied the fair behaviour of P/T-systems. As in the case of live behaviour in section 4 we are interested to find some kind of control to implement fair behaviour. As discussed in the introduction this will be done by introducing two different fair occurrence rules for transitions. These occurrence rules may be thought of to be implemented in hardware or in the compiler of some programming languages. On the basis of fair occurrence rules the user of the hardware or the programmer will try to model systems or write programs that behave fair. In other words, fair processes are generated by fair systems.

Let $\Sigma=(S,T,F,W,m_o)$ be a P/T-system and $v\in F_\omega(\Sigma)$ an infinite occurrence sequence producing the infinite sequence $m_o,m_1,m_2,\ldots$ of markings.

- v is productive if any transition $t\in T$ that is enabled permanently from some step on occurs infinitely often in v: $\forall t\in T(\exists_i \forall_{j\geq i} : m_j \xrightarrow{t} \Rightarrow t\in In(v))$
- v is fair if any transition $t\in T$ that is enabled infinitely often occurs infinitely often in v: $\forall t\in T(\exists_\infty j : m_j \xrightarrow{t} \Rightarrow t\in In(v))$

A transition rule that disallows nonproductive and unfair occurrence sequences is called p-rule and f-rule, resp. The p-rule is also known as "finite delay property" and "just transition rule". To give some examples, $(d_1a_1a_1'b_1)^\omega$ is not productive in FDPh1 (Fig. 1.1) and $(ac)^\omega$ is productive but not fair in Fig. 5.1 .

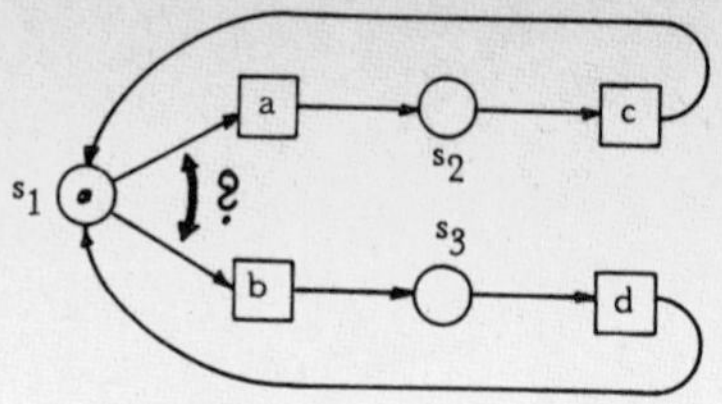

Fig. 5.1: P/T-system with unfair behaviour

Fair occurrence rules are sometimes assumed in unexpected contexts. For instance, in the "alternating-bit-protocol" the noisy half-duplex channel is modelled by two transitions, one for the correct transmission of data items (say, transition a) and another (say, transition b)) for producing an error message. The alternating-bit-protocol is not correct, when the ordinary transition rule is used. In fact, if transition b always occurs from some time one, the transmission of data stops. Hence the occurrences of errors are assumed to be 'fair', i.e. after some finite time the channel works correctly again. Therefore we have to assume the f-rule in all usual implementations of the alternating-bit-protocol.

By $L_\omega^{prod}(\Sigma,h):=\{h(v)\in X^\omega \mid v\in F_\omega(\Sigma) \text{ is productive}\}$ we denote the behaviour of a labelled P/T-system (Σ,h) under the p-rule and $L_\omega^{fair}(\Sigma,h):=\{h(v)\in X^\omega \mid v\in F_\omega(\Sigma) \text{ is fair}\}$. The corresponding families of languages are denoted by $\mathcal{L}_\omega^{prod}$ and $\mathcal{L}_\omega^{fair}$. Since every fair occurrence sequence is also productive, we have for any (Σ,h): $L_\omega^{prod}(\Sigma,h) \subset L_\omega^{fair}(\Sigma,h)$.

On the other hand, by a rather complicated construction in [Carstensen 82] it has been shown that every behaviour under the p-rule can be also obtained by another system under the f-rule:

Theorem 5.1

$$\mathcal{L}_\omega^{prod} \subsetneq \mathcal{L}_\omega^{fair}$$

A more important question is, however, whether every fair behaviour of a P/T-system can be generated by the p-rule. More precisely, given a P/T-system Σ, is there a (labelled) P/T-system (Σ_1,h) such that $L_\omega^{prod}(\Sigma',h) = \text{Fair}(\Sigma)$? This can be interpreted as follows: we assume a given system Σ and a specification of its fair behaviour $\text{Fair}(\Sigma) \subset F_\omega(\Sigma)$, but we have no idea how to implement it. On the other hand, we assume to have a programming environment that allows to run P/T-systems under the p-rule. Then the system (Σ',h) would be an implementation of Fair (Σ) in this environment.

Since Fair (Σ) is a particular case of transitional 4-behaviour, the problem is solved by the following theorem from [Carstensen/Valk 85]:

Theorem 5.2

$\mathcal{K}_\omega^4 \subset \mathcal{L}_\omega^{prod}$

By this theorem and other results from [Carstensen/Valk 85], the hierarchies of Fig. 3.1 obtain $\mathcal{L}_\omega^{prod}$ as common top element, i.e. we also have $\mathcal{L}_\omega^4 \subset \mathcal{L}_\omega^{prod}$ and $\mathcal{L}_\omega^1 \subset \mathcal{L}_\omega^{prod}$. The constructive proof of theorem 5.2 is, however, of less practical value, since the resulting P/T-system is not deadlock free in general, even if the original net has this property. Therefore we now restrict our investigations to deadlock free systems, for which a solution exists too.

A P/T-system Σ is deadlock free if in any reachable marking $m \in R(\Sigma)$ at least one transition is enabled. Equivalently all $m \in R(\Sigma)$ are continual, i.e. $R(\Sigma) \subset CONTINUAL(\emptyset)$. In our next theorem we have to use λ-transitions, i.e. transitions t with $h(t)=\lambda$ (that do not appear in the behavioral description of the system). But we require that after the occurrence of a λ-transition the next transition is λ-free. Such systems are called 1-prompt.

Theorem 5.3

For every P/T-system Σ having the fair behaviour $Fair_E(\Sigma)$ a deadlock free, 1-prompt and labelled system (Σ_1,h) can be effectively constructed that has ω-behaviour $Fair_E(\Sigma)$ under the p-rule: $Fair_E(\Sigma) = L_\omega^{prod}(\Sigma_1,h)$.

The proof in [Carstensen 84] is based on the result on residue sets. It is sufficient to choose $E=\{t\}$ and (since $\mathcal{K}_\omega^4 = \mathcal{K}_\omega^2$, see Fig. 3.1) to prove the theorem for $L= K_\omega^2(\Sigma,\{t\})$ instead of $Fair_E(\Sigma)$. Let $R=\{r_1,\dots,r_k\}$ be the residue set of $CONTINUAL(\{t\})$ which is nonempty. Furthermore by the result on K-restricted P/T-systems in section 4 we can assume that $R(\Sigma) \subset CONTINUAL(\{t\})$. By definition of $CONTINUAL(\{t\})$

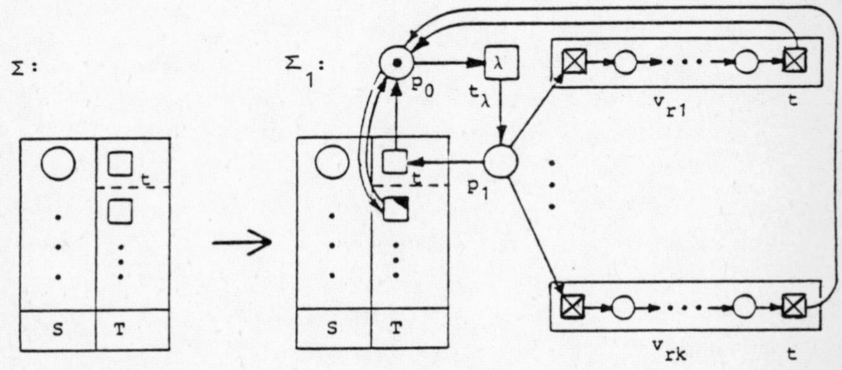

Fig. 5.2: Construction for theorem 5.3

for every marking $r \in R$, some finite occurrence sequence $v_r \in T^*$ can be computed with $\exists r' \in R$: $r \xrightarrow{v_r t} m$ and $m \geq r'$. In the transformation of Σ into Σ_1 in Fig. 5.2 copies (marked by a cross) of all $v_{r_1}t,\ldots,v_{r_k}t$ are introduced. Clearly, besides the additional arcs drawn in Fig. 5.2 all original arcs to places in S are assumed. All transitions of Σ with the exception of t have p_o as side condition. Hence they are blocked when p_o is empty. In Σ_1 every productive occurrence sequence v must contain infinitely often the λ-transition t_λ and hence some of the copies of t must also occur infinitely often. Moreover, every sequence in L is also in $L_\omega^{prod}(\Sigma_1,h)$ and vice versa.

To compare this general result with a wellknown special solution, we consider the fair implementation of distributed mutual exclusion of two processes A and B in

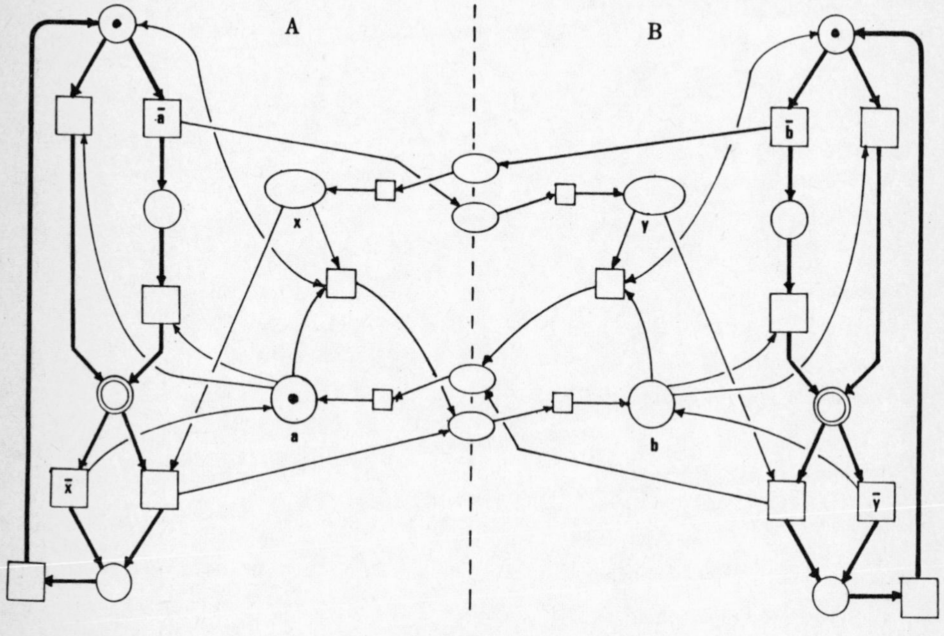

Fig. 5.3: Fair distributed mutual exclusion

in Fig. 5.3 . The critical section is specified by double circles. A and B communicate only by messages via channels on the dashed line. At most one process can have access to the critical region, namely the process that is owning the token in place a or b . To keep the net simple, transitions marked by $\bar{a}$,$\bar{b}$,$\bar{x}$ or $\bar{y}$ are assumed to be enabled only if the corresponding place is unmarked. This can be easily implemented by complementary places for a,b,x and y . In the given marking of Fig. 5.3 process A has access to the critical section, while process B has not. However, process B can fire the transition marked by $\bar{b}$, which sends a request to process A in place x . When leaving the critical section, process A will then pass the token to the place b instead of back to place a , and B has access, too. The net is modelled after an idea in [Raynal 85] modifying the solution of [Ricard/Agrawala 81].

Since the P/T-net of Fig. 5.3 behaves fair under the p-rule, it is of interest to compare it with the general construction of theorem 5.3 . To this end we start by the unfair distributed mutual exclusion of Fig. 5.4 .

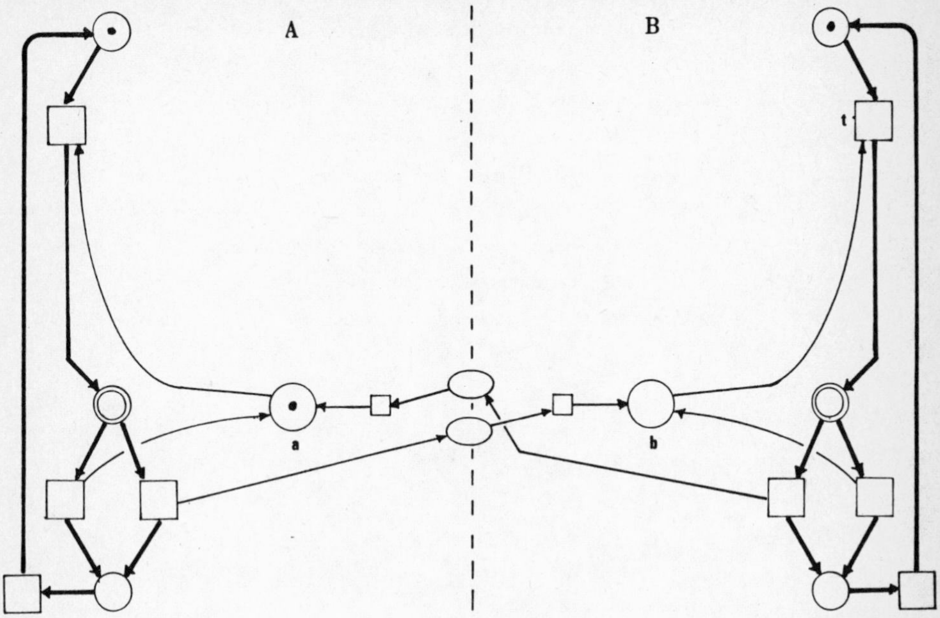

Fig. 5.4: Unfair distributed mutual exclusion

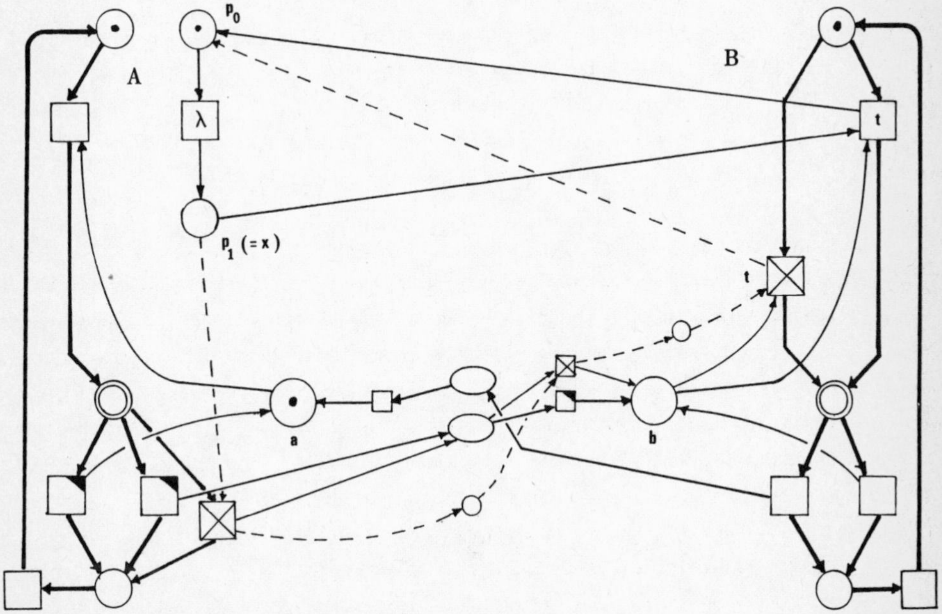

Fig. 5.5: Application of theorem 5.3

Process A can pass the token to B , but also can refuse to do so (under the p-rule). Hence the system is not fair under the p-rule (but would be under the f-rule). Therefore we apply the construction of Fig. 5.2 to transition t in Fig. 5.4 . The resulting net is given in Fig. 5.5 . Again, to simplify the construction only the case is represented, where A is in the critical section. Then after the occurrence of the λ-transition, either transition t can occur (if the token is in b) or a sequence v_1 is enabled, which is marked by a dashed line and crossed transitions. All these transitions are copies of existing ones, which are blocked by the empty side condition p_o . In the construction of theorem 5.3 <u>all</u> transitions having no cross and different from t are to be blocked, but in our case it is sufficient to block only the transitions bearing a black corner in their square symbol. Finally, by the occurrence of the (crossed) copy of t place p_o will be marked again. In the general case, the same construction has to be performed also for other reachable markings, which is not necessary in this particular case.

The similarities of the solutions of Figs. 5.3 and 5.5 are obvious: when leaving his critical section, process A is forced to pass the token to B . The differences lie in the cause of this action: in the first case the action is initialized by a request from B , whereas in the second case by some eventual occurrence of the λ-transition.

In [Roucairol 86] a result similar to theorem 5.3 is given using FIFO-nets. For instance, the example for implementing mutual exclusion can be interpreted in a similar way as the solution of Fig. 5.3 .

At the end of this section we mention some other proposals for fair occurrence rules. We saw in section 1 that the ordinary P/T-system of the five dining philosophers FDPh2 behaves <u>not</u> fair under the fair occurrence rule, i.e. $\mathrm{Fair(FDPh2)} \subsetneq L_{\omega}^{\mathrm{fair}}(\mathrm{FDPh2,id})$. This would not be the case if we also take into account transitions that are enabled after some immediate steps.

Let m be a marking of a P/T-system Σ and $k \in \mathbb{N}$. Then a transition $t \in T$ is called <u>k-enabled in m</u> , if there is some $v \in T^*$ of length at most k such that vt is enabled in m . t is called <u>∞-enabled in m</u> , if v can be of arbitrary length. An infinite occurrence sequence $v \in F_{\omega}(\Sigma)$ is called <u>k-productive</u> and <u>k-fair</u> for $k \in \mathbb{N}_{\infty} := \mathbb{N} \cup \{\infty\}$ if in the definitions of productive and fair, respt., the word "enabled" is replaced by "k-enabled" [Best 83].

<u>Theorem 5.4</u>

For any P/T-system Σ a number $k_o \in \mathbb{N}$ can be effectively computed such that for all occurrence sequences $v \in F_{\omega}(\Sigma)$: (v is ∞-fair) ⇔ (v is k_o-productive) .

Corollary 5.5

For any P/T-system Σ and $v \in F_\omega(\Sigma)$: (v is ∞-fair) $\Leftrightarrow$ ($\forall k \in \mathbb{N}$: v is k-fair) .

The corollary is from [Best 83] whereas the stronger theorem is proven in [Carstensen 86] again by using the theory of residue sets. Note that the sets of all markings for which a transition is k-enabled is right-closed and that the finite residue set R_t can be computed.

By the following program P from [Best 83]

```
program P =                  s := 1
          do  x: true   →  s := s+2
              y: true   →  s := s-1
              t: (s=0)  →  s := s   od.
```

corollary 5.5 is not true for general models of concurrent systems having the power of Turing machines: the infinite occurrence sequence $(xy)^\omega$ is k-fair for any $k \in \mathbb{N}$ but not ∞-fair.

In [Merceron 86] a notion of fairness for occurrence nets is discussed. A process of a P/T-net is considered to be fair if all associated occurrence sequences are fair. Though this may be a useful notion, it can have the drawback that (unfair) occurrence sequences are taken into account which actually do not appear for a participant of the system (e.g. a philosopher). The reason lies in the fact that processes of P/T-systems do not reflect enabled transitions that do not occur. This is another hint that occurrence sequences are more adequate to study fairness problems. The notion of 'objective' case in [Reisig 86] might be able to combine both aspects, but makes sense for some subclasses of nets only.

A further notion of fairness is based on synchronic distances [Lautenbach 77]. Two transitions are in a fair relation if there exists a positive integer k such that neither of them can fire more then k times without firing the other. This approach is further studied in [Murata/Wu 85].

6. References

[Best 83] E. Best: Fairness and Conspiracies, Information Processing Letters 18 (1983, 215-220

[Boasson/Nivat 80] L. Boasson and M. Nivat: Adherences of Languages, J. Comput. System Sci. 20 (1980), 285-309

[Brinch Hansen 73] P. Brinch Hansen: Operating System Principles, Englewood Cliffs: Prentice-Hall 1973

[Carstensen 82] H. Carstensen: Fairness bei Petrinetzen mit unendlichem Verhalten, Univ. Hamburg, FB Informatik, Bericht Nr. 93, IFI-HH-B-93/82, 1982

[Carstensen 84] H. Carstensen: Fairness in Deadlockfree Petri Nets with the Finite Delay Property, Proc. 5th European Workshop on Applications and Theory of Petri Nets, Arhus 1984, pp 234-253

[Carstensen/Valk 85] H. Carstensen, R. Valk: Infinite Behaviour and Fairness in Petri Nets, in G. Rozenberg (ed.): Advances in Petri Nets 1984, Lect. Notes in Computer Sci. 188, Springer, Berlin, 1985, pp 83-100

[Carstensen 86] H. Carstensen: Fairness bei nebenläufigen Systemen, eine Untersuchung am Modell der Petrinetze, Bericht des FB Informatik, Univ. Hamburg, 1986

[Cohen/Gold 77] R.S. Cohen, A.Y. Gold: Theory of ω-languages, Journ. Computer Syst. Sciences 15 (1977), 169-208

[Dijkstra 68] E.W. Dijkstra: Co-operating sequential processes, in F. Genuys (ed.): Programming Languages, Academic Press, London, 1968, pp 43-112

[Dijkstra 71] E.W. Dijkstra: Hierarchical Ordering of Sequential Processes, Acta Informatica 1 (1971),pp 115-138

[Eilenberg 74] S. Eilenberg: Automata, Languages and Machines, Vol. A., Academic Press, New York 1974

[Hauschildt/Valk 86] D. Hauschildt, R. Valk: Safe States in Banker like Resource Allocation Problems, in: G. Rozenberg (ed.), Advances in Petri Nets 1985, Lecture Notes in Computer Science 222, Springer, Berlin, 1986

[Jessen/Valk 86] E. Jessen, R. Valk: Rechensysteme, Springer-Verlag, Berlin, 1986

[Jantzen 86] M. Jantzen: Language Theory of Petri Nets (this volume)

[Landweber 69] L.H. Landweber: Decision problems for ω-automata, Math. Systems Theory 3 (1969), 376-384

[Lautenbach 77] K. Lautenbach: Ein kombinatorischer Ansatz zur Erreichung von Fairness in Scheduling Problemen, Applied Computer Sci. 8, Verlag C. Hauser, München, 1977

[Merceron 86] A. Merceron: Fair Processes, Proc. 7th Europ. Workshop on Application and Theory of Petri Nets, Oxford, 1986

[Murata, Wu 85] T. Murata, Z. Wu: Fair Relation and Modified Synchronic Distances in a Petri Net, Journ. Franklin Institute, 320 (1985) 2, 68-82

[Pelz 86] E. Pelz: ω-languages of Petri Nets and logical sentences, Proc. 7th Europ. Workshop on Application and Theory of Petri Nets, Oxford, 1986

[Reisig 86] W. Reisig: Coexistence: A Refinement of Concurrency, Proc. 7th Europ. Workshop on Application and Theory of Petri Nets, Oxford, 1986

[Raynal 85] M. Raynal: Algorithmes Distribués et Protocoles, Eyrolles, Paris, 1985

[Ricart/Agrawala 81] An Optimal Algorithm for Mutual Exclusion in Computer Networks, Comm. ACM, 24 (1981), 9-17

[Roucairol 86] G. Roucairol: FIFO-Nets (this volume)

[Valk 83] R. Valk: Infinite Behaviour of Petri Nets, Theor. Comput. Sci. 25, (1983), 311-341

[Valk/Jantzen 85] R. Valk, M. Jantzen: The Residue of Vector Sets with Applications to Decidability Problems in Petri Nets, Acta Informatica 21 (1985), 643-674

LANGUAGE THEORY OF PETRI NETS

Matthias Jantzen

Fachbereich Informatik
Universität Hamburg
Rothenbaumchaussee 67
D-2000 Hamburg 13

ABSTRACT Petri nets where multiple arcs are allows and the capacity of the places need not be bounded are here called Place/Transition systems. The restrictions of the possible finite or infinite occurence sequences of a P/T-system to the transitions are called transition sequences and give the basis to define families of formal languages related to classes of P/T-systems.

We introduce the notation and give a survey on methods and results about sets of finite transition sequences. We will compare the classes of Petri net languages we obtain with other families of languages known from automata and formal language theory. We hope to convince that these techniques and results are useful for the formulation and solution of certain questions about P/T-systems, as well as for comparing the underlying systems.

Key words: Petri net language, firing sequence, closure properties, multi-counter languages, intersection closed semi-AFL.

CONTENTS

INTRODUCTION

If one wants to analyze and derive properties of a system modelled by some Petri net, then this requires a great deal of formalism and a decision on which notion is most convenient or adequate. Here we consider P/T-systems - often called Petri nets - as descriptions of the systems and their possible transition sequences, i.e., the sequence of actions a single observer can establish, as partial descriptions of their behaviours.

Many questions about a system can be posed in terms of the sequences of actions that occur and thus may be answered by analyzing the underlying Petri net language. For instance, if a new and better system is designed to replace an existing one, then of course its behaviour should be identical to that of the old system. This can only happen if the languages of the underlying Petri net models are identical. Thus, in order to prove inequivalence of the two systems it is sufficient to exhibit one transition sequence that does not occur in both Petri net languages.

Transition sequences are surely not adequate to fully describe all aspects of a concurrent system and therefore trace languages [Mazurkiewicz 77], partial languages [Grabowski 79 b], semi-languages [Starke 81], and subset languages [Rozenberg/ Verraedt 83] have been defined. Also infinite transition sequences offer a possibility to define and study properties of systems like fairness and starvation.

All these approaches are discussed in several contributions to this volume and we therefore concentrate on the presentation of the traditional approach to study Petri net languages that began with the work of H. Baker [Baker 72], M. Hack [Hack 75] and J.L. Peterson [Peterson 74] and was continued by T. Etzion, A. Ginzburg, M. Jantzen, P.H. Starke, R. Valk, G. Vidal-Naquet, M. Yoeli and others.

The advantages of using the string language approach are based upon the following observations: With the help of Petri net languages we can classify and easily distinguish syntactically defined classes of Petri nets, and thus the underlying systems, by the classes of languages they can define. In some cases, properties of the reachability sets can be deduced from the transition sequences.

The methods used in formal language and automata theory which are applicable here sometimes provide simpler proofs for expected results and allow to formalize some of the folk-theorems. Also, most proofs are constructive and as such provide constructions and design principles. This remark applies especially to closure properties of Petri net languages that are proved by transforming the underlying nets. On the other hand, characterizations of Petri net languages via closure operations open the window to a direct comparison with other families of languages studied in theoretical computer science. For instance, the usual L-type Petri net languages are easily identified as the class of languages acceptable by one-way multi-counter machines in quasi-realtime while testing each counter for zero only a constant number of times [Greibach 78, Jantzen 79c].

The possibility of hiding or identifying transitions by their labelling opens more descriptive power and allows simpler formulations. Also this is convenient for a direct comparison with other classes of languages.

In what follows we basically use the notation from [Peterson 81] with slight variations (we use vectors instead of bags) and extensions according to [Best/Fernandez 86] and sometimes [Starke 80]. Also, because of lack of space, we do not give full proofs but only hints and the references where these can be found.

BASIC NOTATION AND DEFINITION

Looking at a P/T-system as a single observer it is impossible to record the concurrence of distinct transitions at the very same time and thus the sequence of transitions that occurred is the then basic object of consideration. As described in [Reisig 86] a transition sequence is obtained from an occurrence sequence by omitting all the markings reached. Such a transition sequence is free of labels and the set of all such transition sequences which are enabled at the initial marking of some P/T-system N is usually called a free (P-type) Petri net language. If one is interested in all transition sequences that change the initial marking of N into a final marking then there are various ways of how a final marking as the representative of the distributed state of the system to be reached should be specified.

It can be one marking out of a prescribed set (usually finite) of final markings that must be reached exactly (L-type) or it may suffice if finally a certain marking (or one of a prescribed set) is covered (G-type). This can be an adequate definition if the markings of the places, for instance, describe the number of resources available. A third possibility then could be to collect all transition sequences that yield a dead marking, i.e., one where no transition is enabled (T-type). All these types of languages have been studied by Peterson and Hack and can be equipped with a labelling of some sort. Restricting the otherwise nondeterministic choices of transition occurrences within labelled Petri nets one is lead to the definition of deterministic Petri nets [Vidal-Naquet 81, Pelz 86] which is similar to the notion of determinism as used for usual types of automata. In order to give the formal definitions of these languages and the classes (or families) they belong to we want to include some preliminary notion which is taken from standard text books on automata theory and formal languages and necessary in this context.

Notation

Let X be an alphabet then $X^* := X^+ \cup \{\lambda\}$ denotes the free monoid generated by X, where X^+ is the set of all finite non-empty strings (or words) over X, i.e., finite sequences of symbols from X juxtaposed. The transitive monoid operation in X^* is the concatenation and its application to the two strings u and v yields the string uv. The neutral element of X^* is called the empty string noted by λ. Given a string w and a symbol x then the non-negative integer $|w|_x \in \mathbb{N}$ denotes the number of occurrences of the symbol x within w, whereas $|w|$ is the total length of the string w. Hence for $w \in X^*$ we have $|w| = \sum_{x \in X} |w|_x$. The vector $\psi(w) := (|w|_{x_1}, |w|_{x_2}, \ldots, |w|_{x_n})$ is called Parikh vector of w, where $X=\{w_1, x_2, \ldots, x_n\}$ is ordered in the indicated way.

The homomorphism $\psi : X^* \longrightarrow \mathbb{N}^X$ where $w \longmapsto \psi(w)$ as defined above is called the Parikh mapping. Here, for sets A and B, B^A denotes the set of all total mappings from A to B and if A is an (ordered) finite set any such mapping can be denoted by a vector over B. Usually we use column-vectors but do write them as row vectors for a simpler lay-out. The difference is only important in connection with matrix products and then will become clear from the context. An alternative notation would use multisets or bags and is not done here.

In addition to the definitions in [Best + Fernandez 86] let us define column vectors $t^-, t^+ \in \mathbb{N}^S$ for each transition $t \in T$ by: $t^-(p) := W(p,t)$ and $t^+(p) := W(t,p)$ for all $p \in S$. Recall that $W(x,y)=0$ in case $(x,y) \notin F$. This notation from [Starke 78] is used to define a homomorphism $\Delta: T^* \longrightarrow \mathbb{Z}^S$ by $\Delta(t):=t^+-t^-$ which gives the t-column $C(\cdot,t)$ of the incidence matrix $C(s,t):=W(t,s)-W(s,t)$ for all $s \in S, t \in T$. The $|S|\times|T|$-matrices composed out of all the $t^-(t^+)$ column vectors are often called foreward (backward, resp.) incidence function [Hack 75], Prê (Post, resp.) matrices [Brams 83], and correspond to the input (output, resp.) functions in [Peterson 81]. With this definition of Δ we get for each finite transition sequence $w \in T^*$ the following equality: $\Delta(w)=C\cdot\psi(w)$. The enabling rule for t at m now becomes: $t^- \leq m \leq K - t^+$ and $m[w>m'$ implies $m'=m+\Delta(w)$.

At first, the transition rule [t> as defined in [Best/Fernandez 86] has to be generalized to transition sequences.

Definition

Let $N=(S,T,F,K,W,m)$ be a P/T-system. We then write:

(a) $m[\lambda>m$ for any marking $m \in \mathbb{N}^S$

(b) $m[w>m''$ if $w=ut$ for some $u \in T^*$, $t \in T$ and there exists $m' \in \mathbb{N}^S$ such that $m[u>m'[t>m''$.

(c) A transition sequence $w \in T^*$ is enabled at m, written m[w>, if there exists some m' such that m[w>m' holds. Specifically, this means that the empty transition sequence λ is always enabled .

Any subset $L \subseteq X^*$ is a (formal) language and for free Petri net languages the alphabet used will be the set T of transitions.

However, we also want to deal with whole families of languages and notice that a family of languages $\mathcal{L}$ is a nonempty set of languages which is closed under isomorphisms, i.e. change of alphabets, such that not all elements $L \in \mathcal{L}$ are the empty set. The first important family of Petri net languages, extensively studied in [Starke 78], is the basis for all other language families we consider. It is the class of free Petri net languages with or without final markings.

In order to change the initial marking of a P/T-system without changing the underlying P/T-net structure we use the following notation:

Notation

For any P/T-system $\Sigma=(S,T,F,K,W,m)$ the structure (S,T,F,K,W), or (S,T,F,W) if $K(p)=\infty$ for all $p \in S$, is called (the underlying) P/T-net.

In order to define a Petri net language one has to specify four quantities: the underlying Petri net $N=(S,T,F,K,W)$, the initial marking $m \in \mathbb{N}^S$, a usually finite set of final markings $M \subset \mathbb{N}^S$, and a labelling function $\ell: T \rightarrow X$, where X is an alphabet. Given this information $\Gamma:=(N,m,M,\ell)$ and by extending ℓ to a homomorphism $\ell: T^* \rightarrow X^*$ in the obvious way or omitting ℓ if it is the identity, we define the following types of Petri net languages and the corresponding language families.

Definition

Let $\Gamma=(N,m,M,\ell)$ as described above then

(a) $L(\Gamma):=\{\ell(w)\,|\,\exists w\in T^*\ \exists m'\in M:\ m[w>m'\}$ is the L-type or terminal language of N

(b) $G(\Gamma):=\{\ell(w)\,|\,\exists w\in T^*\ \exists m'\in M\ \exists m''\geq m':\ m[w>m''\}$ is the G-type or covering language of N, also called weak language.

(c) $P(\Gamma):=\{\ell(w)\,|\,\exists w\in T^*:\ m[w>\}$ is the P-type language or the set of all labelled transition sequences of N.

(d) $T(\Gamma):=\{\ell(w)\,|\,\exists w\in T^*\ \exists m'\in \mathbb{N}^S:\ (m[w>m' \text{ and } \forall t\in T:\ m'[t>)\}$ is the T-type or deadlock language of N.

The families of L-type (G-type, P,type, T-type, resp.) languages are abbreviated by $\underline{L}$ ($\underline{G}$,$\underline{P}$,$\underline{T}$, resp.).

Among the many possiblities for choosing certain labelling functions, the most simple is the one where $|T|=|X|$ and ℓ is an isomorphism and may thus be omitted completely by choosing $X:=T$. In this situation the languages of either type are called free Petri net languages. A situation worth introducing an extra notation is the one where the labelling function is extended by allowing the empty word λ as a label of the transitions in order to hide them. Languages obtained from Petri nets this way are called arbitrary Petri net languages or languages defined by using so-called λ-transitions.

Definition

For any family X of Petri net languages of either type $X\in\{\underline{L},\underline{G},\underline{P},\underline{T}\}$ let X^f resp. X^λ denote the corresponding class of free resp. arbitrary Petri net languages.

If we are dealing with capacities that restrict the concession of a transition this obviously changes the free Petri net language. On the other hand, places that are bounded in advance by their prescribed capacity can be modelled by introducing so-called complementary places. The construction is given in [Reisig 85] and allows to consider only P/T-systems without capacities since this construction does not introduce new transitions and thus does not change the language generated. In what follows we thus omit the capacity constraints completely.

Example

Consider the structure $\Gamma=(N,m,\emptyset,\sigma)$ where N,m and σ are displayed in the figure. Then $P(\Gamma)=\{\lambda,a\}$ if the capacity of s is given by $K(s):=3$ and the enabling rule of the transition is that defined in [Best/Fernandez 86]. If $K(s)=\infty$, then $P(\Gamma)=\{a\}^*$.

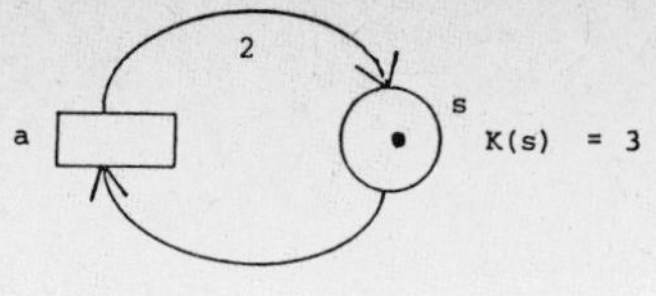

The labelled P/T-system simulating Γ with unbounded capacities and complementary place $\bar{s}$ and initial marking as displayed looks as follows:

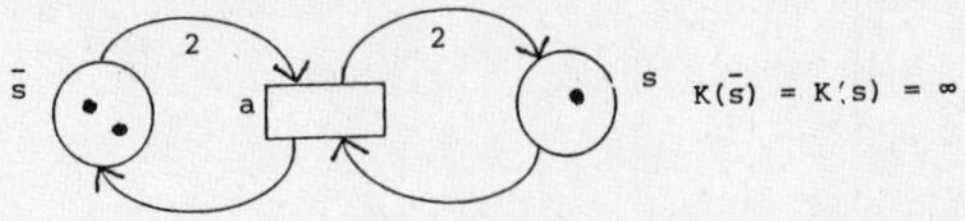

It should be clear from the definition that any P-type Petri net language L has the <u>prefix property,</u> which means that $L= Pref(L):=\{u\in T^* \mid uv\in L\}$. This is no longer the case if we introduce final markings to be reached, covered or being a dead end.

Also the Petri net language, even if it is free of labels, by no means gives enough information to recover the Petri net it came from, unless the Petri nets are selfloop-free and the languages are free ones. However, this is not - and has historically never been - the aim for studying Petri net languages.

The following example shows a Petri net where its free terminal language is just a single word but the free P-type language is larger than just the set of all its prefixes.

<u>Example</u>

The structure Γ consists of the following Petri net N together with initial marking m=(2,1,3) and a single final marking m'=(5,4,0) as indicated. One obtaines $L(N,m,m')=\{aba^2ba^3b\}\neq P(N,m,\emptyset)=G(N,m,\underline{0})=Pref(aba^2bab,aba^2ba^2b,aba^2ba^3b)$.

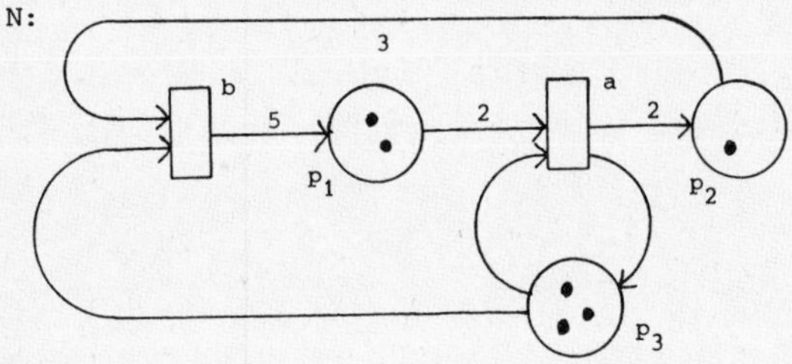

By extending the automata theoretic notion of deterministic machines to Petri nets G. Vidal-Naquet introduced deterministic Petri nets:

<u>Definition</u>

A labelled Petri Net N=(S,T,F,W) with initial marking m_o , i.e., the structure $\Gamma=(N,m_o,\ell)$, is called deterministic if $\forall t,t'\in T\ \forall m\in(m_o>$: $m(t>$ and $m(t'>$ implies $(\ell(t)\neq\ell(t')$ or $t=t')$ and $(\ell(t)=\lambda$ implies $t=t')$.

Definition

If $\Gamma=(N,m_o,\ell)$ is deterministic then $L(\Gamma)$ $(T(\Gamma), G(\Gamma), P(\Gamma)$, resp.) are deterministic Petri net languages of the corresponding type.

For any family $X \in \{\underline{L},\underline{T},\underline{G},\underline{P}\}$ X_{det} (or $X^{\lambda}_{det}, X^{f}_{det}$) denotes the family obtained by using deterministic Petri nets as the underlying structure where non-erasing (arbitrary, injective, resp.) labelling homomorphisms are used.

COMPARING PETRI NET LANGUAGES

Most of the results concerning free Petri net languages are contained in [Starke 78] where Starke corrects a statement by Hack [Hack 75]. The classes $\underline{G}^f$ and $\underline{T}^f$ are not so well studied so far, mostly because the free Petri net languages do not have very nice closure properties and closure operations are an important tool to compare families of languages and are usually considered in formal language theory.

Notice that any P-type language can be written as an G-type language by using the structure $(N,m,\underline{0})$ instead of (N,m) since any marking reachable from m exceeds the zero marking $\underline{0}$ of appropriate size. The preceding example already used this.

It is also not difficult to verify that the covering languages are also terminal Petri net languages which , however, are usually not free. The construction adds new transitions to the old structure in the following way: For each transition t one adds transitions $t_i, 1 \leq i \leq k$, where $t_i^+ \leq t^+$ and each such possibility has to be used, which determines k to the product of all entries in t^+ .

The following table of basic inclusions if from [Peterson 81] and mainly follows from considerations similar to those above. An exception is the proof of $\underline{T}=\underline{L}$ from [Parigot/Pelz 85] which is not contained in Peterson's work.

Theorem

The following inclusions (in general not strict) are valid for the families of Petri net languages defined so far.

$$
\begin{array}{ccccc}
\underline{L}^{\lambda} & \supset & \underline{L} & \supset & \underline{L}^{f} \\
\| & & \| & & \\
\underline{T}^{\lambda} & \supset & \underline{T} & \supset & \underline{T}^{f} \\
\cup & & \cup & & \\
\underline{G}^{\lambda} & \supset & \underline{G} & \supset & \underline{G}^{f} \\
\cup & & \cup & & \cup \\
\underline{P}^{\lambda} & \supset & \underline{P} & \supset & \underline{P}^{f}
\end{array}
$$

A first comparison of some deterministic Petri net languages was given in [Vidal-Naquet 81] and yielded the following strict inclusions.

Theorem

$\underline{L}^f \subset \underline{L}_{det} \subset \underline{L} \subset \underline{L}^{\lambda}_{det}$ and $\underline{P}^f \subset \underline{P}_{det} \subset \underline{P} \subset \underline{P}^{\lambda}_{det}$

Except for this result not much is known when comparing Petri net languages with the deterministic families directly. More information can be obtained by studying their closure properties.

CLOSURE PROPERTIES

In order to understand the properties and limits of Petri net languages as well as to see some of the design methods for new systems from old ones we now consider closure properties of the various Petri net languages, first looking closer to the family of free (terminal) Petri net languages.

When we are given two descriptions of systems and we want to design a system that behaves as either one, then we simply take the union of the two systems and a non-deterministic choice of which to begin with. If we look at Petri net languages, the situation is not always that simple, since the union of free Petri net languages may not be a free language of some other Petri net since we cannot label distinct transitions equally. Thus the following result from [Starke 78] is not surprising:

Lemma

The families $\underline{L}^f, \underline{T}^f, \underline{G}^f, \underline{P}^f$ are not closed with respect to union.

This follows, since the languages {baa} and {aab} are elements of either class but their union is not even contained in $\underline{L}^f$, see [Starke 78].

For the non-free labelled Petri net languages closure with respect to union is trivially true since disjunct union of the systems is always possible.

Also for product the situation for free Petri net languages is not so easy since there are even singletons which are not free terminal Petri net languages, such as the set $L:=\{aba^2ba^3ba^4b\}$, for which P. Starke showed $L \notin \underline{L}^f$. Since we already know from the example before that $\{aba^2ba^3b\}$ is an element of $\underline{L}^f$ we can quickly conclude the following:

Lemma

The family $\underline{L}^f$ of free terminal Petri net languages is not closed with respect to product.

There are only a few operations that can be used to define new free Petri net languages from given ones. Among those that may not be very common is that of taking a quotient from the left or from the right by finite or arbitrary sets.

Definition

For any languages A,B the left (right, resp.) quotient $B^{-1}A$ (AB^{-1}, resp.) of A by B is the set

$B^{-1}A := \{v \mid \exists w \in A, u \in B: w = uv\}$

$AB^{-1} := \{u \mid \exists w \in A, v \in B: w = uv\}$

If $B=\{w\}$ is a singleton, then the quotient is called the derivative of A by w . Often these operations are denoted by $B\backslash A$ for $B^{-1}A$ and A/B for AB^{-1}.

If we want to take the left-derivative of some free Petri net languages by the transition sequence w , then we take the unique marking reached from the initial marking m_o by this sequence as a new initial marking. A similar consideration for the final markings gives the following result:

Lemma

The family $\underline{L}^f$ is closed with respect to left-derivative and right-quotient by finite sets.

Almost all closure properties which are valid for free Petri net languages are at the same time true for all other families of labelled Petri net languages of the same type. The proofs need only minor modifications.

The closure with respect to intersection is easily proved by an effective construction that identifies the transitions of two P/T-systems that are equally labelled or identical.

For proving closure with respect to inverse homomorphisms consider a given P/T-system $N = (S,T,F,W,m)$, a set of final markings $M \subset \mathbb{N}^S$ and a homomorphism $h: X^* \to T^*$. The new P/T-system $N' = (S',X,F',W',m')$ for $h^{-1}(L(N,m,M))$ is constructed as follows: Let $S' := S \cup \{q\}$, where $m'(q) := 1$ and $m''(q)=1$ for each final marking $m'' \in M'$. Now transitions x with $h(x)=\lambda$ get q as its only input and output place, i.e., $^\bullet x = x^\bullet = \{q\}$. If $h(x)=w \in T^+$, then we take x^- as the smallest marking that enables w , the so-called hurdle $H(w) := \min\{m \in \mathbb{N}^{S'} \mid m[w>\}$ and define $x^+ := \Delta(w)+x^-$ so that finally $\Delta(x) = \Delta(w)$, F' and W' are defined accordingly. Also $\forall s \in S$: $m'(s)$ and the final markings differ exactly in the new place q . It is not hard to verify that $L(N',m',M') = h^{-1}(L(N,m,M))$.

Example

Let N be the P/T-net drawn below together with its initial marking m , $X:=\{A,B\}$, and $h: X^* \to T^*$ given by $h(A):=a$, $h(B):=ab$, then $h^{-1}(T(N,m))=\{BB,ABB,BAB\}$ since $T(N,m)= \{a^2b^2, abab, aba^2b, a^2bab\}$.

N:

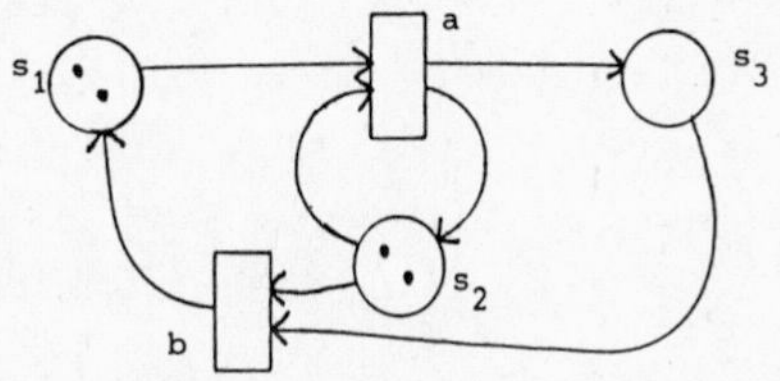

The construction, if applied to this P/T-net would give the net together with its initial marking m' as displayed below. However, T(N',m') = {AA,ABA,ABB,BB,BAB,

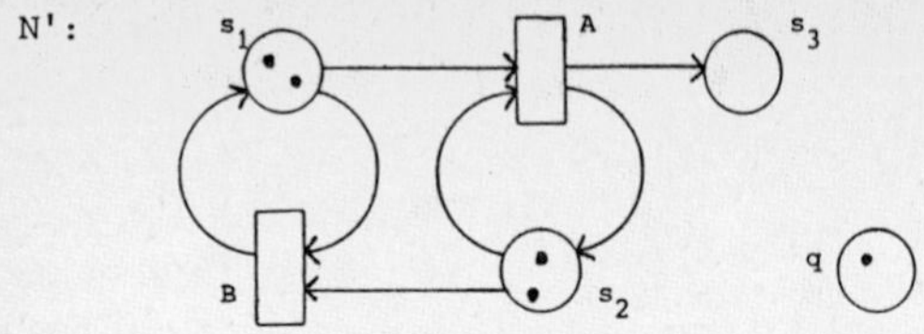

BAA} $\neq h^{-1}(T(N,m))$. This shows that the construction should be modified if the dead-lock languages are to be used. This is sometimes possible by taking appropriate <u>final markings</u> but will not be discussed here in more detail.

It is interesting to see that the family $\underline{L}^f$ of free terminating Petri net languages obtainable from the one-sided Dyck set $D_1:=\{w\in\{a,b\}^* \mid |w|_a=|w|_b$ and $w=uv$ implies $|u|_a \geq |u|_b\}$ also generated as $D_1=L(N,\underline{0},\underline{0})$ by the following simple P/T-net:

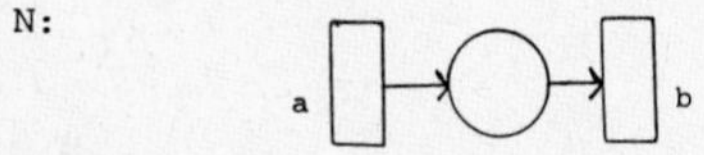

<u>Theorem</u>

$\underline{L}^f$ is the smallest class of languages containing the one-sided Dyck set D_1 and closed with respect to the operations left derivative, right quotient by finite sets, inverse homomorphism, and intersection. $\underline{L}^f$ is <u>not</u> closed with respect to the following operations: union, product, intersection by regular sets, Kleene star, homomorphism.

The free Petri net languages have been seen to form a very weak family of languages which do not even contain all the regular sets. It is therefore appropriate to use the non-free labelled languages from the classes $\underline{L},\underline{T},\underline{G}$ or $\underline{P}$. It is easy to see that all but the class $\underline{P}$ contain the regular sets but still we have not seen whether these families are closed with respect to arbitrary or at least nonerasing homomorphisms.

Since we know from the preceeding results and observations that $\underline{L}$ is closed with respect to intersection, intersection by regular sets, inverse homomorphisms, and codings, i.e., length preserving homomorphisms, by definition it follows from the results in formal language theory that this family is also closed with respect to nonerasing homomorphisms, while $\underline{L}^\lambda$ is closed with respect to arbitrary homomorphism. In order to give an idea of how such a proof would be given directly using Petri net constructions we will give the basic steps without all the formal details.

<u>Lemma</u>

The family $\underline{L}$ (respectively $\underline{L}^\lambda$ is closed with respect to nonerasing (arbitrary, resp.) homomorphism.

For a proof replace the transition t of a P/T-system by $|h(t)|$ new transitions together with the proper codings to yield (h(t) if they occur in sequence. In order to make sure that no other transition in the system can occur inbetween, these transitons must form a sequence and its first transition must disable all other transitions not occurring in this sequence. This is usually done by first introducing a so-called run place which is an input and output place to all transitions in the original P/T-system, and they replace the transition t with $h(t)= x_1,x_2...x_n$ as indicated in the figure below.

Replace

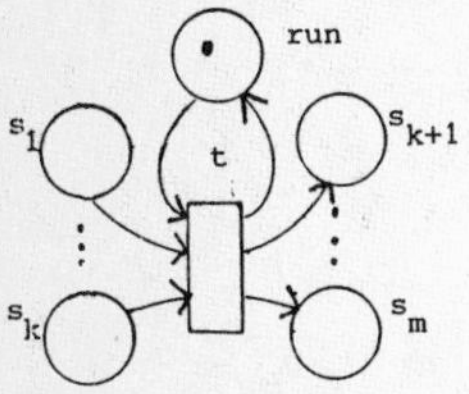

by

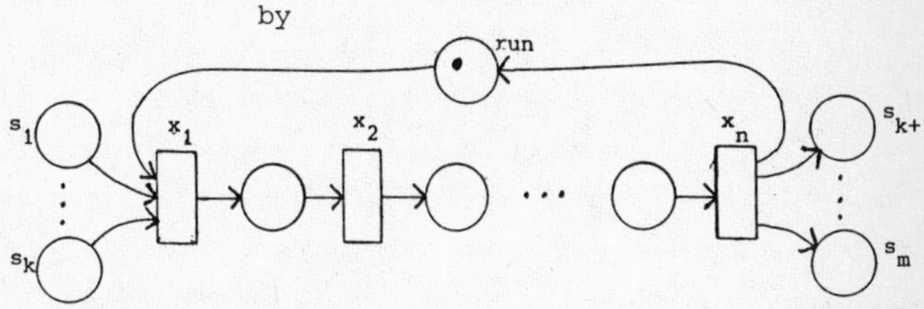

Constructions like this obviously change the concurrent behaviour of the underlying nets but they are appropriate for the string language approach. The question as to which operations on languages give raise to closure operators that do not change the various families of Petri net languages is an important one for a comparison with other known families.

For instance, we already know that $\underline{L}$ ($\underline{L}^\lambda$ resp.) is a union and intersection closed trio, i.e., an intersection closed semi-AFL (full semi-AFL, resp.). Moreover, we can identify the parenthesis language D_1 as the single generator from which we can obtain every terminal Petri net language $L \in \underline{L}$ by using the trio operations: inverse homomorphisms, intersection by regular sets, and non-erasing homomorphisms in connection with intersection.

This characterization follows immediately from the following theorem about free (terminal) Petri net languages:

Theorem

Any language $L \in \underline{P}^f$ or $L \in \underline{L}^f$ can be presented in the form $L= L_1 \cap L_2 \cap \ldots \cap L_k$, where each $L_i, 1 \leq i \leq k$, $k \in \mathbb{N}$ is a deterministic weak one-counter language, i.e. $L_i = g(h^{-1}(D_1) \cap R)$ for some homomorphism h, non-erasing homomorphism g, and a regular set R.

The proof is essentially contained already in [Hack 75] and [Crespi-Reghizzi / Mandrioli 77] but not formulated in this form. For the proof consider those subnets defined by a single place and containing all transitions. The transitions not connected with that place can occur at any time and can be modelled by the finite state control of the deterministic counter automaton which performs the change of its counter according to $\Delta(t)$ for all transitions.

As a consequence of this result we get

Corollary

The complement of a free Petri net language in $\underline{L}^f$ or in $\underline{P}^f$ is a one-counter language but not necessarily a weak one-counter language and not deterministic.

Similar as for deterministic pushdown automata this follows, since the complement of a deterministic weak one-counter language is again one-counter, though in general not deterministic and not weak, see [Harrison 78].

This result does no longer hold if we consider non-free Petri net languages.

From the observation that each place of a given P/T-system behaves like a (weak) counter which cannot be tested for zero except at the end by the final marking, it is not surprising that weak counter languages play the crucial role in those characterizations. In fact, the least intersection closed trio generated by D_1 is known as the family of all languages acceptable by weak (or partially blind) multicounter machines in quasi-real time, [Greibach 78] and thus a machine characterization of (terminal) Petri net languages can easily be given, see also [Jantzen 79 a,b,c].

Since their definition by G. Vidal-Naquet, not many new results were obtained for the class of deterministic Petri net languages. That this family $\underline{L}_{det}$ is not closed with respect to union, product and coding, is widely known among those working in this area but references are not easy to find. The construction used for the intersection of Petri net languages also works for deterministic nets so that $\underline{L}_{det}$ is closed with respect to intersection.

The recent work by E. Pelz [Pelz 86] not only contains proofs for the forementioned but also shows that the complements of deterministic (terminal) Petri net languages are terminal Petri net languages, though not deterministic ones.

Theorem

If $L \subset X^*$ and $L \in \underline{L}_{det}$ or $L \in \underline{P}_{det}$ then $X^* \setminus L \in \underline{L}$.

We will close this section by a table about closure and non-closure properties of the main families of Petri net languages. For the missing proofs see [Hack 75, Peterson 81, Starke 80] and those already mentioned.

operation	$\underline{L}^f$	$\underline{L}$	$\underline{L}_{det}$	$\underline{L}^\lambda$	$\underline{P}^f$	$\underline{P}$	$\underline{P}_{det}$	$\underline{P}^\lambda$
union	-	+	-	+	-	+	-	+
product	-	+	-	+	-	+	-	-
intersection	+	+	+	+	+	+	+	+
intersection by regular sets	-	+	+	+	-	prefix	prefix	prefix
Kleene star	-	-	-	-	-	-	-	-

cont.

operation	$\underline{L}^f$	$\underline{L}$	$\underline{L}_{det}$	$\underline{L}^\lambda$	$\underline{P}^f$	$\underline{P}$	$\underline{P}_{det}$	$\underline{P}^\lambda$
inverse homomorphism	+	+	+	+	+	+	+	+
regular substitution	-	λ-free	λ-free	+	-	prefix	λ-free prefix	prefix
homomorphism	-	-	-	+	-	-	-	+
non-erasing homomorphism	-	+	-	+	-	+	-	+
complement	-	-	-	-	-	-	-	-

COMPARISON WITH OTHER FAMILIES

That $\underline{L}$ is incomparable with the class CF of context-free languages has been shown by Peterson who proved that the language $\{ww^R | w \in \{a,b\}^*\}$ is not in the class $\underline{L}$ by counting the number of different markings that are reachable by transition sequences of length k . Since these are only polynomially many but there are exponentially many different strings of length k , this yields a contradiction. A similar method was used in [Jantzen 81] to show that $\underline{L}$ is not closed with respect to iterated shuffle.

Theorem

(a) Rev:= $\{ww^R | w \in \{a,b\}^* \notin \underline{L}$

(b) $\{ab^n cde^n f | n \geq 1 \quad \notin \underline{L}$

(c) The family $\underline{L}^\lambda$ does not contain all context-free languages, not even the set Rev.

(d) None of the families $\underline{L}$ and $\underline{L}^\lambda$ is closed with respect to Kleene star.

(e) None of the families $\underline{L}$ and $\underline{L}^\lambda$ is closed with respect to complement.

The proofs for (c) and (d) use the decidability of the reachability problem, [Mayr 80, 84], and known results from formal language theory: The family RE of recursively enumerable languages is known to be the smallest intersection closed full AFL containing $L_1 := \{a^n b^n | n \geq 1\}$, and if $\underline{L}$, and consequently then $\underline{L}^\lambda$, would be star-closed, the latter would equal RE . The same would happen if Rev $\in \underline{L}^\lambda$ by results in [Baker/Book 74].

The non-closure with respect to complement can be shown without recursing to the reachability problem. It is easy to show that the complement $\overline{\text{Rev}}$ of Rev is an element of $\underline{L}$, thus if $\underline{L}$ would be closed under complement, then this contradicts (a). If $\underline{L}^\lambda$ would be this family, then by the proof for (c) $\underline{L}^\lambda$ = RE , but this contradicts the non-closure of RE with respect to complement.

What is clear from the characterization is the inclusion of $\underline{L}$ in the family CS of context sensitive languages, which, by the preceeding result, must be proper. $\underline{L}^\lambda$ was shown to be strictly included in the family of all recursive sets in [Greibach 78] using the decidability of the reachability problem.

The type of proof, showing Rev $\notin \underline{L}$ was used in [Jantzen 79 a,b] to prove that the set BIN:= $\{wa^k | w\in\{0,1\}^*, o\leq k\leq n(w)\}$, where n(w) is the integer represented by w as a binary number, is not an element of $\underline{L}$. Since BIN $\in \underline{L}^\lambda$ we have the following comparison between these classes:

<u>Theorem</u>

$\underline{L} \subsetneq \underline{L}^\lambda$ and $\underline{P} \subsetneq \underline{P}^\lambda$

From this result it becomes apparent that hiding transitions by λ-labels not only is a handy concept for simple formulations, but at the same time it increases the expressibility, at least in terms of Petri net languages.

SPECIFIC PROPERTIES

Apart from the direct comparison of the language families in question, other properties can be used for a classification. Very often languages are considered simple when they are commutatively equivalent to a regular set. A set with this property has a semilinear set of vectors as its image under the Parikh mapping and is sometimes called a slip language (has the semilinear property).

<u>Definition</u>

A set $M \subset \mathbb{N}^k$ is called <u>semilinear</u> if there exists a regular set $R \subset \{X_1, \ldots X_k\}^*$ such that $\psi(R)=M$. A language L as well as a family $\mathcal{L}$ is called <u>slip</u> if $\psi(L)$ is a semilinear vector set (for each $L \in \mathcal{L}$, resp.).

The family CF is such a slip family and there exist slip languages not in $\underline{L}$, see [Jantzen 81], and $\underline{L}$ is not a slip family since the set $\{a^n b^m | 0\leq m\leq 2^n, n\geq 0\}$=h(BIN) is an element of $\underline{L}$ which is obviously not slip.

The connection between Petri net languages and reachability sets is simple and not very strong. The Parikh image of $L \in \underline{L}^f$ needs only be transformed lineary according to the transition rule:

$[m\rangle = m + C\cdot\psi(L) = m+\Delta(L)$, then, if L is slip, so is $C\cdot\psi(L)$ and consequently $[m\rangle$. The converse is in general not true.

On the other hand, many subclasses of P/T-systems have semilinear reachability sets and actually generate slip languages. These are, among others, the folloiwng classes of P/T-systems the definitions of which are contained in [Araki/Kasami 77], [Grabowski 80], [Jantzen/Valk 79], [Landweber/Robertson 78] and [Mayr 81].

A P/T-system has a semilinear reachability set and a free Petri net language that is slip, if it is

- bounded
- reversible

- persistent
- persistent-reversible
- can be transformed into a pure P/T-system with at most 5 places

This last result is from [Hopcroft/Pansiot 79] and uses the equivalent formulation of pure P/T-systems by vector addition systems.

The full marking class [m] of a P/T-system is always a semilinear set that can be constructed effectively so that it may be presented as the projection of the reachability set of a P/T-system with only bounded or reversal bounded places (see [Jantzen/Valk 79]). However, this is of purely theoretical interest. Let us close this paper by a recent result about Petri net languages and reachability sets of P/T-systems with final markings.

If no final marking is specified, then the following result can be deduced from the covering graph, see [Burkhard 81]:

Theorem

Let N= (S,T,F,W,m) be a P/T-system, then its reachability set [m> contains a linear subset which is simultaenously unbounded in exactly the places that are simultaneously unbounded in N .

For languages $L \in \underline{P}^{\lambda}$ we have a pumping lemma similar to that for regular sets.

Theorem

For each $L \in \underline{P}^{\lambda}$ there exist numbers k,l such that each $w \in L$ with $|w| \geq k$ has a decomposition $w = xyz$ with $1 \leq |y| \leq l$ such that $xy^{i+1}z \in L$ for all $i \in \mathbb{N}$.

This pumping cannot occur in systems where a certain final marking must be reached. However, T.L. Lambert as recently observed the following by using - if not reproving - the decidability of the reachability problem [Lambert 86 b]. Actually, this is already contained but somehow hidden in [Mayr 80].

Theorem

Let N= (S,T,F,W,m) be a P/T-system, $M \subset \mathbb{N}^S$ a finite set, then there exist $k_o \in \mathbb{N}, u_i, v_i, w_i, x_i \in T^+$ for $1 \leq i \leq n = |T|$ such that $u_o^k v_o w_o^k x_o^k t_1 u_1^k v_1 w_1^k x_1^k t_2 \ldots t_n u_n^k v_n w_n^k x_n^k \in L(N,m,M)$ for all $k \geq k_o$.

Consequently any infinite language $L \in \underline{L}^{\lambda}$ has a Parikh image which contains an arithmetic series, which is a special type of semilinear set, and languages like $\{a^n b^m \mid m=2^n \geq 1\}$, $\{a^n b^m c^k \mid k=n \cdot m \geq 0\}$ or $\{a^n b^m \mid m \geq 2^n \geq 1\}$ are not elements of the family $\underline{L}^{\lambda}$ of arbitrarily labelled Petri nets.

Since Lambert's work is not yet available we can only be vague about the details but it seems that this will be a nice application of solvability of the reachability problem.

Because of the lack of space we could not include the characterizations of $\underline{L}$ and $\underline{G}$ by certain logical first-order formulas. This characterization has as one consequence that this logic might be used as a specification language of a desired behaviour and at the same time a construction of the corresponding labelled Petri net could be constructed.

What we also did not consider here is any enlargement of the classes $\underline{L}$ and $\underline{L}^{\lambda}$ by generalizing the transition rule as done in [Burkhard 81a], [Etzion/Yoeli 81], [Hack 75], [Valk 78], and by others. Usually the extension is that powerful that $\underline{L}^{\lambda}$ becomes the whole class RE . The best known generalizations are probably inhibitor arcs and priority rules.

As shown in [Jantzen 81] the same happens to the family $\underline{L}^{\lambda}$ if powerful closure operations are used, as for instance inverse shuffle or cancellation. Complexity arguments also allow for a classification of the language families but more so for the problems one has to deal with when using Petri nets. The undecidable problems definitely are limitations for the questions that must be solvable effectively.

REFERENCES

The references to this contributio are combined with those of the next one: "Complexity of Place Transition Nets".

COMPLEXITY OF PLACE / TRANSITION NETS

Matthias Jantzen
Fachbereich Informatik
Universität Hamburg
Rothenbaumchaussee 67
D-2000 Hamburg 13

ABSTRACT This is a survey of results about the complexity of decision problems for various questions about Petri nets that arise in the analysis of systems. The border between undecidable and decidable problems is discussed first and then problems are presented by decreasing complexity. As a consequence of the results presented it will follow that one has to concentrate on very restricted classes of systems in order to get practically relevant algorithms that work well for all cases, since even seemingly simple classes of Petri nets have simple problems with a provable high lower bound for the complexity of their solution.

Key words: Complexity classes, complete problems for P, NP, PSPACE, log-space reductions, weak Petri net computer, coverability graph, reachability.

CONTENTS

INTRODUCTION

Now that we learned that the reachability problem for Petri nets is decidable as shown first by Mayr in his Dissertation [Mayr 80], one might hope that many more problems we have about Petri nets can now be solved algorithmically. But this is obviously not possible, since we can identify questions which are too complex as to allow any algorithmic solution. However, even if a problem allows an effective procedure for solving it, this solution may still not be practicable because of its high complexity. Fortunately, knowing that a problem can be solved in general only by an ineffective algorithm does not mean that one should not put his or her hands on it. There are many situations to overcome this bad situation: Either the solution searched for needs not be at 100 per cent exact or one observes that an algorithm, though not guaranteed to run quickly in all cases, may do so for most of your applications. Also, it might be possible and appropriate to relax the problem somewhat and then better algorithms might be found, or to restrict the problem domain to a suitable subclass which still covers most of the cases one is confronted with.

What we will do here is to go step by step through the complexity classes, starting with the undecidable problems, and identifying problems about Petri nets that fall into these classes. Our aim is definitely not to provide the best algorithms in form of a computer program. In general, any existing algorithm would only give an upper bound for the complexity of the problem. Proving lower bounds and optimality of an upper bound is usually an ingenious and difficult problem. As we will see, even very restricted questions are decidable only by using an astronomically large amount of space and time and thus can practically not be solved without the indicated modifications.

BASIC NOTIONS AND DEFINITIONS

When we speak about problems we have to specify the generic instance of the problem and then the yes/no question to be asked. We thus specify a problem in the format used in [Garey/Johnson 79] . This is an informal, encoding-independent approach which only requires polynomially related measures of the input size in order to classify the inherent complexity of the problem and makes it possible to compare complexity classes which all include the class of problems solvable deterministically in polynomial time. Here the time needed by some algorithm is measured as the number of basic steps performed by the algorithm, which usually is represented by some Turing machine. As we are dealing with P/T-systems as inputs for an algorithm solving a problems, we provide the common definition of size, [Garey/Johnson 79], which, roughly speaking, is the length of the binary representation of all the relevant information. For a P/T-net this would be the following:

Definition

Let $N=(S,T,F,W)$ be a P/T-net with unbounded capacities, then

$$\text{size}(F) := \sum_{e \in F} \lceil \log(W(e))+1 \rceil ,$$

$$\text{size}(N) := \text{size}(F) \cdot \lceil \log(|S|)+1 \rceil ,$$

and if an initial marking is used, then

$$\text{size}(N,m) := \text{size}(N)+|S|\cdot\lceil \log(1+\max\{m(s) \mid s \in S\}) \rceil .$$

In principle, the problems we are dealing with are yes/no problems and as such can be formulated as formal languages which contain all the encodings of problem instances for which the problem question is answered yes. This formal language then is the input to a Turing machine and the time (number of single steps) or space (number of cells visited) needed by that machine to accept this language determines the complexity of the problem. Thus, if we say that a problem is in a specific complexity class we do not mean a single generic problem instance but in fact the whole infinite set of all instances of the same problem. More details on this can be found in the first chapters of [Garey/Johnston 79] and in [Hopcroft/Ullman 79].

Notation

P(NP) denotes the class of problems solvable deterministically (non-deterministically) in polynomial time

PSPACE denotes the class of problems solvable in polynomial space (deterministically or non-deterministically)

EXSPACE denotes the class of problems solvable in space bounded by 2^{poly}, where poly is any polynomial.

We know that $P \subseteq NP \subseteq PSPACE$ but cannot tell which of the inclusions is proper, if any at all. Any algorithm for a problem in the class NP known to us works with an exponential amount of time (single steps) and thus if a problem is classified to be NP-complete this definitely means that we cannot use an algorithm that works good for all problem instances.

Definition

A problem L is called complete for a complexity class Q (with respect to log-space reductions) if $L \in Q$ and each $L' \in Q$ can be (log-space) reduced to L by a Turing machine M that uses logarithmic space and maps L' into L such that $x \in L'$ iff $M(x) \in L$.

This log-space reduction is only one possible reduction one can formulate but the most common one and will do for our purpose. Log-space reductions need only deterministic polynomial time and we could use polynomial-time reductions as well. Since we cannot give full proofs in most cases, the reader will have to fill out the missing details and useful references for this are [Hopcroft/Ullman 79] and [Garey/Johnson 79].

UNDECIDABILITY RESULTS

It is obviously important to know which problems should never be attacked because one can prove that no general algorithm for the problem exists and one would otherwise definitely fail.

The first results are quite easy to prove since they can use results known from formal language theory and are related to Petri net languages as described in [Jantzen 86].

Definition

The coemptiness problem for languages from a family $\mathcal{L}$ is the following:
INSTANCE: A finite specification for a language $L \in \mathcal{L}$, an alphabet X such that $L \subseteq X^*$.
Question: Is $L = X^*$?

The equality problem for languages from a family $\mathcal{L}$ is the following:
INSTANCE: Finite specifications for languages $L, L' \in \mathcal{L}$, an alphabet X such that $L \subseteq X^*$; $L' \subseteq X^*$.
QUESTION: Is $L = L'$?

Theorem

The coemptiness and the equality problem is undecidable for languages from the class $\underline{L}$.

The proof in [Jantzen 79b] uses ideas from [Greibach 69] also used in [Baker/Book 74] to show, among others, that this problem is undecidable for the class of reversal-bounded counter automata operating in quasi-realtime, which define a subfamily of $\underline{L}$, thus cannot be solved for the larger class. Compare also [Valk/Vidal-Naquet 81].

Using this result it is easy to show undecidability of other problems related to Petri net languages. For instance, the problem as to whether a given language $L \in \underline{L}^{\lambda}$ is already an element of $\underline{L}$ is undecidable as is the problem as to whether a given language $L \in \underline{L}$ can be obtained by a labelled Petri net with fewer places. The proofs are elegant and short and the method is due to S. Greibach, [Greibach 69]. The same methods are there used to show that if we could decide the semilinearity of some language $L \in \underline{L}$, then we would at the same time have a procedure to decide the reachability problem. Unfortunately the solvability of the latter does not seem to imply that one can decide whether the reachability set is semilinear, see [Mayr 84]. Not much is known about the complexity of the known algorithms that decide the reachability and thus still there remains work to do. The only thing we can say right now is that the complexity is incredible high and thus is of no use in program systems, if the question is not restricted further.

Definition

The regularity (context-freeness, resp.) problem for languages from a family $\mathcal{L}$ is:

INSTANCE: A finite specification for a language $L \in \mathcal{L}$.

QUESTION: Is L a regular set? (Is L context-free, resp.?)

We can easily reduce the regularity problem for the classes $\underline{L}$ and $\underline{P}$ to the coemptiness problem by the forementioned proof technique, which is presented by the following proof.

Theorem

The regularity problem is undecidable for the families $\underline{L}$ and $\underline{P}$.

Proof

Let N be some P/T-net and $L:=L(N,M_1,m_2) \subseteq X^*$. Now, from N one constructs N' such that $L':=L(N',m_1',m_2')=L\{\$\}X^* \cup X^*\{\$\}D_1$, where $\$ \notin X$, which is easy since $\underline{L}$ is closed with respect to union and product. Suppose we could decide whether L' is regular or not, then we could also decide the coemptiness problem for L as follows: If L' is regular, then $L'=X^*\$X^*$ and $L=X^*$ is necessary since otherwise, i.e., L' regular and $L\neq X^*$, implies that $L'':=L' \cap \{w\$\}X^*$ should be regular but indeed we have $L''=\{w\$\}D_1 \notin$ REG. If L' is not regular, then consequently $L\neq X^*$. The same construction works for the class $\underline{P}$, thus proving the theorem.

On the other hand, the regularity problem becomes decidable for the classes of free Petri net languages $\underline{P}^f$ as shown in [Ginzburg/Yoeli 80] and [Valk/Vidal-Naquet 81]. Recently the problem of context-freeness for the class $\underline{P}^f$ was solved in the affirmative by S. Schwer [Schwer 85] . All these proofs use the construction of the coverability tree and cannot be fast in general as will be shown later.

Theorem

The context-freeness and regularity problems for languages from the class $\underline{P}^f$ are decidable.

However, we will see that not only questions about labelled Petri net languages become undecidable, also problems about reachability sets resist any algorithmic solution. For the formulation of their proofs (at least their sketches) we need a notion of week computability by Petri nets.

There are various possiblities to define how a Petri net computes a function, compare [Bramhoff/Jantzen 83], however, the most useful concept due to M. Rabin, see [Baker 73b] and M. Hack [Hack 74] is that of a weak Petri net computer. Also this concept is versatil enough to allow further results concerning the complexity of other decidable problems. Also it allows to compare Petri net classes by the classes of functions they can define. We choose here a presentation similar to that in [Hack 74] which is easy to understand even though it is a bit larger in its exposition. A more concise notation can be found in [Müller 85 a,b], where H. Müller used vector addition systems with states, i.e., pure P/T-nets with only unbounded places and a finite automaton that controls its behaviour.

Definition

A P/T-net $N_f := (S,T,F,W)$ with r distinguished input places (usually denoted by in_i, $1 \le i \le r$), one extra output place (out), one extra start place (on), one extra stop place (off), and possibly a finite number of internal places ($s_i, i \in \mathbb{N}$) is called a weak Petri net computer for the function $f: \mathbb{N}^r \to \mathbb{N}$ iff there exists for each vector $x \in \mathbb{N}^r$ with components x_1 to x_r a proper initialization $m_x \in \mathbb{N}^S$ such that (1) to (5) holds:

(1) $m_x(on) = 1$ and $m_x(in_i) = x_i$ for $1 \le i \le r$.

(2) $m_x(out) = m_x(off) = m_x(s_i) = 0$ for all internal places s_i .

(3) $\forall m \in (m_x>, m \ne m_x>: m(on) = 0 \wedge 0 \le m(off) \le 1 \wedge m(out) \le f(x_1,\ldots,x_r)$.

(4) $\forall m \in (m_x>: m(off) = 1 \Rightarrow m$ is dead.

(5) $\forall 0 \le k \le f(x_1,\ldots,x_r)\ \exists m \in (m_x>: m(out) = k \wedge m(off) = 1$.

The following figures provide examples of weak Petri net computers for the functions add, mult: $\mathbb{N}^2 \to \mathbb{N}$ defined by $add(x_1,x_2) := x_1 + x_2$ and $mult(x_1,x_2) := x_1 \cdot x_2$.

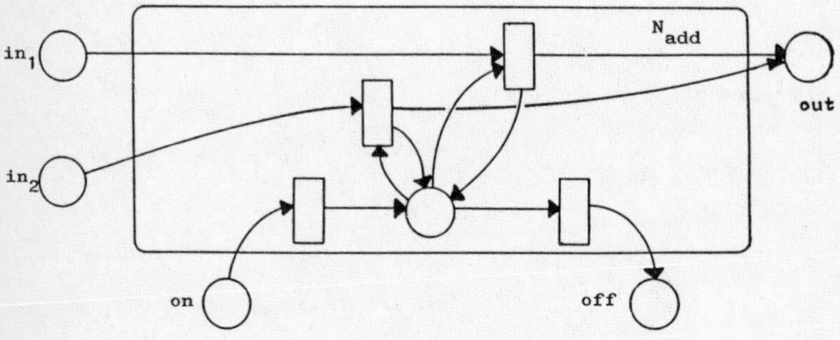

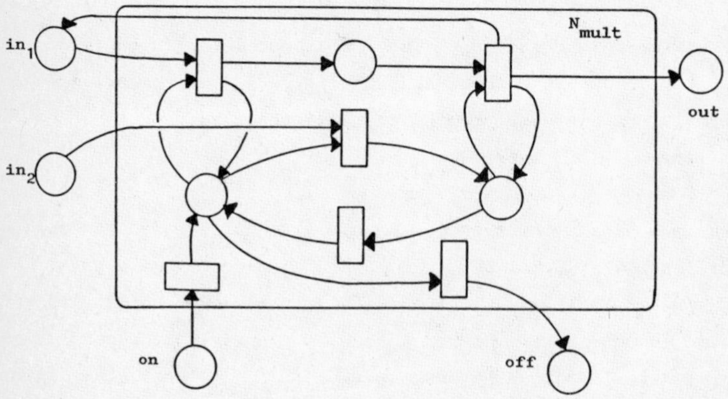

All the functions that are weakly computable by Petri nets have the following monotonicity property: for all inputs $x,y \in \mathbb{N}^r$, $x \leq y$ implies $f(x) \leq f(y)$ which directly follows from the same property of P/T-systems. This excludes a number of simple functions from being weakly computable, such as even:

$\mathbb{N} \longrightarrow \{0,1\}$ defined by even (x):= if x even then 1 else 0 .

On the other hand, as announced by Hack, each function that is weakly computable by some Petri net is primitive recursive, compare [McAloon 84] . Since substitution and identity functions can also be performed by weak Petri net computers, the next result is easy to prove.

Theorem

Polynomials p: $\mathbb{N}^r \longrightarrow \mathbb{N}$ with non-negative integer coefficients are weakly computable by Petri nets. Using the P/T-nets for add, multiplication and substitution, this can be seen from the figure below. The P/T-system shown there weakly computes g correctly even if all the internal places are forced to be bounded by $max(c,x_i)$. Thus it is possible to construct a weak Petri net computer for an arbitrary polynomial p , where each internal place is bounded by $max(x_i,c(p))$, c(p) being the greatest coefficient of p .

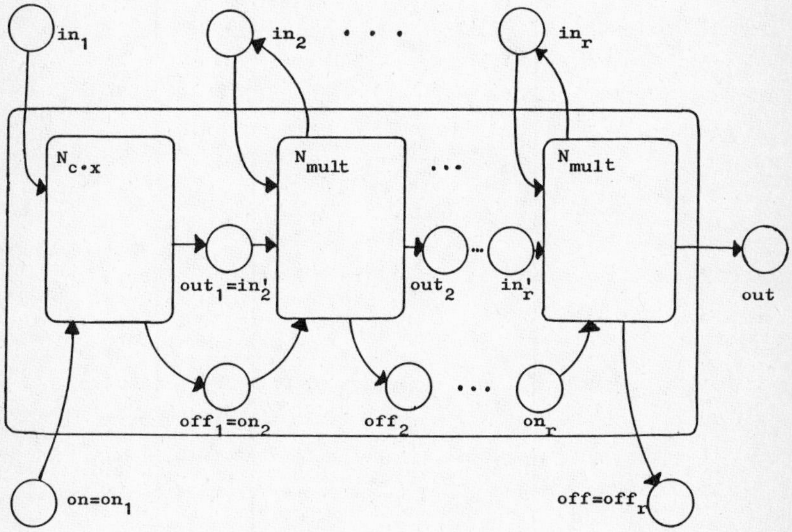

Since weak Petri net computers in addition to the precise result f(x) also obtain any number of tokens less than f(x) the following graph of a diophantine polynomial can be used to reduce the undecidability of Hilbert's tenth problem to the graph inclusion and later to the inclusion problem for Petri net reachability sets.

Definition

Let p be a diophantine polynomial of the graph of p . G(p) is given by $G(P):=\{(x_1,\ldots,x_r,y) \mid o\leq y\leq p(x_1,\ldots,x_r)\}$.

The first reduction uses the fact that any diophantine polynomial p has a solution in $\mathbb{Z}$ iff one of the 2^r polynomials obtained from p by replacing some variables by their negative has a solution in $\mathbb{N}$. Since p(x) has a solution iff $p^2(x)$ has a solution we can restrict attention to polynomials whose range is in $\mathbb{N}$. Now, to any polynomial $p:\mathbb{N}^r \longrightarrow \mathbb{N}$ with integer coefficients we assign two polynomials Q_1,Q_2 with coefficients in $\mathbb{N}$ by a mere separation of positive and negative . Then $p=Q_1-Q_2$ has a solution if $Q_1(x)=Q_2(x)$ for some $x\in\mathbb{N}^r$. Looking carefully at the graphs $G(Q_1)$ and $G(Q_2)$ with integral points, [Hack 76] , one verifies that the polynomial p has no solution iff $G(Q_2+1)\subset G(Q_1)$.

From this one imeediately sees that the subspace inclusion problem for Petri net reachability sets will be undecidable. By adding places in order to level their number and with suitable modifications as described in detail in [Hack 76] the following problems are shown to be undecidable.

Definition

The <u>subspace inclusion</u> (<u>equality</u>, resp.) <u>problem</u> for Petri nets is the following:
INSTANCE: Two P/T-systems $N_1=(S_1,T_1,F_1,W_1,m_1)$, $N_2=(S_2,T_2,F_2,W_2.m_2)$, a number $r\leq\min(|S_1|,|S_2|)$, two projections $q_1:\mathbb{N}^{S_1}\longrightarrow\mathbb{N}^r$, $q_2:\mathbb{N}^{S_2}\longrightarrow\mathbb{N}$ ($|S_1|=|S_2|$ for the equality problem).
QUESTION: $q_1((m_1>) \subseteq q_2((m_2>)$? ($(m_1> = (m_2>$?, resp.)

Theorem

The equality problem as well as the subspace inclusion problem both are undecidable.

However, if we use certain nice subclasses of Petri nets this problem will become decidable. For instance if we look for bounded nets, the reachability set of which is always finite, then the equality problem is definitely decidable. But what is the complexity in terms of the P/T-nets that define these finite sets?

EXTREMELY HIGH COMPLEXITY OF DECIDABLE PROBLEMS

In order to get a grasp on this problem we again look at the computational power of weak Petri net computers.

Definition

Let $A(n):\mathbb{N}\longrightarrow\mathbb{N}$ be recursively defined through $A_n(m)$ by $A_o(m):=2m+1$, $A_{n+1}(0):=1$, $A_{n+1}(m+1):=A_n(A_{n+1}(m)$ and finally $A(n):=A_n(2)$.

The function A(n) majorizes the primitive recursive functions and we will see that it is indeed possible to weakly compute each A_n by some small Petri net, almost proportional in size to n . An exact computation of the relation between n and the size of the net computing A_n seems unnecessary when dealing with this high complexity. The weak Petri net computer for the strictly increasing function $A_o(m)$ is simple and depicted in the figure below:

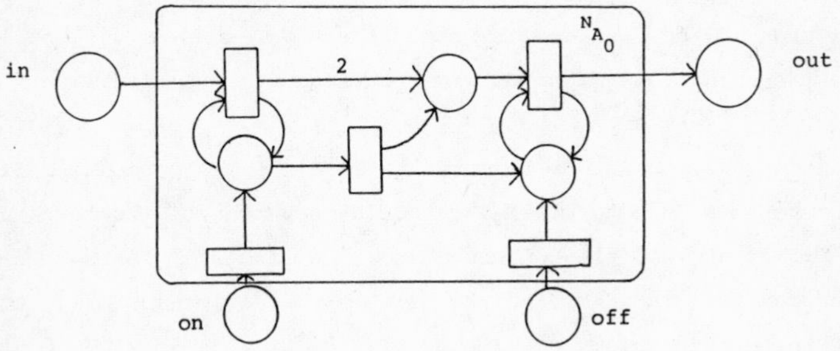

In order to use this Petri net computer iteratively many times the following general construction is used and works correct if the Petri net computer N_f for the strictly increasing function f has the iteration property, which means that not too much tokens are left inside the Petri net computer when restarting it by transferring the token from the 'off' place back to the 'on' place and putting the output tokens back onto the input place. The construction for iterating the weak Petri net computer with iteration property for a strictly increasing function f is given by the net N_g below:

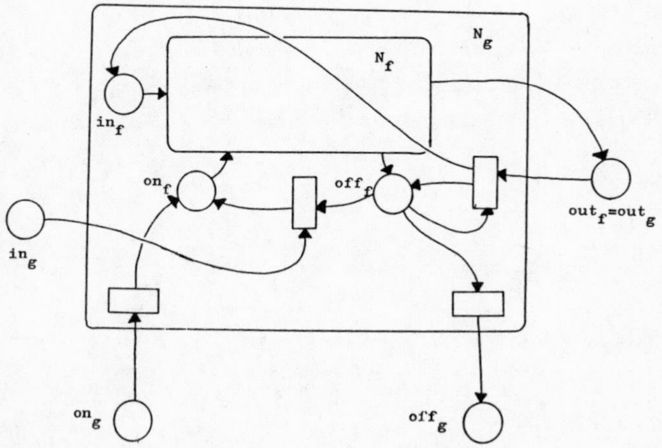

N_g is a weak Petri net computer that has the iteration property and weakly computes the strictly increasing function g defined by $g(n+1):=f(g(n))$ and $g(0):=f(0)$. If we choose $f\equiv A_0$, then $g(m+1)=A_0(A_1(m))$ and applying this construction n-times, then one obtains a weak Petri net computer for each $n\in\mathbb{N}$ computing the function $A_n:\mathbb{N}\longrightarrow\mathbb{N}$, the size of which is growing slowly with n and its reachability set [m> is finite and very large for any proper initialization.

As a consequence we see that the space and time complexity of the coverability graph construction is not primitive recursive as a function of the size of the P/T-system, since it constructs the whole reachability set, if it is finite. Compare the discussion in [McAloon 84].

Theorem

The construction of the coverability graph for a P/T-system N is not primitive recursive in the size of N , but is primitive recursive if $k=|S|$ is fixed.

Since this result was obtained by looking at small P/T-systems with finite but large reachability sets it is not surprising that a reduction of the containment problem for finite reachability sets to the bounded version of Hilbert's tenth problem for which no algorithm can work in primitive recursive space yields a similar statement for the finite containment problem, see [Mayr/Meyer 81].

Theorem

The complexity of any decision procedure for the equality or inclusion problem of finite reachability sets exceeds any primitive recursive function infinitely often.

This problem retains this incredible complexity even if the information that the nets are bounded is given for free.

From [McAloon 84] we know that the inclusion problem for finite reachability sets of k-place P/T-systems for k fixed is primitive recursive, but this still does clearly not mean that this problem then becomes tractable.

But even knowing that we can decide the boundedness of any P/T-system without using the coverability graph construction which we know has this astronomic complexity will not help much. The best algorithms we know to decide boundedness all work in exponential space.

Definition

The boundedness problem for P/T-systems (for P/T-nets, resp.) is

INSTANCE: A P/T-system N=(S,T,F,W,m) (P/T-net (S,T,F,W), resp.)

QUESTION: Is [m> finite? (Is [m> finite for all $m\in\mathbb{N}^S$, resp.?)

Theorem

The boundedness problem for P/T-systems N can be decided in space

$2^{d\cdot size(N)\log(size(N))}$ but not within space $2^{c\cdot\sqrt{size(N)}}$ for suitable constants c and d.

The upper bound was given in [Rackoff 78], while the lower bound is from [Lipton 76]. A detailed analysis of the boundedness problem was given in [Rosier/Yen 85].

Knowing all these horrible bounds for general algorithms it is really not surprising that the reachability problem has a provable lower bound which is low compared with the non-primitive recursive coverability graph construction.

Definition

The reachability problem for P/T-nets is:

INSTANCE: A P/T-net (S,T,F,W) and two markings $m,m' \in \mathbb{N}^S$.

QUESTION: Does $m' \in [m\rangle$ hold?

The result from [Cardoza/Lipton/Meyer 76] shows that reachability is at best decidable within exponential space. Can we do much better if we restrict ourselves to nice subclasses of P/T-systems?

Definition

A P/T-system N=(S,T,F,W,m) is reversible if $m' \in [m\rangle$ implies $m \in [m'\rangle$ for all $m,m' \in \mathbb{N}^S$.

Theorem

The reachability problem for reversible Petri nets is complete in exponential space, i.e. it can be decided within exponential space and each problem which is decidable within this space bound can be reduced to it using only logarithmic space.

Reversible P/T-systems have reachability sets which are semi-linear subsets of $\mathbb{N}^S$ and correspond to presentations of commutative semigroups as studied recently also by D.T. Huynh.

It is also decidable whether a given P/T-system is reversible or not, [Araki/Kasami 77], but its complexity is that of constructing the coverability graph which is used there. It is not clear whether this is needed.

Since the complexity of the inclusion problem for reversible nets is decidable because they have effectively computable semilinear reachability sets one is lead to ask this and similar questions for classes of P/T-nets with the same property, such as P/T-systems with at most two unbounded places. Those systems can be written as vector addition systems with states (VASS) and are studied in great detail in [Howell/Huynh/Rosier/Yen 86]. Stepping down the ladder of complexity classes we must still look for results on lower space bounds which are always worse than the time bounds for the same class of functions. The following list of results is from [Jones/Landweber/Lien 77] which is still an important work in this area.

Theorem

The following problems are complete for polynomial space:

(a) To decide for a given P/T-net and a fixed $k \in \mathbb{N}$ whether each place of the net is bounded by k .

(b) To decide the reachability problem for a given P/T-net which is known to be k-bounded for a given $k \in \mathbb{N}$.

(c) To decide the reachability problem for a given P/T-net, where the number of input places of each transition equals the number of its output places.

Now that we are already shocked by these complexity bounds that forbid any general algorithmic procedure, for instance built in a programming system without restricting the input, we might be pleased to find some NP-complete problem because of the procedures solving them run well in practice.

DECIDABLE PROBLEMS THAT ARE NP-COMPLETE

Let us return to the question of boundedness of a P/T-net for all its possible initial markings which we did not answer until now. We give a proof in detail in order to show how a typical reduction of one problem to another is carried out, and since this answer cannot be looked up in [Garey/Johnson 79] or the Ongoing Guide.

A P/T-net $N=(S,T,F,W)$ is (intrinsically) bounded iff there is no solution $x \in \mathbb{N}^T$ for the inequality $C \cdot x \gneq \underline{0}$. This is seen as follows: any such solution corresponds to a string $w \in T^*$ with $\psi(w)=x$, and $m'=m+\Delta(w)$ shows that a marking m large enough to enable w gives raise to an infinite transition sequence that produces increasing markings. The converse is also true. We know that the following problem is NP-complete, but this is not exactly what we are looking for:

INSTANCE: An integral matrix $A \in \mathbb{Z}^{n \times m}$

QUESTION: Does there exist a vector $x \in \mathbb{Z}^m$ such that $A \cdot x \geqq \underline{0}$?

The NP-completeness of this problem is well known, see [Garey/Johnson 79]. Less known might be that the question as to whether $A \cdot x=b$ for $b \subseteq \mathbb{Z}^m$ has an integral solution x is solvable in deterministic polynomial time. This is described in [Kannan/Bachem 79], and [Chou/Collins 82], improving the former. Consequently, the question whether the inequality $Ax > \underline{0}$ admits an integral solution must be NP-complete, too.

Thus we can try to reduce the boundedness problem for P/T-nets to the following problem in polynomial time or logarithmic space.

INSTANCE: An integral matrix $A \in \mathbb{Z}^{n \times m}$

QUESTION: Is there a solution $x \in \mathbb{Z}^m$ for $Ax > \underline{0}$?

To do so, we define a new integral matrix $B \in \mathbb{Z}^{n \times 2m}$ by

$$B(i,j) := \begin{cases} A(i,j) \ , \text{ if } 1 \leqq j \leqq m \ . \\ -A(i,j) \ , \text{ if } m < j \leqq 2m \ . \end{cases}$$

Now, if $x \in \mathbb{Z}^m$ is a solution for $Ax > \underline{0}$, then $y \in \mathbb{Z}^{2m}$ defined by

$$y(i) := \begin{cases} x(i) \text{ , if } x(i) \geq 0 \text{ .} \\ -x(i-m) \text{ , if } x(i) \leq 0 \text{ .} \\ 0 \text{ in all other cases.} \end{cases}$$

is a solution for $By > \underline{0}$ with non-negative entries, $y \in \mathbb{N}^{2m}$. On the other hand, any solution $y \in \mathbb{N}^{2m}$ for $By>0$ transforms into an integral solution for $Ax > \underline{0}$, namely by $x(i) := y(i) - y(i+m)$.

Notice that the vector $\underline{1}$ with $y(i)=1$ for all i gives the trivial equality $B \cdot \underline{1} = \underline{0}$ and is not allowed as a valid solution.

To show that this boundedness problem is solvable nondeterministically in polynomial time consider the matrix $B' := \begin{pmatrix} A \\ E \end{pmatrix}$, where E is the m×m unit-matrix. Then $B' \cdot y > \underline{0}$ has a solution in $\mathbb{Z}^m$ iff $y \in \mathbb{N}^m$ and $A \cdot y > \underline{0}$ so that the former problem is in NP .

We have thus shown that both problems are reducible to each other and therefore the following is proved. The problems listed below frequently occur when dealing with algebraic methods in connection with Petri nets and thus are worth to be collected in one theorem.

<u>Theorem</u>

Given an integral matrix $A \in \mathbb{Z}^{n \times m}$ and a vector $b \in \mathbb{Z}^m$, the following problems are NP-complete:

(a) $\exists\, x \in \mathbb{Z}^m : Ax \geq \underline{0}$?   (b) $\exists\, x \in \mathbb{Z}^m : Ax > \underline{0}$

(c) $\exists\, x \in \mathbb{Z}^m : Ax \geq b$?   (d) $\exists\, x \in \mathbb{Z}^m : Ax > b$

(e) $\exists\, x \in \mathbb{N}^m : Ax = b$?

(f) $\exists\, x \in \mathbb{N}^m : Ax > \underline{0}$?

For a proof of (a) to (e) see [Garey/Johnson 79] and [Hopcroft/Ullman 79]. The proof of (f) was just explained before. It is known that the problem whether $Ax = \underline{0}$ has an integral solution $x \in \mathbb{N}^m$ can be solved in polynomial time but we have no really practicable algorithm to use. Compare the results of Kachiyan as used in [Kannan/Bachem 79], [Kannan 85], and [Chou/Collins 82] or [Garey/Johnson 79, p. 299].

This question is important when invariants for P/T-systems are searched. The maximal support solution, where support( ) $:= \{i \mid 1 \leq i \leq m,\ x \in \mathbb{N}^m - \{\underline{0}\} : Ax = \underline{0} \text{ and } x(i) > 0\}$ can be obtained in P as shown recently by J.L. Lambert, [Lambert 86a].

The non-liveness problem for free-choice nets was shown to be NP-complete by N.D. Jones et al. by reducing it to the satisfiability problem.

Having seen that the reachability problem is NP-complete for restricted P/T-systems where the number of tokens in the markings is never changed, too, one may ask for simpler classes of nets having a reachability problem which is easier to solve.

Consider the following problem:

INSTANCE: A P/T-system $N=(S,T,F,W,m)$ where $\forall t \in T : |{}^\bullet t| = 1$.

QUESTION: Is $m' \in [m\rangle$?

This problem, the uniform word problem for commutative context-free grammars has been shown also to be NP-complete by D.T. Huynh, [Huynh 83].

If we consider the boundedness problem for P/T-systems that are known to be conflict-free then this can be solved quite fast as shown recently in [Howell/Rosier 86].

Theorem

The boundedness problem for conflict-free P/T-systems is complete for P and in particular for such a system N can be solved deterministically in time of order $(\text{size}(N))^2$.

The references give many more examples of problems related to Petri nets that all show that one cannot expect to construct programs or algorithms that automatically solve these problems in more than one or only simple cases. The question which subclasses of P/T-systems are simple with respect to the complexity of the algorithms used and still are useful in practice is still an important one.

REFERENCES to Language Theory of Petri Nets and Complexity of Place Transition Nets.

[Araki/Kasami 77]
Araki, T./Kasami, T., Decidable properties on the strong connectivity of Petri net reachability sets, Theoret. Comput. Sci., 4 (1977) 99-119.

[Baker 72]
Baker, H., Petri nets and languages, C.S.G. Memo 68, Project MAC, M.I.T., (1972).

[Baker 73a]
Baker, H.G., Equivalence problems in Petri nets, S.M. Thesis, Dept. Electr. Engin., MIT (1973).

[Baker 73b]
Baker, H., Rabin's proof of the undecidability of the reachability set inclusion problem of vector addition systems, Comput. Struct. Group Memo 79, Proj. MAC, MIT (1973).

[Baker/Book 74]
Baker, B. S./Book, R. V., Reversal-bounded multipushdown machines, J. Comput. Syst. Sci., 8 (1974) 315-332.

[Berstel 79]
Berstel, J., Transductions and Context-Free Language, Teubner (1979).

[Best/Fernandez 86]
Best, E./Fernandez, C., Notations and terminology on Petri net theory, Arbeitspapiere der GMD 195, Gesellschaft für Mathematik u. Datenverarbeitung (1986), also this volume.

[Borosh/Flahive/Treybig 86]
Borosh, I./Flahive, M./Treybig, B., Small solutions of linear diophantine equations, Discrete Math., 58 (1986), 215-220.

[Bramhoff/Jantzen 83]
Bramhoff, H./Jantzen, M., Durch Petrinetze definierte Klassen zahlentheoretischer Funktionen, Techn. Rept. IFI-HH-B 98/83, FB-Informatik, Univ. Hamburg (1983), preliminary version: Jantzen, M., Notions of computability by Petri nets, Informatik Fachberichte 66, Springer (1983), 149-165.

[Brams 83]
Brams, G.W., Réseaux de Petri: Théorie et Pratique, Tome 1: Théorie et Analyse, Masson (1983).

[Burkhard 81 a]
Burkhard, H.-D., Ordered firing in Petri nets, EIK, 17 (1981) 71-86.

[Burkhard 81 b]
Burkhard, H.-D., Two pumping lemmata for Petri nets, EIK, 17 (1981) 349-362.

[Cardoza/Lipton/Meyer 76]
Cardoza, E./Lipton, R./Meyer, A., Exponential space complete problems for Petri nets and commutative semigroups, Proc. 8th ACM Sympos. Theory of Comput. Conf., (1976), 50-54.

[Chou/Collins 82]
Chou, T.-W.J./Collins, G.E., Algorithms for the solution of systems of linear diophantine equations, SIAM J. Comput., 11 (1982), 687-708.

[Clote 86]
Clote, P., On the finite containment problem for Petri nets, Theoret. Comput. Sci., 43 (1986) 99-105.

[Crespi-Reghizzi/Mandrioli 77]
Crespi-Reghizzi, S./Mandrioli, D., Petri nets and Szilard languages, Inform. and Control, 33 (1977) 177-192.

[Etzion/Yoeli 81]
Etzion, T./Yoeli, M., The hierarchie of labelled super-nets, Techn. Rept. # 226, Dept. of Comput. Sci., Technion, Haifa, (1981).

[Etzion/Yoeli 83]
Etzion, T./Yoeli, M., Super nets and their hierarchie, Theoret. Comput. Sci., 23 (1983) 243-272.

[Garey/Johnson 79]
Garey, M.R./Johnson, P.S., Computers and Intractability - A Guide to the Theory of NP-Completeness, Freeman, San Francisco (1979).

[Ginsburg 75]
Ginsburg, S., Algebraic and Automata-Theoretic Properties of Formal Languages, North-Holland (1975).

[Ginzburg/Yoeli 80]
Ginzburg, A./Yoeli, M., Vector addition systems and regular languages, J. Comput. Syst. Sci., 20 (1980), 277-284.

[Grabowski 79a]
Grabowski, J., On Hack's conjecture concerning reachability in Petri nets, EIK, 15 (1979) 339-354.

[Grabowski 79b]
Grabowski, J., On partial languages, Preprint No 40/79, Sekt. Mathematik, Humboldt-Univ. Berlin, (1979), and Fundamenta Informatikae 4, (1981) 427-498.

[Grabowski 79c]
Grabowski, I., The unsolvability of some Petri net language problems, Info. Processing Lett., 9 (1979), 60-63.

[Grabowski 80]
Grabowski, J., Lineare Methoden in der Theorie der Vektoradditionssysteme, I, II, III, Seminarberichte 24, 26, 28, Sekt. Math., Humbold-Univ., Berlin (1980)

[Greibach 69]
Greibach, S.A., An infinite hierarchie of context-free languages, J. Assoc. Comput. Mach., 16 (1969) 91-106.

[Greibach 78]
Greibach, S. A., Remarks on blind and partially blind one-way multicounter machines, Theoret. Comput. Sci., 7 (1978) 311-324.

[Hack 74]
Hack, M., Decision problems for Petri nets and vector addition systems, C.S.G. Neno 95-1, Proj. MAC, MIT (1974).

[Hack 75]
Hack, M., Petri net languages, C.S.G. Memo 124, Project MAC, MIT (1975).

[Hack,76], The equality problem for vector addition systems is undecidable, Theoret. Comput. Sci., 2 (1976), 77-95.

[Harrison 78]
Harrison, M.A., Introduction to Formal Language Theory, Addison-Wesley (1978).

[Hopcroft/Ullman 79]
Hopcroft, J. E./Ullman, J. D., Introduction to Automata Theory, Languages, and Computation, Addison-Wesley (1979).

[Hopcroft/Pansiot 79]
Hopcroft, J.-E./Pansiot, J. J., On the reachability problem for 5-dimensional vector addition systems, Tech. Rept. 76-280, Dept. of Comput. Sci., Cornell Univ.Ithaka, New York (1976), and Theoret. Comput. Sci., 8 (1979) 135-159.

[Howell/Rosier/Yen 86]
Howell, R.R./Rosier, L.E./Yen, H.-C., An $O(n^{1,5})$ Algorithm to decide boundedness for conflict-free vector replacement systems, Internal Rept., Dept. of Comput. Sci., Univ. Texas at Austin, Texas, (1986).

[Howell/Huynh/Rosier/Yen 86]
Howell, R.R./Huynh, D.T./Rosier, L.E./Yen, H.-C., Some complexity bounds for problems concerning finite and 2-dimensional vector addition systems with states, Techn. Rept. TR-86-08, Univ. Texas at Austin, Texas (1986).

[Huynh 83]
Huynh, D.T., Commutative grammars: the complexity of the uniform word problems, Information and Control, 57 (1983), 21-39.

[Huynh, 85a]
Huynh, D.T., Complexity of the word problem for commutative semigroups of fixed dimension, Acta Informatica, 22 (1985), 421-432.

[Huynh 85b]
Huynh, D.T., The complexity of the equivalence problem for commutative semigroups and symmetric vector addition systems, Proc. 17th ACM Symp. on Theory of Comput., (1985), 405-412.

[Jantzen 79a]
Jantzen, M., On the hierarchy of Petri net languages, R.A.I.R.O., Informatique thêorique, 13 (1979) 19-30.

[Jantzen 79b]
Jantzen, M., Eigenschaften von Petrinetzsprachen, Ph.D. Dissertation and Techn. Rept. IFI-HH-B-64/79, FB-Informatik, Iniv. Hamburg (1979).

[Jantzen 79c]
Jantzen, M., On zerotesting-bounded multicounter machines, Lecture Notes in Comput. Sci., 67 (1979) 158-169.

[Jantzen/Valk 79]
Jantzen, M./Valk, R., Formal properties of place transition nets, Proc. Advanced Course on GNT of Processes and Systems, Hamburg (1979), also: Lecture Notes in Comput. Sci. 84, Springer (1980) 165-212.

[Jantzen 81]
Jantzen, M., The power of synchronizing operations on strings, Theoret. Comput. Sci., 14 (1981) 127-154.

[Jantzen 86]
Jantzen, M., Complexity of Place/Transition nets, this volume.

[Jones/Landweber/Lien 77]
Jones, N.D./Landweber, L.H./Lien, Y.E., Complexity of some problems in Petri nets, Theoret. Comput. Sci., 4 (1977), 277-299.

[Kannan/Bachem 79]
Kannan, R./Bachem, A., Polynomial algorithms for computing the Smith and Hermite normal forms of an integer matrix, SIAM J. Comput., 8 (1979), 499-507.

[Kannan 85]
Kannan, R., Solving systems of linear equations over polynomials, Theoret. Comput. Sci., 39 (1985), 69-88.

[Keller 72]
Keller, R. M., Vector replacement systems: a formalism for modelling asynchronous systems, Techn. Rept. 117, Comput. Sci. Lab., Princeton Univ. (1972), revised (1974).

[Kosaraju 82]
Kosaraju, S.R., Decidability of reachability in vector addition systems, Proc. 14th ACM Symp. on Theory of Computing, (1982), 267-281.

[Lambert 86a]
Lambert, J.L., On finding a partial solution to a linear system of equation in positive integers, Techn. Rept. no. 263, L.R.I. Univ. Paris-Sud, Orsay (1986).

[Lambert 86b]
Lambert, J.L., Consequences of the decidability of the reachability Problem for Petri nets, Techn. Rept. no 313, L.R.I. Univ. Paris-Sud, Orsay (1986).

[Landweber/Robertson 78]
Landweber, L.H./Robertson, E. L., Properties of conflict free and Persistent Petri nets, J. Assoc. Comput. Mach., 25 (1978) 352-364.

[Lipton 76]
Lipton, R.J., The reachability problem requires exponential space, Research Rept. No. 62, Dept. Comput. Sci., Yale Univ. (1976)

[Mayr 80]
Mayr, E. W., Ein Algorithmus für das allgemeine Entscheidbarkeitsproblem bei Petrinetzen und damit zusammenhängende Probleme, Dissertation, Tech. Rept. TUM-I 8010, TU München (1980).

[Mayr 81]
Mayr, E., Persistence of vector replacement systems is decidable, Acta Informatica, 15 (1981) 309-318.

[Mayr 84]
Mayr, E. W., An algorithm for the general Petri net reachability problem, Siam J. Comput., 13 (1984) 441-460

[Mayr/Meyer 81]
Mayr, E.W./Meyer, A.R., The complexity of the finite containment problem for Petri nets, J. Assoc. Comput. Mach., 28 (1981), 561-576.

[Mayr/Meyer 82]
Mayr, E./Meyer, A., The complexity of the word problem for commutative semigroups and polynomial ideals, Adv. in Math., 46 (1982), 305-329.

[Mazurkiewicz 77]
Mazurkiewicz, A., Concurrent program schemes and their interpretation Techn. Rept., DAIMI PB 78, Univ. Aarhus (1977).

[McAloon, 84]
McAloon, K., Petri nets and large finite sets, Theoret. Comput. Sci., 32 (1984) 173-183.

[Müller 85a]
Müller, H., The reachability problem for VAS, in: Advances in Petri Nets 1984, Lecture Notes in Comput. Sci. 188, Springer (1985).

[Müller 85b]
Müller, H., Weak Petri net computers for Ackerman-functions, EIK, 21 (1985) 236-245.

[Parigot/Pelz 85]
Parigot, P./Pelz E., A logical approach of Petri net languages, Theort. Comput. Sci., 39 (1985) 155-169.

[Pelz 86]
Pelz, E., Closure properties of deterministic Petri nets, Techn. Rept. 297, L.R.I. Univ. Paris-Sud, Orsay (1986) and Proc. 4th Symp. on Theoretical Aspects of Comput. Sci., Passau (1987), to appear.

[Peterson 74]
Peterson, J., Modeling of parallel systems, Tech. Rept. STAN-CS-74-410, Comput. Sci. Dept., Stanford Univ. (1974).

[Peterson 76]
Peterson, J., Computation sequence sets, J. Comput. Syst. Sci., 13 (1976) 1-24.

[Peterson 81]
Peterson, J. L., Petri Net Theory and the Modeling of Systems, Prentice-Hall, (1981).

[Reisig 85]
Reisig, W., Petri Nets, An Introduction, EATCS Monograph on Teoret. Comput. Sci., Brauer, Rozenberg, Salomaa (Eds), Springer-Verlag (1985).

[Reisig 86]
Reisig, W., Place transition systems, this volume

[Rackoff 78]
Rackoff, C., The covering and boundedness problems for vector addition systems, Theoret. Comput. Sci., 6 (1978), 223-231.

[Rosier/Yen 85]
Rosier, L.E./Yen, H.-C., A multiparameter analysis of the boundedness problem for vector addition systems, Proc. F.C.T. '85, Lecture Notes in Comput. Sci. 199, Springer (1985) 361-370 and J. Comput. Syst. Sci., 32 (1986) 105-135.

[Rozenberg/Verraedt 83]
Rozenberg, G./Verraedt, R., Subset languages of Petri nets Part I: The relationship to string languages and normal forms, Theoret. Comput. Sci., 26 (1983) 301-326;
Part II: Closure properties, Theoret. Comput. Sci., 27 (1983) 85-108.

[Schwer 85]
Schwer, S.R., Décidabilité de l'algébricité de langages associes aux reseaux de Petri, These 3ème Cycle, Univ. Paris VII (1985).

[Schwer 86]
Schwer, S.R., On the rationality of Petri net languages, Info. Processing Letters, 22 (1986) 145-146.

[Starke 78]
Starke, P. H., Free Petri net languages, Proc. 7th Symp. MFCS 78, Winkowski (Ed.), Lecture Notes in Comput. Sci., 64 Springer (1978) 506-515.

[Starke 79]
Starke, P.H., On the languages of bounded Petri nets, Proc. 8th Symp. MFCS 79, Becvar (Ed.), Lecture Notes in Comput. Sci. 74, Springer (1979), 425-442.

[Starke 80]
Starke, P.H., Petri-Netze, VEB Deutscher Verlag der Wissenschaften, Berlin (1980).

[Starke 81]
Starke, P.H., Processes in Petri nets, EIK 17 (1981) 389-416.

[Valk 78]
Valk, R., Self-Modifying nets, a natural extension of Petri nets, Lecture Notes in Comput. Sci. 62, Springer (1978).

[Valk/Vidal-Naquet 77]
Valk, R./Vidal-Naquet, G., On the rationality of Petri net languages, in Proc. Theoret. Comput. Sci., Lecture Notes in Comput. Sci. 48, Springer (1977), 319-328.

[Valk/Vidal-Naquet 81]
Valk, R./Vidal-Naquet, G., Petri nets and regular languages, J. Comput. Syst. Sci., 23 (1981), 199-325.

[Valk 86]
Valk, R., Infinite behaviour and fairness, this volume

[Vidal-Naquet 81]
Vidal-Naquet, G., Rationalité et déterminisme dans les réseaux de Petri, Thêse d'Etat, Univ. Pierre et Marie Cuvie, Paris (1981)

[Yoeli/Ginzburg 78]
Yoeli, M./Ginzburg, A., Petri net languages and their applications, Research. Rept. CS-78-45, Dept. of Computer Science, University of Waterloo, (1978).

SECTION 5

OTHER PETRI NET MODELS

G. Roucairol: *FIFO – Nets*

A. Pagnoni: *Stochastic Nets and Performance Evaluation*

FIFO - NETS

Gérard Roucairol
Bull S.A.
68, route de Versailles, 78430 Louveciennes, France

ABSTRACT : This paper presents a survey of applications and theoretical properties of FIFO-nets, i.e. Place-Transition nets in which places behave as FIFO-queues rather than counters. In the first part, the adequacy of FIFO-nets for solving generic synchronization problems is shown and their impact on the fairness property of a concurrent system is discussed. The second part is devoted to the study of the computational power of this model as well as the characterization of some sub-classes for which some classical properties become decidable (liveness, boundedness). Finally, the notion of T-invariant for FIFO-nets is introduced.

Keywords : FIFO-nets, computational power, fairness, liveness, boundedness, invariants, process synchronization, parallelization of programs, serializability, resource allocation.

CONTENTS OF THE PAPER

INTRODUCTION

FIFO-nets are place-transition (Petri) nets in which places behave as FIFO-queues rather than counters. The main paradigm which illustrates the use of FIFO-nets consists of modelling the following specification of behaviour of a concurrent system : whenever an event precedes another one, then some action must take place before another action. Such a requirement which, as a matter of fact, concerns conflict resolution between concurrent transition firings, is very frequently encountered in many realistic systems. In chapter 2 of this paper several examples are discussed and the impact of the use of FIFO-nets on the fairness property of a system is pointed out. These examples include the control of maximal parallelism extracted from sequential programs, the optimal control of the serialization property among transactions accessing a common data base as well as resource allocation problems.

The FIFO principle extends the computational power of place-transition nets to that of a Turing machine, even if the number of different types of items which can occur in a queue (the queue alphabet) is restricted to 2. This increase of descriptive and computational power implies of course a lack of general algorithmic methods to check some properties of a net like boundedness or liveness. However two sub-classes of FIFO-nets are exhibited for which these properties are decidable.

The first sub-class generalizes the notion of free-choice in such a way the usual structural conditions for liveness of free-choice nets are still valuable. The second sub-class implies some regularity (rational) constraints over the possible configurations of the queues. These contraints allow the use of the classical procedure for checking boundedness. Of course these FIFO-nets increase the computational power of ordinary place-transition nets.

1. BASIC DEFINITIONS AND NOTATIONS

Before introducing the notion of FIFO-net, we define some notations we shall use along this paper.

Definition 1.1

Let X be an alphabet ; X^* denotes the free monoid generated by X ; e is the empty word ; X^ω is the set of infinite words over X. Let u be in $X^* \setminus \{e\}$, u^ω is the infinite word obtained by catenating u infinitely often with itself.

Let x belonging to $X^* \cup X^\omega$.

Y being a non empty subset of X :

- $proj_Y(x)$ is the erasing homomorphism which suppresses from x the symbols not in Y
- u being an item of X^*, $u \leqslant x$ means u is a prefix of x.

Definition 1.2 (FIFO-net)

A FIFO-net N = (P, T, B, F, Q) is defined by :

a finite set P of places, also called queues,

a finite set T of transitions, disjoint from P,

a finite queue alphabet Q and two mappings $F : P \times T \to Q^*$

$B : P \times T \to Q^*$

called respectively forward and backward incidence mappings.

Up to now, the only difference with a place-transition net relies on the fact that the incidence mappings take value in Q^* instead of $\mathbb{N}$. The main change appears in the definition of a transition firing.

Definition 1.3

A marking M is a mapping $M : P \to Q^*$

A transition t is fireable in M, written M (t>, iff for every place p $B(p,t) \leqslant M(p)$.

For a marking M, we define the firing of a transition t, written M (t> M', iff M(t> and for every place p the following equation between words holds :

$$B(p,t)\, M'(p) = M(p)\, F(p,t)$$

In other words the firing of a transition t removes B(p,t) from the head of M(p) and appends F (p,t) to the end of the resulting word.

Definition 1.4

A FIFO-net N together with an initial marking M_o is also called a FIFO-net and is denoted (N, M_o).

As usual the firing of a transition can be extended to the firing of a sequence of transitions and we note FS (N, M_o) the set of firing sequences of this net. The firing of a sequence u of transitions from a marking M to a marking M' is written M (u> M'.

The set of markings reachable from M_o will be denoted by $Acc(N, M_o)$.

The graphic representation of a FIFO-net follows the one of a regular P/T-net, except for the marking of the places and the labels of the edges which become words over the queue alphabet Q.

Example 1.1

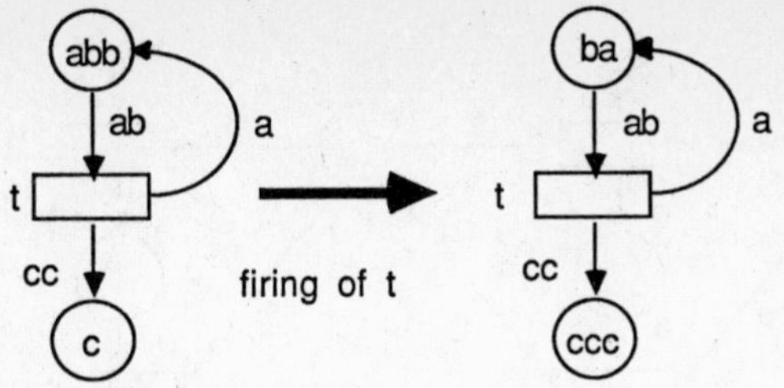

t is fireable

2. APPLICATIONS OF FIFO-NETS

Three applications are successively described.
We start with a very classical problem allowing the reader to be more familiar with the use of FIFO-nets and which points out the interest of these nets in order to obtain a fair solution to synchronization problems.
(In ROUCAIROL [15], several classical synchronization problems are solved using a programming view of FIFO-nets).

2.1. The critical-section problem

Let us consider two processes P_a and P_b mutually exclusive for the access to their own, so-called critical section.

Using ordinary Petri-nets, the classical solution is :

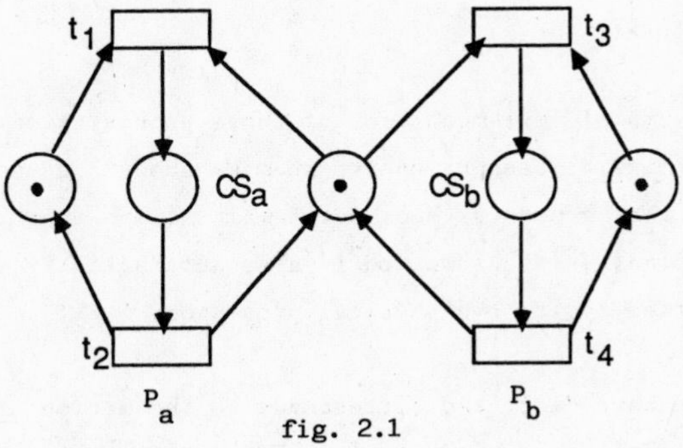

fig. 2.1

Using a FIFO-net a possible solution is :

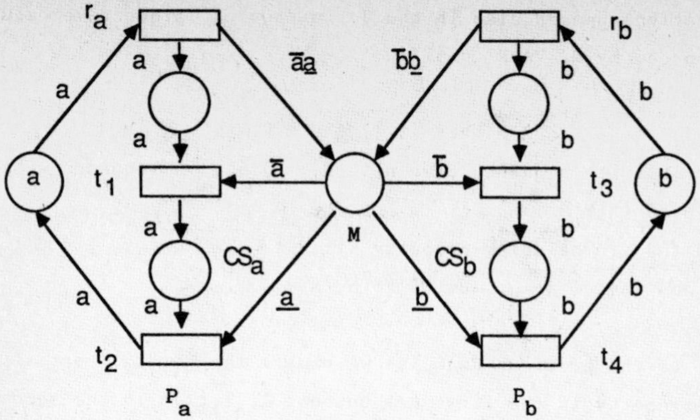

fig. 2.2

In that solution, firing transition r_a (resp. r_b) can be interpreted as the deposit of a request to enter critical section CS_a (resp. CS_b).

It is remarkable to see that just looking at the current marking at the place M, all information can be given about the state of the system of processes, i.e. the current marking of the remaining places.

Let us compare these two solutions from the point of view of their infinite behaviours.

In the net of figure 2.1 $x = (t_1t_2)^\omega$ is a possible infinite firing sequence. We can remark that along this sequence t_3 becomes alternatively fireable and <u>not fireable</u>. It is intrinsic to the solution.

Let us consider now the sequence $y = (r_at_1t_2)^\omega$ of the net in figure 2.2. Along this sequence r_b remains always fireable and there is no reason a priori for not firing it.

If we think in terms of implementation of these processes on a single processor machine, the <u>minimal</u> assumption we can make about a scheduler of these two processes is that a process does not remain always in a ready state without being executed. This assumption is also automatically satisfied if each process is supported by its own physical processor.

The assumption we have described corresponds to the notion of <u>finite delay property</u> in [11]. This is a kind of minimal property to impose to infinite sequences in order to represent realistic infinite concurrent behaviours.

A similar notion appears also in the definition of "productive occurrence rule" introduced by R. VALK in [17].

Definition 2.1 (KARP and MILLER [11])
Let x be an infinite sequence of a net (N, M_o) i.e. a sequence whose every prefix is in FS (N,M_o) :
x satisfies the finite delay property iff $\forall\, t \in T,\ \forall\, u \leqslant x,\ \exists\, v \in T^*$ s.t $uv \leqslant x$ and ($uvt \leqslant x$ or $uvt \notin FS(N, M_o)$).

Coming back to the previous examples we remark that $(t_1t_2)^\omega$ satisfies the finite delay property in the first net but not $(r_at_1t_2)^\omega$ in the second. We can also verify that every infinite sequence of the second net which satisfies the finite delay property contains an infinite number of transitions of both P_a and P_b. This means that this net represents a fair solution of the critical section problem with respect to the two processes and corresponds to the intuitive role a FIFO-queue can play in conflict arbitration.

As a matter of fact, the first net models a Dijkstra's semaphore. But nothing is represented in that net about the management of the process queue of the semaphore, so there is no reason a priori for this solution to be fair.

Finally let us remark that fairness in the second solution can be proved using the fact that the corresponding net is persistent i.e. every choice between transition firings is reversible.

Definition 2.2.
A net (N, M_o) is persistent iff $\forall\ M \in Acc\ (N, M_o)$
$\forall\, t, t' \in T \quad M\,(t\rangle$ and $M\,(t'\rangle$ implies $M\,(tt'\rangle$ (and $M\,(t't\rangle$).

Generally, Petri nets are not persistent (except for marked graphs). Using FIFO-nets conflicts can be modelled with persistent nets (or sub-nets). In many cases that property implies that a live net is also fair with respect to every transition. It is still an open problem to characterize these cases.

2.2. Parallelization of flowchart programs

In [12] R. KELLER has pointed out the use of a notion of queue-automaton in order to control the maximal concurrency extracted from sequential flowchart programs. This notion of queue-automaton can be very elegantly expressed in terms of FIFO-nets. We describe the parallelization procedure by an example.

Let us consider the following program which computes the quotient of the integer division of A by B.

Q: = 0 (a) ;
<u>while</u> A ⩾ B (p) <u>do</u> Q: = Q + 1 (b) ; A: = A - B (c) <u>od</u> ;
<u>write</u> (Q) (d)

(we shall use the letters between brackets in order to refer to the operations in the program).

This program is modelled by a sequential schema which expresses on one hand the sequential control flow of operations and which retains on the other hand from the operations themselves a conflicting use of shared variables.

The sequential control flow is described by a finite automaton :

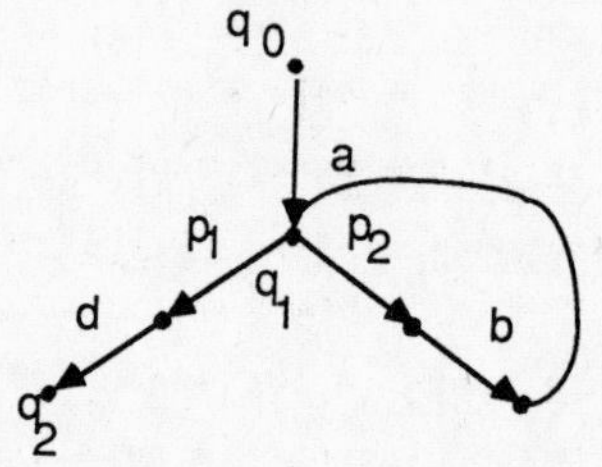

(P_1 and P_2 represent the two alternatives of the test operation p).

To this control flow is associated a <u>symetric "conflict" relation R</u> deduced from the fact that two operations have in common either an output variable or a variable which is both an input variable for one operation and an output variable for the other operation.

For the previous example R is the symmetric closure of the relation

$\bar{R} = \{(a, b), (a, d), (p, c), (b, d)\}$

The parallelization procedure now proceeds in three steps in order to allow concurrent execution of non conflicting operations while retaining from the sequential schema the basic control issued from test operations.

<u>Step 1</u> (control flow of test operations)
The sequential control flow is reduced to the control flow of test-operation only ; this leads to obtain a kind of state-machine representing the reduced control flow.

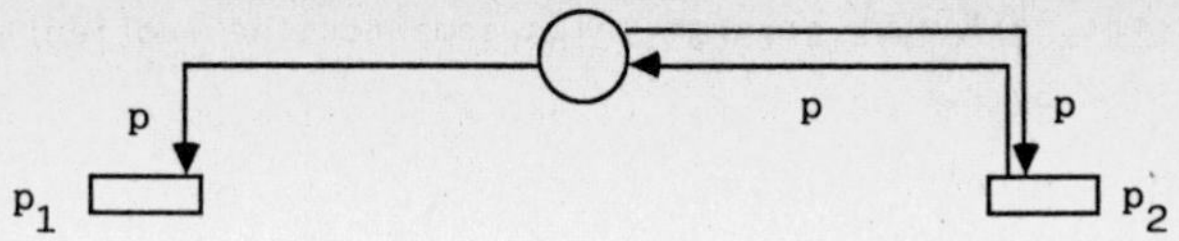

Step 2 (conflict arbitration)

To each remaining operation in the schema is associated a corresponding transition. These transitions as well as test operations have input places defined as follows :

. for every pair (a, b) in $\overline{R}$, P_{ab} is an input place of only both transitions a and b such that

$B\ (P_{ab},\ a) = \text{'a'}$ and $B\ (P_{ab},\ b) = \text{'b'}$

if b is a test-operation with two alternatives b_1 and b_2 then we have $B\ (P_{ab},\ b_1) = B\ (P_{ab},\ b_2) = \text{'b'}$ and $B\ (P_{ab},\ a) = \text{'a'}$

. if an operation c does not appear in any pair of $\overline{R}$, then the corresponding transition has an unique input place P_{cc}, s.t $B(P_{cc},\ c) = \text{'c'}$.

From the previous example, we obtain :

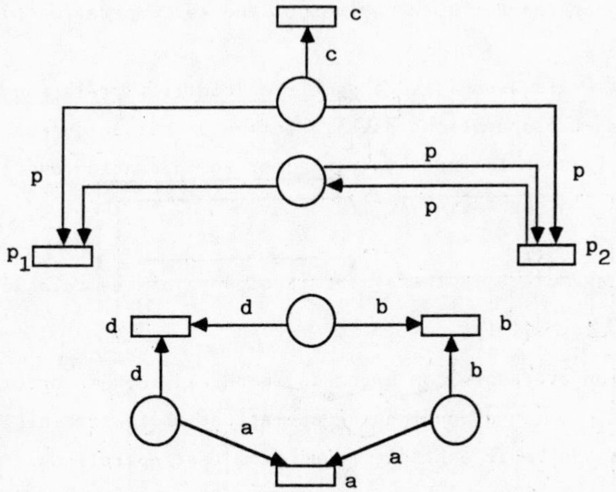

fig. 2.3

<u>**Step 3**</u> (control induced by test operations)
In this step it is explained how the places are filled by the transitions as well as the construction of the initial marking.

Let us consider the sequential control flow of operations. This control flow is a composition of three linear sequences of operations called segments :

s_o = ap, s_1 = bcp, s_2 = d

s_o is called the initial segment, and we can remark that the execution of operations in s_1 (resp. s_2) is governed by p_1 (resp. p_2).

It will be the responsability of the transitions corresponding to the alternatives of a test-operation, to fill the input places of the other transitions.

Let P_{ab} be a place, p_i be an alternative of a test-operation and s_i the segment governed by p_i, then we have :

$$F(P_{ab}, p_i) = \underset{\{a,\,b\}}{\text{proj}}(s_i)$$

The initial marking of P_{ab} being $\underset{\{a,\,b\}}{\text{proj}}(s_o)$

We obtain finally from the previous example the following concurrent schema :

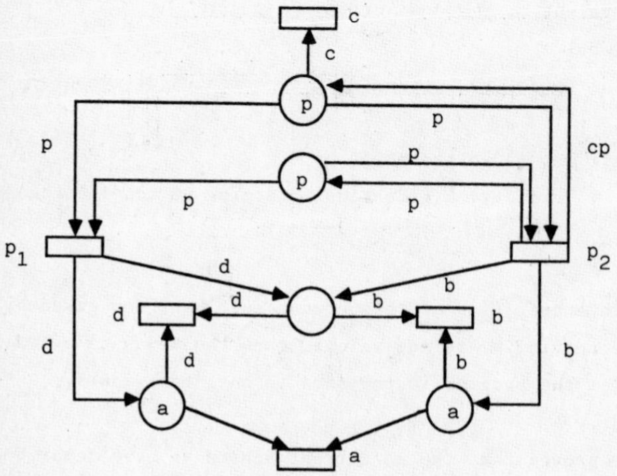

fig.2.4.

Remark that for this example the number of reachable markings is infinite, even though the number of states of the initial schema was finite : the sequence of operations pc can take an unbounded advance over the operation b.

Let us examine now the equivalence which exists between the initial schema and the one we have built. Due to the construction, the equivalence is such that for one behaviour of one schema there exists a behaviour of the other schema such that the relative ordering of conflicting operations is the same in both behaviours.

Let us state this more formally :

- a behaviour of the sequential schema is either a finite word accepted by terminal state (q_2 in the example) or an infinite word whose every prefix is accepted by the control flow automaton ;

- a behaviour of the concurrent schema is either a complete firing sequence (i.e. it cannot be extended into another firing sequence) or an infinite firing sequence (i.e. a sequence whose every prefix is a firing sequence) satisfying the finite delay property (definition 2.1).

Then the equivalence between behaviours we consider is :

<u>Definition 2.3</u>

Let x and y be two behaviours.

x is said equivalent to y and we write $x \equiv y$ iff

- for every symbol a :

  $\text{proj}_{\{a\}}(x) = \text{proj}_{\{a\}}(y)$ (identical occurrences of symbols)

- for every pair (a, b) in the relation R :

  $\text{proj}_{\{a,b\}}(x) = \text{proj}_{\{a,b\}}(y)$ (identical ordering of conflicting symbols)

A semantical interpretation of this equivalence has been given by KELLER [12] : if two behaviours are equivalent, then the sequence of values taken by each variable of the program is the same in both behaviours.

It can also be proved that the concurrent schema we have described is <u>maximally concurrent</u> in the following sense : any word equivalent to a behaviour of the sequential schema is a behaviour of the concurrent schema.

Moreover, as a corollary of a result of KELLER, it can be shown that no place-transition net or even no counting automaton can control the amount of concurrency we have exhibited especially when there are imbedded loops in the sequential schema.

Finally, let us indicate to the interested reader that ROUCAIROL in [16] has considered parallelization of flowcharts under a weaker definition of equivalence for which a slight extension of the notion of FIFO-queue is necessary.

2.3. Serializability of iterated transactions

The serializability problem is a synchronization problem which has been mainly studied in the framework of concurrent accesses to a Data Base [2]. Being given a so-called consistency predicate over the content of a Data Base and a set of transactions - i.e a finite sequence of operations - each one preserving individually the consistency predicate, the serializability problem consists in synchronizing the transactions in order to allow concurrent behaviours which are equivalent to some serial composition of the transactions. Hence, these behaviours preserve also the consistency predicate and are called correct behaviours.

Let us remark that this problem represents an instance of a fundamental phenomenon in the control of concurrent systems which turns to be the achievement of the global correctness of a system of concurrent processes being supposed the individual correctness of each of its component.

In [8], [9], [10] FLE and ROUCAIROL have characterized, in terms of language theory, a generalized version of the serializability problem for transactions which can be infinitely often repeated on more generally for iterative programs as might behave for instance preexisting service processes in an operating system. Their results show that serializability can be controlled by a finite automaton and that resource allocation problems can be modelled as a serializability problem. However, infinite behaviours allowed by this automaton are not necessarily fair i.e. not every transaction or process is repeated infinitely often.

In [7], FLE and ROUCAIROL have pointed out a synchronization algorithm valuable for iterated transactions which guaranties fairness of infinite behaviours. This algorithm is based upon the use of FIFO-nets.

We are going to describe this algorithm with an example.

Let us consider the two following transactions, each one preserving individually the predicate "A = B".

T_1: A: = A * 2 (a) ; B: = B * 2 (b) (T_1 = ab)

T_2: A: = A + 10 (c) ; B: = B + 10 (d) (T_2 = cd)

The iterated behaviour of each transaction is modelled by the following net :

(The numbers 1 and 2 represent the characters '1' and '2' and not the corresponding values).

Let us call a behaviour x of the previous transaction system, an infinite firing sequence such that for $i \in [1, 2]$ $\text{proj}_{A_i}(x) \in T_i^* \cup \{T_i^{\omega}\}$ (any occurrence of transaction in x is completed in x) where A_i is the alphabet of the operations occurring in the transaction T_i. If we consider a prefix y of a behaviour such that each occurrence of transaction is completed in that prefix, the sequence of operations designated in y does not lead necessarily to values in variables A and B such that A = B.

Consider for instance the prefix y = acdb.

As we have already said we are going to consider correct behaviours, i.e. behaviours equivalent to serial behaviours, a serial behaviour being in our case an item of the set $\{T_1, T_2\}^{\omega}$

It is remarkable to observe that the equivalence which is generally used in the literature on serializability is exactly the one we have introduced in the previous section.

For the example we consider the conflict relation is then the symmetric closure of the relation :

$$\overline{R} = \{(a, c), (b, d)\}$$

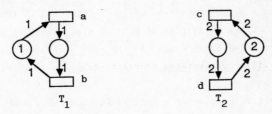

One can verify that the prefix y = acbd of a behaviour is equivalent to the prefix abcd of a serial behaviour ; the operations performed in y lead to a situation where "A = B".

Now we are going to build a control of the two previous nets allowing only correct and fair behaviours. The procedure is somewhat similar to the one of the previous section.

For every pair in the $\overline{R}$ relation we build a place which is an input place of the transitions whose names appear in the pair (the edge leading to a transition being labelled by the index of the transaction to which the transition belongs).

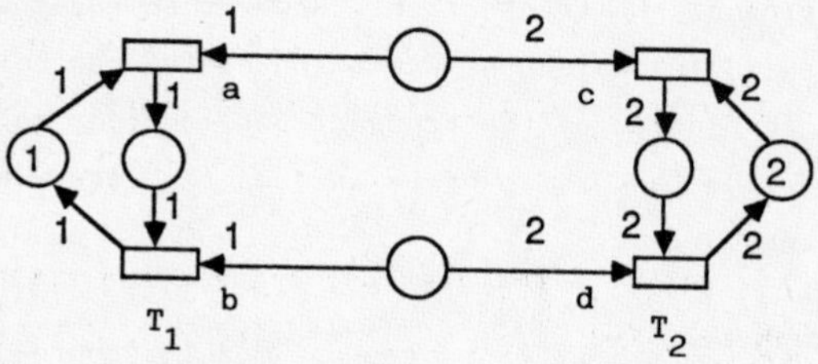

Then to each transaction is attached a <u>controller</u> :

A single loop which appends simultaneously to every place of the transaction, previously created, the index of the transaction.

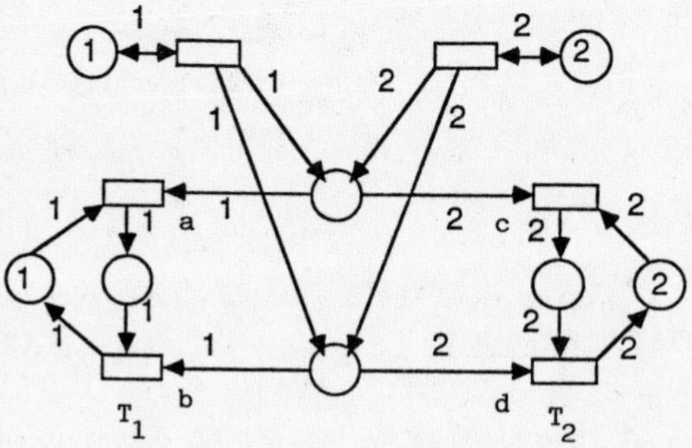

Let us call A the alphabet of the operations performed by the transactions (A = A1 U A2).

The following completeness and soundness results have been shown :

- proj_A (FS(N,Mo)) is exactly the set of prefixes of correct behaviours.
- let us call FDB the set of infinite sequences satisfying the finite delay property.
  - . FS (N, Mo) is exactly the set of prefixes of FDB
  - . For any item x of FDB, for every transaction T_i

    $\text{Proj}_{A_i}(x) = T_i^{\omega}$: fairness

One can remark that the synchronizing places between the two transactions are unbounded. As a matter of fact it has been shown that in order to achieve completeness of the previous construction, the controllers must be independent of the evolution of the transactions. However some particular cases have been identified in [7] for which the evolution of the controller can be synchronized with the evolution of the transactions in order to obtain only bounded places. (Notice that these cases include the case where only two transactions are considered).

We have said that serializability problem can model resource allocation problem. As an exercise the reader is invited to give a fair solution to the very classical "dining philosophers" problem.

The transactions to be considered are :
for each philosopher i :

$(\text{think})_i$; $(\text{takefork}_i)_i$; $(\text{takefork}_{i+1})_i$; $(\text{eat})_i$; $(\text{releasefork}_i)_i$; $(\text{releasefork}_{i+1})_i$

where operation $(\text{takefork}_{i+1})_i$ conflicts with operation $(\text{releasefork}_{i+1})_{i+1}$ and operation $(\text{takefork})_{i})_i$ conflicts with operation $(\text{releasefork}_{i-1})_{i-1}$ (additions and substractions are supposed to be mod n).

3. THEORETICAL PROPERTIES OF FIFO-NETS

In the first section of this chapter we state that FIFO-nets have the computational power of Turing machines. Of course the price to pay to this degree of generality is the undecidability of classical properties for Petri-nets, like liveness or boundeness. However we point out two classes of FIFO-nets for which these properties can be decided. Further work remain to do to charactize other classes of interest from the point of view of decidability results and possibilities of applications. A good candidate seems to be the class of nets obtained by the parallelization procedure we have explained in the previous sections.

The application of the classical invariant technique is faced to the problem of non commutativity of the operations performed on the FIFO-queues. However significant invariant properties can be found by considering the content of a place as a bag of letters instead of a word. See the lecture of MEMMI and VAUTHERIN in this course. Nevertheless, concerning the invariant of transitions (T-invariant) we point out a structural characterization of cyclic firing sequences.

Finally let us notice that a software tool exists in order to analyse the properties of a system of concurrent processes communicating by FIFO places (BEHM [1]).

3.1. Computational power of FIFO-nets

FIFO-nets extend strictly the computational power of Petri nets and reach the computational power of Turing machine. As a matter of fact it is enough that the queue alphabet contains two letters and edges are labelled by at most one letter, to reach the computationnal power of a Turing machine.

Let us call alphabetical, a FIFO-net whose edges are labelled by one letter at most, then we have :

Theorem 3.1

Alphabetical FIFO-nets with a queue alphabet Q, such that $|Q| > 1$, have the computational power of Turing machines.

A constructive proof of this result has been given by MEMMI [13], another proof based upon language theory has been found by FINKEL [6].
These authors have also shown that FIFO-nets can be simulated by alphabetical ones up to an homomorphism.

Definition 3.1

A labelled FIFO-net is a pair (N, Mo, h) such that (N, Mo) is a FIFO-net and and h a labelling function of the transitions h : T ---> X'U {e} where X is a finite alphabet. h is naturally extended to words in order to define the the language of a labelled net :

$$L((N, Mo), h) = \{ h(x) / x \in FS(N, Mo) \}.$$

Theorem 3.2

For every labelled FIFO-net ((N, Mo), h) there exists an alphabetical labelled FIFO-net ((N', M'o), h') where

$Q \subseteq Q'$, $P \subseteq P'$, $T \subseteq T'$

$\forall t \in T \quad h(t) = h'(t)$

$\forall t \notin T \quad h'(t) = e$

and such that L((N, Mo), h) = L ((N' M'o), h')

3.2. Free choice FIFO-nets

The following definition extends the initial definition of free-choice Petri-nets.

Définition 3.2

A FIFO-net is free choice iff for every place p the following holds :

- for every transition t $|B(p, t)| \leqslant 1$ - every output edge of p is labelled by at most one letter.
- $\{a \in Q / \exists t \in T, \mathrm{proj}_{\{a\}}(B(p,t)) \neq e\} = \{a \in Q / \exists t \in T, \mathrm{proj}_{\{a\}}(F(p,t)) \neq e\}$

  the set of letters which can be added to p is the set of letters which can be extracted from p.
- for any pair of transitions sharing p as an input place, p is the only input place.

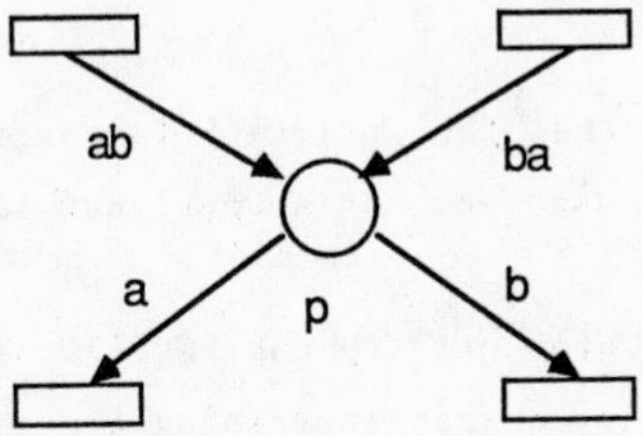

Like free-choice Petri-nets, free-choice FIFO-nets have nice structural properties from the point of view of liveness. As a matter of fact the FIFO principle does not play a role for the liveness property.

Let us call the associated coloured net of a FIFO-net, a net with an identical structure but with the marking of a place considered as a bag of letters instead of a word ; the firing of a transition requiring only the presence of a necessary number of occurrences of letters in a place and not some specific ordered list of these occurrences.

Then we have (FINKEL [6]) :

Theorem 3.3

A free-choice FIFO-net is alive iff its associated coloured net is alive.

It is interesting to remark that the associated coloured net of a free-choice FIFO-net can be unfolded into an ordinary free-choice Petri-net (a place being split into as many places as there are different letters which may enter in the initial place). It can be shown that this new net is also equivalent to the coloured net from the point of view of liveness. FINKEL [6]. Hence the usual Commoner's condition concerning traps and deadlocks can be applied in order to decide about the liveness of a free-choice FIFO-net.

From the reasonning above, we could think that free-choice FIFO-nets have nothing more than the computational power of usual free-choice nets. This is not the case.

Let us call $L(\mathcal{N})$) the language of a class $\mathcal{N}$ of nets - i.e. the set of sets of firing sequences of nets belonging to this class.

FINKEL [6] has shown.

Theorem 3.4

L (free-choice Petri nets) $\not\subseteq$ L (free-choice FIFO-nets) $\not\subseteq$ recursively enumerable sets.

(This is due to the fact that the anti-DYCK language (VAUQUELIN [18]) is a free-choice FIFO-net language and not a Petri-net language).

Another kind of nice features of free-choice FIFO-nets comes from the fact that properties are preserved when increasing the initial marking.

First of all let us define an order relation between words and markings.

Définition 3.3

Let u and v be two words of Q^*. We say that u divides v, u/v, iff there exists a word w of Q^* such that :

$v = w_1 u_1 w_2 \dots w_n u_n w_{n+1}$ with $w = w_1 w_2 \dots w_{n+1}$ and $u = u_1 u_2 \dots u_n$.

Then we say that a marking M divides a marking M', M/M', iff for every place p M(p)/M'(p).

Theorem 3.5

Let (N,M) be a free-choice FIFO net and M' a marking such that : M/M' and the set of letters occurring in M' (p) is the same as the set of letters occurring in M(p) for every place p.

1) (N,M) unbounded --> (N,M') unbounded
2) FS (N,M) infinite --> FS (N,M') infinite
3) (N,M) is alive --> (N,M') is alive

3.3. Monogeneous FIFO-nets

This category of nets has been characterized by FINKEL [4] in order to define a class of FIFO-nets containing at least a class isomorphic to Petri-nets and for which the boundedness problem is decidable using the classical KARP and MILLER procedure [11].

Definition 3.4

A language L $\subseteq$ Q^* is monogeneous if there exist two words u and v of Q^* such that L is included in the set of prefixes of uv^*.
A language L is said semi-monogeneous (shortly s-monogeneous) if it is a finite union of monogeneous languages.
Now we say that a FIFO-net is (s-) monogeneous if for every place the set of sequences of words which can be added to a place whenever firing sequences of transitions is a(s-) monogeneous language. In other words :

Definition 3.5

For each place p we consider the mapping Ip : T --> Q^*, such that Ip(t) = F(p,t). This mapping is naturally extended to words and we say that a FIFO-net is (s-) monogeneous iff for every place p Ip(FS(N,Mo)) is (s-) monogeneous. Ip(FS(N,Mo)) is called the input language of p.

The following net models an example of communication protocol between two processes, given by VUONG and COWAN [19].

The processes exchange messages via the FIFO-queues f12 andf21.

This net is a monogeneous net : If12 (FS(N,Mo)) is the set of prefixes of $(12)^*$.

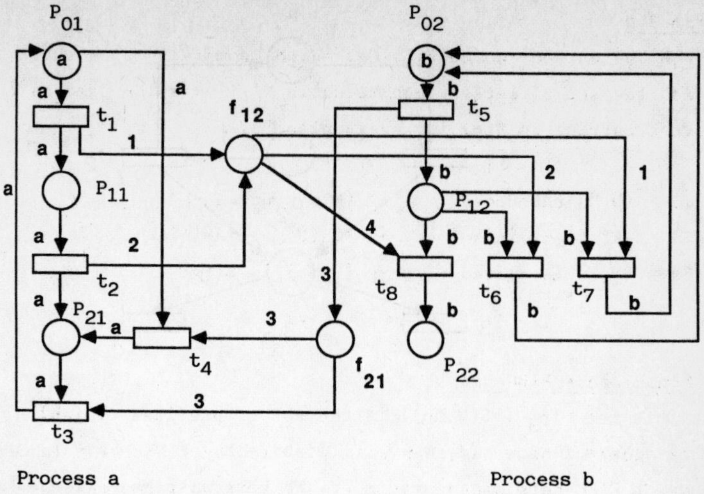

In order to decide if a FIFO-net is bounded, using the KARP and MILLER procedure, a "good" order relation between markings has to be defined.

Definition 3.6

Let N = (P,T,Q,F,B) be a FIFO-net and M, M' be two markings.
We say that M << M' iff for every place p, for every firing sequence x of FS (N,M)

$$M(p).\ Ip(x) \leqslant M'(p).\ Ip(x)$$

For (s-) monogeneous nets this relation can be proved to be an order relation such that every infinite sequence of markings contain a non decreasing infinite subsequence. Moreover we have the classical monotony property :

$$M << M' \dashrightarrow Acc(N,M) \subseteq Acc(N,M')$$

Finally this order relation can be shown to be decidable.

Then we obtain :

Theorem 3.6

The boundedness problem is decidable for (s-) monogeneous FIFO-nets using the KARP and MILLER procedure.

Let us consider the following example :

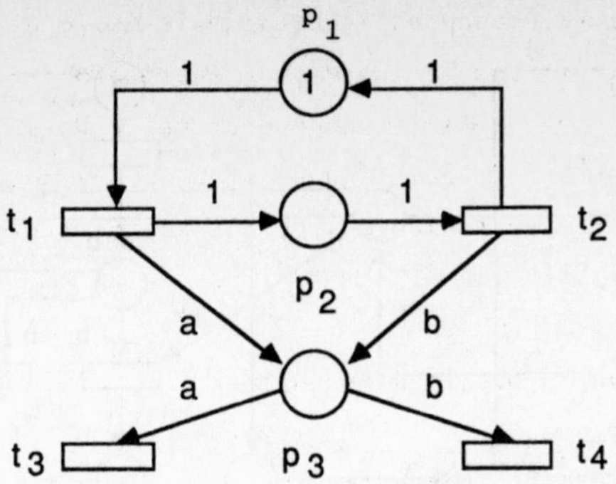

For this net Ip_3 (FS(N,Mo)) is the set of prefixes of $(ab)^*$
We have Mo = (1,e,e) $(t_1\ t_2 >$ (1,e,ab) = M_1
Hence Mo << M_1 and p_3 is unbounded. We have also Mo = (1,e,e)$(t_1 t_3 t_2>$ (1,e,b) = M_2 $(t_1 t_2>$ (1,e,bab) = M_3;
M_2 << M_3

While building the reachability tree for the KARP and MILLER procedure, M_1 will be replaced by M'_1 = $(1,e,(ab)^{\omega})$ and M_3 by M'_3 = $(1,e,b(ab)^{\omega})$. Using this convention, the construction of this reachability tree is finite providing the fact $x^{\omega}.\ u = x^{\omega}$ and $x^{\omega} = xx^{\omega}$ for any finite words x and u.
From the previous example the beginning of the construction of the reachability tree is :

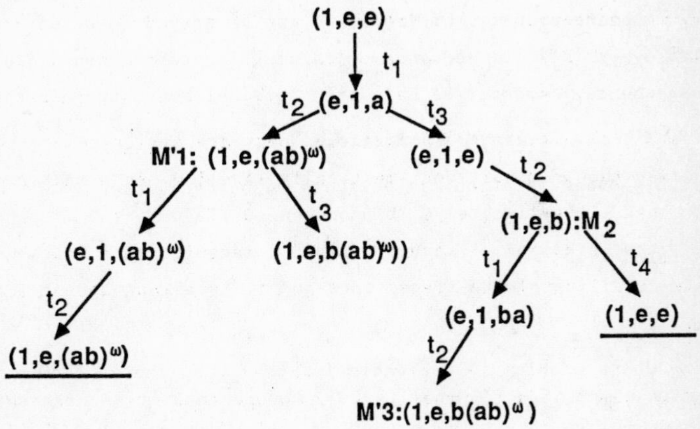

As an exercise the reader is asked to check whether places f12 and f21 in the protocol example are bounded or not.

Like for Petri-nets the boundedness problem is decidable for (s-) monogeneous nets. More generally it can be shown that every problem decidable for Petri-nets is also decidable for (s-) monogeneous nets. This can be proved by pointing out that the set of firing sequences of a (s-) monogeneous set is the intersection of a regular language with the set of firing sequences of a usual Petri-net.

The regular language is obtained as follows :

the reachability tree is converted into a reachability graph by merging into only one node two identical markings on the same branch of the tree ; then we obtain the graph of a finite automaton whose accepted prefix language is designated by RL(N,Mo).

The usual Petri-net is obtained as follows :

the graph of the net is the one of the FIFO-net, but edges are labelled by the number of letters which are added or removed from a place of the original FIFO-net ; the initial marking of a place is just the number of letters existing in the initial marking of the same place of FIFO-net ; let us call $(\overline{N},\overline{Mo})$ such a net.

Then we obtain :

Theorem 3.7

For a (s-) monogeneous net (N,Mo) :

$$FS\ (N,Mo) = FS\ (\overline{N},\overline{Mo}) \cap RL\ (N,Mo)$$

Let us remark also that (s-) monogeneous nets are strictly more powerful than Petri-nets without transitions identically labelled. As a matter of fact it is clear that L (Petri-nets) $\subsetneq$ L (monogeneous FIFO-nets).
But the set of prefixes of $(abba)^*$ is not a language of a Petri-net with an injective labelling of the transitions and it is a language of a monogeneous FIFO-net.

In order to check if a FIFO-net is (s-) monogeneous it is necessary to express the input language of each place. There is no general procedure to do it. But in [6] the reader will find several necessary or sufficient conditions for a net to be (s-) monogeneous.

3.4. About invariant of transitions

Invariants of transitions (T-invariants) characterize cyclic firing sequences i.e. sequences which reproduce their source marking.

In order to characterize such sequences for FIFO-nets we first extend the firing equation of definition 1.3 to sequences of transitions.

Let $s = t_{i_1} \ldots t_{i_m}$ be a sequence of transitions and M,M' be two markings such that M(s>M'.
Then it is easy to show that for every place p the following equation holds :

$$B(p,t_{i_1})\ldots B(p,t_{i_m})\ M'(p) = M(p)\ F(p,t_{i_1})\ldots F(p,t_{i_m}).$$

For cyclic firing sequences we then obtain an equation of the form :

$$xy = yz$$

It is noteworthy to observe that this equation over the free-monoïd Q^* has a solution which is : there exist two words w and w' such that

$$x = ww' \ , \ z = w'w \quad \text{and} \quad y \in w(w'w)^*$$

This solution links together the word which is input in a place and the word which is output from a place as well as the marking of this place in a very particular way. Exploitation of this result remains to be done.

BIBLIOGRAPHY

[1] P. BEHM
"RAFAEL : a tool for analyzing parallel systems in the L environment". 6th European Workshop on applications and Theory of Petri-nets. Espoo 1985 pp227-254.

[2] P.A. BERNSTEIN and N. GOODMAN
"Concurrency Control in Distributed Data Base Systems", Computing Surveys 13 (2) (1981) 185-221.

[3] G.W. BRAMS
"Réseaux de Petri : Théorie et Pratique". Tome 1. Masson. Paris 1982

[4] A. FINKEL
"Control of a Petri net by a finite automaton".
3rd Conf.on Fond. of Soft. Techn. and Theor. Comp. Sci. Bangalore 1983.

[5] A. FINKEL
"Boundedness and liveness for monogeneous FIFO nets and for free choice FIFO nets. Applications to analysis of protocols". Internal report L.R.I. Universite Orsay Paris-Sud 1985.

[6] A. FINKEL
"Contrôle du parallélisme par file". Thèse d'Etat Université Orsay Paris-Sud 1986.

[7] M.P. FLE, G. ROUCAIROL
"Fair Serializability of iterated Transactions using FIFO-nets", Advanced in Petri-nets 84 Lect. Notes Comput. Sci. 188 (1984). 154-168.

[8] M.P. FLE, G. ROUCAIROL
"Multiserialization of iterated Transactions", information Processing Letters 18 (1984) 243-247.

[9] M.P. FLE, G. ROUCAIROL
Maximal Serializability of iterated Transaction", Theoret. Comput. Sci. 38 (1985) 1-16.

[10] M.P. FLE, G. ROUCAIROL
"A language Theoretic Approach to Serialization Problem in Concurrent Systems", Fundamentals of Computation Theory, (1985), lect. Notes Comput. Sci. 199 pp.128-145.

[11] R. M. KARP and R.E. MILLER
"Parallel Program Schemata", J.Comput, System Science. 3 (1969) 147-195.

[12] R.M. KELLER
"Parallel Program Schemata and Maximal Parallelism", J. Asso, Comp, Mach 20 (3)(1973)514-537.

[13] G. MEMMI and A. FINKEL
"An introduction to FIFO-nets ; monogeneous nets : a subclass of FIFO-nets". Theoret, Comp. Sci. 35 - 1985 pp.191-214.

[14] G. MEMMI
"Méthode d'analyse de Réseaux de Petri, Réseaux à Files, et Application aux systèmes temps réel". Univ. Pierre et Marie CURIE, Paris, Thèse de Doctorat d'Etat (1983).

[15] G. ROUCAIROL
"Mots de synchronisation". RAIRO informatique 12 (4) 1978 pp.227-290.

[16] G. ROUCAIROL
"Transformations of sequential programs into parallel programs". Parallel Processing Systems. An advanced course . D.J. EVANS ed. Cambridge University Press 1982. (see also Thèse d'Etat. Paris. 1978).

[17] R. VALK
"Infinite behaviour and fairness". In this course (1986).

[18] B. VAUQUELIN and P. FRANCHI-ZANNETACCI
"Automates a files". Theoret. Compu. Sci. 11-1980 pp.221-225.

[19] T.VUONG and D. COWAN
"Reachability analysis of protocols with FIFO channels". ACM SIGCOMM Symp. on Comm. Archi. and Protocols. Austin 1983.

STOCHASTIC NETS AND PERFORMANCE EVALUATION

ANASTASIA PAGNONI

Dipartimento di Scienze dell'Informazione
Università di Milano, Italy

ABSTRACT This paper is an introduction to the so-called stochastic Petri nets. It contains a critical overview of the most representative stochastic Petri net classes (Stochastic Petri Nets, both in Florin-Natkin and in Molloy form, Generalized Stochastic Petri Nets, Extended Stochastic Petri Nets). Their application to performance evaluation is discussed. A bibliograhy for furthering the subject is given in the appendix.

Key Words: stochastic Petri net, generalized stochastic Petri net, extended stochastic Petri net, immediate transition, timed transition, exponentially distributed firing time, arbitrarily distributed firing time, probabilistic arc, random switch, performance evaluation

CONTENTS

1. Introduction

We wrote this paper as an agile and rather informal guide for people who want to approach the so-called stochastic Petri nets.

The great number of net classes of this sort which have arisen here and there in the last few years meet a twofold requirement of the production world: on the one hand, people have an active interest in using Petri nets for designing and analyzing complex systems; on the other, they do not intend to renounce reasoning about time, probability and related questions.

The underlying idea of every stochastic Petri net model is to represent the concrete system to be analyzed by means of a Petri net - also representing the indeterminancy of the system - and then to apply the methods of stochastic processes theory to the net.

In this paper we present an overview of the stochastic Petri net classes which seem most representative to us (Stochastic Petri Nets, both in Florin-Natkin and in Molloy form, Generalized Stochastic Petri Nets by Ajmone Marsan, Balbo, Conte and Extended Stochastic Petri Nets by Dugan).

We will not give a list of formal definitions, but simply show the construction of these net classes. It will then be easy to relate the various models and to compare their computational power.

Furthermore, we will consider application to performance evaluation , and show the calculus procedures in detail on an example. After some conclusive remarks, as an appendix, we will present a bibliography for those who want to examine the subject in greater depth.

In the sequel we make the supposition that the reader is familiar with basic notions of both Petri net and stochastic processes theory: for them we refer to (Rei82) and (How71), respectively.

2. Construction of some representative stochastic net classes

The stochastic net classes which we want to illustrate here are:

- ° The SPNs (Stochastic Petri Nets) by Florin and Natkin ;
- ° The SPNs (Stochastic Petri Nets) by Molloy ;
- ° The GSPNs (Generalized Stochastic Petri Nets) by Ajmone Marsan, Balbo, Conte ;
- ° The ESPNs (Extended Stochastic Petri Nets) by Dugan .

These are the better known models, as well as those which seem to us best suited for illustrating the different approaches.

These net classes are all defined as from an ordinary place/transition net, and differ, in substance,in the way they alter the firing rule.

The introduced changes are:

(1) Association of a random firing time with the transitions

The time between the instant in which a transition becomes enabled and the instant in which it fires is considered to be a continuous random variable X_t taking real non-negative values, and having associated a distribution function

$$F_t(x) = P\ \{ X_t \leq x \}\ .$$

This is done substantially in three different ways:

(a) To each transition t an exponential distribution function

$$F_t = 1 - e^{-\lambda_t x}$$

is associated, with $\lambda_t > 0$ real parameter and where $x \geq 0$, so that it can be shown (Mol81) that:

° The probability of firing two transitions at the same instant is zero ;

° The reachability graph of the stochastic net is isomorphic to an homogeneous Markov chain , and as such it can be solved .

The exponential ones are the only distribution functions of continuous random variables which satisfy Markov property. So, the fact that an exponential distribution function is associated with every transition is a necessary and sufficient condition for applying the methods of Markov chains theory to the reachability graph of a stochastic net .

(b) The distribution functions associated to the transitions are arbitrary except for :

° All transitions concurrently enabled under some reachable marking, which are exponentially distributed;

° All transitions in conflict at some reachable marking, which are distributed so that if one of them becomes disabled, the probability distribution at a subsequent enabling is independent of the preempted firing time .

In this way, the reachability graph of the stochastic net can be regarded as a semi-Markov process , and as such be solved .

(c) The distribution functions associated to the transitions are completely arbitrary : in this case no general solution method exists and we have to turn to simulation .

(2) Immediate transitions

These are transitions which fire as soon as they are enabled, without any consumption of time. They may be defined explicitly, or implicitly by allowing the parameter λ_t of an exponentially distributed transition t to assume the value $+\infty$.

Graphically, immediate transitions are often represented by a thin bar while timed ones are by a thick one :

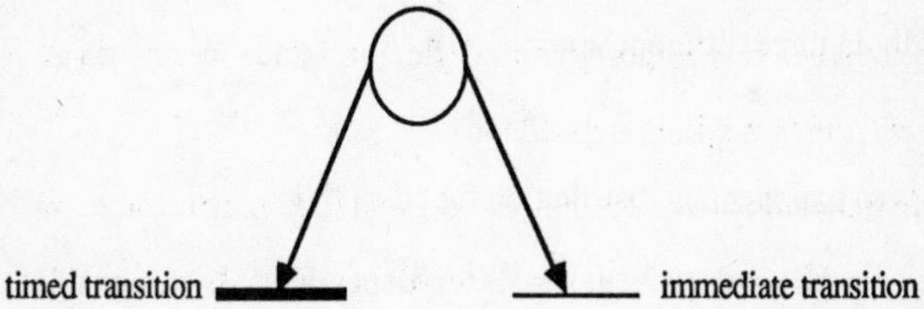

The use of immediate transitions is problematic in case of conflicts .Some authors request, by convention, that:

° Conflicts between immediate transitions are forbidden (Dug81) - because they would be contradictory ;

° Conflicts between an immediate and a timed transition are always solved in favor of the first one (Dug81,ABC84) - be thus no longer conflicts .

(3) Probabilistic Arcs - Random Switches

A probabilistic arc is a two-headed arc going out of a transition in the following way :

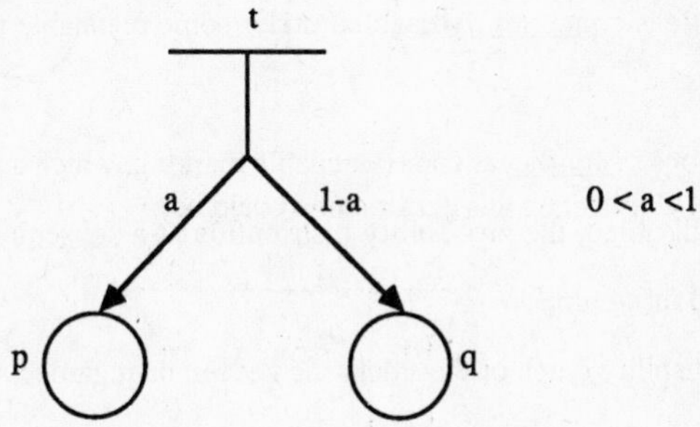

The firing of t produces , with probability a, a token in p and no token in q , or, with probability 1-a , a token in q and no token in p .

A probabilistic arc can be seen as a short form for a conflict between two immediate transitions where a probability is associated to the choice between the two.

A random switch is a probability distribution associated with the choice of the transition to be fired among a set of more immediate transitions in conflict at a certain reachable marking. This distribution is in general marking-dependent.

The characteristic difficulty for the use of random switches is that random switches can be defined only after having detected a conflict at a reachable marking. That is, during the construction of the reachability graph.

When using random switches it is impossible to define an incidence matrix reflecting the net structure, because the net structure is then marking-dependent.

The use of random switches destroys the notion of incidence matrix and, with it, those of S- and T-invariants, even if the random switch is not marking-dependent. E.g., consider the following small net having a marking-independent random switch (the probability of firing each transition is written on the corresponding arc):

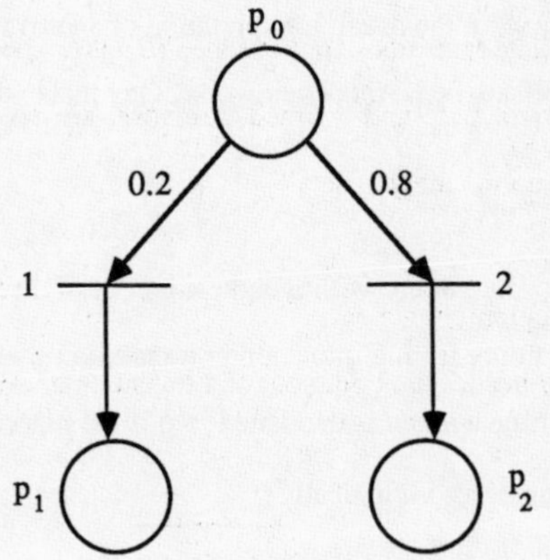

An "incidence matrix" reflecting this net structure could be:

	1	2
p_0	-0.2	-0.8
p_1	1	0
p_2	0	1

and we see immediately that there are no S-invariants, in contrast to the fact that the number of tokens which mark the net is conserved whatever the behaviour of the net.

Of course, the underlying Petri net has, as it is expected, an S-invariant.

Indeed, its incidence matrix is:

	1	2
p_0	-1	-1
p_1	1	0
p_2	0	1

and $[1, 1, 1]^T$ is the S-invariant corresponding to the observed token conservation.

(4) Abnormal Arcs

° Inhibitor Arcs. They are arcs from a place p to a transition t which modify the firing rule of t so: t is enabled only if p is not marked.

The firing of t does not change the marking of p. Graphically :

Such arcs are contradictory w.r.t. the usual interpretation of a Petri net: a pre-condition of an event has not to be satisfied in order to be satisfied. And, even worse, they make the main part of concepts and results of net theory inapplicable.

° Counter-Alternate Arcs. Let an arc with weight k go out of a place p into a transition t_1. A counter-alternate arc is then an arc going from p into another transition t_2, and which changes the firing rule of t_2 so: t_2 may fire once each time a token is deposited in p if the marking of p is $M(p) < k$. The firing of t_2 does not change the marking of p. Graphically :

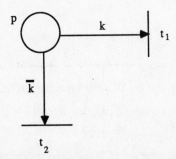

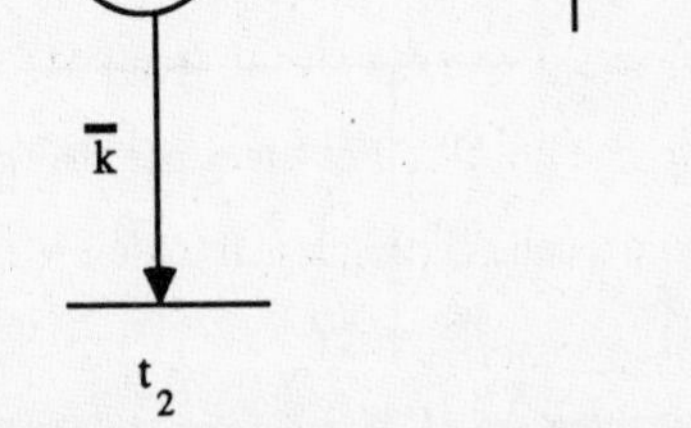

The same remarks regarding inhibitor arcs can be made also for these arcs.

Now we are prepared to show the construction of the four cited stochastic Petri net classes. The following Petri net represents it in an easy way:

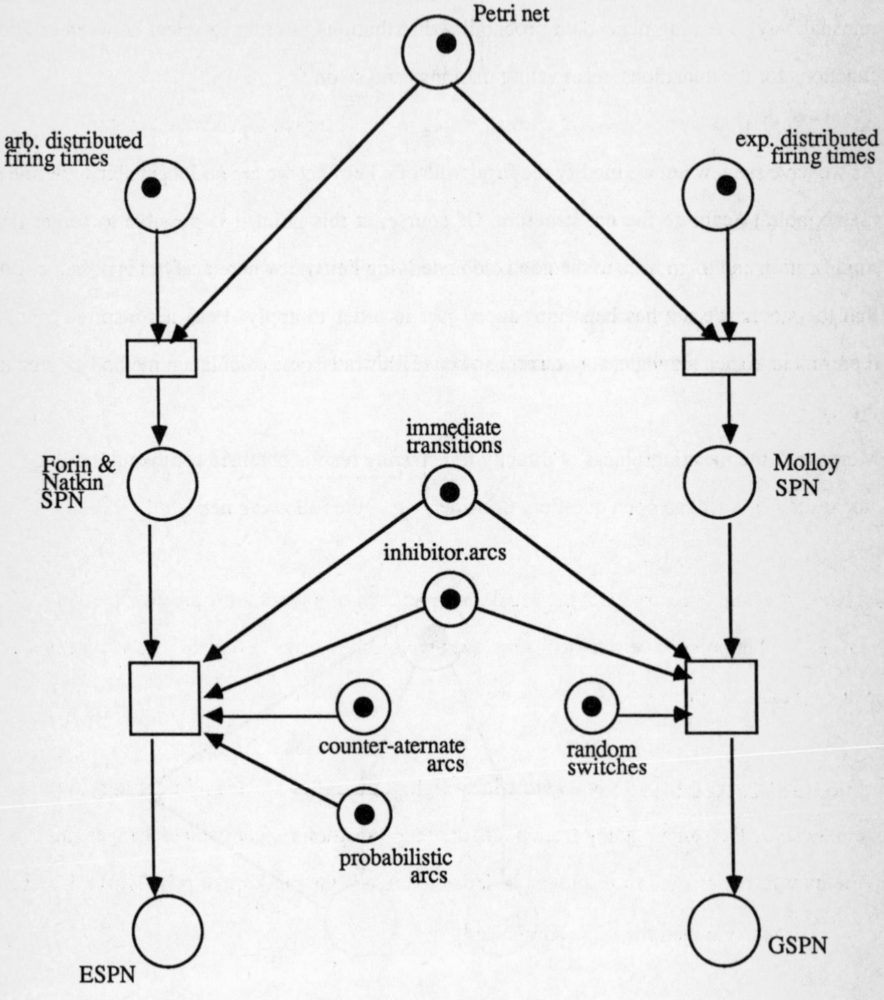

It is obvious that it is possible to give a Markovian (semi-Markovian) version of both the Florin-Natkin SPNs and the ESPNs : to this end it will suffice to restrict the firing time distribution functions adequately. In this way, the Florin-Natkin net class coincides with Molloy's.

Besides these four, there exists a plethora of other net classes, each with its own modifications of the firing rule and its own concepts.

The SANs (Stochastic Activity Networks) by Meyer and Movaghar represent an emblematic example. In addition to arbitrarily distributed firing times and immediate transitions, they have gates, cases (in a very unusual way), marking dependent probability distributions in order to select between cases, reactivation functions for the transitions, reactivating markings and so on.

As we have seen, when we modify the firing rule of a Petri net we are no longer able to define an incidence matrix able to capture the net structure. Of course, at this point it is possible to forget the introduced modification and to go back to the good old underlying Petri net where analysis is possible. But this means that the stochastic net has been introduced just in order to apply Petri net-inspired graphics either to represent, and then simulate, a system, or to better illustrate some calculation method of stochastic process theory .

Moreover, the meaningfulness of directly transferring results obtained for the underlying Petri net to the stochastic net is still an open question. Consider, e.g., the following net:

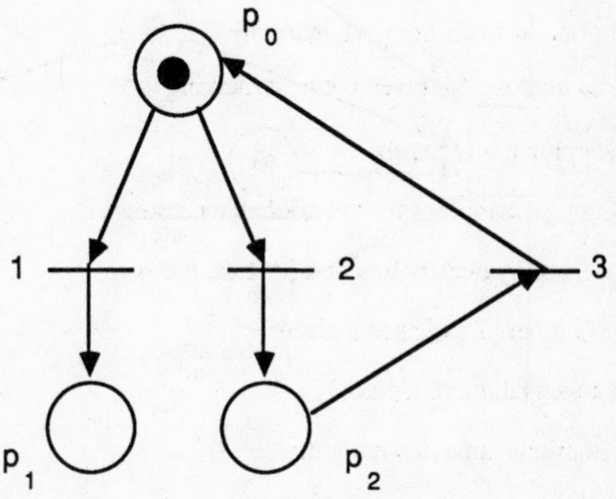

and let a random switch be defined for the transitions 1 and 2 so that at the current marking the probability of firing transition 1 and 2 is, respectively, ε and $1-\varepsilon$, where ε is an arbitrarily small real number s.t. $0< \varepsilon <1$. How meaningful is it to state, sic and simpliciter, that this stochastic net is not live ?

3. Performance evaluation

The application of stochastic Petri nets to performance evaluation can be schematized in the following way :

° The system is represented by means of a stochastic Petri net;

° The reachability graph of the net is constructed;

° The firing time distribution functions associated with the transitions are considered.

There are two possibilities :

*Hypothesis (a) or (b) of the case (1) of the former paragraph holds true.

Then:

° Abnormal arcs and immediate transitions, if there are any, are eliminated by using reachability graph reduction techniques (see, e.g. , in (Dug84)) ;

° The reachability graph is solved, either as a Markov chain or as a semi-Markov process.

We get (Dug84, Mol81) :

If (a) holds, and the net is live and bounded :

° unconditional sojourn time in a marking

° waiting in marking M_i given the next marking is M_j

° next-state probability matrix

° steady state probabilities for the reachable markings

° token probability density function for each place

° average number of tokens in a place

° flow of tokens through a place

° mean recurrence time of a marking

If (b) holds :

° sojourn time in a marking M_i , given that we know the next marking is M_j

° next- state probability martix

° waiting time distribution in marking M_i , given that we know the next marking is M_j

° unconditional sojourn time in a marking

* The hypothesis (c) of case (1) of the former paragraph holds true.

Then the only thing to do is to simulate the net .

Two types of simulation are applied:

- ° Transient simulation: for getting values such as exiting probabilities, time-to-exit distribution ;
- ° Ergodic simulation: for getting long term or average measures, such as average token count or transition utilization.

The whole procedure has been automatized. E.g., package DEEP - Duke University ESPN Evaluation Package (Dug84) - first receives a graphically input ESPN, then classifies it either as Markovian, semi-Markovian or neither, and finally either solves it adequately or simulates it.

References to applications of stochastic Petri nets to performance evaluation can be found in the appendix .

4. An example of calculation

We consider the following self-explanatory Petri net representing a sender-receiver system together with its environment - slightly modified version of an example in (Rei82).

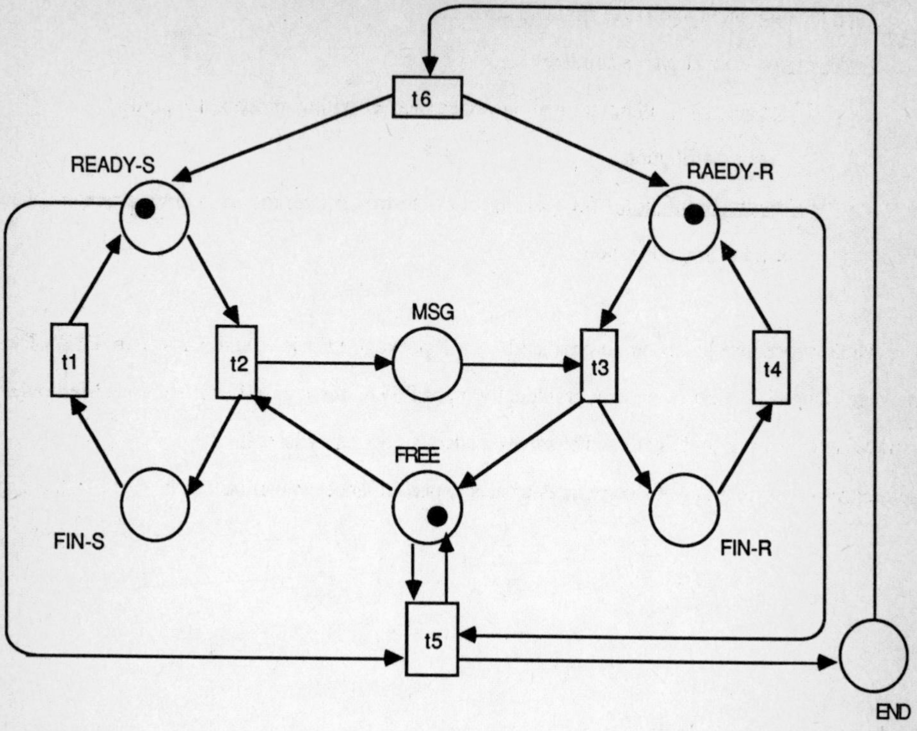

READY-S := sender ready; READY-R := receiver ready; FIN-S := sender finished ; FIN-R := receiver finished; MSG := message in the message channel; FREE := message channel free

We associate an <u>exponential</u> firing time distribution function with each transition. Let the corresponding <u>rates</u> be:

transition	rate (firings/time unit)
t_1	10
t_2, t_3	4
t_4	2
t_5, t_6	1

Let the set of places be ordered so:

(READY-S , FIN-S , FREE , MSG , READY-R , FIN-R , END) .

The <u>reachability graph</u> is (recall that the firing of two transitions at the same instant has probability zero) :

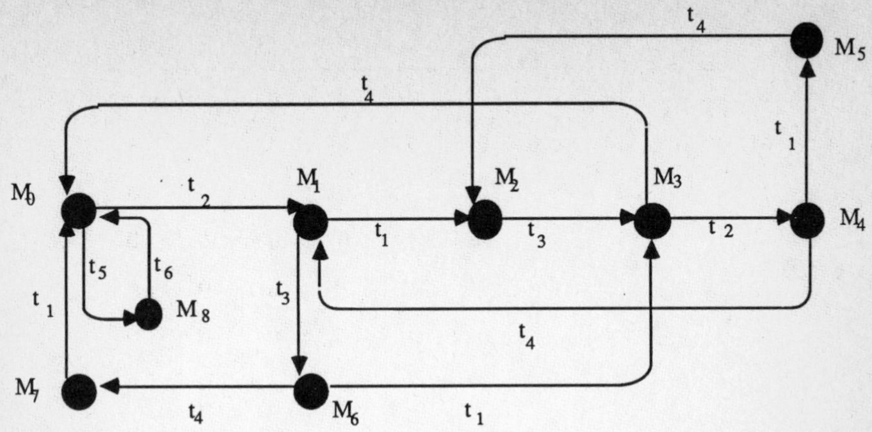

where : $M_0 = (1,0,1,0,1,0,0)$, $M_1 = (0,1,0,1,1,0,0)$, $M_2 = (1,0,0,1,1,0,0)$,
$M_3 = (1,0,1,0,0,1,0)$, $M_4 = (0,1,0,1,0,1,0)$, $M_5 = (1,0,0,1,0,1,0)$,
$M_6 = (0,1,1,0,0,1,0)$, $M_7 = (0,1,1,0,1,0,0)$, $M_8 = (0,0,1,0,0,0,1)$.

The <u>matrix</u> $R = [\, r_{ij} \,]$ of <u>instantaneous transition rates</u> is defined as follows (we make the supposition that the reachability graph does not contain double arcs) :

For $i \neq j$

<u>if</u> $\exists\; t \,\varepsilon\, T : M_i\,[t > M_j$ <u>then</u> $r_{ij} = d\,(1 - e^{-\lambda\tau}\,)\,/\,d\tau\,\big|_{\tau=0} = \lambda$

where λ is the parameter of the exponential distribution function of the transition t

<u>else</u> $r_{ij} = 0$;

<u>For i = j</u> $r_{ii} = d\,\Pi_k\,(\,1 - (\,1 - e^{-\lambda_k\tau}\,)\,/\,d\tau\,\big|_{\tau=0} = d\,e^{-\tau\,\Sigma_k\,\lambda_k}\,/\,d\tau\,\big|_{\tau=0} = -\Sigma_k\,\lambda_k$

where k takes every value $\neq i$ such that $\exists M_k\; \exists t_k : M_i\,[t_k > M_k$ and λ_k is the rate of t_k

<u>Then:</u>

° The <u>unconditional sojourn time in M_i</u> is exponential with parameter $-r_{ii}$

° The <u>waiting in state M_i , given the next state is M_j</u> , is exponential with parameter r_{ij}

° The <u>steadystate probabilities of markings</u> are obtained (How71) by solving the linear equation system

$$\mathbf{x}\,R = \mathbf{0} \quad , \quad \Sigma_i\, x_i = 1$$

(*)

In our example, R is:

	M_0	M_1	M_2	M_3	M_4	M_5	M_6	M_7	M_8
M_0	-5	4	0	0	0	0	0	0	1
M_1	0	-14	10	0	0	0	4	0	0
M_2	0	0	-4	4	0	0	0	0	0
M_3	2	0	0	-6	4	0	0	0	0
M_4	0	2	0	0	-12	10	0	0	0
M_5	0	0	2	0	0	-2	0	0	0
M_6	0	0	0	10	0	0	-12	2	0
M_7	10	0	0	0	0	0	0	-10	0
M_8	1	0	0	0	0	0	0	0	-1

and the solution of system (*) is

$$\mathbf{x} \cong [\ 0.094,\ 0.035,\ 0.235,\ 0.176,\ 0.059,\ 0.293,\ 0.012,\ 0.002,\ 0.094\ ]^T.$$

° The <u>next-state probability matrix</u> $A = [\ a_{ij}\ ]$ is defined by:

$$a_{ij} = -r_{ij} / r_{ii} \quad \text{for } i \neq j$$

$$a_{ij} = 0 \quad \text{else .}$$

a_{ij} is the probability that the marking M_j will be reached at the next transition firing, given that the actual marking is M_i.

Here we get :

$$A = \begin{bmatrix} 0 & 0.8 & 0 & 0 & 0 & 0 & 0 & 0 & 0.2 \\ 0 & 0 & 0.71 & 0 & 0 & 0 & 0.29 & 0 & 0 \\ 0 & 0 & 0 & 1 & 0 & 0 & 0 & 0 & 0 \\ 0.33 & 0 & 0 & 0 & 0.67 & 0 & 0 & 0 & 0 \\ 0 & 0.17 & 0 & 0 & 0 & 0.83 & 0 & 0 & 0 \\ 0 & 0 & 1 & 0 & 0 & 0 & 0 & 0 & 0 \\ 0 & 0 & 0 & 0.83 & 0 & 0 & 0 & 0.17 & 0 \\ 1 & 0 & 0 & 0 & 0 & 0 & 0 & 0 & 0 \\ 1 & 0 & 0 & 0 & 0 & 0 & 0 & 0 & 0 \end{bmatrix}$$

° The steady-state token probability density function assigns the probability of having a certain number of tokens in a place in steady-state.

It can be calculated directly from **x** . E.g., here, the steady-state probability of a message in the channel is :

$$P\{1 \text{ token in MSG}\} = x_1 + x_2 + x_4 + x_5 \cong 0.622$$

° The average number of tokens in a set of places is the mean of the number of tokens in that set of places at the different markings, weighted by the corresponding steady-state probabilities.

Here, e.g., :

$$\text{Average number of tokens in } \{\text{FIN-S, FIN-R}\} = x_1 + x_3 + 2x_4 + x_5 + 2x_6 + x_7 \cong 0.648$$

° The flow of tokens through a transition is given by the transition firing rate multiplied by its steady-state probability of being enabled.

E.g., :

$$\text{Flow through } t_2 = \lambda_2(x_0 + x_3) \cong 1.08 \quad \text{(tokens/time units)}$$

° The mean recurrence time of a marking M_i is:

$$\tau_m(M_i) = (\Sigma_j \lambda_j)^{-1}$$

where j varies over the set of transitions enabled under M_i .

Here, e.g., :

$$\tau_m(M_6) = (\lambda_1 + \lambda_4)^{-1} \cong 0.0833$$

5. Concluding remarks

In short, our opinion on the state of the art of stochastic Petri nets, which we hope to have sufficiently justified in this paper, is that:

- There are many different stochastic Petri net classes, sometimes very similar or even equivalent (cfr.appendix);
- All these models alter in some way the firing rule of Petri nets, and make it so the main part of net theory is no longer applicable ;

° The contribution of Petri nets in such models is rather restricted: often constrained to graphical representation and reachability tree analysis;

° No stochastic element is inserted in the structure of the Petri net: a certain stochastic behaviour is simply postulated for the aspects of indeterminacy of the net (when does a transition fire?).

On the other hand, we think that the request of the industrial world of dealing with the time involved in a process should not be further ignored. But we are convinced that any fruitful research in this area should observe some guidelines :

° The firing rule of Petri nets is based on solid theoretical arguments, and should not be altered ;

° In order to benefit from the results of Petri net theory , it is necessary to introduce the stochastic elements into the net structure (see, as a very first attempt, (Pag85)).

The work still has to be done. But the time to do it seems right.

6. References

(ABC84) AJMONE MARSAN M., BALBO G. , CONTE G., A Class of Generalized Stochastic Petri Nets for the Performance Evaluation of Multi-Processors Systems; ACM Trans. on Computer Systems, Vol.2 , N.2, May 1984

(Dug84) DUGAN J.B., Extended Stochastic Petri Nets: Applications and Analysis; Ph. D. Dissertation, Department of Electrical Engeneering, Duke University, July 1984

(Fel50) FELLER W., An Introduction to Probability Theory and its Applications; Vol. I,2, J. Wiley & Sons, Inc., 1950

(FN81) FLORIN G., NATKIN S., Evaluation Based upon Stochastic Petri Nets of the Maximum Troughput of a Full Duplex Protocol; in: Girault C., Reisig W., eds., Informatik Fachberichte 52, Springer-Verlag, 1982

(How71) HOWARD A.R., Dynamic Probabilistic Systems; Vol. I,2, J. Wiley & Sons, Inc., 1971

(Mol81) MOLLOY M., On the Integration of Delay and Throughput Measures in Distributed Processing Models, UCLA Computer Science Department Report N.CSD-810921, University of California, Los Angeles, 1981

(Pag85) PAGNONI A., Stochastic Invariance in Predicate/Transition Nets; Proc. of the 6th Workshop on Application and Theory of Petri Nets, Helsinky, 1985

(Rei85) REISIG W., Petri Nets, An Introduction; Springer-Verlag 1985

Appendix. A bibliography of stochastic Petri nets

This bibliography is meant to help people interested in furthering their knowledge in stochastic Petri nets. Sometimes the form of the publications is rather raw, expecially when regarded from a Petri net theoretical point of view.
This is not surprising: research in this field was initiated only in 1979, and in environments which are rather removed from Petri net theory.
Nevertheless, these attempts of associating time and probability to a Petri net correspond to concrete user needs, and are worthy of thoughtful consideration.

Chronological inventory:
(The publications marked by * are those suggested for a first reading.)

1979 SHAPIRO S.D., A Stochastic Petri Net with Application to Modeling Occupancy Times for Concurrent Task Systems; Networks, Vol. 9, 1979

1980 SYMONS F.J.W., Introduction to Numerical Petri Nets; ATR, Vol.14, N.1, January 1980

1980 NATKIN S., Les réseaux de Petri stochastiques et leur application à l'évaluation des performances et de la sûreté de fonctionnement des systèmes informatiques; Thèse de Docteur Ingenieur, Paris CNAM, June 1980

1981* MOLLOY M., On the Integration of Delay and Throughput Measures in Distributed Processing Models; UCLA Computer Science Department Report N.CSD-810921, University of California, Los Angeles, 1981

BERTONI A., TORELLI M., Probabilistic Petri Nets and Semi-Markov Processes; Proc. of the 2nd Workshop on Application and Theory of Petri Nets, Bad Honnef, 1981

*FLORIN G., NATKIN S., Evaluation Based upon Stochastic Petri Nets of the Maximum Troughput of a Full Duplex Protocol; in: Girault C., Reisig W., eds., Informatik Fachberichte 52, Springer-Verlag, 1982

1982 MOLLOY M., Performance Analysis Using Stochastic Petri Nets; IEEE Transactions on Computers, Vol.C-3, No.9, September 1982

1984 * AJMONE MARSAN M., BALBO G. , CONTE G., A Class of Generalized Stochastic Petri Nets for the Performance Evaluation of Multi-Processors Systems; ACM Trans. on Computer Systems, Vol.2 , N.2, May 1984

AJMONE MARSAN M., BALBO G., CIARDO C., CONTE G., A Software Tool for the Automatic Analysis of Generalized Stochastic Petri Net Models; Int. Conference on Modeling Techniques and Tools for Performance Analysis, Paris, May 1984

FLORIN G., NATKIN S., An Ergodicity Condition for a Class of Stochastic Petri Nets; Proc. of the 5th Workshop on Application and Theory of Petri Nets, Aarhus, June 1984

TRIVEDI K.S., DUGAN J.B., GEIST R.M., SMOTHERMAN M., Modelling Imperfect Coverage in Fault-Tolerant Systems; 14th Int. Conf. on Fault-Tolerant Computing, IEEE Computer Society Press, June 1984

* DUGAN J.B., Extended Stochastic Petri Nets: Applications and Analysis; Ph. D. Dissertation; Department of Electrical Engeneering, Duke University, July 1984

MEYER J.F., Performability Modeling with Stochastic Activity Networks; Proc. 1984 Real-Time Systems Symp., Austin, December 1984

VALLETTE R. et al., PSI: A Petri Net Based Simulator for Flexible Manufacturing Systems; in: Advances in Petri Nets 1984, Rozenberg G. ed., Springer-Verlag, 1985

1985 MOLLOY M., Discrete Time Stochastic Petri Nets; IEEE Trans. on Software Engeneering, Vol. se.11, N.4, April 1985

FLORIN G., NATKIN S., Les réseaux de Petri stochastiques - Théorie, techniques de calcul, applications; Thèse d'Etat, Université Paris VI, June 1985

* PAGNONI A.,Stochastic Invariance in Predicate/Transition Nets; Proc. of the 6th Workshop on Application and Theory of Petri Nets, Helsinky, July 1985

AJMONE MARSAN M., et al., On Petri Nets with Stochastic Timing; Proc. Int. Workshop on Timed Petri Nets, Turin, IEEE Computer Society Press, September 1985

CHIOLA G., A Software Package for the Analysis of Generalized Sochastic Petri Net Models; Proc. Int. Workshop on Timed Petri Nets, Turin, IEEE Computer Society Press, September 1985

DUGAN J.B., BOBBIO A., CIARDO G., TRIVEDI K., The Design of an Unified Package for the Solution of Stochastic Petri Net Models; Proc. Int. Workshop on Timed Petri Nets, Turin, IEEE Computer Society Press, September 1985

FLORIN G., NATKIN S., On Open Synchronized Queuing Networks; Proc. Int. Workshop on Timed Petri Nets, Turin, IEEE Computer Society Press, September 1985

HOLLIDAY M.A., VERNON M.K., A Generalized Timed Petri Net Model for Performance Analysis; Proc. Int. Workshop on Timed Petri Nets, Turin, IEEE Computer Society Press, September 1985

MEYER J.F., MOVAGHAR A., SANDER W.H., Stochastic Activity Networks: Structure, Behaviour and Applications; Proc. Int. Workshop on Timed Petri Nets, Turin, IEEE Computer Society Press, September 1985

ZUBEREK W.M., M-Timed Petri Nets, Priorities, Preemptions, and Performance Evaluation of Systems; Advances in Petri Nets 1985, Rozenberg G. ed., Lecture Notes in Computer Science N.222, Springer-Verlag, 1986

****

ADDRESSES OF THE AUTHORS

Dr. Gérard Berthelot
Université Paris 11
L.R.I.
Bât. 490
91405 Orsay Cedex
France

Dr. Eike Best
GMD-F1
Postfach 1240
5205 St. Augustin 1
West Germany

Prof. Dr. César Fernández
GMD-F1
Postfach 1240
5205 St. Augustin 1
West Germany

Dr. Hartmann J. Genrich
GMD-F1
Postfach 1240
5205 St. Augustin 1
West Germany

Ursula Goltz
GMD-F1
Postfach 1240
5205 St. Augustin 1
West Germany

Dr. Matthias Jantzen
Universität Hamburg, FB Informatik
Rothenbaumchaussee 67-69
2000 Hamburg 13
West Germany

Dr. Kurt Jensen
Aarhus University
Dept. of Computer Science
Ny Munkegade 116
8000 Aarhus C
Denmark

Prof. Dr. Kurt Lautenbach
Universität Bonn
Institut für Informatik
Wegelerstr. 6
5300 Bonn 1
West Germany

Dr. Gérard Memmi
BULL - C.R.G.
68, route de Versailles
78430 Louveciennes
France

Prof. Dr. Anastasia Pagnoni
Via Monte Rosa, 74
20149 Milano
Italy

Dr. Carl Adam Petri
GMD-F1
Postfach 1240
5205 St. Augustin 1
West Germany

Dr. Wolfgang Reisig
GMD-F1
Postfach 1240
5205 St. Augustin 1
West Germany

Prof. Dr. Gérard Roucairol
CII-Honeywell-Bull
68, route de Versailles
78430 Louveciennes
France

Prof. Dr. Grzegorz Rozenberg
Rijksuniversiteit te Leiden
Subfaculteit Wiskunde en Informatica
Postbus 9512
2300 RA Leiden
The Netherlands

Prof. Dr. P. S. Thiagarajan
The Institute of Math. Sciences
Madras, 600113
India

Prof. Dr. Rüdiger Valk
Universität Hamburg, FB Informatik
Rothenbaumchaussee 67-69
2000 Hamburg 13
West Germany

Dr. Jacques Vautherin
Université Paris-Sud
L. R. I.
Bât. 490
91405 Orsay Cedex
France